AF605877

JOE JONES | Radical Painter of the American Scene

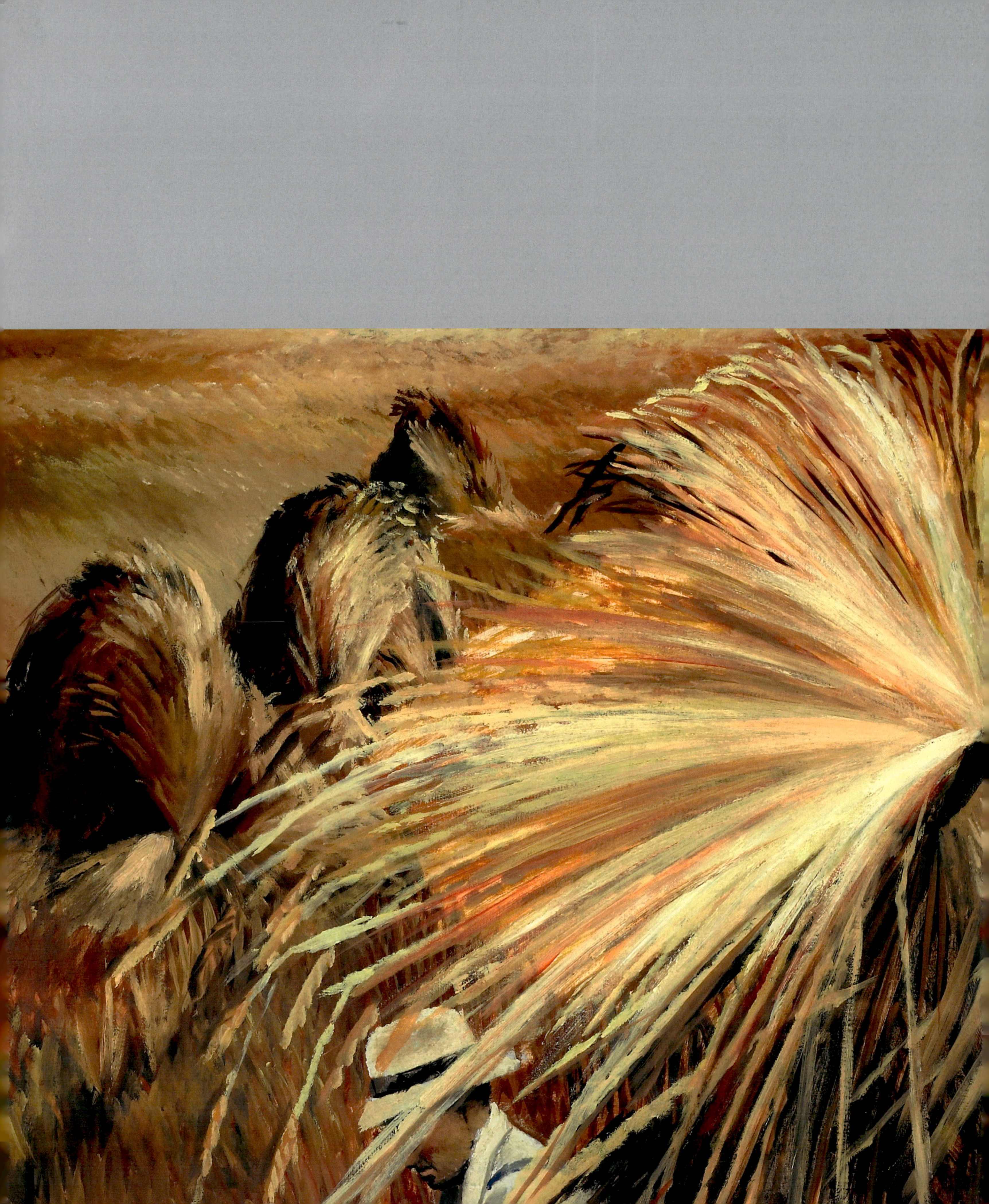

JOE JONES
Radical Painter of the American Scene

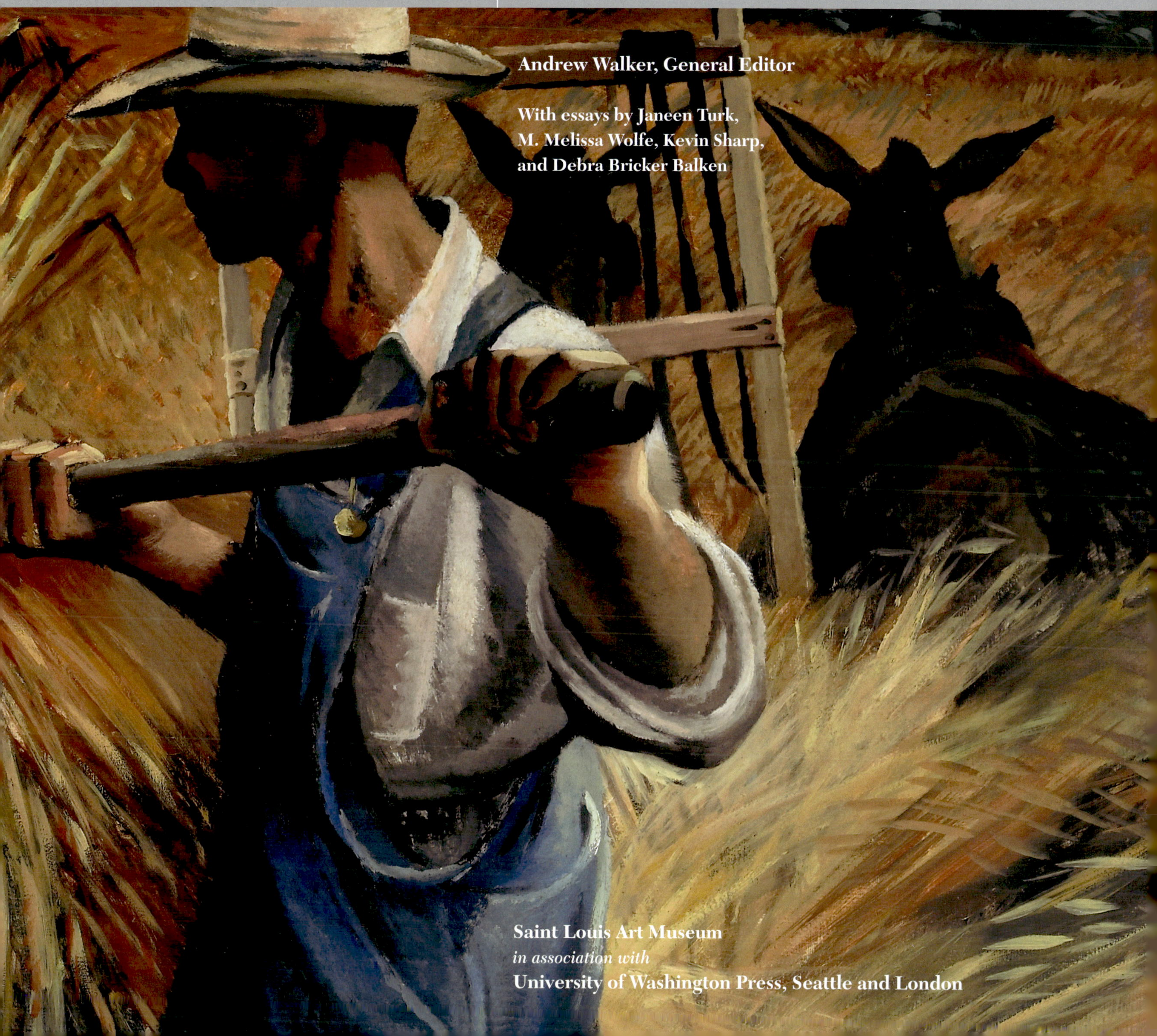

Andrew Walker, General Editor

With essays by Janeen Turk,
M. Melissa Wolfe, Kevin Sharp,
and Debra Bricker Balken

Saint Louis Art Museum
in association with
University of Washington Press, Seattle and London

Published in conjunction with the exhibition *Joe Jones: Painter of the American Scene*, Saint Louis Art Museum, October 10, 2010–January 2, 2011; Dixon Gallery and Gardens, Memphis, Tennessee, January 23–April 17, 2011.

Published by the Saint Louis Art Museum in association with University of Washington Press, Seattle and London.

Saint Louis Art Museum
1 Fine Arts Drive
St. Louis, MO 63110
www.slam.org

Distributed by
University of Washington Press
P.O. Box 50096
Seattle, WA 98145-5096
www.washington.edu/uwpress

Produced by Marquand Books, Inc., Seattle
www.marquand.com

Library of Congress Cataloging-in-Publication Data
Jones, Joe, 1909–1963.
Joe Jones : radical painter of the American scene / Andrew Walker, general editor ; with essays by Janeen Turk . . . [et al.].
p. cm.
Published in conjunction with an exhibition held at the Saint Louis Art Museum, Oct. 10, 2010–Jan. 2, 2011 and at the Dixon Gallery and Gardens, Memphis, Tenn., Jan. 23–Apr. 17, 2011.
Includes bibliographical references and index.
ISBN 978-0-89178-094-6 (hardcover)
ISBN 978-0-89178-093-9 (softcover)
1. Jones, Joe, 1909–1963—Exhibitions. 2. Regionalism in art—Middle West—Exhibitions. 3. Middle West—In art—Exhibitions. 4. Art and society—United States—History—20th century—Exhibitions. I. Walker, Andrew, 1964–. II. Turk, Janeen. III. St. Louis Art Museum. IV. Dixon Gallery and Gardens. V. Title.
ND237.J754A4 2010
759.13—dc22 2010032444

Library of Congress Control Number: 2010926918

All of the following works are by Joe Jones.
Front cover: *St. Louis Riverfront* (detail), c. 1932 (cat. 17).
Back cover: *Missouri Wheat Farmers*, 1938 (cat. 70).
Frontispiece: *Threshing No. 1* (detail), 1935 (cat. 34).
Page 6: *Studio Interior* (detail), c. 1932 (cat. 22).
Page 12: *Working on the Railroad* (detail), 1939 (cat. 73).
Page 14: *Wooded Landscape* (detail), 1931 (cat. 6).
Page 32: *Roustabouts* (detail), 1934 (cat. 32).
Page 54: *Water Hole* (detail), 1936 (cat. 65).
Page 98: *Our American Farms* (detail), 1936 (cat. 42).
Page 116: *Men and Wheat* (detail), 1939–40 (Walker and Turk, fig. 4).
Pages 122–23: *View of St. Louis* (detail), c. 1932 (cat. 24).
Page 178: *Yellow Grain* (detail), c. 1942 (cat. 82).

Edited by Susan F. Rossen, with Susan Weidemeyer
Photography by Nathan Keay, Silvia Ros, Jean Paul Torno, David Ulmer, C. J. Walker, and Karin L. Willis
Designed by Jeff Wincapaw, with Zach Hooker
Typeset by Marissa Meyer
Color separations by iocolor, Seattle

Printed and bound in China by Artron Color Printing Co., Ltd.

Contents

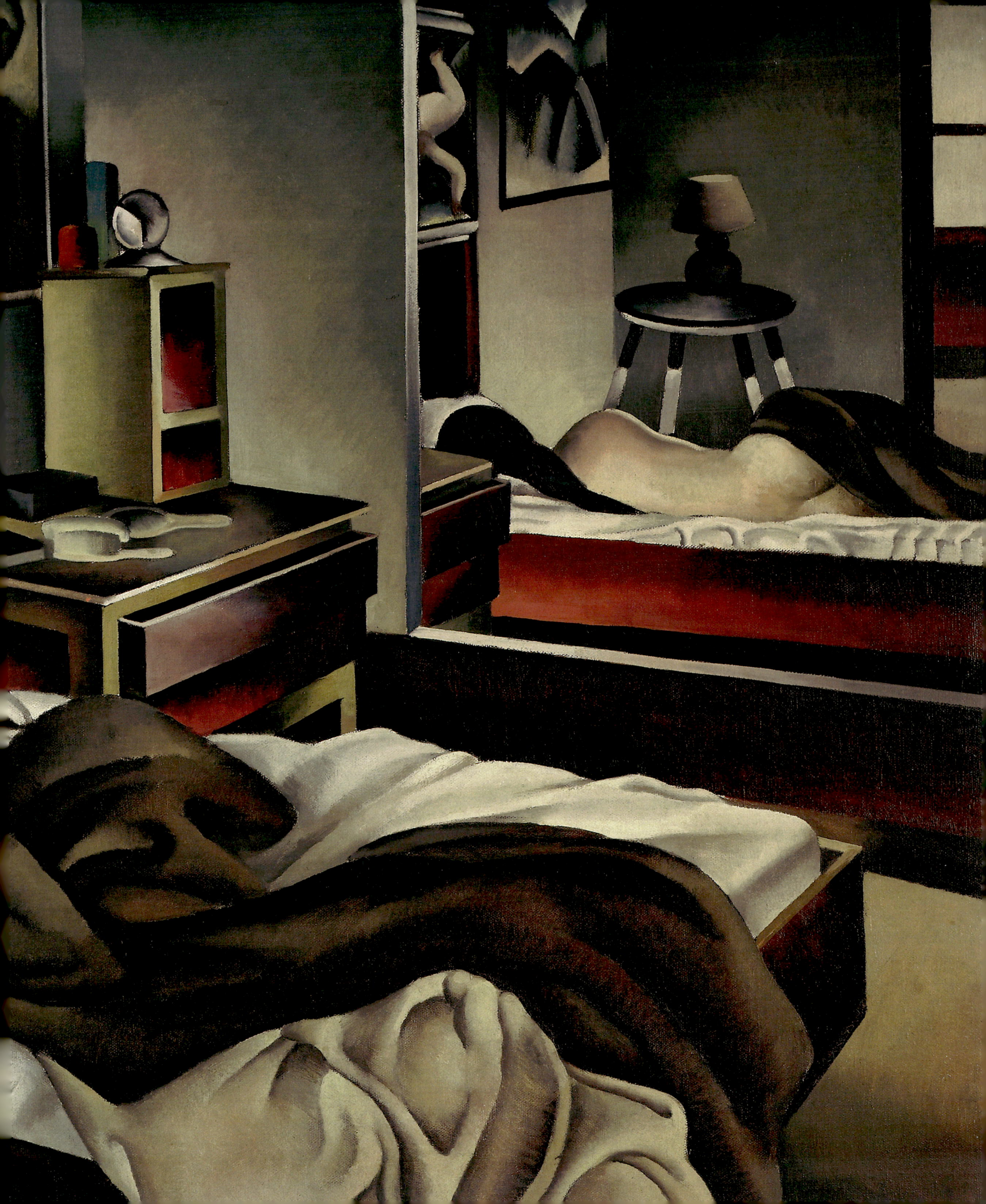

Director's Foreword

Brent R. Benjamin
Director, Saint Louis Art Museum

This catalogue and the exhibition it accompanies represent the culmination of an intensive four-year research project on the St. Louis artist Joe Jones. Jones is hardly a well-known figure in the study of American art of the 1930s and early 1940s. He cannot be easily categorized, either as a regionalist or as a social realist, nor does his work fit into the narrative of the emergence of Abstract Expressionism. He is most remembered now, as he was even in his own day, as a tremendously talented painter with a fierce belief in social justice. Beginning in 1933, Jones was a card-carrying Communist drawn to socio-political themes ranging from labor unrest on the St. Louis waterfront and controversial anti-lynching subjects at a time of resurging racial injustice and violence to scenes of environmental disaster in the Dust Bowl. Jones also showed an uncanny sensitivity to the farmlands of his native Missouri, painting vibrant images of wheat threshing and other types of farm labor.

Though Jones's work earned him the respect of critics and fellow artists during the 1930s, his standing has ebbed in the intervening years. After 1943 he traded his Midwestern themes of labor and social justice—painted in a bold, realist style—for a decorative, linear modernism of a much more personal nature. This work was well received but did not spark the same interest as had his treatments of socially conscious issues. In addition, the political climate changed dramatically after the end of World War II, and Jones's identity as a Communist during the 1930s became a liability even though he no longer embraced the party's cause.

It is the privilege and responsibility of the Saint Louis Art Museum to celebrate artists from the region who have made a significant contribution to the nation's art, especially when their accomplishments have not been recognized elsewhere. *Joe Jones: Radical Painter of the American Scene* is such an effort. It has resulted in a number of remarkable rediscoveries. Many of Jones's early, precisionist-influenced paintings were in private hands and unfamiliar even to specialists of American Scene painting. Exploring these collections has helped us understand Jones's earliest exhibition history and artistic output. The success of this project depended on committed collectors who have appreciated the worth of Jones's works in advance of many museums. However, the most notable find is the mural Jones made for Commonwealth College in Mena, Arkansas, in 1935. It represents the culmination of Jones's attempt to treat politically significant subjects in a monumental form for public engagement. Scholars had long thought the forty-foot mural lost. In fact it had been housed since the mid-1980s in the archives of the University of Arkansas at Little Rock. Although the mural's condition is compromised, the museum is working with the university to restore it to its original state.

The story of Joe Jones could not have been told without the determination of Andrew Walker, Assistant Director for Curatorial Affairs and Curator of American Art, and his Senior Curatorial Assistant, Janeen Turk. They sought out collectors, mined archives, and interviewed Jones's family and his remaining student from the 1930s. Their work was aided by numerous colleagues. Of particular note is Kevin Sharp, Executive Director of the Dixon Gallery and Gardens, in Memphis, Tennessee, who wrote for the catalogue and offered the Dixon as the second venue for the exhibition. This project also benefits from the extraordinary generosity of individual donors to the exhibition and the private and institutional lenders who have assisted in making this endeavor possible. They are listed on page 13. We believe that *Joe Jones: Radical Painter of the American Scene* will reveal the strength and importance of this under-appreciated artist, opening his career to further study and restoring to his oeuvre the stature it deserves.

Preface and Acknowledgments

Andrew Walker and Janeen Turk

Joe Jones: Radical Painter of the American Scene explores the work of the St. Louis–born artist Joe Jones (1909–1963) during the Great Depression. When we initiated our exploration of this subject in 2006, the American economy had begun to teeter in the face of the high number of failing subprime mortgages, creating a national real-estate crisis of epic proportion. By 2008 the economy was in freefall; economists called the situation the country's worst financial catastrophe since the 1930s. These circumstances added a new level of significance to our undertaking. Though separated by nearly seventy years, the similar political and economic struggles of then and now exposed the ways rampant greed and fiscal malfeasance endanger the American dream, especially for the nation's poor and powerless. Taken together, the paintings, drawings, lithographs, and photographs Jones made between 1930 and 1942 provide a portrait of a country wrestling with an economic disaster that displaced urban and rural poor from their homes and took away their livelihoods. A Communist and social activist, Jones believed that his art could effect real political change by exposing the social, labor, and racial injustices that underlay corporate and government policies, hurting American workers everywhere. In the poverty and labor strife of the Heartland, he found a subject that fed his activist sensibility.

Despite the fame and critical acclaim Jones enjoyed in his lifetime, no book-length consideration of his career has ever been undertaken, and no major exhibition of his work has occurred since those organized to honor his memory at the time of his death. For decades afterward, his name most often appeared as a brief reference in discussions of social realist art of the 1930s or anecdotally in accounts of the New Deal art programs of the era.

Karal Ann Marling first encountered the art of Joe Jones in preparing her 1982 book, *Wall-to-Wall America: A Cultural History of Post-Office Murals in the Great Depression*. In 1987 she went on to produce an article and an essay in an exhibition catalogue celebrating the acquisition of Jones's 1937 murals for the 905 Liquor Store, St. Louis, by the Haggerty Museum of Art, Marquette University, Milwaukee. These were the first focused explorations of Jones's career to grapple with the primary sources relating to his art. In both texts, Marling traced Jones's development, including the shift he made from being a politically engaged Communist artist to one who sought and profited from corporate commissions.

In 1991 Louisa Iarocci described the arc of the artist's career in "The Changing American Landscape: The Art and Politics of Joe Jones," published in *Gateway Heritage*, the Missouri History Museum's journal. She emphasized his reliance on regional subjects and on the enduring importance for him of the American landscape, concluding that his turn from political subjects did not indicate that his political beliefs were superficial. In fact many social realists distanced themselves from radical politics at the end of the 1930s, with the growth of fascism in Europe and world war looming on the horizon. Jones has also received attention from writers interested in the art colony of Ste. Genevieve, Missouri, with which he was briefly affiliated.

The most nuanced examination of Jones in the 1930s and 1940s is that of Andrew Hemingway. In his monumental, pathbreaking 2002 study, *Artists on the Left: American Artists and the Communist Movement, 1926–1956*, Hemingway examined Jones's work in relation to his identity as a Communist artist, arguing that even his later scenes of agricultural bounty resonate with leftist ideals, such as collective farming and the primary importance of labor.

Our project builds upon the work of these scholars. Jones's prodigious output during the period in which he achieved national critical acclaim is examined from five distinct perspectives that knit together his aesthetic development, political activism, local identity, and larger art-world impact.

In her essay "Joseph Jones: A Conservative Modern in St. Louis," Janeen Turk discusses Jones's earliest work in the context of the St. Louis art world of the early 1930s: the city's art museum, galleries, newspaper critics, specialized art publications, and patrons. She analyzes Jones's first successes in his hometown, when he was clearly responding to the strong local preference for a temperate form of modernism.

In "Joe Jones: Worker-Artist," M. Melissa Wolfe focuses on Jones's awakening to issues of labor and racial injustice and how he addressed them in his work and actions. She provides in-depth analysis of Jones's first political painting, *American Justice* (cat. 31), and the recently rediscovered mural *The Struggle in the South* (see cat. 39), which constitute the artist's most charged and direct representations of racial and class conflict.

In "Joe Jones and the Dust Bowl: A Search for Social Significance," Andrew Walker treats the artist's least-studied work of this period: his Dust Bowl–related paintings, drawings, prints, and photographs. Walker explicates the ways in which this material satisfied Jones's quest for compelling and relevant subjects that allowed him to further his engagement with social and economic issues affecting the nation's poor. In the Dust Bowl, Jones found a theme that could convey protest and demand change.

"Joe Jones in Ste. Genevieve," by Kevin Sharp, investigates the artist's involvement with the Ste. Genevieve, Missouri, art colony and summer art school, of which he served as a director for a season. In addition to exploring Jones's relationship to his colleagues and their work, Sharp evaluates the appeal to Jones of the colony as a site where he could further his desire to establish himself as a leading artist of the Midwest.

Debra Bricker Balken's "Joe Jones's New York Interactions" examines Jones's experiences in New York as both a part-time and permanent resident (after 1937). In the nation's art capital, Jones struggled to find his place within polemical discussions such as regional versus national identity and socio-political intent versus formal concerns. Balken looks at Jones's solo exhibitions in New York galleries, his successes and failures with the city's museums, his reviewers in both leftist and mainstream publications, and his involvement in artists' activist organizations. The essay section ends with an overview by Andrew Walker and Janeen Turk of Jones's post-office murals.

We hope that this catalogue and the exhibition it accompanies accomplish our goal: to tell the story of one of Missouri's most important twentieth-century artists and convey his significant contribution to American art during the 1930s and early 1940s.

◦ ◦ ◦

Joe Jones: Radical Painter of the American Scene has involved the assistance and collaboration of many individuals in museums, archives, historical museums, galleries, and auction houses, as well as devoted collectors who have sustained Jones's reputation through the purchase of his work.

At the Saint Louis Art Museum, Brent R. Benjamin, Director, offered constant support throughout the genesis and implementation of the project. His dedication to Jones as one of St. Louis's unsung art heroes initiated the process that resulted in this show and book. We are grateful to Kevin Sharp, Executive Director at the Dixon Gallery and Gardens, Memphis, for giving the exhibition a second venue. He has long been an advocate of Jones's oeuvre and has recognized the importance of sharing the artist's contributions with his community.

Chief among those who helped to conceive and tell Jones's story are our coauthors, Debra Bricker Balken, Kevin Sharp, and M. Melissa Wolfe, whose essays present new scholarship in frameworks that reflect the writers' significant expertise in their field. We are very grateful to them for their hard work and belief in the project. Special thanks go to Bryna R. Campbell, who worked tirelessly to compile a very detailed chronology of Jones's life; and to Emily Allred, our tenacious research assistant, who dug deep into all of the sources to make discovery after discovery.

A project of this nature would not be possible without the assistance of those who knew Jones, who studied with him, and whose relatives were early patrons. We are very grateful to the members of Jones's family who assisted us in our research and understanding of the artist's character and career: Katharine Allen, James and Karen Jones, Raya Koren and Peter Jones, Shirley A. Jones, and Kami Mulzet. We also appreciate the support of the family of Jones's most faithful St. Louis supporter, Elizabeth Green: John Green, Bill Lindsley, Carolyn Malecek, and Ann Verdi. Jones's student Martyl (Schweig Langsdorf), an accomplished artist in her own right, offered memories of Jones's personality and his dedication to art with grace and forthrightness. We further appreciate the assistance of George and Dolores Friesen, Martin Schweig, Judith and Ernest Stix, and Tim and Ruth Wood, all of whom had unique perspectives on Jones based on stories passed down by family members.

Inevitably, a recovery project of this scale depended on an array of Jones scholars and enthusiasts who have helped keep his story alive. Without the groundbreaking research of Karal Ann Marling, Professor Emeritus of Art History at the University of Minnesota, our work would not have been possible. Professors Andrew Hemingway (University College of London) and Angela Miller (Washington University, St. Louis) have offered insight and support along the way. Carrying Jones's torch from a more personal perspective are Susan Barrett, Hunt Bonan, Robert Dick, Rory Ellinger, Lloyd Greif, John Horseman, Scott Kerr, Jonathan and David Kodner, James and Virginia Moffett, Elliot Nelson, Jack Parker, Kara Pollnow, Jason Schoen, Rex Sinquefield, Catherine Spaeth, Robert Ventimiglia, and Deedee Wigmore, along with others who contacted us to offer insights, recollections, and collections related to Jones's career in St. Louis.

We would also like to thank those who provided valuable research support and advice: Eric Baumgartner, Hirschl & Adler; Cecilia H. Chin, Smithsonian Institution Libraries; Barb Driesner, Edwardsville Public Library; Linda Honeyman, Seneca Downtown Impact, Inc.; Emily Jones, Woodstock Artists Association and Museum; Mary Kiffer, John Simon Guggenheim Memorial Foundation; Anna Kirchner, Ste. Genevieve Art Guild; Todd D. Smith, Farmers Bank & Trust; the staff of the St. Louis Public Library; and others too numerous to name here.

At the Saint Louis Art Museum, many staff members contributed to the success of this project. Carolyn Schmidt, Deputy Director; Linda Thomas, Assistant Director for Exhibitions and Collections; Bill Appleton, Assistant Director for Education and Public Programs; Sheila Manion, Acting Assistant Director for Development; and Jennifer Stoffel, Acting Assistant Director for Audience Development provided expertise and support on a number of levels. We are especially appreciative of our research team over the years: Emily Allred, Bryna R. Campbell, Rhonda Lally, Erika Rogers, Lauren Staub, and Elizabeth Wolfson. Many of the works in the exhibition required conservation treatment and benefitted from the skills of the museum's Conservation Department members Paul Haner, Nancy Heugh, and Art Rogers. We are particularly grateful to Jeanette Fausz and her talented and dedicated staff in the Registrar's Office, including Angie Carter, Natalie Musser, Ella Rothgangel, and Rachel Shoup Swiston. The distinctive design for the exhibition is due to our creative Design Department, headed by Philip Atkinson and including Jon Cournoyer, Lauri Kramer, and Nick Smith. In the Richardson Memorial Library, Norma Sindelar, Clare Vasquez, and Bryan Young spent much time finding obscure resources. The exhibition was expertly managed by Molly Perse and its interpretation by Louise Cameron. We were also pleased to be able to work with St. Louis–based photographer Jean Paul Torno.

Joe Jones: Radical Painter of the American Scene would not have been possible without the support of over forty lenders, both institutions and private collections. Their names are listed on page 13. We are immensely grateful to all of them for agreeing to part with works in order to share them with a broad, new audience. Among the private collectors, we must single out the exceptional generosity of Jeanne and Rex Sinquefield. Our colleagues at the lending institutions have earned our deepest gratitude: Louise Dompierre and Patrick Shaw Cable, Art Gallery of Hamilton, Ontario; Louis A. Zona, The Butler Institute of American Art; Deborah Gribbon and Mark Cole, The Cleveland Museum of Art; Nannette V. Maciejunes and M. Melissa Wolfe, Columbus Museum of Art; Christoph Heinrich and Timothy Stranding, Denver Art Museum; James Mundy and Mary-Kay Lombino, The Frances Lehman Loeb Art Center, Vassar College; Walter Mason and Annemarie Sawkins, Haggerty Museum of Art, Marquette University; Michael E. Shapiro, High Museum of Art; Kathryn Thomas, Jennifer R. Clark, and Tom Dewey, Jefferson National Expansion Memorial; Andy Abbott, John Burroughs School; Jonathan and David Kodner, Kodner Gallery; Sabine Eckmann, Mildred Lane Kemper Art Museum, Washington University; Robert Archibald, Anne Woodhouse, Dennis Northcott, Molly Kodner, and Linda Landry, Missouri History Museum; Paul D. Schweizer, Munson-Williams-Proctor Arts Institute, Museum of Art; Mary Sue Sweeney Price and Beth Venn, Newark Museum; James K. Ballinger, Phoenix Art Museum; Elizabeth Broun and Eleanor Harvey, Smithsonian American Art Museum; John Hoover, Julie Dunn-Morton, and Deborah Cribbs, St. Louis Mercantile Library at the University of Missouri–St. Louis; Brad Cushman and Linda Pine, University of Arkansas at Little Rock; Dona Bachman and Lori Huffman, The University Museum, Southern Illinois University Carbondale; Adam D. Weinberg and Barbara Haskell, Whitney Museum of American Art; Kimberly Bergen, Marianne Lamonaca, and Cathy Leff, The Wolfsonian–Florida International University; and James A. Welu and William Rudolph, Worcester Art Museum.

We owe a debt of thanks for the editorial know-how and personal commitment of Susan F. Rossen, our tireless editor and advisor, who worked with us to find our voices and to ensure that we gave Jones the comprehensive treatment that he and his art deserve. She was ably assisted by Susan Weidemeyer. We thank our team at Marquand Books, Seattle, for managing the typesetting, design, and production of this book: Ed Marquand, President; Sara Billups, Media Manager; Jeremy Linden, Production Coordinator; Adrian Lucia, Managing Director; Keryn Means, Production Manager; Brynn Warriner, Managing Editor; and Jeff Wincapaw, Design Director. The book's elegant design is by Zach Hooker; it was typeset by Marissa Meyer. We are also grateful to Pat Soden and Denise Clark at the University of Washington Press for their enthusiasm for Jones.

Finally we could not have persevered through the complicated process of rehabilitating Jones's career without the moral support of our families, especially Paula Lupkin and Jason Turk.

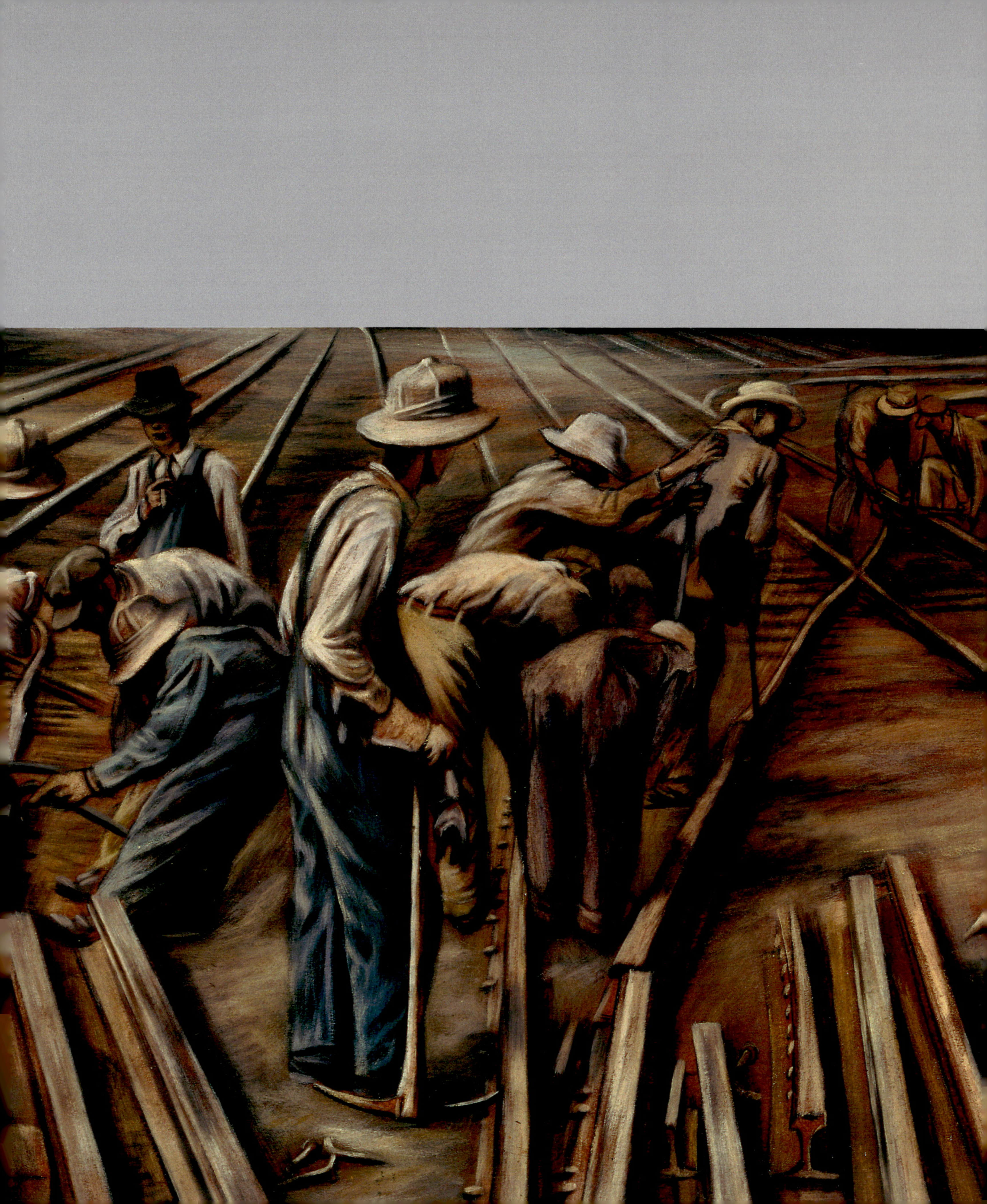

Lenders

Hunt and Donna Bonan
Constance and Henry Christensen
Sarah Dearry
Rory Ellinger and Linda Locke
Richard and Eileen Epstein
George and Dolores Friesen
Estate of Miss Elizabeth Green
Renée and Lloyd Greif
John and Susan Horseman
Jones Family Collection
Shirley A. Jones
Raya Koren and Peter Jones
Michael Lawlor
James and Virginia Moffett
Jeanne and Rex Sinquefield
Otto L. Spaeth, Jr.
Keith and Bobbie Wedge
Ruth and Tim Wood
Four anonymous lenders

Art Gallery of Hamilton, Ontario
The Butler Institute of American Art
The Cleveland Museum of Art
Columbus Museum of Art
Denver Art Museum
The Frances Lehman Loeb Art Center, Vassar College
Haggerty Museum of Art
High Museum of Art
Jefferson National Expansion Memorial
John Burroughs School
Kodner Gallery
Mildred Lane Kemper Art Museum, Washington University in Saint Louis
Missouri History Museum
Munson-Williams-Proctor Arts Institute, Museum of Art
Newark Museum
Phoenix Art Museum
Saint Louis Art Museum
Smithsonian American Art Museum
St. Louis Mercantile Library at the University of Missouri–St. Louis
University of Arkansas at Little Rock
The University Museum, Southern Illinois University Carbondale
Whitney Museum of American Art
The Wolfsonian–Florida International University
Worcester Art Museum

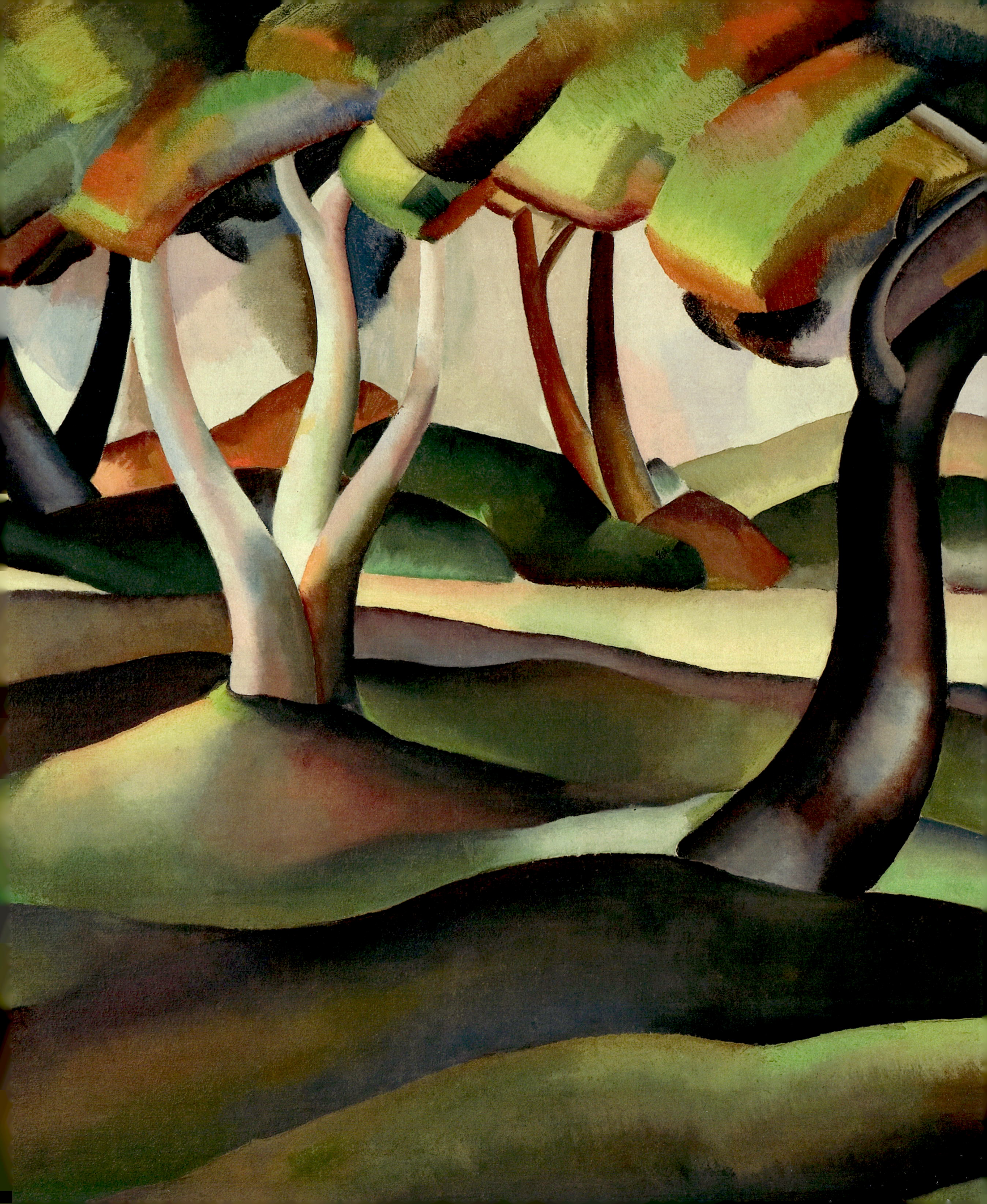

Joseph Jones: A Conservative Modern in St. Louis

Janeen Turk

By early 1930, twenty-year-old Joseph Jones was on the brink of enjoying the first major successes of his artistic career in his hometown, St. Louis. He aspired to leave behind his house-painting job and make a name for himself as an artist. In 1930 he showed work at the city's most prestigious venue, the City Art Museum (now the Saint Louis Art Museum), and won $100 from the local professional artists' society. Over the next three years, Jones became a fixture on the local exhibition circuit. His name regularly appeared on lists of exhibitors and recipients of prizes and honorable mentions, alongside artists decades his senior. He had his first three solo shows and made significant sales, receiving private and corporate commissions for large-scale projects. His works were illustrated repeatedly in the local papers and also appeared in the nationally circulated *Art Digest*. He secured the attention of a devoted patron in Elizabeth Green and a broader show of support in the founding of the Co-operative Art Society (or Joe Jones Club), dedicated to subsidizing his artistic development.[1] Examination of Jones's career from 1930 to 1933 demonstrates that the through line of his success was his perceived modernism. Jones himself encouraged this understanding by affiliating himself and his work with the character traits and formal qualities identified with modern art, as recognized and emphasized by the local media. He also deliberately worked in a particular mode that was especially attractive to his hometown audience: conservative modernism. His approach resembled that of other modernists of broad appeal.

As long as Jones's accessible brand of modernism was understood to be the driving force of his art, many St. Louisans embraced him and his output. He drew the approbation of the bohemian set, art-world insiders, and the well-to-do who believed that supporting him was part of being socially and culturally progressive. This congeniality lasted until Jones turned his focus from the formal concerns of modernism to the representation and indictment of social injustice, a change coincident with his conversion to Communism in 1933. After he announced his political affiliation, Jones lost much of his local backing and began to see that his best chances for future success lay in New York.

MODERNISM IN ST. LOUIS

In St. Louis, "modern" art, at its most basic level, denoted work that rejected artistic tradition as embodied in the teachings of conservative East Coast art academies (see fig. 1).[2] It was understood to be a form of individual self-expression rather than an attempt to naturalistically reproduce appearances. Advocates of progressive art believed that it was the best reflection of "modern times and modern life," visualizing what was "felt to be most germane and essential to the age," defined in these years by industrialization and the ubiquity of technology and the machine.[3]

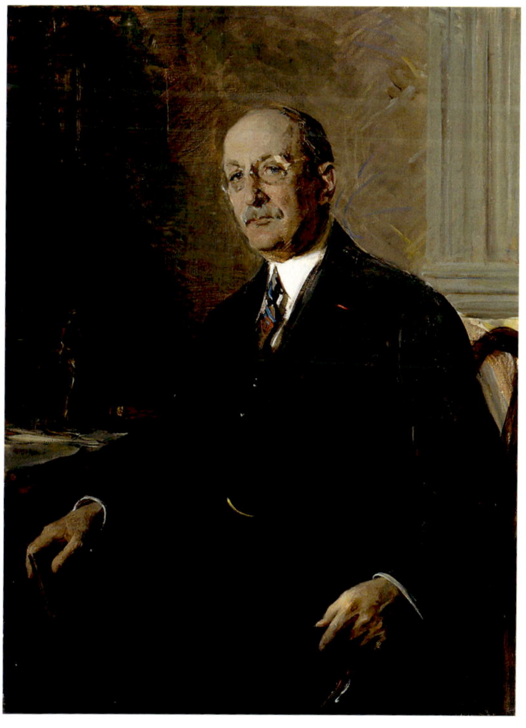

Fig. 1. Ernest L. Ipsen (1869–1951). *Mr. Cass Gilbert*, 1927. Oil on canvas; 48⅛ × 36 in. (122.2 × 91.3 cm). Smithsonian American Art Museum, Bequest of Emily Finch Gilbert through Julia Post Bastedo, executor. All artists whose works appear in this book are American, unless otherwise specified.

Not surprisingly, given its emphasis on independence and individual self-expression, modernism encompassed a broad range of styles, including but not limited to those of quintessential European moderns such as Paul Cézanne, Henri Matisse, and Pablo Picasso.[4] A few key words and phrases appear in local media and publications as recognized hallmarks of the movement: bold color, distortion, some level of abstraction, and the tipped perspectives typical of Cubism.[5]

While a history of early modernism in St. Louis is beyond the scope of this essay, a brief overview will situate the cultural climate in which Jones and his art developed. In 1913 a selection of modernist paintings, including Marcel Duchamp's *Nude Descending a Staircase (No. 2)* (fig. 2), was displayed at one of the city's leading department stores. Duchamp's painting had prompted especially strong negative responses from viewers when it was included that same year in the Armory Show, a widely publicized exhibition of international modern art that introduced a significant slice of Americans to various avant-garde styles, from Post-Impressionism to Cubism. St. Louisans were shocked by the work as well.[6]

In St. Louis, the art-going public had ample opportunity to view and explore modern art in a number of other contexts. In 1928 the city's main library mounted a display of fifty color prints of modern paintings. Visitors saw, in reproduction, works from the early 1900s through 1927.[7] While the holdings of the free-entry, "encyclopedic" City Art Museum were such that Louis LaBeaume, vice president of the institution's board of control, could boast that it had "acquired no modernistic pieces," the museum and an array of local galleries maintained rigorous exhibition schedules, regularly featuring examples of modern art from the United States and abroad.[8] St. Louis's daily papers closely covered important exhibitions, sometimes with illustrations (see fig. 3). The city boasted several arts periodicals, including the *Saint Louis Review* and the *St. Louis Art World*. Other interested parties included a growing number of artists' organizations, committed collectors and patrons, and the faculty and students of the St. Louis School of Fine Arts at Washington University.

By the 1920s, although modern art had achieved a certain degree of critical, if not public, acceptance in the United States, the St. Louis art world was by no means in agreement on the topic. City Art Museum director Meyric Rogers, writing in the *Saint Louis Review* in 1932, acknowledged that, while the modern movement had "definitely conquered the creative field . . . in comparison it [had] gained little basic hold on the involuntary interest of the receiving public." Rogers suggested that the problem lay in too many viewers' attempts to read paintings like books; he asked them to set aside preconceived ideas and focus on looking, feeling, and thinking: "Let us . . . look boldly at the most fantastic and literally unreasonable canvas for what entertainment of color and pattern it can give us."[9]

In effect, critics and the art-viewing public of 1930s St. Louis found conservative modernism, sometimes called modern classicism, the most palatable form of the new. It was firmly representational and not as abstracted or bewildering as the Cubist work of Picasso, for example, which could be seen in the national art publications to which the City Art Museum library and the public library

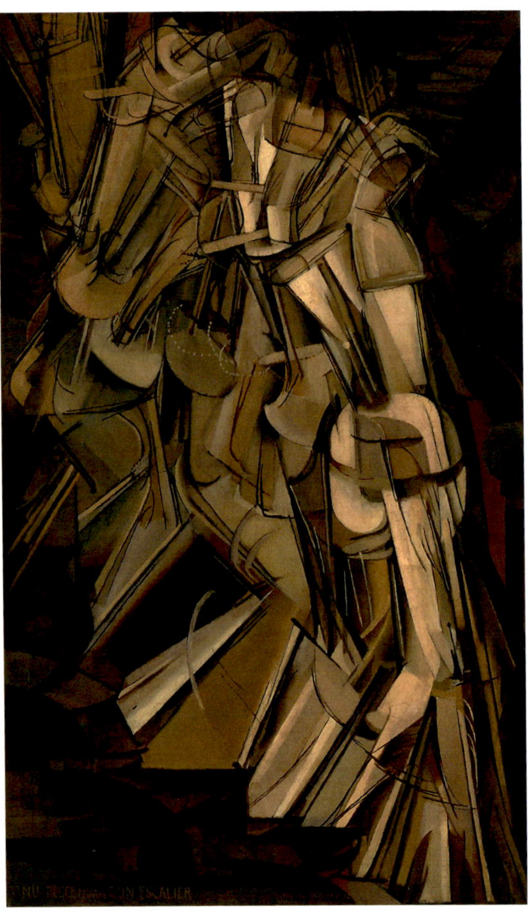

Fig. 2. Marcel Duchamp (French; 1887–1968). *Nude Descending a Staircase (No. 2)*, 1912. Oil on canvas; 57⅞ × 35⅛ in. (147 × 89.2 cm). Philadelphia Museum of Art: the Louise and Walter Arensberg Collection, 1950.

subscribed. Conservative modernism did not shock; rather, it seemed fresh and suited to the vigor of modern life. The qualities associated with this strain of modernism included "simplification," "highly organized design," and a "sculpturesque rather than naturalistic" quality.[10]

St. Louis's preference for moderation was evident in a poll taken during the St. Louis showing of the Foreign Section of the 1930 Carnegie International Exhibition of Paintings, the country's premier exhibition of international contemporary art. Voters gave first place to the fashionable Polish modernist Tamara de Lempicka for her striking depiction of the French microbiologist Pierre Boucard, entitled *Portrait of Dr. B.* (fig. 4).[11] Reviewers identified her style as "modern classicism" and "conservative modern." Rogers declared, "The voting shows St. Louisans appreciate the modern quality in art." But he noted, significantly, "None of the extremely radical pictures have been given public approval."[12]

Although the terms modern classicism and conservative modern conveniently categorized Lempicka's work, St. Louis critics did not consistently invoke these labels to describe moderate forms of modernism, nor did

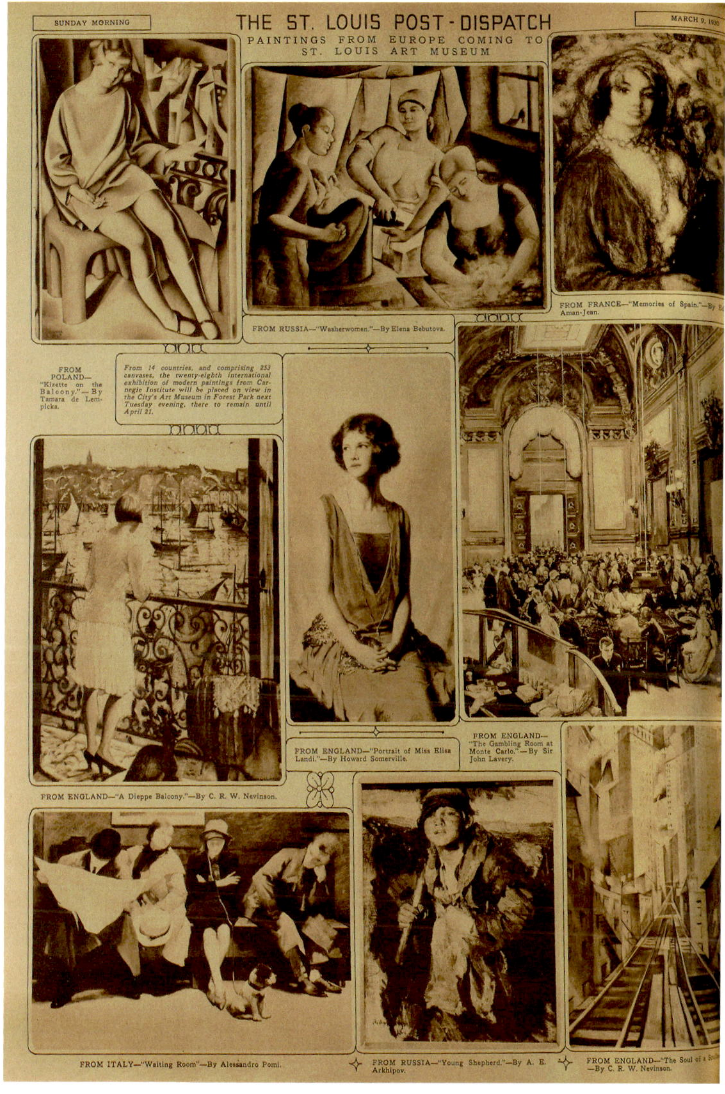

SUNDAY MORNING

THE ST. LOUIS POST-DISPATCH

MARCH 9, 1930

PAINTINGS FROM EUROPE COMING TO ST. LOUIS ART MUSEUM

FROM RUSSIA—"Washerwomen."—By Elena Bebutova.

FROM FRANCE—"Memories of Spain."—By Ed Aman-Jean.

FROM POLAND—"Kizette on the Balcony."—By Tamara de Lempicka.

From 14 countries, and comprising 253 canvases, the twenty-eighth international exhibition of modern paintings from Carnegie Institute will be placed on view in the City's Art Museum in Forest Park next Tuesday evening, there to remain until April 21.

FROM ENGLAND—"Portrait of Miss Elisa Landi."—By Howard Somerville.

FROM ENGLAND—"The Gambling Room at Monte Carlo."—By Sir John Lavery.

FROM ENGLAND—"A Dieppe Balcony."—By C. R. W. Nevinson.

FROM ITALY—"Waiting Room"—By Alessandro Pomi.

FROM RUSSIA—"Young Shepherd."—By A. E. Arkhipov.

FROM ENGLAND—"The Soul of a S…—By C. R. W. Nevinson.

Fig. 3. "Paintings from Europe Coming to St. Louis Art Museum," *St. Louis Post-Dispatch*, March 9, 1930. This page reproduces works from the 1930 Carnegie International Exhibition, including, at top left, one by Tamara de Lempicka.

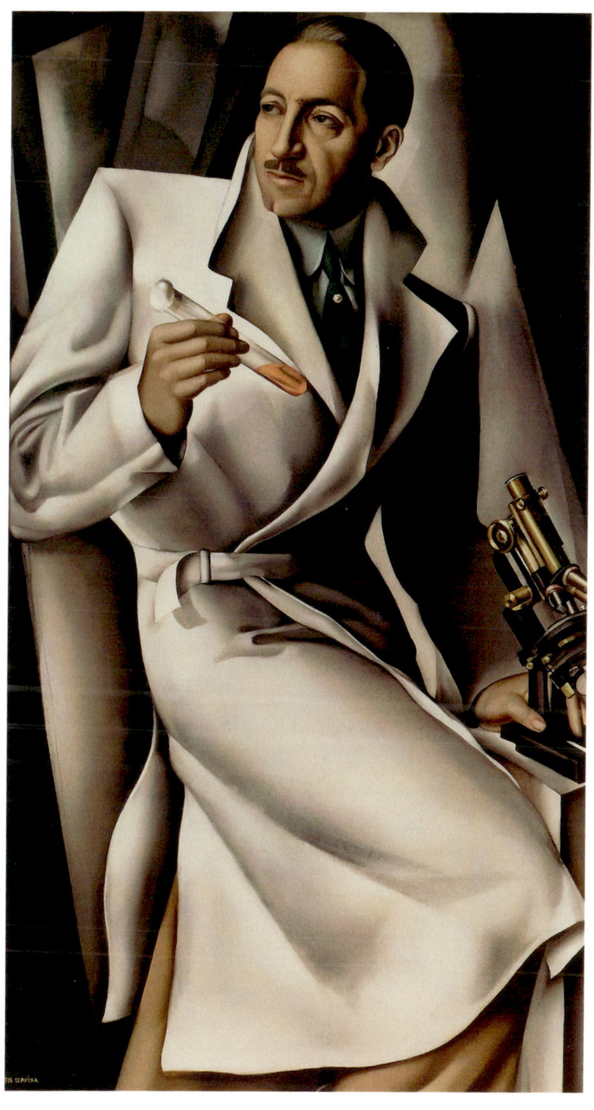

Fig. 4. Tamara de Lempicka (Polish; 1898–1980). *Portrait of Dr. B.*, 1928. Oil on canvas; 53⅛ × 29½ in. (135 × 75 cm). Private collection, Salzburg.

they use a specific vocabulary to refer to the "extremely radical pictures" Rogers cited. Instead, they typically employed hyphenated phrases, descriptions, references to imagined audience responses, and hyperbolic imagery to differentiate between tempered and extreme forms of modernism.

This can be seen in critics' responses to local exhibitions, in which they echoed public opinion on the superiority of conservative versions of modernism. For example, a 1930 installation of American art at the City Art Museum was praised for presenting "a thought-provoking collection of pictures rather than a startling one."[13] "Modernism sits in a high place," a second critic wrote, ". . . but there are no what-is-it paintings."[14] Works that seemed too extreme or "grotesque" were ridiculed. Writers invented examples to emphasize the absurdity they saw in modern art. A *St. Louis Post-Dispatch* reviewer referred to "pinwheels and guitars floating in lurid space."[15] The reviewer for the *St. Louis Star-Times* imagined an extremely radical picture with "rampant curlicues and half a lady's leg in a field of asparagus."[16]

EARLY EDUCATION

Jones would have been aware of the limitations of local taste for modern art. Thus it is not surprising that, from early on in his career, he worked in a reductive but representational manner that he seems to have deliberately selected to appeal to his audience.[17] In fact, before 1930, when he took his first major steps toward an art career (see fig. 5 and cat. 3), he had already experimented with and rejected several styles.

In the early 1920s, a young Jones drew a naturalistic scene of a St. Louis neighborhood (Chronology, fig. 2) and copied images he saw in magazines and advertisements.[18] In 1927, while working as a housepainter with his father, Jones enrolled in some decorative-painting classes, possibly at the nearby David Ranken, Jr., School of Mechanical Trades.[19] Surviving sketches by Jones of decorative motifs (see Chronology, fig. 3) dating from this time conform to the lessons outlined in the course description in the school's 1927–28 catalogue. A photograph in the catalogue shows students decorating a ceiling with motifs similar to those Jones sketched. Ranken students also learned lettering and "styles of alphabets," which interested Jones as he refined his signature throughout the early years of his career (see Signature Analysis).[20] Jones's sketches demonstrate that he was conversant with the illusionistic effects decorative painting demanded and adept at using highlights and shading to suggest volume and depth.

Around 1928/29 Jones executed his first self-portrait, *Self-Portrait of the Artist at Age Nineteen* (cat. 1). Its pronounced impasto, visible brushwork, and strong color indicate that Jones might have been familiar with the art of Post-Impressionists such as Vincent van Gogh, then still considered a modernist by many Americans. But by the time he was ready to exhibit in earnest, Jones's art reflected an entirely different type of currency.

MODERN IDENTITY

The formal approach Jones embraced from 1930 through 1933 is embodied in his 1932 painting *Industrial Landscape* (cat. 19). This work shows a complex of factory buildings and tanks defined by simplified planes and shapes in contrasting tones. The featureless surfaces are rendered sculpturesque by the absence of fine detail or texture, and the rooflines and swirling ridges of the landscape are depicted in a distorted perspective.

Jones also spoke about himself and his art as rejecting academic tradition and embracing individualism. He

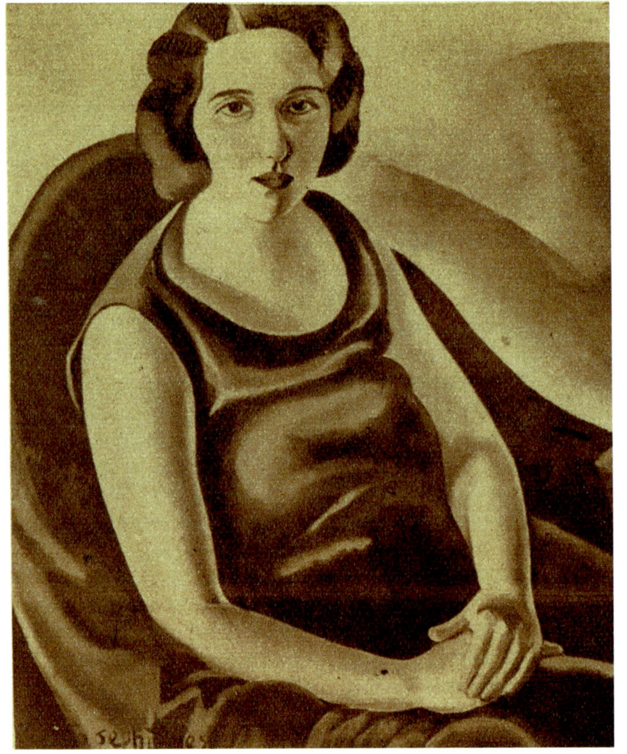

Fig. 5. Joe Jones, *Marg* (or *Maarg*), 1930. Location unknown. Reproduced in the *St. Louis Post-Dispatch*, December 21, 1930.

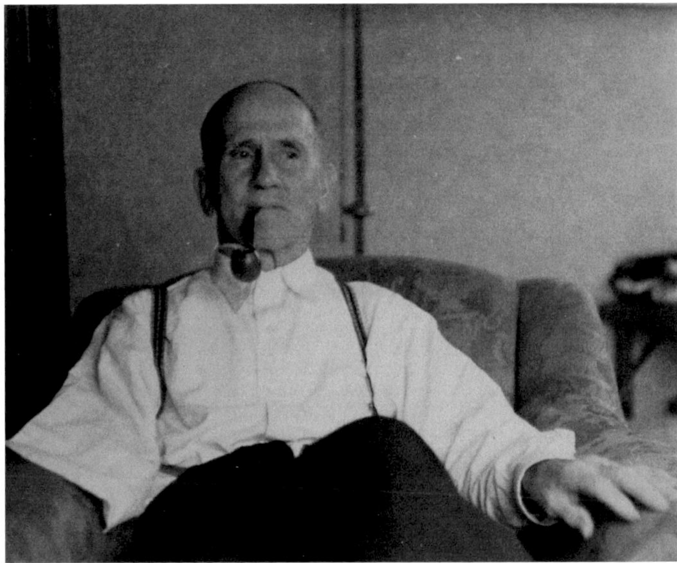

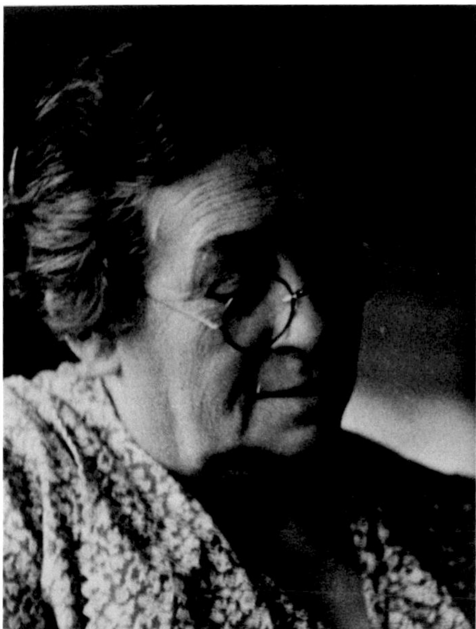

Fig. 6. Frank Jones, father of the artist, c. 1932. Courtesy of James and Karen Jones.

Fig. 7. Anna Jones, mother of the artist, c. 1932. Courtesy of James and Karen Jones.

emphasized the influence of modern art on his work and associated himself with like-minded artists. A June 14, 1931, article was the first to chronicle Jones and his story. A full-page feature including large illustrations of five of his paintings, as well as a photograph of him posed in his studio before *Aspirations* (location unknown; see Chronology, fig. 1), the article must have been a breakout moment for the fledgling artist. Perhaps it served as the impetus for Jones's first one-person show just a few months later. He revealed to his interviewer, Guy Forshey, that an exhibition of modern art had inspired him to paint in the first place; modernism "seemed to offer an opportunity for free expression. It chucked overboard all of the old rules and restrictions of academicians." Further emphasizing his individuality and his distance from academic training, Jones explained that he was self-taught. He said he was glad he had not attended art school, declaring, "When I set out to paint a picture . . . I don't have to remember a lot of rules. . . . I don't have to say . . . 'so and so told me to do it this way.' I am painting to please myself."[21]

Jones elaborated on this point in a 1932 interview about a series of family portraits, including ones of his father and mother (see figs. 6–7; cats. 27–28). He used the portrait of his father as an example of how he "violates accepted rules in painting to please himself." Some criticized it for the absence of a central focus, in accordance with conventional practice. Instead, "the composition revolves about an empty corner . . . the eye of the observer is led into the corner and left there with nothing of particular interest to fasten upon." Jones argued that "the eye does not . . . need any central object to fasten upon because it is caught up . . . by the swing of the circular composition."[22]

In the fall of 1931, Jones became a founding member of a new group dedicated to modern art. The first of its kind in St. Louis, the New Hats consisted of eight artists (including two who would buy his work, Sarah Bloom and Jessie Beard Rickly), two honorary members (Lisbeth Ebers Hoops and Walter Hoops, who would also support him), and one associate. Unlike larger organizations, such as the St. Louis Artists' Guild and the Independent Artists of St. Louis, the New Hats was a select assembly, devoted specifically to encouraging and publicizing contemporary "liberal" trends in art in the Midwest. These goals were to be achieved through exhibitions of members' work and biweekly sketching classes. The name New Hats was apparently selected to underscore the group's opposition to "old hat" art.[23] Conservative art columnist Emily Grant

Hutchings wryly surmised that the term "old hat" applied "when you can guess what the artist had in mind" and covered "practically all the art of the past 500 years."[24] Indeed, the New Hats sought to distinguish their work from art of the past, which they dismissed as dated and unoriginal. By joining the New Hats, Jones allied himself with local devotees of modern art.

RECOGNITION AS MODERN

Writers and critics responding to Jones's work acknowledged him as a "thorough modernist," both explicitly and by drawing to the fore the correlation between his art practice and the traits associated with modern—especially conservative modern—art.[25] According to Forshey, *Marg* (fig. 5), the painting that won Jones his first cash prize, in December 1930, sparked "much notice and controversy," but both admirers and critics of the work recognized it as modern. Admirers found it "a bold canvas done in modern style . . . [with] fine simplicity of design, . . . direct, frank, and bold treatment, . . . representing a fresh and original point of view." Detractors, Forshey continued, objected to the painting's rounded, sculpturesque forms and lack of prettiness, and found it "well, just too modern."[26]

Forshey noted Jones's independence from tradition and his individualistic pursuit of self-expression: "[If] his method does not agree with established rule and precedent then let rule and precedent go hang. . . . Every painting is a new experiment. He is working out his own manner of expression, unhampered by tradition." Forshey praised the formal features that distinguished Jones's painting at this time: "bold, sweeping outlines and a disregard for details of texture, . . . simplicity and strength."[27] He could have been describing *Tower Tops* (c. 1931; cat. 8), which was reproduced in the article. This painting—a view of rooftops from the artist's garage studio on Lindell Boulevard—is an arrangement of the strong, simplified shapes of chimneys and spires, raking rooflines, and the large arc of the city cathedral's dome. The forms are unified not only by this geometry but by the smooth, textureless surfaces throughout. It is as if the artist had been trying to follow Cézanne's famous precept of reducing nature to "the cylinder, the sphere, and the cone."[28]

In November 1931, Jones's first solo show took place at a non-traditional venue, the School of Dancing and Modern Body Culture owned by New Hats member Lisbeth Ebers Hoops, a practitioner of "the Modern Art dance."[29] Jones may have met her through his first wife, Freda Sies (fig. 8), who was also interested in aesthetic dance (although no record of her studying with Madame Hoops can be found).[30] Jones displayed twenty-five paintings, including portraits of family members and patrons, industrial scenes and cityscapes, and four images of Freda. These included *Nude with Red Robe* (c. 1931; location unknown), *Nude Reclining* (1931; cat. 12), and *Freda* (1931; cat. 14). She also served as the model for *Nude* (1931; cat. 13), one of three lithographs in the show (see also cats. 10–11).

Carl Benn, reviewer for the *St. Louis Art World*, found the works in Jones's solo debut appealingly restrained and reasonably modern. Benn characterized his art as "modern in the sense that there are bold contrasts, that design is emphasized," but, he qualified, Jones did "not resort to primitive grotesqueness and senseless distortion." Nor did he resort to the "tricks, inherited in bygone days by disciples of the academic." Benn quoted Jones, who could see no reason "for anything other than

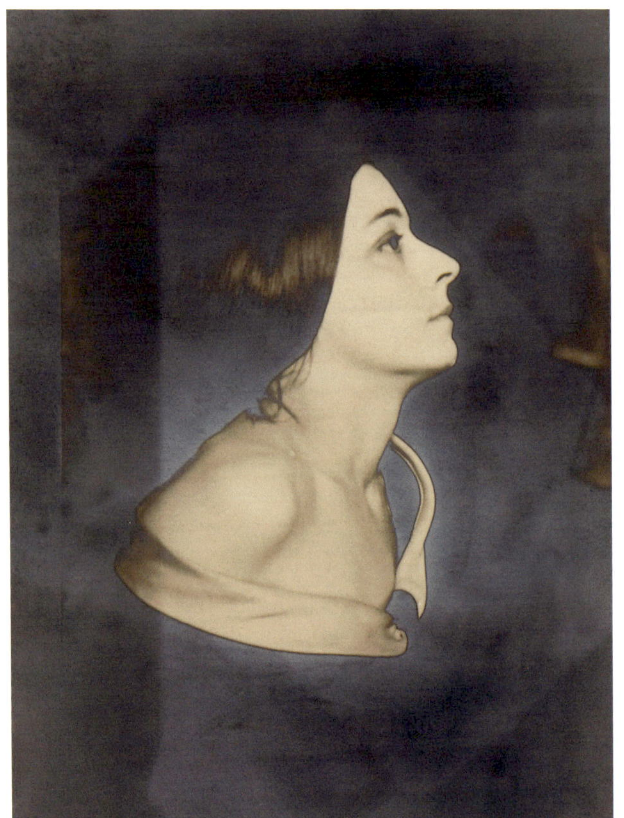

Fig. 8. Freda Sies Jones, first wife of the artist, c. 1932. Courtesy of James and Karen Jones.

a three dimensional composition of forms and color in rhythm, whether it is a study of an ash pit or a likeness of Lady Astor." In *Mrs. Thomas B. Sherman* (1931; cat. 5), in particular, rhythm plays a key role. Chloe Sherman sits quietly, her expression one of unruffled composure, while the zippy pattern on her jacket seems to vibrate in frenetic zigzags of blue. In the lithograph *Laclede Christy Clay Co.* (c. 1931; cat. 11), the stark, assertive verticals of the smokestacks stand out against the curved ridges of earth, the cubistic buildings, and the faceted foliage of the trees. As Benn observed, Jones was able to capture "the attractive forces which an industrial plant offers . . . and yet bring out a definite design . . . carried out in sheer simplicity."[31]

In 1932 Jones's work received official and widely publicized sanction as modern when the St. Louis Artists' Guild jury awarded the $100 Otto L. Spaeth Prize for Modern Painting to one of his still lifes (unidentified).[32] Jones (now calling himself Joe rather than Joseph) held his second one-person show in 1933 at a more conventional venue, the St. Louis Artists' Guild Hall. Benn reviewed this exhibition too, declaring that Jones's work proved false the opinion, apparently offered by a national critic, that the year 1932 had marked the death of modern art. Benn admired the artist's "interpretation in harmonious passages of contrasting tones, with a striving for the utmost simplicity and solidity of forms and masses [that] bring to his work the message of the technological age in which we live." This style, Benn understood, opposed the naturalistic approach of more tradition-bound artists who resorted to "all the artifices of the nineteenth century to obtain representation of romantic subjects in a photographic manner."[33]

Benn singled out as particularly outstanding *Miss Elizabeth Stix* (c. 1933; cat. 29) and *Studio Interior* (c. 1932; cat. 22). In the former, Jones employed a limited palette, with the harmonious contrasts that Benn had commented on. The sitter's pale arm, hands, and face stand out against the dark contours of her hair and dress, and the abstracted, sinuous forms of the background. In this portrait, Jones eschewed texture: the sitter's hair and skin, the folds of her dress, and the background elements appear equally smooth and sculpturesque and, therefore, abstracted.

The ambitious *Studio Interior*, which Jones also reproduced as a lithograph (1932; cat. 21), exhibits a complexity and dynamism that make it the zenith of Jones's engagement with the brand of modernism that absorbed him during these years. In the foreground is the ostensible subject, Freda Jones sleeping so deeply and heavily that she seems to have become one with the mattress and sheets on which she lies. But, primarily, the painting demonstrates Jones's facility with visual play and formal structure. A large mirror on the far wall reflects Freda's back, which appears in much higher relief across the bed than in the view from the front. The mirror expands the studio as it shows the opposite side of the room, where artist and viewer stand. A sliver of window visible in the mirror seems to open the space even more, but is in fact behind the viewer. The artist's *Nude Reclining*, for which Freda also posed, hangs over the bed and serves as a second mirror. In both the painting and the painting within the painting, Freda lies on her stomach, with one arm folded at her chest and the other at her head. *Nude Reclining* appears in the wall mirror as well, allowing the viewer to see the left edge of the composition, which is not visible in the view of the studio. Next to *Nude Reclining* hangs one of Jones's still lifes, a painting of drapery swirled around a table. This resonates with one of the focal points of *Studio Interior*: the elaborate ripples and folds of the blankets on the bed.

In her review of the show, Hutchings noted the works' "decidedly modernistic twist." She saw in Jones's art the influence of "the opponents of 'Naturalism,'" those "devotees of tipped perspective, strident color and [deliberately] incorrect drawing."[34] Hutchings may have been reacting to *Still Life with Mallard Wing* (fig. 9), in which the top of a stool angles toward the viewer. A critic for the *St. Louis Post-Dispatch* noticed Jones's tipped perspective as well, describing the "table top, aslant" in *Still Life with Atlas* (see fig. 10).[35]

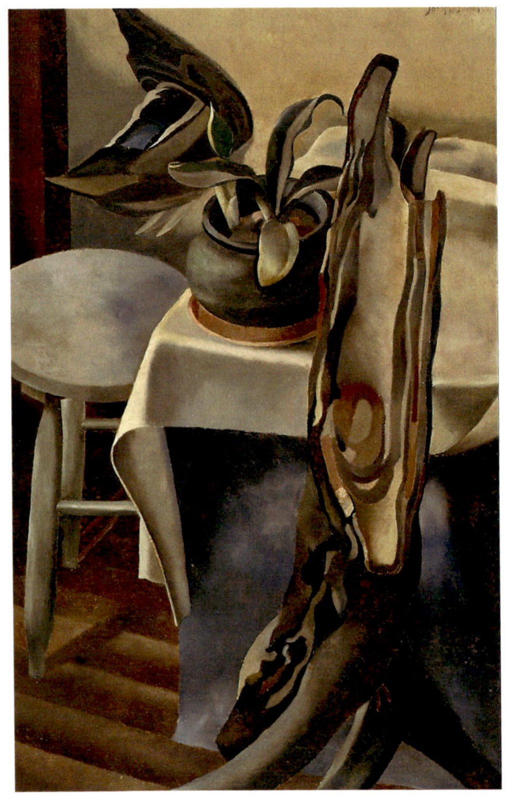

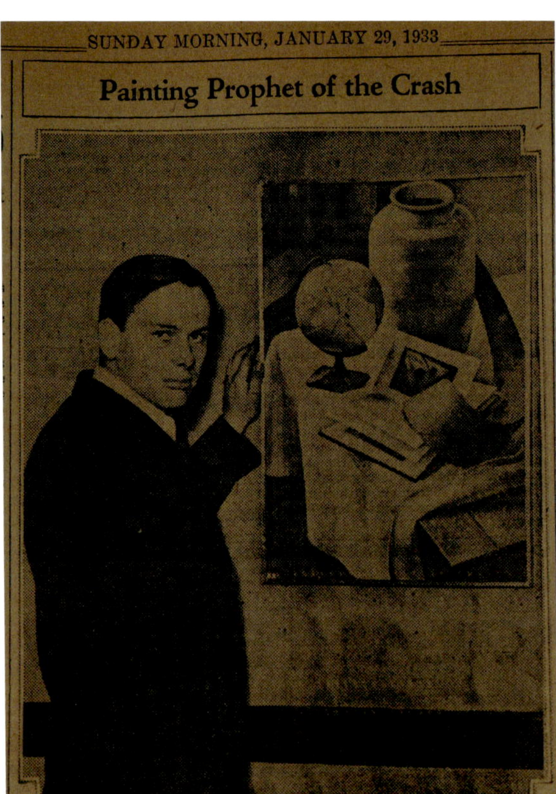

SUNDAY MORNING, JANUARY 29, 1933

Painting Prophet of the Crash

Fig. 9. Joe Jones, *Still Life with Mallard Wing*, c. 1933. Oil on canvas; 40 × 24 in. (101.6 × 61 cm). Photograph courtesy of Ivey-Selkirk Auctioneers, St. Louis.

Fig. 10. "Painting Prophet of the Crash," *St. Louis Post-Dispatch*, January 29, 1933. This clipping shows Jones standing before his *Still Life with Atlas* (location unknown). Courtesy of the *St. Louis Post-Dispatch*.

FOLLOWING AN AUDIENCE FAVORITE

Between the execution of his c. 1928/29 self-portrait and the 1930 Artists' Guild prize, Jones would see modern artists with a similar approach to representation receiving the kind of accolades he desired. One of them was Lempicka. Although she was not unique in her use of hard-edged, reductive forms and smooth surfaces, her particular prominence in St. Louis at the moment Jones was launching his career makes her sleek, striking formalism a likely influence on the young artist.[36] While Jones's exposure to the art of the Polish painter cannot be documented before 1932 (when he wrote a review in which he called her "the most progressive of Polish artists"[37]), he almost certainly visited the immensely popular 1930 Carnegie show, which set a museum record with over 51,000 visitors, and read the extensive local news coverage of Lempicka and her work (see fig. 3).[38]

Jones's portraits exhibit some of the qualities evident in Lempicka's art. The most striking similarity between two early examples by Jones, *Bessie* (1930; cat. 3) and *Grace* (1931; cat. 4), and Lempicka's *Portrait of Dr. B.* is the treatment of surfaces—whether hair, flesh, or fabric—as smooth, untextured, and hard-edged. And like Lempicka, Jones used abstract backgrounds to frame his subjects. In *Bessie* the sitter is bordered by curving echoes of the line of her shoulder and the flare of her sleeve. In *Grace* angular shapes fan out behind the figure of amateur historian Grace Lewis Miller. In all three portraits, the play of angles and planes both unites figure and background and demarcates one from the other. Finally, although *Portrait of Dr. B.* presents a more elaborate and masterful handling of contrasts than *Grace*, it seems that Jones emulated Lempicka's use of strong light and shadow to define the folds and edges of fabric in this work.

MIRIAM MCKINNIE

Like Jones, the artist Miriam McKinnie became known in St. Louis for her moderate modernism. From nearby

Edwardsville, Illinois, McKinnie was, for several years, a step ahead of Jones in establishing a local reputation. She exhibited at the St. Louis Artists' Guild the year before Jones, winning a modern-art prize three years before he did.[39] When Jones first submitted work to the St. Louis Artists' Guild show in 1930, McKinnie's street scene took the top award for best work of art, an honor Jones would receive in 1933.[40] McKinnie considered "simplicity of mass, color, and design" to be the driving force of her work, saying that it "comes under the general classification of modernism" and that she was "striving chiefly to create the illusion of reality without being photographic."[41] Like Jones, McKinnie was a member of the New Hats, and their work was paired more than once in discussions of the St. Louis art world.[42] In fact they worked in similar styles, both favoring clean lines, gradations of shading, and simplified planes. Comparison of two of McKinnie's paintings, *Commerce* and *Mill at Alton* (figs. 11–12), with works like Jones's *Industrial Landscape*, *View of St. Louis* (c. 1932; cat. 24), and *St. Louis Riverfront* (c. 1932; cat. 17) demonstrates the striking overlaps in their themes and approaches, suggesting McKinnie's possible influence on Jones. In his *View of St. Louis*, showing the Eads Bridge tunnel, Jones depicted an industrial scene and a series of blocky buildings in a reductive, stylized manner.[43] Many of these elements appear in McKinnie's *Commerce*. Both artists selected an area where the ground was dug up in order to lay railroad tracks and accommodate the transportation of industrial materials. Jones's view is from a low point, on level with the train tunnel, so that the buildings tower above, while McKinnie adopted an elevated perspective so that the roof planes function as part of the design. Both artists also represented factories and the riverfront with its attendant steamboats and bridges; their compositions similarly feature geometric forms, minimized details, and smooth surfaces. Jones's handling of landscape elements, especially in *Industrial Landscape*—using strong highlights and shadows that emphasize each rill and rise in the earth—resembles McKinnie's treatment of similar subjects in *Commerce* and *Mill at Alton*.

RESONANCE WITH OTHER AMERICAN MODERNISTS

Between 1931 and 1932, Jones produced a number of land- and cityscapes that suggest an awareness of the work of various prominent American modernists. The largest of these, *Wooded Landscape* (1931; cat. 6), was

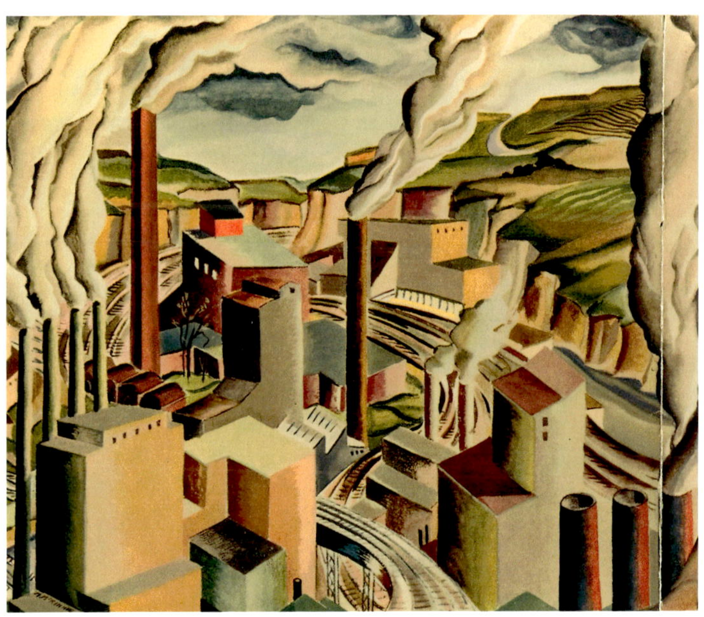

Fig. 11. Miriam McKinnie (1906–1987). *Commerce* (date and location unknown). Reproduced in an advertisement for West Virginia Pulp and Paper Company. Courtesy of the St. Louis Public Library.

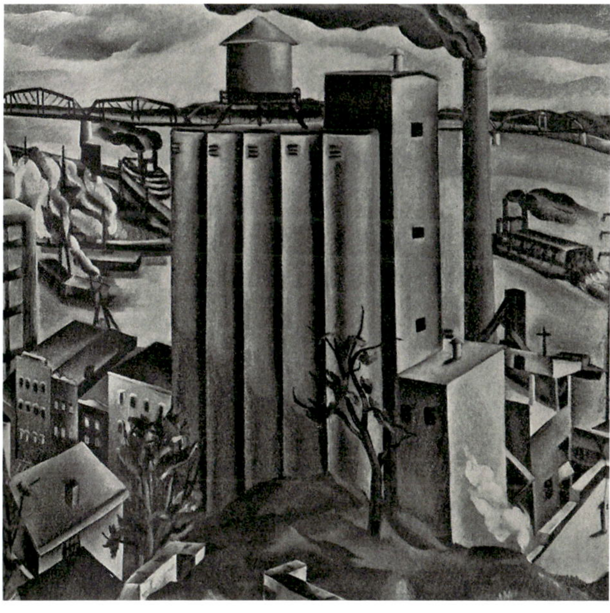

Fig. 12. Miriam McKinnie. *Mill at Alton* (date and location unknown). Reproduced in *Magazine of Art* 28, 8 (August 1935), p. 485.

commissioned for the living room of Elsie Rauh, wife of Aaron Rauh, president of the dry-goods company Rice-Stix. Another landscape (1932; cat. 16) was acquired by Erma Stix, a friend of the Rauhs and sponsor of a St. Louis Artists' Guild modern-art prize.[44] The Rauh and Stix works, along with a third example (c. 1931; cat. 15), share several formal elements: the foliage lies heavily on the architecture of the trees, like sloping rooftops, and simplified trunks and branches seem almost polished smooth, with swells of earth at the bases of the trees. The compositions' components are further defined by a dynamic play of color and alternating lights and darks that combine to create pattern and a sense of movement.

These compositions evoke contemporaneous work by Georgia O'Keeffe, whose popularity was sometimes attributed to the temperate version of modernism she embraced, which made her art accessible and appealing.[45] O'Keeffe depicted abstracted plant forms and sharply delineated landscape elements, and preferred a smooth articulation of forms (see fig. 13). Jones might have known of O'Keeffe's art through magazines, which he later credited for providing much of his information about other artists during his Missouri years. But Jones also encountered O'Keeffe's work in the collection of his patron Marguerite Kauffman Fischel. She had owned O'Keeffe's *Shell and Old Shingle VI* since 1929, and around that time, the painting was on view at the City Art Museum, where it excited a great deal of interest and discussion.[46] Several years later, Jones restored the painting for Fischel.[47] In addition, since 1926 Jones's patrons Erma and Ernest W. Stix had owned O'Keeffe's *Birch Trees at Dawn on Lake George* (fig. 14), which he could have seen in their home.[48] *Birch Trees* focuses on a cluster of monumental trunks that seem to bend and extend in arabesques as they fan out from the center of the composition's lower edge. The careful rendering of forms, outlined with dark edges and shadows, and the use of color gradations to build a sense of volume appear to have impacted Jones's *Wooded Landscape*. Here the groupings of trees with three light-pink trunks at left, in the middle ground and background, practically quote O'Keeffe's birch tree trunks.

O'Keeffe's landscape and flower paintings have long been associated with the human figure.[49] Jones's land-scapes evoke similar associations with the body, as well as with other living forms. In the Stix composition, for

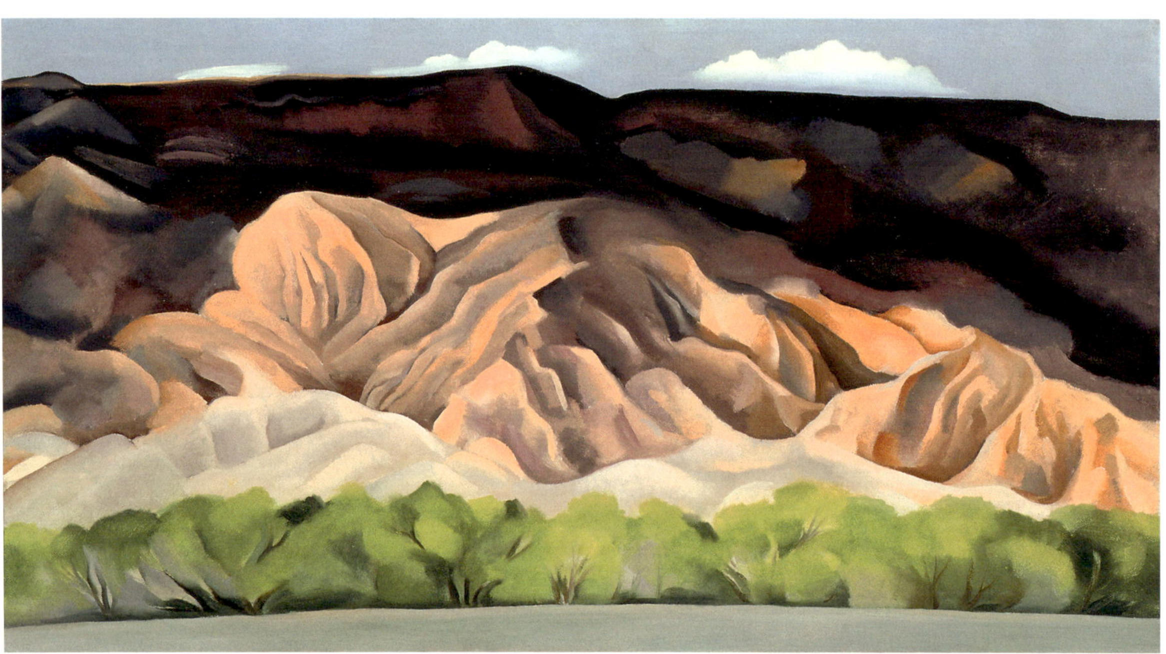

Fig. 13. Georgia O'Keeffe (1887–1986). *Back of Marie's No. 4*, 1931. Oil on canvas; 16 × 30 in. (40.6 × 76.2 cm). Georgia O'Keeffe Museum, Gift of the Burnett Foundation.

example, the contours of the earth might easily be read as soft folds of flesh.[50] The boneless forms of the trees in the Rauh canvas resemble marine organisms. And the stump in *Landscape*, with its curving roots, suggests a sea creature brushing the ocean floor. The visual conflation of landscape and flesh is reversed in Jones's 1931 *Nude Reclining*. The painting depicts a prone Freda lying on layers of brown blankets, near two green cushions, her head on a low pillow. However, the texture and creases of the folded green cushions are akin to those of the shrubbery in the Stix *Landscape*, and their conical shape is congruent with that of the evergreen tree in *Landscape* (cat. 15). Additionally, Freda's hand is as smooth and boneless as the tree trunks in the landscapes, and the tipped-up perspective, combined with the layers of blankets, produces a high, ridged horizon, evoking a mountain range.

In approach and content, Jones's work of this period also resembles that of a group of modern artists now known as precisionists.[51] The precisionists were not affiliated with one another, but shared a purist style characterized by simplification and crisp geometric forms influenced by the "mechanization [and] standardization" of the Machine Age.[52] Louis Lozowick (see fig. 15) and Charles Sheeler (see fig. 16), among others, regularly portrayed depopulated industrial sites and urban views, carefully and elegantly composed. (Works by Lozowick in particular appeared regularly at the City Art Museum.[53]) Their art was recognized in subsequent decades as achieving a balance between abstraction and realism.[54]

Jones also favored uninhabited factory views; he portrayed the Laclede Christy Clay Company in various media and exhibited images of the facility at least four times between 1930 and 1933 (see cat. 11). He painted other industrial facilities as well, such as the Missouri Portland and Alpha Portland Cement companies and the group of buildings and tanks seen in *Industrial Landscape* and *Coal Sheds* (c. 1931; cat. 9). He repeatedly turned to views of St. Louis, representing its skyscrapers, warehouses, garages, and freight-train tracks. Like Lozowick and Sheeler, Jones reduced skyscrapers, smokestacks, warehouses, and factories to meticulously defined planes and geometric volumes, eliminated texture and details, and emphasized pattern. This can be seen in Jones's 1931 mural for the reception room of the KMOX radio station (see Chronology, fig. 4), as well as in *Alley* (1932; cat. 23), with its planar garage doors, walls, and fences; and in *View of St. Louis*, with its repeated configurations of tracks, iron railings, and railroad ties. *St. Louis Riverfront*, exhibiting a sophisticated combination of vertical and diagonal forms, possesses these qualities as well. Jones's use of a familiar style associated with Precisionism was so recognizable that in 1933 Benn wrote about him in terms that could as easily be applied to its practitioners: "[Jones is] striving for the utmost simplicity and solidity of forms and masses [which] bring to his work the message of the technological age in which we live."[55]

SUPPORTIVE COMMUNITIES

Jones's art drew the support of a series of communities in St. Louis. The artist's first backers were his bohemian friends, writers and artists who frequented a makeshift café near the riverfront, the Blue Lantern Inn (see Wolfe, fig. 1). They published a literary magazine called *Vagaries*,

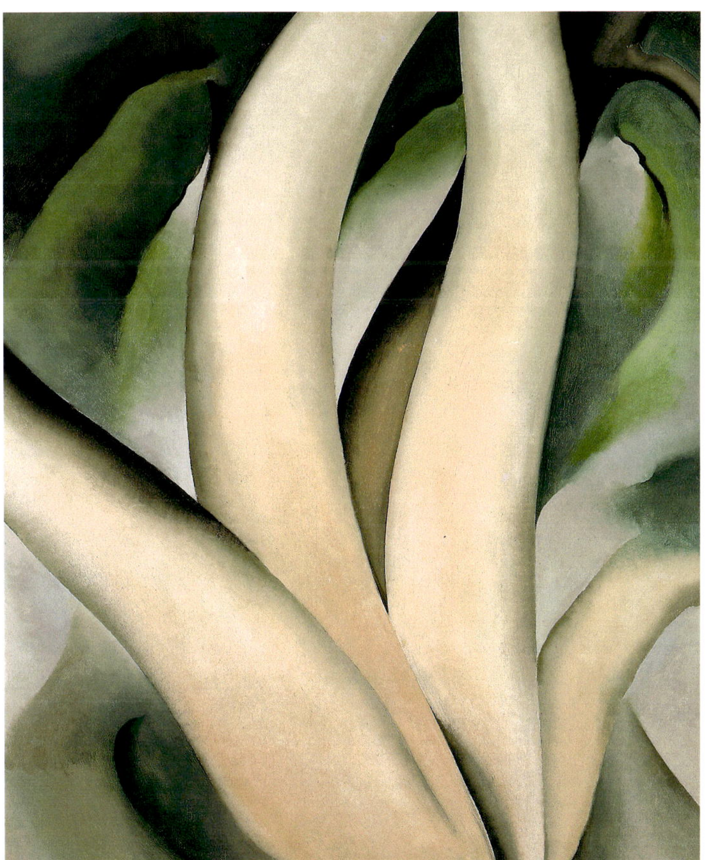

Fig. 14. Georgia O'Keeffe. *Birch Trees at Dawn on Lake George*, 1925. Oil on canvas; 36 × 30 in. (91.4 × 76.2 cm). Saint Louis Art Museum, Gift of Mrs. Ernest W. Stix.

threw fancy-dress balls, and wrote ballads about the inn. Jones's economic difficulties in the early 1930s bonded him with others who saw poverty as a stimulus for pursuing an artistic life. He resided in a series of apartments across the city, including one in a warehouse and another in or above a garage, before eventually moving to a houseboat on the river to cut costs.[56] His lack of instruction in these years affected his art, and many of his earliest paintings suffer from flaking and instability. Jones's identity as a struggling, self-taught artist naturally drew the sympathies of a group of individuals who styled themselves on the cover of an issue of *Vagaries* as youthful ruffians riding a cloud of art, music, and literature while thumbing their noses at a crowd of wealthy people below. Jones's camaraderie with this bohemian cohort continued even as he moved into the limelight. Herbert Friesen, a friend whose name appeared with Jones's on the magazine's "Roll of Scribes" (list of contributors) was a lender to the artist's 1931 first solo exhibition. Friesen's brother Paul bought a work from that show.[57]

Jones's 1931 exhibition caught the attention of art-world insiders as well. Meyric Rogers acquired Jones's *Nude with Red Robe* for his private collection. Rogers became the young artist's advocate after this, advising him as he searched for a New York gallery, writing the preface to the catalogue for his first New York show, and serving as a reference when he applied for a Guggenheim fellowship. The hosts of Jones's first solo foray, Lisbeth Ebers Hoops and her husband, Walter Hoops, were also lenders to the event. The couple was deeply engaged in St. Louis's cultural scene. Madame Hoops, as she was called, was a performer and instructor of dance; her husband managed an arts center that provided local artists with studio and exhibition space. Artists Sarah Bloom and Jessie Beard Rickly purchased work from the 1931 exhibition as well. In addition, Tanasko Milovich, a leading local painter who was president of the Independent Artists of St. Louis, acquired *Studio Interior*.[58]

Jones and his art also interested a number of comfortably middle-class and affluent St. Louisans who were culturally progressive and active in the city's arts circles. Among them was Chloe Sherman, who lent her portrait to Jones's solo debut. Sherman served as the associate editor of the liberal *Saint Louis Review*, one of several arts periodicals that flourished and faded in the city between 1930 and 1933. The review's editorial-board members stated that they chose to found their journal "in the toils of this depression" because they felt the economic climate created a new openness to questioning the status quo, an openness that, in their opinion, was no longer linked solely with socialists or Bolsheviks.[59] The journal published articles as well as short notices on a range of

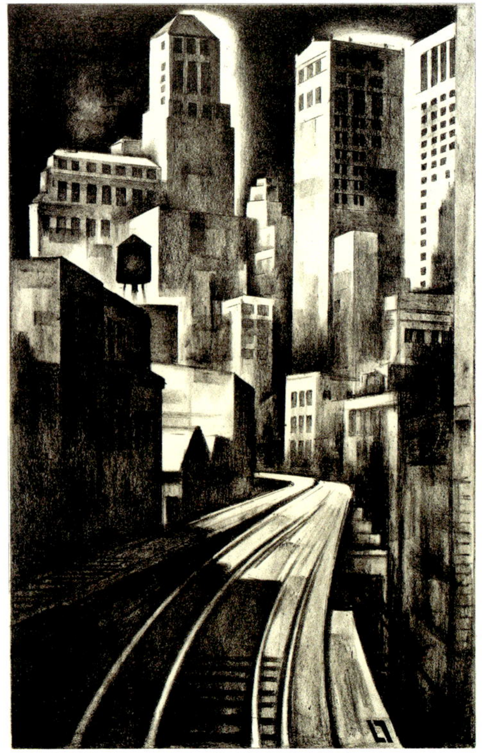

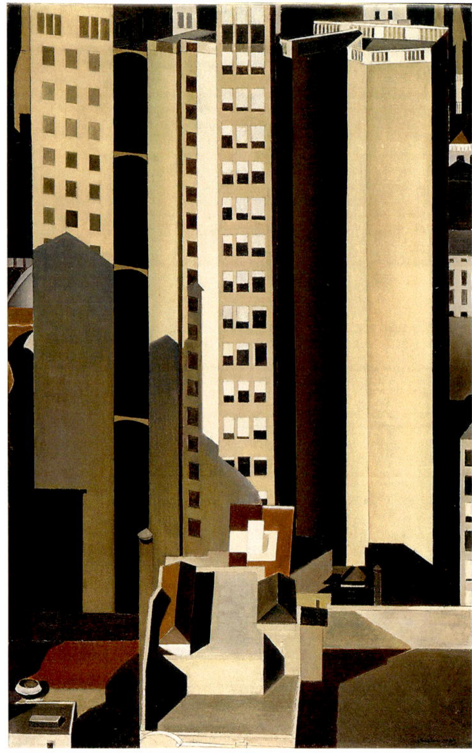

Fig. 15. Louis Lozowick (1892–1973). *Third Avenue (Third Avenue El)*, 1929. Lithograph; 12⅜ × 8 in. (31.3 × 20.2 cm). Smithsonian American Art Museum, Gift of Adele Lozowick.

Fig. 16. Charles Sheeler (1883–1965). *Skyscrapers*, 1922. Oil on canvas; 20 × 13 in. (50.8 × 33 cm). The Phillips Collection, Washington, D.C.

subjects, from political radio broadcasts and art exhibitions to the Socialist Party and the founding of the local chapter of the Communist-based John Reed Club (see Balken). The *Saint Louis Review* steadfastly endorsed Jones and his work. Even though the magazine's premiere issue appeared in March 1932, Jones's November 1931 solo was the first exhibition addressed, and it was described as "one of the most exciting of the season."[60] In subsequent issues, the *Saint Louis Review* reported on more of Jones's shows (at one point illustrating his work above the headline "American Masters"). It even asserted that the existence of the St. Louis Artists' Guild was justified by the fact that the organization drew attention to him. Jones served the journal as a reviewer of gallery exhibitions as well.[61]

In addition to Sherman's involvement with the *Saint Louis Review*, she and her husband, Thomas, collected work by European modernists such as Gino Severini and Maurice de Vlaminck.[62] The couple lived in a house designed and outfitted by two local modernists, architect Frederick Dunn and designer Victor Proetz.[63] Their home and its furnishings combined modern and conventional elements, corresponding to the conservative modernism of Jones's work. Indeed, Meyric Rogers, in a book on interior design, described the Shermans' residence as integrating traditional elements into a "conservative contemporary design."[64]

PROGRESSION TO POLITICAL ENGAGEMENT

The support Jones received from various segments of the St. Louis community endured until he turned his attention to politically charged subject matter. Later in the summer of 1933, he declared himself a Communist. From this point on, press coverage of his work dealt more and more with his radical beliefs. Jones's shift in theme actually dates to early 1933, when he mounted his second solo show, at the St. Louis Artists' Guild. Jones included in it several depictions of workers, "sad-eyed men and women who have labored much, and suffered much," as one writer observed.[65] Another noted that these figures seemed to have experienced "a hard struggle, a resignation, a frustration."[66]

In the context of these images of working-class suffering, the critic for the *St. Louis Post-Dispatch* considered the still lifes Jones included in the exhibition in a similar light. Reproducing an image of Jones with his *Still Life with Atlas* under the headline "Painting Prophet of the Crash" (fig. 10), the anonymous writer interpreted the tipped perspectives in these compositions as suggestive of social unrest. The article characterizes them as "cynical, hard-bitten effusions of one influenced deeply by the inequalities of modern social organization and keenly sympathetic with the struggles of the common man." The writer noted the instability in *Still Life with Atlas*, describing "the cover [of the table] sliding off, an atlas perched perilously near the edge. . . . The atlas needs only a slight jar to send it crashing, any sort of tug on the table would upset the whole business."[67] *Still Life with Mallard Wing* (fig. 9) exhibits the same qualities.[68] Here a stool seems to rest on just two legs, while the shading of the floorboards suggests a deeply grooved surface rather than a smooth one. The mallard wing floats at the upper left, its spatial relationship to the potted plant left ambiguous. One critic saw the rotted log, with its unresolved position, as another sign of Jones's desire to "symbolize the world upheaval he anticipates."[69] Extending nearly the entire height of the painting, the log teeters on uneven stumps, its open core revealing growth rings that dissolve into a pattern of lights and darks.

An article published in the *Post-Dispatch* at the time of the 1933 exhibition indicates that Jones did intend at least one of his still lifes to convey a philosophical message. In the piece, Jones discussed the meaning of a composition he was planning, a kind of alternative *vanitas* that would "depict the timelessness of things and their victory over ephemeral man."[70] The painting, *Still Life with Crystal* (1933; cat. 26), exhibits a palette similar to that of the still lifes in his Artists' Guild solo show, which a critic had described as having "nacreous whites [and] delicate blues and greens . . . with objects arranged in the spirit of a slow dance."[71] The painting features a fossilized fish and a seashell, as well as a book, open to two plates, one showing the ruin of a colonnaded classical building and the other a careful rendering of a modern skyscraper. Thus, on the

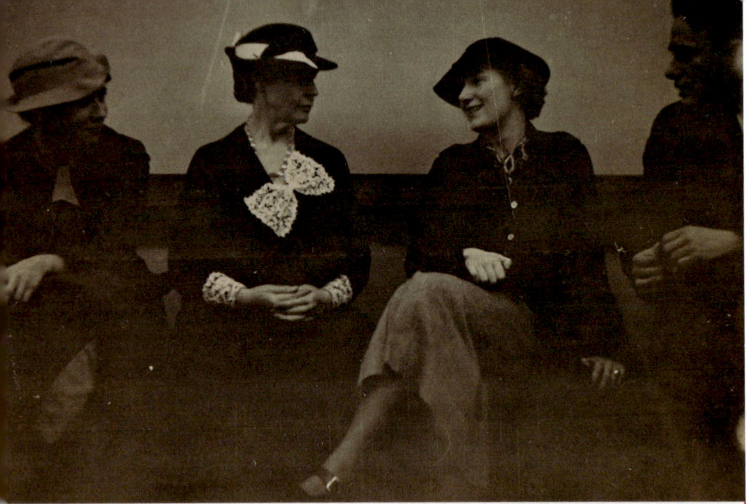

ELIZABETH GREEN (1878–1965)

Elizabeth Green, a prominent St. Louis arts patron, was Joe Jones's greatest supporter and close confidante. Though it remains unclear exactly when and how the two met, they knew each other well enough by May 1933 to travel together to the East Coast. Green would remain a central figure in Jones's life until after World War II.

Green supported Jones in myriad ways, funding his stay in Provincetown in the summer of 1933, purchasing magazine subscriptions for him, shipping works to New York at her expense, enlisting support for many of his endeavors, and lobbying vigorously to secure federal art commissions for him. Perhaps most important, though, was their friendship. At the most difficult moments in his career, Jones often turned to Green for advice and encouragement. He wrote to her almost daily at times. Their correspondence, in the Dr. John Green Collection at the Missouri History Museum, St. Louis, is the primary source for information on Jones's life and career.

Green and Jones did not see eye to eye on every issue. She was distressed by his embrace of Communism, which she believed stood in the way of his artistic development and success; and she did not approve of his public involvement with a married woman, Grace Adams Mallinckrodt, who eventually became his second wife. Nonetheless, Green and Jones shared a deep concern for the less economically fortunate and a passion for furthering opportunities for artists in their hometown. Significantly, Green bought supplies for Jones's Unemployed Artists Class and helped him, and others, establish the Vanguard Gallery, which was devoted to socially engaged contemporary art.

Bryna R. Campbell

Elizabeth Green (second from left) with (from left to right) St. Louis artists Peter Keep, Helen Beccard, and Joe Jones, c. 1936. Courtesy of the Estate of Miss Elizabeth Green.

one hand, we see a structure that has survived, albeit in fragments, long after the fall of the ancient world, and, on the other, contemporary engineering feats that may outlast the current civilization. A globe lends the composition the weight of the universal, while the crystal ball suggests contemplation. It reflects an inverted image of a print of the Crucifixion, embodying a critique of religion on the part of the artist, a corollary to his exploration of the primacy of matter.

A cityscape in the show, a version (location unknown) of *St. Louis Riverfront*, was also interpreted as a critique of "a world of dislocation and paradox . . . need in the midst of plenty."[72] At first glance, *St. Louis Riverfront* is a dynamic Mississippi River scene of excursion steamers passing beneath the dramatic diagonal of Eads Bridge, with an imaginary arrangement of the city's skyscrapers, including the new Civil Courts building, in the background. However, reviewers of the show interpreted the composition as irrational, presaging disaster, and illustrating Jones's social philosophy. "When he turns to his canvas it is to record through the symbols at his command [the] injustices and inequalities which reach to his studio door," one review reads. "The result is . . . a pair of steamboats needlessly, yet deliberately, heading for each other."[73] Another review describes the scene as "two river packets, with belching smokestacks, tossing about violently . . . careening toward a collision. In the background . . . smoking chimneys of the city. From some the smoke blows north, from others south. Crazy enough. But any crazier, the picture asks you, than millions in want because the world has too much of everything?" Jones apparently agreed with this interpretation of his work. "That's what I'm groping toward and what I think I'm beginning to express," he told the reviewer. "I'm not interested in painting pretty pictures to match pink and blue walls. I want to paint things that knock holes in walls."[74]

The same review announced the formation of the Cooperative Art Society, or Joe Jones Club. The ten-member group sympathized with Jones's goals and planned to subsidize him "while he goes on knocking holes out of walls."[75] Each member agreed to pay monthly dues, which would be turned over to the artist in exchange for the paintings he produced. The group committed to arrange exhibitions of Jones's art in St. Louis and beyond, as well as to sell his work in order to compensate members for their investment in him. Jones was elated by the prospect of this regular income. The official announcement of the club's formation, in February 1933, specified that this experiment would extend over seven months, giving Jones time to "create a market for his works."[76] But the group did not decide what would happen at the conclusion of that time frame, whether it would extend the arrangement with Jones, disband, or take up the cause of another struggling artist.[77]

During that period, Jones met Elizabeth Green, a St. Louis art patron thirty years his senior (see "Elizabeth Green," p. 28). Although she was not wealthy, Green would become Jones's most faithful and influential advocate over the following decade. The correspondence between them (today in the Dr. John Green Collection, Missouri History Museum, St. Louis) provides trenchant insight into Jones's life, experiences, and psyche. Before they began to correspond, Jones, along with Freda, went to Provincetown, Massachusetts, with Green, who had painted there in years past and still had a cottage in the area.[78] She hoped that spending time in the famous art colony, known for the teachings of conservative artists such as Charles Hawthorne and St. Louisan Richard Miller, would help Jones advance artistically. As the *St. Louis Art World* noted, the plan was for Jones to "paint boats, fishing smacks, and other subjects."[79] However, his most profound experience in Provincetown proved to be the time he spent discussing Karl Marx with writers, artists, and workers he met. Although he had begun to speak about his sympathy for "those in revolt against . . . capitalistic society" at the time of the founding of the Joe Jones Club, it was not until he returned to St. Louis from the East Coast that he identified himself as a Communist and declared that he would employ his striking style to explicitly convey his politics (see Wolfe).[80]

In September the Joe Jones Club attempted to sell his work by staging an exhibition at Stix, Baer & Fuller, the department store owned by Jones's patron Ernest W. Stix. This seems to have been the only exhibition the club arranged for Jones. A brochure highlighting the artist's connections to modernism accompanied the exhibition. It includes endorsements from fellow New Hats member E. Oscar Thalinger, who stated that Jones had "a keen instinct for design and organization"; and the noted modernist painter Walt Kuhn, who named the St. Louisan "the most promising young American artist." The text only hints at Jones's recent adoption of a radical political position, referring to the connection between Jones's still lifes and "the economic-social condition."[81] However, at the time of the show's opening, the club's members announced their decision to support another artist, using funds raised by the sale of Jones's paintings.[82] Although they had mentioned this possibility before, Jones was shocked and considered the decision a betrayal. In short order, he reported to Green that the club was not paying him according to the terms of the agreement and was refusing to return his unsold paintings to him.[83]

As 1933 drew to a close, two paintings that Jones had executed in Provincetown served to introduce him to the East Coast art world. The first was a straightforward, but critically admired, landscape, *Road to the Beach* (1933; cat. 30), which was included in the exhibition "Painting and Sculpture from 16 American Cities" at the Museum of Modern Art, New York.[84] The other (cat. 31) was a searing anti-lynching painting depicting a slain African American woman and the Ku Klux Klan members who murdered her (see Wolfe). This painting appeared in "American Painting Today" at the Worcester (Massachusetts) Art Museum. The positive reception of these works was the first indication that Jones's fortune would lie beyond St. Louis.[85] As his politics began to receive more press coverage than the formal qualities of his art, support for him in St. Louis waned. Jones himself recognized the shift. In the fall of 1933, he wrote to Green, "I sincerely believe that I am as far as I can go in St. Louis [as] far as recognition is concerned and still the people stand off, convinced sufficiently but without enough courage to follow their own convictions."[86]

NOTES

1. For a detailed narrative, see Chronology. See also Louisa Iarocci, "The Changing American Landscape: The Art and Politics of Joe Jones," *Gateway Heritage* 12, 2 (Fall 1991), pp. 68–75; and Karal Ann Marling, "Workers, Capitalists, and Booze: The Story of the 905 Murals," in *Joe Jones & J. B. Turnbull: Visions of the Midwest in the 1930s*, exh. cat. (Haggerty Museum of Art, Marquette University, 1987), pp. 7–25.

2. In their writings, St. Louis commentators did not consistently distinguish between the terms modern, modernism, modernist, and modernistic.

3. [Meyric Rogers] and Homer Saint-Gaudens, "Preface," *Foreign Section of the 28th International Exhibition of Paintings from Carnegie Institute, Pittsburgh*, exh. cat. (City Art Museum [hereinafter CAM], 1930), pp. 7–8; and Meyric Rogers, "Introduction," *Twenty-fifth Annual Exhibition of Paintings by American Artists*, exh. cat. (CAM, 1930), p. xvi.

4. Writing in 1930, Duncan Phillips and Charles Law Watkins noted that modernism "can and should be applied to so many different kinds of technique that it loses most of its value as a critical category"; idem, "Terms We Use in Art Criticism," *Art and Understanding* 1, 2 (Mar. 1930), p. 163. For more on the broad definition of modernism in the 1920s, see Sylvia Yount, "Rocking the Cradle of Liberty: Philadelphia's Adventures in Modernism," in *To Be Modern: American Encounters with Cézanne and Company*, exh. cat. (Pennsylvania Academy of the Fine Arts, 1996), p. 18 n. 77. She wrote about Philadelphia, but I would argue that the same understanding existed in St. Louis well into the 1930s.

5. See for example Emily Grant Hutchings, "Art and Artists," *St. Louis Globe-Democrat*, June 17, 1928 ("distortion"), and Dec. 15, 1929 ("tipped perspective"); "Modern Art Exemplified in Carnegie Collection," *St. Louis Post-Dispatch*, Mar. 7, 1930 ("bold coloring," "simple patterns," "cubism"); and Max Gottschalk, "Young Artists of St. Louis in American Show," *St. Louis Art World* 1, 1 (Oct. 1931), p. 4 ("abstracted").

6. Some fifteen years later, the critic Emily Grant Hutchings recalled the experience of seeing the Duchamp; idem, "Art and Artists," *St. Louis Globe-Democrat*, Feb. 26, 1928.

7. Ibid.; and idem, "Art and Artists," *St. Louis Globe-Democrat*, Feb. 12, 1928.

8. "Washington Crowded Out by Hercules: . . . Miss Suzanne Napton . . . Assails 'Modern Art,'" *St. Louis Star-Times*, Sept. 30, 1931.

9. Meyric Rogers, "Let Us Be Gay," *Saint Louis Review* 1, 4 (Apr. 15, 1932), pp. 5–7.

10. [Meyric Rogers], "Introduction," *Twenty-sixth Annual Exhibition of Paintings by American Artists*, exh. cat. (CAM, 1931), p. 8 ("sculpturesque rather than naturalistic"); and Meyric Rogers, "Foreword, " *Twenty-seventh Annual Exhibition of Paintings by American Artists*, exh. cat. (CAM, 1932), p. 8 ("simplification," "highly organized design").

11. See "Polish Woman's Painting Winner," *St. Louis Globe-Democrat*, Apr. 22, 1930. For information on Boucard, see John Difford, "Pierre Boucard's Legacy," *Biomedical Scientist* 48, 8 (Aug. 2004), p. 828.

12. "Women Gain Notice in Carnegie Exhibit," *St. Louis Post-Dispatch*, Mar. 16, 1930. Rogers is quoted in "Portrait by Polish Woman Leads Poll at Art Show Here," *St. Louis Globe-Democrat*, Apr. 13, 1930.

For other uses of the term modern classicism and its variants, see "The World of Art: Sketches by Masters," *New York Times*, Dec. 13, 1925; and Samuel Kootz, *Modern American Painters* (Brewer and Warren, 1930), pp. 10, 18, 22, 31–32.

13. "American Painting Exhibit Opens at Art Museum Today," *St. Louis Globe-Democrat*, Sept. 20, 1930.

14. Helen Baker, "Worthwhile Art Seen at Exhibit," *St. Louis Star-Times*, Sept. 30, 1930.

15. "A Fine Art Exhibition," *St. Louis Post-Dispatch*, Aug. 16, 1932.

16. Baker (note 14).

17. For references to Jones's modernism, see Andrew Hemingway, *Artists on the Left: American Artists and the Communist Movement, 1926–1956* (Yale University Press, 2002), p. 34; Iarocci (note 1), p. 70; and Marling (note 1), p. 12. See also Louisa Iarocci, "*A View of St. Louis* by Joseph James [*sic*] Jones," May 3, 1990, unpub. MS, Missouri History Museum, St. Louis, artist's file. Bryna Campbell argued that Jones considered the modernist idiom a tool for social engagement; idem, "Joseph Jones, *Landscape*" (Feb. 2008), http://kemperartmuseum.wustl.edu/files/spotlight2.08.pdf (accessed Dec. 11, 2009).

18. Jones took drawing classes in grade school. See Guy Forshey, "From House Painting to Portrait Painting," *St. Louis Post-Dispatch Magazine*, June 14, 1931, p. 5.

19. This is mentioned by Hermon Baron in *Paintings by Joe Jones*, exh. cat. (A.C.A. Gallery, 1937), n. pag. In the records of the 1930 United States Federal Census, St. Louis, Mo., Apr. 7, 1930, Jones is listed as a "decorating" painter, rather than as a painter-contractor like his father.

20. The Ranken catalogue for the 1927–28 school year describes coursework that included drawing "light and shade from casts" and "flowers, ornaments, and moldings"; *Eighteenth Annual Catalogue, 1927–1928* (David Ranken, Jr., School of Mechanical Trades, 1927), pp. 16–17.

21. Quoted in Forshey (note 18).

22. "A St. Louis Artist Discusses His Family on Canvas," *St. Louis Post-Dispatch*, Aug. 28, 1932.

23. The group was first known as the High Hats; "'High Hats,' New Modern Group Is Organized Here," *St. Louis Art World* 1, 2 (Nov. 1931), p. 3. By the time of their first show, in Dec. 1931, the members had adopted the permanent name New Hats; "Forty Paintings in First Show of New Hats," *St. Louis Art World* 1, 3 (Dec. 1931), p. 1. See also "Directory of Art Organizations," *American Art Annual* 32 (1935), p. 237.

24. Hutchings, who admired the art criticized by moderns as "old hat," listed "sound draughtsmanship . . . and old-fashioned sincerity" as identifying traits of art now dismissed as out of date; idem, "Art and Artists," *St. Louis Globe-Democrat*, Mar. 31, 1929.

25. Forshey (note 18).

26. Ibid.

27. Ibid.

28. Joachim Gasquet, "What He Told Me . . . Excerpt from *Cézanne*," in *Conversations with Cézanne*, ed. by Michael Doran and trans. by Julie Lawrence Cochran (University of California Press, 2001), p. 121.

29. "Lisbeth Ebers Hoops Preparing for Three Solo Dance Recitals," *St. Louis Art World* 2, 1 (Sept. 1932), p. 5. An advertisement for Hoops's school is on the same page.

30. Sies and Jones wed in 1930 and divorced in 1935.

31. Carl Benn, "Joseph Jones Holds First One-Man Show," *St. Louis Art World* 1, 2 (Nov. 1931), pp. 1, 4.

32. "Guild Annual Draws Numerous Entries," *St. Louis Art World* 1, 7 (Apr. 1932), pp. 1, 4; and "Artists' Guild First Prize Is Won by Ozark Farmer," *St. Louis Post-Dispatch*, May 1, 1932.

33. Carl Benn, "Joe Jones' Art Goes Forward, Show Reveals," *St. Louis Art World* 2, 5 (Jan. 1933), p. 1.

34. Emily Grant Hutchings, "Art and Artists," *St. Louis Globe-Democrat*, Jan. 22, 1933.

35. "What Young Man Thinks about Life Put on Canvas," *St. Louis Post-Dispatch*, Jan. 29, 1933.

36. Hemingway considered Jones's "decorative flattened forms and upturned perspective" as evidence of the artist's contact with Cubism, perhaps through contemporary American work; Hemingway (note 17).

37. Joseph Jones, "Carnegie International," *Studio Review* (Apr. 1932), in CAM publicity scrapbook, Saint Louis Art Museum, archives.

38. "Some Moderns Kept on View at Museum," *St. Louis Globe-Democrat*, Apr. 29, 1930. One of Lempicka's paintings was reproduced in "Paintings from Europe Coming to St. Louis Art Museum," *St. Louis Post-Dispatch*, Mar. 9, 1930, along with eight works by other artists selected from the 329 in the show (fig. 3). "Photographs of Rare Paintings from the Carnegie Institute, Pittsburgh," *St. Louis Globe-Democrat*, Mar. 9, 1930, included all three of her submissions as part of a two-page spread illustrating the offerings of the exhibition. No other artist was represented with more than a single image. As Lempicka's portrait of Pierre Boucard led and eventually won the St. Louis popularity vote, the results were published and discussed in a series of articles. *Portrait of Dr. B.* was even illustrated again on Apr. 13 in the *Globe-Democrat* (note 12), as well as in "Painting by Woman Voted Best in Art Exhibition Here," *St. Louis Star-Times*, Apr. 21,

1930; and "Polish Woman's Painting Winner" (note 11).

39. "An Interesting Woman Artist," *St. Louis Post-Dispatch*, Oct. 3, 1933.

40. Prize lists, St. Louis Artists' Guild Exhibition Catalogs, 1890–, Richardson Memorial Library, Saint Louis Art Museum.

41. Anita Mueller, "A Kitchen Studio," *St. Louis Globe-Democrat*, July 26, 1931.

42. "'High Hats'" (note 23); Paul B. Corr, "Individuality Is Keynote of New Hats' Show," *St. Louis Art World* 2, 3 (Nov. 1932), p. 1; and Marquis W. Childs, "Three St. Louis Artists," *Magazine of Art* 28, 8 (Aug. 1935), p. 485.

43. See the entry (by Lynn E. Springer) on *View of St. Louis*, in *Currents of Expansion: Painting in the Midwest, 1820–1940*, exh. cat. (Saint Louis Art Museum, 1977), p. 155. For an analysis of the painting as well as the perspective of the view and the identification of the buildings it includes, see Iarocci (note 17).

44. Prize lists (note 40). Some of Jones's landscapes may depict the city's Forest Park, since he lived nearby and is known to have sketched there. For work identified as showing the park, see the sales list for Elizabeth Green's apartment sale, 1934, Dr. John Green Collection, Missouri History Museum, St. Louis (hereinafter Green Papers). See also the recollections of Ernest W. Stix, Jr., in an e-mail from Stix to Sarah Lindgren and Valerie Rudy-Valli, Feb. 20, 2005. Saint Louis Art Museum, document files for *Wooded Landscape*.

45. For a period consideration of O'Keeffe's version of modernism, see Milton W. Brown, "Cubist-Realism: An American Style," *Marsyas* 3 (1945), p. 156.

46. For the late 1920s exhibition of *Shell and Old Shingle VI*, see "Paintings by 28 American Masters in Show at Museum," *St. Louis Post-Dispatch*, Aug. 14, 1932. For Jones's reliance on magazines, see John Selby, "Joe Jones, Who Began as House Painter, Hailed as Promising Artist," *St. Louis Globe-Democrat*, Sept. 11, 1938. For the provenance of the painting, which is in the collection of the Saint Louis Art Museum, see Barbara Buhler Lynes, *Georgia O'Keeffe: Catalogue Raisonné*, vol. 1 (Yale University Press, 1999), no. 545.

47. For documentation of Jones's restoration work, see Jones to Elizabeth Green, June 19 and 28, 1935; and M.K.F. [Marguerite Kauffman Fischel] to Jones, which ends with a note from Jones to Green, Aug. 28, 1935, all letters in Green Papers.

48. The Stix family displayed *Birch Trees at Dawn on Lake George* in their sunroom, along with another of Jones's tree paintings, *Struggle* (1935; cat. 37); interview with Judith and Ernest W. Stix, Jr., and the author and Andrew Walker, Oct. 5, 2009. For the provenance of the O'Keeffe, which is in the collection of the Saint Louis Art Museum, see Lynes (note 46), no. 510.

49. See for example Herbert J. Seligmann, "Georgia O'Keeffe, American," *MSS* 5 (Mar. 1923), p. 10, repr. in Barbara Buhler Lynes, *O'Keeffe, Stieglitz and the Critics, 1916–1929* (UMI Research Press, 1989), pp. 195–96. In addition to discussing such contemporaneous perspectives on O'Keeffe's work, Lynes reprinted a number of the relevant essays in their entirety.

50. For an examination of the elision of landscape and body in one of Jones's landscapes (cat. 16), see Campbell (note 17).

51. As Karen Tsujimoto noted in *Images of America: Precisionist Painting and Modern Photography* (University of Washington Press, 1982), p. 22, a number of precisionists were included in Samuel Kootz's roster of artists whose work fit his definition of modern classicism. Kootz used the term to describe art that unified subject and meaning with elements of style, such as formal design and color; Kootz (note 12). The parallels between Jones's work and that of the precisionists are examined in Iarocci (note 17), pp. 13–16. Julia R. Myers used the label in discussing Jones; idem, "Joe Jones," in *American Paintings and Sculpture to 1945 in the Carnegie Museum of Art*, ed. by Diana J. Strazdes (Hudson Hills Press, 1991), p. 278.

52. Gail Stavitsky, "Introduction," *Precisionism in America, 1915–1941: Reordering Reality* (Harry N. Abrams, 1994), p. 8.

53. Lozowick showed at CAM twice annually from 1930 to 1932. Artist Exhibition Index, 1909–2000, CAM and Saint Louis Art Museum, Richardson Memorial Library, Saint Louis Art Museum.

54. John I. H. Baur, *Revolution and Tradition in Modern American Art* (Harvard University Press, 1951), pp. 7–8.

55. Benn (note 33).

56. Jones to Green, Sept. 1933, Green Papers.

57. For documentation of the condition issues of Jones's early work, see Saint Louis Art Museum, Conservation Department files. For lenders to the exhibition, see "Exhibition by Joseph Jones," 1931, typescript, Saint Louis Art Museum, document files for *Mrs. Thomas B. Sherman*. For sales from the exhibition, see "Jones Commissioned to Decorate KMOX in Modern Manner," *St. Louis Art World* 1, 3 (Dec. 1931), p. 4.

58. Milovich received the painting as a gift.

59. "The Reviewer," *Saint Louis Review* 1, 1 (Mar. 1, 1932), p. 1.

60. "In the Art Galleries," in ibid., p. 3.

61. Clyde H. Burroughs, "American Masters," *Saint Louis Review* 2, 1 (Nov. 5, 1932), p. 9; "The Reviewer," *Saint Louis Review* 1, 6 (May 15, 1932), p. 2; and Joseph Jones, "Art, Theatre, Movies," *Saint Louis Review* 1, 2 (Mar. 15, 1932), p. 9.

62. Works by Vlaminck and Severini from the Sherman collection are now in the collection of the Saint Louis Art Museum.

63. See *Mid-Century Modern Architecture in St. Louis County: Outstanding Examples Worthy of Preservation* (St. Louis County Historic Buildings Commission, June 2007), n. pag. For information about the furnishings designed for the Shermans by Victor Proetz, see Saint Louis Art Museum, document files for the pieces now in the museum's collection.

64. Meyric Rogers, *American Interior Design* (W.W. Norton, 1947), p. 270, pl. 34.

65. "What Young Man Thinks" (note 35).

66. Thelma Wiles Thalinger, "Views and Reviews: Paintings of Joe Jones," *St. Louis Art World* 2, 6 (Feb. 1933), p. 4. None of the paintings of workers has been identified.

67. "What Young Man Thinks" (note 35).

68. This work has been extensively restored.

69. "Provincetown Makes Artist a Communist," *St. Louis Post-Dispatch*, Sept. 21, 1933.

70. Described in "10 Persons Pledge Aid to Struggling Artist," *St. Louis Post-Dispatch*, Feb. 19, 1933.

71. Thalinger (note 66).

72. "A Young Man with a Will," *St. Louis Post-Dispatch*, Feb. 3, 1933.

73. Ibid. The version exhibited in 1933 showed the two steamers positioned closer to each other than in cat. 17.

74. "What Young Man Thinks" (note 35). For a discussion about the compatibility of this statement with the Marxist perspective on the role of art, see Richard D. Wells, "Elizabeth Green: A Patronage Portrait," Ph.D. diss. (St. Louis University, 1985), p. 65.

75. "What Young Man Thinks" (note 35).

76. "Society to Finance Young Artist Here," *St. Louis Globe-Democrat*, Feb. 19, 1933.

77. "10 Persons Pledge" (note 70).

78. Wells (note 74), pp. 18, 64.

79. "Joe Jones Going to Provincetown," *St. Louis Art World* 2, 9 (May–June 1933), p. 4.

80. "Provincetown Makes Artist a Communist" (note 69); for Jones's pre-Provincetown radical sympathies, see "10 Persons Pledge" (note 70). Iarocci believed that Jones's first overt pro-Communist statements must have seemed to Joe Jones Club members like a "slap in the face"; idem (note 1), p. 70.

81. "Joe Jones—A St. Louisan and One of America's Most Promising Young Artists," exh. brochure (Stix, Baer & Fuller, 1933), n. pag.

82. The group's announcement was reported in "Young Artist's Work on Sale," *St. Louis Post-Dispatch*, Sept. 15, 1933. In fact, no paintings were sold. Jones to Green, n.d. (Sept. 1933), Green Papers. Iarocci posited that Jones's political activities, along with the failure of his works to sell, led his patrons to withdraw their support; idem (note 1), p. 70; and (note 17), p. 4.

83. Jones to Green, n.d. (Sept. and c. Oct. 1933), Green Papers.

84. *Painting and Sculpture from 16 American Cities: Atlanta, Baltimore, Boston, Buffalo, Chicago, Cleveland, Dallas, Detroit, Los Angeles, Minneapolis, Philadelphia, Pittsburgh, St. Louis, San Francisco, Santa Fe, Seattle*, exh. cat. (Museum of Modern Art, 1933), cat. 81.

85. *Exhibition of American Painting Today*, exh. cat. (Worcester Art Museum, 1933), cat. 61. For praise of Jones's painting in this show, see Edward Alden Jewell, "The Realm of Art," *New York Times*, Dec. 17, 1933.

86. Jones to Green, n.d. (c. Oct. 1933), Green Papers.

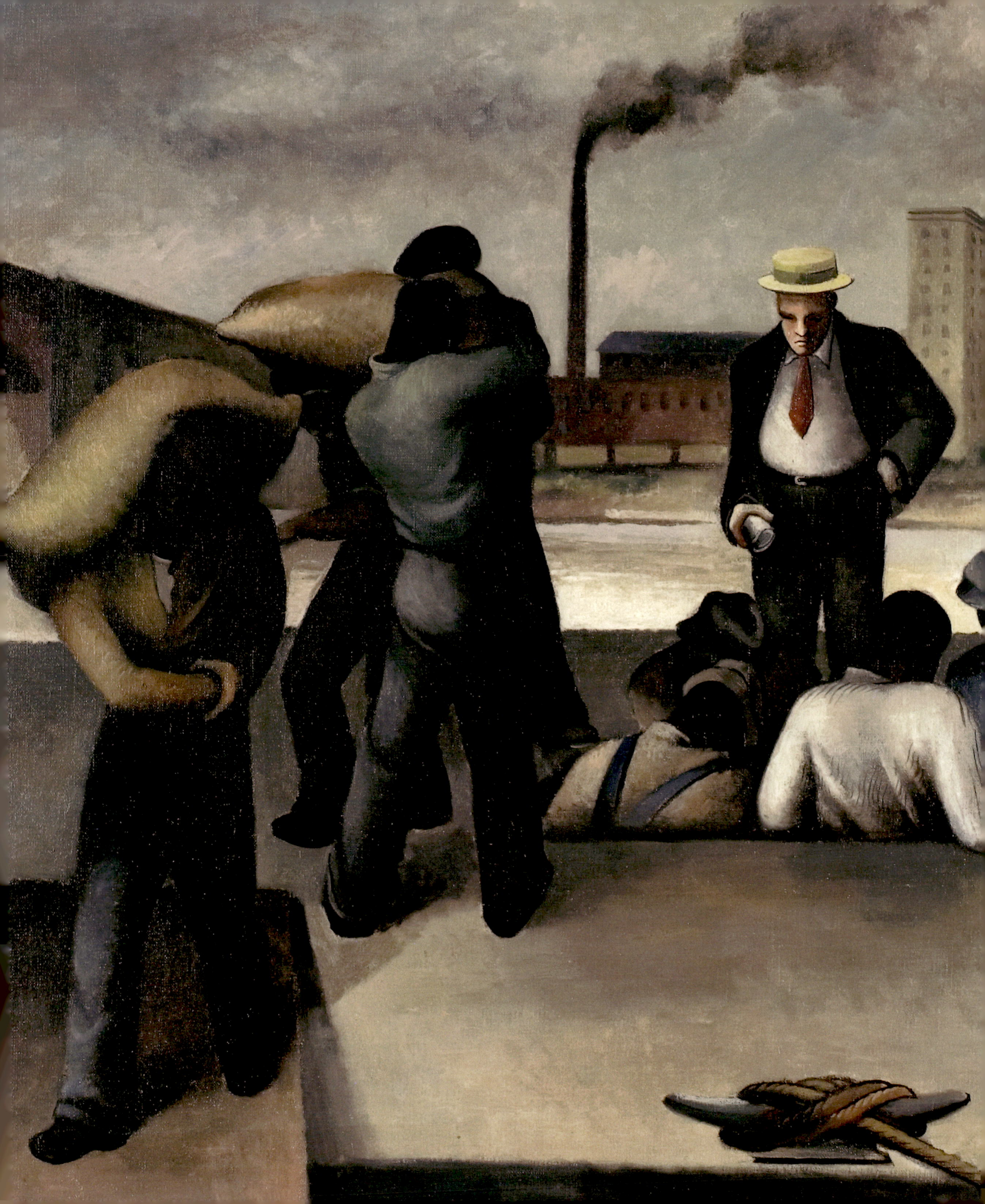

Joe Jones, Worker-Artist

M. Melissa Wolfe

> *I'm not interested in painting pretty pictures to match pink and blue walls. I want to paint things that knock holes in walls.* Joe Jones, 1933

"Provincetown Makes Artist a Communist" proclaimed an article in the September 21, 1933, issue of the *St. Louis Post-Dispatch*. Certainly, the news of yet another figure in the nation's cultural or intellectual world making such a commitment during the "'Red' Decade" of the 1930s was hardly shocking. The artist was Joe Jones, one of St. Louis's up-and-coming native sons. In May he had made his first trip to New York City, en route to Provincetown, Massachusetts, one of the most renowned art colonies in the country, where he spent the rest of the summer. While it was assumed, or at least hoped for, by those interested in his career that the experience would mark a significant development in the twenty-three-year-old artist's life, this was not exactly the turn they had expected. This essay addresses the nature of the consequent urban-protest works Jones produced and, especially, the proscriptive and descriptive role played by Communist ideology in the racial, political, and economic issues that these images engaged.

Jones did not *find* Communism in Provincetown as much as he *settled* on it there. The artist's social outlook had been formed in the gregarious camaraderie of bohemian radicals who gathered alongside local wharf workers in the grimy haunts of the Mississippi River levee. The Blue Lantern Inn (fig. 1), situated in a rat-infested warehouse near the foot of Washington Avenue, was favored by "local neophytes of the arts, the theoretical rebels and young iconoclasts."[1] There Jones, ex-housepainter-turned-artist; Orrick Johns, poet and former drama critic; Jack Conroy, ex-miner-turned-writer-and-editor; and William Sentner, architect-turned-union-organizer (and Jones's grade-school playmate), joined others of a similar disposition who dismissed Prohibition-era sobriety as they wrestled with the profound issues overwhelming a country in the throes of the Great Depression. In 1932 twenty thousand businesses went bankrupt, and wages were cut by forty percent. In St. Louis, over thirty percent of the population was out of work, with over eighty percent of African Americans either un- or underemployed; the city's relief system spent thirty-eight percent less per capita than any other city its size.[2] Johns later remembered that mile-long Hooverville, where the most desolate of St. Louis's residents lived,

> hung over the river bank, south of the bridges, and was cut off from the city by a network of railroad tracks. I had seen many similar shanty towns in the west, stalked by hunger. . . . But . . . I had never seen such stark destitution as that on the river front of South St. Louis. The people were practically imprisoned there, discouraged by police and watchmen from going into the city.[3]

Strikes and demonstrations became more and more common. The activities of the Communist Party on behalf

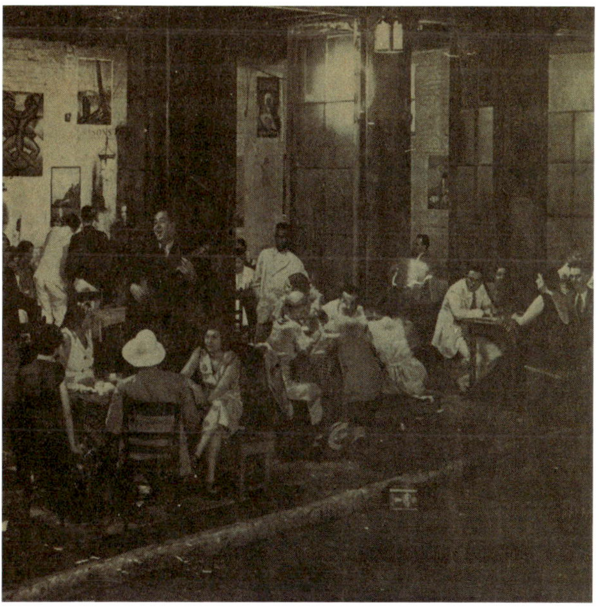

Fig. 1. Gathering, including Joe Jones (in a white suit seated at a table at the right), at the Blue Lantern Inn, St. Louis, c. 1930. Reproduced in Helen Seevers, "Blue Lantern Bohemians," *St. Louis Post-Dispatch*, March 3, 1969. Courtesy of George and Dolores Friesen.

of those suffering in St. Louis gained widespread attention and respect, following the leading role its members played in organizing a massive demonstration on behalf of the city's unemployed in 1932. Many in the arts showed their solidarity with workers by participating in the demonstration, and a local John Reed Club—the cultural arm of the Communist Party and open by invitation to members and nonmembers alike—was established.[4] Conroy, Johns, Sentner, and Jones all joined the organization.

There are clear indications that Jones's increasingly leftist beliefs had begun to dwell uneasily beneath the modernist patina of his pre-Communist canvases. A reviewer of his first one-person show, in 1933, noted the underlying tension in a version of *St. Louis Riverfront* (c. 1932; cat. 17): "Two river packets, with belching smoke-stacks, tossing about violently on the calm waters of the Mississippi, careening toward a collision. . . . From some the smoke blows north, from others south. Crazy enough. But any crazier, the picture asks you, than millions in want because the world has too much of everything?" The reviewer quoted Jones's explanation that such interpretations were what he was "groping toward. . . . I'm not interested in painting pretty pictures to match pink and blue walls. I want to paint things that knock holes in walls."[5] In Provincetown the artist found a way to make sense of the overwhelming experience of the Depression when he joined "the society of a small group of painters, teachers, and working people who chose to spend their time studying and discussing the economics of Karl Marx." Communism addressed Jones's "undefined yearning . . . [for] a definite philosophy on which to predicate his art. . . . Henceforth his art would be outspoken."[6] In short, Jones's subtext of social revolution had found an explicit voice.

Much of the interpretive framework of Jones's social-protest paintings, drawings, and prints has been lost over time as scholars have identified the work more generally with the broader characteristics of Social Realism of the 1930s.[7] However, to be a Communist artist during the Third Period of the Communist Party (1928–35) entailed not only a more specific agenda than Social Realism, but also one that often acted in opposition to the aims of non-Communist social realists. In essence a Communist artist was a class-conscious worker whose production—art—acted as a weapon in the impending revolution to end fascist structures of power and give laborers control over their production in an ideal Communist state. There was a call for artists especially from the working class. These "worker-artists" had claims of legitimacy as "insiders" in depicting the conditions and concerns of the proletariat. Rather than using their cultural achievements to move up in a class-based society, Communist artists retained their working-class identity in opposition to the elite status of the cultural world. Allied with workers, artists focused on the dynamics of their localities, coupled with the impassioned aim to incite in workers the revolution that would eliminate suffering and injustice.

Jones's working-class background, revolutionary zeal, and Midwestern roots made him an exemplary worker-artist. Though lengthy, two descriptions of the artist convey that his contemporaries understood him and his production in this role. Stephen Alexander, reviewing Jones's first solo show at the American Contemporary Art (A.C.A.) Gallery, New York, in 1935, wrote:

> Jones has come by his Communism as naturally as he has come by the normal heritage of the average worker, manual or intellectual, today—that is, through insecurity, unemployment, class justice and the terrific struggle for existence. His art is a living expression of his participation in this struggle and grows organically out of the environment and the people he knows. . . . But he does not stop at simply giving a faithful visual report. It is when he adds a class-conscious mind to a trained hand and eye, that he achieves his most significant expression.[8]

And Johns's description of Conroy and Jones is equally illustrative:

> Jack Conroy, of Moberly, Missouri, editor of *The Anvil* . . . was the new man, the agrarian-industrial Ulysses of brutalized road life in America, the worker who learned Latin and mathematics by himself to enter the university, who wrote and wrote for years in

obscurity, who corresponds with everybody and reads everything. It is no wonder that he was fearless, that he smashed through the polite timidities and said his say. Joe Jones, son of a one-armed house painter of St. Louis, himself member of a house painters' local, big, rangy, swift and swift-thinking, who almost alone of the PWAP [Public Works of Art Project] in St. Louis challenged the opportunist trickery of the Museum-boss administrators, and who carries on an unemployed art class, in a room of the old Courthouse wrested from the authorities.[9]

Far from being an intellectual ideologue like many leading Communists, Jones embraced the party in an uncomplicated and earnest fashion, as had many rank-and-file workers (he often took too seriously the mockery and high jinks in which Conroy and his band indulged). And, as noted, much was made of his membership in this rank and file. He was the grandson of a stonemason and the son of a housepainter. He quit school at fourteen to help support his family, which ended up among the city's poverty-stricken on relief. He retained his housepainters' union membership, and as a member of the artists' union refused to work on a government project because of pay conflicts.

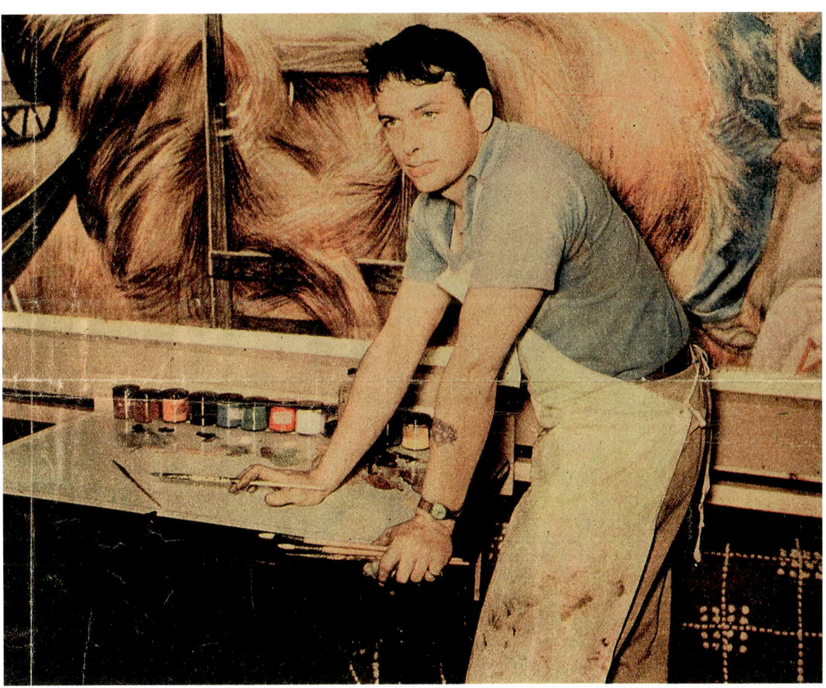

Fig. 2. This photograph of Joe Jones painting *Threshing*, his mural for the Magnolia, Arkansas, Post Office (Walker and Turk, fig. 1), appeared in the *St. Louis Post-Dispatch*, May 29, 1938.

In part Jones constructed his worker-artist identity in opposition to the elitism of the art world. He continued for a while, as a fine artist, to work in his painter's overalls and cap and use "ordinary house painting equipment"; when he exhibited for the first time at the Museum of Modern Art, New York, his biography—the chance to introduce himself to New York's art world—stated starkly: "Joe Jones. Born St. Louis. 1909. Self-Taught."[10] He gained wide notice when he ran his wet finger over Diego Rivera's controversial (and barely finished) mural, *Detroit Industry* (1932–33), in the Detroit Institute of Arts, proclaiming to shocked onlookers that this was how housepainters determined whether paint had been mixed correctly. "If it works with the house painters," he declared, "why shouldn't it work with Rivera?"[11] When Jones returned to St. Louis from Provincetown, he moved into a houseboat "propped on the ruined levee, with black industrial St. Louis all around him [as he] paints fiercely, angrily," asserting his identity with destitute river workers and Hooverville inhabitants over his middle- and upper-class patrons, who would have been more comfortable with the expected bohemian studio.[12] Interviewers described him as virile, turbulent, brash, boisterous, and irrepressible. His rather confrontational approach to the establishment seemed perfectly to embody the revolutionary zeal of his paintings and was complemented by the apparent genuineness of his Midwestern character. A "blue-eyed giant, [he] looks the way his name sounds—of good plain American stock, with an open face, freckles on his wide cheek bones and the hands of a man who can toss hay with the haying crew."[13] His pose in a work apron, showing sweat, muscles, and tattoo, and leaning forward on a simple utility table (fig. 2), suggests why even those not in the sway of leftist sentiment could not help but see something genuine in him. According to an article in *Art Digest*:

A modern novelist inventing a creative figure to express the American scene in these years would logically find him somewhere in the Middle West, would give him a plebeian name and most likely an artisan's background, and would expect him to look a little like a baseball player probably, to grin when he talks and to talk pugnaciously and with wisecracks. Society has forestalled him and invented Joe Jones in exactly that image.[14]

Worker-artists felt compelled to differentiate themselves from the pervasive documentary mode of Social Realism. As artist Jacob Burck wrote, "It is up to the revolutionary artists to help pave the way for a complete break with bourgeois culture by developing new plastic revolutionary expressions which embody the aspirations of the working class for the desired classless state."[15] Proletarian art needed to be performative in order to provoke its audience to act, whether through anger or empathy. It needed to operate in the imperative rather than the declarative: it did not say, "Look at this fight"; it said, "Fight!" Mural painting was considered an effective means of accomplishing these goals, especially given that at the time the three most well-known Mexican muralists—José Clemente Orozco, Rivera, and David Alfaro Siqueiros—were working on projects in the United States. As Milton Brown noted, "The impressive achievements of the Mexicans in creating a public, socially oriented, representational, popular art of international stature under a revolutionary government by drawing on the past as well as on indigenous forms and traditional imagery, converged with and stimulated the interest in mural painting."[16] It is not surprising that the very first visit Jones made on his initial trip to New York was to the New School for Social Research to see murals that had been executed there by Orozco and the American Thomas Hart Benton.[17]

Jones's first chance to paint a mural as a worker-artist occurred within a few months of his return from Provincetown, and it marked his most successful endeavor to bridge art and workers in class struggle. Jones was accepted on the PWAP, and through much wrangling he began to teach an art class two evenings a week for a racially integrated group of unemployed students in St. Louis's Old Courthouse. As a collective unit, Jones and seven of the students, five of whom were African American, created the no-longer extant *Social Unrest in Old St. Louis* (fig. 3), a 16-×-37-foot mural done in chalk pastel that incorporated straightforward visualizations of Communist issues embedded in episodic scenes set along the Mississippi River levee.[18] In the upper left, a freight train loaded with men heads for a veterans' demonstration

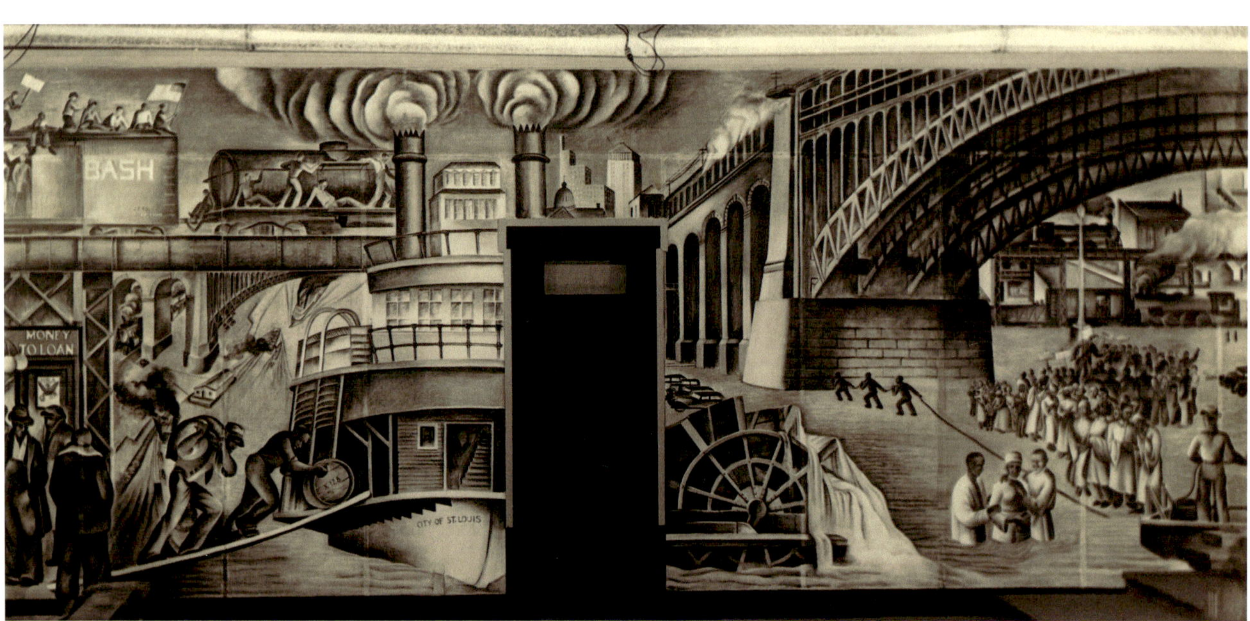

Fig. 3. Joe Jones and members of his Unemployed Art Class. *Social Unrest in Old St. Louis*, 1933–34. Chalk pastel on board; 16 × 37 ft. (4.9 × 11.3 m). Old Courthouse, St. Louis. Destroyed. Image courtesy of the Missouri History Museum, St. Louis.

in Washington, D.C. This scene was intended to remind soldiers, whose loyalty to capitalist democracy was hard to shake, of the aftermath of the 1932 Bonus March. This huge rally was organized by veterans of World War I, many out of work, to demand that bonuses they had been promised, which were to come due in 1945, be paid out now. Army forces, led by General Douglas MacArthur, used bayonets, tear gas, and tanks to clear out the protestors—unarmed veterans—still lingering in the city; hundreds were injured and several killed.[19] In the lower left of the mural, unemployed African Americans loiter in front of a pawnshop as they watch two roustabouts load a river packet named *City of St. Louis*. The pawnshop window displays the Blue Eagle, symbol of the National Recovery Administration (NRA), suggesting that help from New Deal programs was actually encumbering (like a loan), making workers into "pawns." In the lower right is a baptism scene in which African Americans line up to obtain the religious assurance of salvation. They merge with a gathering of agitators who surround a soapbox orator. The messages on the signs they hold—"Save the Scottsboro Boys!," "Hands Off Cuba!," "Down with Fascism!," and "Don't Starve, Fight!"—were all well-known Communist Party slogans.

The party opposed New Deal policies because, in its view, they encouraged the development of fascism out of a crisis in capitalism. Accordingly, depicted on the far left-hand side of the Old Courthouse mural are the short-sighted and insufficient solutions of the New Deal, as represented by the Blue Eagle, whereas on the right are more effective responses to the major issues of the day supported by the party. The group around the pawnshop looks to the right, to the only two figures in the composition who are working, suggesting that the answer to unemployment rested with the Communists' recognition of labor's productive power. As Jones explained, "The baptismal group represents . . . religion as an opiate" and "the group of agitators, the natural evolution of discontent which cannot be appeased by religion."[20] Thus Jones presented New Deal policies and religion as appeasements proffered to mollify the proletariat, allowing the unimpeded growth of fascism and quelling the natural tide of revolution required to establish the workers in their rightful productive state.

While its narrative devices are fairly conventional, the Old Courthouse mural became a "battleground on which to transfer the class struggle."[21] In February 1934, when it was unveiled—surrounded by Soviet propaganda posters—Jones welcomed a fight. A reporter noted that "if it remains presentable for four or five months [Jones] will be satisfied. If objections cause its removal before that time, he will be more than pleased."[22] Over the ensuing ten months, Jones became an "irritating thorn" to city leaders as he maintained a combative dialogue over the mural.[23] In March members of the National American Bands of Action (NABA), a local American Fascist League group, broke into the classroom. They tore up the Soviet posters that decorated it—a warning that they would destroy the mural—and inscribed the following in black letters on a sheet of muslin:

> This is a public building, a building of the American people. We, as Americans, will not tolerate its use for the worship of any foreign idols or fetishes because it is un-American. It destroys homes and separates families, it destroys men as God meant them to be. We say that it must stop. Do you understand? We say [it] must stop.[24]

Johns crowed to Conroy that "after the destruction . . . the workers actually turned out en masse to defend the mural—the best example I know of rallying workers for their own *cultural* rights."[25] The radicals continued their agitation, but when several of the African American members of Jones's class and his wife, Freda, were arrested during a Communist-led unemployment demonstration at City Hall, the conflation of Jones, the mural's topics, and the active protest was too much. On December 14, St. Louis Director of Public Safety George W. Chadsey declared the class a front for Communist meetings and ordered the students and teachers to vacate the building. Jones, still pushing the limits, asked Chadsey to participate in a symposium, "Art—Free or Dictated," an invitation he declined. When Jones showed up for class on the 16th, he found that his classroom had been padlocked.

The conflict over the class and its mural jettisoned Jones to national attention among radicals. His eviction garnered protest letters from the Socialist Party, the American League against War and Fascism, and the Marine Workers' Industrial Union.[26] Photographs of the mural were included in the "National Exhibition of Art by the Public Works of Art Project," held at the Corcoran Gallery of Art in Washington, D.C., in April 1934. During a trip to New York in late 1935, Jones was feted by radicals and accepted several speaking invitations. Most notably, early the following year, he gave a talk, "Repression of Art in America," at the public session opening the First American Artists' Congress in New York (see Balken). And in 1937, he was the only artist from the United States invited to the Congress of Revolutionary Writers and Artists held in Mexico City.[27]

While such explicit Communist agitation certainly brought about the acrimonious assault by city officials and conservatives in St. Louis, the issue of race also played an important, if less publicly acknowledged, role. The Communist Party vigorously encouraged interracial organizing, postulating that racial prejudices were being perpetuated by industrialists and landlords as a way to direct workers' antagonisms against one another rather than at those who controlled the system that oppressed them all, regardless of race. By integrating his class, Jones situated himself against the generally accepted, prejudicial practices of most of the art world—including academic training, museum acquisitions and exhibitions, commercial-gallery representation, and even New Deal programs (which only marginally sought to include blacks). His actions also clearly confronted the deeply embedded racial and class prejudices in St. Louis.[28] NABA's scrawled warning on a white muslin sheet, rather than paper, was a potent and intentionally thinly veiled reminder of the potential for Ku Klux Klan violence. When Jones's class was evicted, Chadsey's defense was that "the place is entirely lacking in the Bohemian atmosphere that you would expect if it were a genuine studio. . . . Jones says they are unemployed, members of the depressed and downtrodden classes, who want to study art. But they don't look like artists to me."[29] At the core of Chadsey's comments was the assumption that true artists are neither working class nor African American; importantly, in acting as such, Jones's students were stepping out of their place. This, one suspects, is exactly what Jones wanted to reveal. Art, class consciousness, and racial oppression merged to incite the downtrodden to revolution.

Roustabouts (1934; cat. 32) locates the Old Courthouse mural issues more specifically in St. Louis's long-established racist structures. The city gained its historical, economic, and political identity from its river trade; yet, as one of the city's African American citizens aptly observed:

> The steamboat was a part of a lazy economic system that was built upon the very backs of black men. . . . Its voracious boilers were fed pitch and wood by black men, its decks loaded and unloaded by black men, its cabin and staterooms served by black servants, its saloon and promenade strutted and enjoyed by white gentlemen. . . . No real attempt to understand the cultural roots of the Negroes of St. Louis can overlook or omit these lowly roustabouts. Indeed, they were the undertow of the monetary commerce that was making St. Louis into a city of major importance.[30]

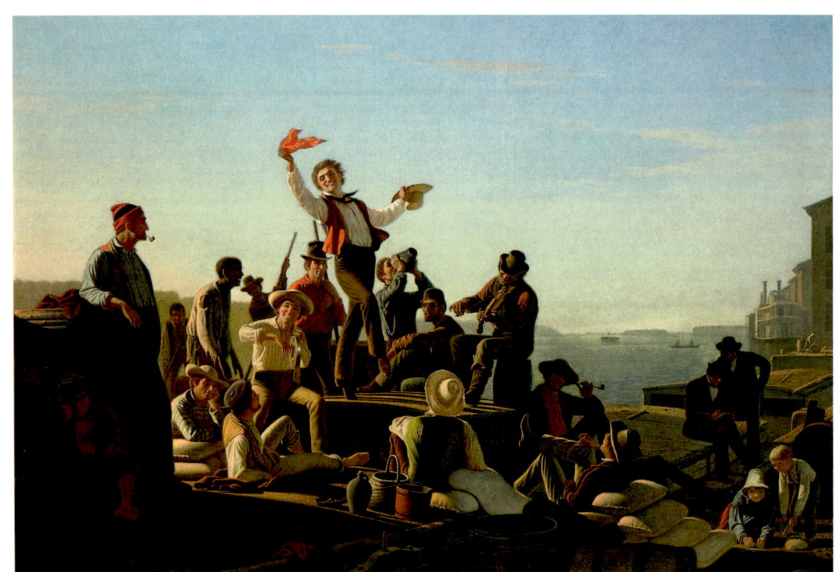

Fig. 4. George Caleb Bingham (1811–1879). *Jolly Flatboatmen in Port*, 1857. Oil on canvas; 47 1/16 × 69 5/8 in. (119.5 × 176.8 cm). Saint Louis Art Museum, Museum Purchase.

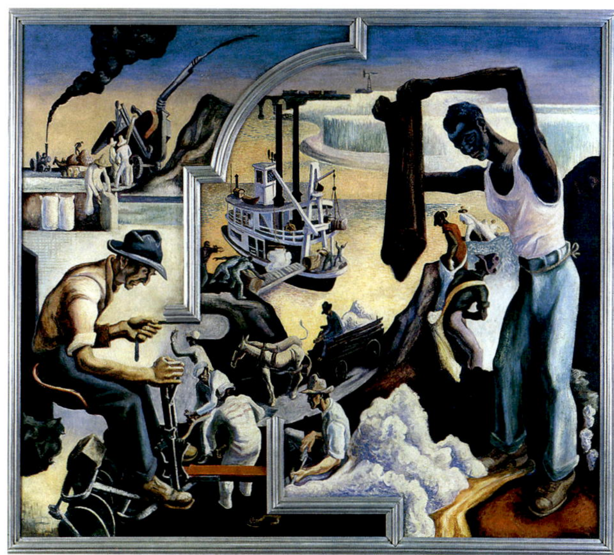

Fig. 5. Thomas Hart Benton (1889–1975). *Deep South*. From *America Today*, 1930. Distemper and egg tempera, with oil glaze, on gessoed linen; 92 × 117 in. (233.7 × 297.2 cm). Collection AXA Gallery, New York.

The politicized nature of *Roustabouts* is clarified when read against works by two other renowned Missouri artists, *Jolly Flatboatmen in Port* by George Caleb Bingham (fig. 4) and *The Deep South* by Thomas Hart Benton (fig. 5). Bingham emphasized the marginalized racial and class position of blacks in the nineteenth century through such details as tattered clothing; however, the figures' limp arms and work-worn, slumped postures reveal the absence of the strength needed to confront their situation. And, although Benton's twentieth-century roustabouts seem vigorous, the energy of their movements does not coalesce into an evocation of discord, but rather constitutes a rhythmic, undulating visual motif that creates a sense of compositional and psychological harmony. At first glance, Jones's narrative seems straightforward, with the dominance of the white boss conveyed in his centrality and position overseeing the black workers who stand below the dock in a barge. However, the repetition of downcast heads could suggest passive-aggressive resistance, and the authority visually vested in the white man's height is in fact subtly challenged by the workers loading goods, especially the black man in the right foreground whose position counters that of the boss. The dynamic between economic and physical power weaves between boss and workers in a crisscross pattern. This pattern is reiterated, in concentrated form, in the foreground knot of rope, which seems to embody these tensions: it could loosen or tighten in response to the fluctuations caused by movement of the figures and the water below. The latent potential for revolution inherent in physical power seems to hover on the brink of erupting in this silent, sullen scene.[31]

The increased racial strife of the early 1930s was signaled by the sharp jump in lynching across the South, from eight documented in 1932 to twenty-eight in 1933. Situating such violence within the problems of the economic inequalities of capitalism, the Communist Party called for art that would "*explain* lynching graphically and plastically. We must attack the social forces responsible for lynching."[32] *American Justice* (1933; cat. 31) is Jones's response to this call. When he created the work during his stay in Provincetown, there were few models upon which he could draw, at least until 1935, when both the NAACP and the John Reed Club held competing anti-lynching exhibitions in New York (see "Anti-Lynching Activism," p. 40) that offered a wide array of visual and conceptual approaches to the topic.[33] Though the painting has often been read as a rather straightforward narrative of a Klan lynching of a black female, a cryptic note to Jones after its inclusion in the 1933 Worcester (Massachusetts) Art Museum's annual exhibition, American Painting Today, suggests that there might be more to the subject: "Your painting has created considerable talk here. One of my friends asked what it was all about, and I was very glad that I knew the reason for its being painted. It solved all my friend's doubts."[34] The only comment Jones made about the painting's content was in a letter to his St. Louis patron Elizabeth Green:

> It is my personal interpretation, of a lynching that brought beauty out of such a fascinating subject—I want to ask a question, why do people who find beauty and love in a picture of a crucifixion painted by an Italian master even to the point of purchasing it, why

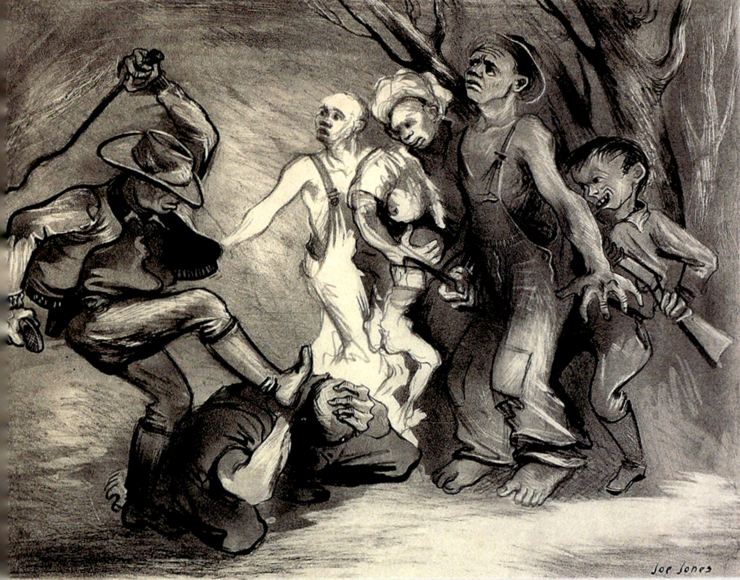

ANTI-LYNCHING ACTIVISM

One of the most significant political movements in which Joe Jones engaged was the campaign to end lynching in the United States. He produced at least five works protesting these white-supremacist mob executions, including the sardonically titled 1933 *American Justice* (cat. 31), featuring a female lynching victim and her killers, and his 1935 Commonwealth College mural (fig. 6; cat. 39; and Chronology, figs. 7–8), a work that includes an African American woman stopping a lynching in progress. Jones's sustained engagement with this issue, along with his labor activism and the interracial group of students he taught at St. Louis's Old Courthouse, demonstrates his deep commitment to racial justice.

Jones's activism can be linked to his membership in the American Communist Party, which he joined in 1933. The party had taken a strong stance against lynching since the beginning of the Great Depression, linking it to other social inequities believed to be the results of the racist and class-based structure of capitalism. By 1934 two competing anti-lynching bills had been introduced into Congress. One mandated prosecution of collaborating local officials, while the other—a more radical, Communist-supported bill—demanded the death penalty for lynchers. Many artists engaged in the cause by exhibiting their works in two anti-lynching exhibitions held in New York in 1935. Jones's work *Lynching* (location unknown) was included in "Struggle for Negro Rights," the show organized in support of the more radical of the two bills. Unfortunately, neither passed. In effect, none of the two hundred anti-lynching bills introduced into Congress from 1909 on ever became law.

Bryna R. Campbell

Joe Jones. *Southern Peonage*, 1937. Lithograph; 11 × 14½ in. (27.9 × 36.8 cm). Columbus Museum of Art, Ohio: Museum Purchase, Derby Fund, from the Philip J. and Suzanne Schiller Collection of American Social Commentary Art, 1930–1970.

do they avoid a lynching? (which is exactly the same thing) and the handling is recognized as beautiful?[35]

Drawing associations between lynching and Christ's crucifixion was a strategy frequently utilized by the African American community to oppose accounts in the mainstream press that typically justified murder as retribution for sexual assault. Though few victims of lynching were actually guilty of the crime—or even accused of it—the association was cemented in the popular imagination. The terror inspired by the idea of a white Christian woman violently ravaged by a bestial black man assured a pervasive, if tacit, support of lynching.[36] To counter the narrative of demonization related by persecutors (the lynchers), African American authors and artists told the story from the perspective of the victim seen as a Christ-like martyr. Countee Cullen, Langston Hughes, and James Weldon Johnson all published poems about a black Christ; Johnson's 1927 publication *God's Trombones* contains an illustration of the Crucifixion by Aaron Douglas.[37]

As Edward Blum noted, "Mapping biblical symbols onto racial violence was a brilliant maneuver. It reversed the sacred symbolic order asserted and upheld by the lynch mob, one that linked whiteness with godliness and blackness with sinfulness. By associating black victims with the biblical Christ, black writers turned this

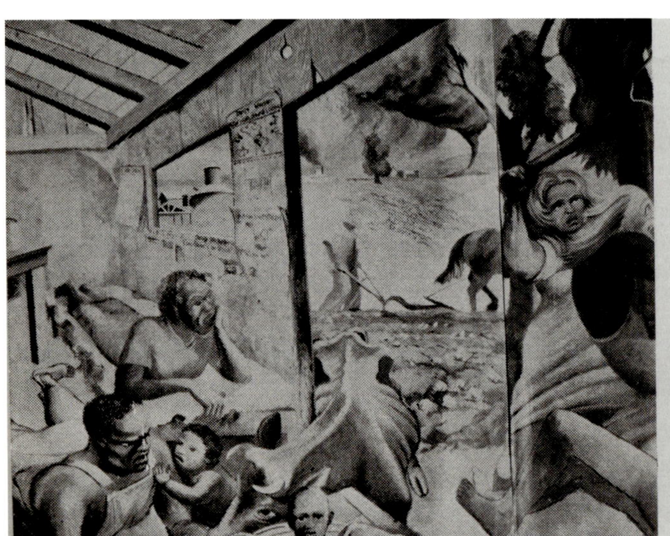

white supremacist cosmology on its head."[38] The African American newspaper *Chicago Defender* published a widely reproduced photograph of the 1930 lynching of Thomas Shipp and Abraham Smith in Marion, Indiana, with the caption "American Christianity" and admonished that "Christian America must know that all the world points with scorn at a country that spends millions to Christianize other countries while at home the barbarians hold their lynching picnic at regular intervals."[39] The caption, like Jones's title, uses the ironic voice to effectively reverse who is the true "barbarian," revealing the distance between the assumed behaviors and beliefs of those who profess Christianity and the actual behaviors in which they engage.

Jones's explanation of *American Justice* suggests that we, at least in part, are to read the figure of the lynched woman as a martyr in the vein of the "black Christ" figure. The unnerving cabalistic circle of silhouetted Klan members, contrasted with the African American woman draped in innocence by a white cloth, supports this strategy. However, Jones did not title the work *American Christianity*, but rather *American Justice*. This difference shifts the context from the religious to the secular and puts the finger on political and judicial systems in accord with Communist Party rhetoric. In so doing, the painting denies the palliative effect of religious texts, in which the community is assured of the victim's redemption in the divine realm, and equally important, in which God alone is allowed to seek retribution on behalf of the wronged. Taken outside of this religious context, there is no salvation for the victim and no punishment for the perpetrator unless individuals act to restore and carry out true justice. To the Communist Party, the onus to restore failed justice fell to the community, which was then responsible for initiating social revolution.

The call to revolution that Jones struggled to voice through the lynching in *American Justice* is made explicit in a 9-×-40-foot mural he completed two years later, in 1935, for Commonwealth College in Mena, Arkansas (fig. 6; cat. 39; and Chronology, figs. 7–8). Described as a "pictorial appraisal of the social forces operating in Arkansas," the mural comprises three thematic sections in five panels that were situated across the walls of an alcove at one end of the Commons Room.[40] The panel on the left depicts the abject economic conditions of a sharecropper's family in a cobweb- and fly-infested abode as floods, dust storms, and a tornado ravage their fields. The two panels on the right show a group of work-worn miners gathered around a leader who pours water from his lunch pail in a well-known signal to strike. The center two panels feature a massive tree around which are conflated three horrific lynching scenes, with one victim

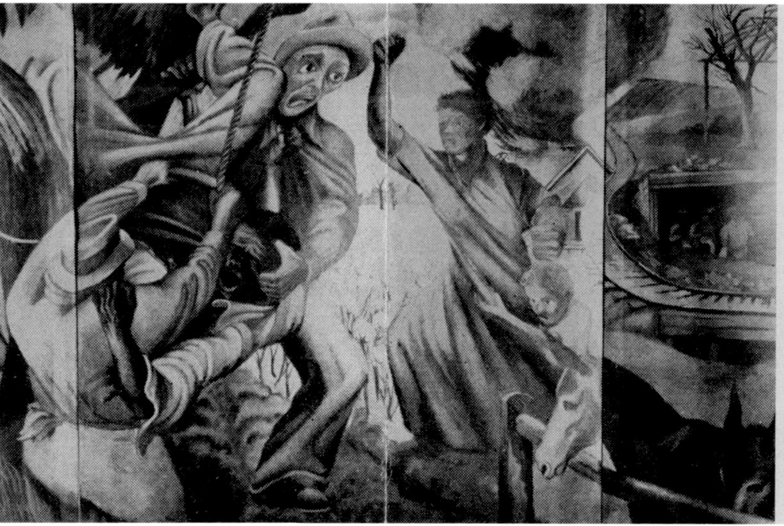

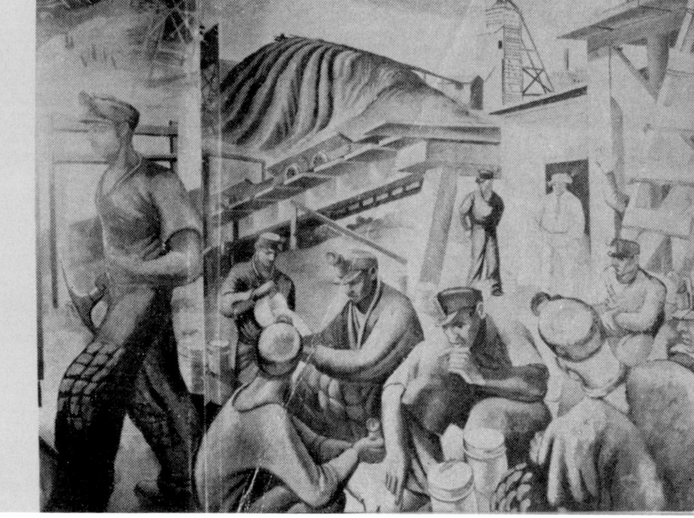

Fig. 6. Joe Jones. *The Struggle in the South,* 1935. Oil on Masonite. Reproduced as it looked originally in *Paintings by Joe Jones*, exh. cat. (A.C.A. Gallery, 1937), n. pag.

mutilated, one burned, and one still in a desperate struggle with his captors.[41] Each section suggests the trials of Arkansas's working class. Lynching is imaged as one of many terrors—be they violence or abject poverty—that result from the failure of capitalism. The inclusion of a farmer who plows under his cotton amid such destitution, in submission to New Deal policies aimed at eliminating overproduction in an effort to stabilize prices, further points to the federal government's culpability in perpetuating such burdensome inequality.

The forthright voice of the mural reflects the heady environment Jones experienced at Commonwealth College, a residential labor school committed to educating working-class individuals to take leadership roles in grassroots socio-economic reforms.[42] The college constituted an invigorating, if eclectic, community of leading radical thinkers and generally uneducated farmworkers and other kinds of laborers. The environment deeply resonated with Jones, who felt he "went down there as one of them. They were my people."[43] He saw the mural as the exemplary achievement of his endeavors as a worker-artist. He made it for workers, in a place accessible to them, and he aimed to speak honestly about their experiences in it. In preparation, he spent two days in the area talking with and taking photographs of sharecroppers and miners. A well-known radical, "Mother" Ella Reeve Bloor, was also at the college that summer. She emphasized the significance of Jones's mural, stating:

> Every worker will know what it means. . . . It is the first picture portraying adequately the struggles of the workers and farmers that I have ever seen. In this mural there is not only struggle and poverty, but hope—and this hope comes from the share-croppers and miners themselves. From their unity, and their realization that they can only be emancipated by helping one another.[44]

As "Mother" Bloor suggested, a significant aspect of the mural is that it does not merely depict, but rather graphically explains the conditions responsible for class inequities and shows workers exactly how to end them. The mural's three scenes of farming, mining, and lynching are visually and ideologically connected through gesture. The reclining sharecropper on the left looks in anger toward the lynching scene. His clenched fist is matched by the fist of the miner on the right, who has left his companions to stride toward the lynchings, suggesting a solidarity between agricultural and industrial workers. This gestural motif is repeated and intensified in the raised fists of the two women who immediately frame the lynchings. Their muscular arms move the conflict to its apex. The woman on the left wields a torch over her head as she pushes her way closer to add her own measure to the violence inflicted on the victims. The woman on the right, however, raises her fist in righteous indignation toward the murderers. Her aggression is given moral rectitude by the child who clings to her side and by the fire that races behind her; having burned her home, it seems to move with her to extinguish whatever blights its (and her) path.

Jones began the mural only months after the two anti-lynching exhibitions opened in New York. They offered models for him to formulate his own visualizations of social injustices that he explored in the Commonwealth mural.[45] Sponsored by the John Reed Club, "Struggle for Negro Rights," in which Jones was represented, encouraged its participants to link lynching to other economic and social inequalities of capitalism. Images focusing on racial solidarity among workers, the Scottsboro Boys trials,

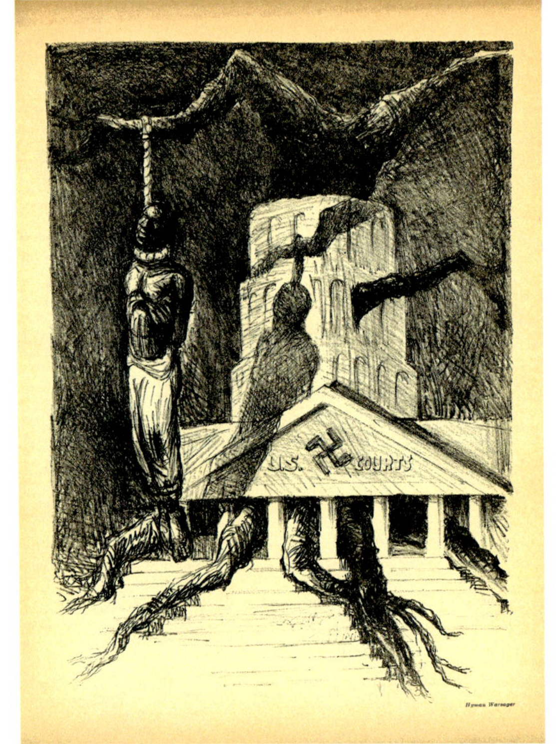

Fig. 7. Hyman Warsager (1909–1974). *The Law*, 1934. Reproduced in *New Masses* 10, 2 (1934), p. 7. Courtesy of the Tamiment Library, New York University.

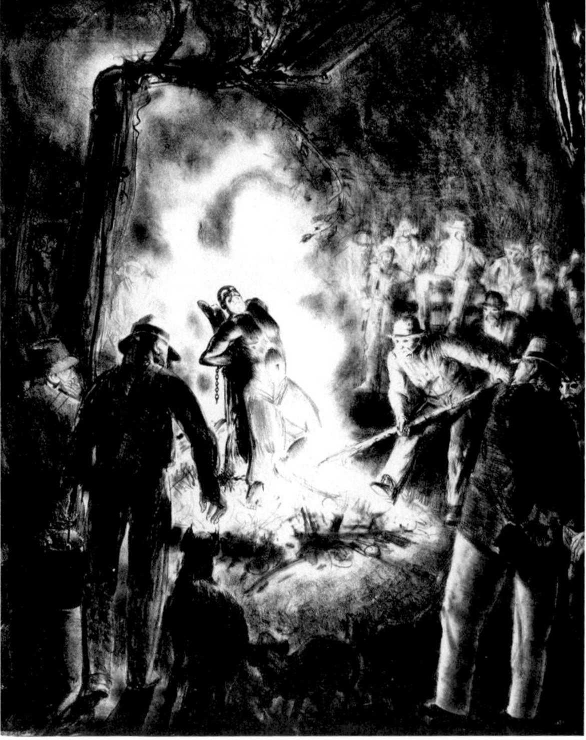

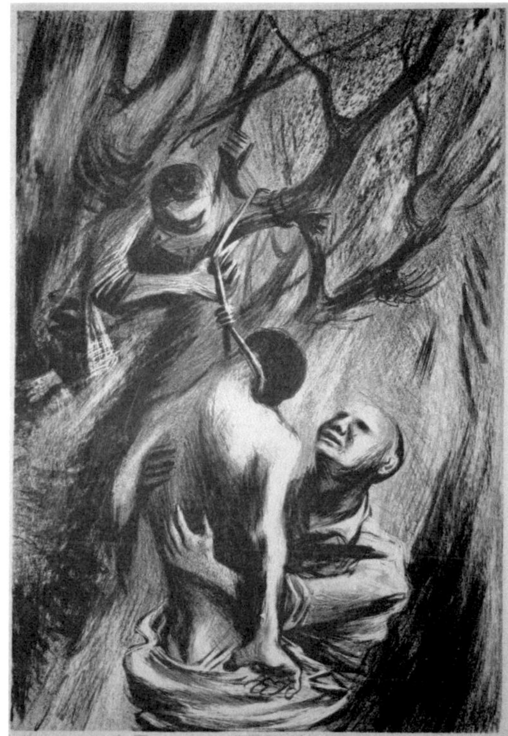

Fig. 8. George Bellows (1887–1925). *The Law Is Too Slow*, 1923. Lithograph; 25⅞ × 19¼ in. (65.7 × 49 cm). Columbus Museum of Art, Ohio: Gift of Jeffrey Shedd.

Fig. 9. Joe Jones. *Three Men and a Tree*, c. 1937. Lithograph. Courtesy of Legend Fine Arts, Wichita.

and the corruption of the legal system were as prevalent as literal lynching images. Typical is Hyman Warsager's *The Law* (fig. 7), in which the roots of the lynching apparatus have infiltrated the judicial system, suggesting that ending lynching was not a matter of controlling local mobs but rather of building a new structure of justice. Drawing on such models for the Commonwealth mural, Jones was more successful at visualizing his understanding of the nature of lynching, as well as the revolution such abuses demanded. The mural is impressive in its direct, plainspoken entreaty to its working-class audience; in it simplicity and indignation join forces to formulate a deeply effective, and affective, work of art that is fully empowered to act as a weapon.

In part, the difference in effectiveness between Jones's two murals and *American Justice* lies in the manner in which he relayed their content. In *American Justice*, there is no explicit action that ties the visual elements together; rather, the symbols act in aggregate to create meaning. The Ku Klux Klan members are Evil; the partly draped dead woman, Justice; the dog, Fidelity; the home, Domesticity. This interpretive strategy was clearly understood by the radical press, which frequently used the draped female as a symbol of the fascistic corruption of the American legal system. Yet the relationship between these signs is oddly unclear and does not seem to satisfactorily explain the composition. An undercurrent of emotion in the painting is out of sync with its pastiche of easily read signifiers, making it difficult to move from the psychological terror and physical violence of lynching to contemplating the systemic political and ideological aberrations responsible for it. This reveals the deeply complicated and unsettling nature of the available sources for such an early depiction of lynching. By the very nature of their purpose, anti-lynching images have their origins in lynching photographs, such as one reproduced in the *Chicago Defender*, in which a thick darkness presses against the crowd. Its inescapable presence can be felt in one of the earliest anti-lynching images, *The Law Is Too Slow* (fig. 8), a 1923 lithograph by George Bellows, in which a mottled darkness swallows any detail of the masked mob not directly lit by the fire's diabolic glare. It also haunts Jones's painting; the hanging noose beckons another victim, and the black void behind conjures a fear-laden unknown, challenging the intellectual rhetoric of ideological symbols layered over the troubling scene.

Jones's decision to embody the virtue of justice in the black female reflects his experience in St. Louis radicalism. Early in the decade, a group of mostly African American workers who had been agitating City Hall for jobs and relief joined the Communist-led Unemployed Council. The council drew on the strong solidarity of black communities to mobilize support for several bloody and deadly demonstrations in July 1932 that constituted the first integrated protest movement in the city. On the heels of this, in May 1933, the local Communist Party organized an electrifyingly successful strike of black and white female workers at the Funsten Nut Company; it achieved nearly all their demands, including equal pay for blacks. Jones thus left for Provincetown at a moment when African American women acted to demand justice, and got it.

While *American Justice* speaks to racial discrimination in a symbolic language readily accessible to radicals of the time, it also offers another message, the crux of which rests on the characterization of the female. In 1935 a reviewer for *Time* described the painting as "a vivid picture of a prostitute who had been lynched by hooded Ku-Kluxers."[46] Yet there is no real evidence to suggest she is a prostitute, and the conclusion seems couched in the pervasive racist refusal to accord a black woman the same innocence and respectability as a white woman. The house and canine, in fact, place the woman in a working-class domestic environment. Additionally, the dog, which howls in mourning, gives a visual presence to and an outlet for the familial and communal grieving that lynching inflicted upon African Americans and that was largely unacknowledged in the mainstream press. Jones was moved to express similar mourning in a later image, *Three Men and a Tree* (fig. 9), in which two men tenderly remove the body of a lynching victim from a tree.

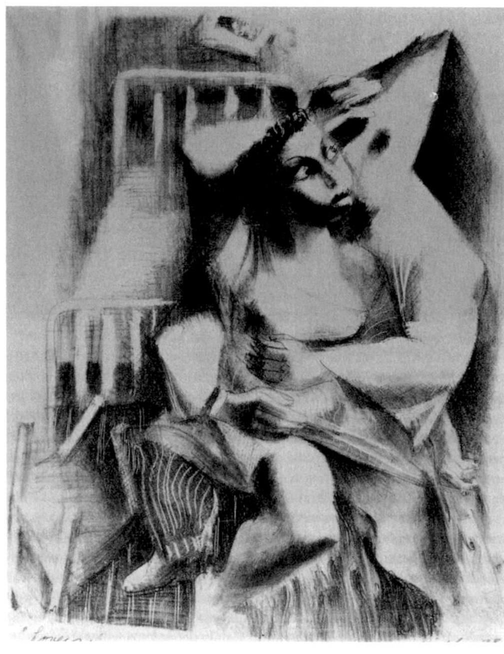

Fig. 10. Ernest Crichlow (1914–2005). *Lovers*, 1938. Lithograph; 14 × 11 11/16 in. (35.6 × 29.7 cm). National Gallery of Art, Washington, D.C., Dave and Reba Williams Collection.

Although most readings of *American Justice* assume the woman has been lynched, the rope hangs evocatively empty. The painting more effectively points to the crime of rape, acting as a vehicle—in support of black women's concerns—to publicly assert the more typical nature of interracial sexual violence that all too often was experienced within the African American community.[47] Frances Pohl convincingly argued this interpretation, pointing to the phallic nature of the men's torches and draped sheets, and to the misogyny implied in the tension of white and brown trees that cross one another over and over throughout the landscape.[48] The men perform their corruption of "blind justice" in hoods that restrict their sight; in turn the denial by the *Time* reviewer of the situation presented reveals a continued choice to remain blind to what is in front of one's eyes, literally and institutionally.

American Justice is rare in its inclusion of the injustice perpetrated against black women as a way to reveal a corrupt legal system. Nonetheless, as many scholars have noted of similar images, the painting constitutes yet another opportunity for privileged access to the black female body which underlies the unspoken condoning of her rape in the first place. Insistently erased from public acknowledgment, such assault is addressed by few images. Ernest Crichlow's *Lovers* (fig. 10) reveals the problematic nature of Jones's painting. In Crichlow's lithograph, the female is not symbolic. She is clothed and fights the Klan member who attacks her, attempting to pull off the hood that hides his identity and thus his accountability. The print effectively speaks to both the insidious underbelly of racialized power inequalities and the imperative to resist through revolution. While Jones clearly desired this same outcome, *American Justice* struggles to negotiate the language of symbolism with the horror of lynching and the power and vulnerability of the nude female body.

The following year, in 1934, Jones painted one of his most successful social-protest canvases, *We Demand* (cat. 33), in which an integrated line of demonstrators is led by four African Americans—a family of three followed by a veteran. The painting's dynamic mix of ideology and narrative can again be located in radical activities in St. Louis, where blacks not only eventually outnumbered whites at many of the demonstrations, but by 1933 comprised one third of the local Communist Party organization. Hershel Walker, an African American active in the 1932 Unemployed Council demonstrations, recalled "the moving effect of 'black and white demonstrating together before city hall, going to jail together, and getting food to eat together' in a city that was still fully segregated."[49] Reflecting the council's community- rather than job-based support, demonstrations had a strong family component; often entire families marched together in protest lines.

The placard Jones's leader holds refers specifically to the Communist-supported Lundeen Bill then before Congress, which called for complete coverage for the unemployed in all occupations. Demands by the integrated female strikers at the Funsten Nut Company resulted in the St. Louis Board of Aldermen passing a resolution in favor of this bill. One of the leaders who emerged from the strike was Jones's close friend William Sentner, who, though white and Jewish, modeled for the lead figure in *We Demand*. Thus Jones depicted the strongest leader in his immediate group of radical colleagues, but then altered his race to better reflect the cumulative nature of labor agitation in St. Louis, as well as the biracial nature of revolution that Communists envisioned.[50] Jones gave his worker-leader accepted traits of manliness in his physical strength, dignity, and courage, and simultaneously challenged accepted prejudices by placing these ideal characteristics on the black male.[51]

In *We Demand*, Jones resolved the problematic pastiche of elements found in *American Justice*. The later composition evolves easily, both formally and ideologically; it begins with a group standing in the background and listening to an agitator, then moves into action with a line of demonstrators, and culminates in the leader's enlarged fist and striding foot, which signal a promise for revolution and change. The ideological underpinning of the painting was missed by one reviewer, who criticized placing demonstrators in an unpopulated industrial landscape rather than in city streets where they would be noticed.[52] However, the interweaving of workers with the steel I-beams of the elevated railroad tracks, the complementary arcs of human and industrial forms, and the power of the train as it moves forward on the tracks combine to make a perfect ideological statement on the production, importance, and strength of the laborer.

The majority of Jones's urban social-protest works are active compositions that attempt to motivate the viewer from status quo to revolution. However, Jones also created paintings that engage the most abject conditions of the Depression in order to inspire through empathy. *Garbage Eaters* (location unknown) was described by a leftist reviewer as "stark and intense—one of the bitterest pictures I have ever seen. Figures stuffing stale garbage down their throats, vomiting from weakness and nausea."[53] Such raw, unmediated vision—a notable difference from most social-realist imagery—was associated with Francisco de Goya's difficult paintings and prints, and its source was attributed to "a powerful reaction to . . . life among the starving and the stunted and the oppressed."[54] Certainly, the decision Jones made in 1933 to live on a houseboat not far from Hooverville, St. Louis's worst slum, seems a somewhat perverse insistence that he immerse himself in the utmost example of the human cost of the country's economic failure—an experience that fueled his anger. This response was not a given, however; three weeks in a mining "dump" gave writer Edward Dahlberg "such a shock from the 'grotesquery' of it that he couldn't make literature out of it."[55]

Part of Jones's compulsion to elicit his anger through contact with the outcast was his own deeply felt identity as marginalized. His career is marked by the difficult balance of remaining true to his working-class roots and his desire to be accepted and successful in the art world. It seems clear that his struggle with social "niceties" and his oft-mentioned buckteeth marked him as working class to many, causing him much insecurity and frustration.[56] When in 1936 Jones was criticized for becoming "too slick" after the success of his second one-man exhibition in New York,[57] he returned to St. Louis and painted *Bottle Dancer* (1936; cat. 46).[58] Originally titled *Human Refuse*, the image is made difficult by its straightforward depiction of a young African American prostitute, the dismal direction of her future indicated by her destitute environment and the syphilis that shows its advanced state on her skin. He explained the painting to his dealer: "That's us. We all prostitute ourselves, anyway."[59] Jones clearly expressed his frustration with a society that uses the marginalized only to discard them without concern when they are no longer interesting or "exploitable." Reviewers noted the care the artist took in executing the painting, inferring that the way by which he showed his empathy with his subjects was, as he himself had confirmed, through his masterful rendering of them.[60]

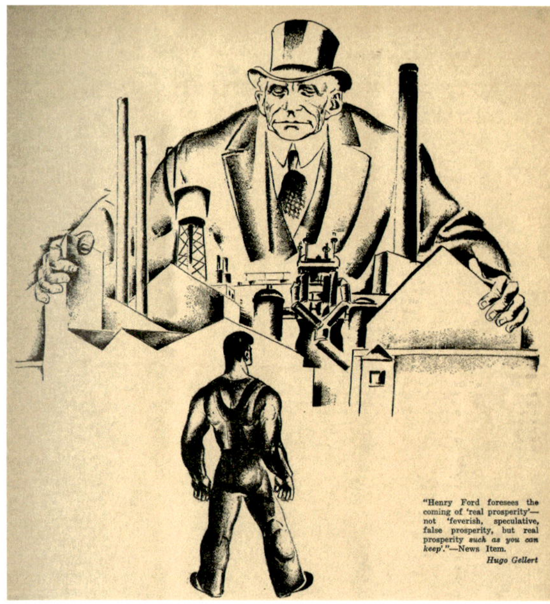

Fig. 11. Hugo Gellert (1892–1985). "Henry Ford foresees the coming of 'real prosperity.'" Reproduced in *New Masses* 7, 7 (December 1931), p. 11. Courtesy of the Newberry Library, Chicago, Fol. J2617.6635.

In a February 1935 letter to Green, Jones speculated about the impact he believed his paintings would have if he had an exhibition in New York: "The revolutionary element in my work, so closely tied up with the rest of my work, is the only thing of its kind so far, and would be (as a show) a very important development in

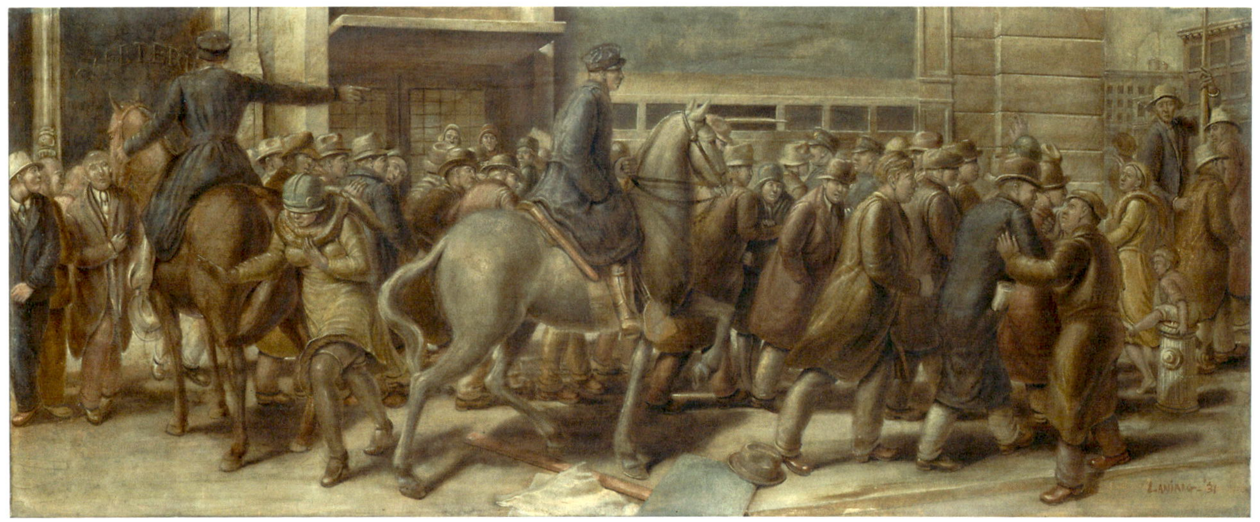

Fig. 12. Edward Laning (1906–1981). *Unlawful Assembly, Union Square*, 1931. Tempera on composition board; 14⅛ × 36 in. (35.9 × 91.4 cm). Whitney Museum of American Art, New York; gift of Isabel Bishop, 84.59.

American art today. . . . The revolutionary pictures here are full of political satire or on the other hand sickles and hammer."[61] In May his wish and prediction came true. Jones's first one-person show in New York opened at the newly established A.C.A. Gallery, run by Herman Baron (see "Herman Baron," p. 103). The exhibit, which featured works such as *Demonstration* (location unknown; it included a vignette of garbage eaters), *We Demand*, *American Justice*, *Roustabouts*, and others, was a surprise hit (see Balken). *New York Times* critic Edward Alden Jewell was among those who noted what Jones's paintings had that those of others did not:

> Socially, this may be called a Left Wing show. . . . In his case one never suspects that painting, as an art, has figured exclusively, for him, as a crude machine by means of which propaganda broadsides may be catapulted into the face of the public. On the contrary, a spectator is pretty sure to feel the artist's intense concern for esthetic content.[62]

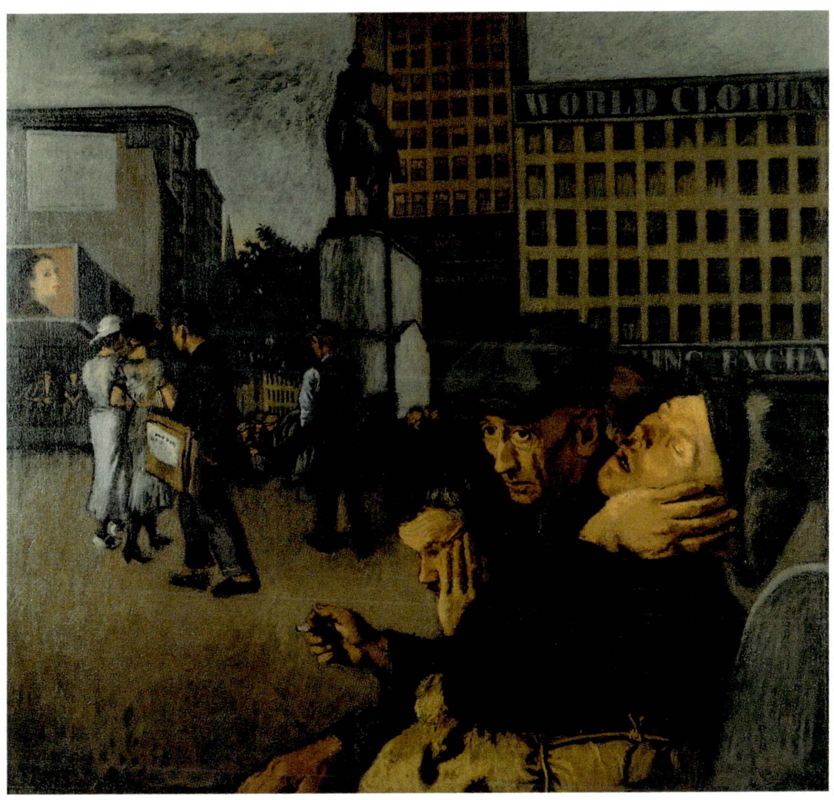

Fig. 13. Raphael Soyer (1899–1987). *In the City Park*, 1934. Oil on canvas; 38 × 40 in. (96.5 × 101.6 cm). Private collection, New York.

Baron was exaggerating somewhat when he claimed that, with the critical acceptance of Jones's exhibition, "propaganda art became respectable overnight."[63] Yet the show both legitimized social-realist painting in the American art capital and, importantly, constituted a powerful model for those who had been struggling to create a new genre of revolutionary art. Most of these pioneering artists were illustrators and/or cartoonists who found it difficult, regardless of how accomplished they were, to move to fine art from the more literal or telegraphic visual language they were used to. Their attempts, displayed in Baron's 1932 show of John Reed Club artists, were derided as "scolding" and "less art than homily." Even Baron thought some of the work was "crude to the point of painfulness."[64] A 1931 cartoon by Hugo Gellert captioned "Henry Ford foresees the coming of 'real prosperity'" (fig. 11), included in the exhibition, is typical in its explicit text and reductive symbolism. (The limits of such visual vocabulary are demonstrated in Jones's problems with *American Justice*.) Artists who produced easel paintings also struggled to meet the call for revolutionary art. Edward Laning's 1931 painting *Unlawful Assembly, Union Square* (fig. 12) was shown in the second John Reed Club members' exhibition, in 1933. The work reveals the skills of someone with academic training; however, it fails to evoke the urgency and conflict in the actions of police breaking up a Communist-led unemployment demonstration.

Jones remained engaged in Communist Party activities for several more years after his 1935 "coming of age" in the art world. However, the content of his work during this period signified a shift in both his radicalism and its relationship to his art. This is due in large part to change in the Communist Party itself. In August 1935, the Seventh World Congress of the Comintern initiated the phase commonly known as the Popular Front (it would later be called the Democratic Front). The rhetoric of proletarianism and revolution—the call for art as a weapon—was abandoned, and a generalized focus on "the people" replaced class consciousness. The party also turned away from the combative, polemical position it had maintained in relation to other leftist systems, such as

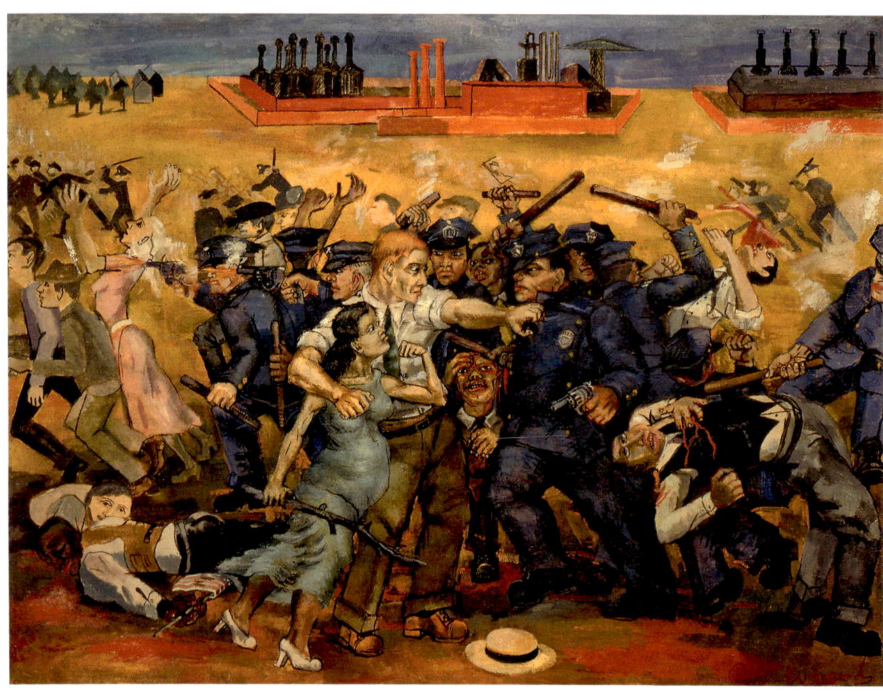

Fig. 14. Philip Evergood (1901–1973). *American Tragedy*, 1937. Oil on canvas; 29½ × 39½ in. (74.9 × 100.3 cm). Private collection, Courtesy Terry Dintenfass, Inc.

the Socialist Party and New Deal programs. Like the *New Masses* editors who now asked illustrators to "play down any signs of aggressive radicalism," Jones's art changed in accord with his party.[65] A review in the *New York Tribune* was one of many Jones's 1937 A.C.A. solo show received that noted his adoption of "a new and simple procedure, none the less effectual for its subtlety and want of propagandist flag-waving."[66]

Without the veneer of radicalism called for by Third Period Communism, however, Jones's work, like that of many other Popular Front artists, is not significantly distinguishable from images by other social-realist contingents. For instance, in accord with earlier Third Period tenets, an *Art Front* reviewer compared concurrent 1935 exhibitions at the Whitney Museum of American Art and the A.C.A. Gallery, singling out a painting by Raphael Soyer (one of three brothers who became notable social realists) entitled *In the City Park* (fig. 13). Such paintings might be considered radical at the Whitney, but at the A.C.A. Gallery, the reviewer chastised, they would be "rearguard action. . . . The Soyers have taken a step to the left," but "to take a further step is to represent the will to struggle."[67] Indeed, the dynamic of revolution that activates a work such as *We Demand* is absent from *In the City Park*. Importantly, however, Soyer's work is not that different from Jones's 1939 *Conversation* (cat. 76), which seems to eschew any explicit social message.

Jones's later paintings became, in effect, genre scenes of the down and out, without the difficult challenges the artist had set for himself in his earlier work, when he aspired to the role of a history painter by addressing social and political conditions on a systemic level. The artist's move away from the turbulent world of the "shouters and the marchers"[68] is especially notable considering that the violence and frequency of labor conflicts grew in the last years of the decade, increasingly engaging other socially aware artists who were close colleagues of Jones, such as William Gropper and Philip Evergood. Evergood executed *American Tragedy* (fig. 14), often cited as an exemplar of Social Realism, in 1937 in response to a brutal attack by police and guards on a group of unarmed multiracial strikers at a Republic Steel mill. The painting boils over with the anger and indignation that Jones eschewed in paintings like *Conversation*.

The shift in Jones's art has also been traced to the artist's employment, in the fall of 1935, by the Resettlement Administration (RA) to record conditions in the Midwest.[69] Taking a cue from tropes used in documentary photography, *Condemned* (1936; cat. 47) depicts a closely cropped figure in a composition much more simplified than one finds in Jones's earlier work. It reflects photographs the artist took, such as *WPA Worker* (1937; cat. 51). While the smiling expression of the man in the photograph does not compare to the worried countenance of the woman in the painting, both compositions show the figures from a low viewpoint. This strategy succeeds in monumentalizing and conferring worthiness on two ordinary individuals, underscoring their significance as representations of "the people." Though the warning of the tattered sign in *Condemned* is readable—"Danger, Building is Unsafe, Condemned, Stay Away"—the implications of the situation it reveals are subordinated to the focus given the female laborer.

Jones's work changed as well because of his increasing identity with New York. The nation's art capital had a tremendous impact on the self-trained painter, who admitted that until 1935 art magazines were his main connection with other artists. On his first extended stay in the city, he made repeated, lengthy visits to the Metropolitan Museum of Art, where he was "overwhelmed by the masses of pictures . . . [and] humble enough to hope he would measure up to the high standard always on exhibition here."[70] The rapidity and depth with which he absorbed lessons from such visits is apparent, as his stature among his artistic peers quickly rose with the critical success of his two one-person shows at the A.C.A. Gallery in 1935 and 1937, and his solo show at the Walker Galleries in 1936. Moreover, in 1937 *Threshing No. 1* (1935; cat. 34) was purchased by the Metropolitan, making him one of the youngest painters whose work had ever been acquired by that august institution.

While he remained in St. Louis through these first few years of success, maintaining close ties with the city's radical set, by the fall of 1937, Jones had settled in the East, never to return permanently to his hometown.[71] One likely reason for this move was his engagement to fellow St. Louisan–turned–New Yorker Jane Kauffman (see "Jane Kauffman Wood," p. 65); by the fall of that year, the couple was living together in the city.[72] Kauffman was a committed radical activist, and it is quite plausible that *Condemned* is a visual expression of the social issue about which she was especially passionate—affordable and safe housing for the poor. The condemned sign suggests that the woman's unfortunate situation is due as much to the issue of housing as to her unemployment.

Even with Kauffman's connections, however, Jones seems to have struggled a bit to find his place among the various communities in his new city, and he never really took the same public role nor found the same close camaraderie within the radical circle in the East that he had in St. Louis.[73] Tellingly, in 1937 Eli Jaffe, who was then a young radical writer, asked Jones to read a draft of a novel he was working on (for which Jaffe had spent hours researching in the New York Public Library) about the struggles of a couple living in Oklahoma's Dust Bowl. Jaffe recalled that Jones

> said he would, but only with the understanding that he would pull no punches. And he didn't. "What you've written is the hysteria of a New York intellectual," he said. "If you want to write honestly about the Dust Bowl, why don't you get your ass out there and get to know the people?"[74]

On one hand, Jones's response is yet another instance in which he positioned his identity counter to that of an intellectual or art-world elite. On the other hand, it suggests that although he understood the need to locate himself in New York, Jones continued to feel that the world and the people with whom his radicalism connected were back in the Midwest.

Certainly part of Jones's tempered engagement was due to the changes in the broader radical community, but it was also clearly due to his increased preference to position himself within New York's rich artistic traditions and broad, dynamic art community. Jones's paintings began to reveal his increasing engagement with aesthetic over social issues; reviewers repeatedly noted the "increase in [his] power as a painter," and praised his "new surface opulence. . . . Every inch of canvas is . . . a color fabric of great complexity and subtlety."[75] For instance, in *Conversation* the overall unity of figure and ground, interweaving of color, facility with glazing, and greater focus on painterly aspects all combine to mediate the painting's introspective character. Such work helps to explain Jones's otherwise surprising complaint in 1938 that the artist "Arnold Blanch said the other afternoon that I was the only artist in NY that [*sic*] wanted to talk about problems of art. . . . He and Doris Lee are the only ones I have been able to find who have time for art—everyone else finds time only for political thought and activity, which should be a part of every artist but never his whole interest."[76]

Concurrent with his increased identification with the art world, Jones moved away from the Communist Party, as many others did later in the decade, as evidence of the Soviet Union's alliance with fascism mounted. In 1938 he asserted he was still a Communist, but that his active political life was "almost negligible."[77] Jones's particular voice as a social realist in these years—how he positioned his radicalism and artistic content—is consolidated in a series of images he made of railroad workers that began with sketches for his submission (which was not chosen) to the 1939 Wellston, Missouri, post-office mural competition.[78] Jones reworked one of these (cat. 73)—a multifigured composition, with a maze of tracks and distant railyards—in a more simplified and focused way in such paintings as *Railroad Workers, St. Louis* (c. 1939/40; cat. 75). Jones's increased interest in artistic practice is evident: his glazing gives noticeable depth to the reduced palette of blue, red, white, and brown; and his quick, angular strokes of color weave the composition together. Gone is the revolutionary impulse of *We Demand*, where the placard and enlarged fists of the workers thrust aggressively out at us. Instead, aided by the lines of the rails, we are drawn quietly into the scene.

However, this change does not necessarily indicate that Jones entirely abandoned his Communist sentiments. He continued to sympathize with and revere workers. As a reviewer of the 1938 Annual Exhibition of Paintings by American Artists at the City Art Museum, St. Louis, observed, "Joe Jones, who has frequently used his art for sharp denunciation of the existing social order, in his canvas *Railroad Workers* has found in perhaps the dreariest of city scenes, a railroad yard, a setting to emphasize the dignity of labor and the virility of the workers."[79] In Jones's painting, the railroad employees do not turn away from us, but face us. We become workers as well, placed in the midst of the tracks and required to stoop in order to meet the men at their eye level, as equals. The canvas is not only a powerful companion to the artist's earlier protest images, but also an equally commanding urban counterpart to his contemporary threshing images, such as *Harvest Scene* (c. 1939/42; cat. 72), in which comrades are similarly engrossed in modern communal labor, sharing a productive goal.[80]

Characterizing the 1930s, Milton Brown wrote, "Class antagonisms, ideological positions, and economic, political, and social actions were sharply delineated. People took sides, made commitments, dreamed dreams."[81] Of the many "sides" to take, Jones aligned himself with the Communist Party, whose positions seemed to best acknowledge his experience of life as a working-class person and, importantly, offered him a clear direction in which to move as an artist committed to helping identify and resolve the era's problems. Rather than haranguing over positions and theories, Jones drew both his self-worth and his world view from action. As he himself stated years later, "Fighting was necessary to keep alive and be young—it was fun and it helped me to think."[82] However, what set him apart from the rank and file of the "shouters and the marchers" to which he felt akin was that his anger and artistic abilities coalesced to make him an exemplar worker-artist who created some of the most individual and powerful visual calls to arms at a very specific, and important, moment for Social Realism. Jones has been criticized at times for the seeming veneer of propaganda in his social-protest images—and indeed he struggled to manage the complicated dynamics of race, class, and ideology within a coherent visual dialogue. It is this very tension of ideology and artistic sensibility in his paintings, however, that both offered a much-needed early model for socially engaged artists, and embodied the similarly unresolved struggle of Americans to understand the profound experience of the Great Depression.

NOTES

1. Helen Seevers, "Blue Lantern Bohemians," *St. Louis Post-Dispatch*, Apr. 3, 1969. The Blue Lantern, operated by Hogarth Riverune and local artist Leon Contristable, faded out with the end of Prohibition. After its demise, Savo Radulovich's bar, Little Bohemia, also near the Mississippi, became a favored haunt. See Douglas Wixson, *Worker-Writer in America: Jack Conroy and the Tradition of Midwestern Literary Radicalism, 1898–1990* (University of Illinois Press, 1994), p. 429.

2. Rosemary Feurer, *Radical Unionism in the Midwest, 1900–1950* (University of Illinois Press, 2006), p. 32.

3. Orrick Johns, *Time of Our Lives: The Story of My Father and Myself* (Stackpole Sons, 1937; reprint: Octagon Books, 1973), p. 338.

4. Bill Jordan to Jack Conroy, Feb. 28, 1932, Jack Conroy Papers, Newberry Library, Chicago (hereinafter Conroy Papers). The Communist Party organized the first John Reed Club in New York in 1929. Its mission was to encourage the expression of party ideals and thereby enrich the nation's arts. By the time of the first national congress of John Reed Clubs in May 1932, the organization was established in ten other cities and boasted 642 members. See Guenter Lewy, *The Cause That Failed: Communism in American Political Life* (Oxford University Press, 1990), p. 9.

5. "What Young Man Thinks about Life Put on Canvas," *St. Louis Post-Dispatch*, Jan. 29, 1933.

6. "Provincetown Makes Artist a Communist," *St. Louis Post-Dispatch*, Sept. 21, 1933. Jones was especially drawn to the class dynamics at the heart of Communism's theory of revolution. In the article, he declared, "Class Consciousness. . . . That's what I got out of my trip to New England. Those people [New Englanders] are like the Chinese—ancestor worshipers. They made me realize where I belong." While it is difficult to ascertain just whom Jones socialized with, Provincetown had a well-established leftist community of artists, writers, and activists who, Communist or not, would have been interested in debating the theories of Karl Marx. It included writers Waldo Frank, George Willison, and Edmund Wilson; and artists Karl Knaths, Dorothy Loeb, Fritz Pfeiffer, Douglas Roach (secretary of the local Communist Party), and Bob Rogers. Both Knaths and Jones attended the First American Artists' Congress, in February 1936, as representatives of Provincetown and St. Louis, respectively. I would like to thank Whitney Smith and Stephen Borkowski for their generous assistance with Provincetown history.

7. Important recent scholarship on artists working in the radical left that addresses this issue includes Andrew Hemingway, *Artists on the Left: American Artists and the Communist Movement, 1926–1956* (Yale University Press, 2002); Helen Langa, *Radical Art: Printmaking and the Left in 1930s New York* (University of California Press, 2004); and Alejandro Anreus, Diana L. Linden, and Jonathan Weinberg, eds., *The Social and the Real: Political Art of the 1930s in the Western Hemisphere* (Pennsylvania State University Press, 2006).

8. Stephen Alexander, "Art: Joe Jones," *New Masses* 15, 9 (May 28, 1935), p. 30.

9. Orrick Johns, "The John Reed Clubs Meet," *New Masses* 13, 5 (Oct. 30, 1934), pp. 25–26. The *Anvil*, founded in 1935, was one of a host of "little magazines" in the 1930s dedicated to publishing leftist and proletarian essays and literary works for a working-class readership. The *Anvil* featured work by writers such as Nelson Algren, Meridel LeSueur, and Richard Wright. The magazine's slogan was "We Prefer Crude Vigor to Polished Banality." After merging with the *Partisan Review* in 1937, it was later republished as the *New Anvil*, edited by Algren and Conroy. Conroy himself discussed the important role of the worker-artist (or worker-writer) in a lecture at the 1934 John Reed Club national convention in Chicago: "Pity or idealizations . . . often distort the efforts of middle-class writers in describing factory life, while few workers possess the literary skills or desire to write of their experience"; see paraphrase in Wixson (note 1), p. 379.

10. Quoted in Louisa Iarocci, "The Changing American Landscape: The Art and Politics of Joe Jones," *Gateway Heritage* 12, 2 (Fall 1991), p. 69. See Joe Jones to Elizabeth Green, Aug. 28 and 30, 1935, Dr. John Green Collection, Missouri History Museum, St. Louis (hereinafter Green Papers). As Jones asserted later, "People will have to accept me for what I am, not what they can make out of me"; Jones to Green, n.d. (Fall 1933).

11. Hayden Martin, "House Painter Artist Gives Views on Rivera Murals," *Detroit News*, [1933], St. Louis Public Library, artist's file. Quoted in Richard D. Wells, "Elizabeth Green: A Patronage Portrait," Ph.D. diss. (St. Louis University, 1985), p. 66.

12. Marquis W. Childs, "Three St. Louis Artists," *Magazine of Art* 28, 8 (Aug. 1935), p. 486.

13. "Joe Jones Never Studied Art, but His Mine Scene Stirs Furor," *New York World-Telegram*, Feb. 1, 1936.

14. Anita Brenner (in the Brooklyn *Daily Eagle*), quoted in "Joe Jones of Missouri: A 'Success Story,'" *Art Digest* 10, 8 (Jan. 15, 1936), p. 15.

15. Jacob Burck, "Sectarianism in Art," *New Masses* 8, 8 (Apr. 1933), pp. 26–27.

16. Milton Brown, in *Social Art in America 1930–1945*, exh. cat. (A.C.A. Gallery, 1981), pp. 9–10.

17. Green noted that on May 22, their first day in the city, she "went out with Joe to see the frescoes in the School of Social Economy and a gallery or two"; Green, "Trip East in 2nd hand Pontiac with Provincetown our objective. Joe Jones, his wife Freda and the dog Snippy. Narrative of our journey," Green Papers. Given Jones's radical proclivities, he must also have studied the work of the Mexican muralists the year before, when an exhibition that included easel paintings by all three was displayed at the City Art Museum. See *Mexican Arts: A Catalogue of an Exhibition Organized for and Circulated by the American Federation of Arts*, exh. cat. (American Federation of Arts, 1930).

18. Descriptions of the mural were published in "Social Unrest Mural in Old Court-House," *St. Louis Post-Dispatch*, Feb. 16, 1934; and Johns (note 9).

19. Jones may very well have seen participants of the Bonus March as they camped overnight in the St. Louis railroad yards on their way to Washington, D.C. See "310 War Veterans Camp Here on Way to Demand Bonus," *St. Louis Post-Dispatch*, May 20, 1932.

20. Quoted in "Social Unrest Mural" (note 18).

21. Jacob Kainen, "Joe Jones, Vital Revolutionary Artist," *Daily Worker*, May 5, 1935.

22. "Social Unrest Mural" (note 18).

23 "Chadsey Takes No Chances on Art, Fears Communism," *St. Louis Star-Times*, Dec. 15, 1934.

24. "Old Courthouse Display of Soviet Art Torn Down," *St. Louis Post-Dispatch*, Mar. 5, 1934.

25. Johns to Conroy, Mar. 5, 1934, Conroy Papers.

26. See "Head of Art Class in Old Courthouse Will Oppose Ouster," *St. Louis Globe-Democrat*, Dec. 14, 1934; "Chadsey Takes No Chances" (note 23); "Unemployed Artists Protest on Lockout," *St. Louis Post-Dispatch*, Dec. 16, 1934; "Civic Rights Body to Try City Officials," *St. Louis Globe-Democrat*, Dec. 17, 1934; and "Chadsey Can't Attend Show by Art Students He Evicted," *St. Louis Post-Dispatch*, Jan. 4, 1935.

27. Jones captured the personalities and revolutionary zeal of the congress in a series of watercolor sketches (location unknown). The sketches were reproduced in "At the Congress of Revolutionary Artists and Writers," *St. Louis Post-Dispatch*, Feb. 14, 1937. Jones joined other invitees: German composer Hans Eisler; writer Waldo Frank (who had been in Provincetown when Jones was); Joseph Freeman, an editor of *New Masses*; and filmmaker Mack Schwab. They all participated in public discussions with Mexican leaders about creating a national arts program that would be embraced by the Mexican masses.

28. Jones publicly played on the history of the courthouse. Slaves had been auctioned on its steps, and the initial decision in the Dred Scott case had been made there. As one reporter noted, "[It is] a rather neat conceit, Jones thinks, that negroes whose forebears were sold as slaves at the Courthouse should find there the ultimate in freedom of artistic expression"; "Social Unrest Mural" (note 18).

29. Quoted in "Chadsey Takes No Chances" (note 23). The reporter countered with his own observations that the students "did not look like the artists of musical comedy. Some were decidedly toil worn, but they were undoubtedly trying to draw." The class ended after the eviction, not because of lack of interest, but rather, it seems, because a building that would host a mixed-race class could not be found. Jones wrote to Green,

"I think I should see what can be done at the painters' hall, but I know the negro problem will raise its head there also"; Jones to Green, Mar. 8, 1935, Green Papers.

30. Nathan B. Young, "From *Your St. Louis and Mine*," in *'Ain't But a Place': An Anthology of African American Writings about St. Louis*, ed. by Gerald Early (Missouri Historical Society Press, 1998), p. 340.

31. The association of the roustabout with revolution was quite topical for a radical audience, which could immediately have made a connection between the painting and a popular Communist-themed play about labor and race relations. *Stevedore*, by Paul Peters and George Sklar, debuted with a black and white cast in April 1934 at the Civic Repertory Theatre, New York.

32. Stephen Alexander, "Art," *New Masses* 14, 12 (Mar. 19, 1935), p. 29.

33. Jones showed *Lynching* in the John Reed Club exhibition; see *Struggle for Negro Rights*, exh. cat. (A.C.A. Gallery, 1935). While he referred to *American Justice* early on by the more generic, descriptive title of *Lynching*, he was using the title *American Justice* by the time he exhibited the work at the Worcester (Mass.) Art Museum in 1933. It seems unlikely that he would have shown it later with the descriptive title, and then again with the current title. Since the exhibition catalogue for the John Reed Club show is not illustrated, it remains unclear whether what was titled *Lynching* is a known work or even if it was a painting or print. For an excellent discussion of the two exhibitions, see Helen Langa, "Two Anti-Lynching Art Exhibitions: Politicized Viewpoints, Racial Perspectives, Gendered Constraints," *American Art* 13, 1 (Spring 1999), pp. 11–39.

34. Ben Stone, secretary at Worcester Art Museum, to Jones, Dec. 30, 1933, Green Papers.

35. Jones to Green, n.d. (1933), Green Papers.

36. In 1939 sixty-five percent of white respondents stated they felt lynching was justified when it involved sexual assault. See Jacquelyn Dowd Hall, "'The Mind That Burns in Each Body': Women, Rape, and Racial Violence," in *Moral Controversies: Race, Class, Gender in Applied Ethics*, ed. by Stephen Jay Gould (Wadsworth Publishing Co., 1993), p. 305.

37. See Langa (note 33), p. 28.

38. Edward J. Blum, "Lynching as Crucifixion: Violence and the Sacred Imagination of W.E.B. DuBois," in *The Souls of W.E.B. DuBois*, ed. by Edward J. Blum and Jason R. Young (Mercer University Press, 2009), p. 190.

39. *Chicago Defender*, Aug. 16, 1930; quoted in Shawn Michelle Smith, "The Evidence of Lynching Photographs," in Dora Apel and Shawn Michelle Smith, *Lynching Photographs* (University of California Press, 2007), p. 20. Lawrence Beitler took the photograph of the lynching.

40. "Joe Jones Starts Murals at Commonwealth College," Commonwealth College press release, Aug. 17, 1935, Green Papers. In most descriptions of the mural, the panels are numbered one through five, from right to left. This suggests that they were arranged along the southern wall in the college's Commons Room so that, upon entering the room, a viewer first encountered the right end of the mural, making the logical reading right to left, rather than left to right, as one would otherwise assume. Descriptions of the mural are found in Al Lehman, "Brilliant Murals by Joe Jones Decorate Labor College Walls," *Daily Worker*, Aug. 31, 1935; and "Joe Jones Made Artistic Boswell of Life in U.S.," *New York Herald Tribune*, Oct. 1935, Green Papers.

41. The extant panels of the mural are now at the University of Arkansas, Little Rock. While the mural has suffered significant losses, it can be reconstructed through photographs from Jones's sketchbook, held by the artist's family, as well as a verbal description accompanied by illustrations in Fielding Burke, "Pelzer: 'Just Another of Those Damned Strike Towns,'" *New Masses* 17, 5 (Oct. 29, 1935), p. 16; and "Art: Southern Labor's Story in Blue, Gray, and Fiery Red," *Newsweek* 6, 9 (Aug. 31, 1935), p. 21.

42. For a history of the college told by two of its leaders, see Raymond and Charlotte Koch, *Educational Commune: The Story of Commonwealth College* (Schocken Books, 1972).

43. Quoted in "Joe Jones Made Artistic Boswell" (note 40). Jones was elated with the mural and spoke of his enthusiasm to create similar ones. See Jones to Green, Aug. 4 and 19, 1935, Green Papers; and John Selby, "Joe Jones, Who Began as House Painter, Hailed as Promising Artist," *St. Louis Globe-Democrat*, Sept. 11, 1938. Jones also credited his Resettlement Administration commission to the success of his murals in the Old Courthouse and Commonwealth College; Jones to Green, Sept. 12, 1935, Green Papers.

44. Quoted in "Mural in Commons Nears Completion," *Commonwealth College Fortnightly* 11, 17 (Sept. 1, 1935), p. 4. Bloor, Conroy, and Jones all lectured at the college that summer. After completing his mural, Jones traveled for nearly a month with Bloor as she gave talks along the way to the East Coast. Bloor, who had investigated child labor for Upton Sinclair and had worked for numerous Communist Party election campaigns, was known for her radical speechmaking, nurturing, and straightforward explanations of Communism. A farmer's wife and mother of eight, she spoke as one with laborers. It seems likely that she was a strong model for Jones. See Sandra J. Sarkela, Susan Mallon Ross, and Margaret A. Lowe, *From Megaphones to Microphones: Speeches of American Women, 1920–1960* (Praeger Publishers, 2003), pp. 85–88; and "Ella Reeve Bloor," in *American Radical and Reform Writers*, ed. by Steven Rosendale (Thompson Gale, 2005), pp. 37–44.

45. The richness of Jones's explorations at the college—perhaps the result of the emotional warmth and inspiration of like-mindedness he found there or of the visual inspiration of the anti-lynching exhibitions—sustained a continued visual dialogue in other works by him. Motifs and vignettes in this mural are also seen in the shared likeness of the heavyset mining boss and the boss in *Roustabouts*; the blighted landscape behind the mine and the landscape of *Our American Farms* (1936; cat. 42); and the group of seated miners in *Miners* (1935; cat. 38).

46. "Housepainter," *Time* 25, 22 (June 3, 1935), p. 32.

47. Hall (note 36), p. 309, noted that, when black and white women active in anti-lynching associations gathered to discuss issues, the former actively talked about the lack of attention paid to the rape of black women by white men. Since many of the participants of the Funsten strike commented on the novelty of whites meeting with blacks in their homes, and vice versa, it seems at least plausible that the radical black women in this group brought the topic of rape to the dialogue such visits engendered. The disparity in racial justice would have been on Jones's mind at this time as well, due to the extensive coverage of the trials of the Scottsboro Boys—nine black teenagers falsely accused of gang-raping two white girls. In what many decried as a "legal lynching," eight received death sentences (later commuted) and one, a mistrial. Just months before Jones created *American Justice*, then, national headlines revealed all too clearly the extent to which a capricious claim of black-on-white rape could put the lives of so many at stake, while innumerable cases of white-on-black rape were ignored.

48. Frances K. Pohl, *In the Eye of the Storm: An Art of Conscience, 1930–70, Selections from the Collection of Philip J. and Suzanne Schiller*, exh. cat. (Pomegranate Art Books, 1995), p. 50.

49. Quoted in Feurer (note 2), p. 33.

50. It seems possible as well that Jones's willingness to place African Americans in leadership roles was due in part to his experience growing up next to the Ville, a mostly working-class African American neighborhood in St. Louis known for the high quality of its leaders, education, and services.

51. For a discussion of manliness in the art of the 1930s, see Barbara Melosh, *Engendering Culture: Manhood and Womanhood in New Deal Public Art and Theater* (Smithsonian Institution Press, 1991); and Erika Doss, "Looking at Labor: Images of Work in 1930s American Art," *Journal of Decorative and Propaganda Arts* 24 (2002), pp. 231–57.

52. Kainen (note 21).

53. Ibid.

54. Lewis Mumford, "The Art Galleries: In Capitulation," *New Yorker* 11, 16 (June 1, 1935), p. 57; repr. in *Mumford on Modern Art in the 1930s*, ed. and with intro. by Robert Wojotiwicz (University of California Press, 2007), pp. 164–67.

55. Johns to Conroy, Apr. 7, 1934, Conroy Papers.

56. See Herman Baron's revealing account of Jones's internal dilemma when, after his second New York solo exhibition, he was invited to show at a museum being boycotted by progressives. "As a young boy," Baron wrote, "[Jones] dreamed of riches when he grew up; success to him meant acceptance into the upper classes." He quoted the artist as saying that he had "always dreamed that some day I would be invited to that exhibi-

tion and win a prize." But, Baron continued, Jones pushed away the "coveted crown because he could not turn 'scab.'" Herman Baron, "Social Art," in "History of A.C.A. Gallery, " unpub. MS, pp. 35–37, A.C.A. Papers, Archives of American Art, Smithsonian Institution, Washington, D.C. Karal Ann Marling also discussed this dilemma in "Workers, Capitalists, and Booze: The Story of the 905 Murals," in *Joe Jones & J. B. Turnbull: Visions of the Midwest in the 1930s* (Haggerty Museum of Art, Marquette University, 1987), pp. 7–25. According to an unsigned article, "sneers of the academicians helped make [Jones] class conscious," and the artist's buckteeth revealed his proletariat roots; "Joe Jones Made Artistic Boswell" (note 40). Jones focused on teeth as a signifier of class in his photographic studies. See "Pages from a Painter's Notebook," *St. Louis Post-Dispatch*, Dec. 13, 1936. When he was finally able to afford the dental work he needed, he declared, "Beginning with the day after the operation, I have had a distinct feeling of starting a new life . . . without the antagonisms which has its roots in one's own inferiority"; Jones to Green, Mar. 18, 1938, Green Papers.

57. Herman Baron, *Joe Jones*, exh. cat. (A.C.A. Gallery, 1937), n. pag.

58. Jones never indicated the specific source of this title. However, in most sexual dictionaries, the bottle dance is described as a striptease specialty that requires gripping a bottle with the vaginal muscles. This would suit Jones's propensity for confronting extreme or abject subjects. The bottle dance is also the most famous folk dance of Paraguay. Female dancers engage in violent movements while balancing one or more water-filled vessels on their heads. During the colonial era of the 1930s and '40s, Cameroonian musicians in palm-wine establishments would strike bottles to create music for dancers. Like European coffee houses, these gathering spots served as sites for debate and artistic creation, as well as places for "sinful behaviour, moral degeneration . . . and passage for men heading for the brothels"; Nicodemus Fru Awasom, *The Emergence of Public Spheres in Colonial Cameroon: The Case of Palm Wine Drinking Joints as lieux de sociabilité in Bamenda Township* (University of The Gambia, 2008), p. 3. Both the Paraguayan and Cameroonian traditions could have been transported to St. Louis, where they were modified by cultural groups.

59. Quoted in Baron (note 56).

60. "Subject matter has always been a thing I have made acceptable by my handling"; Jones to Green, n.d. (1933), Green Papers. Reviewers noted the contrast of the "powerful indictment of society," social disease, and "courageous and tragic and horrifying" content in Jones's work with his careful, "old master's" touch; Baron (note 57).

61. Jones to Green, Feb. 16, 1935, Green Papers. Indeed, Jones proved influential. Baron suggested that it was Jones's example that pushed William Gropper to move from cartoons to painting; Baron (note 56), p. 34.

62. Edward Alden Jewell, "Ex-House Painter in Art Show Here," *New York Times*, May 22, 1935. Jewell had seen Jones's work before his solo show, when the critic had delivered the opening address for the Worcester Art Museum's annual exhibition of 1933.

63. Herman Baron, *31 American Contemporary Artists*, exh. cat. (A.C.A. Gallery, 1959), n. pag.

64. Thomas C. Lin, "A Scolding Show by 20 Artists," *New York Times*, Nov. 13, 1932; and Baron (note 56), p. 8.

65. Hemingway (note 7), p. 105.

66. "Social Documents," *New York Herald Tribune*, Oct. 31, 1937.

67. Jerome Klein, "Twenty-one Gun Salute," *Art Front* 1, 5 (May 1935), p. 6; quoted in Hemingway (note 7), pp. 70–71.

68. Quoted in "Joe Jones of Missouri: A 'Success Story,'" *Art Digest* 10, 8 (Jan. 15, 1936), p. 15.

69. Hemingway (note 7), p. 138. See also Jones to Green, Sept. 12, 1935, Green Papers.

70. Robert Hanna to Green, Feb. 21, 1935, Green Papers. The enthusiasm of a convert is apparent in Jones's letters to Green. "I just returned from 6 hours in the Metropolitan Museum," he wrote in one, "and there is more there that interests me than any other place. This is my 4th visit. Tomorrow will be the fifth"; Jones to Green, Mar. 8, 1935, Green Papers.

71. For a discussion of his milieu in St. Louis between 1935 and 1937, see Wixson (note 1), p. 368.

72. Jones to Green, Sept. 27, 1937, Green Papers.

73. "Getting my feet on the ground here again has been rather difficult, after my visit home, while St. Louis slips into the past it's so hard to build something in its place. Everyday is an effort visiting people"; Jones to Green, Jan. 26, 1938, Green Papers.

74. Eli Jaffe, *Oklahoma Odyssey: A Memoir* (Eli Jaffe, 1993), p. 3. This story is also recounted in Shirley and Wayne Wiegand, *Books on Trial: Red Scare in the Heartland* (University of Oklahoma Press, 2007), p. 43. Jaffe did take Jones's admonition seriously, and by the next year he was in Oklahoma participating in the activities of the radical community there. He also spent time as a writer-in-residence at Commonwealth College, which was located only twenty-two miles from the Oklahoma–Arkansas border. See Jaffe, p. 45.

75. "Increase in power": untitled clipping, *New York Sun*, Nov. 16, 1940, A.C.A. Papers (note 56). "New surface opulence . . .": "New Qualities Appear in Joe Jones' Paintings," *New York World-Telegram*, Nov. 16, 1940.

76. Jones to Green, Mar. 18, 1938, Green Papers.

77. Quoted in Selby (note 43). The viability of the Communist Party essentially ended in late 1939 for most Americans with the Hitler–Stalin Pact.

78. The sketch, titled *Working on the Railroad* (cat. 73), was reproduced on the cover of *Recent Paintings, Joe Jones*, exh. cat. (A.C.A. Gallery, 1939); see "Herman Baron," p. 103.

79. "St. Louis Artists' Show Opens," *St. Louis Globe-Democrat*, Oct. 30, 1938.

80. Not surprisingly, a reviewer of Jones's 1939 A.C.A. Gallery exhibition noted that "violent social protest . . . has been reduced to a definitely minor role. . . . In the current show harvesters are matched in number by railroad workers"; "Joe Jones Matures," *Art Digest* 14, 5 (Dec. 1, 1939), p. 12.

81. Brown (note 16), p. 14.

82. Jones to Jack Boksenbaum, Jan. 10, 1957, Saint Louis Art Museum, archives.

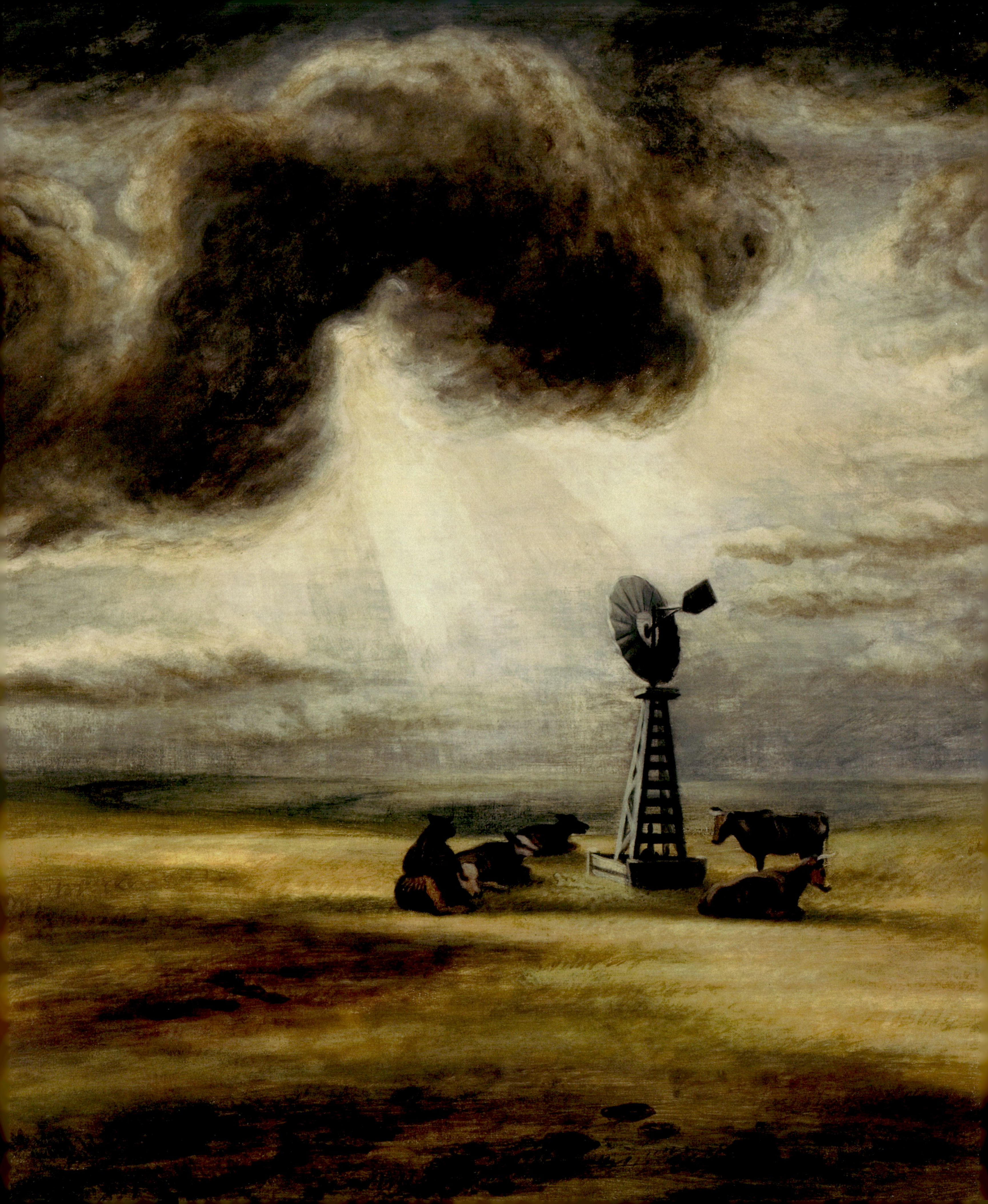

Joe Jones and the Dust Bowl: A Search for Social Significance

Andrew Walker

Joe Jones considered himself not just an artist, but a Midwestern artist. The distinction is important, even essential, to understanding how Jones built his national reputation after he left St. Louis for his first prolonged stay in New York in 1935. Jones recognized that his identity as an artist from the Midwest brought an authenticity to subjects that enjoyed new popularity in the art world of the 1930s. In this way, he was not unlike his Missouri forebear George Caleb Bingham (see Wolfe, fig. 4), who became famous nationally for his antebellum scenes of life along the Mississippi and Missouri rivers. In 1934 Bingham was the subject of a retrospective at the City Art Museum of St. Louis (now the Saint Louis Art Museum). Whether Jones visited the show is not known, though the following year it traveled to the Museum of Modern Art (MoMA), New York, where he could also have seen it.

The coincidence of Jones's artistic introduction and Bingham's revival in New York in 1935 is thought provoking. Though separated by a century, both artists recognized the relevance of the local in choosing their subjects. St. Louis critic Marquis W. Childs, in writing of the Bingham revival, called out the painter's resistance to an "art-for-art's sake" approach. Rather, the nineteenth-century artist played a role in shaping the "trend of the times, not only with his brush, but directly as well," through his active role in the political culture of the region in which he lived. "The revival of interest in Bingham is in part evidence," Childs continued, "of what many critics regard as a radical shift in style and taste back in the direction of representation and narrative value."[1]

When the Bingham retrospective opened at MoMA in 1935, the museum's director, Alfred H. Barr, Jr., echoed Childs's observation in the exhibition pamphlet: "A full generation before Homer and Eakins [Bingham] painted the 'American Scene,' making a vivid record of life in the Mississippi Valley."[2] Clearly, cultural leaders in St. Louis and New York saw Bingham as a forerunner of American Scene painters, whether a regionalist such as Thomas Hart Benton or a social realist such as William Gropper. At the same time, they accepted the importance of New York as the American art-world capital, where high-profile careers were launched and solidified.

Jones followed a parallel path. He shared with other American Scene painters the belief that art has a social purpose, rooted in authentic experience. He was also convinced that, as a painter and advocate of social reform, he needed to be known in New York. Beginning in 1935 and continuing through 1941, Jones sought a platform in the national art world, building on his identity, like Bingham, as a Missourian whose deep connections to the land and its people gave him legitimacy.

1935: ARRIVING IN NEW YORK

When Jones arrived in New York in 1935, he was deeply aware that his life was changing. His marriage to his first wife, Freda Sies, had ended, giving him renewed energy to focus on his art making. "I have managed to meet the widest variety of people who really know about painting," he enthused to his St. Louis patron Elizabeth Green, "from the most conventional reactionary people to the most developed radicals who have a genuine knowledge of the cultural movement [and] who have all showed a real and genuine enthusiasm about my work."[3] His days were filled: when he was not meeting artists or going to museums and exhibitions, he painted (see Balken). As he summed up in a letter to Green, "I've seen so much in the short time I've been here. I'm ready to explode."[4]

That explosion intensified with the positive reception he received from the New York art world for his first major solo exhibition, at the American Contemporary Art (A.C.A.) Gallery in May 1935. The show included several farm scenes, as well as *American Justice* (1933; cat. 31) and other socially concerned works such as *Roustabouts* and *We Demand* (both 1934; cats. 32–33). Given Jones's overt engagement with radical content, what most critics wanted to know was whether he was a painter or a propagandist. Lewis Mumford, writing for the *New Yorker*, and Edward Alden Jewell, the influential critic for the *New York Times*, each lauded Jones as the season's star and praised his ability to present activist subject matter in an artistically sophisticated manner, avoiding the trap of being overly polemical.[5] In fact Jewell's view that Jones's formal strengths trumped his partisan content clearly became a point of debate among the critics taken with this twenty-six-year-old self-taught newcomer. As Mumford cautioned, his overtly political compositions could fall prey to "pulseless propaganda" and thus lose not only compositional subtlety but also authenticity.[6] To prove his point, he pointed to *New Deal* (fig. 1), which critiqued flawed federal agricultural policies. A farmer plows under his cotton on the left. On the right, milk strikers pour the contents of their pails onto a road. And in the center, an emaciated woman holding an eviction notice nurses a sickly baby. Mumford believed that works like this, while ambitious, lacked focus: *New Deal*'s heavy-handed political message overpowered the artist's ability to depict landscape sensitively; rather, it was rendered in undifferentiated patterned surfaces—"like paper cutouts"—that lacked the weight of forms in space.[7]

For Mumford and other writers, Jones excelled as a painter when he stayed true to local topics, especially in his treatment of scenes of rural Missouri. "But it is when the artist forgets his social mission," wrote the critic for the *New York Sun*, "that he seems most thoroughly the painter."[8] And Jewell noted in his review: "Socially, this may be called a Left Wing show—if with important digressions, such as the arresting rural subjects 'Red Earth' and 'Wheat.'"[9] *Wheat*, which Jones had debuted at the Whitney Museum of American Art's annual paintings exhibition of the previous year, is known only through a surviving black and white reproduction (fig. 2). *Wheat* and *Red Earth* (c. 1935; cat. 35) present lively panoramic scenes of rural labor. In the first, a farmer drives a motorized tractor as he harvests an abundant wheat crop; in the second, a man, seated on a horse-drawn plow, tills the reddish earth into deep furrows, preparing the ground for planting. As though meditating on the seasons, Jones imposed upon the land a geometry which reinforces the structure of constant labor that defines a farmer's life.

Although the more conventional press considered these seemingly straightforward landscapes as non-political, reviews in the left-wing *Art Front* and *New Masses* made a particular point of emphasizing their social import. "The textures are rich and firm, the outlines blurred," wrote Clarence Weinstock, one of the most eloquent defenders of Social Realism, "an exuberant romantic merger by means of color brings man, machine, wheat and sky together."[10] Stephen Alexander, another leftist critic, connected both *Wheat* and *Red Earth* to Jones's social mission:

> The stuff of America is deep in these pictures. Jones loves his country and his people, and has written his feeling for them into honest paintings. You will find here none of the slick waxen lies of a Grant Wood prettying up the Middle West in overmantel pictures for drawing rooms. When Jones paints a landscape it

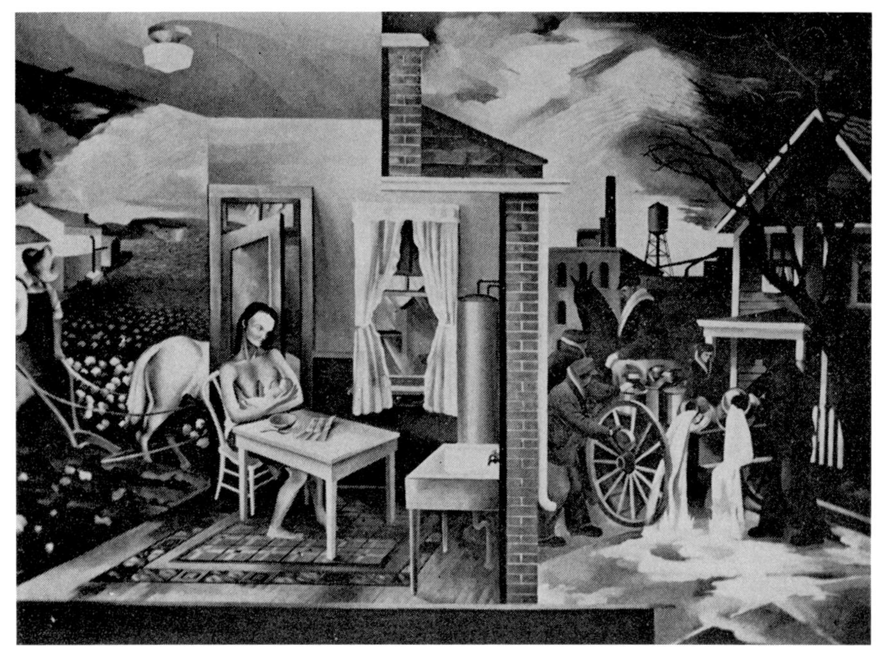

Fig. 1. Joe Jones. *New Deal* (or *Capitalism*), 1933. Oil on canvas. Location unknown. Reproduced in *Joe Jones*, exh. cat. (A.C.A. Gallery, 1937), n. pag.

is a straightforward, honest observation ("Red Earth," "Wheat"). But he does not stop at simply giving a faithful visual report. It is when he adds a class-conscious mind to a trained hand and eye, that he achieves his most significant expression.[11]

For both writers, class consciousness underlay the union of man and nature that Jones captured in his images, as well as in his insistence that he too, as a worker-artist, was subject to the socio-political circumstances of the world in which he lived.[12]

Jones's work struck viewers as truthful; he was able to paint mid-America because of his active participation in Midwestern life. Meyric Rogers, director of the City Art Museum, said as much in the introduction he authored for the A.C.A. exhibition's pamphlet: "He paints what he has lived with and among and knows in so living. Subject matter is important to him as it is part and parcel of what seems visually interesting and, therefore, worth celebrating in pigment."[13] The artist's choices of what to paint were driven by his worldview, both physically and politically. Jones's success as a painter was ultimately, according to Weinstock, the result of "an intelligence which his economic position as a worker, and his political insight as a class-conscious one, furnish him with constantly increasing material."[14]

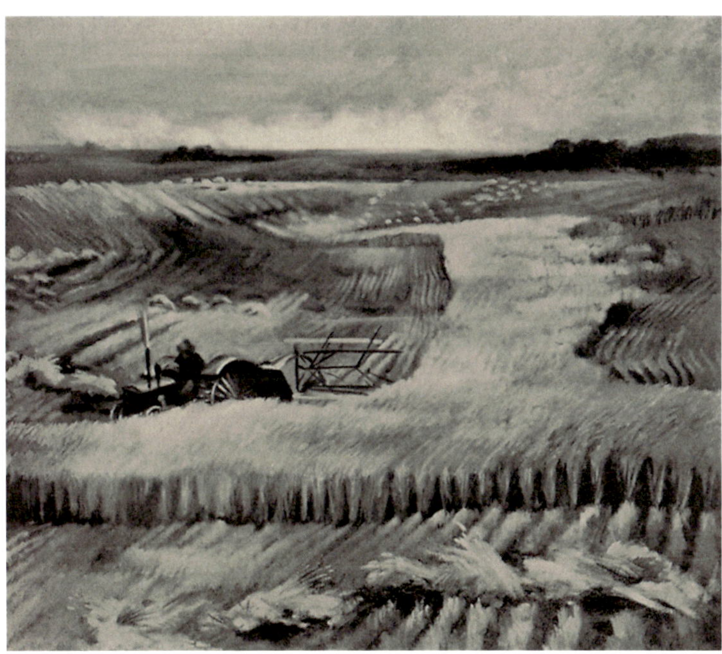

Fig. 2. Joe Jones. *Wheat*, 1934. Oil on canvas. Location unknown. Reproduced in *Magazine of Art* 28, 1 (January 1935), p. 47.

"THE PROFESSOR OF WHEAT"

The success of the 1935 exhibition at the A.C.A. Gallery made Jones something of a celebrity among the set interested in art with a social message. As doors opened to the artist, he sought another subject rooted in his experience, something that would validate his artistic efforts even more. Surprisingly, however, Jones did not find that content in urban subjects, but rather in the labors of Midwestern farmers and sharecroppers, which he encountered firsthand in St. Charles, a farming community just west of St. Louis. His time in the fields that summer resulted in an array of richly colorful and compositionally complex canvases. Although he claimed to have worked alongside the farmers and itinerant laborers mowing across the broad bottomlands of St. Charles, it is not likely that he cut or bundled any wheat himself.[15] Rather his labor involved the paintbrush. In his images of the winter-wheat harvest, he positioned himself deep in the landscape, on the same plane as the field workers. He expressed a bold exuberance for this work, which he described in a letter to Green in early July as the harvest was concluding: "The flowing wheat and puffy clouds goes [*sic*] clear through you and life begins from there."[16] That exuberance is seen in works such as *Farmer with Wheat* (fig. 3) and *Straw Stacks No. 2* (1935; cat. 36), in which Jones situated himself in a sea of cut wheat. In the former, only the heads of a field worker and his horses are visible over the top of the crop. In the latter, the wheat, now harvested, has become an undulating hill. Dominating the composition, this piled-high, golden crop bridges farm and sky to overwhelm the mules and the farmer perched on top of the straw stack.

The work that resulted from that summer became the foundation of Jones's next one-person exhibition in New York, titled "Paintings of Wheat Fields"; it was held at the Walker Galleries, on 57th Street, for two weeks in January 1936. Maynard Walker, director of the Walker Galleries, was well known at the time as the primary supporter of regionalists Thomas Hart Benton, John Steuart Curry, and Grant Wood. Walker mounted Jones's exhibition in cooperation with A.C.A. director Herman Baron. The event afforded a new perspective on the potential for political advocacy in American Scene painting. Jones was not a straightforward regionalist uncritically celebrating the Midwest. His paintings of farm laborers, unlike those of Benton (see Wolfe, fig. 5; and Balken, figs. 4–5), were born out of his empathy for their economic struggle and the dignity their work bestowed upon them. Critics by and large confirmed the exhibition's positive appeal on these terms. Jones's landscapes were "very direct," "forceful," and "essentially American," in the opinion of Bryan Holme, writing for *London Studio*.[17] An announcement of the show in *Forum* made that "essentially American" aspect into a narrative:

> With a directness as characteristic as his name, young Joe Jones retired from the heart-warming success of his New York debut to work in the wheat country bordering St. Louis, his birthplace and his home. There, convinced that his artistic growth and strength must come from a deep actual understanding of the subjects he wanted to paint and not from intellectual concepts, he labored in the fields with farmers, and painted both.[18]

Working alongside his subjects confirmed Jones's artistic authenticity, prompting some to place his work at the same level as that of celebrated artists. In the *New Yorker*, Mumford ranked *Farmer with Wheat* with the best accomplishments of Vincent van Gogh. A notice in *Art News* praised Jones for drawing the figure with the assurance of both Thomas Eakins and Winslow Homer. It continued: "The case of Joe Jones offers a concrete contribution to the widely discussed question of the use of native material by native artists. Naturally his choice of subject matter is not only original but praiseworthy, and his whole work can be heralded as a return by American artists to a content approaching that of Winslow Homer."[19]

Importantly, Knoedler Galleries, New York, had just opened a retrospective exhibition of watercolors by Homer, whose reputation as one of the country's greatest artists was growing at this time. Critics celebrated his focus on American life as an aspect of the revolutionary role he played in shaping the history of American art. Jones was clearly part of a uniquely national tradition linked to indigenous subjects depicted in an innovative style that eschewed the "complexities and abstractions of the whole modern concept."[20]

Jones wrote to Green of the positive response to his show: "I feel as though my work up here has reached a glorious conclusion for the time."[21] In late January, he penned another quick note to her: "I think the show a success, and there is a general feeling now that I am in the first place as an artist in America; this sound[s] incredible[;] but up here its [*sic*] not hard to believe."[22] He relished the fact that he had been dubbed in the media "the Professor of Wheat."[23]

Although many critics at the time interpreted Jones's farm scenes as positive, simple statements of exuberance, largely free of polemics, there were important exceptions. A writer for *Survey Graphic* observed that Jones's decision to work among laborers was related to his "proletarian philosophy," which aligned them with the urban workers he had painted the year before.[24] In an article in *Fortune* magazine extolling the best art of 1935, the poet and writer Archibald MacLeish was circumspect about the

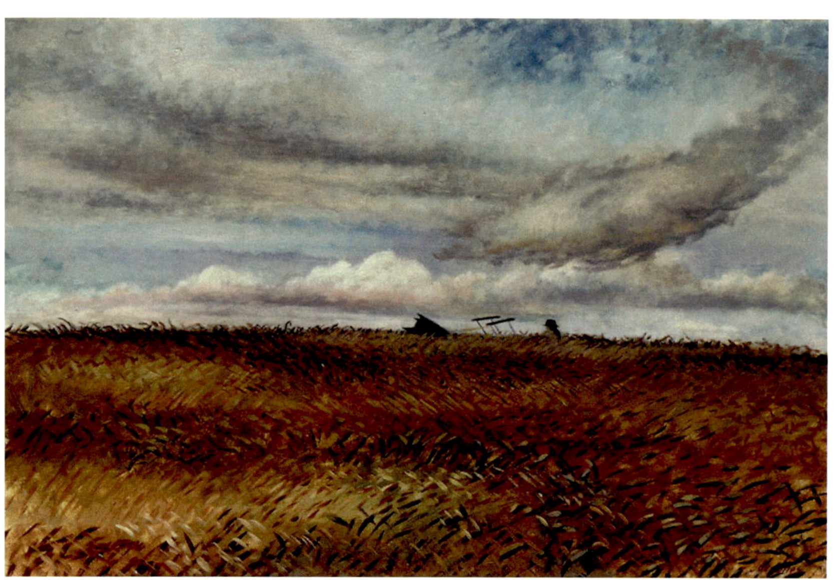

Fig. 3. Joe Jones. *Farmer with Wheat*, 1935. Oil on Masonite; 24 × 36 in. (61 × 91.4 cm). Private collection.

seemingly apolitical nature of Jones's themes. MacLeish had visited Jones's New York apartment-studio in late 1935 and witnessed the progress of his wheat series. His article, which appeared before the artist's exhibition opened at the Walker Galleries, focused largely on *Threshing No. 1* (1935; cat. 34), which the magazine illustrated in full color. "If this picture here seems non-political to you, thank Jones's insistence on objectivity and examine more thoughtfully the face of the farmer and his left fist in yours (a probably deliberate paraphrase of the communist salute) which bring the whole landscape into line."[25]

MacLeish's interpretation of the farmer's raised fist as a deliberate allusion to a Communist symbol relates to what Jones perceived as his success, both in the Walker show and in his career to this point. The writer's suggestion transforms *Threshing No. 1* from a celebration of Missouri's agricultural abundance into a socialist critique of a troubled time for Midwestern farmers, during which overproduction and land policy were severely undercutting their livelihoods. As we have seen with his *New Deal*, Jones understood these circumstances, particularly as dire agricultural problems led to widespread displacement among tenant farmers and sharecroppers. Jones told Green that he considered his depiction of the land in that work vibrant and successful, but this is not to say that the image does not possess a dark side.[26] Under the New Deal's crop-reduction program, farm owners were paid to plow under their fields. The result was that sharecroppers and tenants farmers who actually worked the land were forced to migrate. Jones's awareness of the politics and the hardship that lay just beneath the surface of those farmlands he so richly painted would only deepen as he increasingly confronted the realities of the Dust Bowl.

THE DUST BOWL

From 1930 to 1936 (and in some places to 1940), acute drought and bad land management caused severe ecological and agricultural damage to American prairie lands. These severe conditions affected some 100 million acres in the United States. What came to be known as the Dust Bowl stretched from the Texas Panhandle and adjacent parts of New Mexico and Colorado, to Arkansas, Oklahoma, Nebraska, Kansas, Missouri, Iowa, and into the Dakotas. By 1940 some 2.5 million people had been forced to move from their homes and businesses in these areas, constituting the largest migration within a short period of time that the United States has ever experienced.

While the term Dust Bowl evokes the hardships experienced by farmers during the 1930s due to drought, the factors contributing to such devastation were much more complex. At the end of World War I, the price of wheat and other agricultural commodities plummeted. This sudden drop threatened the stability of farms across the Midwest, forcing a number of owners into tenancy in order to stay solvent. The particular topography of the Great Plains region further aggravated this financial precariousness. Area farmers were unfamiliar with the technique known as "dry farming," whereby arid land without irrigation is planted with drought-resistant crops and a fine ground surface is maintained to protect the natural moisture of the soil from evaporation. As farmers attempted to pull more crops from the land to offset the ruinous consequences of deflation, they actively depleted the soil, making it more vulnerable once the drought began in 1930. Substantially weakened by the stock-market collapse the year before, the banking system was ill-equipped to help people hold onto their farms in the face of this convergence of natural and market calamities. As farmers fell behind on property taxes and mortgages, most banks were unable or unwilling to extend credit or refinance to help alleviate the financial burdens. As a result, the number of forced sales of farms, bankruptcies, and foreclosures from 1932 to 1934 was more than double the number from 1927 to 1929.[27]

The Agricultural Adjustment Act (AAA) of 1933 was intended to tackle the depressed price of wheat, and large landowners in the Midwest enthusiastically embraced the program. In an attempt to raise the price of agricultural commodities by reducing market supply, the federal government offered to pay farmers to not till portions of their fields. The Agricultural Adjustment Administration oversaw the distribution of subsidies to farmers who reduced their crop size. This access to ready cash was a benefit to many farmers who used the subsidy checks to pay off debts and modernize their production processes by purchasing new farm machinery.[28] Since the AAA required farm owners to share their subsidy checks with any tenants working their land, many chose to work around the system by employing transient day laborers with whom they had no obligation to share the subsidies. In fact farm owners frequently chose to evict their workers and keep the government money. Like a perfect storm, the drop in prices, poor farming decisions, and an economic crisis of epic proportions made for a new underclass of tenant farmers and sharecroppers. The resulting social blight was exactly what attracted Jones to the Dust Bowl.

Jones's harvest paintings, such as *Threshing No. 1*, stood in stark contrast to what was, in fact, a depleted, even deadened landscape. The farmer, his pitchfork overflowing with wheat, seems to deny the poverty and desperation that farmers faced daily. Although the St. Charles region was not affected by the ecological devastation of the Dust Bowl, farms there had participated in the widespread problem of overproduction, thereby destabilizing the market. By late 1935, when Jones was in his studio painting his experiences in St. Charles, watching the winter harvest was a somewhat distant memory. He had followed this by traveling in August to Commonwealth College in Mena, Arkansas. The left-leaning college had invited Jones to deliver a series of lectures; he remained there when he was asked to paint a mural for the dining hall (see Wolfe, fig. 6; cat. 39; and Chronology, figs. 7–8). His stay in Mena put him in the midst of the Dust Bowl, where he saw the struggles of sharecroppers evicted from their homes. As M. Langley Biegert noted, by 1934 "landowners had been evicting tenants and sharecroppers throughout the South, with little or no compensation."[29] The school was becoming an outspoken voice for the American labor movement, particularly tenant farmers. One section of Jones's mural focuses on that very issue. An African American family lies on the floor of their cabin, hungry and forlorn, while an emaciated cow enters from the field. Beyond the open doorway, a lone tenant farmer plows under the rich cotton crop to meet the government's buy-out plan at the expense of the family's livelihood.

In order to prepare for his commission, Jones traveled through the Dust Bowl, witnessing heartrending scenes of Depression-wrought devastation.[30] "I have excellent photos to work from," he wrote to Green, "the best I've made so far."[31] Jones could not depict an idealized rural life. He had found a new theme in landscapes of the rural Midwest, one that could promote social commentary. What he needed now was a national platform through which to proffer his work.

WORKING FOR THE NEW DEAL

In fall 1935, Green attempted to connect Jones with Edward B. Rowan, head of the Treasury Relief Art Program (TRAP) so that the artist might find work with this agency. She told Rowan about Jones's youthful spirit and growing reputation: "It is still in the early stages, but I think it important to place Joe Jones's name before the proper person."[32] Indeed, Rowan was that person: he had seen Jones's exhibit at the A.C.A. Gallery and had been particularly impressed with the agricultural images showcased there.[33] He wrote the artist in August 1935 to say that Olin Dows, an artist and TRAP official, wanted to offer him a job painting murals. Under the terms of the program, as an artist from Missouri, Jones would be paid $79 per month, provided that he was eligible for relief. Initially, Jones seemed interested in the offer. Deep into his Commonwealth College project, he believed that murals, the focus of TRAP, offered a momentous opportunity to create socially impactful art with access to a wide public. He also felt that the federal initiative was a worthy jobs program for needy artists.[34] But after weighing the compensation package, Jones rejected the job. He was emphatic. One could not live on the salary being offered. In a strongly worded letter to Green, Jones outlined his position:

> I am not negating the fact that the government can be a patron of the arts, but I do know artists as well as other workers have to be paid a living wage, and when they are not, they will have to fight for a living

wage as other workers do. Also I am not forgetting the necessity of my making my own living. It doesn't seem fair to me that the government should receive my entire artistic output . . . and even then have the chance of having my work destroyed because of its honesty. I will work very carefully with Rowan on this matter but he will have to prove to me the sincerity of our government as a patron of the arts. . . . I want to do murals, which you know, but they will be honest, intelligent and I expect to be paid for them.[35]

Jones's perspective underscored his position regarding art making as a form of labor. The edge of agitation in his tone reveals his identification with radicalized workers, whether on the docks of St. Louis or in the fields of St. Charles.

Conversations with Rowan, whom Jones met in Washington, D.C. in late August, led to a more acceptable option. A new program was getting under way: the Resettlement Administration (RA). The RA was created by executive order in 1935 and brought together a number of initiatives meant to alleviate rural poverty.[36] Rexford G. Tugwell, a professor at Columbia University, New York, served as the RA's director. He defined the interlaced programs' main goal: to effect "sweeping land reform" by removing small and tenant farmers from compromised areas, especially in the Dust Bowl region, and setting them up on more efficient farms with better soil.[37] Moreover, the establishment of rural cooperatives would enable farmers to share the most modern agricultural machinery. As he wrote in the introduction to the first pamphlet describing the RA:

> The fundamental problem is the readjustment of people to the land resources of the Nation. Land must be adapted to its best economic use. Our pioneering policies of exploitation and careless use of the land are no longer possible or feasible and can no longer be continued. Millions of American citizens in rural areas require assistance to enable them to become self-sustaining and to enjoy a decent American standard of living.[38]

Insisting that government land purchase and rural settlement constituted the only viable long-term solution, Tugwell's ardent text reads like a polemic; he was labeled Rexford the Red by opponents who accused him of being a far-left radical. The claims that, under Tugwell, the RA intended to "socialize" America's land and "collectivize" its people prompted controversy and ultimately the dissolution of the organization.[39]

For Jones, however, the RA's plan went right to the heart of his own beliefs. As a telegram distributed by the RA's office in Little Rock, Arkansas, states: "The purpose of Resettlement is not only to help the farmer himself but to help the Nation as a whole by stabilizing that segment of the Nation's population which has been shifting back and forth between country and city—comprising in times of depression a large percentage of the total of unemployed."[40] Not surprisingly, then, Jones rejected Rowan's offer to join the mural project and chose instead to consider a position with the RA's Special Skills Division.

The Special Skills Division was one of two within the RA created to employ artists and photographers. The other, the Historical Section, used them to photograph the economic and social conditions in the Dust Bowl that made the RA necessary. Under the direction of another Columbia University professor, Roy Stryker, this section

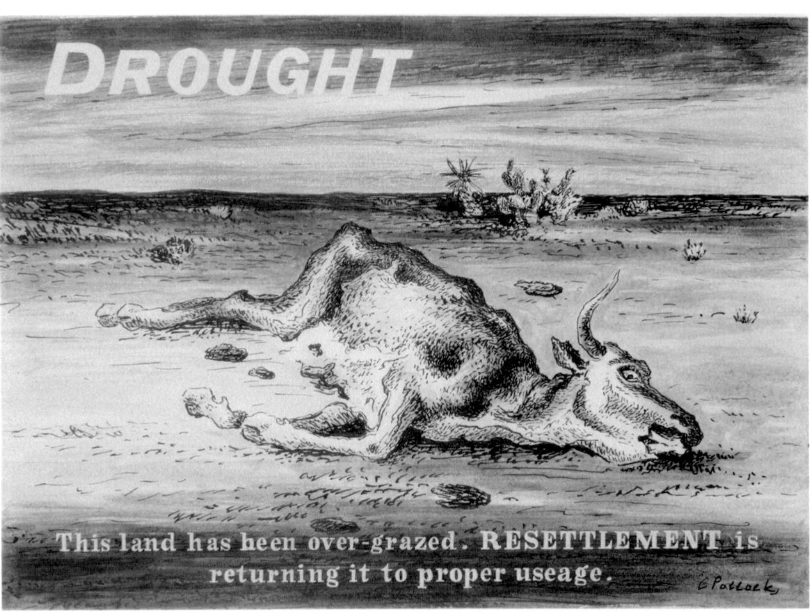

Fig. 4. Charles Pollock (1902–1988). *Drought*, 1937. Photograph from FSA–OWI Collection, Library of Congress, Washington, D.C., LC-USF344-003700-ZB.

became the basis for the Farm Security Administration (FSA), which replaced the RA in 1937.[41] A professor of economics, Stryker had used visual aids in his classroom. Understanding the documentary and expressive power of photography and film, he made these media his division's top priority, and they came to dominate the RA's work.

The staff of the Special Skills Division had a very different brief, that of encouraging rural populations to preserve and continue their vernacular artistic traditions.[42] Jones was hired to produce not only murals but also posters, pamphlets, and displays that underscored the importance of the agency. Jones wrote enthusiastically to Green, "This program starts with a group of 6 artists and technicians to interpret the people in various sections of the country and to exhibit collectively their findings. The exhibit will go all over the country." The possibility of working steadily in Dust Bowl communities would make his experience, and therefore his art, more convincing. "Our subject matter will be the social aspect of these people portrayed honestly—for example 'Roustabouts.'"[43] The job also paid a living wage—$3,200 per year—a sum substantially greater than what the Treasury Department was offering.

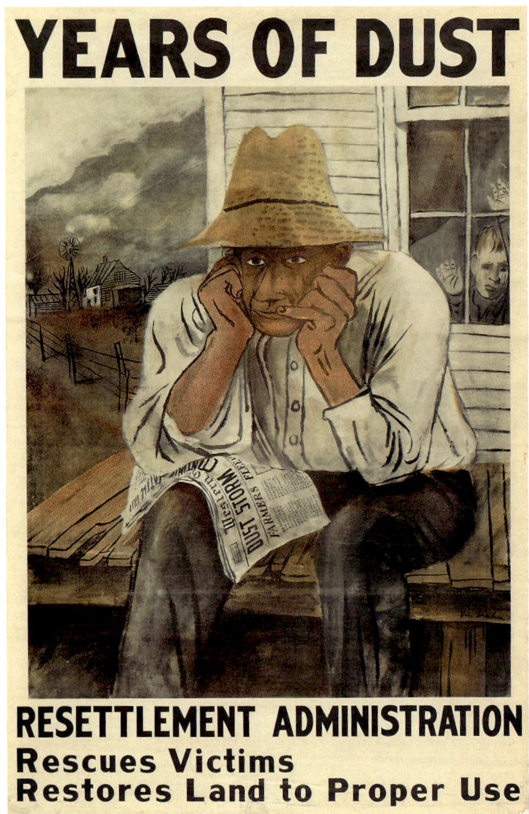

Fig. 5. Ben Shahn (1898–1969). *Years of Dust, Resettlement Administration, Rescues Victims, Restores Land to Proper Use*. Lithograph; 37⅞ × 25 in. (96.2 × 63.5 cm). The Museum of Modern Art, New York, Gift of the Designer, 147.1947.

Jones's singling out of *Roustabouts*—a painting that evokes racial inequities and management-labor issues then current in St. Louis—clearly indicates that he expected the RA to encourage such work. Heading up the artists in the Special Skills Division was Ben Shahn, whose radical politics certainly must have been attractive to Jones. Shahn's duties were broad. In addition to traveling through the South and Midwest documenting the lives of sharecroppers, he designed posters and covers for RA pamphlets; developed displays for clubs and schools throughout the region that graphically defined the agency's role and initiatives; put together an exhibit for the 1936 Democratic Party National Convention in Philadelphia; and directed his artists in creating advertisements for Pare Lorentz's magisterial movie *The Plow That Broke the Plains* (1936).[44] Tugwell had hired the filmmaker as a consultant and then agreed to fund a movie that would highlight the overall goals of the RA. Indeed, the half-hour film features many of the locations, from Montana to the Texas Panhandle, that photographers working for Stryker's Historical Division had captured in work which at the time was on display at the New York Public Library.[45] The film, along with the myriad related graphic, photographic, and fine-art images made by RA artists, gave a face and voice to the plight of agricultural workers throughout the Dust Bowl.[46]

Jones wrote to Rogers in September 1935, "I have just accepted a swell job in Washington as one of eight artists to travel through the country and paint the lives and condition of the people in various sections."[47] The others in the stable he expected to join, while not well known today, were recognized, socially engaged artists. They included Bernarda Bryson (who would marry Shahn), Frank Buffmire, Boris Deutsch, Richard Jensen, Olaf Nordmark, Charles Pollock, and Richard Sargent. The pamphlets and posters they designed feature such titles as *Rural Slum*, *Soil Erosion*, and *Drought* (fig. 4).[48] Shahn's poster *Years of Dust* (fig. 5), inspired by his experiences photographing communities throughout the Dust Bowl region, became one of the most famous of the RA's images. Shahn juxtaposed the figure of an impoverished, pre–New Deal farmer with a list of the RA's bold initiatives. Charles Pollock (the older brother of painter Jackson Pollock) went to the Carolinas to study the region's mostly African American farmworkers. Like his colleagues, he made sketches that he then translated into paintings, posters, and lithographs intended to promote awareness of the conditions of poverty and despair he witnessed, as well as the government's efforts to find practical solutions for these abject conditions. His lithograph *The Harvest—South Carolina* (fig. 6), based on what he saw in South Carolina, was included in an important 1936 exhibition and publication organized by the American Artists' Congress. *America Today: A Book of 100 Prints* not only celebrated a variety of printmaking themes and styles, but also championed, according to critic Elizabeth McCausland, "the contemporary trend toward ever greater democratization of art."[49] In an interview conducted years later, Deutsch called the RA "the highlight of a great democracy." He continued, "We would go out in the field and travel into different states and make sketches, and then come back to Washington and work them over. Either that or paint those things. And all this work belonged to the Government."[50] Deutsch's reminiscence emphasizes the connection between the artists' documentary efforts and the RA's mission and politics.

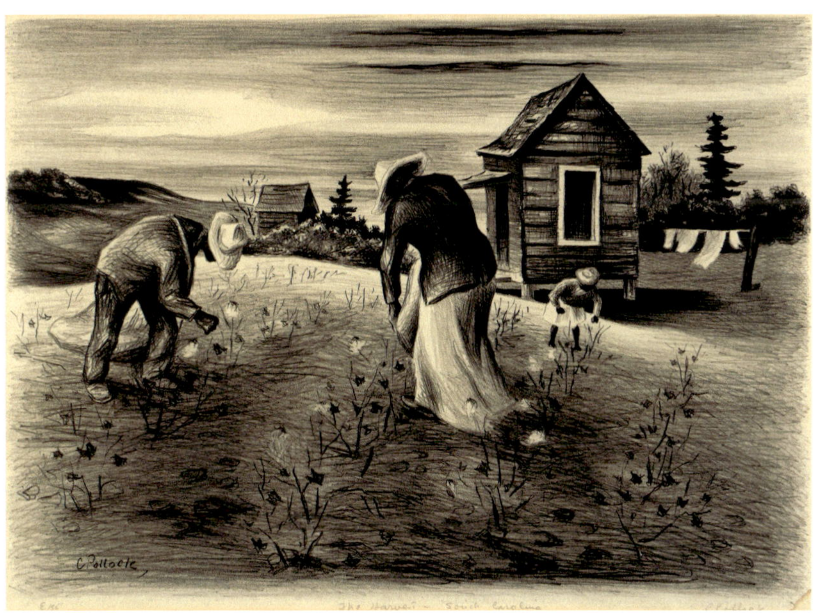

Fig. 6. Charles Pollock. *The Harvest—South Carolina*, c. 1936. Lithograph; 10¼ × 14¼ in. (26 × 36.2 cm). Smithsonian American Art Museum, Gift of Mr. and Mrs. Nelson Allmendinger.

Jones was excited and apparently ready to join the team, which makes it all the more surprising that, in the end, he did not take the job. Exactly why is unclear. Other opportunities, such as a major commission he received to execute a series of mural-size paintings, *The Story of the Grain*, for the 905 Liquor Store (1936; see cats. 40–41), in downtown St. Louis, may have lured him away (see Sharp). But he did not abandon interest in the RA altogether. As Adrian J. Dornbush, director of the Special Skills Division, announced in a July 1936 report, Jones's involvement had become much more focused. "In connection with the emergency situation in the drought areas, Mr. Joe Jones, of St. Louis, Missouri, a well-known American painter, has been given a special appointment for a period of six weeks. . . . Mr. Jones' work will, for the most part, be in Region III" (the country was divided into twelve regions; Region Three included Illinois, Indiana, Iowa, Missouri, and Ohio).[51]

No mere employee then, Jones worked as a special invitee with expertise in the Midwest. Although his itinerary during the six weeks he traveled through Region Three is lost, the work that Jones made in connection with his assignment embraces a variety of media and subjects. As was his habit by now, he used a camera to record the people and landscapes he encountered. This technique was of course of primary importance for other RA artists, including Shahn, whose skill as a photographer actually influenced Stryker's extensive use of the medium in the Historical Section.[52] Jones's photographs from this trip do not survive; only a handful of sketches, gouaches, watercolors, and monochromes exist. Some bring to mind the accidental composition of a snapshot. *To Make Our Daily Bread* (1936; cat. 48) shows two young boys gathering food amid a desolate Dust Bowl landscape. Depicted without sentiment, the children—their faces hidden—embody a moment of pathos wrought by the ecological disaster. Jones's painting, tightly focused on the

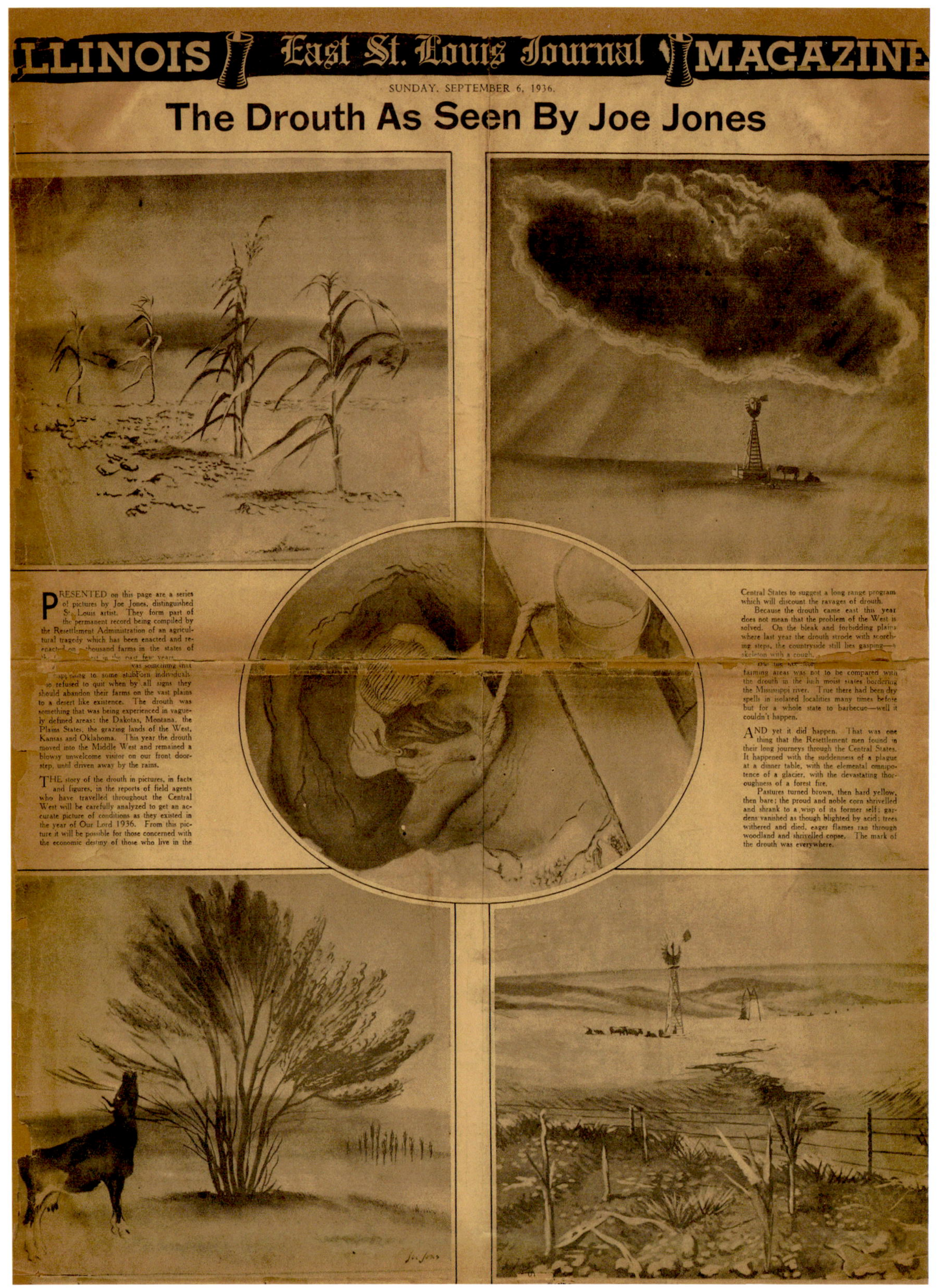

ILLINOIS East St. Louis Journal MAGAZINE

SUNDAY, SEPTEMBER 6, 1936.

The Drouth As Seen By Joe Jones

PRESENTED on this page are a series of pictures by Joe Jones, distinguished St. Louis artist. They form part of the permanent record being compiled by the Resettlement Administration of an agricultural tragedy which has been enacted and re-enacted on [illegible] thousand farms in the states of [illegible] in the past few years. [illegible] was something that [illegible] happening to some stubborn individuals [illegible] refused to quit when by all signs they should abandon their farms on the vast plains to a desert like existence. The drouth was something that was being experienced in vaguely defined areas: the Dakotas, Montana, the Plains States, the grazing lands of the West, Kansas and Oklahoma. This year the drouth moved into the Middle West and remained a blowsy unwelcome visitor on our front doorstep, until driven away by the rains.

THE story of the drouth in pictures, in facts and figures, in the reports of field agents who have travelled throughout the Central West will be carefully analyzed to get an accurate picture of conditions as they existed in the year of Our Lord 1936. From this picture it will be possible for those concerned with the economic destiny of those who live in the Central States to suggest a long range program which will discount the ravages of drouth.

Because the drouth came east this year does not mean that the problem of the West is solved. On the bleak and forbidding plains where last year the drouth strode with scorching steps, the countryside still lies gasping—a skeleton with a cough.

But the [illegible] farming areas was not to be compared with the drouth in the lush moist states bordering the Mississippi river. True there had been dry spells in isolated localities many times before but for a whole state to barbecue—well it couldn't happen.

AND yet it did happen. That was one thing that the Resettlement men found in their long journeys through the Central States. It happened with the suddenness of a plague at a dinner table, with the elemental omnipotence of a glacier, with the devastating thoroughness of a forest fire.

Pastures turned brown, then hard yellow, then bare; the proud and noble corn shrivelled and shrank to a wisp of its former self; gardens vanished as though blighted by acid; trees withered and died, eager flames ran through woodland and shrivelled copse. The mark of the drouth was everywhere.

Fig. 7. "The Drouth as Seen by Joe Jones," *East St. Louis Journal* (*Illinois Magazine*) (September 6, 1936). This article reproduces several of Jones's Dust Bowl works from his time with the Resettlement Administration.

young subjects, brings a human element to the Southern tenant-farmer problem, and shares qualities with innumerable photographs taken for the RA's Historical Section. Others, such as his drawing *On His Last Legs* (1936; cat. 49), are simple studies. The skillful rendition of the forlorn, emaciated mule seen here captures both anatomical detail and expression. The mule was named Missouri's official animal in 1820, because of its superior ability to do fieldwork. The misery of Jones's mule seems to indicate a state in decline.

In the thousands of images of the Dust Bowl, emaciated farm animals achieved symbolic status. Many of Jones's surviving works show how he adopted what was becoming Dust Bowl iconography. In one work, a gouache entitled *Midwestern Landscape* (1936; cat. 43), several cows surround a windmill, likely gathering at the water hole with the hope of getting a drink. A path of eroded soil leads to a single haystack, all that is left of the seemingly endless abundance Jones had painted in St. Charles only one year before. In the foreground, separated from the arid terrain of the farmstead by a still-intact fence, is a struggling crop of corn, a regional staple that was severely affected by the drought. This combination of elements—windmill, apparently abandoned and thirsty cattle, ruined crops, and fence rails—belongs to the lexicon of visual cues that Jones began to use in various compositions and settings. The windmill was especially important to the farms that dotted the Great Plains. It helped pioneers settle the West by capturing the abundant wind as a power source to pump water into moisture-poor areas. Inexpensive and easy to maintain, it also allowed farmers to grind grain. Moreover, the windmill facilitated the expansion of the cattle industry by bringing water to livestock. Any traveler on the Great Plains could not venture far without encountering this functional marvel.[53] However, during the Depression, the windmill came to symbolize the backwardness of rural technology and ineffectual land management.

The bright yellows and blues of *Midwestern Landscape* lend a feeling of optimism to the gouache, but in *Windmill and Two Bulls* (1936; cat. 44) Jones reworked the composition and palette to emphasize the despair of the

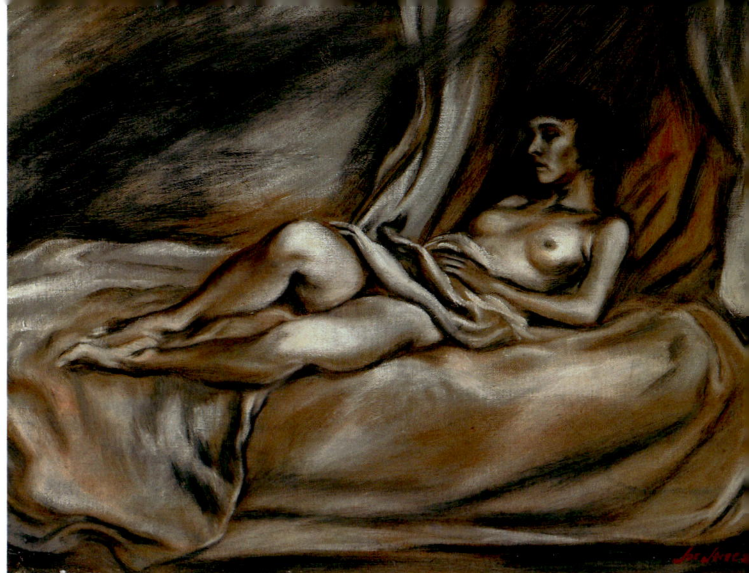

JANE KAUFFMAN WOOD (1907–2004)

In the years between his marriages to Freda Sies, which ended in early 1935, and Grace Adams Mallinckrodt, which began in 1940, Jones developed a romantic relationship with Jane Kauffman, an important leftist activist. In June 1935, the artist helped Kauffman's aunt Marguerite Fischel restore a Georgia O'Keeffe painting she owned. Jones and Kauffman may have met through this connection, if not in New York, where the two were part of the same leftist circles.

Kauffman grew up in circumstances that could not have been more different than those of Jones. She was the only child of Harold Kauffman, an important St. Louis banker and broker, and Mayflower descendant Janet Morton. Her family lived on exclusive Portland Place, a private street inhabited by some of St. Louis's wealthiest and most well-known citizens, including the Busches, Mallinckrodts, and Nagels; and she attended prestigious Smith College, in Northampton, Massachusetts. After graduating in 1929, however, Kauffman chose to reject her background. Compelled by rampant social injustices that were worsened by the Depression, she moved to New York City and devoted her energy to helping the poor, union organizing, and fighting for housing rights. During their relationship, Kauffman was deeply engaged in Jones's career, posing nude for a number of studies. Jones gave her several works from his Dust Bowl period, including *Young Corn* (fig. 12), a version (fig. 21) of *Drought Farmer* (c. 1937; cat. 60), *Dust Storm* (1937; cat. 66), and *Carcass* (c. 1937; cat. 68). Several of these works focus on poverty and labor strife—issues that would continue to motivate the activist long after her relationship with Jones ended. Kauffman, who married fellow leftist Bob Wood in 1947, dedicated herself to such causes until the end of her long life.

Bryna R. Campbell

Joe Jones, *Nude*, c. 1937. Oil on canvas; 16 × 20 in. (40.6 × 50.8 cm). Estate of Miss Elizabeth Green. Jane Kauffman likely posed for this painting.

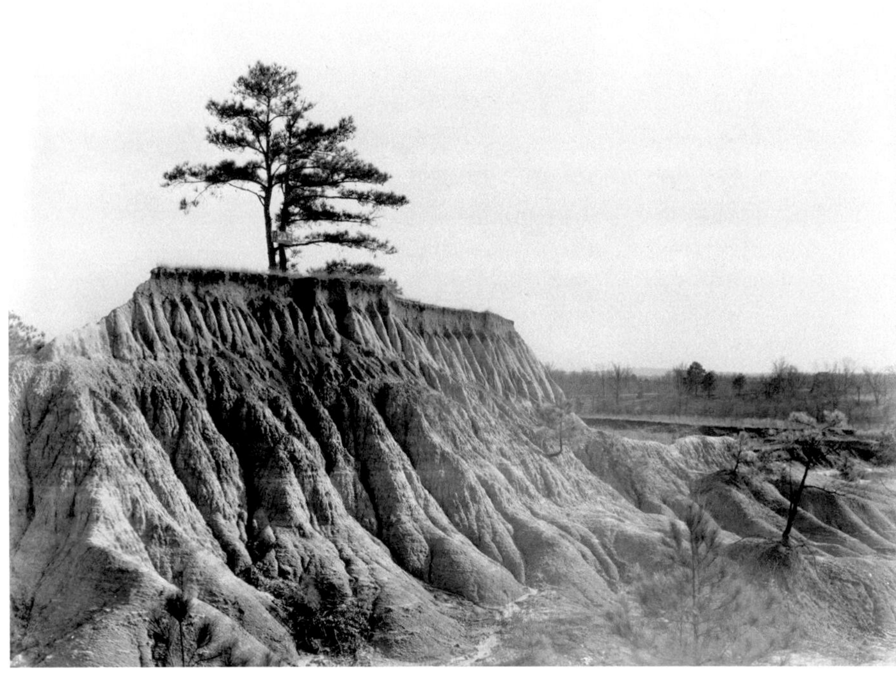

Fig. 8. Walker Evans (1903–1975). *Erosion near Jackson, Mississippi*, 1936. Photograph from FSA–OWI Collection, Library of Congress, Washington, D.C., LC-USF347-003057-C.

region. An ominous, dark cloud, about to explode and stir up the eroded soil, looms over the cows mingling around a windmill. Jones must have intended this painting and others to help effect fundamental change in public policy. In this way, he linked his social concerns with those of the RA. An article entitled "The Drouth as Seen by Joe Jones," which appeared in the *East St. Louis Journal* (*Illinois Magazine*), illustrated five of Jones's works (most of them cropped) as factual evidence (fig. 7). "They form," the writer declared, "part of the permanent record being compiled by the Resettlement Administration of an agricultural tragedy that has been enacted and re-enacted on a thousand farms in the states of the Central West in these past few years."[54]

Jones's contribution to that permanent record established his experience of the Dust Bowl as authentic and made legitimate his political aspirations for this work. At the time, he had just begun a relationship with Jane Kauffman, a young St. Louis socialite who had rejected her blue-blood status to become an ardent and lifelong socialist organizer in New York. Although not much about their relationship is known, Jones did claim in a letter to Green to be engaged to Kauffman. He also painted her and later gave her several works of art he made while traveling through the Dust Bowl in 1936 and 1937 (see "Jane Kauffman Wood," p. 65; figs. 12, 21; and cats. 66, 68).[55] More importantly, however, Jones and Kauffman were part of a group of youthful agitators who viewed the Dust Bowl as a legitimate site of racial and labor injustice. In his memoir, labor organizer and author Eli Jaffe vividly recalled an incident in 1937, when he showed Jones the beginning of a novel he had written about a

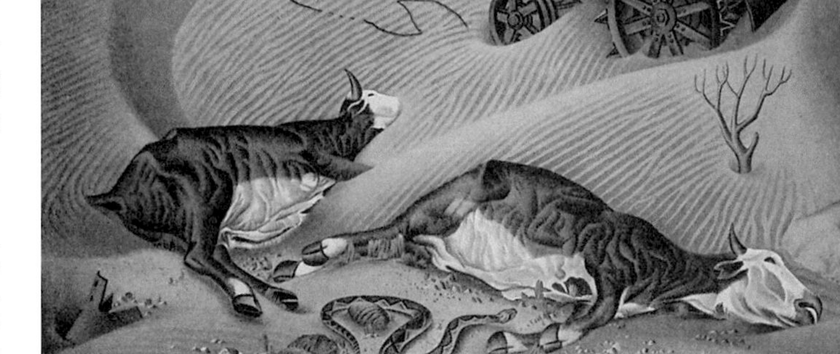

Fig. 9. Alexander Hogue (1898–1994). *Drouth Survivors*, 1936. Oil on canvas; 30 × 48 in. (72.6 × 121.9 cm). Destroyed. Reproduced in *Trois siècles d'art aux États-Unis*, exh. cat. (Éditions des Musées Nationaux, 1938), pl. 55.

young man and his pregnant wife in Dust Bowl Oklahoma. Jaffe had researched the topic at the New York Public Library. Jones's response, when asked his opinion, was succinct: "If you want to write honestly about the Dust Bowl, why don't you get your ass out there and get to know the people?"[56] Veracity and effective activism could not be generated from a library table. Only work in the field, Jones believed, could lead to art capable of effecting social change.

Nowhere was Jones's political advocacy more successful than in *Our American Farms* (1936; cat. 42). The painting was featured in the Whitney Museum of American Art's Third Biennial Exhibition of Contemporary American Painting, which opened in November 1936. Jones must have been pleased by the museum administration's decision to pay artists a rental fee for the paintings included in the show. That same year, Jones, along with fellow artist James Turnbull, helped mount in St. Louis a boycott of the City Art Museum's annual exhibition of local artists because the museum refused to compensate artists in this way.[57] Artists across the nation were agitating museums for this acknowledgment. As Turnbull succinctly stated, "Everybody else gets paid, why shouldn't we?"[58] Jones had gathered material for *Our American Farms* as an RA employee. Thus he considered the painting a product of his labor that should be valued as such.[59]

In *Our American Farms*, the mythically rich soil that produced the cornucopia of crops celebrated in works such as *Threshing* (1936; cat. 40) has literally blown away, leaving farm, windmill, outbuilding, and stock tank teetering on a precipice. Not only had Jones traveled through such landscapes while on assignment for the Special Skills Division, but he was also likely familiar with photographs such as Walker Evans's view of severely damaged land near Jackson, Mississippi (fig. 8). Stryker had sent Evans to Mississippi in March 1936 to document erosion and its impact on housing, in part to show the RA's progress in rectifying the situation.[60] The resemblance of Jones's painting to Evans's photograph is striking. However, unlike Evans's image and the drawings and watercolors Jones made while working for the RA, *Our American Farms* is much more than a visual record of fact. It shares its post-apocalyptic character with a work by Alexander Hogue, also shown in the 1936 Whitney annual, which became a cause célèbre. *Drouth Survivors* (fig. 9) presents the Texas Panhandle as almost devoid of life. An abandoned tractor is buried in a growing mound of eroded soil, providing a backdrop for the dead cattle spread across the foreground. The "survivors" of the painting's title are the snake that slithers toward the belly of the dead cow on the right and the groundhog that emerges from its underground den to survey the destruction. Jeanette Lowe, writing for *Art News*, considered Hogue's painting one of the exhibition's most interesting, praising its "surrealist treatment of a very real theme."[61] For his searing depiction, Hogue was attacked by a chapter of the Texas Chamber of Commerce. The group planned to buy his painting in order to burn it in a street in the town of Dalhart, as a public demonstration of its members' outrage. Hogue himself never claimed the

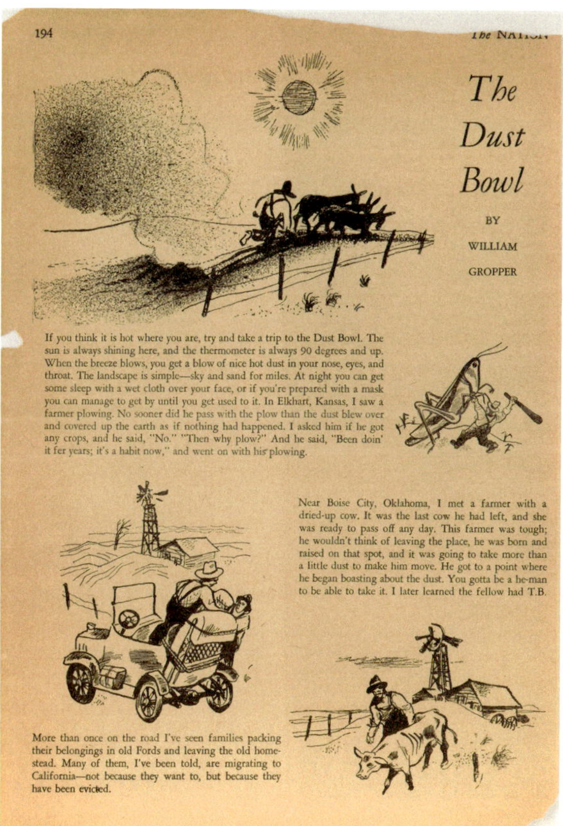

194 *The Nation*

The Dust Bowl

BY WILLIAM GROPPER

If you think it is hot where you are, try and take a trip to the Dust Bowl. The sun is always shining here, and the thermometer is always 90 degrees and up. When the breeze blows, you get a blow of nice hot dust in your nose, eyes, and throat. The landscape is simple—sky and sand for miles. At night you can get some sleep with a wet cloth over your face, or if you're prepared with a mask you can manage to get by until you get used to it. In Elkhart, Kansas, I saw a farmer plowing. No sooner did he pass with the plow than the dust blew over and covered up the earth as if nothing had happened. I asked him if he got any crops, and he said, "No." "Then why plow?" And he said, "Been doin' it fer years; it's a habit now," and went on with his plowing.

Near Boise City, Oklahoma, I met a farmer with a dried-up cow. It was the last cow he had left, and she was ready to pass off any day. This farmer was tough; he wouldn't think of leaving the place, he was born and raised on that spot, and it was going to take more than a little dust to make him move. He got to a point where he began boasting about the dust. You gotta be a he-man to be able to take it. I later learned the fellow had T.B.

More than once on the road I've seen families packing their belongings in old Fords and leaving the old homestead. Many of them, I've been told, are migrating to California—not because they want to, but because they have been evicted.

Fig. 10. William Gropper (1897–1977). "The Dust Bowl," *Nation* 145, 8 (August 21, 1937), p. 194. Gropper's text and illustrations describe his impressions of the Dust Bowl from the time of his Guggenheim Fellowship.

work to be an accurate representation of the Panhandle, but rather a warning: "That's what [the landscape] will be if they don't let the government do its work."[62] Like Hogue's painting, Jones's *Our American Farms* is at once a call to action and a meditation on the loss confronting the nation both ecologically and economically. Its title gave the picture the status of a national icon, suggesting that the lonely, forsaken outpost belonged to every American. In her review, Lowe singled out *Our American Farms* for special praise. The canvas struck her as "a bitter study in soil erosion; here again the consideration of a contemporary social problem. It is a desolate portrayal, handled with imagination and compassion."[63] Jones had found in the Dust Bowl a subject that could convey protest and demand change, though differently than had his more overtly proletarian subjects of the previous year. Now his images of the Midwestern landscape, born out of a type of documentary realism, aspired to revolutionary critique.

GUGGENHEIM FELLOWSHIP

The six weeks Jones spent traveling across Region Three for the RA had a profound effect on him. The question was how to build upon that experience, since long-term employment under the federal program seemed impossible at that moment. Like many other artists, writers, and scholars of the day, he turned to another source of support: the John Simon Guggenheim Memorial Foundation. His close friend Jack Conroy had won a Guggenheim fellowship in 1935 for creative writing; he planned to interview African American migrant workers and convey their experiences in a book, which was eventually published as *They Seek a City* (1945).[64] Jones had been planning to apply for a fellowship in the months after his 1935 A.C.A. Gallery debut, even while he was discussing employment with one of the federal programs. In letters to Green, he regularly mused about how a Guggenheim grant would allow him to work with relative freedom. Jones finally took action in late 1936, alerting Rogers to his plan and his desire to use the museum director as a reference. Describing the work he intended to complete during the fellowship period, he specifically cited his RA experience in the application, avowing that his six-week stint in the Dust Bowl was an inadequate amount of time in which to capture the devastation being wrought there:

> The United States Government has wisely recognized the drought and erosion problems as being tremendously important. Entire populations have been uprooted and impoverished, the land apparently destined to become a desert. . . . It is almost impossible to mirror such a catastrophe and its effect upon the land and the people after only a fleeting trip through by bus or motor car. I feel that, under the unstultifying terms of a Guggenheim fellowship, I could produce a series of drawings and paintings calculated to bring a clearer understanding of the difficulties and problems of an extremely distressed section of America.[65]

Jones's application proved successful, and in 1937 he, along with Gropper and the German émigré George Grosz, were named awardees in the area of Fine Arts. The Guggenheim Foundation evidently recognized the Dust Bowl as a worthy subject of artistic interpretation; both Jones and Gropper planned to travel in the region. Shortly after notification of his selection, Jones wrote to Henry Allen Moe, president of the foundation,

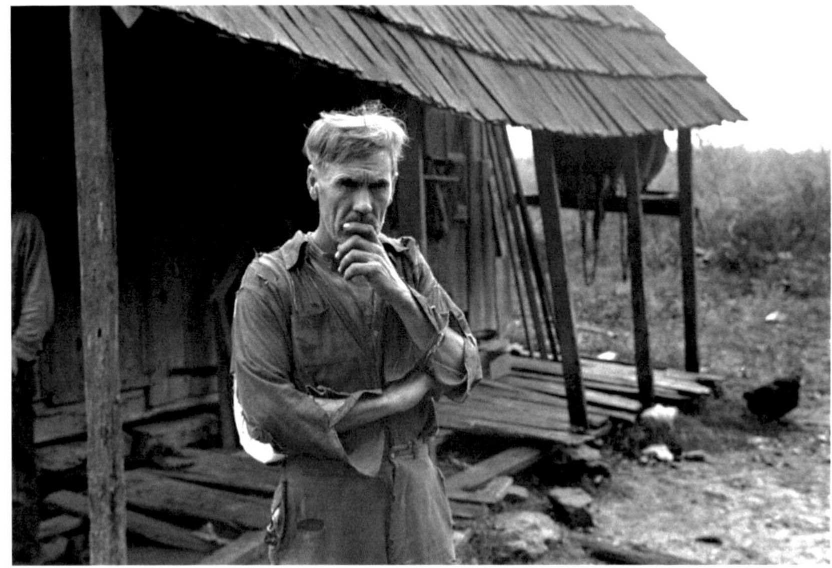

Fig. 11. Ben Shahn. *Sam Nichols, Tenant Farmer, Boone County, Arkansas*, 1935. Photograph from FSA–OWI Collection, Library of Congress, Washington, D.C., LC-USF33-006037-M3.

with a special request. Estimating that his tour would take him to eight different states in the Midwest—a trip nearly impossible to accomplish by train—Jones asked for permission to use some of his stipend to purchase an automobile. "I have a car," he wrote, "worth a couple hundred dollars if [I could trade it] in on a station wagon that could be slept in and I would be able to stay on the job more leisurely. My experience in travelling some of this territory last summer led me to believe this would be the ideal way to work efficiently as well as inexpensively."[66] The foundation approved.

The car allowed Jones to engage meaningfully with families and communities—he could stop, observe, and converse with the intent of deepening what he considered genuine experiences of the people he encountered. As he related in a later letter to Moe, "I went places and saw what had happened to these places. I began to get the 'feel' of both places and events. More important, I saw and talked with the people of these places, the victims of those events."[67] Jones's exact itinerary is not clear. Two postcards he sent to Green situate him in Colorado, Oklahoma, and the Texas Panhandle, though they do not touch upon the nature of his activities. He did describe the usefulness of his car, however: "The car goes fine and I have had a successful sleep in it. I had all the cracks sealed in the back of the body because of the dusty roads."[68] He made no interim reports from the field to the Guggenheim's New York office, unlike Gropper, who not only wrote to the foundation but also authored several articles for the *Nation* that detail his experiences. In "The Dust Bowl," published in the magazine's August 21, 1937, issue (fig. 10), Gropper described encounters he had in various towns: "Near Boise City, Oklahoma, I met a farmer with a dried-up cow. It was the last cow he had left and she was ready to pass off any day."[69] His sparse vignettes capture the desperation of the situations he witnessed, and are accompanied by thumbnail sketches of what had become archetypal Dust Bowl scenes—farmers plowing eroded soil, dilapidated windmills, evicted families, and emaciated cattle.

What does survive from Jones's travels are photographs that have descended through his family and have

Fig. 12. Joe Jones. *Young Corn*, 1937. Oil on canvas; 15⅝ × 10$\frac{5}{16}$ in. (39.7 × 26.2 cm). Collection of Ruth and Tim Wood.

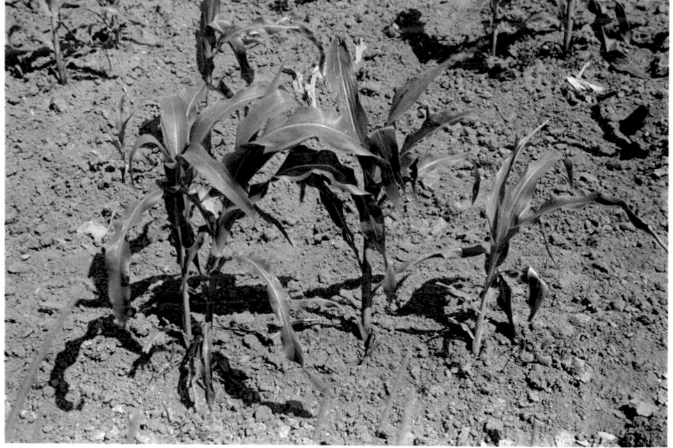

Fig. 13. Ben Shahn. *Field of Young Corn, Central Ohio*, 1938. Photograph from FSA–OWI Collection, Library of Congress, Washington, D.C., LC-USF33-002922-M1.

never been studied in relationship to his fellowship work. They reveal the artist using the camera like a sketchbook, capturing the impact of the Depression and drought on both land and workers. The influence on Jones of the work of FSA photographers such as Shahn (see fig. 11) and Dorothea Lange seems undeniable. Shahn's photographs for the RA were exhibited as early as 1936; he believed, as did Jones, that they were "the raw materials of painting."[70] Jones captured a worker, his arms crossed, by pointing his camera at an upward angle, imbuing the figure with a sense of defiant courage and strength in the face of adversity (1937; cat. 51). This strategy was one that Shahn, and many others, used to enhance his subjects' heroism and humanity, while not diminishing the severity of their plight. Jones would have agreed with Shahn that behind the work of the FSA and the RA was a moral imperative to help the underprivileged.[71]

Relating closely to his work the previous year for the RA, Jones's 1937 photographs are more focused than Shahn's, concerned largely with devastation. Nearly every surviving image—whether of windmills, water towers, or fence posts buried in windswept soil (see cats. 51–54, 56–59, 62–64)—contains the iconography that had been established to express blight in the Dust Bowl. One photograph captures windburned cornstalks (cat. 58), a subject that Jones also transferred to canvas and gave to Kauffman (fig. 12). Along with the windmill and fence post, ruined corn became a symbol of ecological disaster

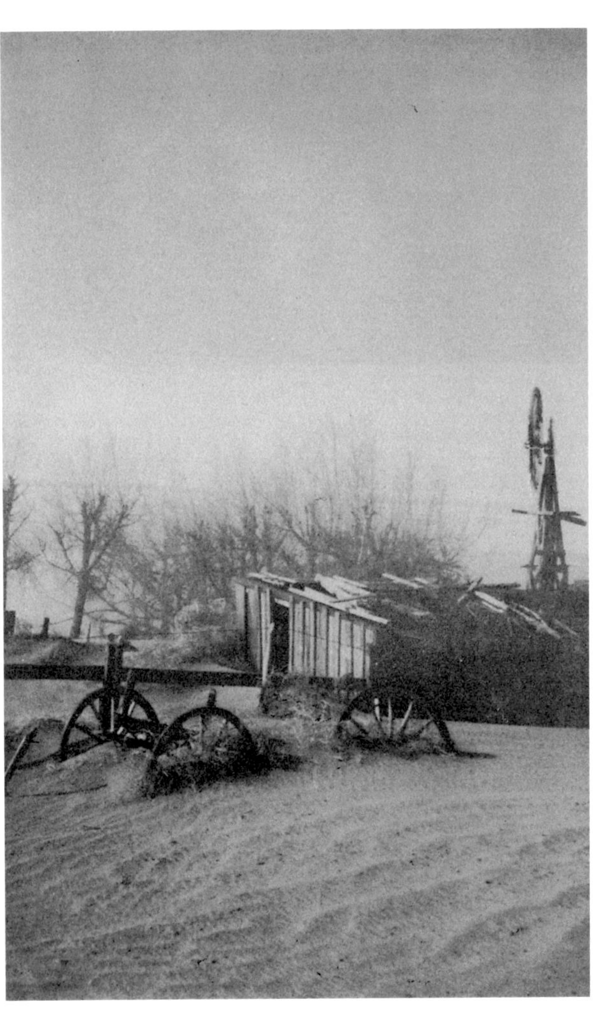

Fig. 14. Arthur Rothstein (1915–1985). *Results of a Dust Storm, Cimarron County, Oklahoma*, 1936. Photograph. FSA–OWI Collection, Library of Congress, Washington, D.C. LC-USF34-004072-E.

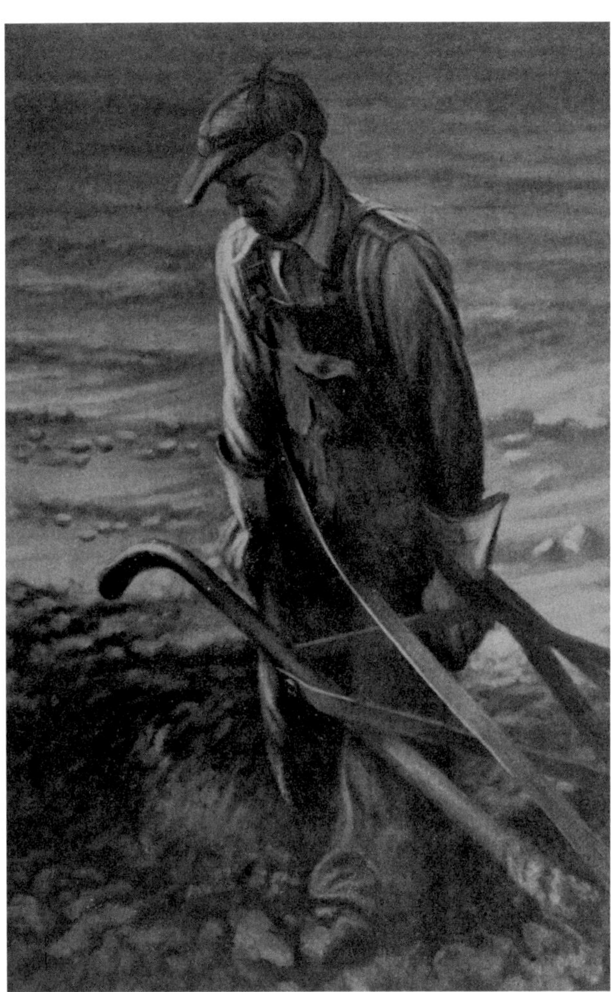

Fig. 15. Joe Jones. *Farmer* or *Ploughing*, c. 1937. Location unknown. Reproduced in *Paintings by Joe Jones*, exh. cat. (A.C.A. Gallery, 1937), n. pag.

not only in photographs, such as Shahn's uncannily similar shot (fig. 13), but also in literature of the day. In his 1939 novel *The Grapes of Wrath*, John Steinbeck wrote vividly about a storm's destructive power: "Men stood by their fences and looked at the ruined corn, drying fast now, only a little green showing through the film of dust."[72]

In another photograph by Jones of abject despair, a dilapidated shack, collapsing from neglect, sits in the midst of a dusty field (cat. 63). Perhaps his most unconventional snapshot (cat. 64) focuses on a wallpapered room of a deserted house, into which soil and tumbleweeds have blown. The door stands ajar and possessions left behind litter the floor. The abandoned farmstead became a symbol of not only the destructive effects of drought and wind but also the massive exodus of sharecroppers, only some of whom were resettled as part of the government's land-reform efforts. Such images often appear in RA publications. One such scene is a 1936 view of a partly buried outbuilding in Oklahoma (fig. 14). This image's later inclusion in Lawrence Svobida's famous 1940 memoir, *An Empire of Dust*, further underscores its iconic potency.[73]

Jones clearly culled imagery from his stock of photographs, a practice, as we have seen, that he employed in making his paintings. In a request for an extension of his Guggenheim Fellowship, Jones in fact likened his understanding of life in the rural locations he visited to snapshots—accurate and authentic. Influenced by these photographs and their focus on Dust Bowl symbols, Jones made a lithograph entitled *Wastelands* (1937; cat. 67) for the American Artists Group.[74] It pictures an eroded field beneath a sky darkened by swirling dust. In the middle ground is a modern-day ruin of fence posts, windmill, and machinery. The American Artists Group, along with Associated American Artists (AAA), produced such prints in large editions during the 1930s, enabling a broad

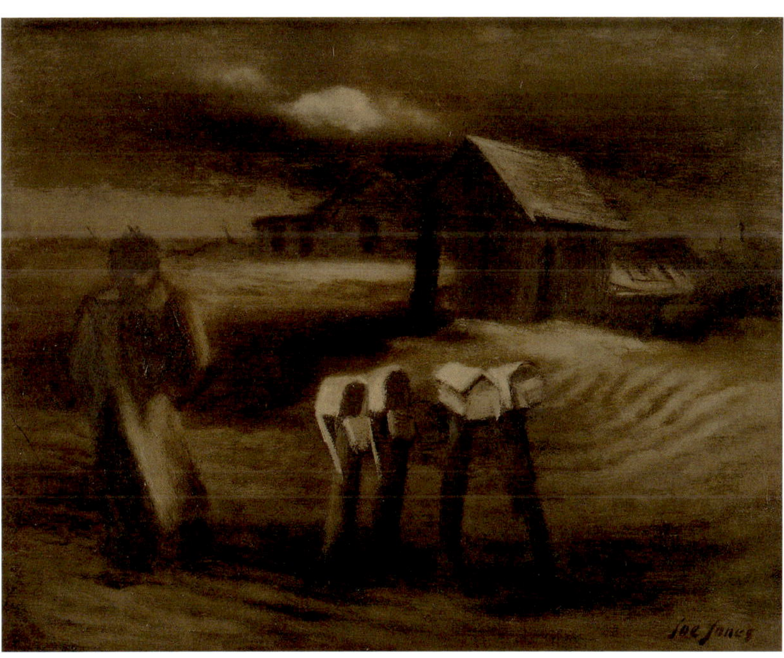

Fig. 16. Joe Jones. *Study for "Departure,"* 1937. Oil on canvas; 16 × 20½ in. (40.6 × 52.1 cm). Courtesy of the Missouri History Museum, St. Louis.

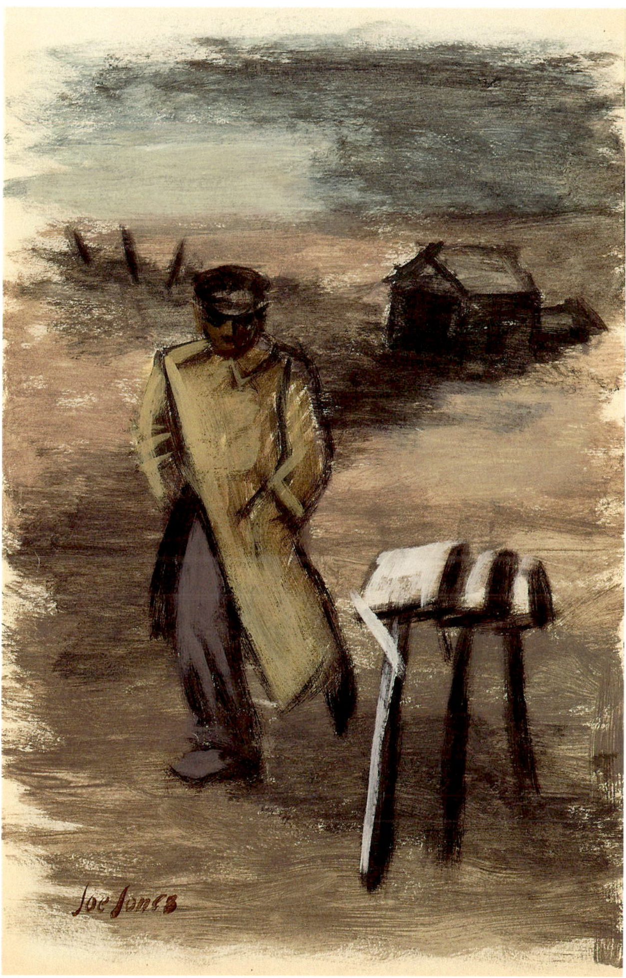

Fig. 17. Joe Jones. *Study for "Departure,"* 1937. Gouache on cardboard; 18 × 12 in. (45.7 × 30.5 cm). Denver Art Museum, Gift of Mrs. Ernest W. Stix.

audience to acquire the graphic art of social realists at affordable prices.[75]

At times the correspondence between a photograph and painting is direct. In a particularly mournful photograph, a tenant farmer pauses to inspect the furrow he has just plowed in a wind-damaged field (1937; cat. 52). The futility of the work recalls an observation Gropper made upon encountering a similar scene in Elkhart, Kansas: "I saw a farmer plowing. No sooner did he pass with the plow than the dust blew over and covered up the earth as if nothing had happened."[76] The man's slumped shoulders, downward glance, and feet sunken into the ruined soil all contribute to a feeling of futility. Jones repeated the image in a painting called variously *Farmer* or *Ploughing* (fig. 15). Although in the painting the farmer seems to have aged and the surrounding landscape appears more desperate than in the photograph, the compositions of both are nearly identical.

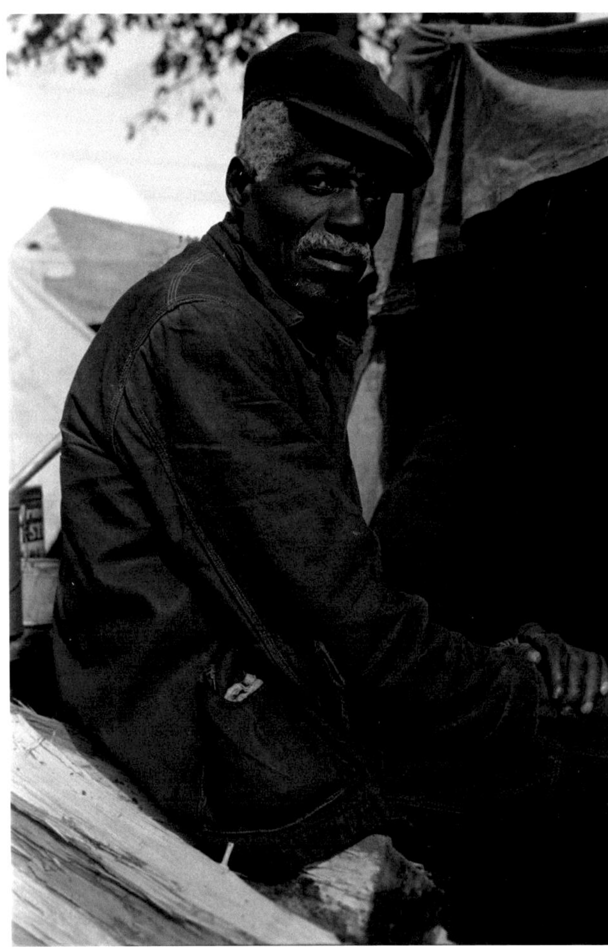

Fig. 18. Arthur Rothstein. *Evicted Sharecropper along Highway 60, New Madrid County, Missouri*, 1939. Photograph courtesy of FSA–OWI Collection, Library of Congress, Washington, D.C., LC-USF33-002922-M1.

Another painting Jones produced during his fellowship is *Departure* (1938; cat. 61). In this large oil, a sharecropper wearing a workman's cap, his hands stuffed in the pockets of a heavy, yellow-tinted topcoat, strides purposefully across a bleak stretch of land. In the lower-right foreground, a cluster of three mailboxes—signals of a time now gone, when people lived there—lines the road the agricultural refugee has been forced to travel. In the background, on the same axis as the mailboxes, a dilapidated shack or dugout appears to sink slowly into the eroded earth. Jones probably used his photographs to develop this composition. A haunting shot of mailboxes along a rural road (1937; cat. 62) may have influenced the artist to include them in his painting. The seeming endlessness of this bleak landscape and the displaced farmer's lonely exit from it are reinforced by the monochromatic brown palette Jones employed.

Indeed, Jones's Dust Bowl paintings share an earth-toned palette that evokes the region's pervasive dusty soil. Two studies he made for *Departure* show him not only working out the composition, but also consistently applying a narrow range of subdued grays, browns, and yellows. An oil (fig. 16), also titled *Departure*, features elements retained in the final work but in a horizontal format; its muted palette makes the image appear as through a haze of dirt. A gouache (fig. 17), which more closely relates to the finished canvas, reveals the artist defining areas of color: he heightened the intensity of the sharecropper's yellow overcoat and made the browns of the fields and the blue of the sky more distinct from one another. Here he also more clearly presented the farmer as an African American, emphasizing the population most dramatically affected by evictions in Missouri and Arkansas.[77]

Only two years later, in January 1939, the Southern Tenant Farmer's Union (STFU) organized a large demonstration in southeastern Missouri by sharecroppers recently evicted from their farms. Newly homeless and angry, they began gathering just south of the town of Sikeston, Missouri, where Highways 60 and 61 meet.[78] Over one thousand farmers from multiple states participated, the

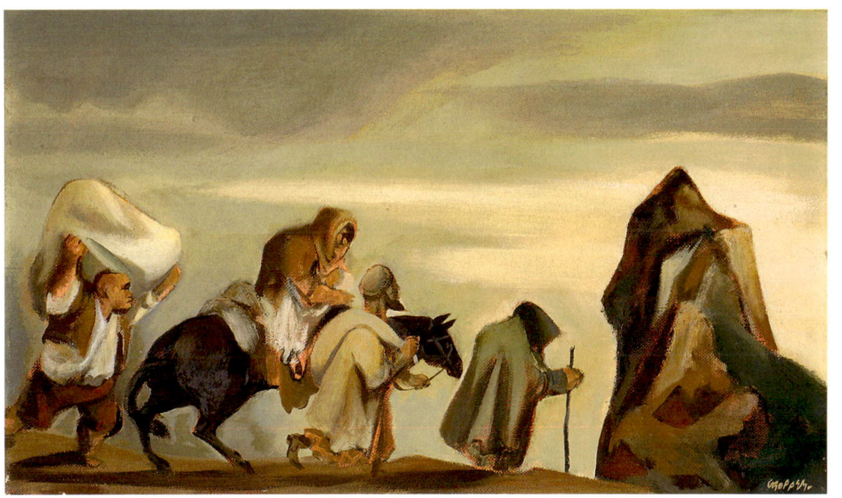

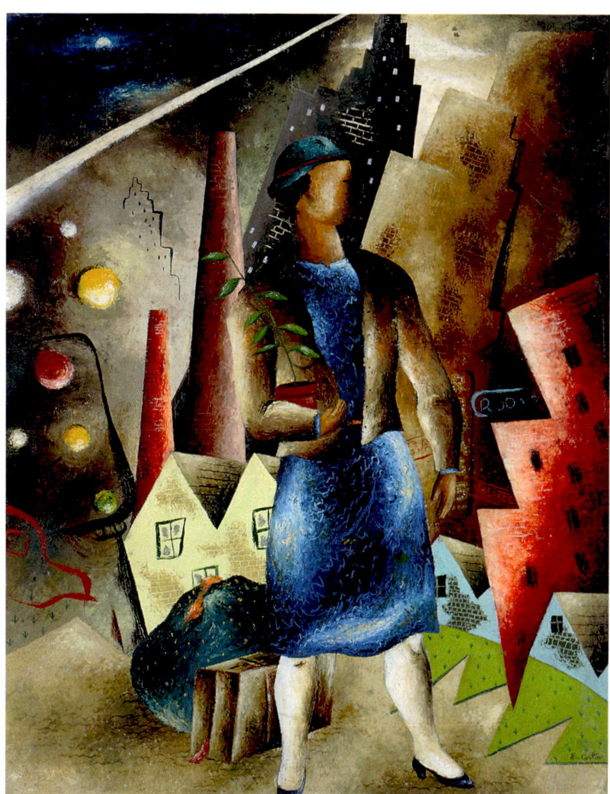

encampment spreading for thirty-eight miles to intersections east and west, from Sikeston to Cairo, and seven miles to the north and south, from Sikeston to Hayti.[79] While the majority of the protesters were black, at least one third were white, making the demonstration decidedly interracial, although most of the white participants congregated just south of Sikeston.[80]

Arthur Rothstein, dispatched by the FSA, documented the event in a series of powerful works, including *Evicted Sharecropper* (fig. 18).[81] Wearing a heavy topcoat and workman's cap, the man bears a striking likeness to Jones's protagonist in *Departure*. While there is no connection between these two works, Jones did write to Rowan in 1939 about the sharecroppers' strike, emphasizing his familiarity with the widespread evictions of black and white farm laborers alike.[82] In his painting, the sharecropper's departure into a literal desert, the beginning of an uncertain journey, offered Jones a means to express the pain caused by government land policies. To the final composition, Jones introduced an important detail absent in the gouache: a telephone pole stands in the darkened background like a cross, lending a spiritual note to this image of suffering. Several years before, in 1933, Jones had planned to paint a crucifixion in "sympathy with those in revolt against the present organization of capitalist society. . . . There have been crucifixions all along the tortuous paths of mankind, . . . they have been milestones on his stumbling road to perfection."[83] Although the composition was never realized, the crosslike form in *Departure* elevates the painting from earnest documentation to a critique of the powerful forces that caused such displacements. The migrant sharecropper is at once the victim of a capitalist system viewed as market-driven and racist, as well as a potential benefactor of a new socialist system as he sets off on a path of recovery.

Gropper made the religious association even more explicit in *Minorities* (fig. 19), a work he completed during his Dust Bowl year. The painting depicts a departing

Fig. 19. William Gropper. *Minorities*, 1938/39. Oil on canvas; 17⅞ × 30⅛ in. (45.4 × 76.5 cm). The Phillips Collection, Washington, D.C.

Fig. 20. Eldzier Cortor (b. 1916). *Eviction*, c. 1939. Oil on canvas; 30⅛ × 24 ¼ in. (76.5 × 61.6 cm). Saint Louis Art Museum, Gift of the Federal Works Agency, Works Projects Administration.

farm family moving in a friezelike formation across a barren landscape. The mother and child are seated on an emaciated mule, led by a bearded patriarch dressed in a white robe. Thus, this journey becomes that of the Holy Family. Despite leftist antipathy to religion, both Jones's and Gropper's evocations of the biblical themes of exile and redemption acknowledge the centrality of faith in the lives of rural families. For this reason, Claude Williams, director of Commonwealth College and a Presbyterian minister, told Jones's friend Eli Jaffe that, to reach Southern laborers, one "had to do it through religion."[84] This aligned the artists with organizations such as the STFU. In fact many rural preachers backed the union's efforts, for they too made a fraction of the salaries paid to their urban counterparts, and many had to work as tenant farmers or sharecroppers to make extra money. Not surprisingly, the STFU sought the support of preachers in part by turning traditional spirituals into union songs.[85] Rather than rejecting religion as "the product of capitalistic exploitation," union organizers and artists such as Jones and Gropper regarded it as an effective strategy to gain and unite members across wide, socially imposed racial boundaries.[86]

Displacement and homelessness plagued urban dwellers as well as rural ones. In 1940 Eldzier Cortor, a Chicago-based African American artist working for the Federal Arts Project, painted scenes of Bronzeville, a neighborhood on the city's South Side. His *Eviction* (fig. 20) features a young black woman carrying a plant and seeking a room for let. Community organizers at the time focused on unaffordable rents and the resulting high number of evictions of working-class families.[87] Jones's *Condemned* (1936; cat. 47) also addresses the problem of housing for the urban poor.

The theme of exile culminated for Jones in a trio of paintings that included *Departure*, the now-lost *Farmer* or *Ploughing*, and a large-format composition of a seated farmer. The location of the latter is unknown, but several sketches (see fig. 21) and a finished smaller version (c. 1937; cat. 60) exist. Jones's goal in this series was to make the figure, not the landscape, the central carrier of meaning. When Jones wrote the report about his fellowship work to the Guggenheim Foundation, he pointed to these paintings as especially significant. "The three panels coming close together express three definite and separate characteristics of basic human nature in all of us." The farmer in the old army coat in *Departure* is the realist, ready to face the future, whatever it requires. In leaving the farm to relocate, perhaps to a city, he advocates for change, whether political or social. The farmer engaged in contour plowing "is the person without a philosophy who does his work because he finds it is ennobling." The seated farmer is the most lost of them all, stuck in indecision and unable to envision a better life.[88]

At this time, Jones requested an extension of his fellowship. While he traveled the Dust Bowl, the artist wrote, "The places, events, and people were as clear in my mind as so many photographs." But he continued, "When I

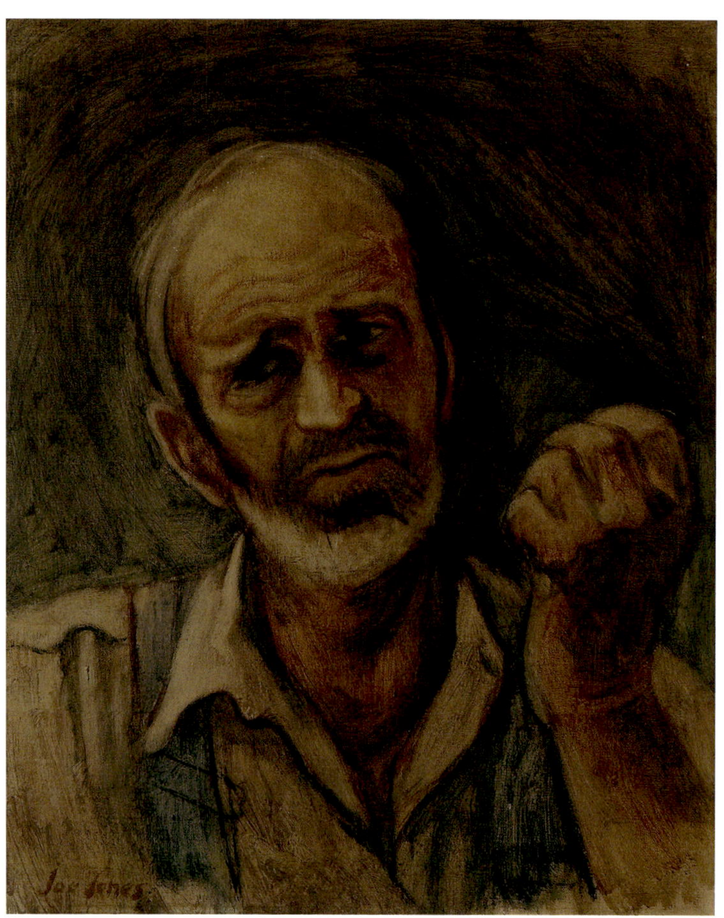

Fig. 21. Joe Jones. *Farmer*, c. 1937. Oil on canvas; 19 5/16 × 15 5/16 in. (49.1 × 38.9 cm). Collection of Ruth and Tim Wood.

came to paint—to put the stuff on canvas—I began to see that they could not be taken as separate . . . as photographs might be viewed. I had to understand the relation, the meaning, behind these separate photographic impressions. It is at this point that the real work lives. This is the work I am now in the midst of."[89] Jones needed more time to synthesize all that he had taken in and recorded. Unfortunately, his request was not granted.

Jones's Dust Bowl experience, however, helped him find content that was both socially engaged and visually compelling. His fellowship paintings constituted the core of an exhibition held at the A.C.A. Gallery in 1937. Meant to demonstrate that his artistic talent was more than a flash in the pan, the show placed the artist at a significant crossroad (see Balken). Was he fulfilling his promise? This was the question that his Dust Bowl paintings seemed to raise. Jewell saw the new works, with their dark palette and ambiguous backgrounds, as representing a regression. "But where," he queried, "is the distinctive personal style that an artist of exceptional promise seemed about to establish?"[90] To Jewell at least, Jones seemed to have traded his authentic Midwestern voice for politics; the exhibition's bleak, proletarian themes made the writer miss the panache of Jones's earlier wheat fields. Other critics, however, embraced Jones's so-called "militancy" as the realization of the artist's social purpose. Like his mural for Commonwealth College, these new works transformed the tragedy of the Great Plains from the conveyance of fact into an impassioned demand for action. Emily Genauer, critic for the *New York World Telegram*, recognized Jones's intent. She contrasted his art with the "message-bearing political posters" of the RA. "Today his

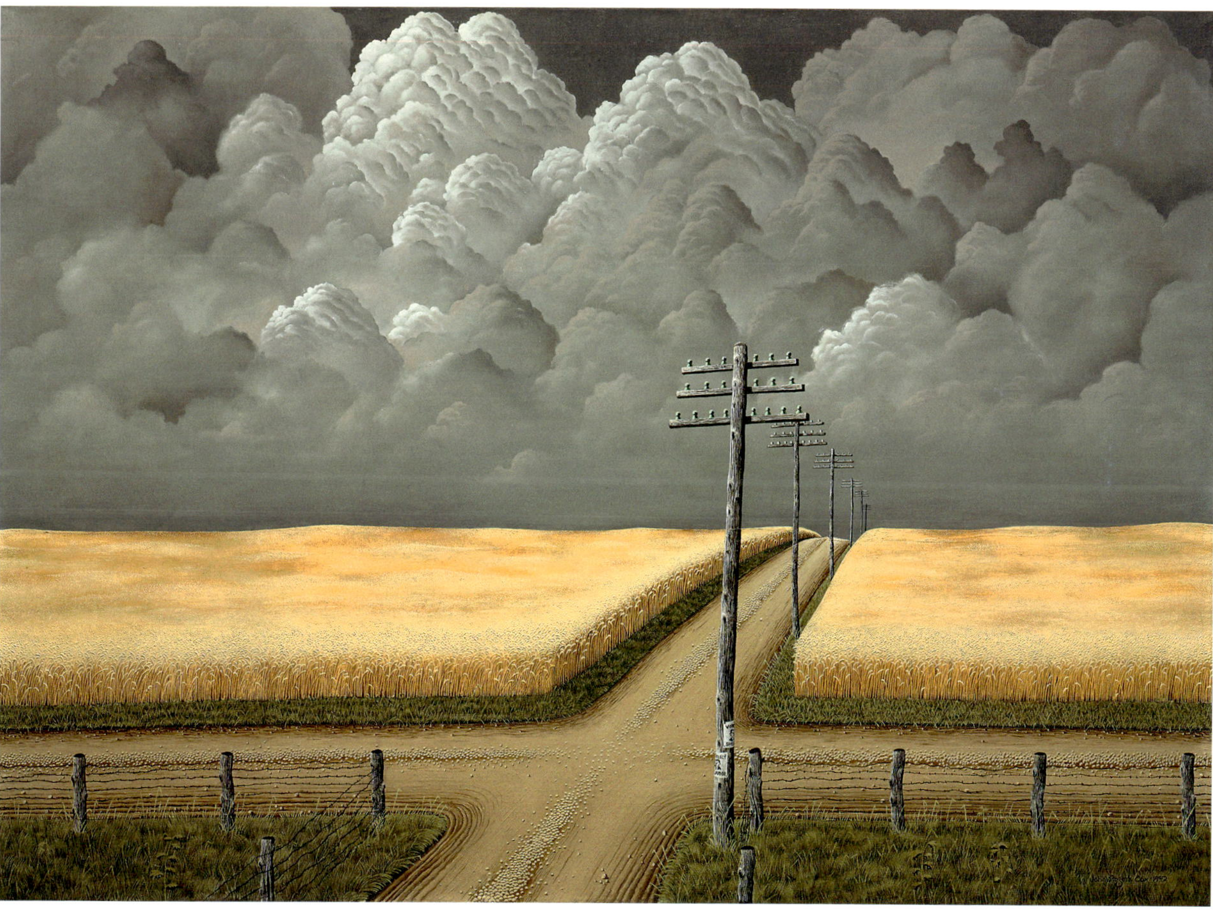

Fig. 22. John Rogers Cox (1915–1990). *Gray and Gold*, 1942. Oil on canvas; 36 × 59⅞ in. (91.5 × 151.8 cm). The Cleveland Museum of Art, Mr. and Mrs. William H. Marlatt Fund, 1943.62.

pictures have a much more profound human content. There is in them cosmic perspective, passionate insight . . . painted with the brilliance, the exquisite poignance, the profound compassion of an El Greco, or a Goya."[91]

Significantly, Jones completed his Dust Bowl series in St. Louis. But just as the exhibition that introduced the series opened in New York, the artist made a decision that would change his life and his approach to subject matter in the ensuing years. As the *St. Louis Post-Dispatch* reported: "Joe Jones, young St. Louis artist, will leave the city within a few weeks to make his home in New York."[92] In the nation's artistic capital, opportunities to work and participate in a vital creative scene outstripped those in his hometown. For Jones, however, moving from St. Louis and the Midwest would also mean no longer being in direct contact with the place that had empowered his art.

Jones's more or less permanent departure from St. Louis, however, did not indicate a rejection of heartland subjects. The five designs that he would complete for the Treasury Department's mural program all focused on agricultural themes for rural post offices in Missouri, Arkansas, and Kansas (see Walker and Turk). For that work, he traveled to the communities, met with local leaders, and observed local farming techniques. As Jones stated often, to paint a scene authentically one had to get to know the land and the people. A landscape of social commentary required firsthand experience. Moreover, as a Midwesterner from a working-class background, Jones claimed deep understanding of the challenges faced by the tenant farmers and sharecroppers who dominated his subject matter between 1935 and 1940.

Away from St. Louis and increasingly distanced from the Communist beliefs he had first embraced in 1933, Jones produced agricultural landscapes that exhibit clear differences from his Dust Bowl works. In January 1942, he submitted *Yellow Grain* (c. 1942; cat. 82) to the "Artists for Victory" exhibition at the Metropolitan Museum of Art, New York. The show was organized by the Artists for Victory, Inc., which included nearly ten thousand artists representing twenty-three societies with widely varying political and artistic points of view.[93] Avoiding left- or right-wing ideologies, the umbrella organization espoused a singular goal: to assist the national war effort through a show of unquestioned unity. A. Hyatt Mayor, the Metropolitan's curator of prints, asserted in the museum's bulletin: "This vast exhibition comes aptly at a time that stirs our country more deeply than it has been stirred since the Civil War. . . . Today, in another such hour that seems almost to show the shape of the victory to come, the vitality of this exhibition gives us one more affirmation of the strength that we are throwing into man's most far-flung struggle."[94]

In *Yellow Grain*, Jones harkened back to the more jubilant depictions of harvesting that he had painted after his 1935 summer in the wheat fields of St. Charles. Positioned atop a large pile of wheat, a farmer watches over an elaborate symphony of activity. The field workers, whose faces are largely obscured and who wear a variety of work hats, are engaged in tasks from pitching hay and manning the threshing machine, to driving a smoke-belching tractor and loading a hay wain. *Yellow Grain* celebrates the harvest as an example of worker cooperation akin to that of teams building ships or forging steel. Such an approach was appropriate for the exhibition's strong patriotic premise. Here is America at work in a scene of modern collective labor that emphasizes the Midwest as the nation's breadbasket. As an affirmation of Jones's success, the Cleveland Museum of Art purchased *Yellow Grain* along with five other American Scene paintings, including John Roger Cox's eerie take on Midwestern wheat fields, *Gray and Gold* (fig. 22). The overt patriotic goals of the exhibition do not undermine the social content of *Yellow Grain*. The cooperative nature of the farming, in line with government policies resulting from farm reform, underscores the promise of collectivized agriculture. Additionally, as Andrew Hemingway suggested, representing agricultural practice in this manner recalls what the Soviet Union had promoted in its first and second Five Year Plans, as well as its state-sponsored boosterism of farm practice during World War II.[95]

Whatever the social content of *Yellow Grain*, by 1943 Jones's enthusiasm for the Communist project had pretty much dissipated (see Wolfe, and Balken). His second submission to "Artists for Victory," *Winter in Dutchess County* (location unknown), was set far from the socio-political landscape of the Midwest. Jones was actively painting a new subject, the scenery around his Fishkill, New York, home. He submitted such a work, *Spring Plowing* (1942; cat. 83), to the Whitney's 1942 annual contemporary art exhibition. He would also include the canvas in a solo show that March at his new New York gallery, AAA, along with twenty-five other oil paintings, mostly agricultural scenes. In the carefully composed *Spring Plowing*, with its conventional spatial arrangement, a lone farmer tills his field with an antiquated hand plow pulled by two horses. Jones's muted palette of browns and yellows captures the early spring atmosphere. In contrast to a work like *Yellow Grain*, the Fishkill scene embraces the serenity of simple, peaceful farm life, eschewing cooperative mechanized labor for a return to the yeoman ethos of an earlier time. Clearly, Jones's interests were shifting. In the wake of World War II, the federal arts programs had all but stopped. For Jones something stopped as well. Now remarried and a father, he had other priorities. His engagement with the local was not about political advocacy for a community, but rather about his personal attachment to his family and to views outside his studio window. As he wrote in October 1942 to Green:

> I'm having a whirl of a time up here. I'm in the midst of 5 paintings and they are all coming off well. We are near the end of the fall color here and it is a fine year after a summer of plentiful rain . . . Pete [Jones's eldest child] loves the colored leaves and hugs them, and flowers, he likes to eat them. He laughs when the tree branches touch his face and thinks they are playing games with him.[96]

NOTES

1. Marquis W. Childs, "Rediscovering a Forgotten Missouri Painter," *St. Louis Post-Dispatch*, Mar. 11, 1934.

2. Alfred H. Barr, Jr., "George Caleb Bingham: The Missouri Artist, 1811–1879," exh. brochure (Museum of Modern Art, 1935), p. 5.

3. Joe Jones to Elizabeth Green, Feb. 25, 1935, Dr. John Green Collection, Missouri History Museum, St. Louis (hereinafter Green Papers).

4. Jones to Green, Feb. 11, 1935, Green Papers.

5. Lewis Mumford, "The Art Galleries: In Capitulation," *New Yorker* 11, 16 (June 1, 1935), p. 57; repr. in *Mumford on Modern Art in the 1930s*, ed. and with intro. by Robert Wojtowicz (University of California Press, 2007), pp. 164–67; and Edward Allen Jewell, "Ex-House Painter in Art Show Here," *New York Times*, May 22, 1935.

6. Mumford (note 5). It is worth noting that the introduction to the exhibition pamphlet by Meyric Rogers ends with a statement acknowledging the artist's shortcomings: "The errors in these canvases, and many can be found, are those of abundance and choice rather than emptiness." Meyric Rogers, "Foreword," *Joe Jones*, exh. brochure (A.C.A. Gallery, 1935), n. pag. A.C.A. director Herman Baron was not happy with this sentence, as it seems to have prompted a number of critics to see Jones as a promising but as yet unrealized talent; Baron to Jones, Apr. 30, 1935, Green Papers.

7. Mumford (note 5). See also "Provincetown Makes Artist a Communist," *St. Louis Post-Dispatch*, Sept. 21, 1933.

8. "Two Painters Make Debuts," *New York Sun*, May 23, 1935.

9. Jewell (note 5).

10. Clarence Weinstock, "Joe Jones," *Art Front* 1, 6 (July 1935), p. 6. For a discussion of Weinstock's influence, see Andrew Hemingway, *Artists on the Left: American Artists and the Communist Movement, 1926–1956* (Yale University Press, 2002), pp. 39, 113–14.

11. Stephen Alexander, "Art: Joe Jones," *New Masses* 15, 9 (May 28, 1935), p. 30.

12. Jones said as much in a review he wrote in 1932: "[It] is always refreshing to find painters that [*sic*] dare paint what they see and feel around them"; Joseph Jones, "Carnegie International," *Studio Review* (Apr. 1932), in CAM publicity scrapbook, Saint Louis Art Museum, archives.

13. Rogers (note 6).

14. Weinstock (note 10).

15. News release from the Walker Galleries, 106 E. 57th St., Jan. 9, 1936, Maynard Walker Papers, Archives of American Art, Smithsonian Institution, Washington, D.C.

16. Jones to Green, n.d. (July 8, 1935), Green Papers. I am grateful to Kevin Sharp for his observations regarding this series of wheat paintings by Jones.

17. Bryan Holme, "America," *London Studio* 11, 61 (Apr. 1936), p. 239.

18. "Wheat Fields: Three Scenes from the Plains," *Forum* 95 (Apr. 1936), pp. 224–25.

19. Lewis Mumford, "Goya, Homer and Jones," *New Yorker* 11, 52 (Feb. 8, 1936), pp. 58–59; repr. in *Mumford on Modern Art* (note 5), pp. 187–90. "Joe Jones Celebrates Missouri's Wheatfields," *Art News* 34, 17 (Jan. 25, 1936), p. 9.

20. Ann Hamilton Sayre, "A Centennial of Homer Watercolors," *Art News* 34, 17 (Jan. 25, 1936), p. 12.

21. Jones to Green, n.d. (c. Jan. 20, 1936), Green Papers.

22. Jones to Green, n.d. (late Jan. 1936), Green Papers.

23. Jones to Green, n.d. (c. Jan. 1936), Green Papers.

24. "Wheat—Four Paintings," *Survey Graphic* 25, 8 (Aug. 1936), p. 474.

25. Archibald MacLeish, "U.S. Art: 1935," *Fortune* 7, 6 (Dec. 1935), p. 69.

26. Jones to Green, n.d. (c. summer 1933), Green Papers.

27. Paul E. Parker, *A Portrait of Missouri, 1935–1943: Photographs from the Farm Security Administration* (University of Missouri Press, 2002), p. 5.

28. Ibid., pp. 7–8.

29. M. Langley Biegert, "Legacy of Resistance: Uncovering the History of Collective Action by Black Agricultural Workers in Central East Arkansas from the 1860s to the 1930s," *Journal of Social History* 32, 1 (Fall 1998), p. 73.

30. For a discussion of this contrast in Midwestern scene painting, see Joni L. Kinsey, Rebecca Roberts, and Robert F. Sayre, "Prairie Prospects: The Aesthetics of Plainness," in *Recovering the Prairie*, ed. by Robert F. Sayre (University of Wisconsin Press, 1999), pp. 20–25.

31. Jones to Green, Aug. 10, 1935, Green Papers.

32. Green to Edward B. Rowan, July 14, 1935, Green Papers.

33. Rowan to Green, Aug. 5, 1935, Green Papers.

34. Transcription of letter from Jones to Rowan, Aug. 25, 1935, in Jones to Green, Aug. 27, 1935, Green Papers.

35. Jones to Green, Aug. 28, 1935, Green Papers.

36. R. Douglas Hurt, *The Dust Bowl: An Agricultural and Social History* (Nelson-Hall, 1981), p. 94.

37. Donald Worster, *The Dust Bowl: The Southern Plains in the 1930s* (Oxford University Press, 1979), p. 159.

38. R. G. Tugwell, "Foreword," *Resettlement Administration Publication* 1 (Sept. 1935), n. pag.

39. Sarah T. Phillips, *This Land, This Nation: Conservation, Rural America and the New Deal* (Cambridge University Press, 2007), pp. 128, 143.

40. Resettlement Administration [hereinafter RA] handout attached to letter from O. E. Jones, Information Advisor, Region Six, to John F. Carter, Director of Information, RA, Oct. 11, 1935; Record Group 96, Records of the Farmers Home Administration, 1918–1975, General Correspondence from the Washington Office, Heading 168 (Exhibits), Box 32; National Archives, College Park, Md.

41. When Stryker joined the RA, his purpose was unclear, but his interest in photography led him to direct the documentary project that would transform the medium. See F. Jack Hurley, *Portrait of a Decade: Roy Stryker and the Development of Documentary Photography in the Thirties* (University of Louisiana Press, 1972).

42. Jake Milgram Wien, "Art, Progressive Politics and the Idea of the Frontier: Bernarda Bryson Goes to Washington," in *The Vanishing American Frontier: Bernarda Bryson Shahn and Her Historical Lithographs Created for the Resettlement Administration of FDR* (Wien America, 1995), p. 1.

43. Jones to Green, Sept. 12, 1935, Green Papers.

44. Adrian J. Dornbush to Grace E. Falke, RA, Apr. 15, 1936, interoffice communication; Records of the Farmers Home Administration, 1918–1975, General Correspondence from the Washington Office, Heading 986 (Special Skills, Correspondence by Name), Box 67; National Archives, College Park, Md..

45. Ibid.

46. Debra Bricker Balken, *After Many Springs: Regionalism, Modernism and the Midwest*, exh. cat. (Des Moines Art Center/ Yale University Press, 2009), p. 167. The documentary represented a milestone in filmmaking, combining social awareness and the Roosevelt administration's liberal causes. By July 1936, *The Plow That Broke the Plains* had been shown at hundreds of theaters in Arkansas, Illinois, Ohio, Tennessee, Texas, and other states. See also Robert L. Snyder, *Pare Lorentz and the Documentary Film* (University of Oklahoma Press, 1968), pp. 40–47.

47. Jones to Meyric Rogers, Sept. 21, 1935, Green Papers.

48. Dornbush to Falke, RA, Jan. 24, 1936 (note 44). Dornbush noted, "Messrs. Ben Shahn, Olaf Nordmark, and Boris Deutsch are continuing their work on sketches, depicting the dust storm and soil erosion areas, which sketches will be used for poster material."

49. Elizabeth McCausland, quoted in Helen Langa, *Radical Art: Printmaking and the Left in 1930s New York* (University of California Press, 2004), p. 20.

50. Boris Deutsch, oral-history interview, June 1–5, 1964, Archives of American Art, Smithsonian Institution, Washington, D.C., pp. 11–12.

51. Dornbush to Falke, RA, July 18, 1936, report for week ending July 11, 1936 (note 44).

52. Hurley (note 41), pp. 36–54.

53. Approximately six million American windmills were in operation in the Great Plains region and the West between 1880 and 1930.

54. "The Drouth as Seen by Joe Jones," *East St. Louis Journal (Illinois Magazine)* (Sept. 6, 1936).

55. Jones to Green, Sept. 27, 1937, Green Papers.

56. Eli Jaffe, *Oklahoma Odyssey* (Eli Jaffe, 1993), p. 3.

57. For a cogent and thorough discussion of this protest, see Karal Ann Marling, "Workers, Capitalists, and Booze: The Story of the 905 Murals," in *Joe Jones & J. B. Turnbull: Visions of the Midwest in the 1930s*, exh. cat. (Haggerty Museum of Art, Marquette University, 1987), pp. 15–16.

58. J. B. Turnbull, quoted in ibid., p. 15. Jones participated in another protest in 1936, at the Gillespie Galleries, Pittsburgh, against the Carnegie International. Jones exhibited a now-lost canvas, *Sharecropper's Family*, evidently derived from his RA experience. See Alice Graeme, "Artists Boycott Carnegie Show over Rental Issue," *Washington Post*, Nov. 8, 1936.

59. Earlier that year, Jones had delivered a speech at the First American Artists' Congress against War and Fascism entitled "Repression of Art in America" (see Balken). Jones made it clear that, while he had earned his stripes as a social realist representing the unskilled urban laborers, he was now pursuing a corresponding subject in the rural regions of the Midwest, in part as a government worker. He was one of many: a number of the artists showing at the Whitney had also found their subjects while working for the Works Progress Administration. See Joe Jones, "Repression of Art in America," in *Artists against War and Fascism: Papers of the First American Artists' Congress*, intro. by Matthew Baigell and Julia Williams (Rutgers University Press, 1986), pp. 75–77.

60. Belinda Rathbone, *Walker Evans, A Biography* (Houghton Mifflin, 1995), p. 115.

61. Jeannette Lowe, "Painting and Literature at the Whitney," *Art News* 35, 7 (Nov. 14, 1936), p. 19.

62. Alexander Hogue, quoted in Hurt (note 36), p. 63.

63. Lowe (note 61), p. 20.

64. The book was published by Doubleday, Doran, and Co. See Jack Conroy, Jack Salzman, and David Ray, *Jack Conroy Reader* (Burt, Franklin and Co., 1979), p. 177.

65. Joe Jones, Guggenheim Fellowship application, 1936, Guggenheim Foundation Archives, New York.

66. Jones to Henry Allen Moe, Mar. 1937, Guggenheim Foundation Archives, New York.

67. Jones to Moe, Dec. 28, 1937, Guggenheim Foundation Archives, New York.

68. Jones to Green, Apr. 15, 1937, Green Papers.

69. William Gropper, "The Dust Bowl," *Nation* 145, 8 (Aug. 21, 1937), p. 194.

70. Seldon Rodman, *Portrait of the Artist as an American* (Harper and Brothers, 1951), p. 91.

71. See John D. Morse, "Ben Shahn: An Interview," *Magazine of Art* 37 (Apr. 1944), pp. 136–41.

72. John Steinbeck, *Grapes of Wrath* (Viking Press, 1940), p. 6.

73. Lawrence Svobida, *An Empire of Dust* (Caxton Printers, Ltd., 1940), opp. p. 67. The caption for the photograph reads: "Wheels that no longer turn."

74. Aline Kistler, "Prints of the Moment," *Prints* 8, 2 (Dec. 1937), p. 94. The lithograph was priced at $2.75.

75. See Erica Doss, "Catering to Consumerism," *Winterthur Portfolio* 26, 2–3 (Summer/Autumn 1991), p. 143.

76. Gropper (note 69). The other three short essays by Gropper that appeared in this magazine are "Gropper Visits Youngstown," 145, 1 (July 3, 1937), pp. 14–15; " Out West," 145, 4 (July 24, 1937), p. 96; and "Gipsy Labor," 145, 13 (Sept. 25, 1937), p. 321.

77. See Nicholas Natanson, *The Black Image in the New Deal: The Politics of FSA Photography* (University of Tennessee Press, 1992), p. 113.

78. Richard S. Kirkendall, *A History of Missouri*. Vol. 5, *1919–1953* (University of Missouri Press, 1986), p. 197.

79. Ibid.; and Bonnie Stepenoff, *Thad Snow: A Life of Social Reform in the Missouri Bootheel* (University of Missouri Press, 2003), p. 92.

80. Ibid.

81. Natanson, "The Photo-Series: Arthur Rothstein and the Missouri Bootheel," in idem (note 77), p. 124.

82. Jones to Rowan, n.d. (c. Oct. 8, 1938); Record Group 121, case files concerning embellishment of federal buildings, 1934–43; Records of the Section of Fine Arts, Public Buildings Administration; Entry 133, Box 56 (Charleston, Mo., file); National Archives, College Park, Md.

83. "10 Persons Pledge Aid to Struggling Artist," *St. Louis Post-Dispatch*, Feb. 19, 1933.

84. Jaffe (note 56), p. 47.

85. Mark Fannin, *Labor's Promised Land: Radical Visions of Gender, Race, and Religion in the South* (University of Tennessee Press, 2003), pp. 101, 295.

86. Ibid., pp. 288, 299.

87. Rebecca O. Johnson, "Lonesome Refugees," *Callaloo* 30, 3 (Summer 2007), p. 843.

88. Joe Jones, General Report, Feb. 8, 1938, Guggenheim Foundation Archives, New York.

89. Jones to Moe, Dec. 28, 1937, Guggenheim Foundation Archives, New York.

90. Edward Allen Jewell, "One-Man Shows by Benton, Biddle, and Joe Jones," *New York Times*, Oct. 31, 1937.

91. Emily Genauer, "Joe Jones Takes Rank with the Masters," *New York World-Telegram*, Oct. 30, 1937.

92. "Artist Joe Jones to Move to New York," *St. Louis Post-Dispatch*, Aug. 19, 1937.

93. For a discussion of Artists for Victory, Inc., see Cécile Whiting, *Anti-Fascism in American Art* (Yale University Press, 1989), pp. 135–36.

94. A. Hyatt Mayor, "The Artists for Victory Exhibition," *Metropolitan Museum of Art Bulletin*, n.s. 1, 4 (Dec. 1942), p. 141.

95. Hemingway (note 10), p. 37.

96. Jones to Green, Oct. 12, 1942, Green Papers.

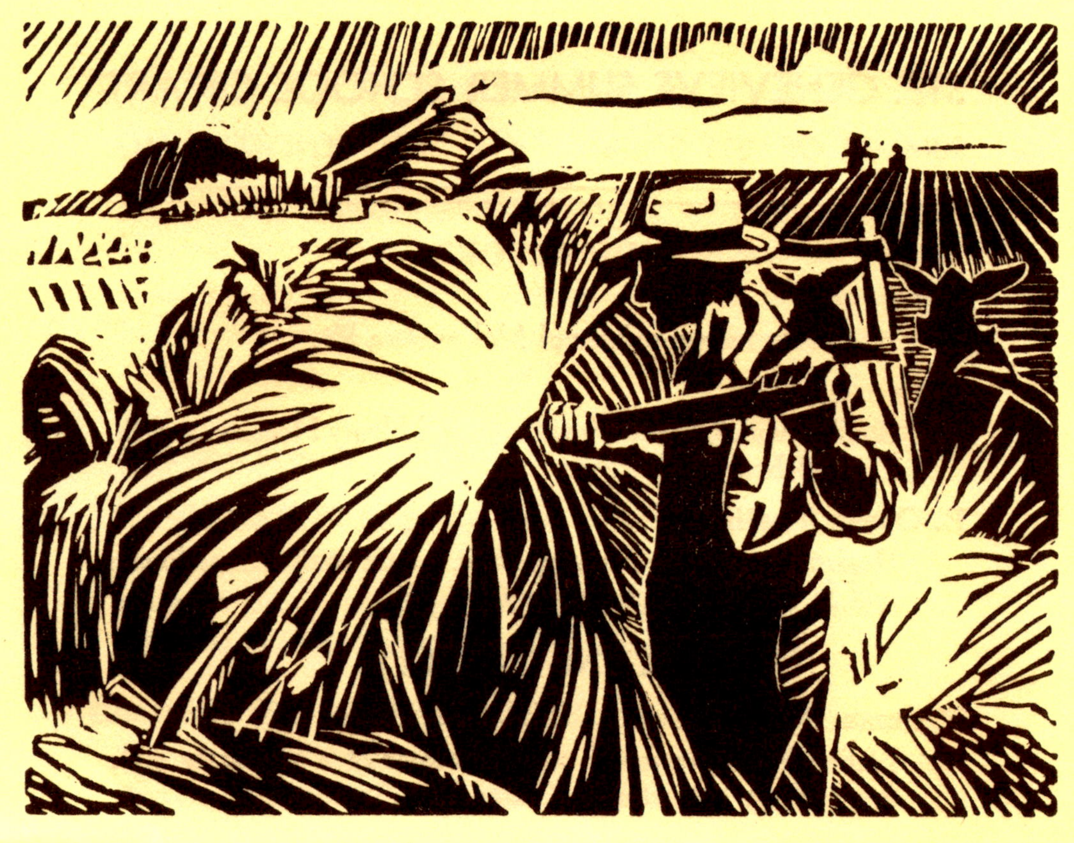

STE. GENEVIEVE SUMMER SCHOOL OF ART

Joe Jones in Ste. Genevieve

Kevin Sharp

When Joe Jones arrived in Ste. Genevieve, Missouri, in early July 1936, to be part of the art colony that had started there, he was only twenty-seven years old, but already an established painter on the American scene. He had by then explored most of the Depression-era themes upon which his reputation rested, and he was well known to leading American artists, critics, dealers, and museum officials. Jones was young to have achieved so much and to have had his achievements so well recognized. But youthful exuberance, experiential wonder, and a powerful sense of righteousness were perhaps the greatest strengths he brought to his art in the 1930s. Each new place Jones visited, each new person he met—and they were all new to him then—seemed to bring out some different quality in his art and his expectations for it. However, in going to Ste. Genevieve in the summer of 1936, Jones was seeking not so much new experiences as to be surrounded by people, places, and purposes that were familiar. A new leader in the American art world, he was intent on using his elevated position as a platform to influence and assist others.

Like many people in St. Louis, Jones may have first taken notice of Ste. Genevieve in the autumn of 1930. On October 12, the small Mississippi River town some sixty-five miles south of the city found itself on the brink of widespread racial violence. The village erupted that Sunday morning after word spread among its 2,800 residents that a pair of African American men and a female companion had shot and killed two white lime-kiln workers in the aftermath of a brawl. The shooter insisted that he was protecting the woman's honor against unwanted sexual advances by one of the white men, but it did not quell the anger of Ste. Genevieve residents, some intent on lynching. Later that night, armed white men drove through the African American sections of Ste. Genevieve, demanding that every person of color prepare to leave. By the following morning, nearly all of Ste. Genevieve's two hundred black residents, including some whose families had lived in the town for more than a century, had begun their exodus.[1]

The following week, Ste. Genevieve civic leaders invited seventy "native, property owning blacks" to return, and nearly all reclaimed their homes. But the palpable threat of mob violence effectively decimated the town's African American population, and many families that had been lured by work in the lime quarries and kilns never came back. The two black men charged with the murders were eventually tried and sentenced to life in prison; charges against the woman were dismissed. Meanwhile, the leaders among the white vigilantes, including six who had kidnapped an African American postal worker, were fined and paroled without serving jail time.[2]

The violence in Ste. Genevieve was damaging on a number of fronts. The relative racial harmony that had existed for decades was compromised and not easily restored. The town would see its population of black laborers, consumers, renters, homeowners, and neighbors dwindle. The incident also precipitated a fundamental shift in the public perception of Ste. Genevieve, as newspapers nationwide picked up the story. Residents were startled to hear their town characterized as a seat of racial tension. A local newspaper reported in the immediate aftermath of the clash that Ste. Genevieve had always considered itself a community of "gracious and cultured people." Its residents were descended from "founding fathers whose very nature was an artistic one," another local writer insisted.[3] But that identity was now cast into reasonable doubt.

Newspaper coverage of the episodes in Ste. Genevieve finally subsided in 1932. Gradually, tourists returned. Among the first to arrive in the summer of 1932 were two well-known St. Louis painters, Jessie Beard Rickly (see

Fig. 1. Cover of *Ste. Genevieve Summer School of Art*, July 6–August 15, 1936, with a woodcut (artist unknown) after Joe Jones's *Threshing No. 1* (1935; cat. 34). Dr. John Green Collection, Missouri History Museum, St. Louis.

fig. 2) and Bernard E. Peters (see fig. 3), along with their families. They rented the Mammy Shaw House, an early-nineteenth-century residence near Second and Merchant streets in the old part of Ste. Genevieve. The two painters planned a season of work and relaxation, and they asked artist friends to join them on weekends. Vera Flinn, a teacher at Washington University, St. Louis; Miriam McKinnie, a gifted painter based in Edwardsville, Illinois, just across the river from St. Louis; Aimee Schweig (see fig. 4), a prominent St. Louis artist; and Aimee's precocious teenage daughter, Martyl, visited and produced images in and of Ste. Genevieve. In late September and early October, Flinn, McKinnie, Peters, Rickly, Schweig, and two interested locals—Matthew Ziegler (a farmer and amateur painter who rented houses in Ste. Genevieve) and his aunt Sister Cassiana Marie (born Martha Vogt, she was an Order of St. Joseph nun trained in art)—held an exhibition of their summer work in the Mammy Shaw House (see fig. 2). Staged over two consecutive weekends, the show drew as many as 350 visitors. More than 150 made the drive or train ride down from St. Louis, and virtually every leading citizen of Ste. Genevieve signed the guestbook.[4]

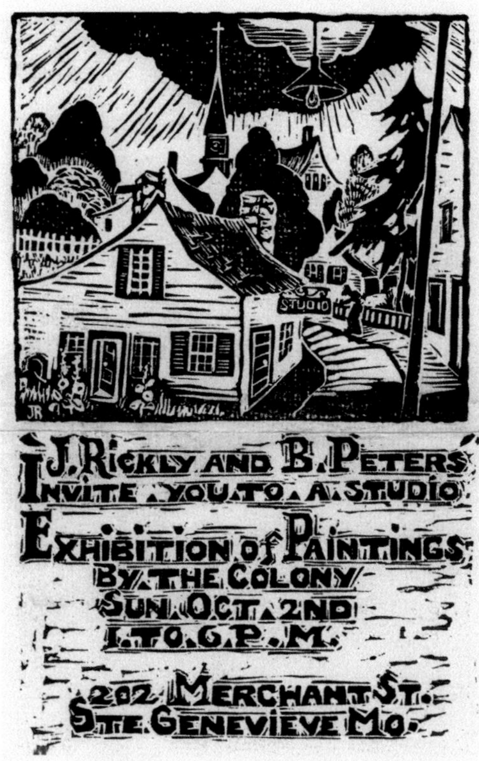

Fig. 2. Jessie Beard Rickly (1895–1975). Invitation to exhibition at the Mammy Shaw House, Ste. Genevieve, 1932. Woodcut. Photo courtesy Martin Schweig Studios.

Apart from its recent past, the town acquitted itself well to artists in 1932. It had the appealing patina of age, picturesque scenery, welcoming but not especially nosy residents, and a very rich history. The people of Ste. Genevieve believed that the town had been founded in about 1735 (the date was later determined to be closer to 1750). Following traders, trappers, and missionaries who had explored the region in the seventeenth century, French-speaking pioneer farmers from Canada entered the Illinois Country in the early eighteenth century and eventually crossed the Mississippi River in search of arable soil, salt deposits, and lead. When the outpost of Ste. Genevieve was erected just south of where the town now stands, it became one of the first permanent settlements established by people of European ancestry west of the Mississippi.[5] Agriculture was the basis of Ste. Genevieve's prosperity, but mining entrepreneurs, tons of extracted ore, and the ready transportation provided by the river promised to bring expansion and even wealth to the budding village. Lead drawn from mines along the nearby St. Francis and Big rivers and iron extracted from the rolling Ozark Mountains further west were transported along a plank road to Ste. Genevieve and the Mississippi. As the hamlet flourished and grew, its local gentry built sturdy houses of masonry and wood in the Southern Creole manner.[6] A significant number of Ste. Genevieve's early-nineteenth- and even some eighteenth-century houses survived in the 1930s, and some still stand.

The expansion of the railroads west of the Mississippi in the late 1850s marked the beginning of the town's decline as a transportation hub. When the Iron Mountain Railroad chose St. Louis rather than Ste. Genevieve as its base of operation, the great age, or at least the promise of a great age, for the lower-river community effectively ended. By the late nineteenth century, it had become a quiet, yet generally prosperous, agricultural center. The arrival of large lime companies in the early twentieth century further enriched the community and brought steady employment to many of its townspeople, even as it left large gashes in the earth where the limestone was quarried. Through it all, Ste. Genevieve never forgot its proud early history. Its impressive domestic architecture, distinctive French character, and small-town charm made it an attractive destination for leisure travelers, including artists from the big city sixty-five miles to the north.[7]

From early on in his career, Jones was no doubt acquainted with the founders of the incipient Ste. Genevieve art colony. Flinn, Peters, Rickly, and Schweig were well known in St. Louis. They in turn would have been intrigued by the brash, young one-time housepainter elbowing his way into local art exhibitions and attracting the attention of journalists. Jones had certainly crossed paths with these artists by March 1930, when he exhibited an Art Deco–influenced depiction of a clay factory (possibly cat. 11) at the St. Louis Artists' Guild, to which most of the city's consequential painters and sculptors belonged. In late 1931, Rickly bought a painting depicting Jones's wife, Freda Sies (possibly cat. 14, from 1931), and he joined an artists' group she cofounded called the New Hats (see Turk). The name was probably a tongue-in-cheek reference to "High Hats," a term young progressives at the art colony in Provincetown, Massachusetts, derisively assigned to the more traditional painters who summered on Cape Cod.[8] Before the stock market crashed in October 1929, Rickly and Schweig (fig. 5) had spent summers together in Provincetown, studying with Charles Hawthorne at his Cape Cod School of Art, and with his protégé Henry Hensche. When the Depression made long-distance travel and extended stays on the Cape prohibitively expensive, the two resourceful women began searching for ways to re-create Provincetown's artistic esprit de corps close to home.

The St. Louis artists' first summer in Ste. Genevieve had been a spontaneous success, and in 1933 they returned with a more focused program in mind. Rickly had exhibited eighteen of her Ste. Genevieve paintings at the St. Louis Artists' Guild in February and was beginning to realize that the colony experience had commercial as well as aesthetic and collegial value.[9] She spent nearly the whole summer of 1933 in Ste. Genevieve. Schweig generally traveled down on weekends, riding with Rickly's husband, Francis. Visitors came and went, and the conversations at the Mammy Show House about art, lasting well into the night, were lively and at times intense. Peters had been drawn to Ste. Genevieve more for solitude than for socio-aesthetic debate, and that second summer he and his wife, Ord, bought a large house

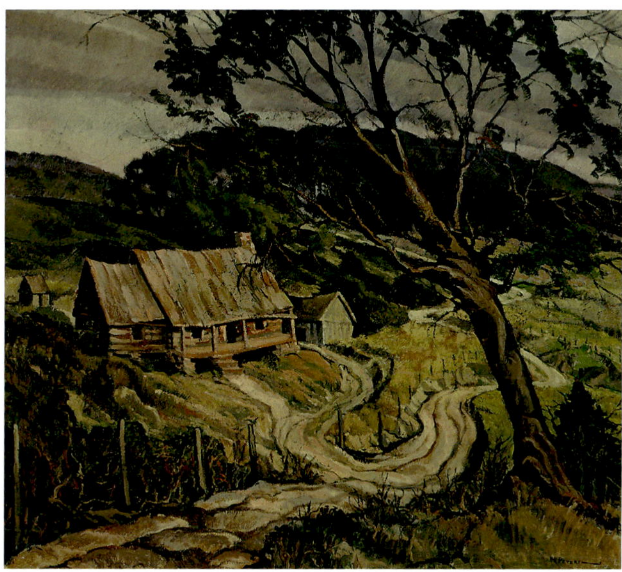

Fig. 3. Bernard E. Peters (1893–1949). *Untitled (Landscape)*, c. 1930s. Oil on canvas; 36 × 39½ in. (91.4 × 100.3 cm). Collection of John and Susan Horseman.

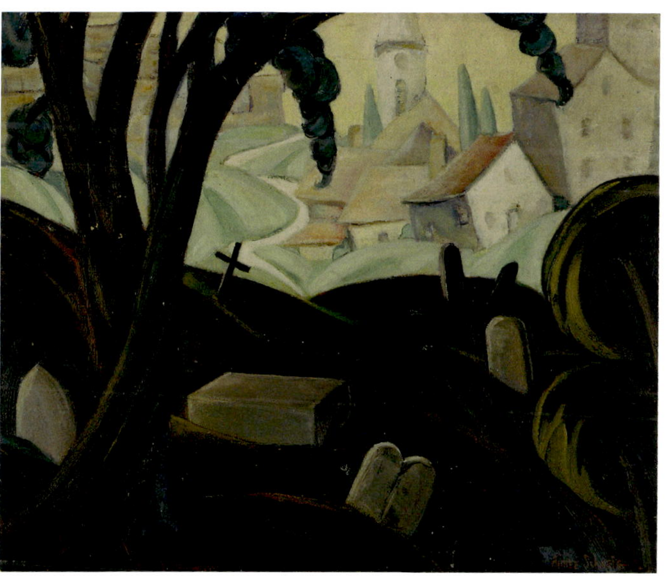

Fig. 4. Aimee Schweig (1897–1987). *Graveyard*, c. 1930s. Oil on panel; 20 × 24 in. (50.8 × 61 cm). Courtesy of Missouri History Museum, St. Louis.

overlooking the Mississippi, just a few miles south, near the town of St. Mary. For the remainder of his career, he painted scenes of village life and the rugged Ozarks landscape, but he kept to the edges of the colony.[10] Schweig moved into the quarters in the Mammy Shaw House that the Peterses vacated, sharing the rental with Rickly. The arrival of summering painters for the second year in a row confirmed to locals that Ste. Genevieve had not lost its artistic pedigree after all. Signaling their embrace of the colony, town officials invited Rickly and Schweig to stage an exhibition of their work at the inaugural event of the new Ste. Genevieve Museum.[11]

During their second summer in Ste. Genevieve, Rickly and Schweig began to think about the town as the site of an art school, one that would serve artists and art students of the Midwest as Provincetown attracted those in the East. They were aware of a similar endeavor launched in the summer of 1932 by Marvin Cone, Adrian J. Dornbush, Edward B. Rowan, and Grant Wood in another old quarry town, Stone City, Iowa. Dozens of artists, young and old, mainly from Illinois, Iowa, Kansas, and Minnesota, poured into the village, most hoping to work alongside Wood, whose *American Gothic* (The Art Institute of Chicago) had made him famous when it debuted in Chicago in 1930. The founders of the Stone City Art Colony and School created a summer academy with structured classes, trained faculty, and formal critiques. In its second year, the school was accredited under the authority of Coe College in nearby Cedar Rapids.[12] Rickly and Schweig's friend and fellow St. Louis painter E. Oscar Thalinger sent his talented son Jean to study in Stone City, and he must have brought home practical information that proved useful to the women in developing their plans for Ste. Genevieve. In fact, Wood was in St. Louis in the spring of 1933, serving as a juror of the St. Louis Artists' Guild annual exhibition at the City Art Museum. Along with two other judges (Dixie Selden and Neil Ives), he awarded Jones's *Clay Mine* (location unknown) the prize for best work of art in the show.[13]

Rickly and Schweig became convinced that an art school would add purpose to their artistic ambitions and generate interest in the work they produced in Ste. Genevieve. Cooperative town officials believed it would help attract visitors. Even as the Stone City experiment was already collapsing in August 1933 under the weight of unrealized (and unrealistic) financial expectations, Rickly and Schweig continued planning and promoting their venture (see fig. 6). By early the following summer, their ideas had taken shape. At the end of June 1934, the *Ste. Genevieve Fair Play* announced the formation of a summer art academy and the mission it would pursue: "The School, established in the third year of the Art Colony, is a natural outgrowth of its founders' desire to increase the appreciation of art in the Middle West. Its purpose is to perpetuate contemporary Midwestern life by the preservation of its scenes and types in paint."[14]

The educational program Rickly and Schweig imagined for Ste. Genevieve was inspired by their experience at the Cape Cod School of Art. Moreover, the Mississippi River town's French pedigree paralleled the Old World feel long perpetuated by the Portuguese American fishermen

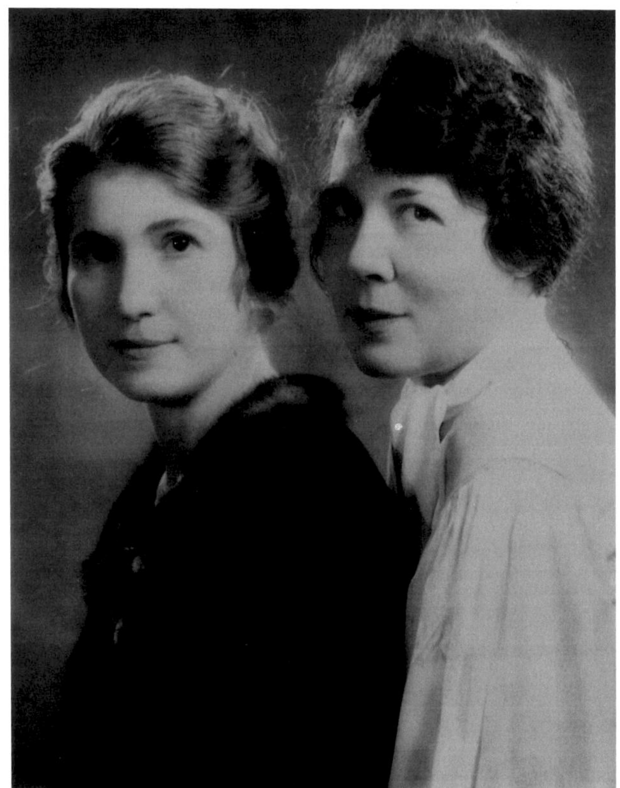

Fig. 5. Jessie Beard Rickly and Aimee Schweig, c. 1930. Courtesy of Martin Schweig.

of Provincetown. But in its dedication to the emerging aesthetic of the Midwest, the school Rickly and Schweig founded in southeastern Missouri was very different from the one they had known on the Cape. They were consciously aligning themselves with a model of American painting that many considered indigenous, and therefore more authentic than the imported Impressionism and European modernism generally favored in Provincetown. They had taken their position before the loudest polemics for Midwestern art were sounded in the 1930s: before Wood published his *Revolt against the City* (1935), which called for "growth of non-urban and regional activity in the arts and letters"; before Thomas Hart Benton's self-portrait appeared on the cover of *Time* in December 1934, signaling the arrival of Regionalism as a major force in American art, and well before he made a blustery return to his native Missouri from the East Coast in September 1935; and just as critic Thomas Craven was polarizing the American art world with his assault on European modernism in his 1934 *Modern Art: The Men, the Movements, the Meaning*.[15] In advance of these significant events, Rickly and Schweig brought tiny Ste. Genevieve into the national discussion about Regionalism, American Scene painting, and Midwestern art.

Rickly and Schweig's Midwest boosterism echoed comments young Jones had been making to reporters in St. Louis for as long as they had been listening to him. In the first major interview he gave, in June 1931, Jones chided St. Louis colleagues who spent their summers in seaside artist haunts in the East: "If there's anything that galls me, it's the way they go to Gloucester or some place and copy somebody and then come back here talking down to us who have stayed here and painted what we saw in nature of St. Louis." To his thinking, "enough fishing smacks have already been painted anyway." If he had gone East to art school or to find patrons, it would have "killed everything I have that is worth while," he insisted.[16] The young proletarian pledged to remain in St. Louis and stay true to his Midwest origins. It "is as good as anywhere else, and if an artist has something to say he can say it here as well as anywhere."[17] Even after a visit to Provincetown in the summer of 1933, Jones held to his promise. Back in St. Louis, he told a reporter that he could not understand the outsized attraction of the Massachusetts colony's painters to "those gaudy French things, as if there was nothing happening here and now that was worthy of painting."[18]

But Jones had been more affected by his 1933 travels in the East than he either realized or let on. He found himself beginning to doubt whether he still belonged in St. Louis. That fall he wrote to his patron, confidante, and advisor Elizabeth Green from the houseboat in which he and Freda were now residing on the Mississippi River, "I don't think the depressive atmosphere I have returned to has exactly been a very beneficial one." He was ready to admit that "the keen interest in doing things such as there was in Provincetown is utterly lacking in St. Louis, everything seems so well pleased with itself you feel like an intruder."[19] In another letter to Green written around the same time, he confessed that he had gone "as far as I can go in St. Louis."[20]

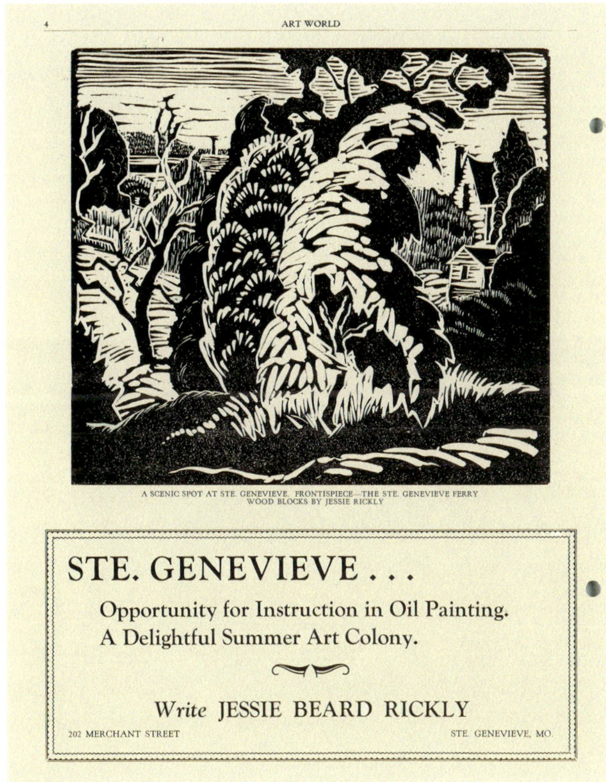
4 ART WORLD

A SCENIC SPOT AT STE. GENEVIEVE. FRONTISPIECE—THE STE. GENEVIEVE FERRY
WOOD BLOCKS BY JESSIE RICKLY

STE. GENEVIEVE . . .
Opportunity for Instruction in Oil Painting.
A Delightful Summer Art Colony.
Write JESSIE BEARD RICKLY
202 MERCHANT STREET
STE. GENEVIEVE, MO.

Fig. 6. Advertisement for Ste. Genevieve Art Colony, *St. Louis Art World* 2, [10] (Summer 1933), p. 4. This ad features Jessie Beard Rickly's *Scenic Spot at Ste. Genevieve*. Woodcut. Location unknown.

Jones may not have fully grasped then the degree to which the American art world and the federal government were becoming interested in Midwestern art and artists. He was distracted by renovations to the houseboat, and not selling enough pictures even to keep fuel in the stove, much less eke out a living. The challenges of that winter on the Mississippi (at one point, he and Freda were out of money and down to their last six eggs) only magnified his doubts about St. Louis and the career path he was charting.[21] Apart from starting a free class for unemployed artists (notable for its racial mix of the students) at St. Louis's Old Courthouse (see Wolfe), his only successes in late 1933 and early 1934 were in the East. A powerful lynching painting, *American Justice* (1933; cat. 31), appeared in the Worcester Art Museum, in Massachusetts, and one of his landscapes (1933; cat. 30) was on view in New York at the Museum of Modern Art's "Painting and Sculpture from 16 Cities" exhibition.[22] The two shows were less confirmation that Jones belonged in the East than recognition of what he and others were producing in American Scene incubators like St. Louis. He may not have seen it that way yet, but others did. Edward Alden Jewell wrote in his *New York Times* review of the Museum of Modern Art show: "America seems suddenly to have gone regional, and a good thing it is."[23]

The Ste. Genevieve Artists' Colony and Summer School of Art officially opened on July 9, 1934. In addition to the founders, the faculty and visiting lecturers included Flinn, McKinnie, Thalinger, the esteemed St. Louis sculptor Victor S. Holm, and Gregory Ivy, a Missouri-born painter then teaching at a small college in Pennsylvania. Like its now-defunct counterpart in Stone City, the summer school drew its share of mature artists as well as students. Helen Beccard, a noted St. Louis–based social realist and teacher, made her way to Ste. Genevieve, as did Joseph P. Vorst, a German émigré who had family in the town and had settled in St. Louis by 1929 or 1930. Vorst was then transforming his native New Objectivity (Neue Sachlichkeit) style into an expressive form of American Scene painting, focusing on such subjects as life along the Mississippi River and the region's poverty (see fig. 7). On July 21, the *Ste. Genevieve Fair Play* reported that "Mr. and Mrs. Joe Jones of St. Louis" had dropped in that week.[24] The Joneses arrived via the river and the houseboat that was becoming a source of ever-escalating tension. The couple would abandon their floating home in Arkansas City, Arkansas, just a few weeks later, when it became clear that it would never get them back upriver to St. Louis.[25] (They abandoned their marriage a few months after that.) In late October, the colony's close-of-season exhibition at the Mammy Shaw House attracted over two hundred visitors during the eight days it was open. More than one hundred made the trek from St. Louis.[26]

Rickly and Schweig were determined to repeat the experiment. The following summer, classes started on July 8, involving mostly the same visiting artists, with guest lecturers coming and going. That summer the town was more lively than it had been in past years, as residents and civic leaders prepared for its bicentennial celebration in August. Planned for more than a year, the anniversary was marked by four days of ceremonies, speeches, concerts, parades, historical re-enactments, and theatricals. The festivities culminated on August 22 with the broadcast of telephone greetings from Franklin D. Roosevelt over a private line. The president saluted "the fortitude of the pioneers who built their homes on the western bank of the Mississippi and wrested minerals from the hills, furs from the forest, and a plentiful harvest from the plain." He remained confident that the present-day

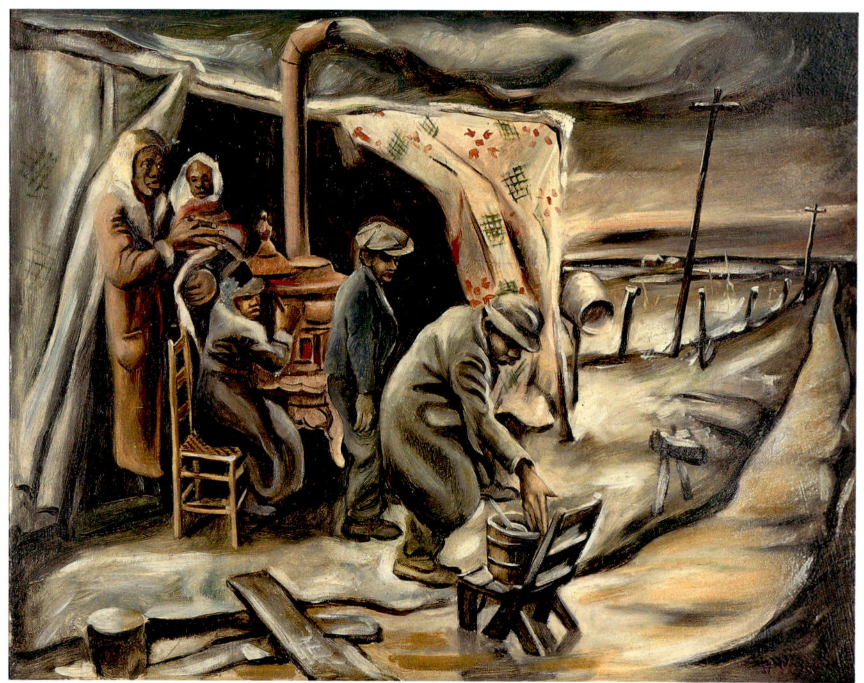

Fig. 7. Joseph P. Vorst (1897–1947). *Sharecroppers' Revolt*, c. 1940. Oil on panel; 24 × 31 in. (61 × 78.7 cm). Collection of John and Susan Horseman.

residents had "not lost the stalwart qualities of frontier days" and extended "hearty wishes for a happy and prosperous future."[27]

Clearly, Ste. Genevieve had put the violence of 1930 behind it. Five years later, it not only jubilantly observed a bicentennial, but also witnessed its nascent tourist economy grow beyond expectations. More than fifteen thousand visitors flocked to the village to participate in the festivities.[28] The steady influx of tourists might have promoted the art colony as well as the community, but it proved a missed opportunity. Rickly and Schweig had a falling out at some point in early August that pushed their Ste. Genevieve project to the brink of dissolution. The precise circumstances that ended the women's long friendship are unknown.[29] Whatever occurred, they could not overcome their differences. The colony's regular news briefs and updates ended abruptly in mid-August, just as the celebration and largest crush of visitors arrived. There was no triumphant exhibition at the close of the season. When Rickly left Ste. Genevieve at the end of the summer, she would never return in any capacity related to the colony and school. If these were to continue, it fell to Schweig alone to organize them.[30]

As the Ste. Genevieve art colony stumbled, Jones was in the midst of his meteoric rise to national prominence. Having reconciled his Midwest identity and East Coast ambitions, he had gone to New York in early February 1935, spent six weeks rubbing shoulders with artists and writers, and laid out for them an impressive body of work that captured the current social foment in Middle America. Before returning home in late March, he had secured a solo exhibition at the American Contemporary Art (A.C.A.) Gallery in Greenwich Village, which opened in May and was so successful that it was restaged later in the summer. Jones saw neither installment. He was studying the wheat fields near St. Charles, Missouri, during the show's first incarnation, and lecturing and painting a mural at Commonwealth College in Mena, Arkansas (see Wolfe, fig. 6; cat. 39; and Chronology, figs. 7–8), during its second.

Jones had intended to return to St. Louis when he left Mena in September 1935, but he changed his plans at the last minute and journeyed to New York instead. By no later than November, he had met Maynard Walker, an ambitious New York art dealer who had just lured Benton, John Steuart Curry, and Wood from Ferargil Galleries, his former employer, to the new Walker Galleries on 57th Street, in midtown Manhattan. Walker's stock was very much on the rise, and so it seemed was Jones's.[31]

Walker agreed to give Jones a solo exhibition in January 1936 of the wheat-harvest paintings inspired by his previous summer in St. Charles. Jones understood that, in presenting his work with Walker, he was about to experience a level of critical scrutiny and possibly commercial success beyond anything he had known thus far. He dared to imagine becoming a nationally recognized figure and had little difficulty summoning the image. He considered not only what his elevated stature in the art world might mean to his painting and activism, but also how he might use it to help other artists back home. En route to New York for the Walker Galleries opening, he wrote to Green, who had subsidized his train ticket and the relative luxury of his travel: "I don't think I shall ever be completely happy about my own success untill [*sic*] my fellow artists have a decent chance to prove their usefullness [*sic*] to society."[32] It was, like most of his utterances, a completely guileless expression of selflessness and a foretelling of his next efforts in self-promotion.

The presentation of Jones's wheat-field paintings at the Walker Galleries was by no means an unqualified success (see Balken). Some critics who had been on the fence about the artist the previous spring and summer were even less convinced of his abilities now, and others who had appreciated the audacity of the socially charged imagery they had seen at the A.C.A. Gallery were not certain he had sustained it in his fields of golden wheat.[33] But the show more than met Jones's own expectations, and to his thinking it represented a "glorious conclusion" to all he had been trying to accomplish.[34] Work sold for good prices, he sent newspaper clippings home to his mother, and he relayed to Green that "there is a general feeling now that I am in the first place as an artist in America[;] this sound[s] incredible but up here its [*sic*] not hard to believe."[35]

Jones did not wait for the opening of the Walker Galleries show to begin leveraging the influence he expected to derive from it. The mere promise of success on 57th Street was enough to convince Herman Baron, director of the A.C.A. Gallery, to allow Jones and four colleagues from St. Louis—Fred Conway, Thalinger, James Turnbull, and Vorst—to organize an exhibition of Midwestern art at the gallery in the spring of 1936. The typewritten call for entries was probably authored by Jones himself and certainly spoke to his experience of the last year:

> A committee of five St. Louis artists has as its purpose the desire to reach a representative and alert group of Middle-western artists who are vitally responsive to the socio-economic, environmental, and natural forces of life about them, and who are making use of this material for the subject matter of their art.
>
> Because of the vitality, the significance, the fertility, of this subject matter of the interior, the East is now looking toward this part of the country for the nucleus of an American art—a genuinely native and typical art.[36]

The May 1936 exhibition "Paintings by Midwestern Artists" was the fulfillment of Jones's expressed desire to help like-minded colleagues working in the center of the United States. It featured examples by twenty-three painters from Arkansas, Illinois, Kansas, Missouri, Tennessee, and Texas; the majority were from Jones's home state, and of these most were based in St. Louis (a few may have been Jones's students from his Unemployed Art Class). Ten of the artists represented had—or soon would have—ties to the colony in Ste. Genevieve.

Jones and most of his Missouri colleagues in the A.C.A show contributed works rooted in social commentary, reflective of their immediate surroundings, or both. Jones showed *We Want More* and *Cropper Family* (both location unknown), a return to imagery of social unrest and protest after the pastoral interval of his wheat-harvest compositions. Lawrence Adams, a graduate of the Yale School of Fine Arts and a teacher at the University of Missouri, showed five paintings, including *Missouri Farmer* and *Serving an Eviction Notice*. Beccard presented a canvas called *An American Scene*. Conway's *Early Bird* was a wry meditation on class struggle. McKinnie exhibited *Saturday Auction* and *Old Cider Press*, the latter a rural landscape possibly painted near Ste. Genevieve. Joseph Meert, a former student of Benton's, sent two paintings, *Picking up Coal* and *Join the Picket Line*. Schweig sent *Wheat*, which depicted a subject now indelibly associated with Jones. Frederick Shane, another instructor at the University of Missouri, offered five works, among them *The Scavenger*. Bernice Singer, an African American painter from St. Louis, showed *Worn Out* and *W.P.A. Worker*. Thalinger sent *Mining Town*, no doubt painted somewhere near Ste. Genevieve; and Vorst exhibited *Missouri Mules*, *Hill Farmers*, and *Cotton Pickers*.[37]

In the *New York Times*, critic Howard Devree penned a mostly laudatory review of the show, impressive for being the first of twenty new exhibitions opening in the city that he discussed. Devree was grateful that, among the paintings on display, there were "no imitations of Benton, Curry and Wood." He liked that the work seemed "very local, close at hand, emotionally conceived and expressed." Jones was the only artist of the group with whom the critic was familiar, but he appreciated much of what he saw by the others, even allowing for "certain immaturities, even crudeness." The work, he felt, was "all-purposeful, intelligent, indigenous expression." Devree approved of Schweig's *Wheat* and saw "humor and shrewd observation" in the examples by Conway and Shane.[38] A large illustration of Vorst's *Missouri Mules* appeared in the center of the article.

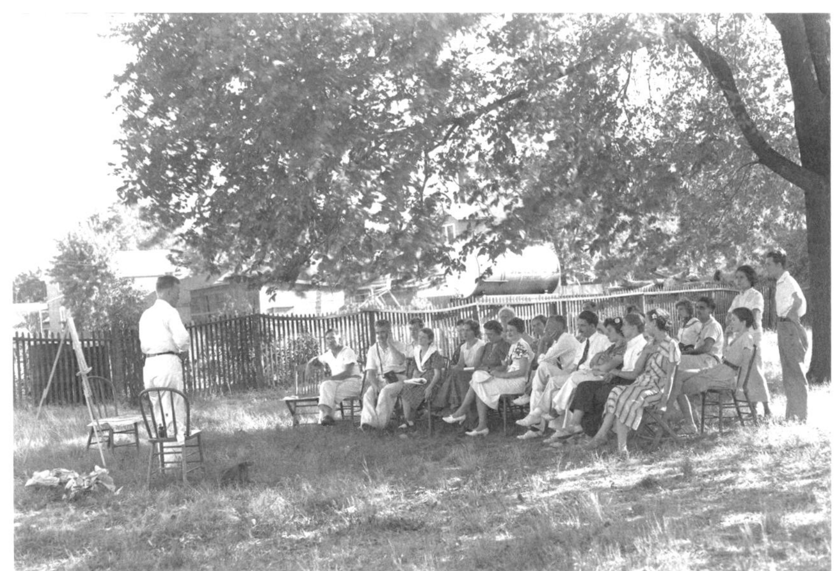

Fig. 8. Ste. Genevieve Summer School of Art class, c. 1936. Courtesy of Martin Schweig.

The heady experience of the A.C.A. exhibition must have boosted Schweig's confidence that the 1936 season (July 6–August 15) of the Ste. Genevieve Summer School of Art would attract enough students to remain viable. The inclusion in the show of so many artists already associated with the school helped validate the art colony in the context of the rising visibility and importance of American Scene painting. That point was literally and figuratively driven home to prospective enrollees when the A.C.A. show moved in June to St. Louis's new Vanguard Gallery, which Jones and Green had a hand in founding.[39] But the status conferred by the New York exhibition and its St. Louis redux were not the only inducements Schweig had to offer potential students. By the time the A.C.A. show opened in New York, she had persuaded Jones to teach at and serve as a co-director of the school.

In addition to giving the 1936 session star power, Jones would bring solid teaching experience to Ste. Genevieve. He had worked with advanced art students in 1932 and with unemployed students in the Old Courthouse beginning in late December 1933, a class he taught twice a week for a year. At the time of his Walker Galleries exhibition, he had presented four lectures in the New York area, including one at the Art Students' League, and another in Philadelphia.[40] He was no doubt aware that Benton and Wood had enhanced their own positions as leading American artists by building followings of students and acolytes. Moreover, he saw teaching as a way of helping others and spreading his beliefs, and he seemed to genuinely enjoy it (see Chronology, fig. 5).

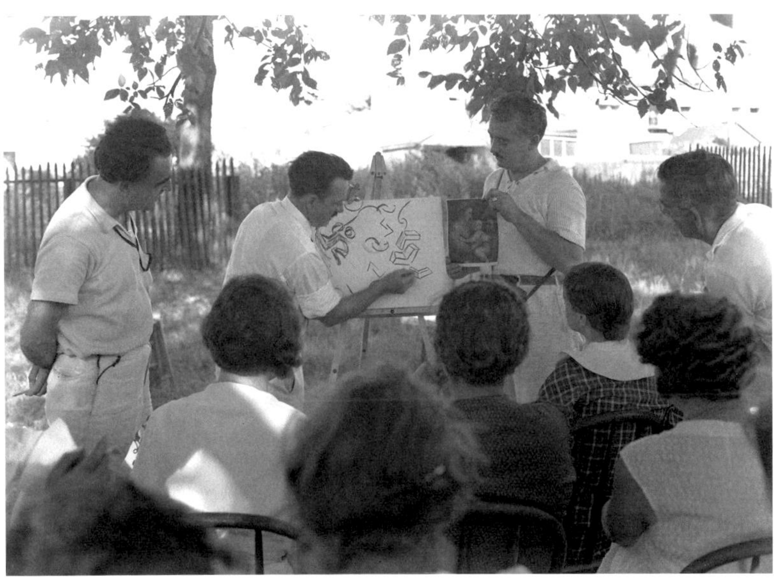

Jones was so crucial to Schweig's Ste. Genevieve strategy that, for the cover of the school's publicity brochure, she cut (or had someone cut) a block print of his *Threshing No. 1* (fig. 1), a painting that was quickly becoming the artist's signature work (1935; cat. 34). But for all his incandescence, Jones turned out not to be Schweig's largest attraction, even though he may have been responsible for attracting the artist who was. Benton—now back in Missouri—had agreed to make an appearance at the school. It is unclear whether Jones knew Benton at that point; Schweig almost certainly did not. But Jones could have called on any number of mutual acquaintances to invite the titan of Regionalism to spend a day or two along the Mississippi River. He had met Benton's friends Craven, Curry, and Wood at the opening of his wheat-paintings show (see Balken), and of course he now knew Benton's dealer Maynard Walker quite well.[41] The contact could have been made as well through Lawrence Adams, who was included in the Midwestern show at the A.C.A. Gallery and that summer would help Benton with a large cycle of murals for the Missouri state capitol building in Jefferson City.[42] However the invitation was extended, by mid-May Benton had committed to teach at Ste. Genevieve at a not-yet-determined point in the summer, depending on the progress he was making on his murals. Adams planned to accompany him to the art colony.

Jones visited Ste. Genevieve briefly in the second week of June, probably on his way back to St. Louis from Forrest City, Arkansas, where he had been arrested, along with the Pulitzer Prize–winning novelist Josephine Johnson, on suspicion of inciting sharecroppers to strike.[43] Jones insisted to Green that the incident had been much exaggerated in the press, but when Johnson produced an article for *New Masses* voicing her outrage at the treatment of tenant farmers and those trying to organize them, it was accompanied by his illustrations.[44] Toward the end of the month, he wrote to Schweig, informing her of another possible student, promising to get together with Thalinger about publicity, and preparing her for the likelihood that he would not arrive in Ste. Genevieve until July 5, the day before classes were to begin. The registration of students was to occur two days before that, and

Fig. 9. Thomas Hart Benton (at easel) teaching a Ste. Genevieve Summer School of Art class, 1936. Courtesy of Martin Schweig.

Schweig may have counted on his assistance. He knew his tardiness would be a concern, but he had been sick, he said, and "work here is kinda pressing."[45]

By the time Jones rolled into Ste. Genevieve, the entire state of Missouri was suffering a heat wave. It only grew worse the following week; newspapers reported that it was 107 degrees in St. Louis on July 13, and that to date fifteen people had died of heat prostration. Jefferson City, where Benton was working, was even hotter, at 110 degrees. The scorching temperatures and their effect on crops—particularly the wheat harvest—were rapidly becoming a cause of national alarm.[46] Jones had planned from the outset to teach a class in mural painting that summer "for those interested in public art,"[47] and he knew that the timing of his arrival coincided perfectly with the ripening of Missouri's winter wheat, however diminished it might be. Despite the heat, he apparently introduced his pupils to the culture of wheat harvesting, which he had come to know the summer before in St. Charles. The *Ste. Genevieve Fair Play* noted on July 11 that "a group of students have already found an ideal subject for sketching in the wheat threshing scenes on the farms near Ste. Genevieve."[48]

Within days of his arrival in Ste. Genevieve, Jones learned from Adrian J. Dornbush, formerly part of the Stone City Art Colony and now a coordinator with the federal government's Resettlement Administration, that he had received a six-week appointment to "prepare a pictorial report of the drought."[49] His plans to help "fellow artists have a decent chance to prove their usefullness [*sic*]" in Ste. Genevieve evaporated in his pursuit of an opportunity all his own. He left sometime in mid-July, stopping first in Champaign, Illinois. He found that he would have to venture deeper into the Great Plains to witness the drought's most devastating effects.[50] He had traveled as far as Mitchell, South Dakota, by July 22, when he ran out of money, but that was far enough. He was deeply moved by the ruin and desolation he found. He asked Green to wire him twenty-five dollars so he could return home, and he was apparently back in St. Louis before the end of the month. Jones was again in Ste. Genevieve on or before Sunday, August 9, when he led an evening discussion.[51]

Schweig must have been concerned by Jones's absence in the middle of the term and by the fact that there was as yet no sign of Benton. He was still working in Jefferson City, immersed in his murals for the capitol building, and increasingly testy about interruptions.[52] Perhaps in part to compensate for his own imminent or recent departure from the river town, Jones had written to Benton, urging him to inform Schweig of his expected arrival date. Benton had promptly dashed off a note, around Monday, July 20, signaling his intentions: "My dear Mrs. Schweig, Joe Jones has written me asking that I inform you of the time that Lawrence Adams and I propose to arrive in Ste. Genevieve. Doing the best we can we should be in town by Sat. morn. Sincerely yours, Thomas H. Benton."[53]

Saturday, July 26, came and went, and Benton was nowhere near Ste. Genevieve. Another weekend passed without sight of him, and then another. He finally found his way to the art colony on Wednesday or Thursday, August 12 or 13, just days before classes ended. Despite the lateness and brevity of his visit (it appears he spent only one day there), it stirred considerable excitement. The students recognized the honor his appearance represented, and more than one artist, including Vorst, traveled from St. Louis just to meet him. In one photograph (see fig. 9) of his busy day in Ste. Genevieve, Benton is seen working intently at an easel, boldly marking a canvas or panel with a piece of charcoal to demonstrate his approach

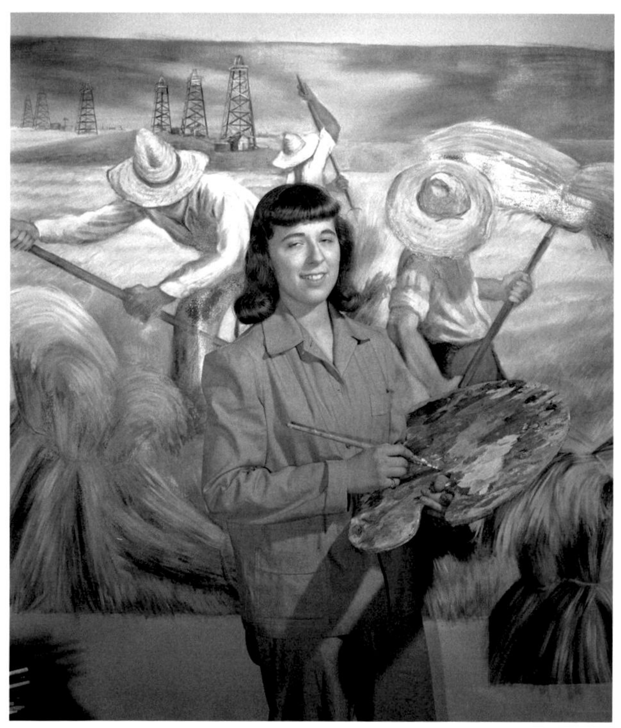

Fig. 10. Martyl Schweig standing before her mural *Wheat Workers*, 1940, executed for the Russell, Kansas, Post Office. Arthur Witman Photograph Collection; Western Historical Manuscript Collection, University of Missouri–St. Louis.

to organizing form and developing compositions. On the left, Thalinger cocks his head for a better view, Ziegler leans in from the right, and the helpful Vorst holds up a reproduction of Raphael's *Madonna of the Chair* (Palazzo Pitti, Florence) as a group of female students look on. In another photograph, Schweig and Benton pose side by side, grinning at the camera, with what may be one of Benton's compositional studies on an easel to their right. This photograph appeared in the *St. Louis Star-Times* on Friday, August 14, announcing Benton's visit and Schweig's triumph in luring him to Ste. Genevieve.[54] The school closed for the summer the next day with a lecture by Jones's friend Turnbull and an "impersonation party."[55] Apparently, no exhibition of summer work occurred at the colony that year.

While the Ste. Genevieve wheat-harvest mural, if it was ever completed, is apparently lost or destroyed, it played a part in the creation of many others. Just a few weeks after the close of the 1936 session, Jones was asked by liquor retailer Morris Multin to produce five murals for his new 905 Liquor Store in downtown St. Louis. The cycle, called *The Story of the Grain*, includes *Threshing* (cat. 40), *Binding the Wheat*, *Shipping to Market*, and *A Market for Wheat* (all Haggerty Museum of Art, Marquette University, Milwaukee); the fifth is a riverfront subject (cat. 41). The wheat murals derived from Jones's work in the fields near St. Charles during the summer of 1935, but his ability to imagine them in a large format was certainly aided by his teaching in Ste. Genevieve. In *Threshing* Jones assembled a group of ten custom cutters and field hands, most dressed in blue overalls, around a stationary thresher and a mule-drawn wagon loaded with sheaves of cut wheat. A man in the foreground, his back turned and his knee resting on a fat burlap sack, winds binding twine around his left arm and watches a cascade of wheat shoot from the thresher out beyond the composition's edge. To his left, another man leans over a sack filled with grain and cinches it closed. Behind him, two men confer over some unseen object they are holding in their hands. It could be the plumpness of the grain or possibly the thinness of their pay; Jones offered no indication. In a remarkably serene image, given the intensity of the labor, each man quietly and efficiently performs his role in the harvest.

Jones completed the 905 commission by December, and the large paintings were installed in Multin's store in early 1937. The aesthetic and critical success of *The Story of the Grain* doubtless persuaded Jones to reexamine the theme of wheat in four of the five murals he completed for post offices in Arkansas, Kansas, and Missouri between 1938 and 1941, at a time when he was exploring the subject in his easel paintings less and less frequently (see Walker and Turk).[56] The pair of men in *Threshing* appears again in the mural Jones did for the

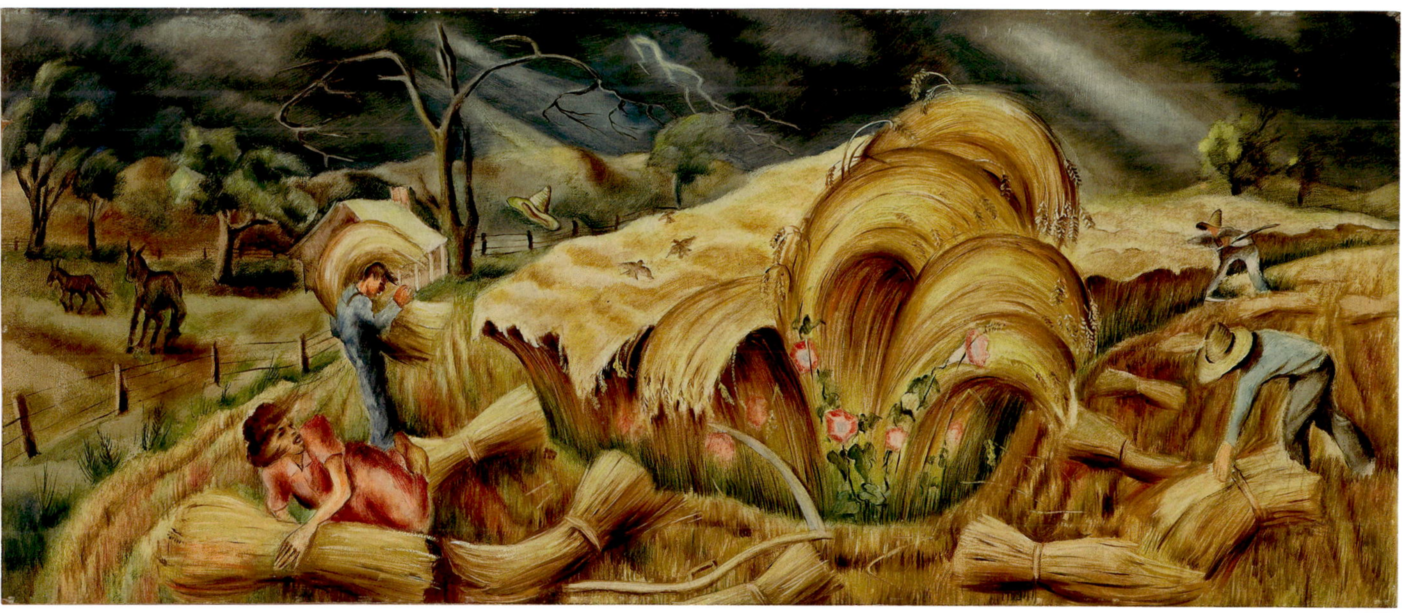

Fig. 11. Joseph P. Vorst. *Binding the Wheat*, 1940. Oil on laminated paperboard; 16 × 36 in. (40.6 × 91.4 cm). Collection of Hunt and Donna Bonan.

Magnolia, Arkansas, Post Office, in 1938. Anchoring the lower-right corner, one winds twine and the other closes a sack. They also turn up, on a smaller scale, and without their comrades or machines, in one final canvas called *Missouri Wheat Farmers* (1938; cat. 70) and in a lithograph of the same title (1938; cat. 69).

A number of the artists who spent time in Ste. Genevieve in the mid-1930s intensified their aesthetic connection to Jones later in the decade. More than a few found meaningful expression and paying commissions by employing his signature wheat-harvest themes. They would never have called themselves Jones's followers; by then he would not have thought of them that way either. But there is no question that his influence deepened in the aftermath of the 1936 A.C.A. exhibition and his participation in the art colony. Schweig had been among the first to understand the advantage in aligning herself with Jones, starting with her presentation of a wheat-field scene in the A.C.A. show. Her daughter, Martyl, only eighteen years old in 1936, was clearly taken with Jones's work. The style, as well as the subjects, of her early windblown Midwest townscapes, images of working-class struggle, and, of course, the harvesting of wheat can be traced to formative experiences with Jones in Ste. Genevieve. In *Wheat Workers* (see fig. 10), Martyl's impressive 1940 mural for the Russell, Kansas, Post Office, and other paintings in the same idiom, his influence was still evident, even though he had long ago left her immediate orbit.[57]

Even more mature painters seemed to keep a close eye on Jones after his summer in Ste. Genevieve. McKinnie, an artist Jones had looked to in his formative years (see Turk), later returned the compliment. *Harvest*, her 1938 mural for the post office in Marshall, Illinois, just west of Terre Haute, Indiana, features sturdy field workers cutting and binding wheat.[58] For the Jackson, Missouri, Post Office, Conway painted cows grazing among mighty stacks of chaff left over from the wheat harvest.[59] Vorst produced a stylized oil sketch of a family binding wheat into brilliant arabesques of grain (fig. 11). He hoped it would earn him the post-office commission in Seneca, Kansas, that ultimately went to Jones. In other works (see fig. 7), Vorst intensified the social engagement of his

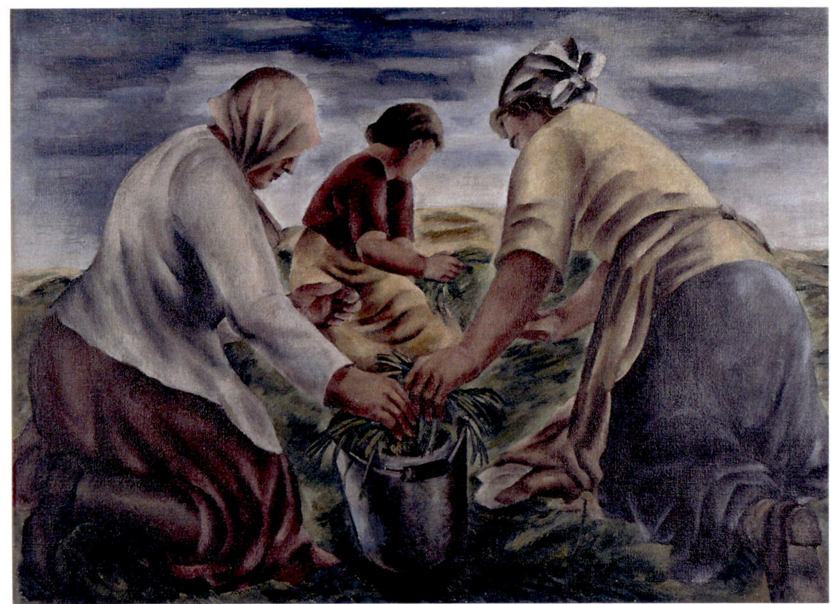

art in another subject reminiscent of Jones at his most outspoken. Ziegler, the Ste. Genevieve native, was commissioned in 1940 to paint a mural in Flandreau, South Dakota, and, not surprisingly, he chose to depict a field of cut, bound, and stacked wheat.[60] Even Benton became interested in the wheat harvest. He completed *Cradling Wheat* (Balken, fig. 4) in 1938 and *Threshing Wheat* (Sheldon Swope Museum of Art, Terre Haute, Indiana) in 1939. He later translated *Cradling Wheat* into a lithograph, which he described as a "scene in the hill country of East Tennessee in 1928. . . . I doubt whether this kind of harvesting can be found anymore—anywheres."[61] The claim of prior ownership of the theme by Benton may have been intended to preempt complaints from Jones, "the Professor of Wheat," as he had been dubbed at the time of his Walker Galleries opening.

In June 1937, the A.C.A. Gallery staged a second "Exhibition of Midwestern Artists," which featured examples by twenty-one painters from Illinois, Indiana, Iowa, Minnesota, and Missouri. Jones showed two gouaches "of dust bowl farmers" that he may have produced the previous summer as he tracked the drought in South Dakota.[62] He was again the only artist in the show most local reviewers knew, even though Adams, McKinnie, Meert,

Fig. 12. Miriam McKinnie (1906–1987). *Women Gathering Greens*, c. 1937. Oil on canvas; 23 × 31 in. (58.4 × 78.7 cm). Collection of John and Susan Horseman.

Schweig, Singer, Turnbull, and Vorst were returning to the A.C.A. for the second consecutive year. All but Singer were involved in some way with the Ste. Genevieve colony. Vorst's *Drifters on the Mississippi*, a large painting of two Missouri mules taking refuge on rooftops from the floods of January 1937, was reproduced in Emily Genauer's glowing notice in the *New York World-Telegram*.[63] McKinnie contributed a painting of "flood refugees hovering over a stove" and the powerful *Women Gathering Greens* (fig. 12), which Howard Devree admired for its "sculptural reality."[64]

The *New Yorker* offered the most triumphant review of the A.C.A. show. It was also the most alert to Jones's leadership within what seemed to be a growing movement of like-minded Midwestern artists. These painters, the writer remarked, sent their work to New York:

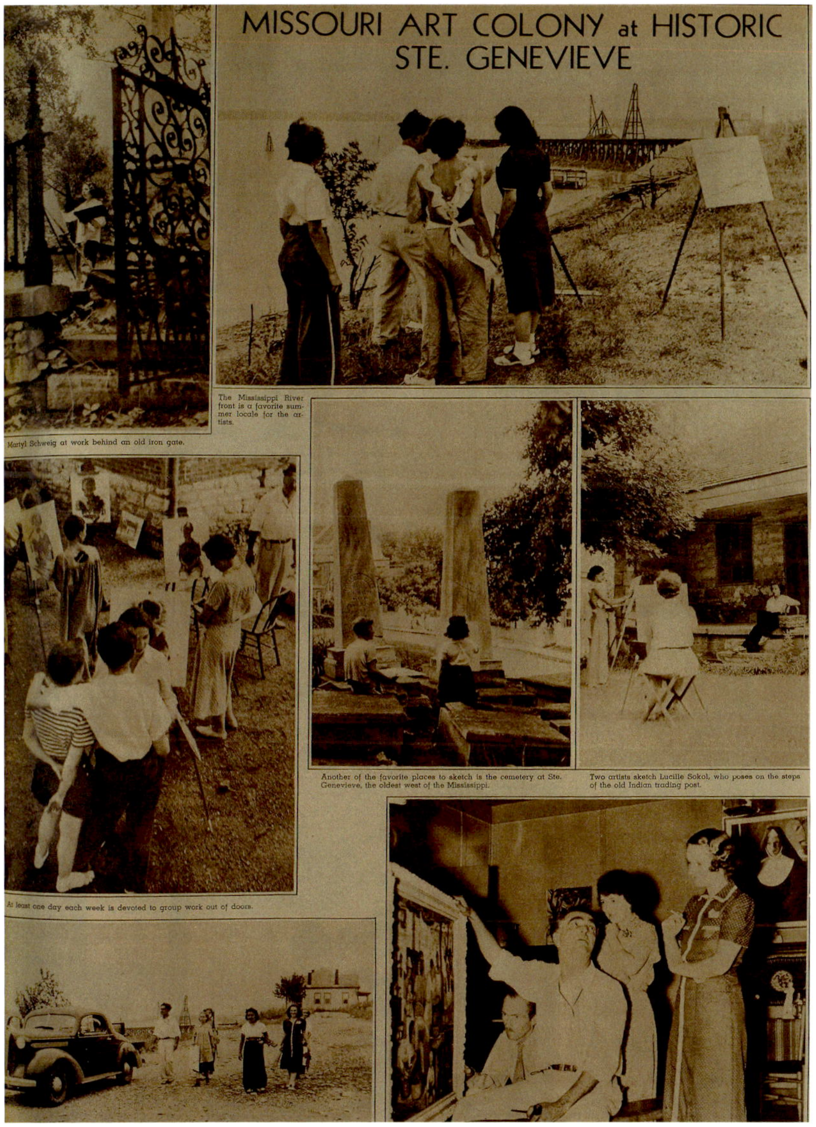

> not so much to be shown as to show us. They demonstrate that Joe Jones . . . is no lonely phenomenon. His candid observation of the world he lives in is no personal idiosyncrasy, but the expression of a growing consciousness of a whole group of mid-western artists, acutely sensitive to their environment and to the social factors which produce it.[65]

Jones was not working in isolation, and it appeared that he was gathering momentum and followers in Missouri, much as Wood was in Iowa and Benton was in Kansas City. It seemed a reasonable expectation, but it would prove not to be the case.

To Schweig's delight, both Jones and Benton agreed to return to Ste. Genevieve for the summer session in 1937. She featured the photograph of Benton surrounded by artists and students on the school's publicity material (fig. 9). While publicity about that summer was upbeat (see fig. 13), enrollment was not appreciably larger than it had been the previous year; only twenty-one students signed up.[66] Jones had received a Guggenheim Fellowship in March to paint scenes of the Dust Bowl. He spent part of the summer in the panhandles of Texas and Oklahoma and further west in Colorado, taking stock of the devastation and ruined farms (see Walker). He made an appearance at the school, but his role in establishing a vision and curriculum for it was much diminished from the previous year. There is no evidence that Benton showed up at all that summer.[67]

The first of the lime workers' strikes began in Ste. Genevieve in the summer of 1937. Martyl recalled that the parks and squares were filled with idle men whose sullen presence drained much of the small town's charm. It was said that Jones himself incited the workers, but given the relatively scant time he spent in Ste. Genevieve, it would seem unlikely that he caused anyone to walk off the job.[68] By early June 1938, workers at the Bluff City, Peerless, and Ste. Genevieve lime companies were all on strike. Schweig by now had fully given up the idea of continuing the school. There would be no summer session in 1938 or ever again. Artists from St. Louis, including Schweig, continued to gather in Ste. Genevieve until 1941, if in

MISSOURI ART COLONY at HISTORIC STE. GENEVIEVE

Martyl Schweig at work behind an old iron gate.

The Mississippi River front is a favorite summer locale for the artists.

At least one day each week is devoted to group work out of doors.

Another of the favorite places to sketch is the cemetery at Ste. Genevieve, the oldest west of the Mississippi.

Two artists sketch Lucille Sokol, who poses on the steps of the old Indian trading post.

Fig. 13. "Missouri Art Colony at Historic Ste. Genevieve," Sunday Photogravure Picture Section, *St. Louis Post-Dispatch*, August 22, 1937. This spread, which highlights activities of the school's 1937 season, includes, at the upper left, a photo of teenage Martyl Schweig painting; and, at the lower right (from left to right), artists Fred E. Conway, E. Oscar Thalinger, Aimee Schweig, and Mrs. Conway.

fewer numbers and with diminishing collective purpose. But once the United States entered World War II at the end of the year, they stopped going altogether.[69]

Jones did not go back to Ste. Genevieve after the summer of 1937. He moved to New York in late August, and remained in the East more or less permanently for the rest of his life. His successful invasion of New York in 1935, his return there in 1936 with Midwest colleagues in tow, and his willingness to renew the effort in 1937 stirred some of the artists associated with the Ste. Genevieve colony to dream beyond the banks of the Mississippi. A few months after the second A.C.A. group show closed, Vorst sent his *Drifters on the Mississippi* to the Art Institute of Chicago's Annual Exhibition of American Paintings and Sculpture. It won the M.V. Kohnstamm Prize of $250, and was reproduced in the exhibition catalogue. By the fall of 1938, Vorst had attracted a one-person exhibition of his own in New York at the Charles Morgan Gallery. But he asked his new friend Benton, whom he had met in Ste. Genevieve in 1936, to write the introductory essay for the catalogue rather than Jones, even though the latter had been the first to open Manhattan's galleries to him.[70] McKinnie took part in both A.C.A shows as well, and in between, she sent *The Cider Press* to the forty-sixth annual exhibition of the National Association of Women Painters and Sculptors in New York. The painting won the Celine Baekeland Prize for the best American landscape, earning McKinnie $150 and the pleasure of seeing her work reproduced in the *New York Times*.[71]

Of all the Missouri painters who spent time with Jones in Ste. Genevieve, the young and impressionable Martyl Schweig (who eventually decided to be known professionally by her first name) was most enamored with him and followed his advice and example most earnestly. She was taken with his good looks and charisma as well as his talent, and saw herself as something of a protégé. In 1936 and 1937, she may have been one. As she was completing her *Wheat Workers* mural in Russell, Kansas, in early June 1940, she told Clarissa Start of the *St. Louis Post-Dispatch* about her development as a young painter and her education. She described the training she had received from her mother and their early trips to Provincetown. "Then I started going down to Ste. Genevieve," she recalled, "and since such artists as Joe Jones and Thomas Hart Benton were there, the constant association with good artists taught me a lot. We had discussions and we painted from seven each morning till five at night." But looking back years later, it was the counsel of Jones, not Benton, that she remembered as best serving her ambitions.[72]

That same summer and again the following year, Martyl studied with Boardman Robinson and Arnold Blanch in Colorado Springs. Jones had probably visited the city during his Dust Bowl travels in 1937. That summer his *Sharecropper Family* (location unknown) was on view at the Colorado Springs Fine Arts Center, which Robinson had founded. Jones would have been drawn to Robinson, a socially engaged artist who had traveled to Russia with John Reed in 1915.[73] He could have described Robinson in colorful detail to Martyl when he returned to Missouri, encouraging her to hone her art under his tutelage. Three years later, she seems to have heeded his advice.

Jones apparently saw the Schweigs from time to time as he passed through St. Louis in 1938 and 1939 on his way to install murals in post offices in Magnolia, Arkansas; Anthony, Kansas; and Charleston, Missouri. In early 1940, he fell into a romance in St. Louis with Grace Adams Mallinckrodt, who had married into a prominent local family. The liaison was discovered in April; her divorce proceedings in June were widely reported in the St. Louis papers; and the scandal surrounding the affair further complicated the artist's relationship with

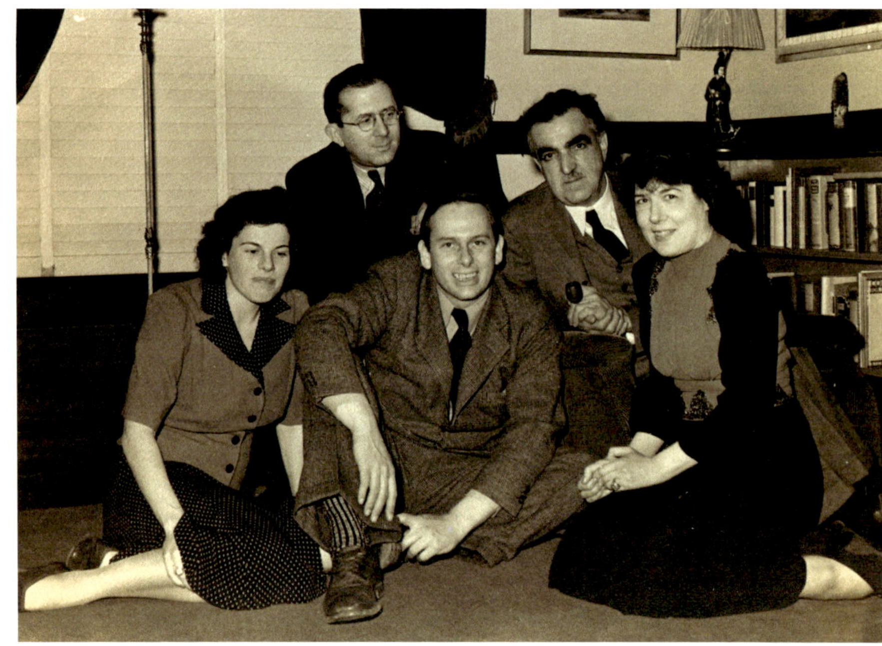

Fig. 14. Grace and Joe Jones with Aimee Schweig (front row, left to right) and Martin Schweig and E. Oscar Thalinger (back row, left to right), c. 1940. Saint Louis Art Museum, archives.

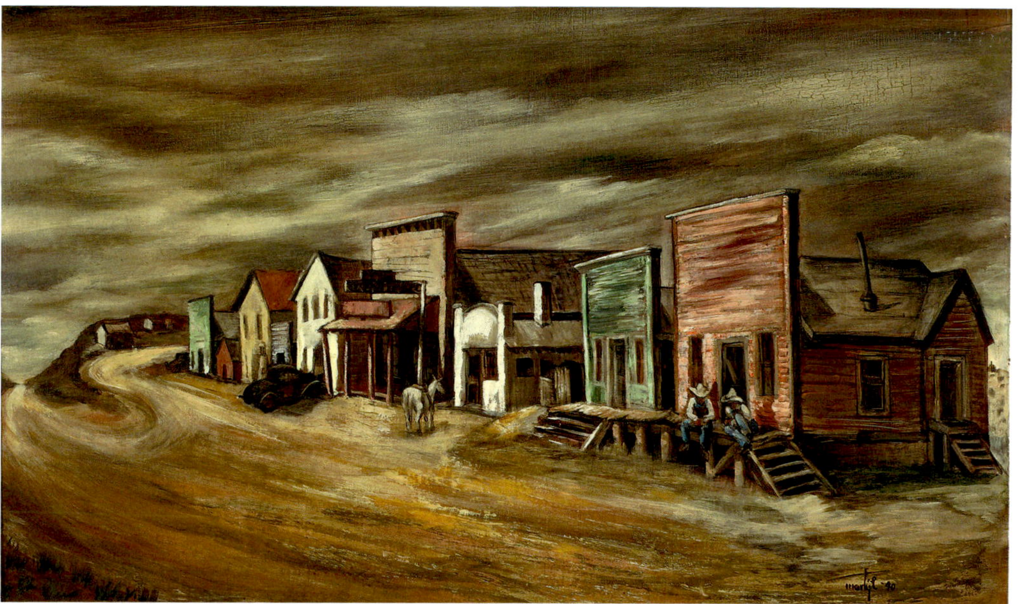

Fig. 15. Martyl (born 1918). *The Town*, 1940. Oil on Masonite; 21½ × 36¼ in. (54.6 × 92.1 cm). Collection of John and Susan Horseman.

his hometown. Martyl remembered that Jones was still welcomed in the Schweig home (see fig. 14), but once he and Grace were married back East in October, his visits to St. Louis became more infrequent. Martyl, however, continued to value and act on the advice she had received from him.[74]

Jones had urged Martyl to enter the annual competitive exhibitions for young artists at the A.C.A. Gallery, and she submitted the painting *Sun Valley* (location unknown) to the June 1941 show.[75] On the strength of this work, Baron gave her a one-person show at the gallery late the following year, which included *The Town* (fig. 15), a painting that still bore the influence of Jones. At twenty-four Martyl was even younger than Jones had been when he received his first New York solo exhibition; it was the highlight of her career thus far. Perhaps because Jones had distanced himself from her world, she asked Robinson and Blanch to pen brief introductory notes for her A.C.A. catalogue. Jones was, however, aware of the exhibition: "Martyl Schweig is one man showing at the A.C.A. Gallery opening Sunday and they tell me she has become a very good painter," he wrote Green.[76] He lived only a short train ride from lower Manhattan, but Martyl later recalled that he did not attend the opening event. He never saw the show, but he did not see his own first exhibition in New York either.[77]

The choices made by Vorst, Martyl, and the other Ste. Genevieve painters to advance their careers underscore the increasingly tenuous nature of Jones's relationships with them. In the wake of his exciting rise to prominence, he was surrounded by artists who hungered for opportunities and success identical to his own. Even as those colleagues began to embrace his signature themes in 1936 and beyond, even as they looked to him for leadership, he did not remain in Ste. Genevieve long enough to establish the kind of following he may have imagined when he accepted Schweig's invitation. Jones could have aided his Missouri colleagues and at the same time elevated his own stature in the American art world simply by exerting his presence in Ste. Genevieve. But youthful enthusiasm and attraction to experiential wonder did not always serve his career ambitions in the same way that they served his art. Jones raced off to the Dust Bowl, and that was that.

NOTES

1. Philip Marchand, *Ghost Empire: How the French Almost Conquered North America* (Praeger, 2007), pp. 323–25.

2. Patrick Huber, "Sainte Genevieve (Missouri) Riot of 1930," *Encyclopedia of American Race Riots*, ed. by Walter C. Rucker and James N. Upton, vol. 2 (Greenwood Press, 2007), pp. 579–83.

3. Marchand (note 1), p. 324.

4. James G. Rogers, Jr., *The Ste. Genevieve Artists' Colony and Summer School of Art, 1932–1941* (Foundation for Restoration of Ste. Genevieve, 1998), pp. 12–14, 37–40.

5. Carl J. Ekberg, *Colonial Ste. Genevieve: An Adventure on the Mississippi Frontier*, 2nd ed. (Patrice Press, 1985), pp. 11–12.

6. Ibid., pp. 436–48.

7. Ibid., pp. 9, 126–76. See also Robert Sidney Douglas, *History of Southeast Missouri: A Narrative Account of Its Historical Progress, Its People and Its Principle Interests*, vol. 1 (Lewis Publishing Co., 1912), p. 251.

8. Rogers (note 4), pp. 96–97.

9. Ibid., pp. 42–44.

10. Ibid., pp. 44–45.

11. Ibid., pp. 46–47.

12. On the colony and school, see James M. Dennis, *Grant Wood: A Study in American Art and Culture* (Viking Press, 1975), pp. 137–38; and *When Tillage Begins: The Stone City Art Colony and School* (Mount Mercy College, May 20, 2008), www.mtmercy.edu/busselibrary/schome/artists.html (accessed Sept. 14, 2009).

13. "Artists' Guild Award Goes to Joseph Jones," *St. Louis Post-Dispatch*, May 28, 1933. Dixie Selden was an Impressionist painter from Cincinnati and a former student of Frank Duveneck; by 1933 she was nearing the end of her career. Neil Ives is most often associated with the art colony in Woodstock, N.Y.

14. Quoted in Rogers (note 4), p. 51.

15. Grant Wood, *Revolt against the City* (Clio Press, 1935). Quoted in *Art in Theory, 1900–2000: An Anthology of Changing Ideas*, ed. by Charles Harrison and Paul Wood (Blackwell, 2003), p. 436. Thomas Craven, *Modern Art: The Men, the Movements, the Meaning* (Simon and Schuster, 1934). On Benton, Craven, and Wood, see Henry Adams, *Thomas Hart Benton: An American Original* (Alfred A. Knopf, 1989), pp. 236–51.

16. See Guy Forshey, "From House Painting to Portrait Painting," *St. Louis Post-Dispatch Magazine*, June 14, 1931, p. 5. Quoted in Karal Ann Marling, "Joe Jones: Regionalist, Communist, Capitalist," *Journal of Decorative and Propaganda Arts* 4 (Spring 1987), p. 48.

17. Quoted in Forshey (note 16).

18. Quoted in "Provincetown Makes Artist a Communist," *St. Louis Post-Dispatch*, Sept. 21, 1933.

19. Joe Jones to Elizabeth Green, n.d. (c. Oct. 1933), Dr. John Green Collection, Missouri History Museum, St. Louis (hereinafter Green Papers).

20. Jones to Green, n.d. (c. Oct. 1933), Green Papers.

21. Jones to Green, n.d. (c. Dec. 1933), Green Papers.

22. See *Exhibition of American Paintings Today*, exh. cat. (Worcester Art Museum, 1933), cat. 61; and *Painting and Sculpture from 16 American Cities: Atlanta, Baltimore, Boston, Buffalo, Chicago, Cleveland, Dallas, Detroit, Los Angeles, Minneapolis, Philadelphia, Pittsburgh, St. Louis, San Francisco, Santa Fe, Seattle*, exh. cat. (Museum of Modern Art, 1933), cat. 81.

23. Edward Alden Jewell, "A Nation-Wide Challenge," *New York Times*, Dec. 17, 1933.

24. "Art School Notes," *Ste. Genevieve Fair Play*, July 21, 1934. See also Rogers (note 4), p. 54.

25. Jones to Green, Aug. 29, 1934, Green Papers.

26. Rogers (note 4), p. 56.

27. Ibid., p. 58. For Roosevelt's greetings, see John T. Woolley and Gerhard Peters, *The American Presidency Project* (University of California at Santa Barbara; 1996 on), http://www.presidency.ucsb.edu/ws/?pid=14920 (accessed Sept. 15, 2009).

28. Gregory W. Franzwa, *The Story of Old Ste. Genevieve* (Patrice Press, 1998), pp. 106–08.

29. Many years later, Schweig's daughter, Martyl, suggested that Rickly was temperamentally difficult and jealous of her mother's talent. See "Martyl Interview Transcript," Andrew J. Walker and Martyl, Feb. 12, 2009, Schaumburg, Ill., n. pag., Saint Louis Art Museum, archives.

30. Rogers (note 4), pp. 58–60. See also Scott Kerr and R. H. Dick, *An American Art Colony: The Art and Artists of Ste. Genevieve, Missouri, 1930–1940* (McCaughen and Burr Press, 2004), p. 63.

31. See Patricia Junker, *John Steuart Curry: Inventing the Middle West* (Hudson Hills Press, 1998), p. 227.

32. Jones to Green, n.d. (c. Jan. 1936), Green Papers.

33. See for example Malcolm Vaughan, untitled clipping, *New York American*, n.d., Missouri History Museum, St. Louis, artist's file; and Lewis Mumford, "Goya, Homer, and Jones," *New Yorker* 11, 52 (Feb. 8, 1936), pp. 58–59; repr. in *Mumford on Modern Art in the 1930s*, ed. and with intro. by Robert Wojtowicz (University of California Press, 2007), pp. 187–90.

34. Jones to Green, n.d. (c. Jan. 1936), Green Papers.

35. Jones to Green, n.d. (late Jan. 1936), Green Papers.

36. "Midwest, ACA, 1936," typescript to which the title was added in an unidentified hand and the date, Jan. 15, 1936, in another hand, Green Papers.

37. *Paintings by Midwestern Artists*, exh. cat. (A.C.A. Gallery, 1936). While no one in New York noticed Rickly's absence from the show, it was a telling exclusion.

38. Howard Devree, "In Local Art Galleries," *New York Times*, May 10, 1936.

39. "Midwest Art Display at Vanguard Gallery," *St. Louis Post-Dispatch*, June 18, 1936.

40. Jones to Green, n.d. (late Jan. 1936), Green Papers.

41. See Jones to Green, n.d. (c. Jan. 1936), Green Papers.

42. On these murals, see Adams (note 15), pp. 252–75.

43. See "Josephine Johnson Arrested in Strike," *New York Times*, June 6, 1936.

44. Jones to Green, June 6, 1936, Green Papers; and Josephine Johnson, "The Arkansas Terror," *New Masses* 20, 12 (June 30, 1936), pp. 12–14.

45. Jones to Aimee Schweig, n.d. (postmarked June 26, 1936), Martyl Langsdorf Papers, Reel 2992, frames 85–87, Archives of American Art, Smithsonian Institution, Washington, D.C.

46. "Missouri's Crop Loss Runs High," *New York Times*, July 14, 1936.

47. *Ste. Genevieve Summer School of Art* (Ste. Genevieve Summer School of Art, July 6–Aug. 15, 1936), n. pag.

48. "Art School Has Fine Enrollment as Term Begins," *Ste. Genevieve Fair Play*, July 11, 1936.

49. Jones to Green, July 23, 1936, Green Papers.

50. Jones to Green, July 22, 1936, Green Papers.

51. Rogers (note 4), p. 67.

52. Adams (note 15), pp. 255–56.

53. Thomas Hart Benton to Schweig, n.d. (postmarked July 20, 1936), Martyl Langsdorf Papers (note 45), frames 82–83.

54. "Gathering Ideas for Murals," *St. Louis Star-Times*, Aug. 14, 1936.

55. Rogers (note 4), p. 68.

56. Marling (note 16), pp. 46–59.

57. For more on Martyl's mural, see Barbara Melosh, *Engendering Culture: Manhood and Womanhood in New Deal Public Art and Theater* (Smithsonian Institution Press, 1991), p. 216; and video interview, Andrew J. Walker and Martyl, Nov. 3, 2009, Schaumburg, Ill., Saint Louis Art Museum, archives.

58. For a reproduction of the Marshall, Illinois, mural, see New Deal Art During the Great Depression (2006 on), www.wpamurals.com/sld023.htm (accessed Mar. 7, 2010).

59. A sketch for Conway's mural is reproduced in Karal Ann Marling, *Wall-to-Wall America: A Cultural History of Post-Office Murals in the Great Depression* (University of Minnesota Press, 1982), p. 124.

60. For Vorst's *Sharecroppers' Revolt*, see Julie Novarese Pierotti, *Regional Dialect: American Scene Paintings from the John and Susan Horseman Collection*, exh. cat. (Dixon Gallery and Gardens, 2008), p. 46. For Ziegler's mural in Flandreau, S.D., see Marling (note 59), pp. 84, 119–20.

61. For Benton's *Threshing Wheat*, see Adams (note 15), p. 311. Benton is quoted in Creekmore Fath, *The Lithographs of Thomas Hart Benton* (University of Texas, 1979), p. 74. For more on antiquated farm equipment in contemporaneous works by Benton and other regionalists, see Balken.

62. See for example Jerome Klein, "Art Comment: Depression Topic in Two Exhibitions," *New York Post*, June 5, 1937.

63. E[mily]. G[enauer]., "Sudden Deluge of New Art Exhibitions Takes the Critics by Surprise," *New York World-Telegram*, June 5, 1937. On the flooding, see "The Mississippi, Flowing over Levees, Drives 40,000 from Homes in the South," *New York Times*, Jan. 25, 1937.

64. Howard Devree, "A Reviewer's Notebook: Comments on Some of the Newly Opened Group Exhibitions and One-Man Shows," *New York Times*, June 6, 1937; quoted in Pierotti (note 60), pp. 42, 88.

65. "Sights and Sounds," *New Masses* 23, 12 (June 15, 1937), p. 29.

66. See Rogers (note 4), p. 64.

67. Ibid., pp. 69–71.

68. Ibid., pp. 70–71.

69. Ibid., pp. 71–73. For an interview with Martyl in which she described working in the Ste. Genevieve area, see Clarissa Start, "Her Paintings Are Man-Size Jobs," *St. Louis Post-Dispatch*, June 5, 1940.

70. Kevin Sharp, "Edward Alden Jewell, Joseph Vorst, and the End of American Scene Painting," in Pierotti (note 60), pp. 13–15.

71. "13 Prizes Awarded in Women's Art Show. Artists Represent Nearly Every State," *New York Times*, Jan. 26, 1937.

72. Start (note 69).

73. Jones wrote to Green, n.d. (c. July 1937), Green Papers, from the West. See *Third Annual Exhibition of Paintings by Artists West of the Mississippi*, exh. cat. (Colorado Springs Fine Arts Center, 1937), no. 40. *Sharecropper's Family* was loaned by the A.C.A. Gallery. On Boardman's Russian trip with Reed, see "Writer Criticizes Marye. John Reed Says Ambassador Failed to Protect Him in Russia," *New York Times*, Apr. 24, 1916.

74. On the affair between Jones and Grace Adams Mallinckrodt, see for example, "Joe Jones Named in Mallinckrodt Divorce Trial," *St. Louis Post-Dispatch*, June 14, 1940; and Martyl interviews (notes 29, 57). Martyl continued to credit Jones with her success after her direct contact with him had ended. Because she won the coveted Frank G. Logan Medal at the annual Artists of Chicago and Vicinity show at the Art Institute of Chicago in 1950, she was given a brief biography in the unpaginated exhibition catalogue, which notes: "She studied in the Sainte Genevieve Summer School of Art under Aimee Schweig (her mother) and Joe Jones."

75. For a reference to *Sun Valley*, see Howard Devree, "A Reviewer's Notebook," *New York Times*, June 22, 1941.

76. Jones to Green, Dec. 5, 1942, Green Papers.

77. *Martyl*, exh. cat. (A.C.A. Gallery Publication, Dec. 6–19, 1942). See also Martyl interview (note 57).

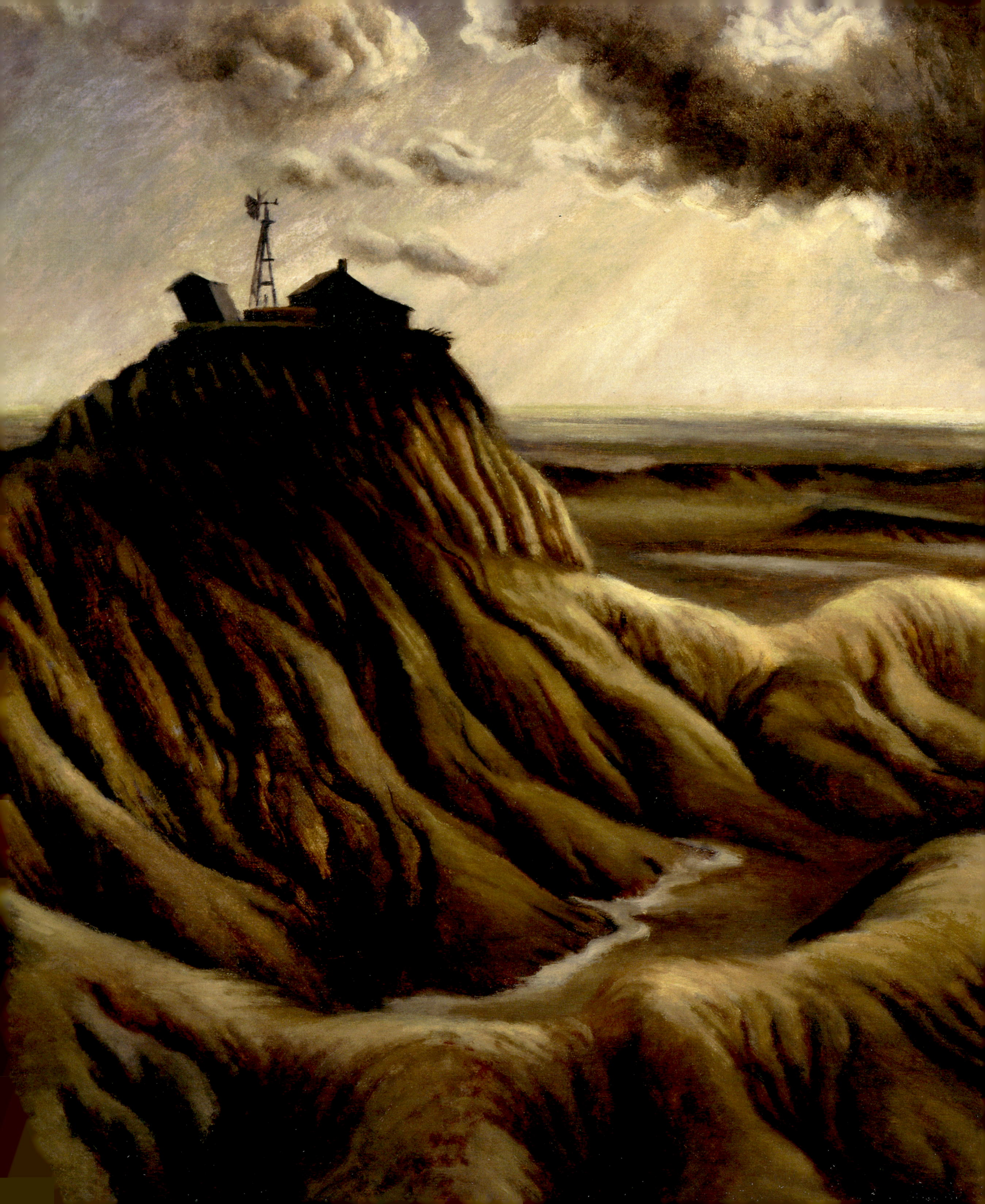

Joe Jones's New York Interactions

Debra Bricker Balken

When Joe Jones made a commitment in 1937 to live in New York, he did not give up on his Midwest identity. While he had earlier bemoaned to Elizabeth Green, his primary patron and friend, that St. Louis had never fully acknowledged him as an artist, stating, "I sincerely believe that I am as far as I can go in St. Louis [as] far as recognition is concerned and still the people stand off,"[1] his relationship to the Heartland would remain complex, an integral ingredient of his work into the early 1940s. Whatever professional limitations he experienced in St. Louis, as he immersed himself in Depression-era New York, his aesthetic ties to Missouri would become particularly urgent, driven by his desire to incorporate Midwestern responses to unemployment and racial and social injustice, as well as the state of agrarian labor, into a national aesthetic discussion. Jones never defined himself as a regionalist and would always insist upon some modicum of formal invention in his work, having had his start as a modernist painter.[2] And while his involvement in the Communist Party (he had declared his allegiance to the party after an epiphany in Provincetown, Massachusetts, in 1933; see Wolfe) ironically coincided with his desire for increased visibility and a bigger platform for his work, he would never entirely succumb to its realist strictures, deeming that type of visual strategy to be one-sided and arid. In contrast to the party line, he always assumed that the declaration of one's originality, with all of its connotations of formal risk, was not the offshoot or territory of capitalism. As his interactions in New York would reveal, Jones would initially crusade for the Midwest and its subjects with zeal. He would argue for making them part of the critical discourses waged at various public forums such as the Artists' Union and the First American Artists' Congress. In Manhattan he would become acutely aware that any representation of the prairie had to be tied to the radical components of modernism to be efficacious and current. Yet politics would be an equal component of his studio practice, vying with his interest in recasting entrenched pictorial conventions and subjects.

° ° °

Jones made two initial trips to New York, in 1935 and 1936, to prospect for a gallery to represent him, as well as to scout the cultural landscape. He arrived in the city just after Thomas Hart Benton had relocated to his native Missouri to teach at the Kansas City Art Institute. In this safe haven, Benton hoped to be spared the "degenerate" modernism that he thought had infiltrated contemporary European and, especially, American art, which in his opinion had given up on its rich legacy of history painting.[3] Benton had long been rabid on the topic of avant-garde developments, disaffected with what he considered the modernists' fussing with form and alliance with abstraction. Once he made it onto the cover of *Time*, in December 1934 (the magazine described him as the "most virile of U.S. painters of the U.S. Scene"[4]), he wagered that his presence was now required in the Midwest to consolidate its authority as a bona fide wellspring for art. With Regionalism—named for its revival of vernacular narratives—having coalesced into a movement in the mid-1930s, Benton knew that he could lobby most effectively for the cause of the Heartland and its imagery in situ. His new notoriety and continued access to New York through publications such as *Commonwealth*, *Saturday Review of Literature*, and *Scribner's*, in which he would now proselytize for the lost virtues of a Renaissance tradition and its emphasis on the figure, enabled a recasting of Midwestern themes that related both to the rectitude of and nostalgia for rural life. Moreover, Benton's return home was helped by a powerful advocate, Thomas Craven, a critic who hailed from Kansas and had multiple writing

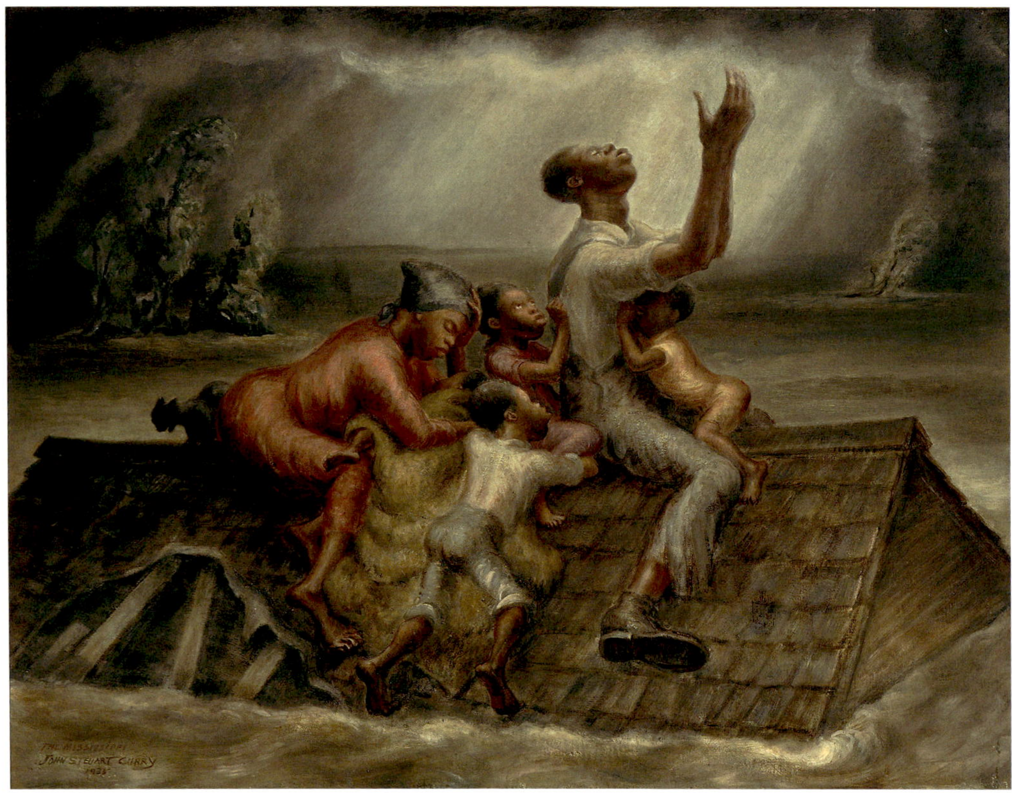

Fig. 1. John Steuart Curry (1897–1946). *The Mississippi*, 1935. Tempera on canvas, mounted on panel; 36 × 48 in. (91.4 × 121.9 cm). Saint Louis Art Museum, Museum Purchase.

posts in New York, including ones at *Scribner's* and the *Nation*. He touted Benton as a "great artist . . . [whose] art is too specifically real, too deeply impregnated with . . . the *collective American spirit*, to touch the purists, methodists, and doctrinaire—those whose idealism kneels to international panaceas and European formula."[5]

Jones's trajectory reversed that of Benton. He left home believing that the infrastructure of a marketplace and informed critical media or press was too minuscule in the Midwest to advance serious discussion of the region's authenticity and indigenous traits. Jones was never an artist whom Craven could integrate into his regionalist canon; his urban scenes relating to labor unrest, exploitation, and protest countered Benton's bucolic renditions of farm life. In short, Jones's radical politics and progressive ethos were anathema to the pert idealizations of agricultural bounty that became part of Benton's imagery once he returned to Missouri. There was nothing about Jones's work that tied him to the representations of Regionalism by Benton or his confreres John Steuart Curry (see fig. 1) and Grant Wood. Their adumbrations of productivity emanated from nostalgia for a premodern era of agricultural practice: the harvesting devices and equipment in their paintings were the property of a pre-industrialized culture. During the height of the worst economic calamity to beset the twentieth century, Jones had little truck for such wistful longing. In a work such as *Men and Wheat* (1939; cat. 71), a sketch for the Treasury Department's "Forty-eight State Mural Competition," he acknowledged the mechanization of agriculture. He sensed that New York was preoccupied with realpolitik, demanding art with hard-hitting subjects revealed through new strategies.

Jones's first solo show in New York, at the American Contemporary Art (A.C.A.) Gallery in 1935, happened almost instantaneously, in contrast to Benton's experience. Benton waited for commercial representation in the city for more than a decade, spurned first by Alfred Stieglitz, the doyen of American dealers and an arch-modernist who could never reconcile Benton's ambivalence toward abstraction. (Benton responded to this rejection by writing to Stieglitz, "I am of the opinion that making pretty little lines and spots over canvas or paper is a waste of time and that it is either stupid or degenerate."[6] (The word degenerate became his catchall for any overbearing trace of subjectivity in art, despite its presence in his own painting; he had become too blinded by the new ideology of Regionalism to allow any balance between form and content.)

Shortly after he arrived in Manhattan in 1935, Jones conveyed to Green, with whom he corresponded regularly, often daily, that he was not only fully immersed in work in his makeshift studio but also taken by what he was seeing. His day-to-day routine during those winter months alternated between visiting with artists, studying collections at the city's multiple art museums, attending special exhibitions of work by his contemporaries, and painting. Green's friend Robert Hanna spent time with Jones in New York and reported back to her that Jones was surprised and impressed by a visit to the Biennial Exhibition of Water Colors, Pastels, and Drawings by American and Foreign Artists at the Brooklyn Museum: "He wanted to see everything else [but was, he said], 'not interested in water colors.' When we got to them dead tired he realized that he had never before seen what could be done with water color. 'Got a great kick!' He is receptive and wide awake."[7]

Jones's museum experiences inspired in him an emboldened self-confidence as to the superiority of his work. For, after he made the rounds of the collections at the Metropolitan Museum of Art and the contemporary holdings of the Museum of Modern Art (MoMA) and the Whitney Museum of American Art, he was left with the certainty that his own painting was unique and stood out. As he explained to Green, "The revolutionary element in my work, so closely tied up with the rest of my work, is the only thing of its kind so far, and would be (as a show) a very important development in American art today."[8] While Jones's inaugural stint in New York (he had stopped there briefly with his first wife and Green en route to Provincetown in 1933) was complicated by the emotional fallout from his recent divorce (which explains part of his need to escape from St. Louis), the progress that he soon made in his temporary studio would result in an exhibition at the A.C.A. Gallery that generated widespread praise.[9]

Founded in 1932 by the artists Stuart Davis, Adolf Dehn, and Yasuo Kuniyoshi, along with Herman Baron (see "Herman Baron," p. 103), the A.C.A. Gallery had a decidedly socialist agenda formulated to accommodate the radical politics of artists nationally. Baron, the only non-artist in this collaborative venture, soon became the ascendant partner. As the gallery's director, he made the calculated decision to downplay abstraction in his programming in favor of literal explications of class inequity. Baron located progress in representations that disclosed palpable evidence of a social conscience. Such subjects became the stock of artists such as Philip Evergood (see fig. 2 and Wolfe, fig. 14), William Gropper (see Walker, figs. 10, 19), Reginald Marsh, and the Soyer brothers (see Wolfe, fig. 13), whose art was concerned either with corporate corruption or its human toll. As a result, Davis, an ardent leftist who did not believe that art should be polemical, would eventually defect to Edith Halpert's Downtown Gallery, where formal ingenuity was still upheld as an aesthetic standard. Even though the A.C.A. Gallery seemed like a tight fit for Jones, the prospect of showing there was something of an initial letdown for him.

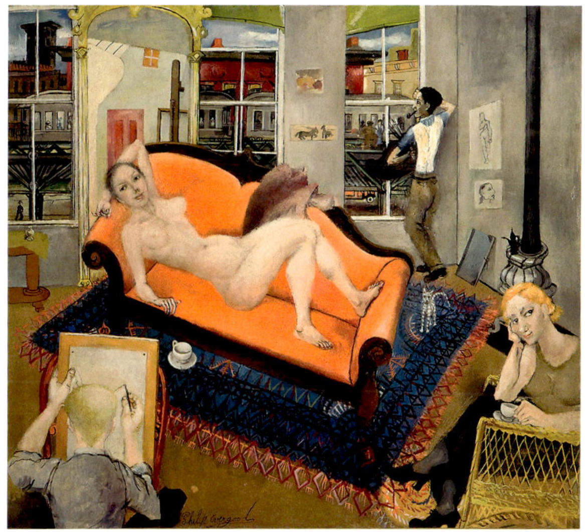

Fig. 2. Philip Evergood (1901–1973). *Nude by the El*, 1933. Oil on canvas; 37⅜ × 42⅞ in. (94.9 × 108.9 cm). Hirshhorn Museum and Sculpture Garden, Smithsonian Institution, Gift of the Joseph H. Hirshhorn Foundation, 1966.

He had hoped for a more established setting for his new realist take on the Midwest. In fact, he naively wrote to Green soon after he assessed New York's exhibition scene, "I will try to get my show in the Modern Museum, also I will try the Whitney then the galleries."[10]

Jones had exhibited *Road to the Beach* (1933; cat. 30) at MoMA in late 1933 in a sprawling overview, "Painting and Sculpture from 16 American Cities," shortly before he made his recce to Manhattan.[11] This entry was decidedly neutral in spirit, a scene of fractured foliage elements that reveal a lingering debt to the Cubist movement. Clearly, though, Jones had misjudged MoMA as a possibility for the new direction of his work, what with the museum's Eurocentric focus and construction of a formalist continuum that spurned narrative subjects, especially those with a political emphasis. The context was obviously wrong for his more gritty handling of figuration. As the Depression stretched into the late 1930s, MoMA occasionally eased up on its cleansed reading of contemporary art in some of the exhibitions it organized. It included Jones's *Without Mother* (fig. 3), in a broad survey, "Paintings for Paris." A somewhat modified version of the show, "Trois siècles d'art aux États-Unis," circulated to the Jeu de Paume, Paris, in 1938. It included Jones's *We Want More Pay* (1936; location unknown).

MoMA may not have been in the offing for Jones, but the Whitney, with its broad allegiance to the diverse strains of American modernism, did make a commitment to his art through the mid-1940s. After *Wheat* (see Walker, fig. 2) was highlighted in its second annual exhibition of contemporary art in 1934, his work became a staple in these surveys.[12] Jones had an advocate at the Whitney in Lloyd Goodrich, a young writer and curator, who saw that he was consistently integrated into and made a fixture of these exhibitions. (Goodrich, a pioneering supporter of American art who wrote significant studies on artists such as Eakins, Homer, Hopper, O'Keeffe, and Ryder, went on to serve as the Whitney's director from 1958 to 1968.) Goodrich advised Jones on options for commercial representation by spelling out the predilections of the few New York galleries that would take on progressive American artists, such were the constant setbacks and limitations for the art of homegrown radicals. Two of Goodrich's recommendations were the Downtown and Rehn galleries. Goodrich, no doubt, had picked up on the equal importance that Jones had assigned to form and content in his painting, as well as his particular resistance, as Jones had called it, to the "political satire or . . . sickles and hammers" that drove most work exhibited at the New York branch of the John Reed Club.[13] His muting of an ideological agenda, along with his desire to retain a modicum of invention in his painting, must have convinced Goodrich that Edith Halpert, the Downtown Gallery's director, would be predisposed to his art. After all, she had shown the work of Ben Shahn, a Communist sympathizer, who had similarly rejected party sloganeering in acerbic political statements in which injustice is melded with terse design. In addition, Halpert carried the paintings of Max Weber, an artist whose style had undergone profound transformation by reneging on its Cubist origins. By the mid-1930s, Weber would caution that "art for its own sake is doomed to suffocation and extinction" and thereby required the balance of a recognizable subject, preferably one given to the uneasy tension between factory owners and disenfranchised workers.[14] While Jones had initially dismissed Downtown's and Rehn's programming as "on an artistic downgrade" and Downtown's

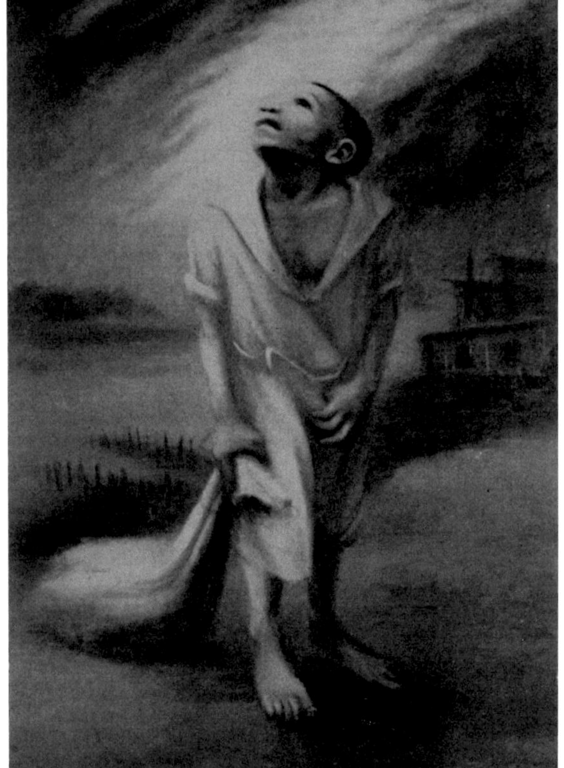

Fig. 3. Joe Jones. *Without Mother*, c. 1937. Location unknown. Reproduced in *Paintings by Joe Jones*, exh. cat. (A.C.A. Gallery, 1937), n. pag.

stable of artists as "decadent," he apparently approached them.[15] He did hold out some hope for Halpert, once he was privy to Goodrich's insider take. But Halpert never visited Jones's studio, and Goodrich's proposed alliance between Jones and her failed to materialize.

The John Reed Club, a Communist Party–affiliated organization founded in 1929 to encourage leftist sentiments in America's artistic and literary worlds, would have embraced Jones as one of its brethren, but it was never a recourse for him. He considered its interests too partisan and restrictive, even though he had briefly served as the art editor of the *Anvil*, an organ of the John Reed Club, along with his friend the proletariat writer Jack Conroy.[16]

Hence, the A.C.A. Gallery emerged as a fallback for Jones, who entered into the relationship uncertainly, not convinced that Baron could successfully market his work. As the artist wrote to Green, "The manager [Baron] is terrible [*sic*] sympathetic and wants to push my work but he does not have the selling contacts Halpert and Rehn does [*sic*]."[17] Baron, however, would not disappoint him. Jones's first New York exhibition was a considerable success. As Archibald MacLeish, a lapsed modernist who came to construe the avant-garde movement as narcissistic and out of step with the Depression, would write in *Fortune* in late 1935, Jones "pretty much stole the season . . . having more scope, vitality, more fecundity, and more promise as well as mastery than most artists a decade senior."[18]

Lewis Mumford of the *New Yorker* named Jones the "season's most promising young artist." Mumford's acclamation emanated from what he discerned as Jones's "earnestness, a fierceness, [and a] powerful reaction to the sombreness of life among the starving and the shunted and the oppressed." Nonetheless, he hedged his bets on Jones's future in this otherwise effusive piece by positing reservations on the finite range of Jones's themes. Mumford deemed that Jones ran the same aesthetic risk as his regionalist counterparts, such as Benton, Curry, and Wood, whose frequently escapist images contained dogmatic underpinnings. Mumford concluded that Jones "works with as narrow a set of political symbols as the

RECENT PAINTINGS JOE JONES

NOV. 12 TO DEC. 2

1939

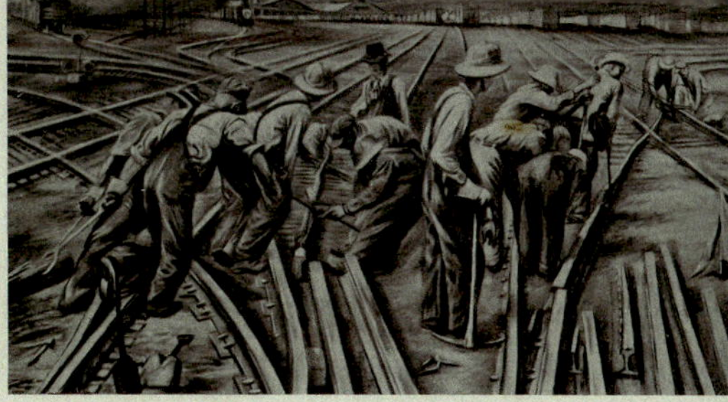

A. C. A. GALLERY

52 WEST 8 STREET • NEW YORK CITY

HERMAN BARON (1892–1961)

One of Joe Jones's greatest champions in New York was Herman Baron, director of American Contemporary Art (A.C.A) Gallery and tireless advocate for artists on the left. Jones and Baron first met in the spring of 1935, during the artist's first extended trip to America's art capital. An enthusiastic supporter of the radical content in the St. Louisan's work, Baron quickly arranged Jones's first solo exhibition on the East Coast. The show received rave reviews. Jones would enjoy four more one-person exhibitions and participate in numerous group exhibitions at the gallery before moving permanently to the Associated American Artists (AAA) Galleries, New York, in 1942.

Baron, a Lithuanian immigrant who had served in World War I, developed an interest in leftist politics in the early 1920s while studying at New York University. In 1932 he and his wife, Ella Block, joined several artists—Stuart Davis, Adolf Dehn, and Yasuo Kuniyoshi—in establishing the A.C.A. Gallery as a space devoted to the work of struggling artists.

Jones's relationship with Baron developed at a critical time for the artist, only weeks after his Unemployed Art Class in St. Louis's Old Courthouse had been shut down. Through Baron, he met some of the most important leftist artists in New York. Jones's participation in the First American Artists' Congress, in February 1936, was also likely the result of his ties to the gallery, since it served as the main meeting space for the Congress' organizers. After Jones left the A.C.A. Gallery and turned away from political themes, his friendship with Baron endured. The dealer continued to name Jones as one of the most important artists he had ever represented.

Bryna R. Campbell

Recent Paintings by Joe Jones, exh. cat. (A.C.A. Gallery, 1939). The cover reproduces Jones's *Working on the Railroad* (1939; cat. 73). Dr. John Green Collection, Missouri History Museum, St. Louis. Courtesy A.C.A. Galleries, New York.

painters of Americana."[19] The critic's inference that Jones took up the cause of labor exploitation with little or no critical distance, especially in works such as *Roustabouts* and *We Demand* (both 1934; cats. 32–33), was a cautionary reminder that his imagery could easily devolve into enactment of Marxist doctrine, and thereby perpetuate needless pictorial tedium.

Mumford was not alone in his qualified approbation of Jones's first exhibition at the A.C.A. Gallery. Some writers either tempered their analysis with reserve or ventured that Jones's unmitigated renditions of labor exploitation operated as propaganda. For example, an anonymous journalist in *Time* magazine capitalized on Jones's early training as a housepainter in St. Louis, a background that he noted was shared with Adolf Hitler (apparently connecting their early amateur-artist status and working-class origins). The *Time* writer acknowledged Jones's "unmistakable talent and power," traits that, he explained, derived from the artist's independence from supporters such as the Communist Party. Yet the implication remained that a stylistic connection obtained between Jones's political pieces and the conformist agitprop produced by artists who served totalitarian governments. The rhetorical comparisons between Jones and the man who "thought up Naziism" were intentionally charged and polemical.[20] Whatever these unsettling associations, *Time* would cover Jones's work through the mid-1940s with sustained interest and enthusiasm. Jones might have been a "onetime St. Louis housepainter,"[21] as he was dubbed in a later issue, but his background also pressed *Time*'s case for the relevance and currency of his material. His transformation into an artist was a handy metaphor for the social role now expected of creative workers and their subjects by the mass media. (This expectation would shift after World War II. In 1949, when Jackson Pollock was featured in *Life* magazine, his non-figurative compositions were mined for traces of his interior life, his subjectivity emerging as a trope for mid-century American ingenuity.)

Most of the reviews that grew out of Jones's first exhibition at the A.C.A. Gallery centered on the issue of his artistic identity and pondered whether he should be tagged either as a regionalist or proletarian painter.[22] Mumford maintained that Jones combined aspects of both traits in his work, and that he forged a hybrid expression which surmounted the specificity of both of these labels.[23] By contrast, Clarence Weinstock, an editor of *Art Front* (the publication of the Artists' Union, a non-sectarian organization formed in 1933 to lobby for federal relief programs for artists and later, in the wake of the Works Progress Administration, reconstituted to arbitrate labor issues for its members), argued that Jones's compositions were the antipode of the sylvan landscapes that Benton and others continued to produce into the mid-1930s, even after vast areas of the Great Plains were afflicted by drought. Rather, Weinstock lobbied for the realism that pervaded Jones's work, reading it as reinforcement of his social commitment. He noted that, "instead of conceiving of society as a far away province of art, he sees himself subject to society, bonded by enmities and alliances, member of a class, a worker." But there was overlap and unity in both writers' positions. Like Mumford, Weinstock knew that Jones's unembellished representations of protest, such as *We Demand*, and of the victimization of workers, such as *Roustabouts*, were not mere illustrations and that his "technique" or style was highly considered, albeit a secondary feature aiding the conveyance of meaning.[24]

There would be no critical consensus as to an appropriate name or designation for Jones's work. The issue was further compounded by Jones's exhibition of a series of wheat-field paintings at the Walker Galleries, New York, in January 1936. Maynard Walker, the gallery's proprietor, had originally used the term "Regionalism" in 1933 to describe, as he stated, "an art which really springs from the American soil and seeks to interpret American life. . . . Much of the most vital modern art in America is coming out of our long backward Middle West."[25] Walker ascribed a certain modernity to the paintings of Benton, Curry, and Wood (whom he would consciously construct into a triumvirate), in contrast to the advocacy of Craven, who emphasized these artists' resuscitation of Renaissance formats, resulting in a style in which verisimilitude had become a paragon. However immoderate and narrow Walker's declarations about the state of European modernism (he deemed Cubism to be "just rubbish"[26]), his boosterism of an art that emanated from the Heartland appropriated aspects of the discourses that had been used to interpret the work of American artists associated with the circle of Stieglitz, such as Dove, Marin, and O'Keeffe.[27] For example, the word virility became part of Walker's language to denote the progressive content of Regionalism, inferring that it took a certain aesthetic courage, if not masculine resourcefulness, to introduce a cornfield or Missouri farmer into the visual lexicon.

Jones's Walker Galleries exhibition demarcated yet another dramatic aesthetic shift or about-face, in that scenes of social injustice now co-existed alongside pictures of agricultural bounty. The latter category, as *Time* noted, constituted "the main part of his show," and overshadowed the more overt political zeal that informed a work such as *Miners* (1935; cat. 38), also on view. *Threshing No. 1* (1935; cat. 34), for instance, with its lush expanse of tall wheat, captures the moment of harvest, unwittingly extending the mythology of nature's endless productivity. Walker clearly felt that he had found another regionalist artist to integrate into his pantheon.

However, Jones would purposefully resist such typecasting. Salient differences would remain between Benton and Jones, even though both depicted whatever pockets of verdancy were left in the Midwest. Unlike the regionalists, Jones was more interested in the archetype of the laborer: the farmer in *Threshing No. 1* becomes a rural analogue for a Promethean figure. While the mythic reference is not highly original, the laborer here also emerges as a surrogate for the artist. The worker in the central foreground, his profile obscured by the rim of his broad hat, powerfully wields his pitchfork, which bears a robust profusion of wheat like a loaded paintbrush articulating an abstract composition. Benton depicted his farmhands in a similar anonymous fashion in works such as *Cradling Wheat* (fig. 4), where their faces remain masked and unarticulated. Yet Benton's visual agenda was clearly unrelated to Jones's Marxist-inspired vision, in which all workers are equal and part of a collective. There is a distinct sense of community in Benton's harvest portrayals. His workers operate as tropes for the shared values of American culture and experience, their antiquated machinery underscoring a sentimental yearning for a bygone era. And while Benton had once been predisposed toward Marxism, questioning capitalist monopolies and their control of work forces in the late 1910s, his socialist leanings had receded by the time he assumed the mantle of the "most virile [painter] . . . of the U.S. scene" in late 1934. Yet his thinking was not solely constricted by nationalism, at least as it pertained to the empowerment of a

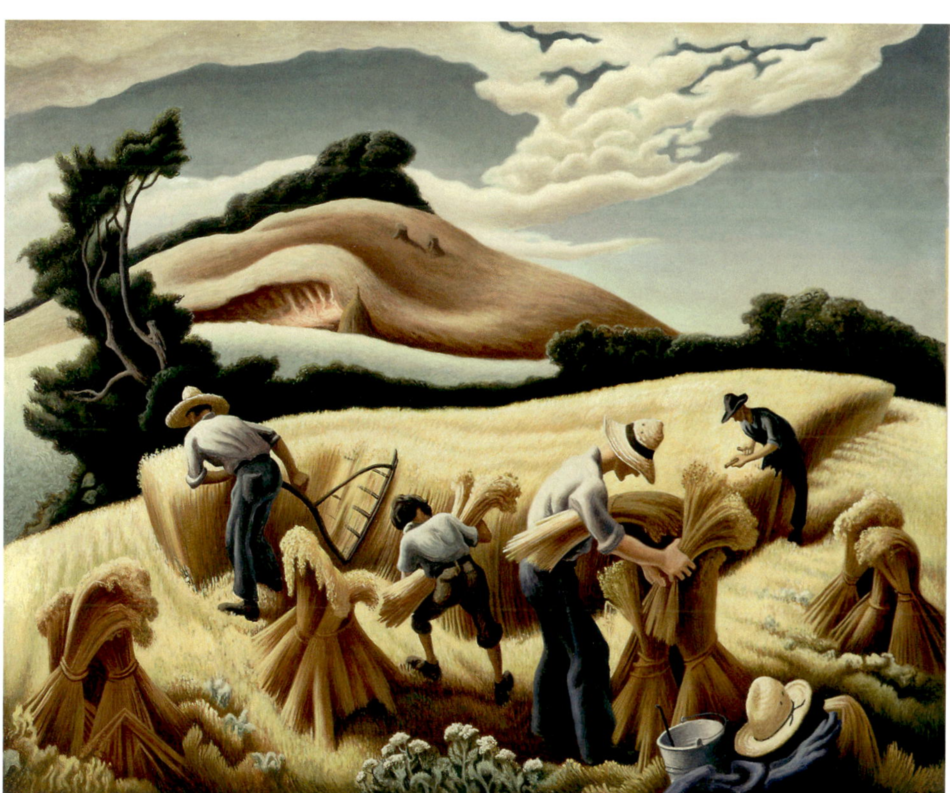

Fig. 4. Thomas Hart Benton (1889–1975). *Cradling Wheat*, 1938. Tempera and oil on board; 31¼ × 39¼ in. (79.4 × 99.7 cm). Saint Louis Art Museum, Museum Purchase.

disenfranchised working class. In fact, he avowed at the end of his life, "I could see no conflict between American democratic ideals and the ideals of Soviet Russia. . . . I was convinced that the American dream had been continually discounted by capitalist organizations which had grown beyond the people's control."[28]

The ideological incongruities in Benton's character would color critical approaches to Jones, compounding the issue of his artistic identity. But the young artist's show at the Walker Galleries gave him the exposure and sales he desired. Jones recounted the opening to Green: "The party was swell and among the lesser guys—there was Edward G. Robinson and Kate Hepburn, movie people. Eugene Speicher, Arnold Blanch, Reginald Marsh, Grant Wood, John Steuart Curry, everybody liked it. . . . I forgot Thomas Craven was also there. *I don't like him between us.*"[29] Craven remained silent on his assessment of Jones, publishing nothing about the artist and his exhibitions. As previously noted, the conservative critic was hard-pressed to weave Jones into his analysis of Regionalism, there being no room for images of protest in his reactionary repackaging of American art. Whatever his reliance upon mimetic devices to structure his realistic compositions, Jones knew that he could never uphold Craven's requirement to depict "the collective American spirit,"[30] that its contemporary extensions involved an outmoded capitulation to tradition. (The only avant-garde artists whom Craven thought capable of elaborating upon the "Great American thing," as the adage went, were John Marin and Georgia O'Keeffe.[31]) Hence, Jones's need to distance himself from the critic. Only in 1939, as Regionalism began to wane, could Craven finally position Jones in his narrative of the "native movement" and its far-reaching presence in contemporary American art. He included Jones's lithograph *Missouri Wheat Farmers* (1938; cat. 69) in an ambitious published compendium of one hundred of the nation's most notable contemporary prints. Not surprisingly, artists like Benton and Curry received multiple entries in the book. The strength of the critic's authority, however, required him to claim the broadest sampling of artistic tendency at the time. Jones's one entry fell into this category. *Missouri Wheat Farmers*, done after an oil painting (1938; cat. 70) featured in a 1939 exhibition at the Associated American Artists (AAA) Galleries, depicts two farmers gathering grain into bags for market. Craven dismissed Jones's Communist leanings as the naïveté of youth and celebrated his talents as a draftsman. Jones's print, with its simplified composition and "brilliant use of light," eschewed the propagandist tendencies of "proletarian art." Quite simply, and in spite of his politics, Craven had to admit that Jones's realism had transformed "two men at rather dull work [into] a beautiful picture to see."[32]

The responses to the second unveiling of Jones's painting in Manhattan were far more mixed than those generated from his first. Some critics, such as E. M. Benson, who wrote for the *Magazine of Art*, were thrown off by his now dual engagement with urgent social themes and Missouri's expansive landscape. Benson did not believe that the latter subject had yielded anything new or innovative in the artist's work. In fact, he thought that Jones's treatment of the wheat field was overly formulaic and represented a setback:

> I was convinced, and still am, that Jones has real talent; that he captures something in the American scene which neither Benton nor Curry nor Grant Wood nor any of what Craven's gold-seal boys have given us—a distinctive, original, unformalized way of seeing and painting our landscape and people. His progress during the past year . . . is disappointing. He may have worked as a farmhand in wheat fields, but he paints them far less convincingly than van Gogh. . . . There is an obvious sameness about the way he composes his wheat field pictures that becomes a trifle tiresome.

Yet Benson praised Jones's images of workers in what he otherwise wrote off as prosaic or "tiresome" landscapes. He still thought of Jones above all as a "proletarian" painter and the cause of the labor movement as his primary pictorial ambition.[33]

Mumford took a tack opposite to Benson's, while similarly drawing upon van Gogh as a comparison. The *New Yorker* critic asserted that Jones "recalls van Gogh at the height of his powers. . . . He has been called a proletarian painter. Perhaps he is. But he is closer to Whitman than to Marx."[34] Mumford found poetry, then, in these scenes of harvest rather than socialist pieties. His view would be corroborated by the Metropolitan Museum of Art, which acquired *Threshing No. 1* after it was showcased at the Walker Galleries.[35] Its entry into a collection in which art history was scripted as an apolitical endeavor, knit together through the axiom of stylistic breakthrough, resulted in a new critical standard for Jones's work. Most writers and collectors would now require greater evenness and conformity from him. But the recalcitrant Jones was not ready to please or appease them.

Thus the question of where to place Jones within the myriad aesthetic movements of the 1930s lingered on. Once he won a fellowship from the Guggenheim Foundation, enabling him to travel to the Dust Bowl in 1937, his painting would dwell on bleak ecological and social realities, such as those that he had already captured in *Our American Farms* (1936; cat. 42), where a windswept terrain is sculpted into an abstract tower of Babel; or on the pathos of a farmer forced to vacate his desolate fields and homestead, as in *Departure* (1938; cat. 61). Jones brought the same unstinting candor to these scenes as he had to *Roustabouts* and *We Demand*, albeit still ensuring that his imagination had the upper hand. He diluted his realism with pronounced exaggerations: the land formation in *Our American Farms*, in particular, emerges as an undulating, heaving mound.

Edward Alden Jewell, a critic for the *New York Times*, would find little formal ingenuity in the work Jones made as a Guggenheim Fellow, which was exhibited in 1937 at the A.C.A. Gallery. He was not taken by the reworking of a once-lush wheat field into an abject landscape. He wrote about Jones's paintings of the parched Great Plains, "Gone is the virtuoso of the dazzle of those earlier *Wheatfields*, one item in which series has entered the Metropolitan. Joe Jones re-emerges an exponent, more strictly of 'proletarian themes.'"[36] Clearly, Jewell's aesthetic comfort level had been challenged by these images of poverty and agricultural ruin. Like the custodians of the Metropolitan, he required evidence of compositional transcendence or uplift.[37] The Whitney Museum's purchase, in 1936, of *Our American Farms* would compound the sense of disparity that ran through Jones's work, whatever its topicality.

No matter that Jones wanted, as he stated in an interview with the *St. Louis Post-Dispatch* in 1937, to create "a pictorial record of just what is happening to the Middle-West, not so much in a record of the floods, droughts, erosion, and those things, but what they are doing to the people, the migration of the farmers and the uncertainty and restlessness that have resulted."[38] The thematic vacillation that characterized his painting proved too confusing for most interpreters, who sought from him more constancy or a more methodical, monolithic unfolding of themes and forms. Consequently, Jones would never achieve the ballast in New York that he craved.

Jones moved to Manhattan in the late summer of 1937 (he retained a studio and residence in St. Louis through 1939). He wrote to Green:

> I finally saw my picture in the MET—and at the Whitney's and went away very much encouraged with my things next to the country's best—to have such a reaction is going to be important to me in connection to moving here. I did feel St. Louis would be a better place to form my work. One thing that impressed me very much was the solidity my two things have

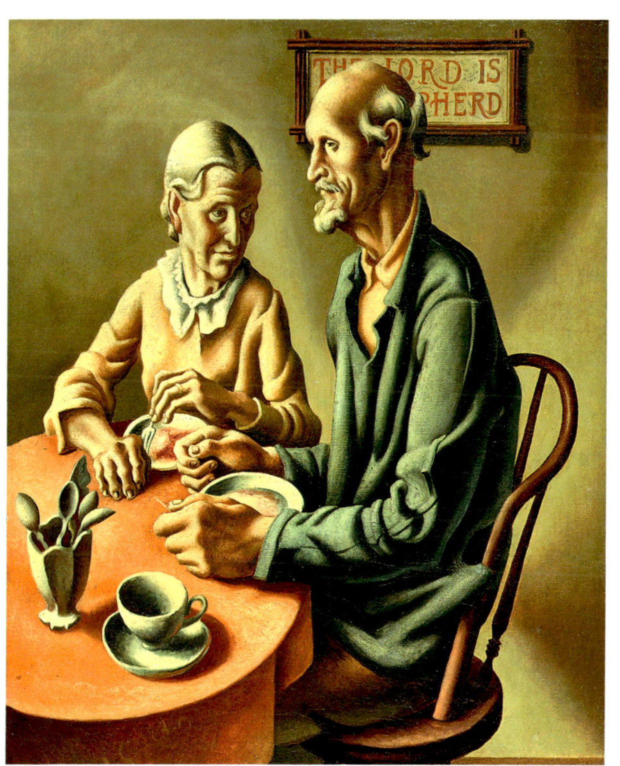

Fig. 5. Thomas Hart Benton. *The Lord Is My Shepherd*, 1926. Tempera on canvas; 33¼ × 27⅜ in. (84.5 × 69.5 cm). Whitney Museum of American Art, New York; Purchase 31.100.

compared with others, and also the freshness of point of view and use of paint, the rest almost entirely are finished technicians following one theory, or school of painting, or another which seems a little mechanical after a while.[39]

Even though the Midwest had given him a significant start, he had outgrown the region, frustrated by its limited exhibition opportunities and chance to make a decent livelihood. His work had finally become part of a national discussion in New York, and the albeit modest sales from the frequent shows that he now had at the A.C.A. reinforced the necessity of his move. (The Walker Galleries would ironically cease to be a venue for Jones's painting once his commitment to the city became permanent. He clearly no longer upheld the geographic terms of its director's construction of Regionalism.)

In deeming his "freshness of point of view and use of paint" a counterpoint to the more "mechanical" compositional formulas that had been devised by his contemporaries, Jones may have been referring to Benton, whose painting *The Lord Is My Shepherd* (fig. 5) had become a mainstay of the Whitney collection from the time of its acquisition in 1931. Its abundant humility and emphasis on the virtues and simplicity of a life associated with hard work reveal the almost-religious calling Benton brought to such art. The fervor of Benton's image contrasts with the unemotional ritual of labor in *Harvest Scene* (c. 1939/42; cat. 72), signaling what Jones considered the modernist foundation of his work and its repudiation of the sentiment involved in the recasting of Renaissance conventions.

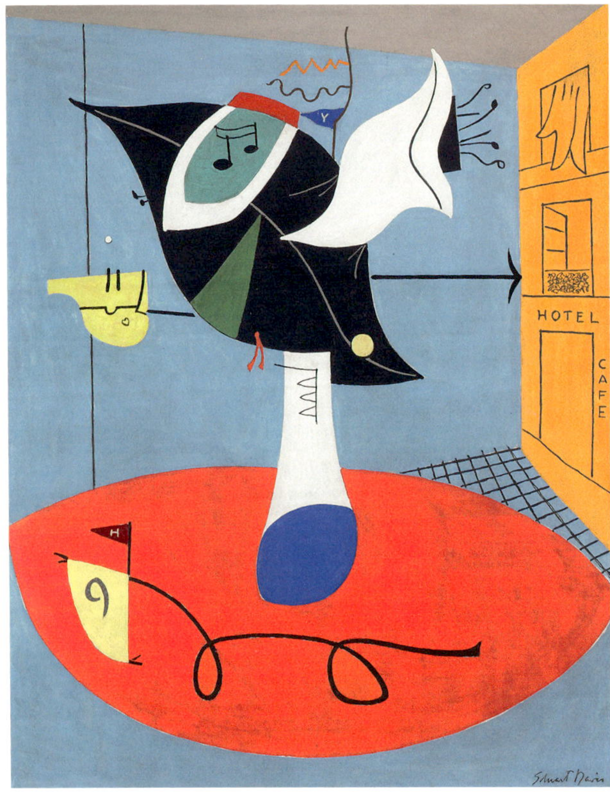

Fig. 6. Stuart Davis (1892–1964). *Still Life with Flowers*, 1930. Oil on canvas; 40 × 32 in. (101.6 × 81.3 cm). Crystal Bridges Museum of American Art, Bentonville, Arkansas.

But even before Jones established his studio in Manhattan and ensconced himself in its artistic scene, he was an ardent public defender of the Heartland. Both he and Benton felt that the Midwest had become a crucible for the renewal of art, but Jones made the additional calculation that New York was an indispensable platform for the promulgation of his ideas, and he insisted on inserting Midwestern subjects into the debates that were waged at the frequent meetings of the Artists' Union.

While the Artists' Union was untethered from the John Reed Club and recharted as a non-partisan organization in 1934, it was quickly infiltrated by the Communist Party, which made its modernist faction particularly vulnerable and imperiled. (Very few modernists who attended union meetings, such as Arshile Gorky, Willem de Kooning, Ibram Lassaw, and Mark Rothko, were card-carrying party members. By the time they became central figures in the New York School—the ascendant art movement in the United States after 1945—socialism had suffered a phenomenal setback domestically, its ideology the target of Cold War politics.) On his periodic visits to New York, Jones had participated in the frequently charged and rancorous exchanges at the union, where the aesthetic priorities of art were contested, along with more practical issues that related to unemployment and union representation. During the run of his show at the Walker Galleries, for example, he felt emboldened enough to introduce himself at a large union gathering as a spokesperson for the Heartland, to which Harold Rosenberg, an editor of *Art Front* (the union's official publication), responded, "Who the hell made you the representative of artists of the Midwest?"[40]

In order to understand Rosenberg's acrimonious outburst, some background is necessary. Rosenberg, who would subsequently rival Clement Greenberg as the foremost post–World War II American art critic, had no truck with the Communist Party, let alone with its fellow travelers or Soviet sympathizers. Additionally, he had defied the union's membership by steering the direction of *Art Front* to the more heady place of focusing on the abstract variations of modernism, as well as its social context and components, while spurning the unmitigated realism the party required of art and literature.[41]

Rosenberg had begun his association with *Art Front* as a writer, brought on board by Stuart Davis, its editor. As noted above, despite being an avowed Marxist, Davis consciously kept his politics out of his work. Whatever his belief in the social relevance of art, his Cubist-derived compositions (see fig. 6), which incorporate quirky and at times droll references to popular culture, are unmarked by any euphoria for the labor movement. During his stint as editor of *Art Front*, Davis waged a particularly notorious battle with Benton, who, he claimed, "conceives the Middle West as provincial, he sees it in his own image. I, too, think that great art will come out of the Middle West, but certainly not on the basis of Benton's presumptions. It will come from artists who perceive their environment, not in isolation, but in relation to the whole." Davis went on to contend that "Benton should have no trouble in selling his wares to any Fascist or semi-Fascist type of government that might set itself up. His qualifications would be in general, his social cynicism which allows him to depict social events without regard to their meaning."[42]

Davis saw as irresponsible Benton's use of imagery that, like propaganda, had the potential to become the pawn of a totalitarian regime. Hitler, after all, Davis reminded his readers, had skillfully and seamlessly drawn on the talents of artists to achieve his skewed version of socialism. Thus the Midwest became tainted as a regionalist outpost where the political implications of the use of retrogressive art forms were dismissed and ignored. This explains the acrimony embedded in Rosenberg's subsequent outburst at Jones. (Davis's indictment would have been known to Jones, whose first exhibition at the A.C.A. Gallery, in 1935, had been covered, as mentioned above, in *Art Front*.[43])

That Davis read fascist overtones in Benton's murals, put off in particular by his stereotypical exaggeration of the facial features of African Americans and Jews, would inform part of the content of the First American Artists' Congress against War and Fascism, for which Davis served as executive secretary and later national chairman. The congress' mission was to address the emergence in Europe of totalitarianism, along with its representations and repressions. It also aimed to unite socially and politically concerned artists in order to oppose limits on artistic expression, as well as advocate for programs that could help them achieve financial security.[44] The orchestration of the inaugural American Artists' Congress took place at the A.C.A. Gallery beginning a few months after Jones's first show.[45] And while Jones was not part of the planning committee—by this point, he had returned to St. Louis—he was asked to deliver a paper, becoming an effective "representative of the Midwest," despite Rosenberg's put-down.

Jones had the distinction of appearing at Town Hall in the only public session of the three-day congress, in mid-February 1936, alongside Mumford (who gave the opening address), Davis, Margaret Bourke-White, Aaron Douglas, Rockwell Kent, and others. These speakers discussed a range of subjects related to the goals of the congress. Bourke-White elaborated upon the differences between government patronage of the arts in the United States and the Soviet Union, and Douglas talked about the contributions that African American artists and musicians had made to American culture, as well as the challenges they faced as a result of racism. Jones, who spoke against censorship in the arts, represented the voice of the working class. In his opening remarks, Davis located "a real danger of Fascism in America," one that could be traced and discerned in the reactionary, nationalistic prose of critics, such as Craven, who wrote for William Randolph Hearst's publications.[46] Davis cautioned artists to remain aloof from such patriotism, as well as from any political group. He contended that art was a universal project,

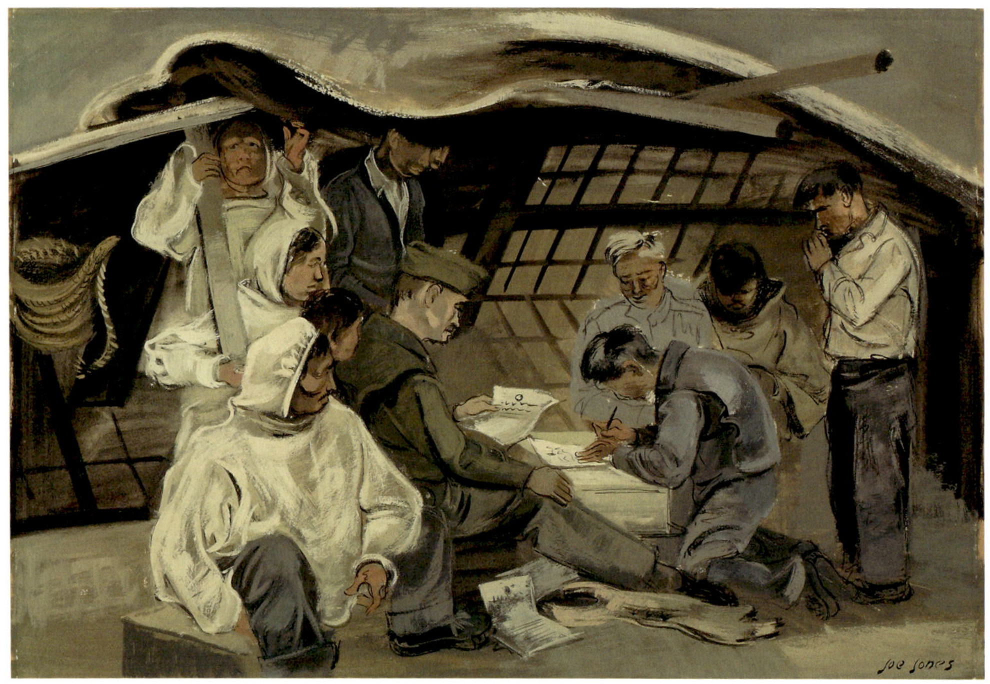

Fig. 7. Joe Jones. *Organizing the ATG*, 1943. Pastel and gouache on paper; 14½ × 21$^{15}/_{16}$ in. (36.8 × 55.8 cm). Courtesy of the Army Art Collection, U.S. Army Center of Military History, Washington, D.C.

ultimately driven by the elaboration of the individual voice, and shaped through the shared priority to advance its media.

Jones's talk, "Repression of Art in America," delivered before a sold-out audience, was brief and tightly scripted, as prescribed for many of the speeches scheduled for the first day of the event.[47] In it he dwelled on the rights of artists in the United States, invoking his firsthand experience of censorship, which he considerd a fascist act, during the now-notorious scandal that had unfolded at St. Louis's Old Courthouse in 1934, when the classroom where Jones and his unemployed students had created a mural with incendiary scenes of labor unrest was padlocked by city officials (see Wolfe). The censure of these murals was seen by congress organizers as an affront to freedom of expression that paralleled the destruction of Diego Rivera's commission for Rockefeller Center in 1933. (An image of Vladimir Lenin that Rivera had brazenly inserted into a panorama of a May Day celebration had incensed his conservative patron.) Such acts were viewed, moreover, by Davis and the congress' organizers as violating the egalitarian ethos implicit in the mural medium, its public access making it a consummate form of democratic expression. Jones had a dim view of Rivera, whose murals he thought were overly dependent upon American corporate sponsors, unlike his own projects, which he achieved without recourse to such financing or intermediaries. By extension, Jones concluded that the progressive content of Rivera's work either willfully incited the ire of its establishment underwriters or was subjugated and manipulated to reinforce their values. Nonetheless, whatever his aversion to Rivera, Jones not only defended him against the actions of Rockefeller, but also observed that the benefactors of museums had similarly enforced their own vested interests on collections and programming, foregoing their role as enlightened, impartial champions. Finally, Jones argued that censorship extended into the domain of easel painting, especially now that art such as his aspired to be socially relevant.

The job of working as an artist in a severely downsized economy had its risks. But were these any different from the ongoing, historic challenges and setbacks to avant-garde culture? The extrapolation was one that Jones could not make in the limited time assigned to discuss his encounter with repression. That type of response was left to other speakers at the congress, such as Meyer Schapiro, who would arguably become the foremost art historian in the postwar United States. In a closed session the following day, Schapiro proffered the idea that all contemporary art is driven by aesthetic concerns, that it issues from individual rather than collective experience and is primarily preoccupied with stretching the known parameters of visual composition. Schapiro's assessment came with the proviso that, "in a society where all men can be free individuals, individuality must lose its exclusiveness and its ruthless and perverse character."[48] That is, without some recognition of the artist's relationship to class structure, his or her work will ultimately land in the privileged and distanced realm of figures who control its destiny.

Baron recalled that, at a rehearsal for the congress at the A.C.A. Gallery, Arnold Blanch, a social realist from Minnesota with little empathy for a renewal of modernism, countered Schapiro's paper by stating, "This is very excellent, I'm sure; but will the artists understand it? *We're* simple people."[49] However, Jones must have absorbed something of Schapiro's thinking: his own painting would gradually ease into less urgent social criticism and return to its early investment in reformulating the pictorial ingredients of art. In fact, his re-transformation as an artist would parallel the evolution of Schapiro's thinking. In 1938 the art historian applied his disclaimer on the "social bases of art" to Benton, in response to the self-aggrandizing rhetoric in Benton's first autobiography.[50] Schapiro wrote in the newly restructured *Partisan Review*—like the *Anvil* (which it had absorbed), once an organ of the John Reed Club but remade into a liberal publication in 1937—that Benton's "idea of a realistic art is expressed as an opposition to two extremes. In criticizing abstract art, he isolates objects as the field of painting; in criticizing a realism guided by radical values and a desire for change, he poses the stable, unpolitical everyday world and the corresponding historical past as the proper subjects for art."[51] Jones worked assiduously to counter and disassociate himself from a staid, retrogressive image of the Heartland. He helped orchestrate and participate in an exhibition of work by artists from the Midwest that opened at the A.C.A. Gallery in June 1936 and moved to the Vanguard Gallery, St. Louis (see Sharp).

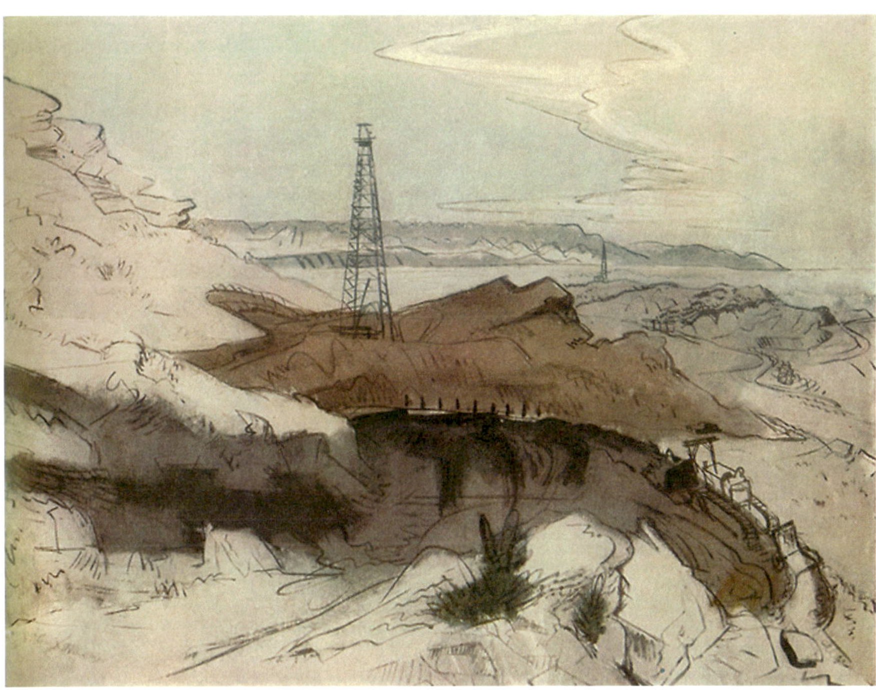

Fig. 8. Joe Jones. *Elk Basin*, 1944. Formerly Collection Standard Oil. Reproduced on the cover of *Art Digest* 20, 8 (January 15, 1946).

As Howard Devree of the *New York Times* stated at the outset of his review of this show, "Let it be said that there are no imitations of Benton, Curry and Wood; and second, that there has been no attempt to glorify the 'American Scene' from without."[52] With the exception of Jones, the artists included in the event were unknown to New York audiences, their engagement of issues that related to social injustice ironically overshadowed by idealist takes on agrarian bounty produced by their regionalist counterparts.

As the Moscow Trials got underway in 1936, shortly after the First American Artists' Congress convened in New York, and numerous Soviet artists, scientists, writers, and intellectuals were either executed or sent to the gulag for their support of Leon Trotsky and Lenin (the original architects of Soviet Communism), the American Communist Party ceased to exert credibility and influence, its power base at institutions such as the Artists' Union vastly eroded. The barbarity of Stalin's incarnation of socialism now emerged as another iteration of totalitarianism. Jones remained mute on this subject, but his own commitment to the party waned, and he gave up on its ability to effect radical reform.

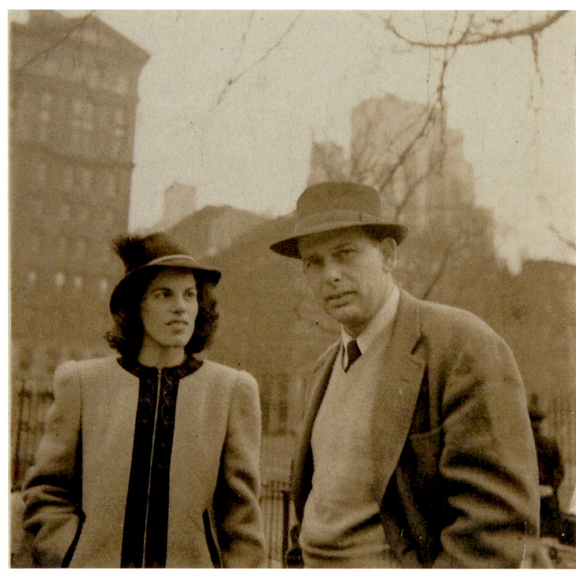

Fig. 9. Grace and Joe Jones in New York, 1943. Courtesy of James and Karen Jones.

From 1937 through 1941, Jones was involved with the post-office mural programs of the U.S. Treasury's Section of Painting and Sculpture (see Walker and Turk). Although the section's administrators quashed his attempts to decorate post offices with representations of poor sharecroppers, Jones was able to communicate his empathy and respect for field laborers in scenes of wheat and corn harvests. He exhibited at the A.C.A. Gallery through 1940, when his last solo show took place there. The gallery continued to represent him through much of 1941. The artist seems to have returned to the

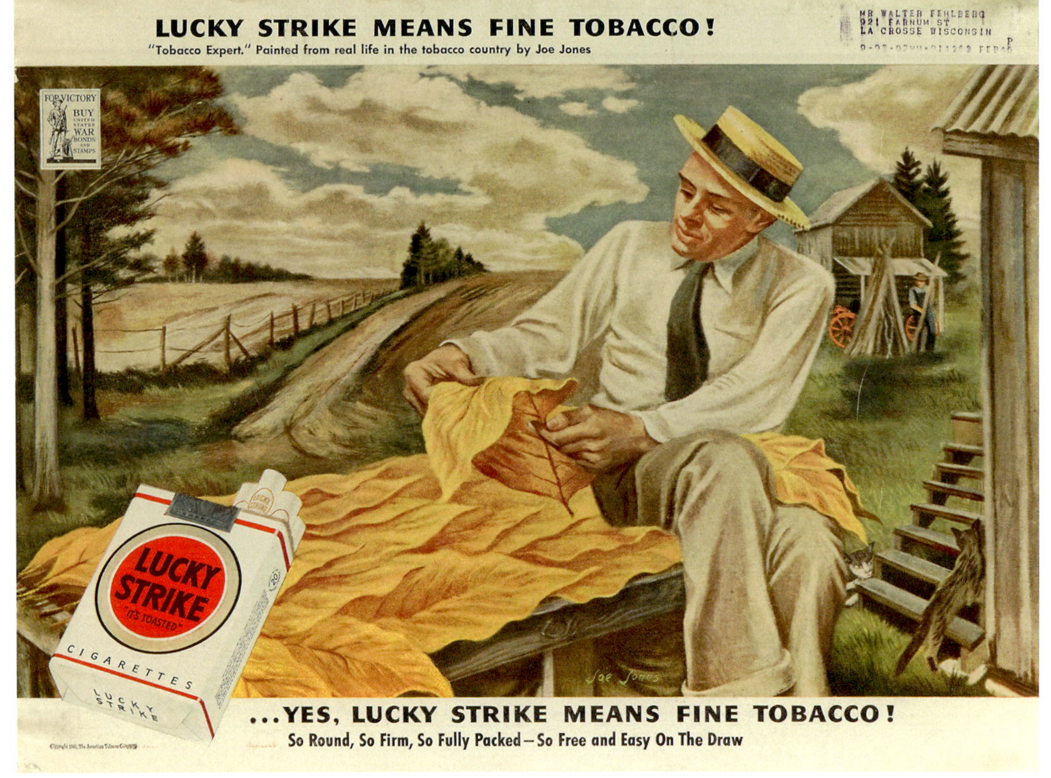

Fig. 10. "Lucky Strike Means Fine Tobacco!" This advertisement for the American Tobacco Company reproduces Jones's *Tobacco Expert*, c. 1943. Oil on canvas; 25 × 40 in. (63.5 × 101.6 cm). Location unknown. Advertisement courtesy of Andrew Walker.

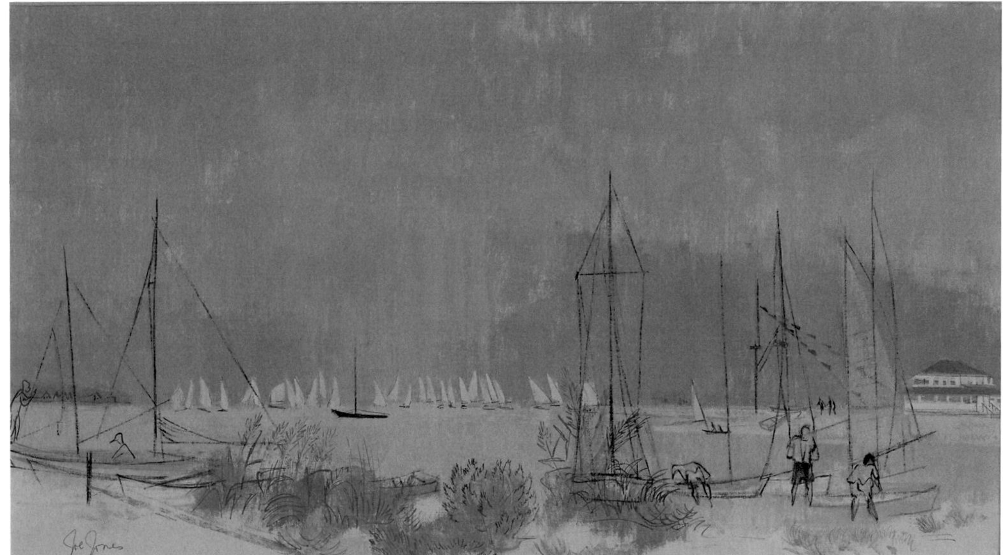

Fig. 11. Joe Jones. *Regatta, Barnegat Bay, New Jersey*, c. 1950. Oil on canvas; 22 × 40 in. (55.9 × 101.6 cm). Courtesy of Robert M. and Mary Ventimiglia.

Walker Galleries for a short time that year, before settling at the commercial AAA Galleries. In 1943 Jones found another governmental position, in the War Art Unit of the United States Engineer Office, which sent him to Alaska to produce images of soldiers (see fig. 7). Jones's political fervor, now attenuated in a distant geographical post, was redirected to the Allied Forces and their fight against fascism.

Elizabeth Green had wondered whether Jones's political epiphany in Provincetown in the summer of 1933, when he declared himself a Communist, would be a momentary diversion or a lasting commitment. Jones had countered her speculation with characteristic irritation:

> Why do you insist I am not making a contribution in art, because you personally don't agree with the political studies? You refer to my aspirations in the past tense—ridiculous! . . . If I have been seeking publicity (as you subtly accuse me) instead of trying to do a worthwhile job with painting, my task would be a very easy one.[53]

However, Green's reservations were not entirely off-base. Jones's personal life settled down. Remarried (see fig. 9) and eventually the father of four, he moved with his family to upstate New York and eventually to the tranquil suburbs of New Jersey. From his permanent abode in the Northeast, the Midwest would eventually recede as a subject in his art. However, his pastoral scenes of wheat fields and laborers would fuel the redirection of his painting, which morphed, as a *Time* writer phrased it, into "graceful handwriting."[54] Jones had ceased to find meaning in political organizations. As he stated in the *St. Louis Globe-Democrat* in 1938, "My active political life is almost negligible."[55]

Yet, another kind of collective, the corporation, stepped in almost immediately as a surrogate subject. Jones's commissions—yes, commissions, whatever his disapproval of Rivera's patrons—for Abbott Laboratories, American Tobacco (fig. 10), and Standard Oil (see fig. 8)—ironically permitted the elaboration of his own voice. His subjectivity surfaced in quasiabstract landscapes, set near his New Jersey home or in far-flung locales such as Bermuda, in which his brushwork and line became more calligraphic, now fully liberated from the constraints of realism (see fig. 11). Jones had indeed returned to his roots as a dedicated modernist. As he said of the last phase of his work, "The secret, if there is a secret, in the development of my painting at the moment, is I am enjoying painting now because I have taken the work out of it and left only the joy."[56]

NOTES

1. Joe Jones to Elizabeth Green, n.d. (c. Oct. 1933). All correspondence from Jones to Green is in the Dr. John Green Collection, Missouri History Museum, St. Louis (hereinafter Green Papers).

2. For a discussion of Jones's conflicted relationship with Regionalism as it played out in New York, see Debra Bricker Balken, *After Many Springs: Regionalism, Modernism and the Midwest*, exh. cat. (Des Moines Art Center/Yale University Press, 2009), pp. 127–37.

3. Thomas Hart Benton to Alfred Stieglitz, May 20, 1923, Alfred Stieglitz and Georgia O'Keeffe Papers, Yale Collection of American Literature, Beinecke Library, Yale University, New Haven, Conn.

4. Allen Jackson, "Art: U.S. Scene," *Time* 24, 6 (Dec. 24, 1934), p. 25. See also Balken (note 2), pp. 73–77.

5. Thomas Craven, *Modern Art: The Men, the Movements, the Meaning* (Simon and Schuster, 1934), p. 335.

6. Benton to Stieglitz (note 3). Benton was referring here to Pablo Picasso, although he would have applied this description to modernist art in general, such was the level of his disdain by 1923 for any iteration of pictorial invention. The irony of his stance is clear when one considers the ongoing originality of his own work.

7. Robert Hanna to Green, Feb. 8, 1934, Green Papers.

8. Jones to Green, Feb. 16, 1935, Green Papers.

9. Jones described himself as "terribly lonesome and confused," "homesick," and "awfully nervous," in a letter to Green on Feb. 11. Two days later, he wrote that he was doing better: "I have only one mental and emotional problem to worry about now. I think you know what I mean" (apparently referring to his ex-wife); Jones to Green, Feb. 13, 1935. Both letters in Green Papers.

10. Jones to Green, Feb. 25, 1935, Green Papers.

11. *Painting and Sculpture from 16 American Cities: Atlanta, Baltimore, Boston, Buffalo, Chicago, Cleveland, Dallas, Detroit, Los Angeles, Minneapolis, Philadelphia, Pittsburgh, St. Louis, San Francisco, Santa Fe, Seattle*, exh. cat. (Museum of Modern Art, 1933), cat. 81.

12. Jones participated in the Whitney's annual exhibitions in 1934, 1936–38, and 1940–46.

13. Jones to Green, Feb. 16, 1935, Green Papers.

14. Max Weber, "The Artist, His Audience, and Outlook," in *Artists against War and Facism: Papers of the First American Artists' Congress*, intro. by Matthew Baigell and Julia Williams (Rutgers University Press, 1986), p. 126.

15. In a letter to Green (Mar. 4, 1935), Jones said that he was going to take his work to Rehn's and that he would be ready to return to St. Louis if things went well with either gallery. He later wrote Green (Mar. 12, 1935) that neither gallery was interested in adding new artists to its stable. For "on an artistic downgrade" and "decadent," see Jones to Green, Feb. 25, 1935. All letters in Green Papers.

16. See Douglas Wixon, *Worker-Writer in America: Jack Conroy and the Tradition of Midwestern Literary Radicalism, 1898–1990* (University of Illinois Press, 1994), p. 384.

17. Jones to Green, Mar. 7, 1935, Green Papers.

18. Archibald MacLeish, "U.S. Art: 1935," *Fortune* 7, 6 (Dec. 1935), p. 69.

19. Lewis Mumford, "The Art Galleries: In Capitulation," *New Yorker* 1, 16 (June 1, 1935), p. 57; repr. in *Mumford on Modern Art in the 1930s*, ed. and with intro. by Robert Wojtowicz (University of California Press, 2007), p. 166.

20. "Housepainter," *Time* 25, 22 (June 3, 1935), p. 32.

21. "Workers and Wheatfields," *Time* 27, 5 (Feb. 3, 1936), p. 46.

22. For an in-depth discussion of the term Regionalism and its application in American art, see Balken (note 2), pp. 105–12.

23. Mumford actually believed that Jones's work combined aspects of "three schools that have dominated the scene during the past season—the neo-romantics, the Americanists, and the proletarians." The "neo-romantics" Mumford alluded to included Eugene Berman and Pavel Tchelitchew. See Lewis Mumford, "The Three Bentons," in *Mumford on Modern Art* (note 19), p. 161.

24. Charles Weinstock, "Joe Jones," *Art Front* 1, 6 (July 1935), p. 6. The issue of whether Jones could be categorized as a regionalist has been addressed by Karal Ann Marling, "Workers, Capitalists, and Booze: The Story of the 905 Murals," in *Joe Jones & J. B. Turnbull: Visions of the Midwest in the 1930s*, exh. cat. (Haggerty Museum of Art, Marquette University, 1987), p. 12. Marling maintained that Jones's work straddled both Regionalism and Social Realism. In contrast, Andrew Hemingway framed Jones as an "anti-regionalist"; idem, *Artists on the Left: American Artists and the Communist Movement, 1926–1956* (Yale University Press, 2002), p. 36.

25. Maynard Walker, quoted in "Mid-West Is Producing an Indigenous Art," *Art Digest* 7, 20 (Sept. 1, 1933), p. 10.

26. Ibid.

27. See Balken (note 2), pp. 79–80; and idem, *Dove/O'Keeffe, Circles of Influence*, exh. cat. (Sterling and Francine Clark Art Institute, 2009), p. 52.

28. Thomas Hart Benton, "American Regionalism, A Personal History of the Movement," in idem, *An American in Art: A Professional and Technical Autobiography* (University Press of Kansas, 1969), p. 167.

29. Jones to Green, Jan. 1936, Green Papers.

30. Craven (note 5).

31. Georgia O'Keeffe talked about the chase for the "great American Thing"; idem, *Georgia O'Keeffe* (Viking Press, 1976), n. pag.

32. Thomas Craven, ed., *A Treasury of American Prints* (Simon and Schuster, 1939), caption for pl. 59.

33. E. M. Benson, "Two Proletarian Artists: Joe Jones and William Gropper," *Magazine of Art* 39, 3 (Mar. 1936), p. 189.

34. Lewis Mumford, "Goya, Homer, and Jones," *New Yorker* 11, 52 (Feb. 8, 1936), pp. 58–59; repr. in *Mumford on Modern Art* (note 19), p. 190. Mumford, it should be noted, had referred to Jones's work as "pulseless propaganda" in his review of the artist's first show at the A.C.A. Gallery (note 19).

35. The Metropolitan Museum of Art deaccessioned *Threshing No. 1* in 1990.

36. Edward Alden Jewell, "One-Man Shows by Benton, Biddle, and Joe Jones," *New York Times*, Oct. 31, 1937.

37. Ibid.

38. Jones, quoted in "Guggenheim Award Won by Joe Jones," *St. Louis Post-Dispatch*, Mar. 29, 1937.

39. Jones to Green, Sept. 20, 1937, Green Papers.

40. Harold Rosenberg, quoted in Gerald Monroe, "Art Front," *Archives of American Art Journal* 13, 3 (1973), p. 17.

41. For an examination of Rosenberg and *Art Front*, see Debra Bricker Balken, *Harold Rosenberg* (University of Chicago Press, forthcoming).

42. Stuart Davis, "Davis Rejoinder," *Art Digest* 9, 13 (Apr. 1, 1935), pp. 12–13. According to Monroe (note 40), p. 13, Davis served as editor of *Art Front* from the second through the tenth issues. According to Hemingway (note 24), p. 87, Davis became president of the union in 1934.

43. Weinstock (note 24).

44. See Matthew Baigell and Julia Williams, "Introduction," *Artists against War and Facism* (note 14), pp. 11–12.

45. For a discussion of the relationship between the American Artists' Congress and the A.C.A. Gallery, see Herman Baron, American Artists' Congress, A.C.A. Papers, Archives of American Art, Smithsonian Institution, Washington, D.C. Baron was hardly objective in his recapitulation of the events that led to the first congress, having developed a particular disdain for Davis because of the artist's refusal to reveal his political beliefs in his highly modernist work.

46. Stuart Davis, "Why an Artists' Congress?," in *Artists against War and Facism* (note 14), p. 68. Davis was talking about the *Daily Mirror*'s art critic, but he could easily have been talking about Craven, who wrote for the *New York American*, a Hearst publication. The year before, Davis had declared that Craven's "critical values may possibly be clouded by a lively sense of commercial expediency. His efforts to bring art values to the place of a Rotarian luncheon are a particularly repellent form of petty opportunism and should be so understood and explained whenever one has the misfortune to slip on them"; Stuart Davis, "The New York

American Scene in Art," *Art Front* 1, 3 (Feb. 1935), p. 6.

47. Jones, "Repression of Art in America," in *Artists against War and Fascism* (note 14), pp. 75–77.

48. Meyer Schapiro, "The Social Bases of Art," in ibid., p. 113.

49. Attributed to Arnold Blanch, in Baron (note 45).

50. Benton (note 28).

51. Meyer Schapiro, "Populist Realism," *Partisan Review* 4, 2 (Jan. 1938), p. 55.

52. Howard Devree, "In Local Art Galleries," *New York Times*, May 10, 1936.

53. Jones to Green, Apr. 19, 1934, Green Papers.

54. "Angry Man Calms Down," *Time* 58, 17 (Oct. 22, 1951), p. 21.

55. John Selby, "Joe Jones, Who Began as House Painter, Hailed as Promising Artist," *St. Louis Globe-Democrat*, Sept. 11, 1938.

56. Quoted in Harry Salpeter, "The New Mister Joe Jones," *Esquire* 23, 6 (June 1945), p. 82.

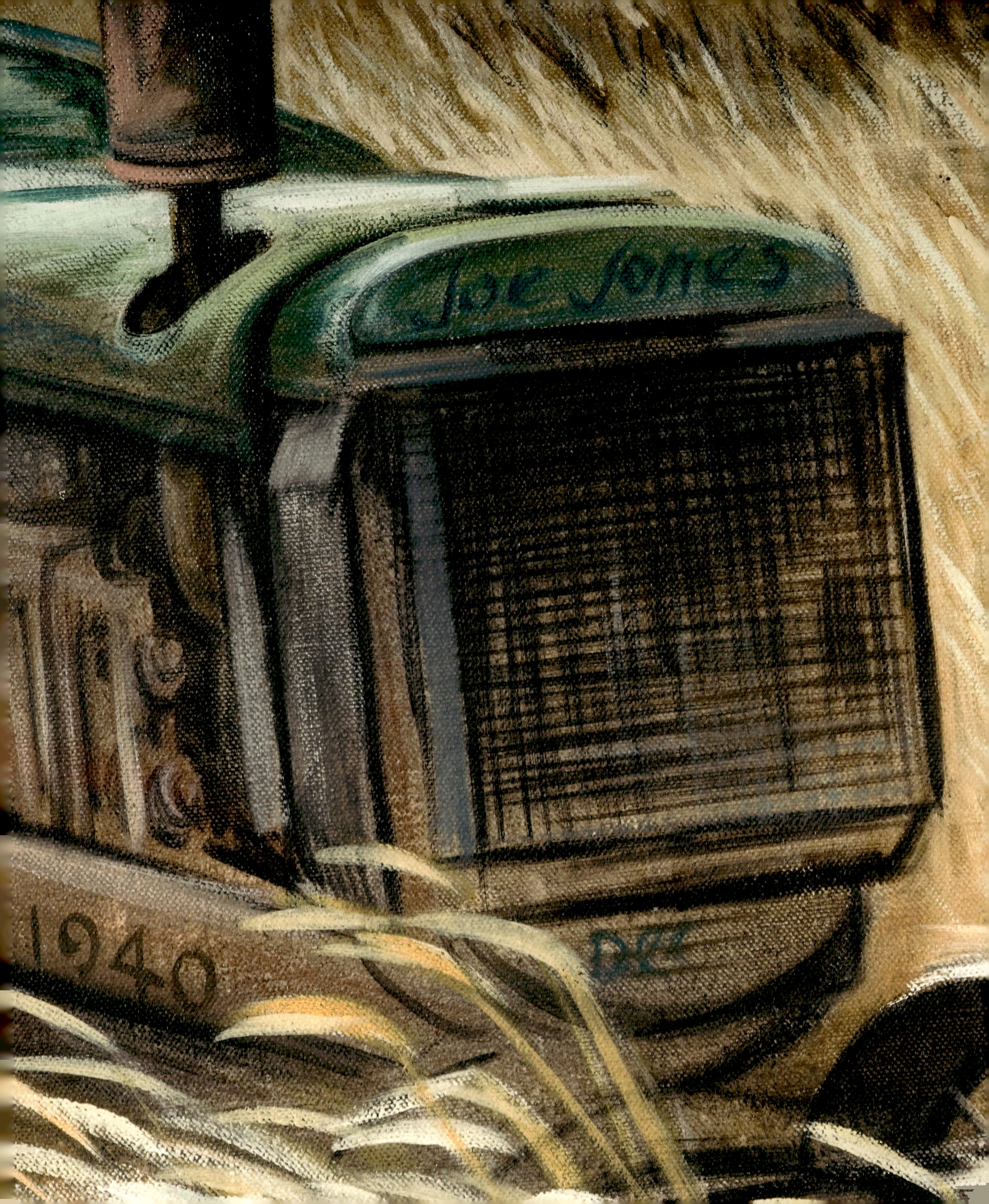

Joe Jones
1940

Joe Jones's Treasury Department Murals

Andrew Walker and Janeen Turk

Between 1937 and 1941, Joe Jones completed five murals for the Section of Painting and Sculpture (later the Section of Fine Arts). A New Deal art program organized under the Treasury Department, the section employed artists to decorate newly constructed federal buildings, largely post offices. The commissions were awarded on the basis of several factors, including success in juried competitions, design submissions, and satisfactory work on previous section projects. An artist was required to submit a series of designs, incorporate any mandated changes, and await approval before proceeding to the next stage. First, a scaled black and white sketch had to be approved, then a scaled design in color, next a photograph of a full-size cartoon, and finally a photograph of the installed mural.[1] Payment (in Jones's case, between $550 and $800) was usually made in installments throughout the process.

Jones's primary contact at the section was superintendent and (later assistant chief) Edward B. Rowan. Rowan had encountered Jones and his work when the artist was employed by the Public Works of Art Project, of which Rowan had served as assistant and technical director. The two met in August 1935, after the artist turned down a low-paying position with the Treasury Relief Art Project. Instead, he accepted an offer from the Resettlement Administration Special Skills Division (see Walker).[2]

The section offered Jones the opportunity to be paid what he felt was a fair wage for the mural work he had been eager to pursue since the success of his Commonwealth College project (see Wolfe). Although the agency used its approval procedures to direct content and even details of composition in the murals it sponsored, Jones was able to negotiate the bureaucratic process to his advantage. The murals he produced satisfied his personal and political perspectives through his choice of subjects that promoted the nobility of workers and their labor. Each of Jones's five section post-office murals presents some aspect of agricultural work, with four depicting scenes of wheat harvest and the fifth presenting the harvesting of corn.

MAGNOLIA, ARKANSAS, 1937–38

For Jones's first section project (fig. 1), a post-office mural for Magnolia, Arkansas, he traveled to that town to generate ideas for his composition. He determined that the African American sharecroppers who worked in the region were "the people who count," and his first design for the mural depicted a group of them on a break. However, his initial idea was summarily rejected by Rowan, who wanted the artist to work with one of his tried-and-true subjects: wheat.[3]

Two months after receiving the initial rejection from Rowan, Jones announced that he had plans for a wheat-threshing mural. Even with the forced change in focus, Jones used the subject of wheat harvest to showcase his interest in the lives of rural laborers. The final composition features a central figure pitching bundles of wheat into a threshing machine, which separates the grain from the chaff and shoots the latter out in a plume while pouring the former into sacks to be tied by the workers at the lower right. One of these men, at the far right, echoes the central figure of Jones's *Threshing* mural for the downtown St. Louis 905 Liquor Store (1936; cat. 40). He rests one knee on a sack of wheat while coiling a length of twine around his arm. Jones must have been intrigued by this figure and the other grouped with him, who bends down to tie a sack, since the artist devoted several works to them. In addition to a preliminary sketch of the two figures, he also produced stand-alone images, including a lithograph and a finished easel painting, both titled *Missouri Wheat Farmers* (both 1938; cats. 69–70); the lithograph would be widely circulated by the Associated

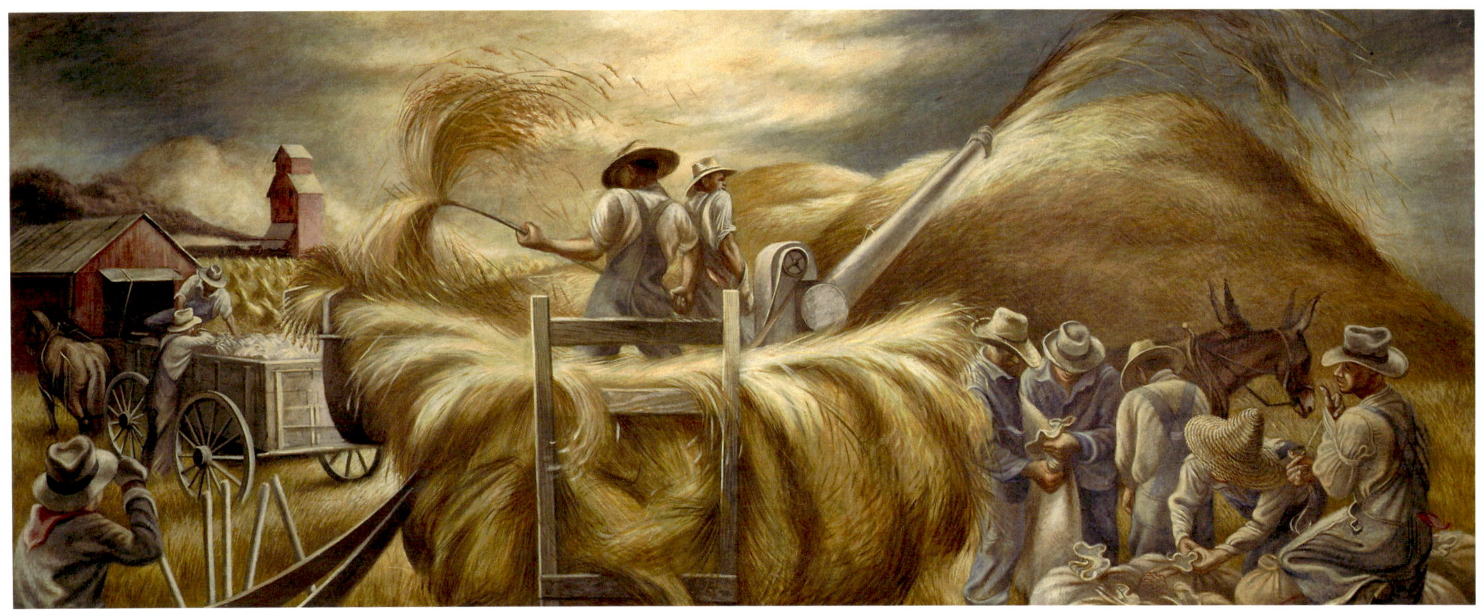

American Artists. As Jones stated to Forbes Watson, editor of the section's bulletin, he was drawn to the activity of performing a task well, as reflected in *Missouri Wheat Farmers*: "The aesthetics of doing ones [*sic*] work is to me the most beautifull [*sic*] rhythms imaginable—the way a man who knows and enjoys his work, pitches wheat or ties sacks . . . or paints as we do, knows the real joy of living a purposefull [*sic*] life."[4]

CHARLESTON, MISSOURI, 1938–39

Because of his excellent work on the Magnolia mural, Jones received a second commission, this time for the post office in Charleston, Missouri (fig. 2). Jones had read about the region in the 1938 Farm Security Administration pamphlet *Rich Land, Poor People* and had learned that wheat farming was on the rise in this area. Thus he planned another wheat-harvest scene; this one shows a team of workers loading bundles of grain onto a hayrack to be hauled to the threshing machine. The mural's primary focus is the abundance of wheat, which is depicted in shades of gold and copper. Massed on the hayracks and seen in a vibrant spray at the end of a pitchfork, the wheat's visual appeal reinforces the beauty Jones found in the harvesters' labor.[5] The artist had, after all, used a similar figural arrangement in his 1935 canvas *Threshing No. 1* (cat. 34). A signal image in Jones's 1936 exhibition "Paintings of Wheat Fields" at the Walker Galleries, it was purchased by the Metropolitan Museum of Art in 1937.

Fig. 1. Joe Jones. *Threshing*, 1937–38. Oil on canvas; 5 × 12 ft. (1.5 × 3.7 m). For Magnolia, Arkansas, Post Office. Courtesy of Farmers Bank & Trust, Magnolia, Arkansas.

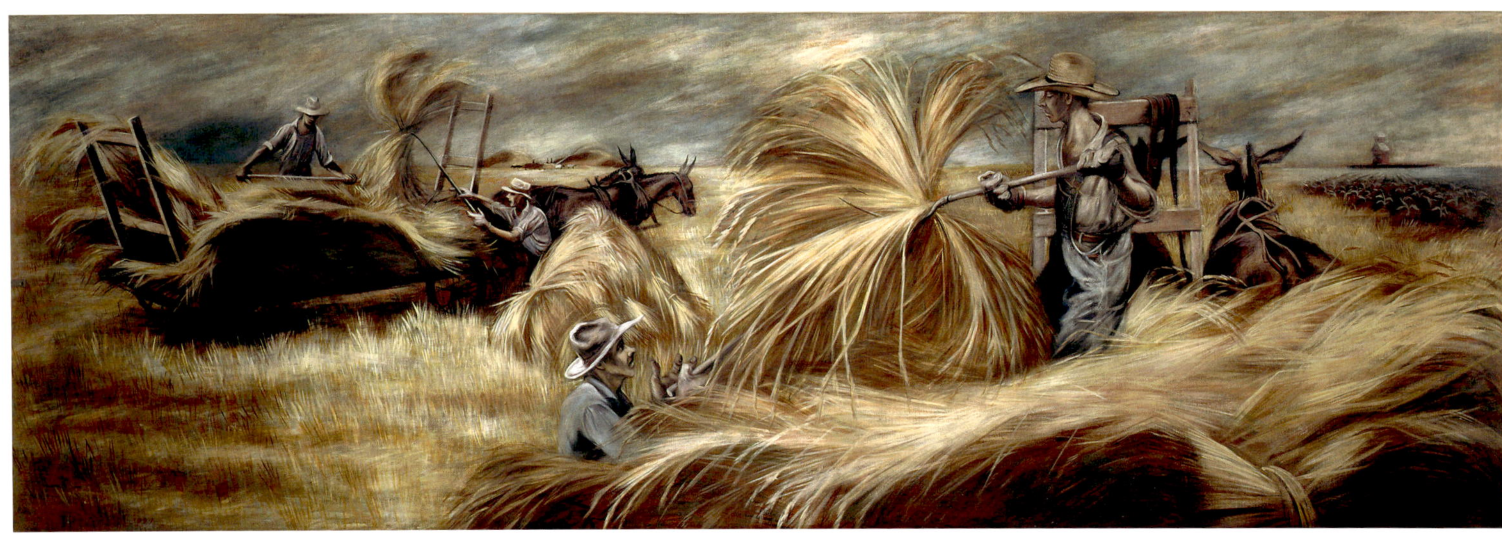

Fig. 2. Joe Jones. *Harvest*, 1938–39. Oil and tempera on canvas; 4 × 12 ft. (1.2 × 3.7 m). Charleston, Missouri. Post Office.

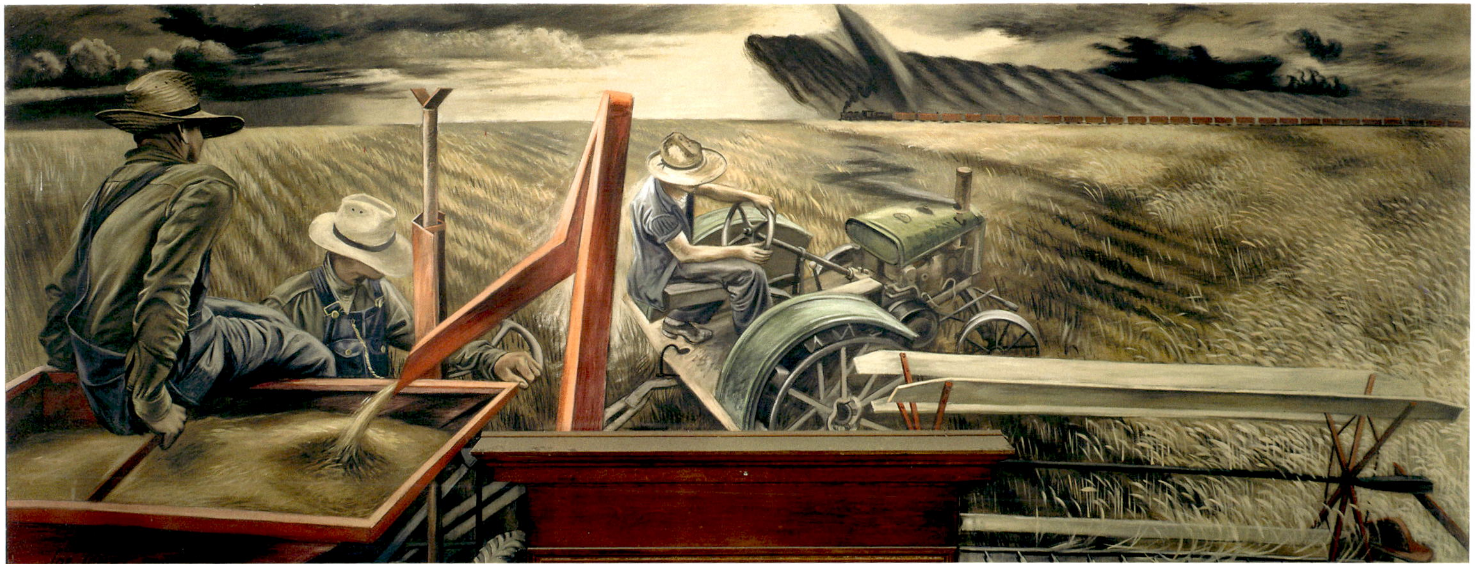

Fig. 3. Joe Jones. *Turning a Corner*, 1939. Oil on canvas; 5¼ × 14 ft. (1.6 × 4.3 m). Anthony, Kansas, Post Office.

Fig. 4. Joe Jones. *Men and Wheat*, 1939–40. Oil and tempera on canvas; 5⅙ × 12 ft. (1.6 × 3.7 m). Seneca, Kansas, Post Office.

ANTHONY, KANSAS, 1939

Jones's third mural (fig. 3), for the Anthony, Kansas, Post Office, depicts a tractor maneuvering a combine around the corner of a wheat field. Jones had seen combines, machines that both cut and threshed wheat, in use in the Anthony area when he visited to prepare for the mural. He spent time in the fields alongside workers, and he took photographs of the implements they used. Jones emphasized that he intended his composition to acknowledge the value and importance of labor: "My interest was in portraying man at work, his job before him and how he goes about it with his tools—man creating. . . . Man doing his work efficiently and under control is beautiful to look at to other men and this is my chief concern."[6]

SENECA, KANSAS, 1939–40

In 1939 Jones participated in the section's largest nationwide contest: the "Forty-eight State Mural Competition." The ambitious program, designed to put a mural in a rural post office in every state, attracted 972 artists, who submitted 1,477 designs.[7] Meant to revitalize the mural program, the competition focused on rural community values and attempted through the jury process to assure that each town had a voice in determining the final design. Artists were encouraged to visit the towns selected for the program and to discuss possible subjects with residents.

Jones won the competition for Seneca, Kansas, a farming town northwest of Kansas City that had just finished constructing a new post office.[8] Entitled *Men and Wheat*,

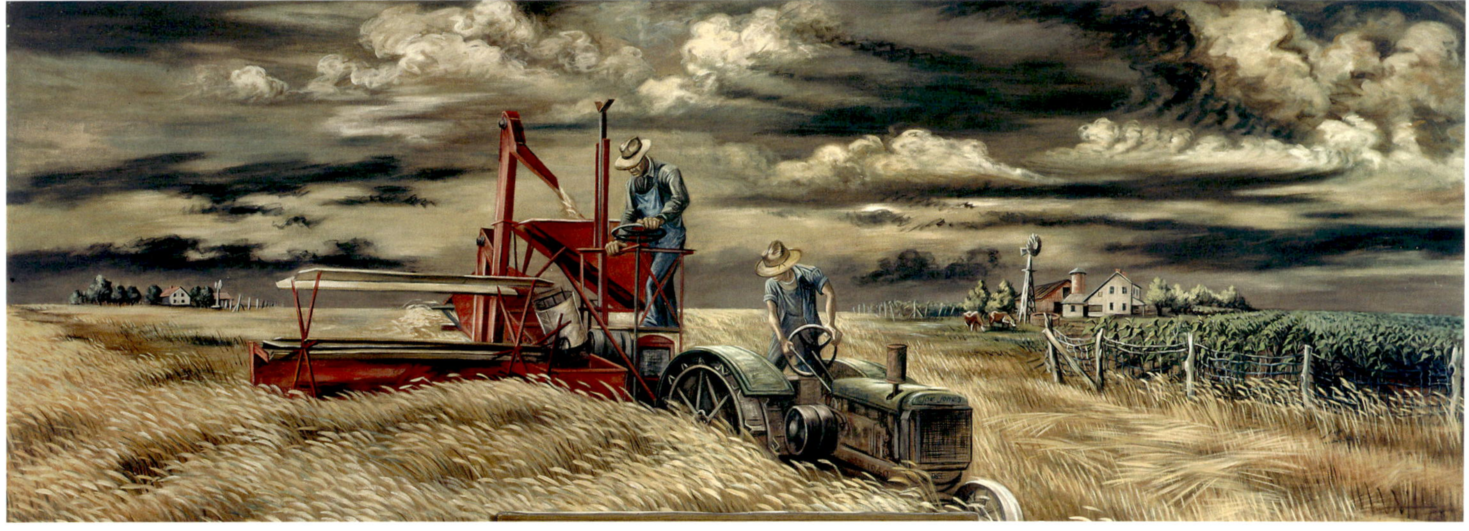

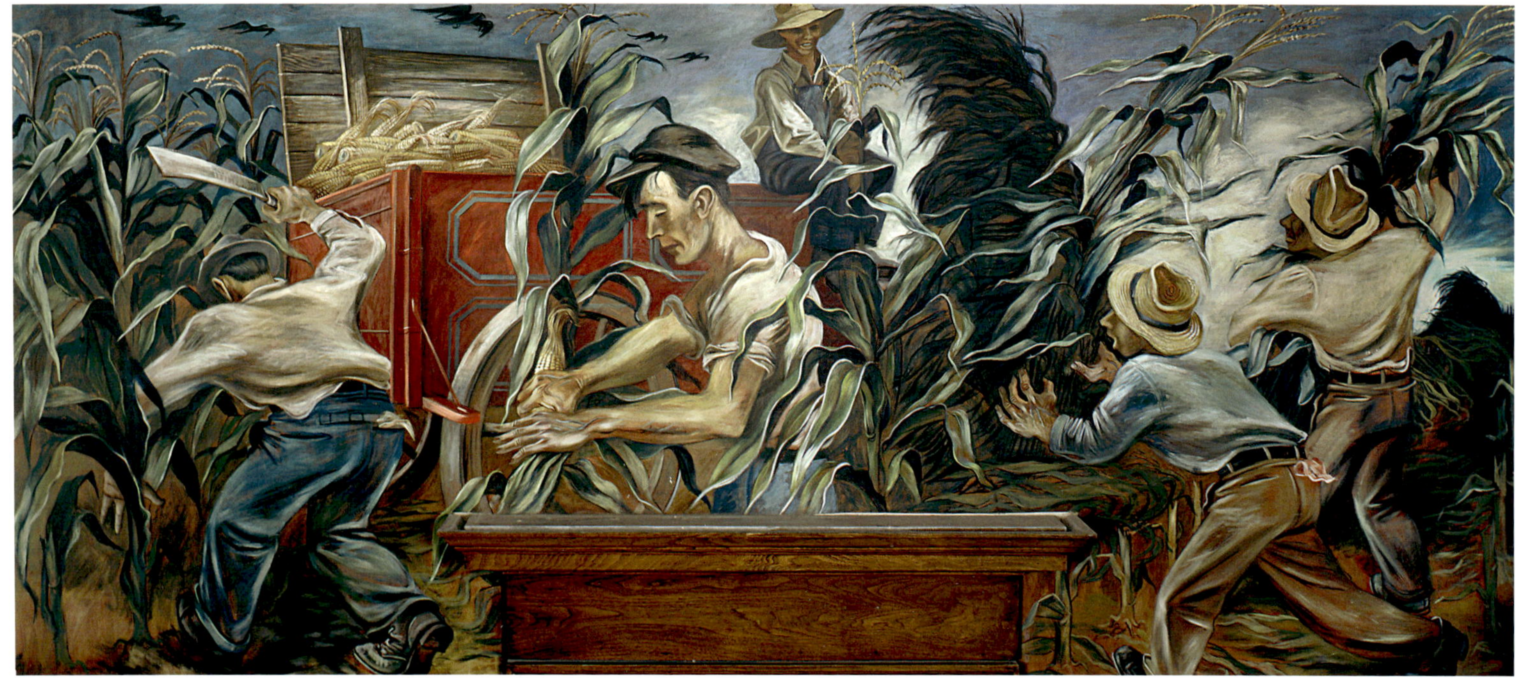

the painting (fig. 4) illustrates Jones's experience working in the wheat fields of Missouri. Jones's initial design (cat. 71) shows a modern tractor and combine cutting the crop in what appears to be an endless golden field. Although Jones felt positive about the mural, the design prompted local criticism. The Seneca postmaster felt that Jones had represented the region as one vast wheat field rather than as a site of smaller plots (truck farms), which were more typical of the area surrounding the town.[9] In addition, the postmaster objected to the machinery represented, declaring that it was not up-to-date and that it referenced a specific manufacturer—Massey-Harris—which, he declared, was tantamount to advertising in a government space.

The criticism justifiably rankled Jones and pointed to the difficulties underlying a national mural competition in which local input—rule by committee—could limit artistic license. As Rowan stated in a letter to Jones, however, the view of the section was clear: "You are quite right in stating that a mural need not be a cross section for a community to be a vital work of art, but we have found in this new program of painting for the public that those murals which most truthfully reflect the activities, life and aspirations of the people are the ones which seem to have greatest meaning for the public."[10] Jones made the changes necessary to meet the needs of the Seneca community, and the mural was unveiled in February 1940.

DEXTER, MISSOURI, 1940–41

For his final section mural (fig. 5), located in Dexter, Missouri, Jones chose the subject of corn harvesting. In this composition, he depicted the "three most exciting actions of the harvest, husking, cutting, and shocking." As always, Jones wanted to draw attention to the workers and their tasks. To accomplish this, he presented most of the figures in the foreground, into which he compressed the various steps of the harvest—even though they did not take place in physical or temporal proximity—so that they could be viewed together. Jones stated, "In this way I have been able to indicate a maximum of human activity in relation to the crop, this I believe to be (human activity) most important in public art."[11]

Fig. 5. Joe Jones. *Husking Corn*, 1940–41. Oil and tempera on canvas; 5⁵⁄₁₂ × 11⅚ ft. (1.7 × 3.6 m). Dexter, Missouri, Post Office.

NOTES

1. For an account of the administration of the section, see Richard D. McKinzie, "The Art of Bureaucracy," in *The New Deal for Artists* (Princeton University Press, 1973), pp. 53–73.

2. The primary sources documenting Jones's involvement in this project are the records of the section in the National Archives. For the events and correspondence related to Jones's section projects, see Record Group 121, case files concerning embellishment of federal buildings, 1934–43; records of the Section of Fine Arts, Public Buildings Administration; Entry 133, Box 3 (Magnolia, Ark., file), Box 24 (Seneca, Kans., file), Box 32 (Anthony, Kans., file), Box 56 (Charleston and Dexter, Mo., files); National Archives, College Park, Md.

For Rowan's earliest correspondence regarding Jones and his work, see Louis LaBeaume to Edward B. Rowan, Mar. 30, 1934, Public Works of Art Project selected administrative and business records, 1933–34, Archives of American Art, Smithsonian Institution; and the 1935 correspondence between Jones, Green, and Rowan, Dr. John Green Collection, Missouri History Museum, St. Louis.

3. Joe Jones to Meyric Rogers, [Sept.] 21, 1937, Saint Louis Art Museum, archives. Rowan to Jones, Oct. 15, 1937, Record Group 121 (note 2), Box 3.The subject of wheat was considered at the time Jones was invited to submit, perhaps at the suggestion of Rowan, since the artist's first letter to him about the Magnolia mural questions the appropriateness of wheat for a region that produced so little of it; Jones to Rowan, July 30, 1937, ibid.

4. Jones to Rowan, Dec. 2, 1937; Jones to Forbes Watson, c. 1938, both ibid.

5. Jones to Rowan, received Oct. 4, 1938, Record Group 121 (note 2), Box 56.

6. Jones to Forbes Watson, Aug. 17, 1939, Record Group 121 (note 2), Box 32.

7. Karal Ann Marling, *Wall-to-Wall America: A Cultural History of Post-Office Murals in the Great Depression* (University of Minnesota Press, 1982), p. 81.

8. The jury that selected Jones's design comprised Olin Dows, Edgar Miller, Henry Varnum Poor, and Maurice Sterne. See Rowan to Jones, Oct. 16, 1939, Record Group 121 (note 2), Box 24.

9. Rowan to Jones, Dec. 20, 1939, ibid.

10. Rowan to Jones, Dec. 11, 1939, ibid.

11. Jones to Rowan, Feb. 6, 1941, Record Group 121 (note 2), Box 24.

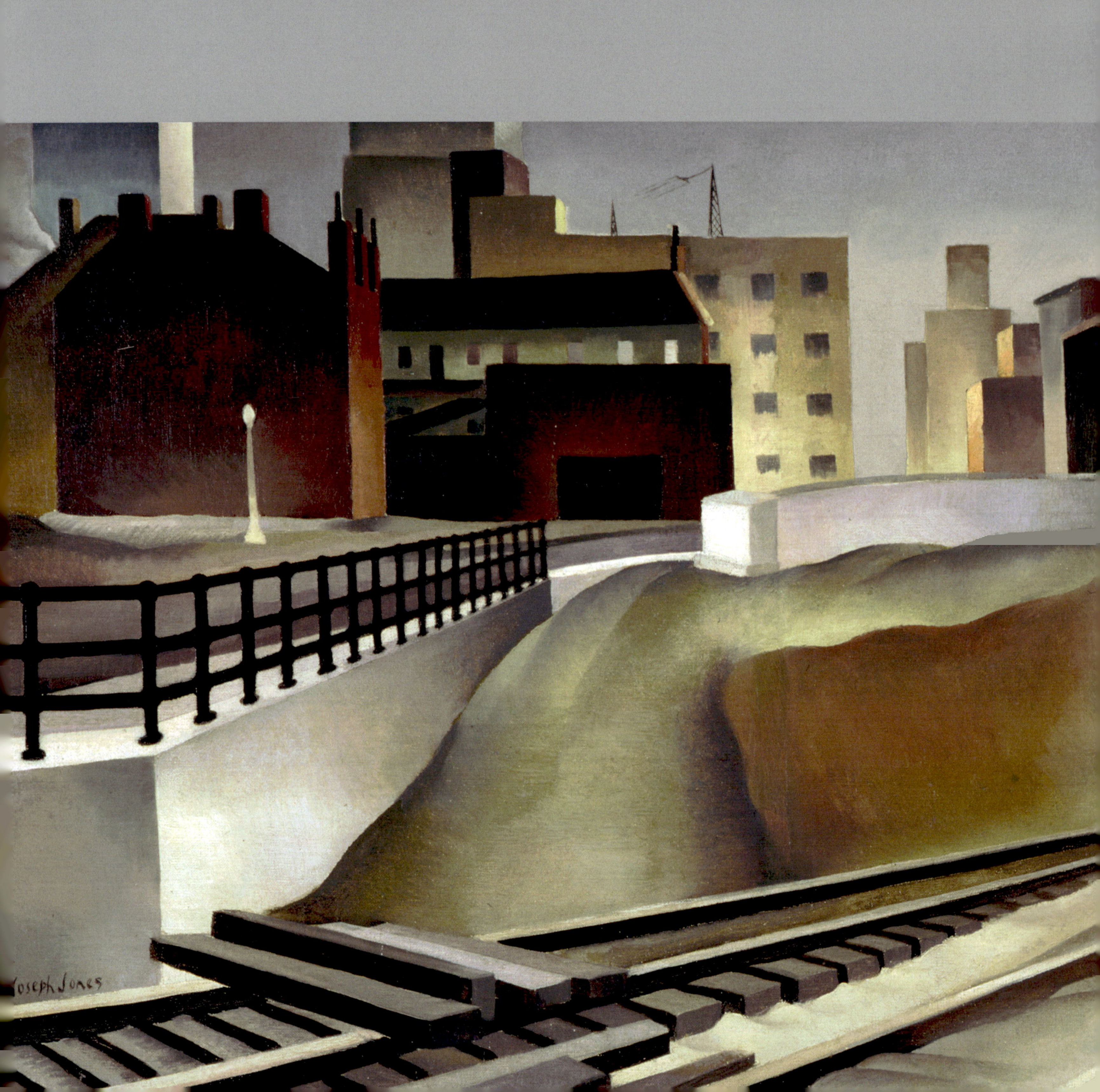
Joseph Jones

Plates

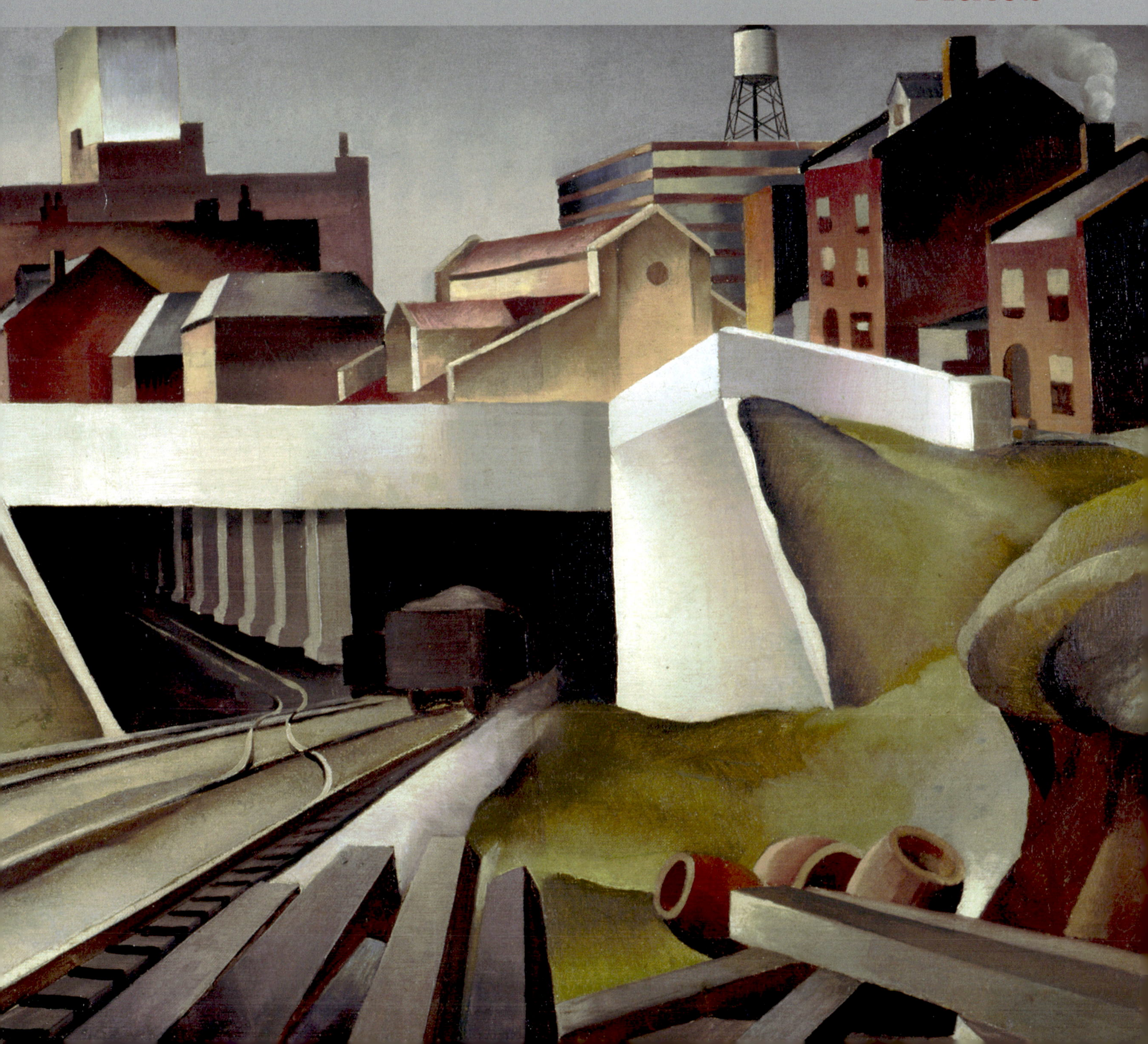

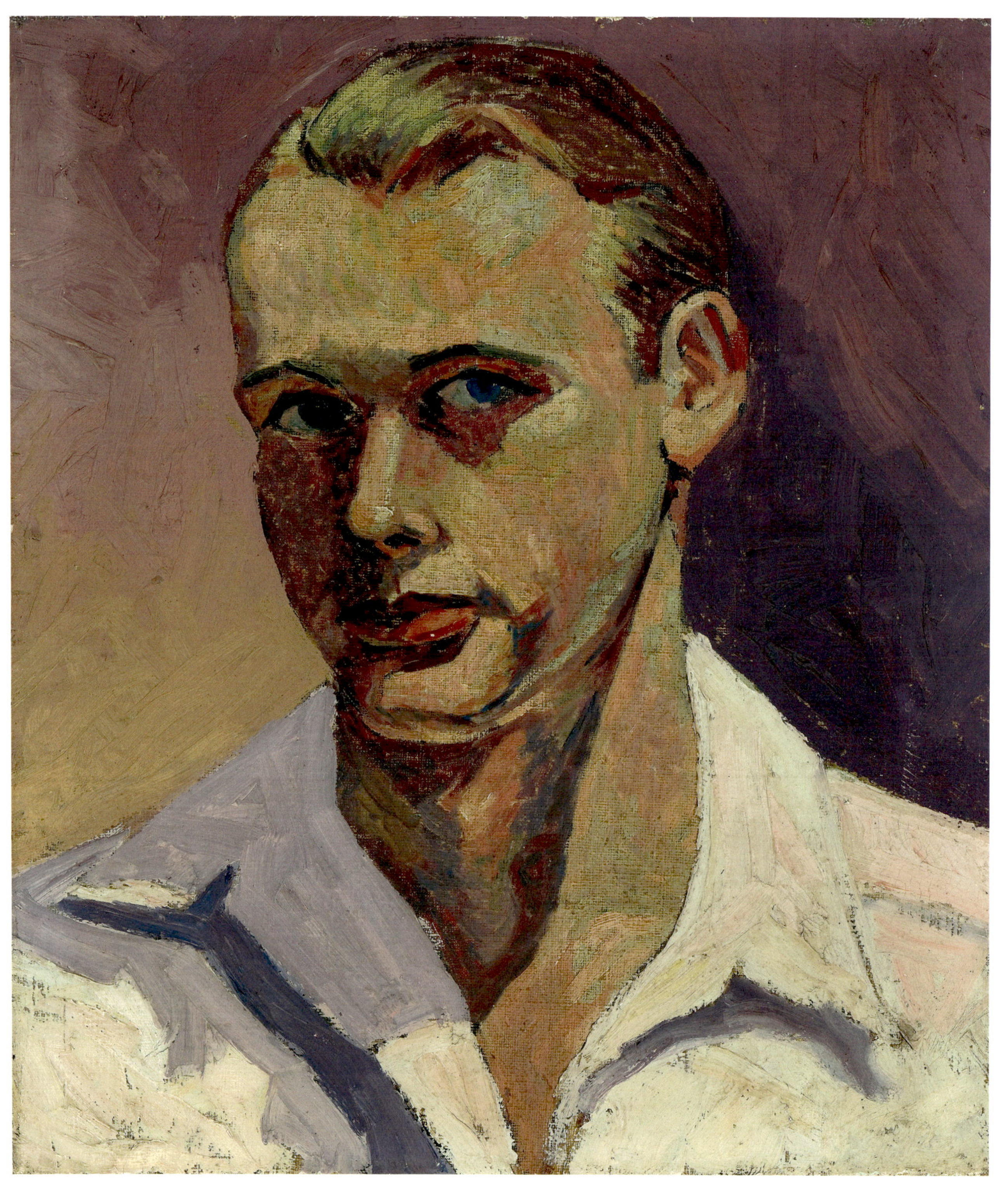

1 *Self-Portrait of the Artist at Age Nineteen* c. 1928/29
Oil on canvas; $18\frac{1}{8} \times 16\frac{1}{8}$ in. (46 × 41 cm)
Collection of Shirley A. Jones

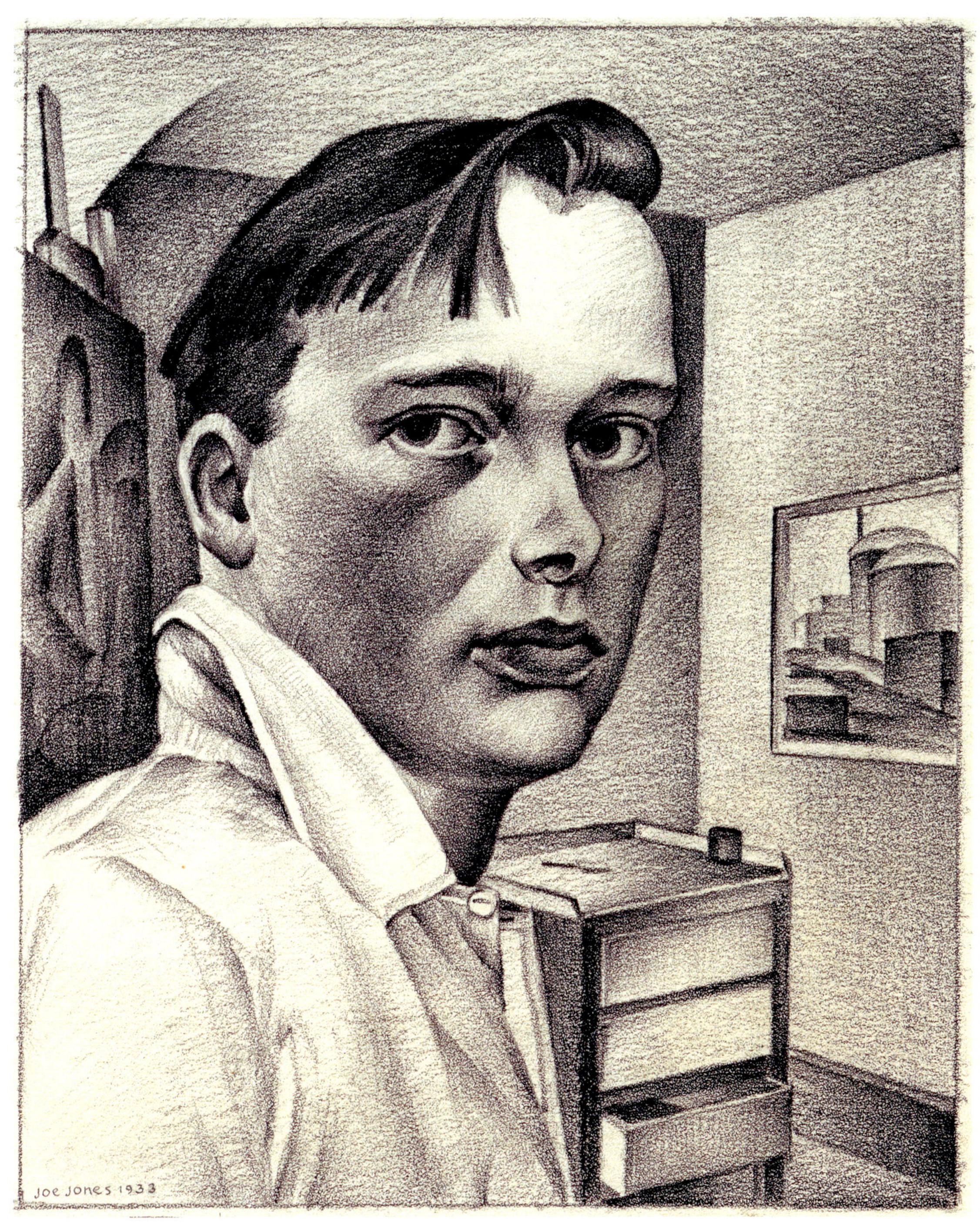

2 *Self-Portrait* 1933
Pencil on paper; 15 × 12⅞ in. (38.1 × 32.7 cm)
The Wolfsonian–Florida International University, Miami Beach, Florida,
The Mitchell Wolfson, Jr., Collection

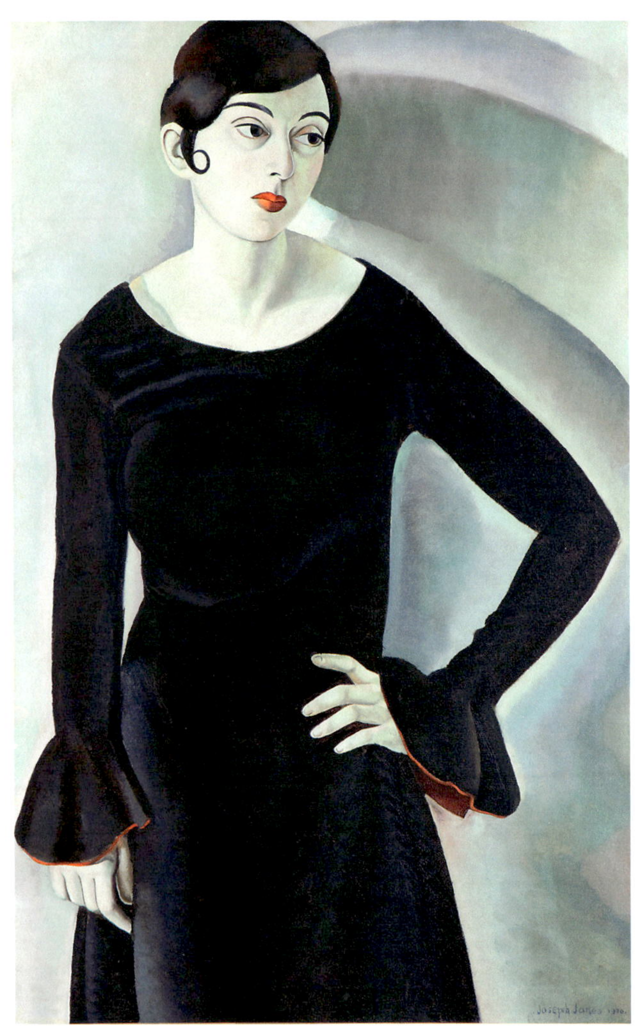

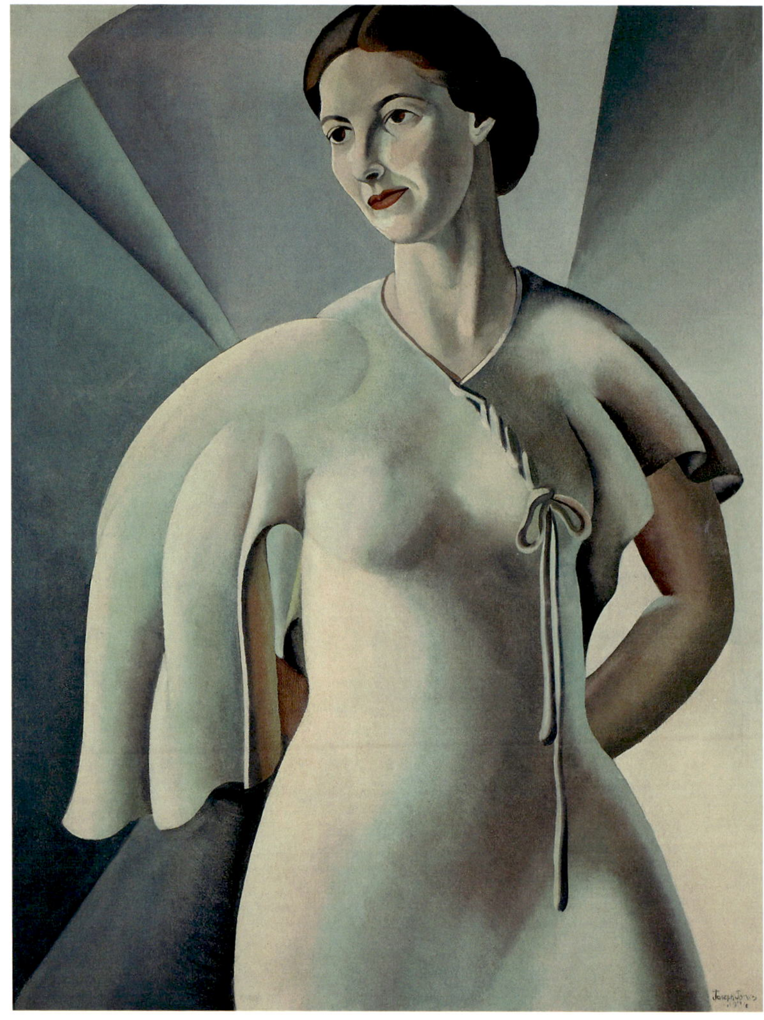

3 *Bessie* 1930
Oil on canvas; 44 × 28 in. (111.8 × 71.1 cm)
Collection of Richard and Eileen Epstein

4 *Grace* 1931
Oil on canvas; 44 × 34 in. (111.8 × 86.4 cm)
Private collection

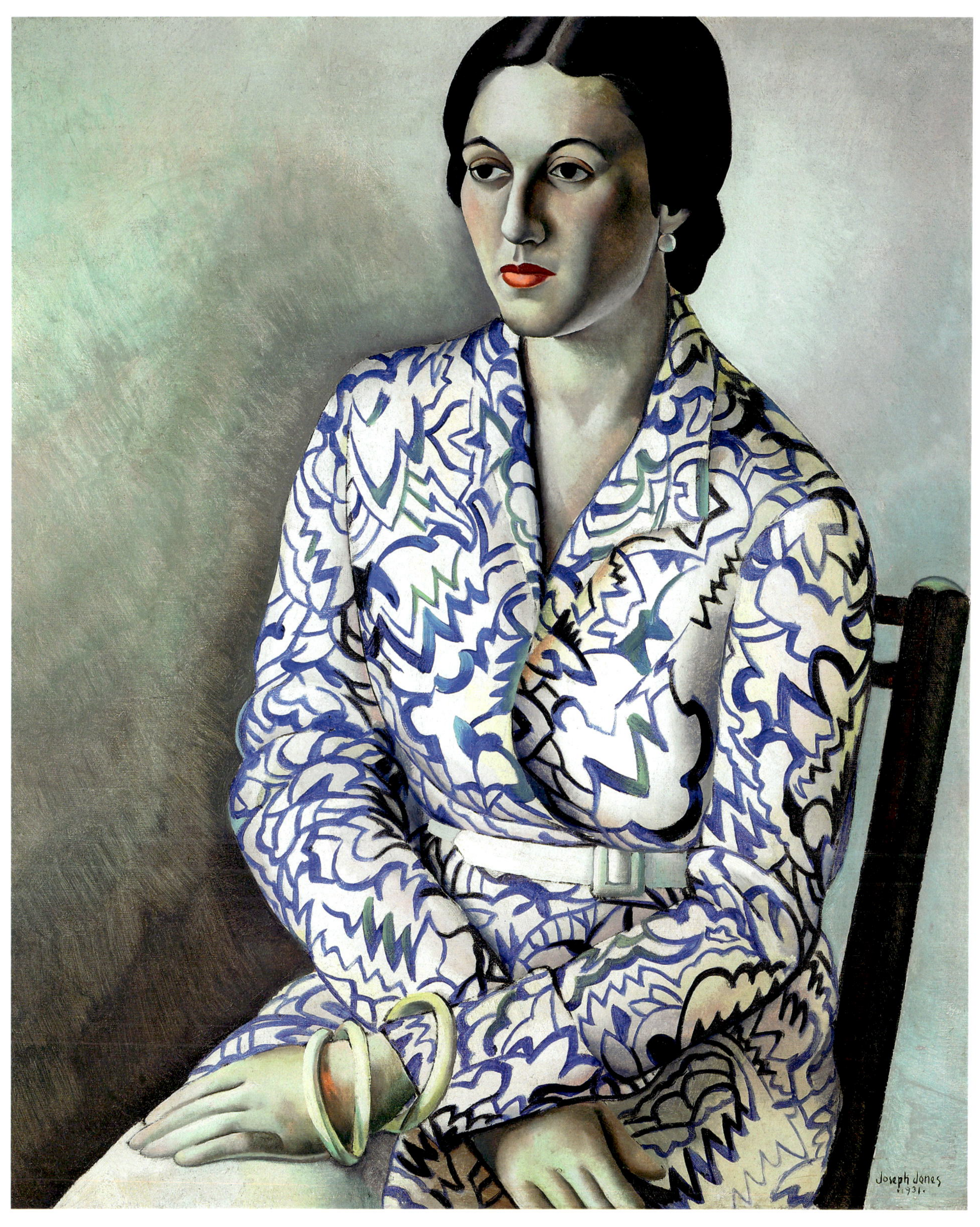

5 *Mrs. Thomas B. Sherman* 1931
Oil on canvas; 36⅛ × 30¼ in. (91.8 × 76.8 cm)
Saint Louis Art Museum, Gift of William C. Sherman
in memory of his parents, Mr. and Mrs. Thomas B. Sherman

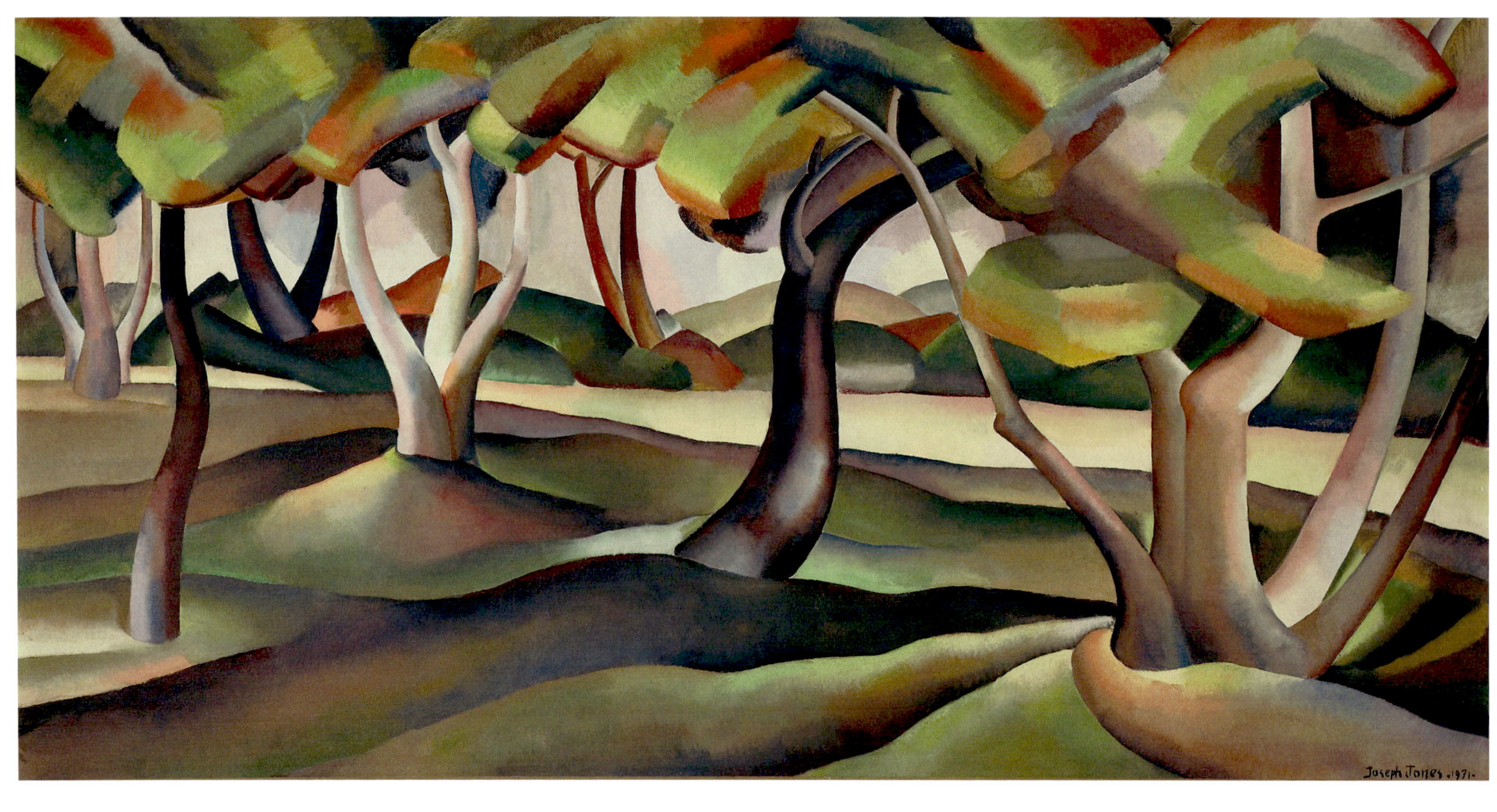

6 *Wooded Landscape* 1931
Oil on canvas; 37¼ × 72¼ in. (94.6 × 183.5 cm)
Saint Louis Art Museum, Gift of Jean Rauh Block and
Elsie Rauh Scherck in memory of Mr. and Mrs. Aaron S. Rauh

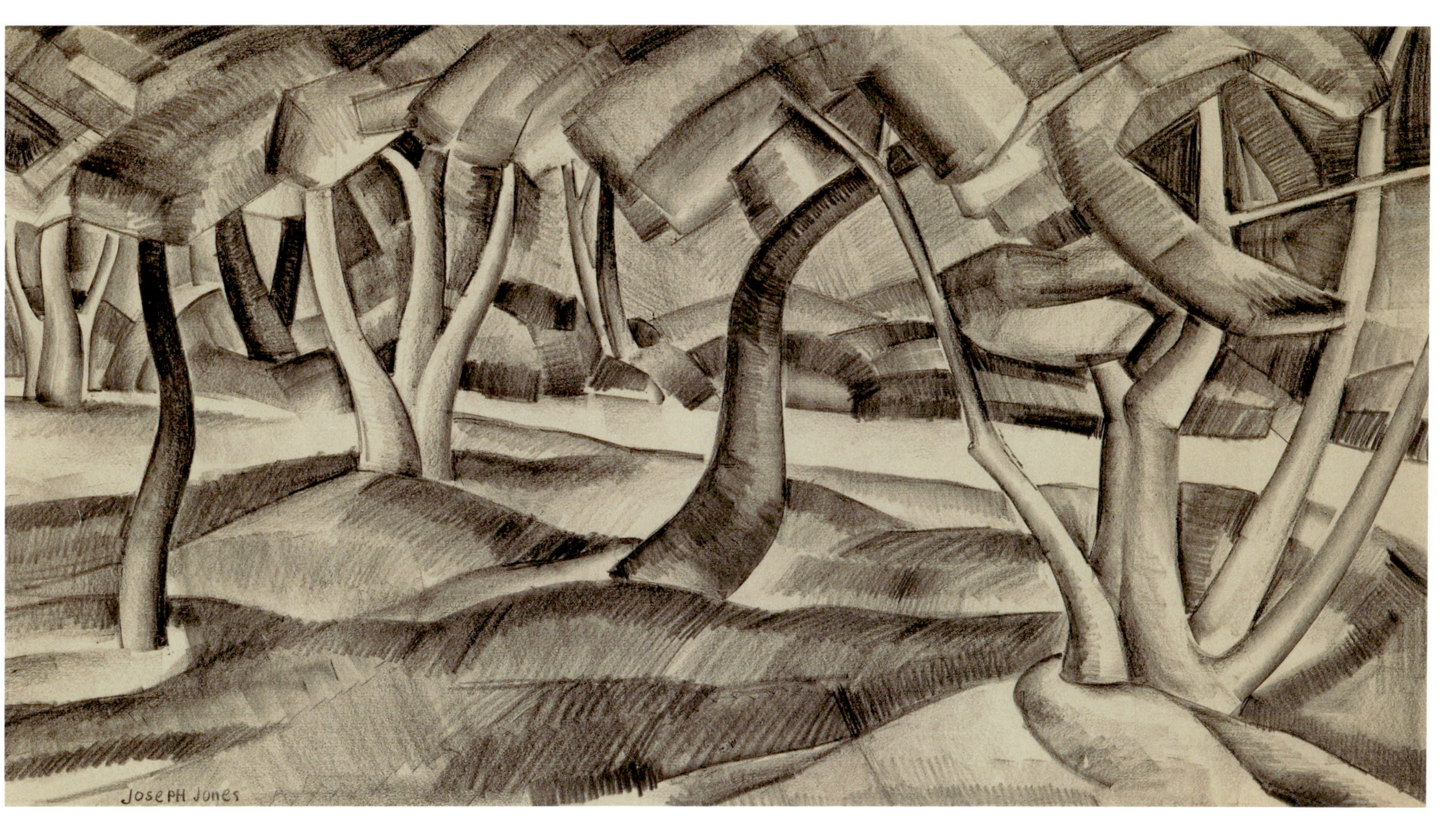

7 *Landscape* c. 1931
Crayon on thin beige wove paper, mounted on board;
20⅞ × 38⅞ in. (53 × 98.7 cm)
Mildred Lane Kemper Art Museum, Washington University in St. Louis, University Acquisition, 1981

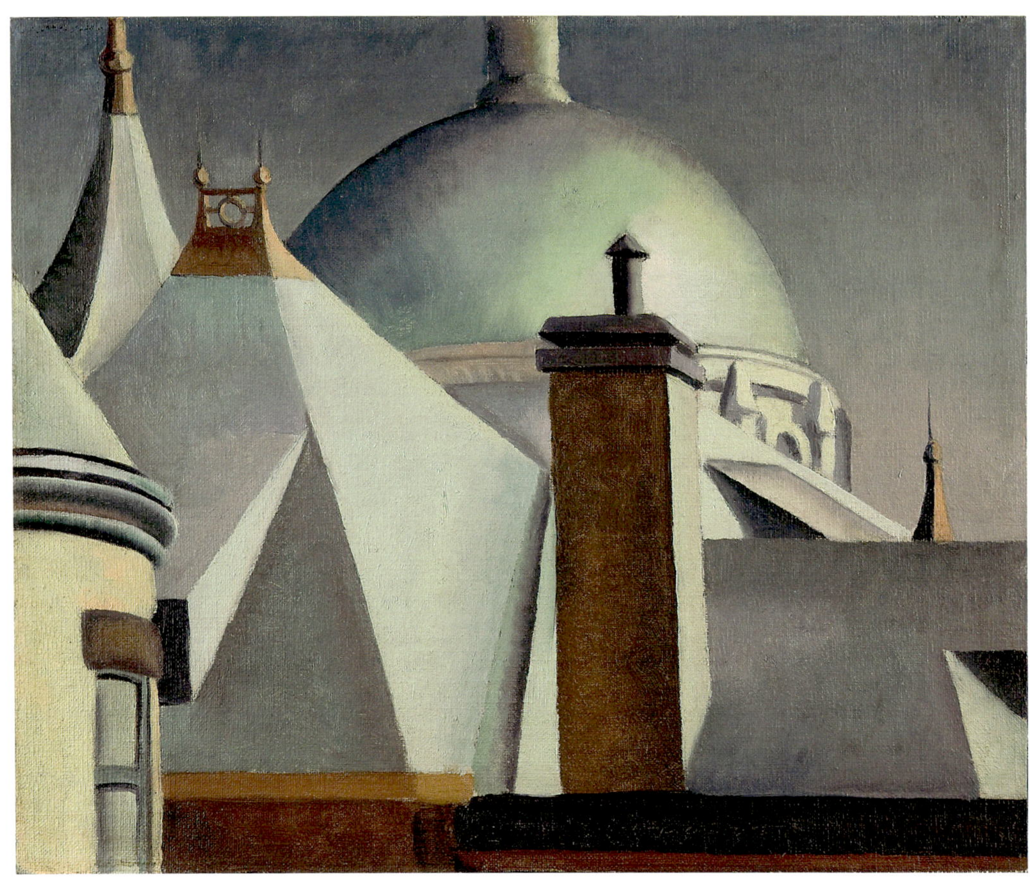

8 *Tower Tops* c. 1931
Oil on canvas, mounted on laminated paperboard; $14\frac{1}{16} \times 17$ in. (35.7×43.2 cm)
Courtesy of the Missouri History Museum, St. Louis

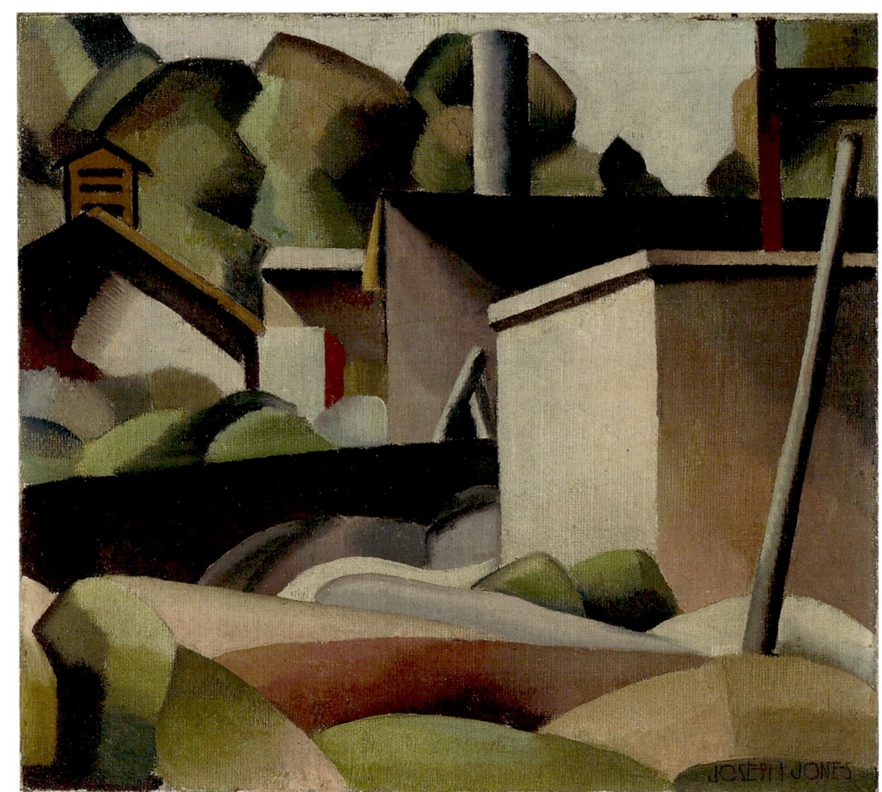

9 *Coal Sheds* c. 1931
Oil on canvas; $16\frac{3}{16} \times 18\frac{1}{4}$ in. (41.1×46.4 cm)
Collection of George and Dolores Friesen

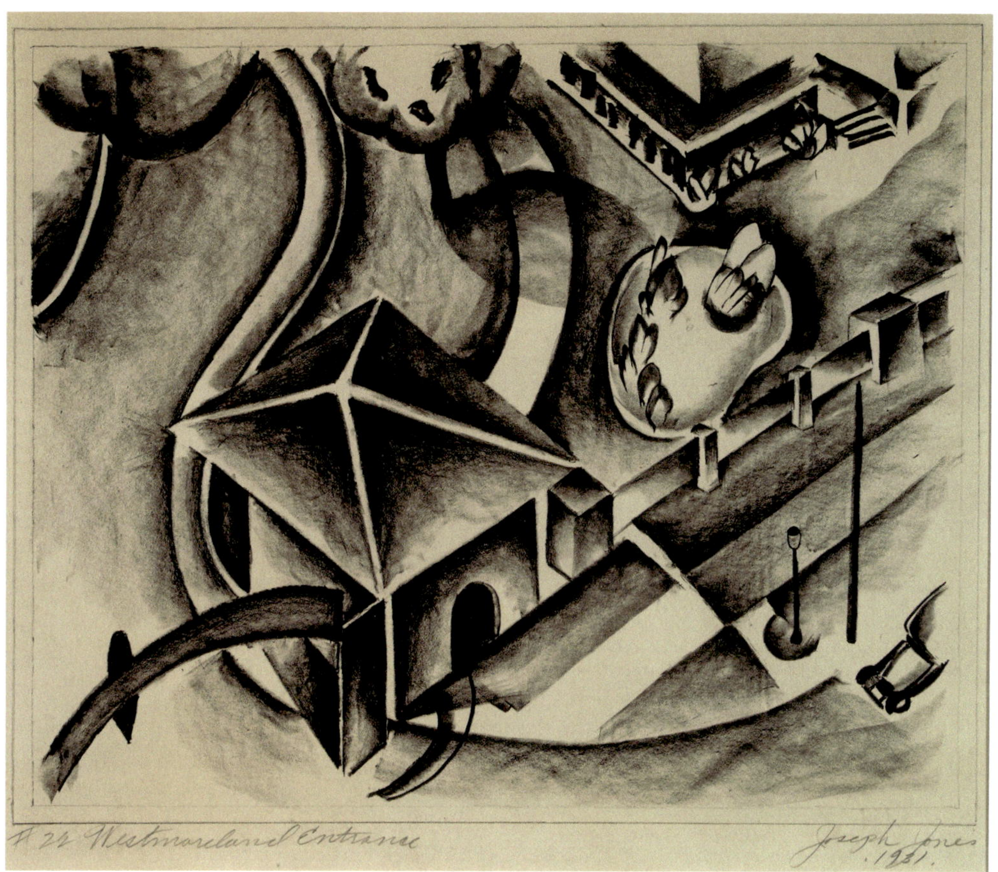

10 *Westmoreland Entrance* 1931
Lithograph; image: 13 × 15 in.
(33 × 38.1 cm)
Collection High Museum of Art, Atlanta,
Gift of Michael and Lisa Shapiro

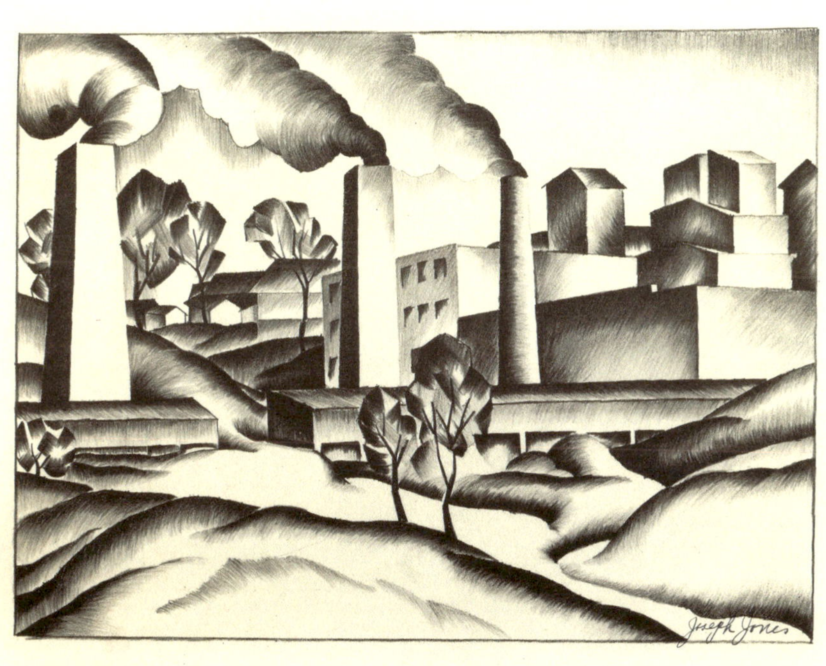

11 *Laclede Christy Clay Co.* c. 1931
Lithograph on beige wove paper;
image: 9 × 12⅛ in. (22.9 × 30.8 cm),
sheet: 12½ × 15¾ in. (31.8 × 40 cm)
Saint Louis Art Museum, Bequest of
Horace M. Swope

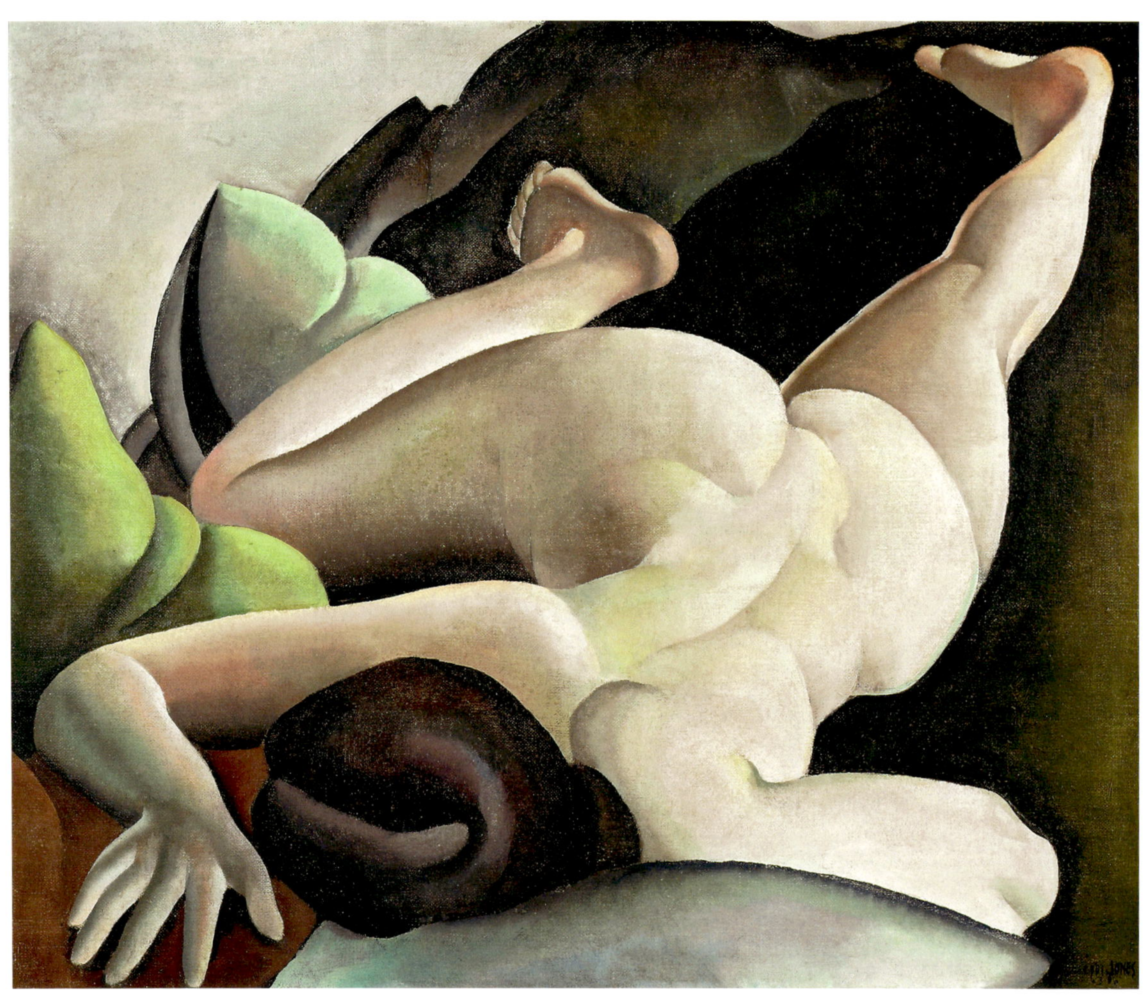

12 *Nude Reclining* 1931
Oil on canvas; 25 × 30 in.
(63.5 × 76.2 cm)
Collection of Jeanne and
Rex Sinquefield

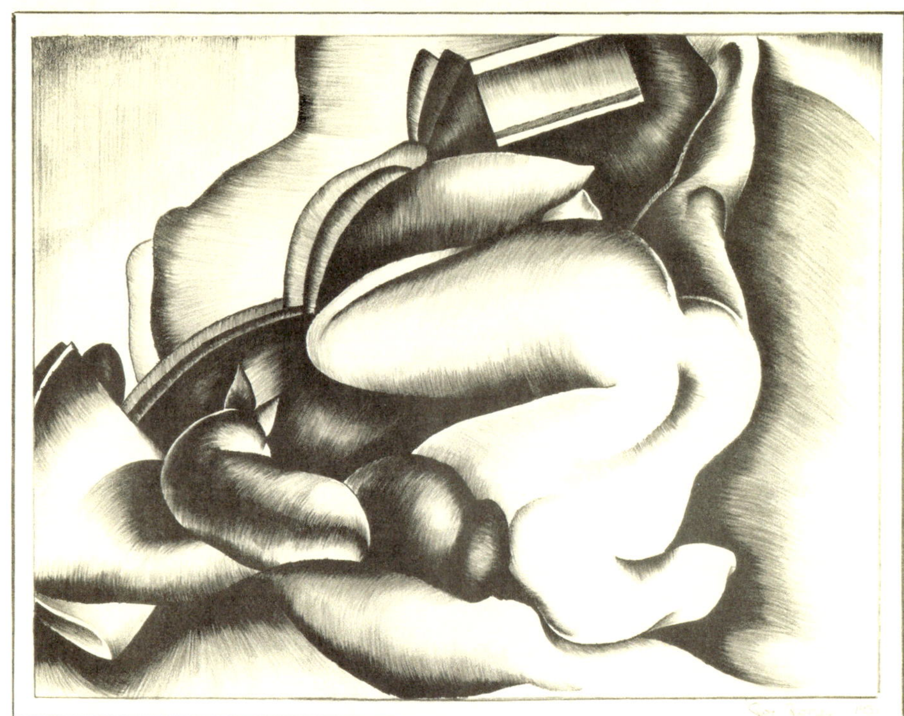

13 *Nude* 1931
Lithograph on off-white wove paper;
image: 11¾ × 15⅛ in. (29.8 × 38.4 cm),
sheet: 13⅞ × 18 in. (35.2 × 45.7 cm)
Collection of James and Virginia Moffett

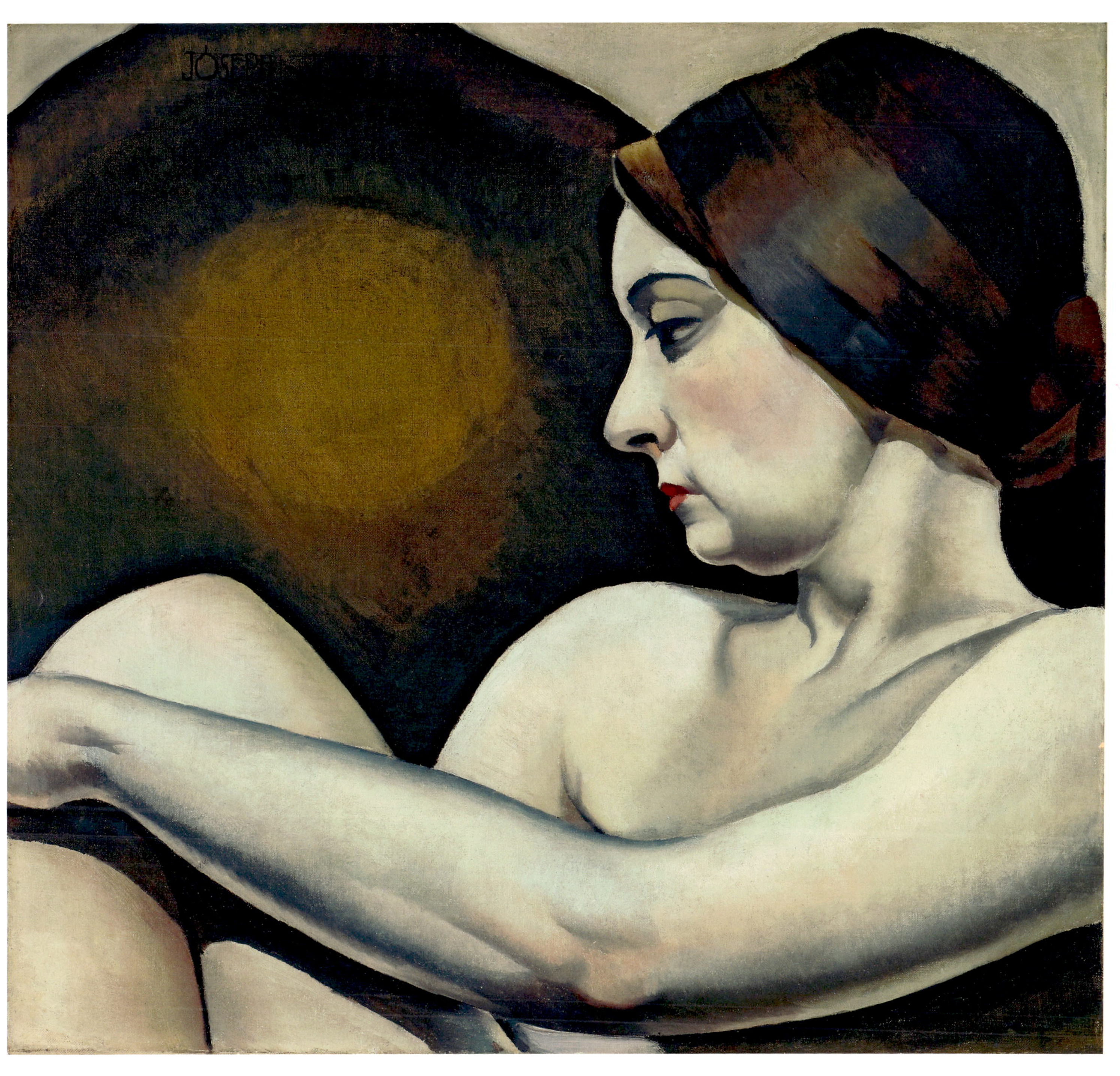

14 *Freda* 1931
Oil on canvas; 20 × 22 in. (50.8 × 55.9 cm)
Collection of James and Virginia Moffett

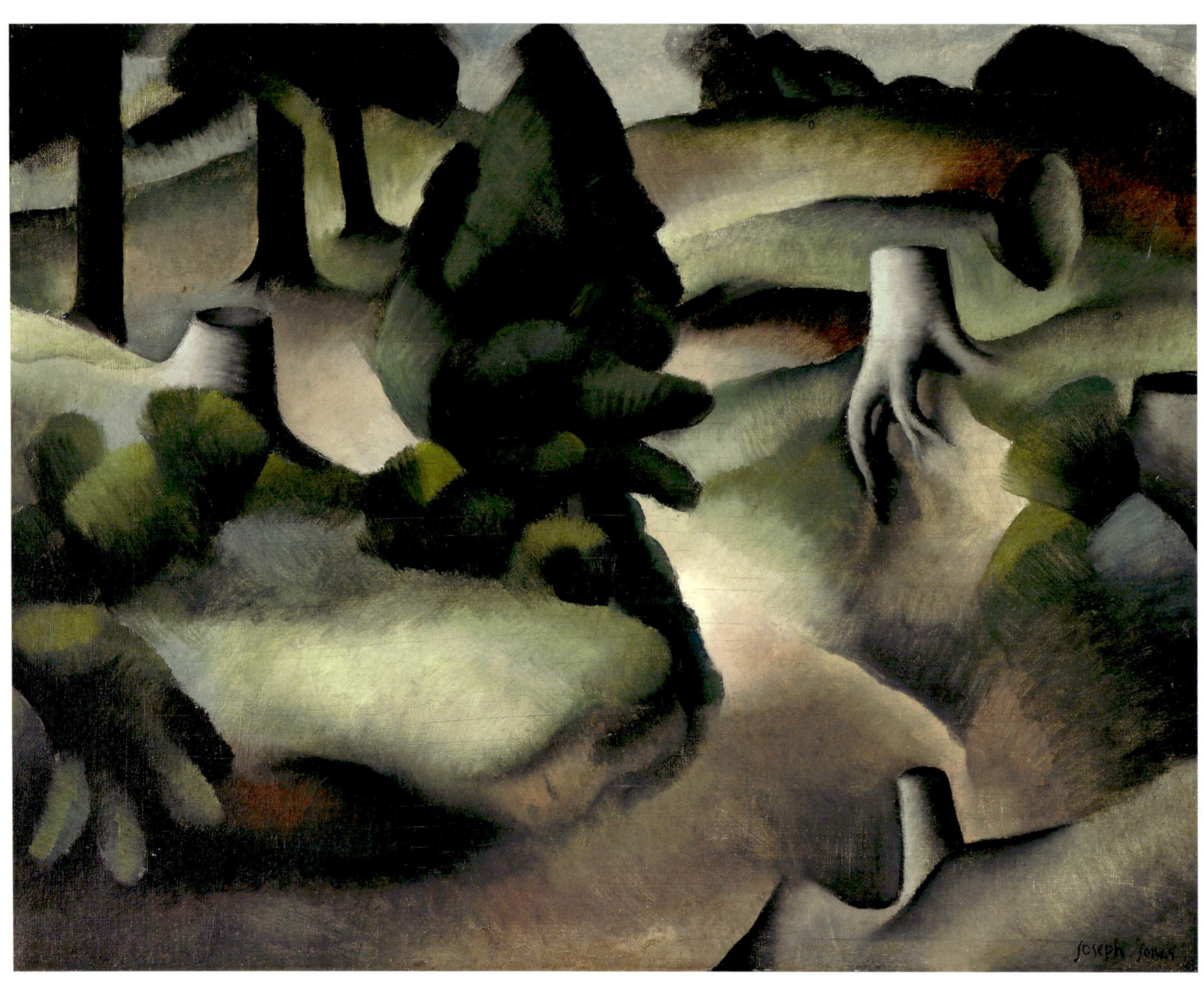

15 *Landscape* c. 1931
Oil on canvas; 20 × 26 in. (50.8 × 66 cm)
Collection of John and Susan Horseman

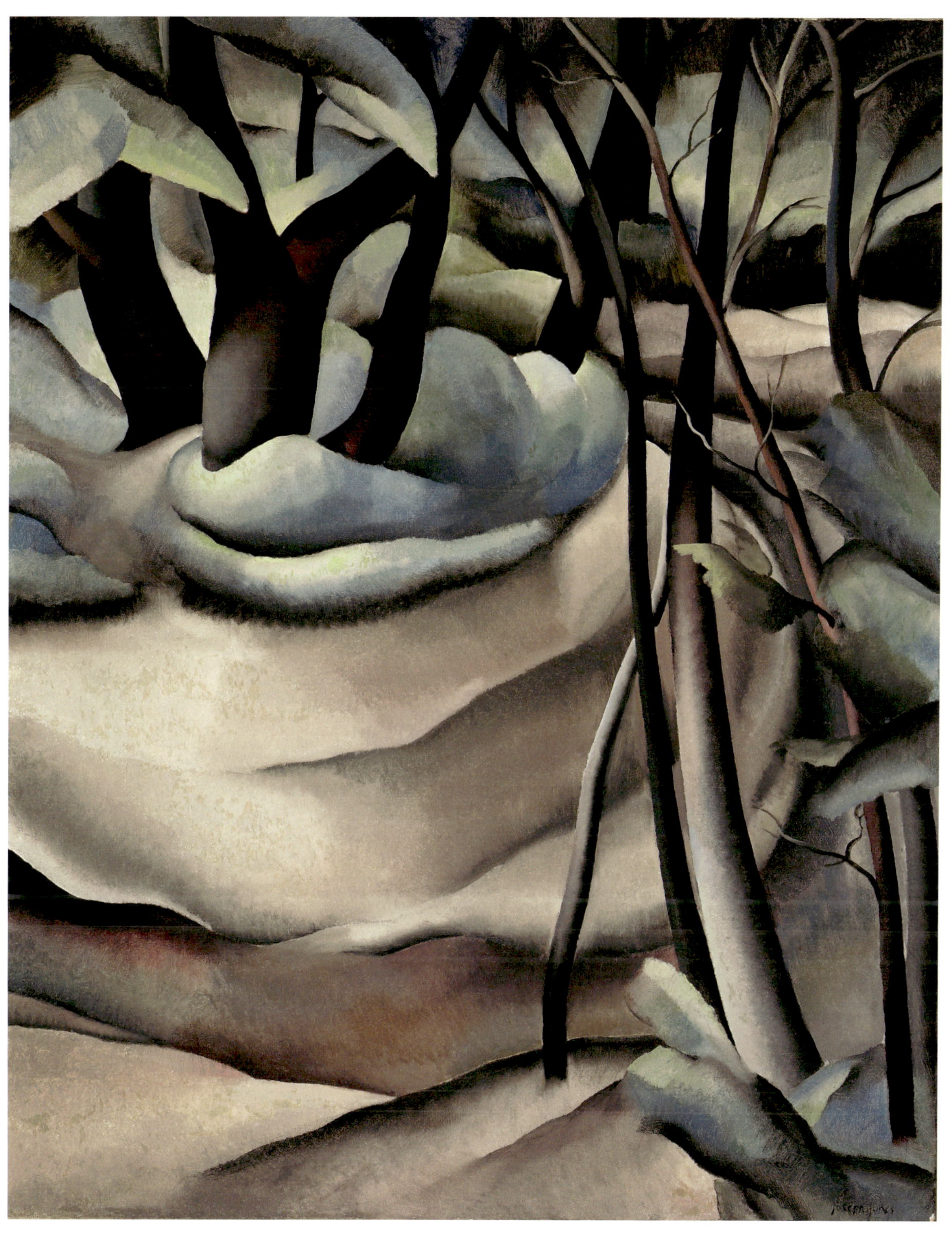

16 *Landscape* 1932
Oil on canvas; 40 × 32⅛ in. (101.6 × 81.6 cm)
Mildred Lane Kemper Art Museum, Washington University in St. Louis,
Gift of the Estate of Mrs. Ernest W. Stix, 1970

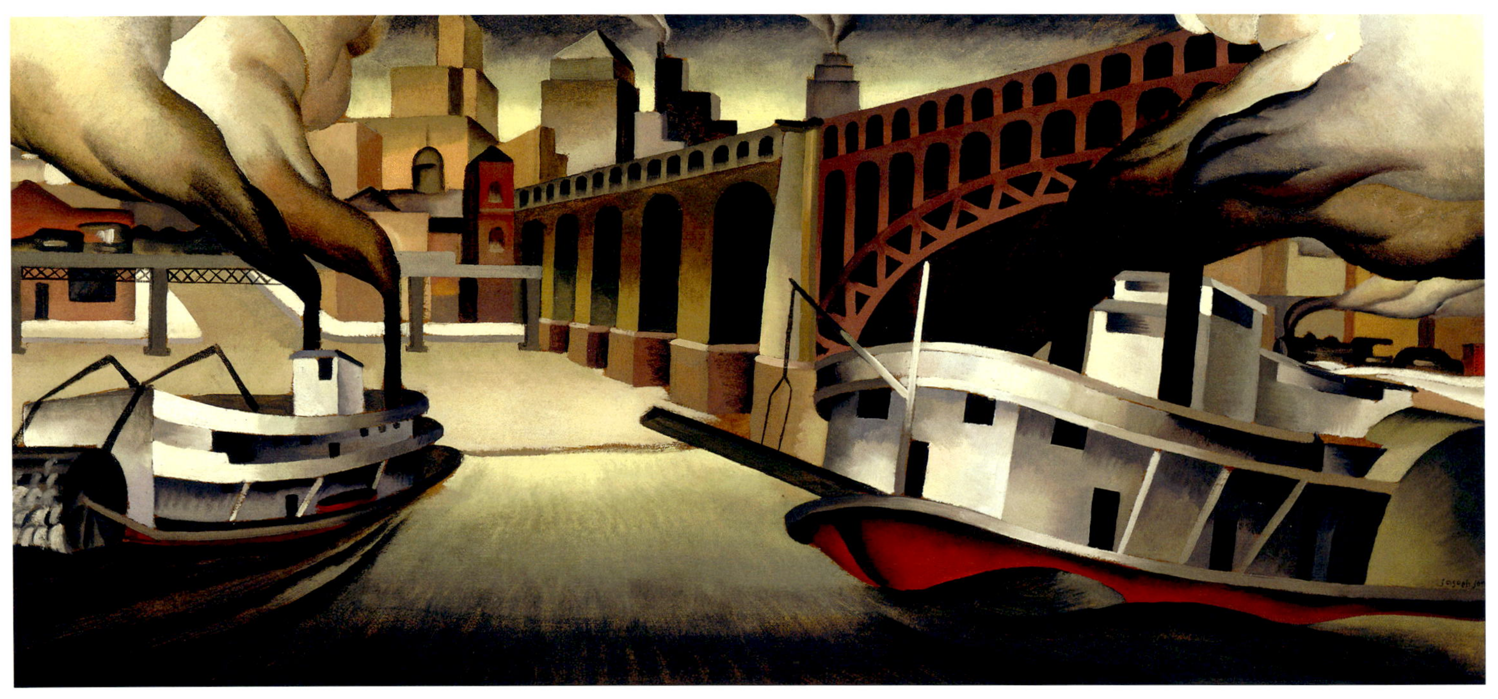

17 *St. Louis Riverfront* c. 1932
Oil on paperboard; 23 × 48 in. (58.4 × 121.9 cm)
Collection of Renée and Lloyd Greif

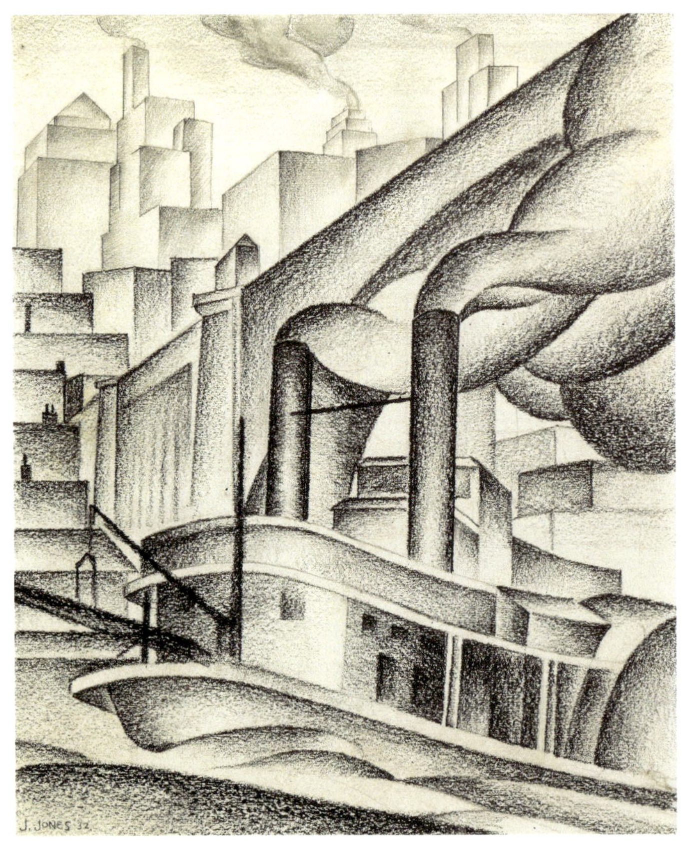

18 *St. Louis Riverfront* 1932
Pencil on cream paper; 8½ × 7 in.
(21.6 × 17.8 cm)
St. Louis Mercantile Library at the University of Missouri–St. Louis, Gift of Ruth Ferris

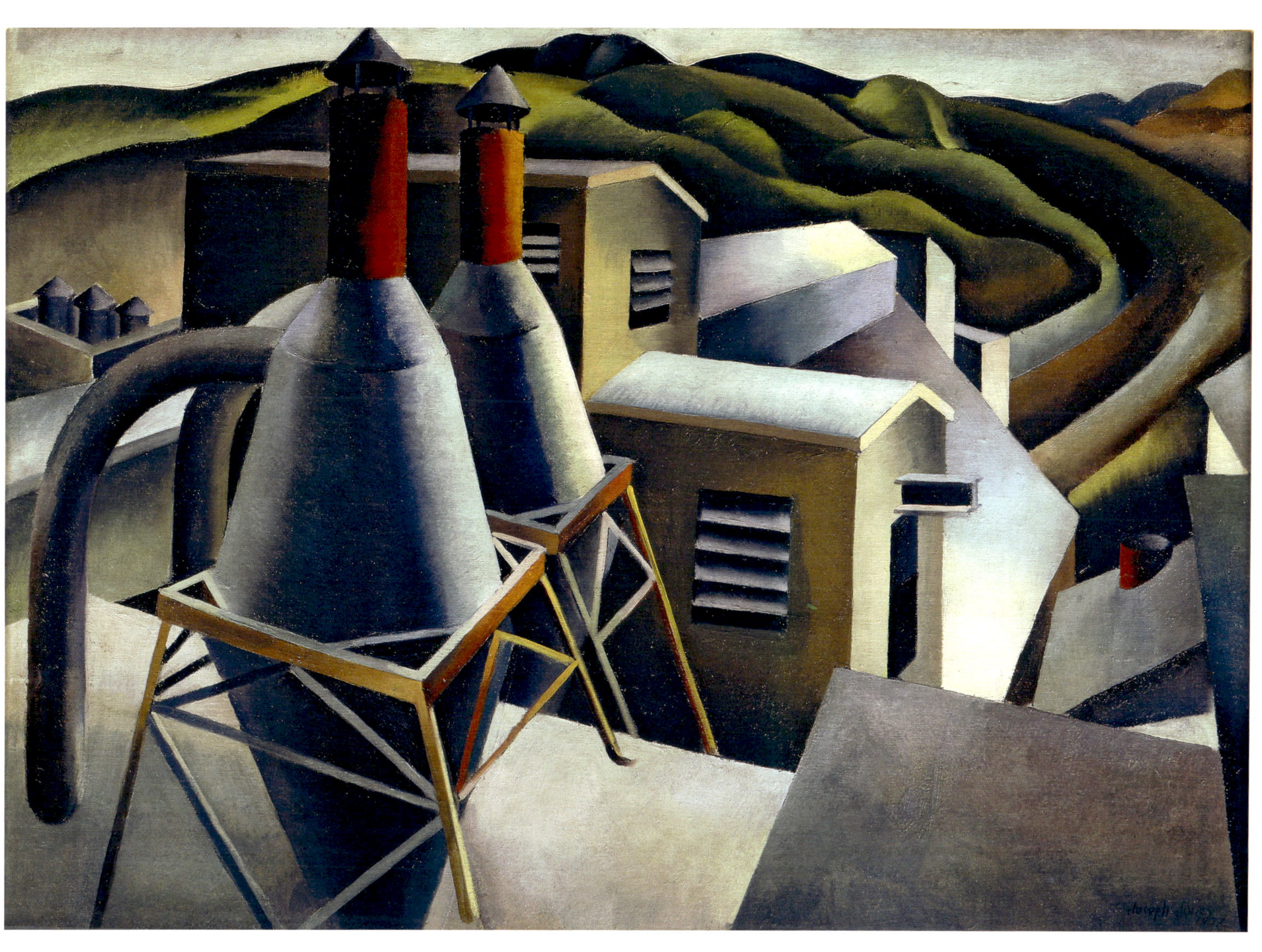

19 *Industrial Landscape* 1932
Oil on canvas; 20 × 28 in. (50.8 × 71.1 cm)
Collection of Michael Lawlor

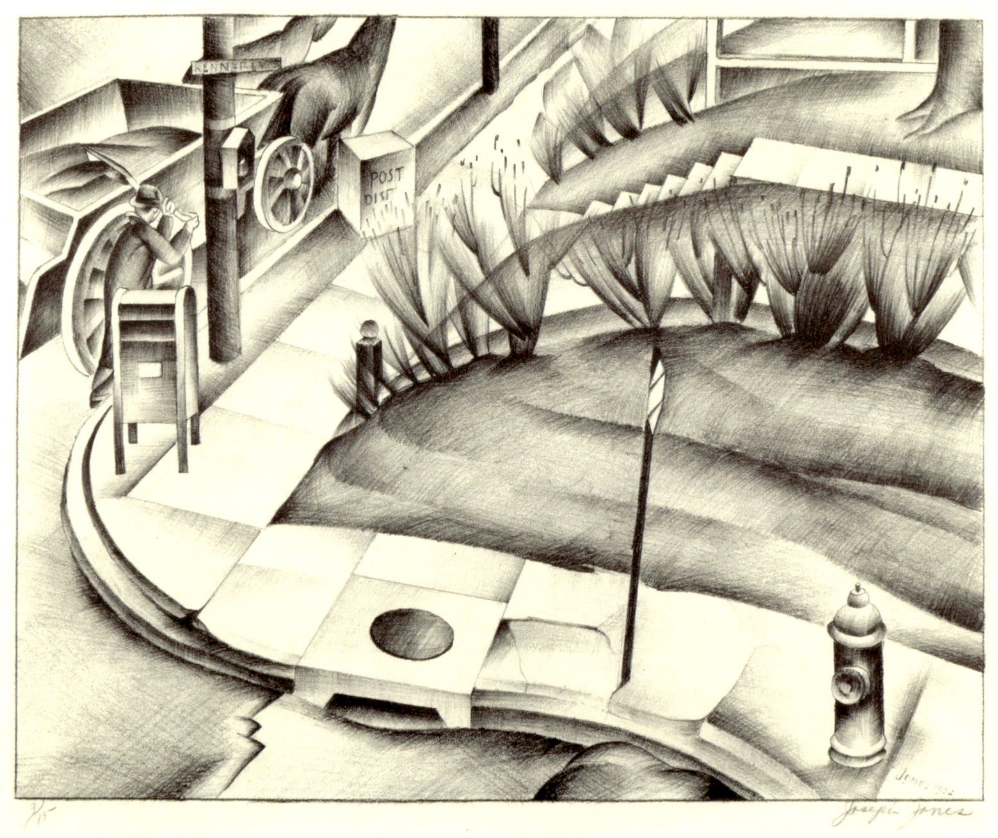

20 *Kennerly and Marcus* 1932
Lithograph on Oriole Linen Bond paper; image: $11\frac{7}{16} \times 14\frac{9}{16}$ in. (29.1×37 cm), sheet: $16\frac{1}{4} \times 21\frac{1}{4}$ in. (41.3×54 cm)
Collection of Keith and Bobbie Wedge

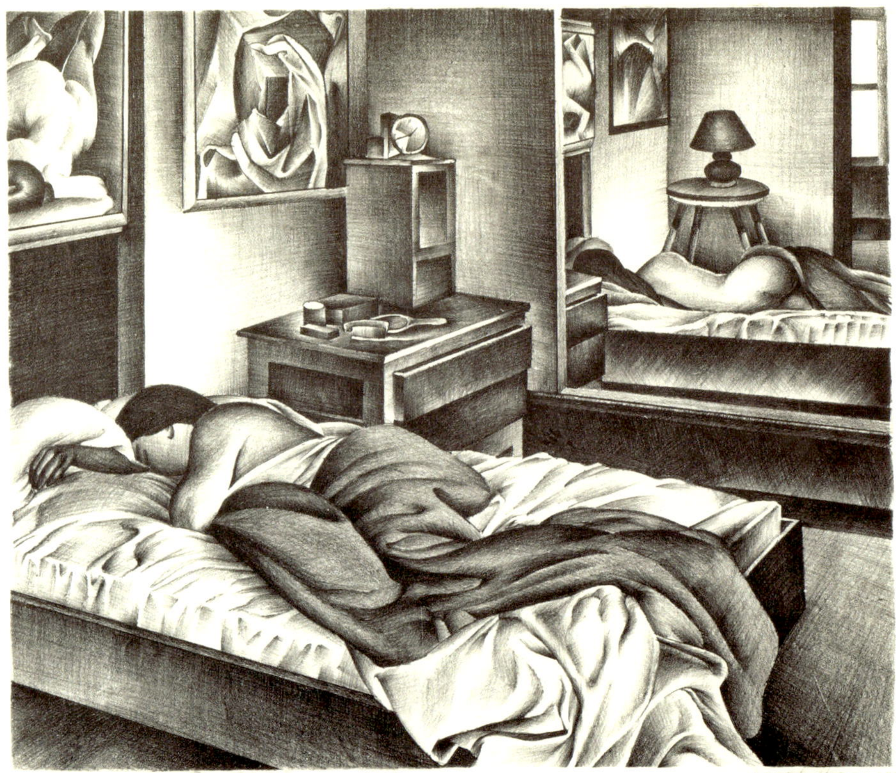

21 *Studio Interior* 1932
Lithograph on Oriole Linen Bond paper; image: $10\frac{3}{4} \times 12\frac{7}{8}$ in. (27.3×32.7 cm), sheet: $20\frac{1}{8} \times 17\frac{1}{16}$ in. (51.1×43.3 cm)
John Burroughs School, St. Louis

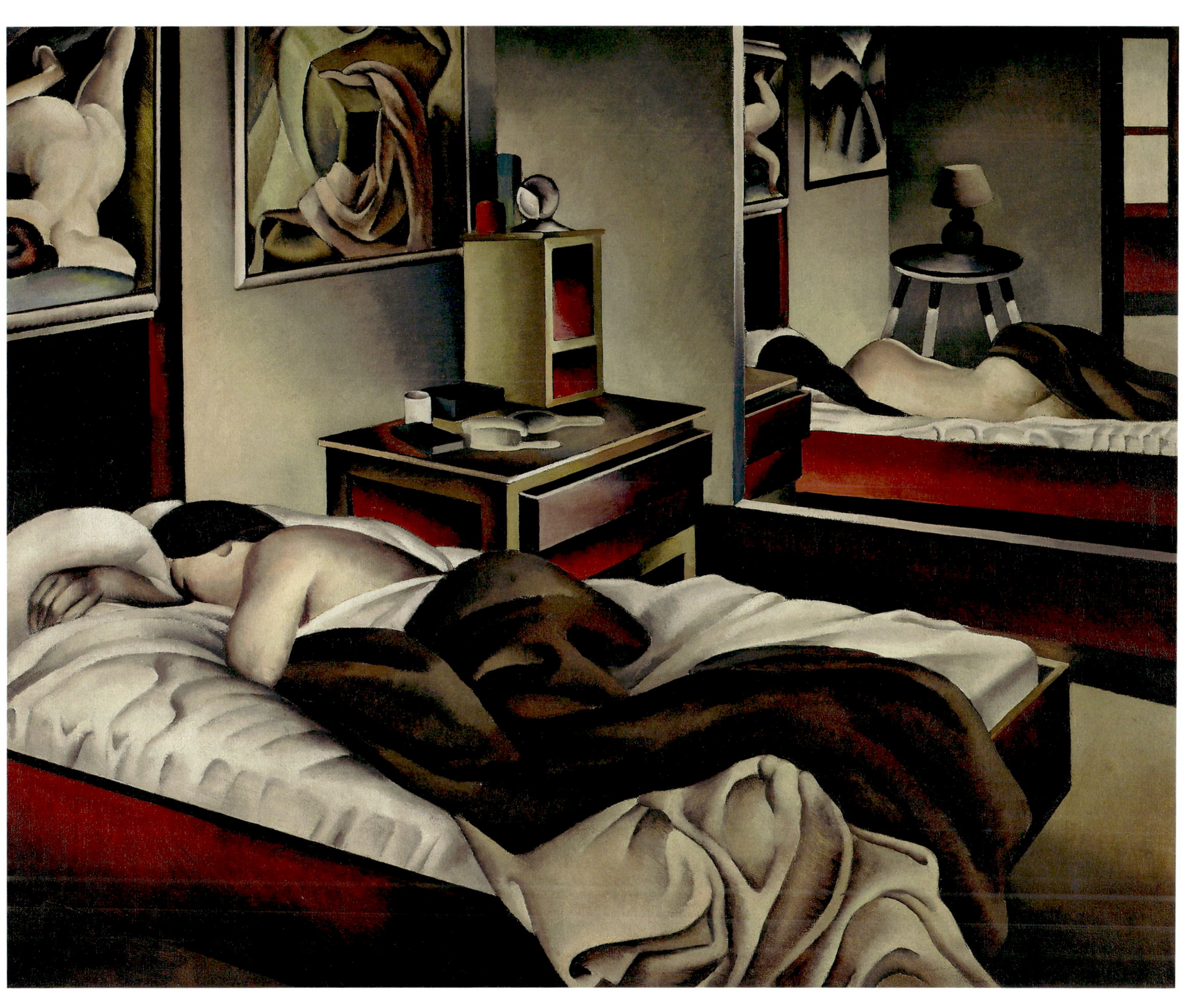

22 *Studio Interior* c. 1932
Oil on canvas; 40 × 50 in.
(101.6 × 127 cm)
Collection of Jeanne and
Rex Sinquefield

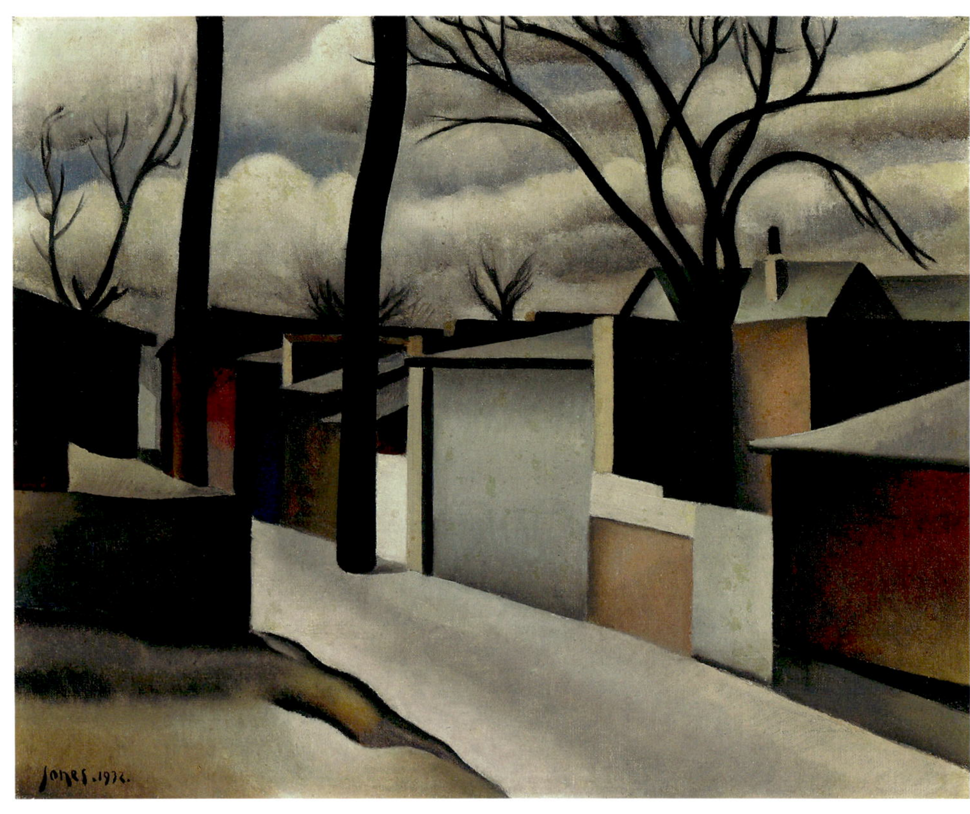

23 *Alley* 1932
Oil on canvas; $16\frac{3}{16} \times 20\frac{1}{8}$ in. (41.1×51.1 cm)
Collection of Otto L. Spaeth, Jr.

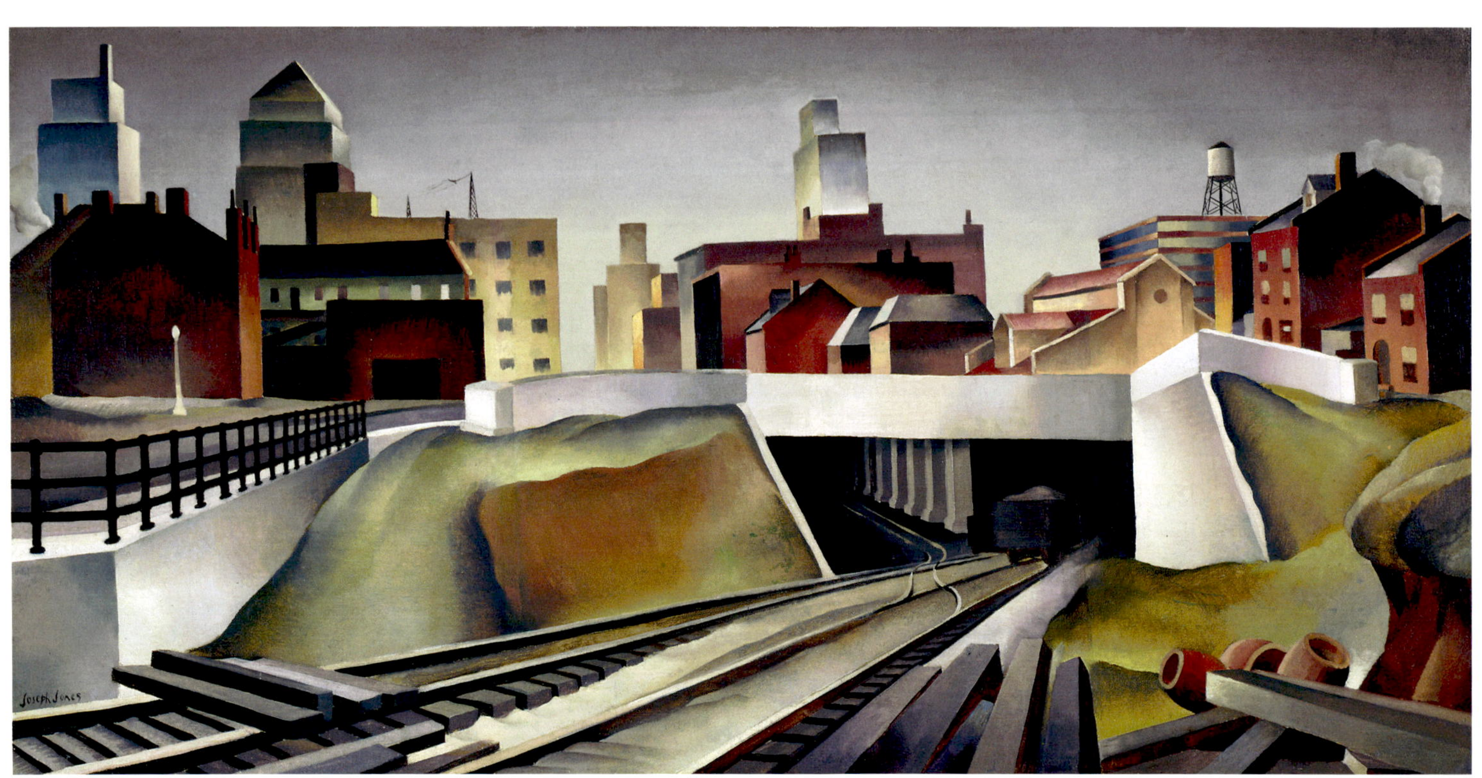

24 *View of St. Louis* c. 1932
Oil on canvas; $25\frac{1}{4} \times 50\frac{1}{2}$ in. (64.1×128.3 cm)
Saint Louis Art Museum, Gift of Mrs. Robert Elman

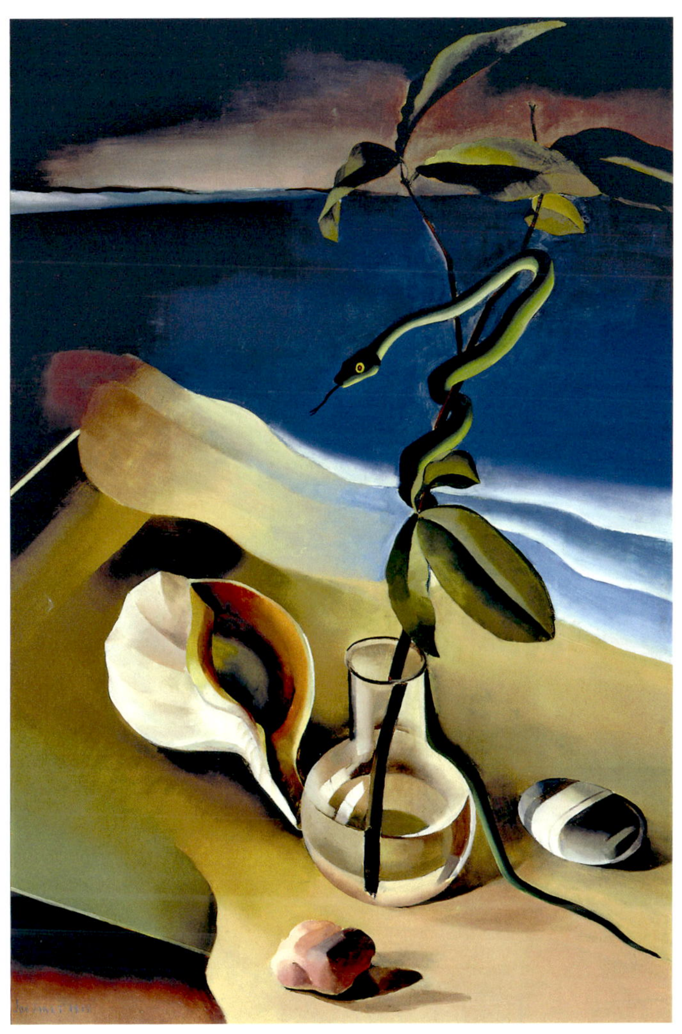

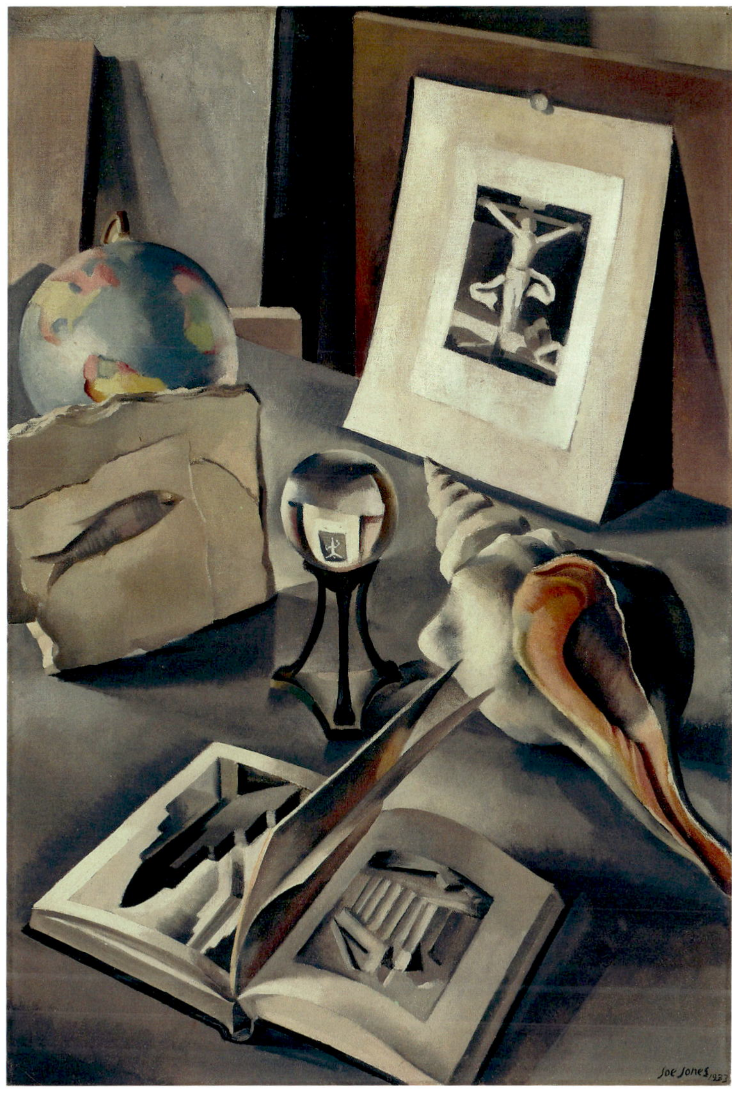

25 *The Green Snake* 1933
Oil on Masonite; 30 × 20 in. (76.2 × 50.8 cm)
Collection of Phoenix Art Museum, Gift of Richard Anderman in honor of Lorenz and Joan Anderman

26 *Still Life with Crystal* 1933
Oil on canvas; 36 1/16 × 25 in. (91.6 × 63.5 cm)
Private collection

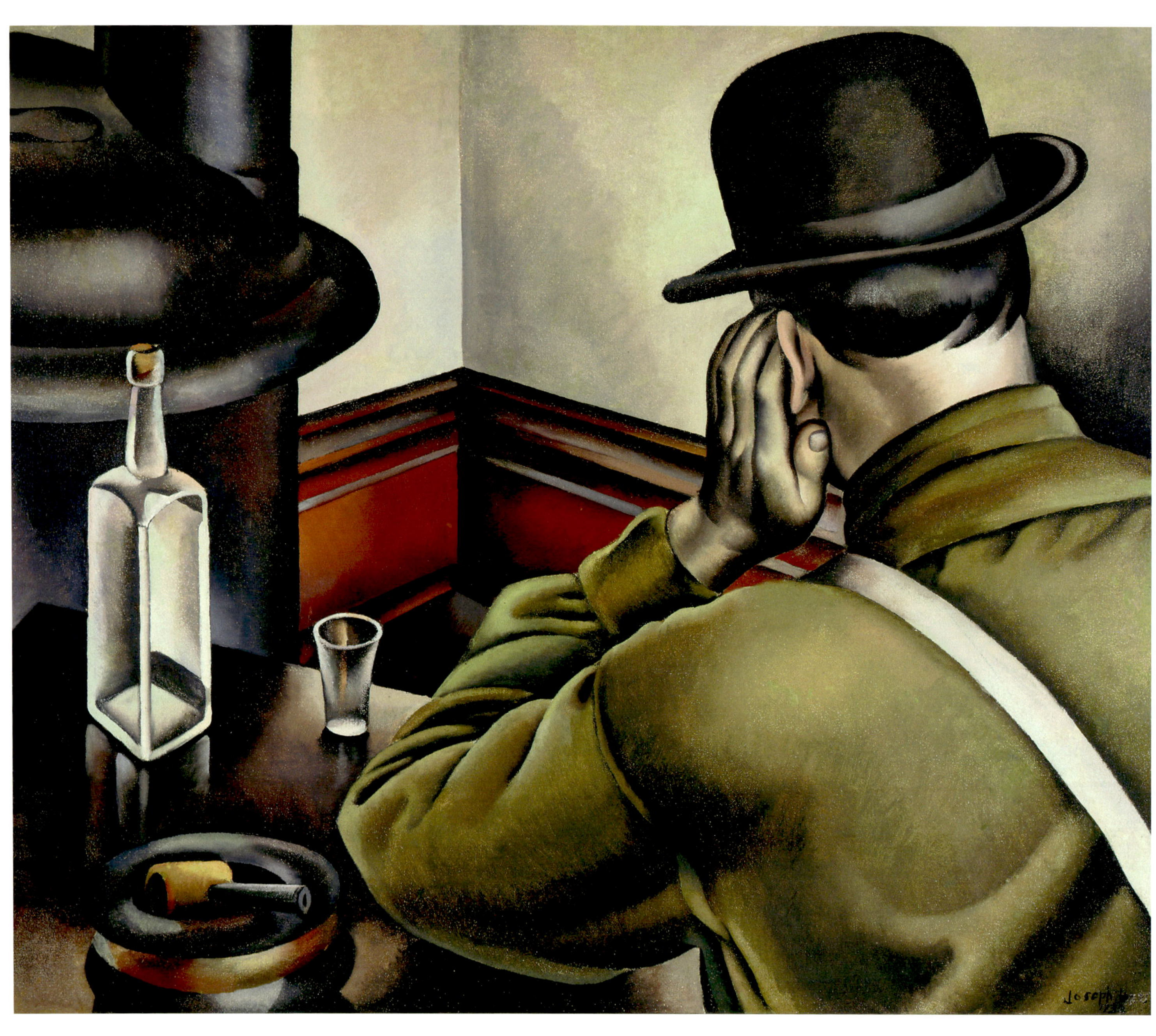

27 *My Father* c. 1932
Oil on canvas; 30 × 36 in. (76.2 × 91.4 cm)
Munson-Williams-Proctor Arts Institute, Museum of Art, Utica, New York

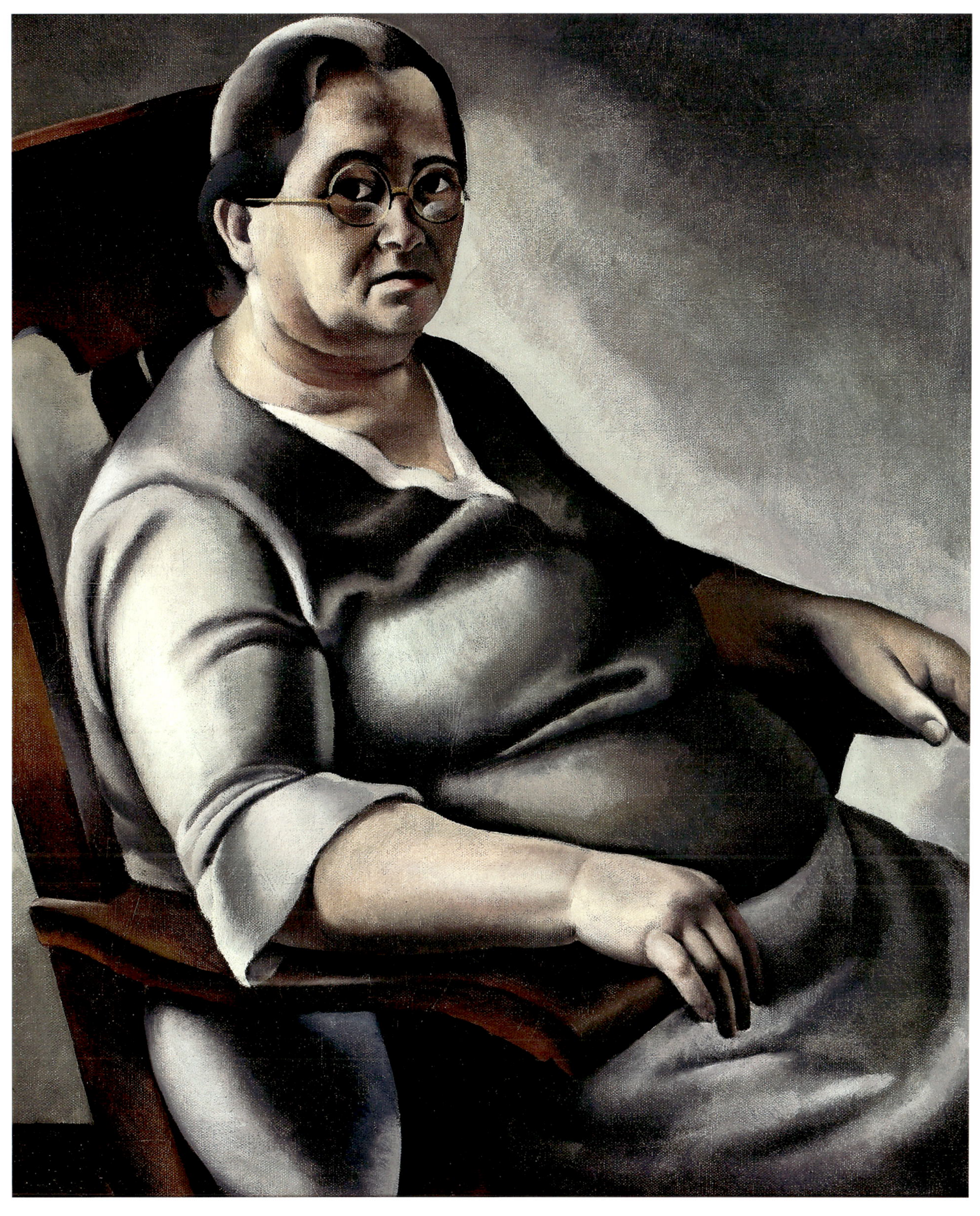

28 *My Mother* c. 1932
Oil on canvas; 36½ × 30 in. (92.7 × 76.2 cm)
Private collection

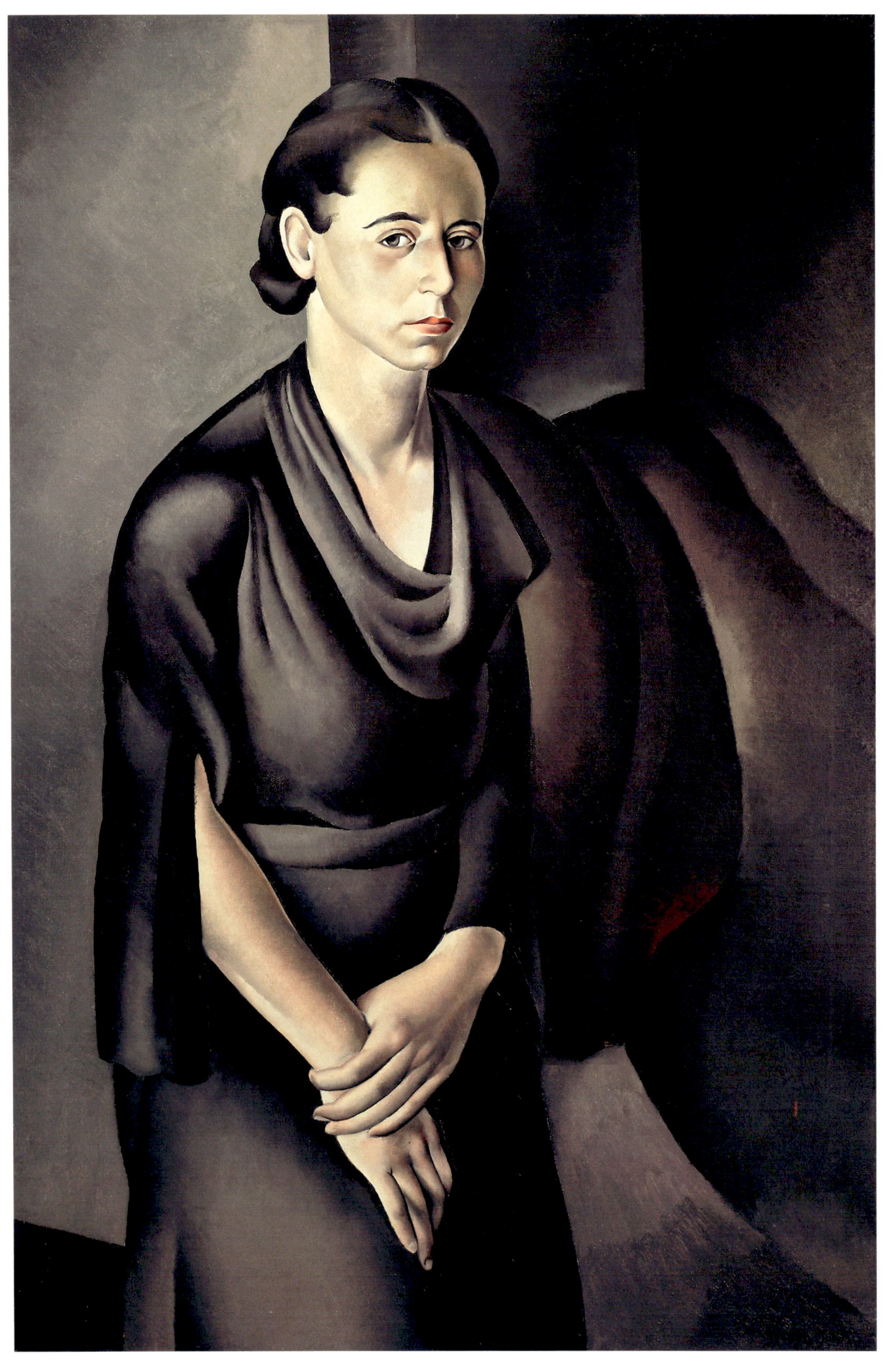

29 *Miss Elizabeth Stix* c. 1933
Oil on canvas; 48 × 32 in. (121.9 × 81.3 cm)
Collection of Jeanne and Rex Sinquefield

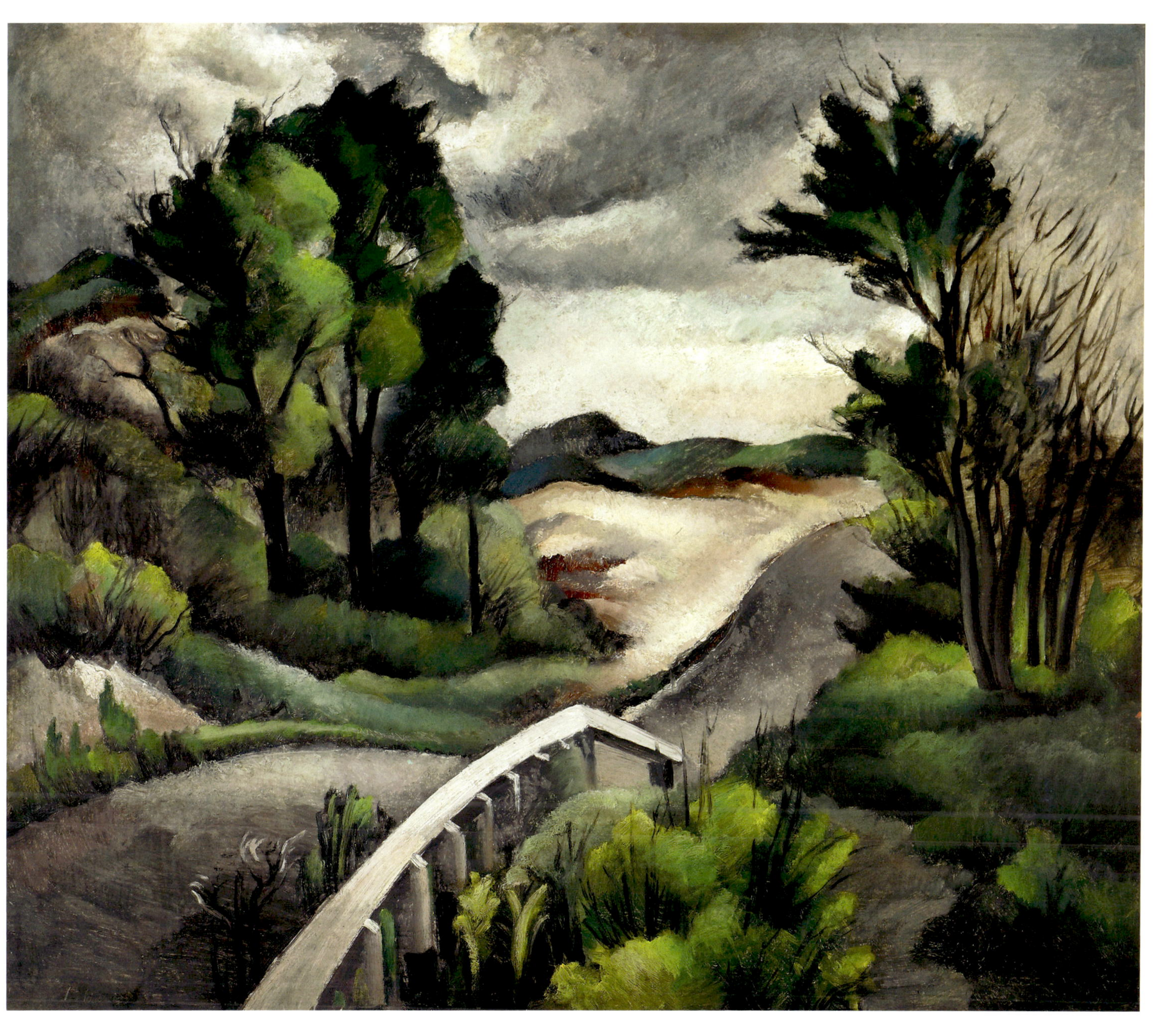

30 *Road to the Beach* 1933
Oil on Masonite; 25 × 30 in. (63.5 × 76.2 cm)
Collection of John and Susan Horseman,
courtesy of Kodner Gallery, St. Louis, Missouri

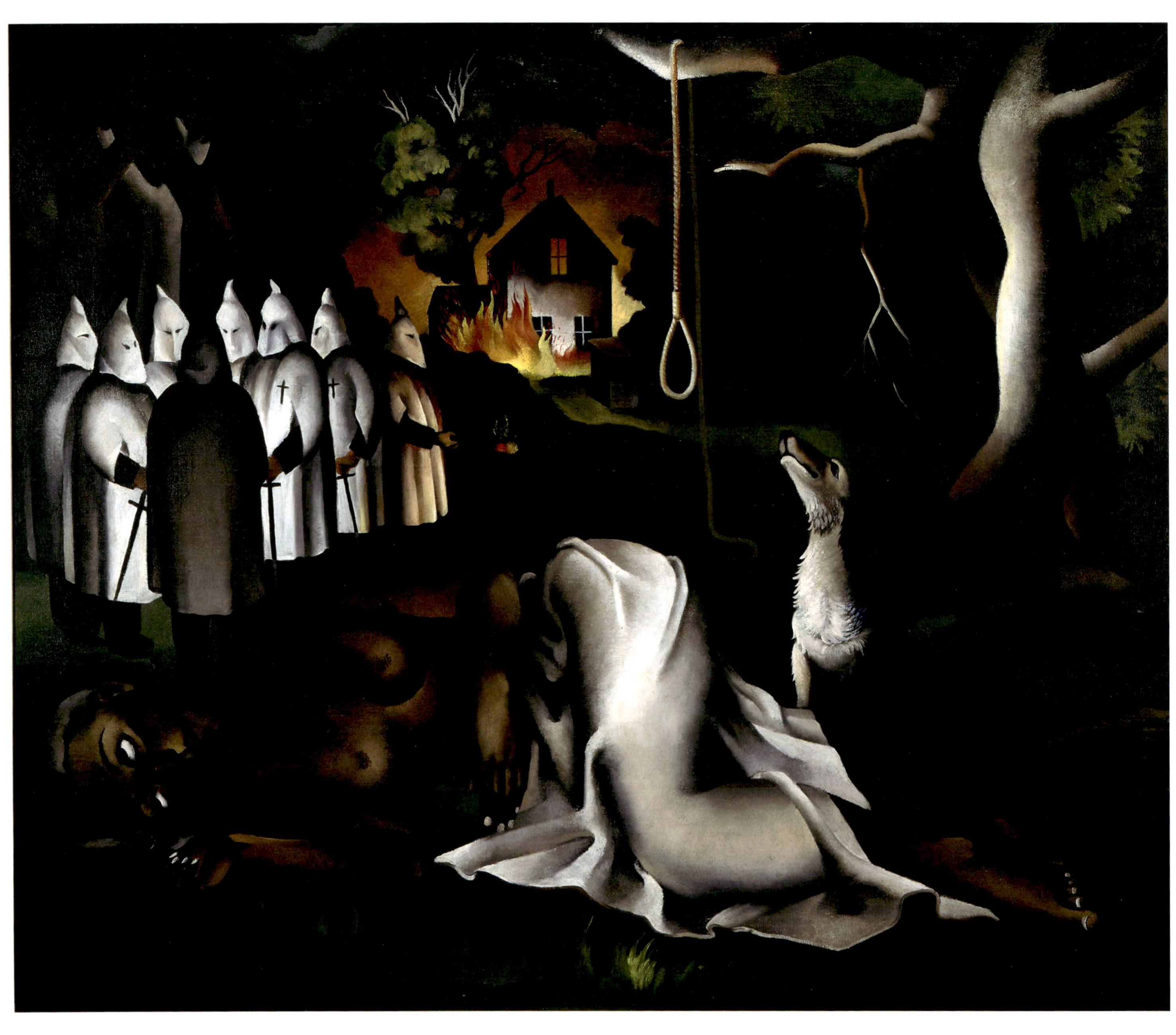

31 *American Justice* 1933
Oil on canvas; 30 × 36 in. (76.2 × 91.4 cm)
Columbus Museum of Art, Ohio: Museum Purchase, Derby Fund, from the Philip J. and Suzanne Schiller Collection of American Social Commentary Art 1930–1970

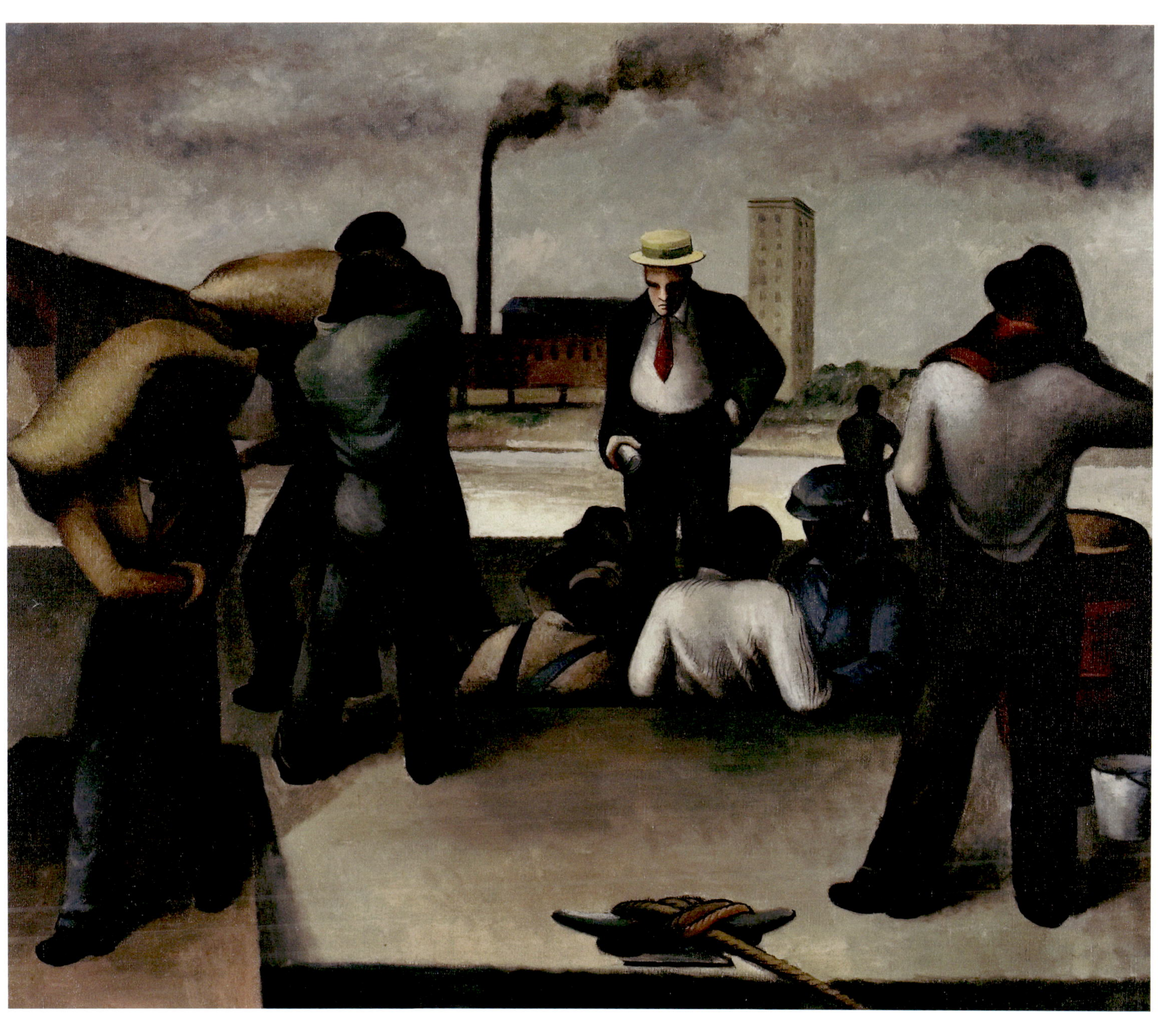

32 *Roustabouts* 1934
Oil on canvas; 25 × 30 in. (63.5 × 76.2 cm)
Worcester Art Museum, Worcester, Massachusetts,
Gift of Aldus C. Higgins

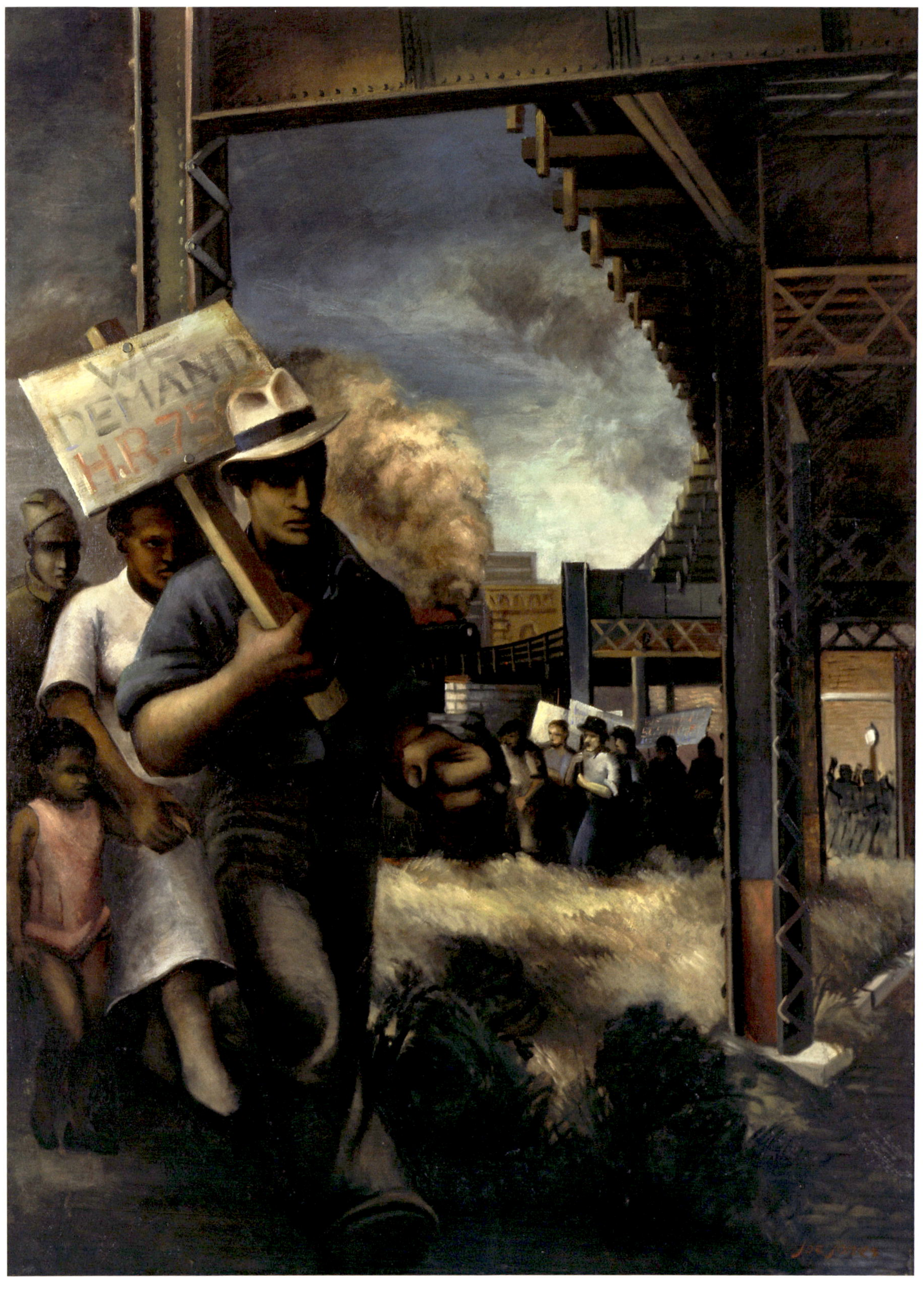

33 *We Demand* 1934
Oil on Masonite; 48 × 36 in. (121.9 × 91.4 cm)
Collection of The Butler Institute of American Art, Youngstown, Ohio, Gift of Sidney Freedman 1948

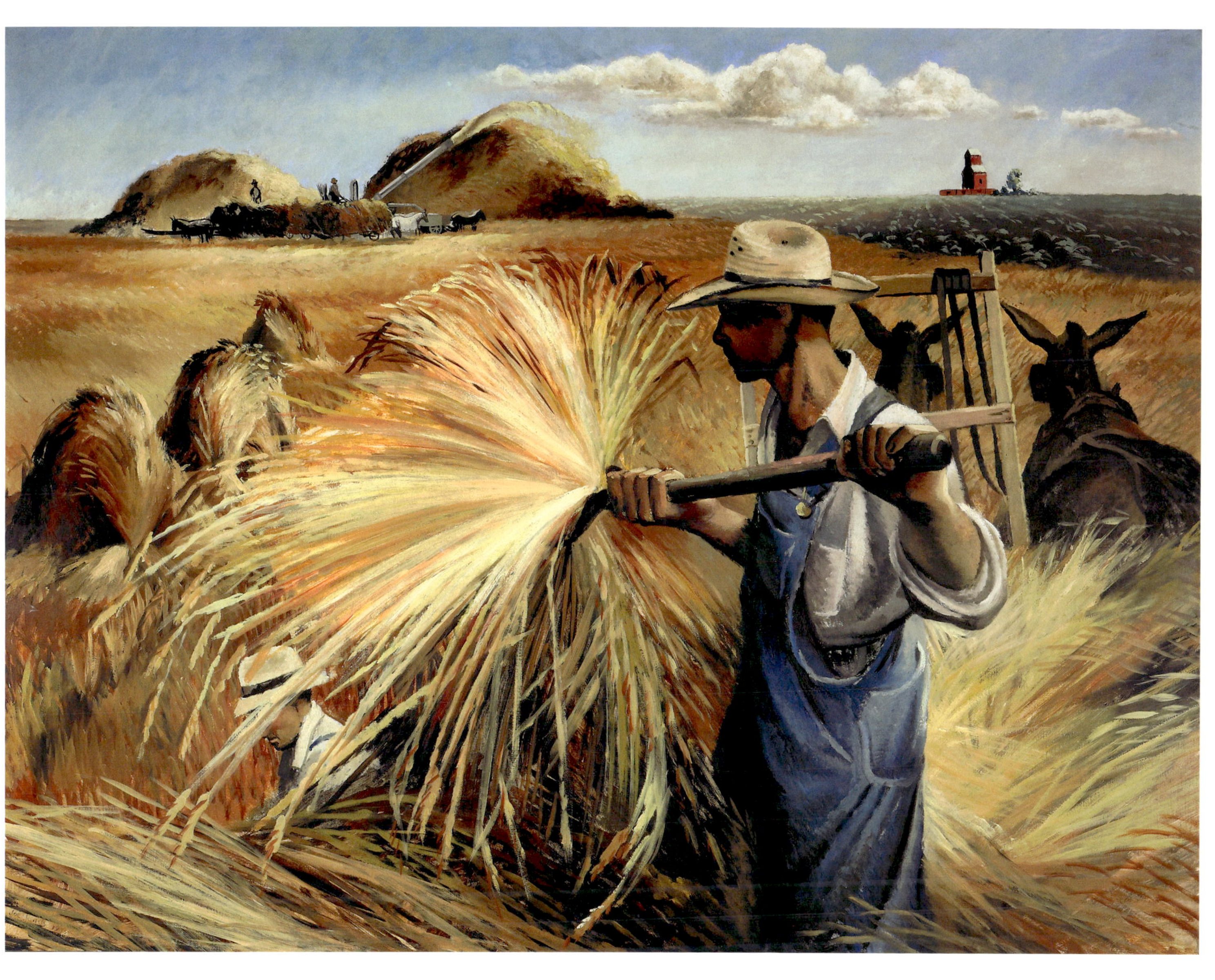

34 *Threshing No. 1* 1935
Oil on Masonite; 35¼ × 47¼ in. (89.5 × 120 cm)
Private collection

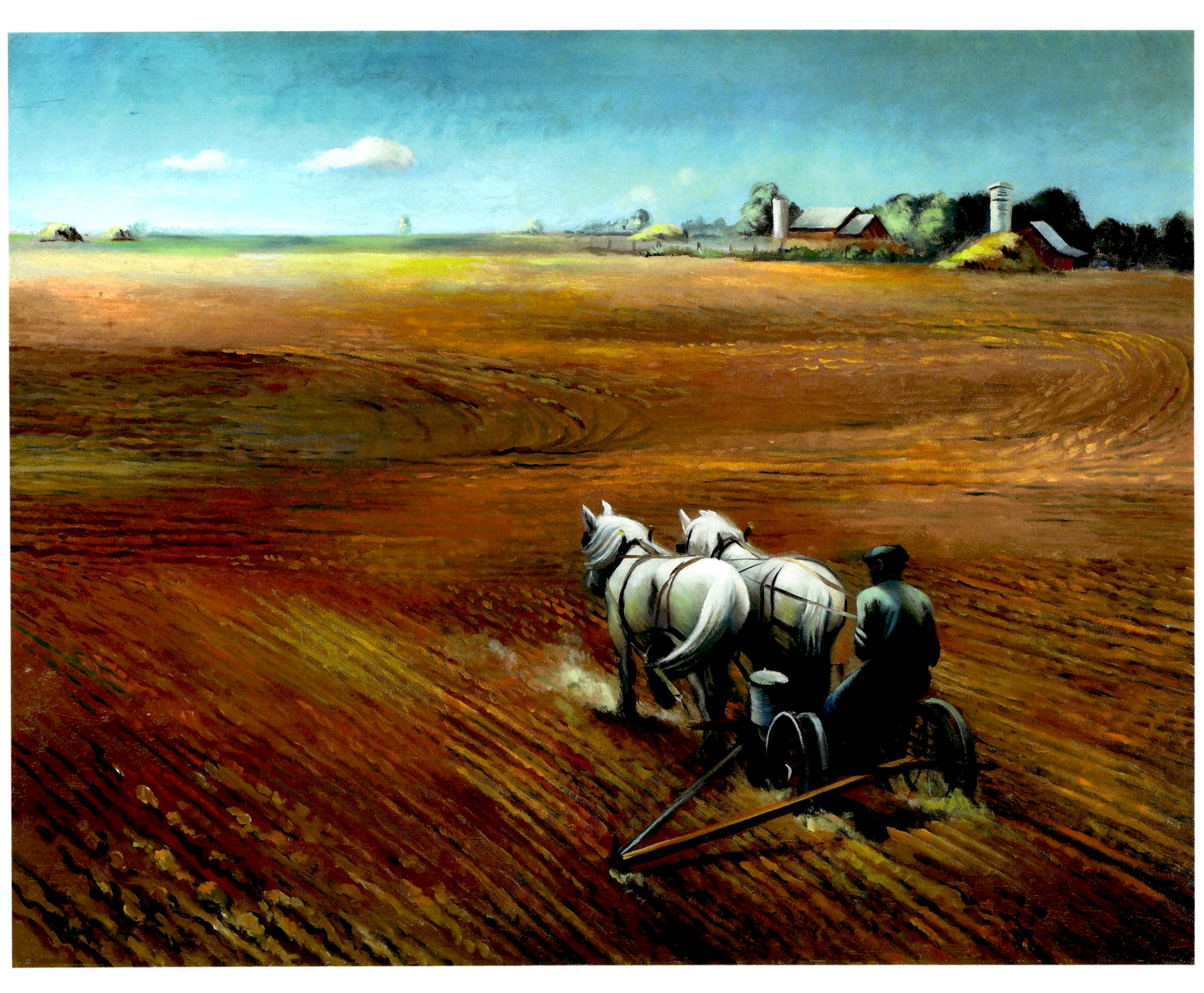

35 *Red Earth* c. 1935
Oil on panel; 36 × 48 in. (91.4 × 121.9 cm)
Collection of Jeanne and Rex Sinquefield

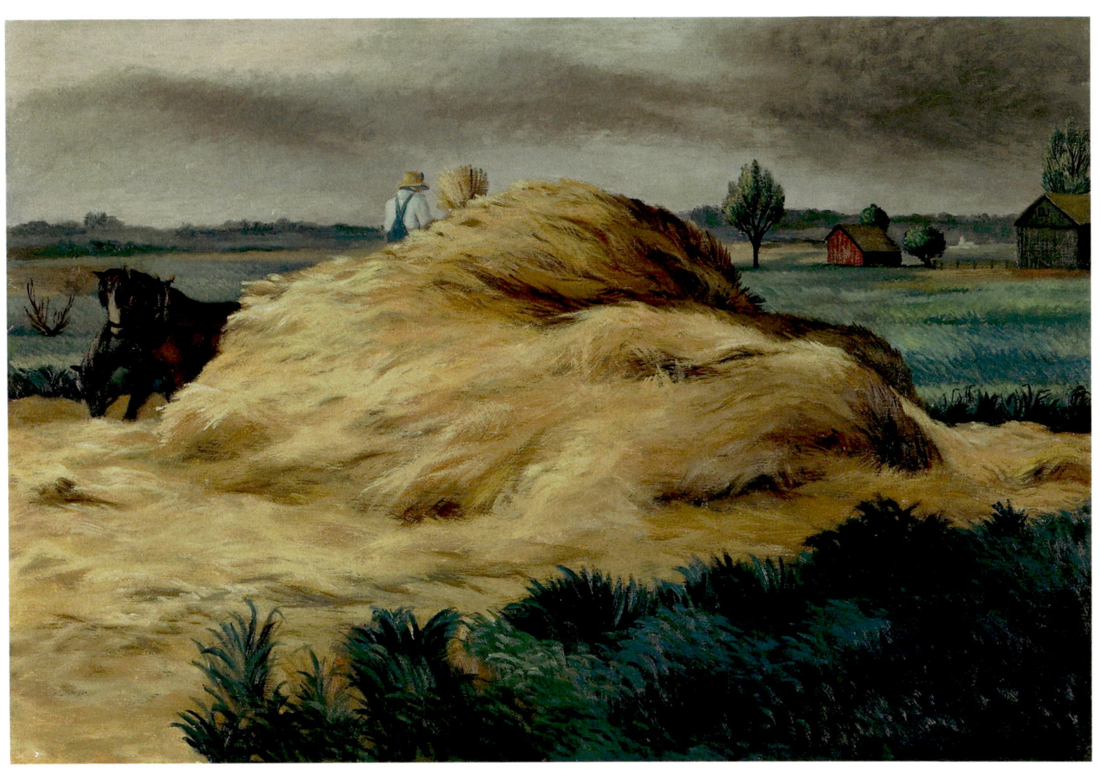

36 *Straw Stacks No. 2* 1935
Oil on canvas; 22 × 33¼ in.
(55.9 × 84.5 cm)
Collection of Jeanne and
Rex Sinquefield

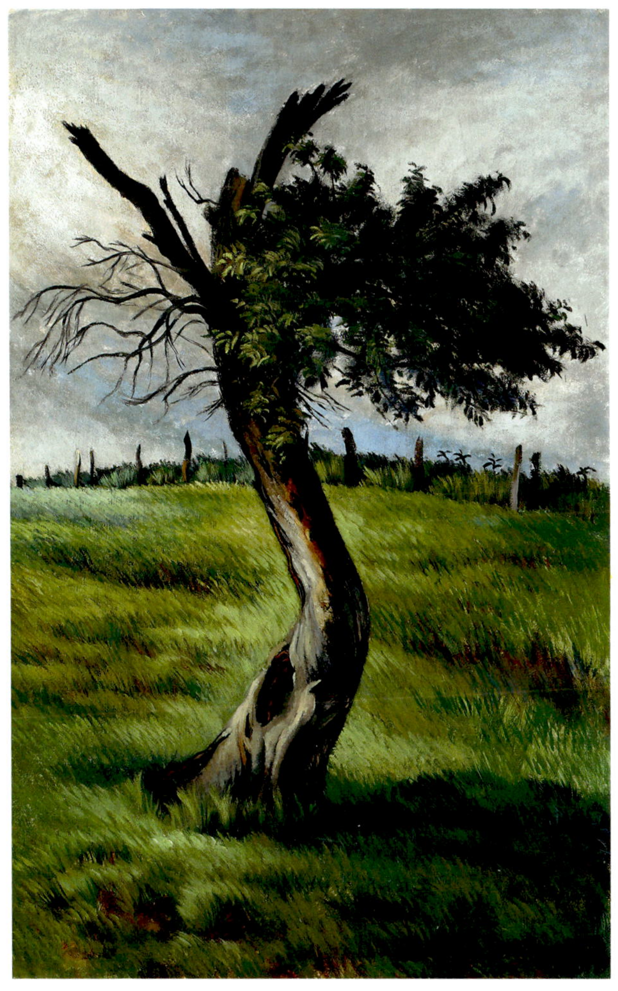

37 *Struggle* 1935
Oil on Masonite; 35⅞ × 24 in. (91.1 × 61 cm)
Courtesy of Kodner Gallery, St. Louis, Missouri

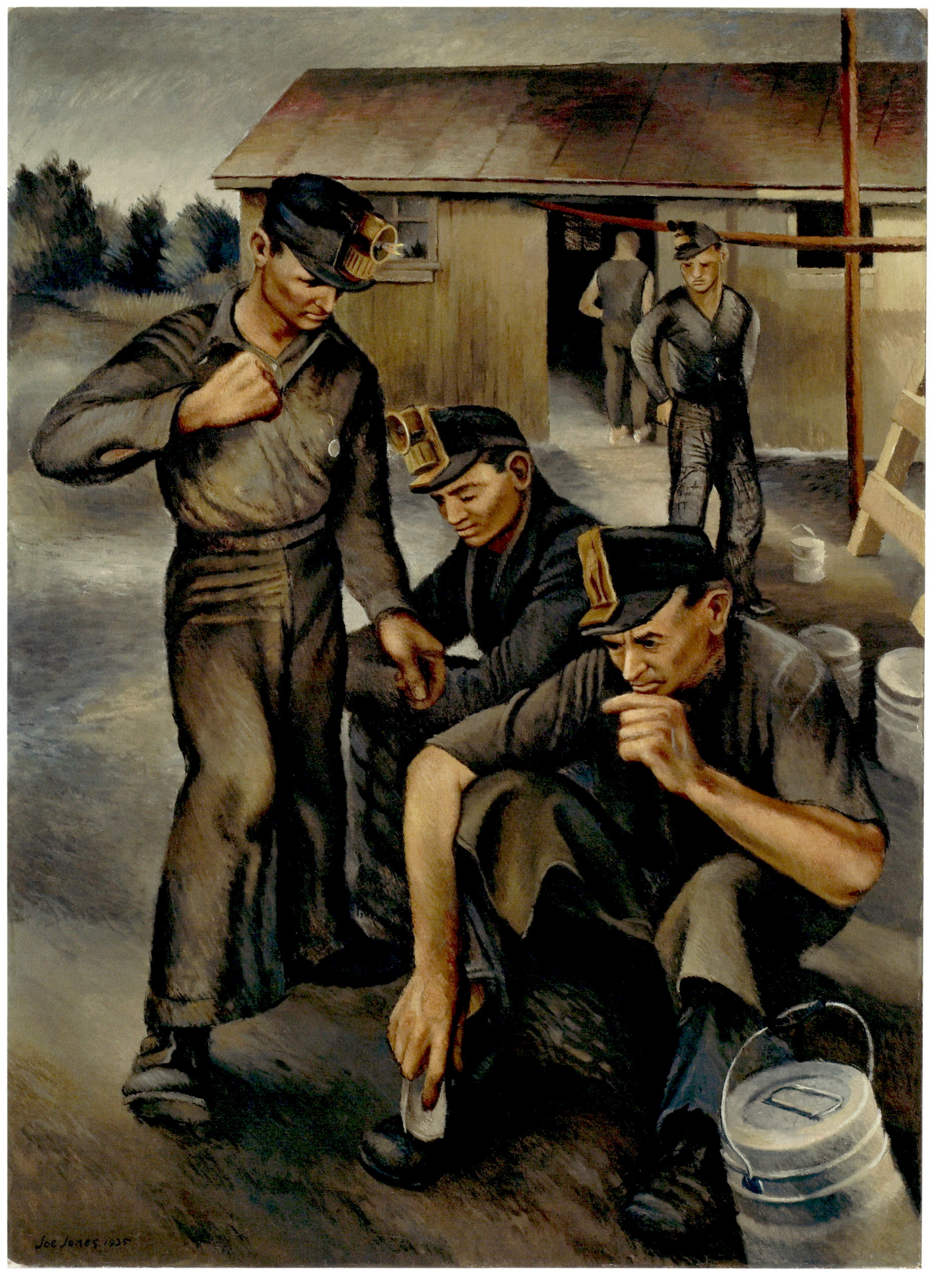

38 *Miners* 1935
Oil on paperboard; 47¾ × 36 in. (121.3 × 91.4 cm)
Collection of Rory Ellinger and Linda Locke

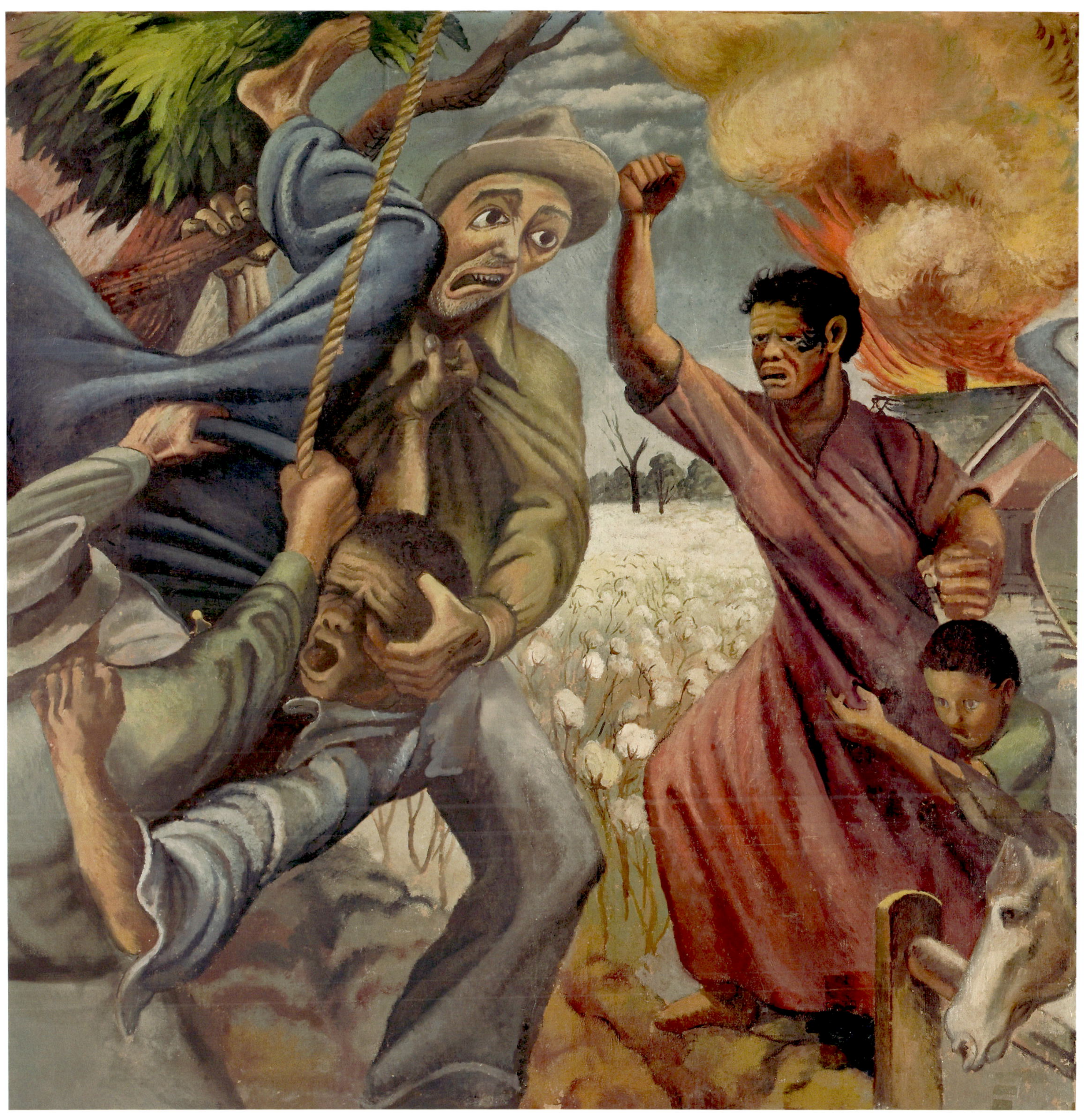

39 *The Struggle in the South* 1935
(Reconstructed image of a segment of the mural)
Oil on Masonite; section 9: 74 × 6¾ in. (188 × 17.1 cm),
section 10: 91⅞ × 36½ in. (233.4 × 92.7 cm),
section 11: 91¼ × 48 in. (231.8 × 121.9 cm)
Collection of the University of Arkansas at Little Rock

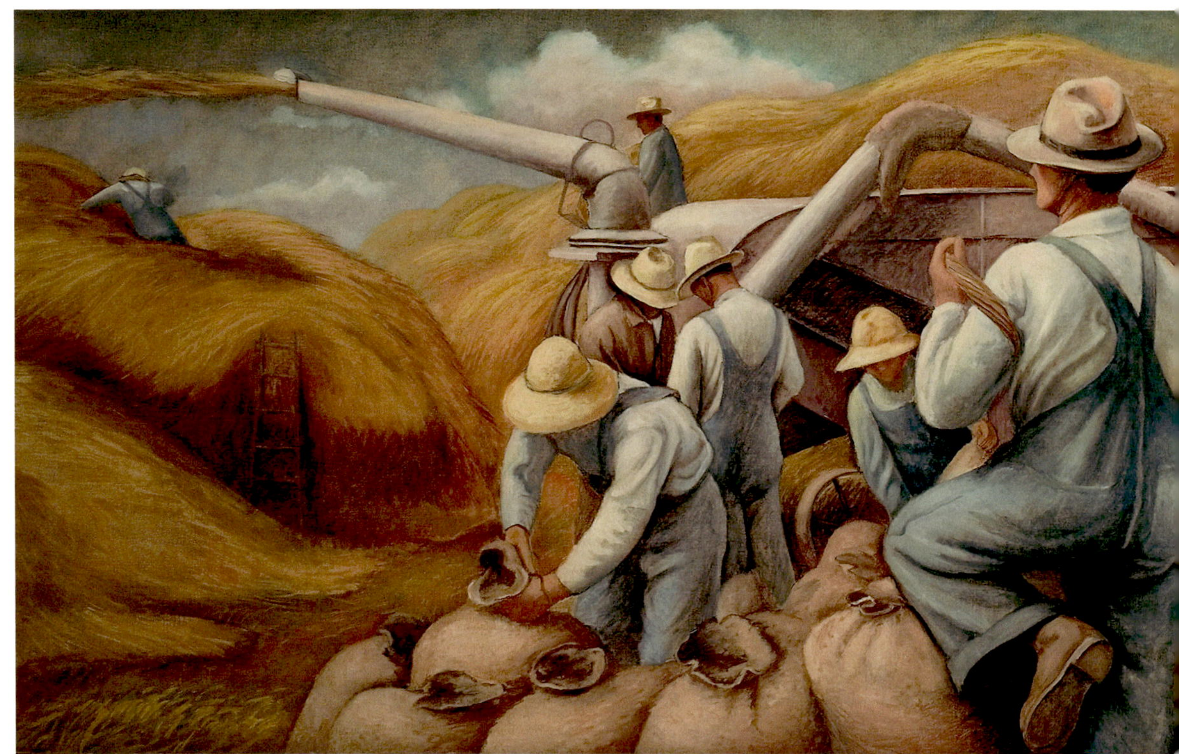

40 *Threshing (905 Mural)* 1936
Oil on canvas, mounted on Masonite;
38¼ in. × 145½ in. (97.2 × 369.6 cm)
Haggerty Museum of Art, Gift of
Mr. and Mrs. Victor Packman and
Mr. and Mrs. Leo Rothbarth

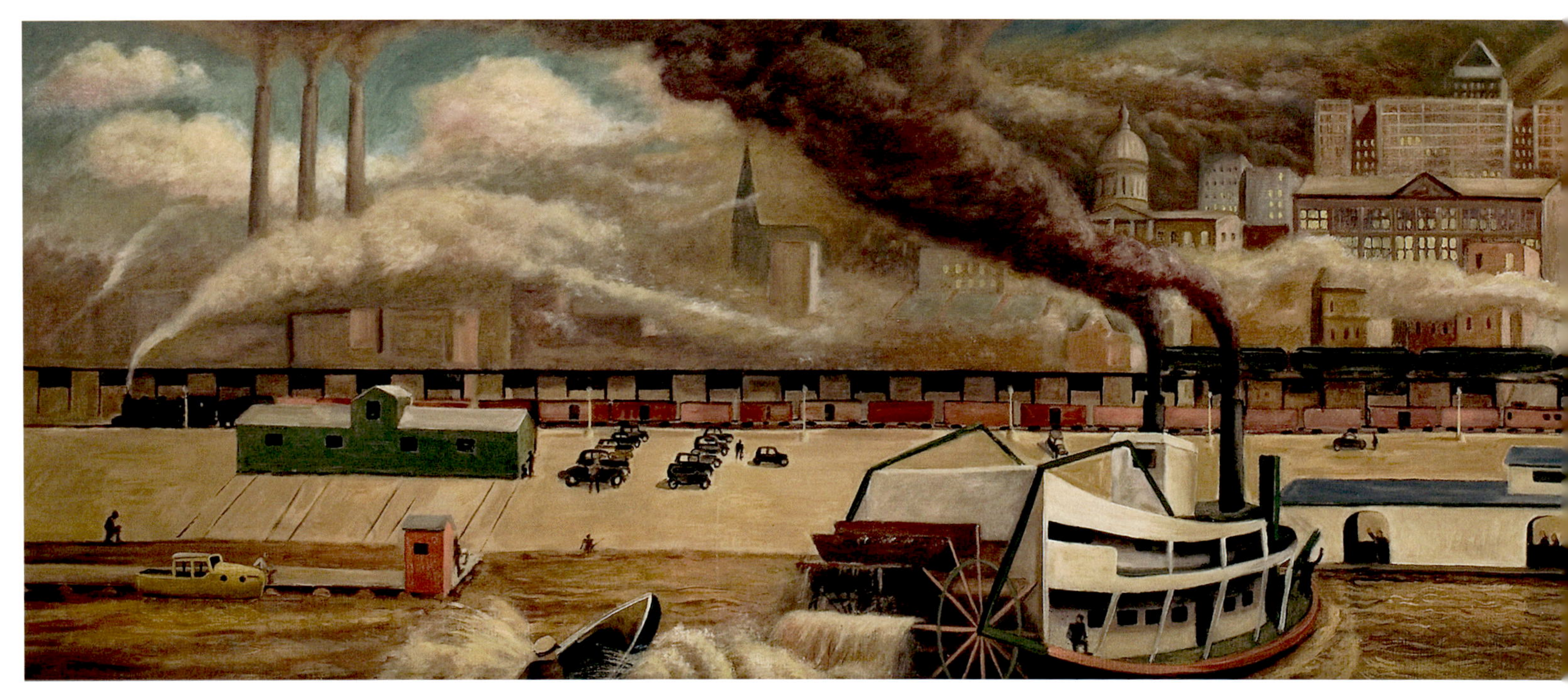

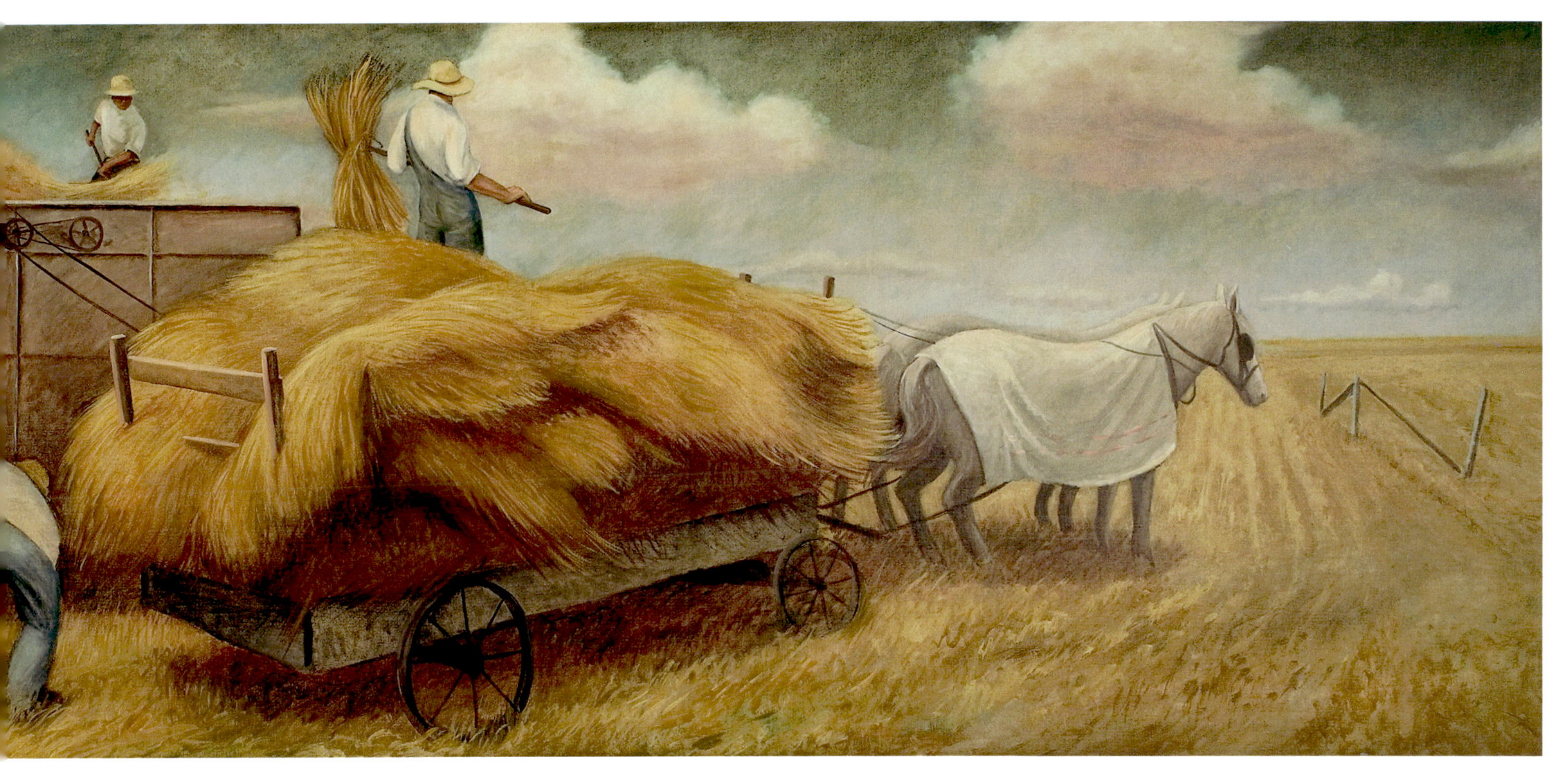

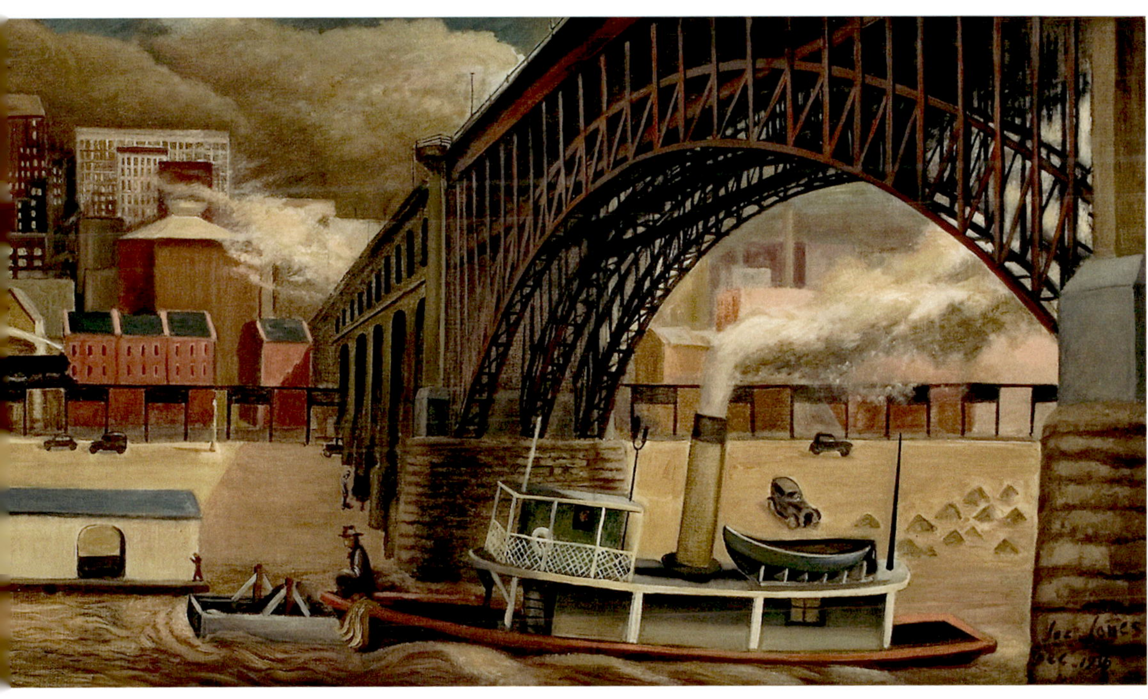

41 *Riverfront (905 Mural)* 1936
Oil on canvas, mounted on Masonite;
34⅞ × 136 in. (88.6 × 345.4 cm)
Jefferson National Expansion
Memorial / National Park Service

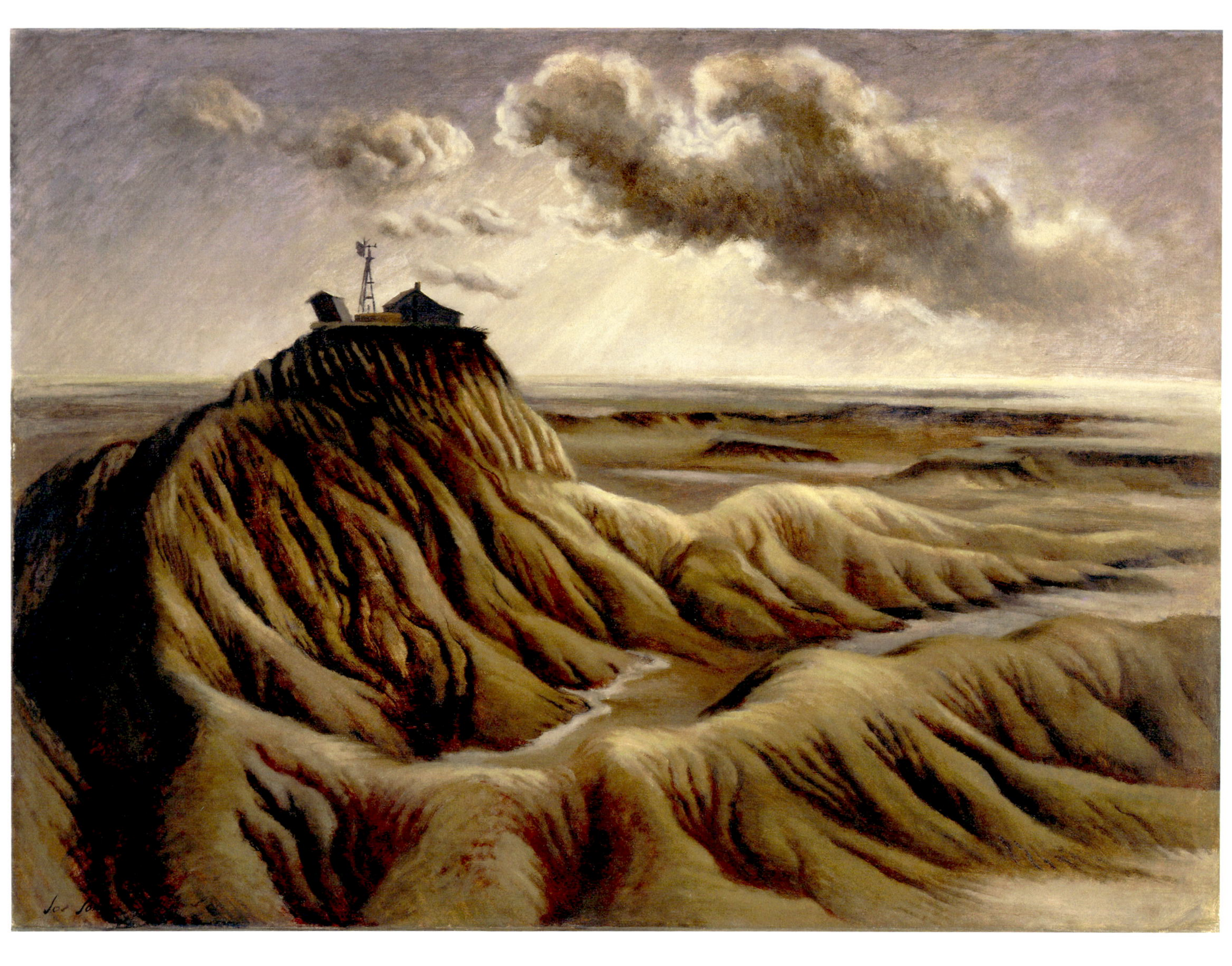

42 *Our American Farms* 1936
Oil and tempera on canvas; 30 × 40 in. (76.2 × 101.6 cm)
Whitney Museum of American Art, New York, Purchase

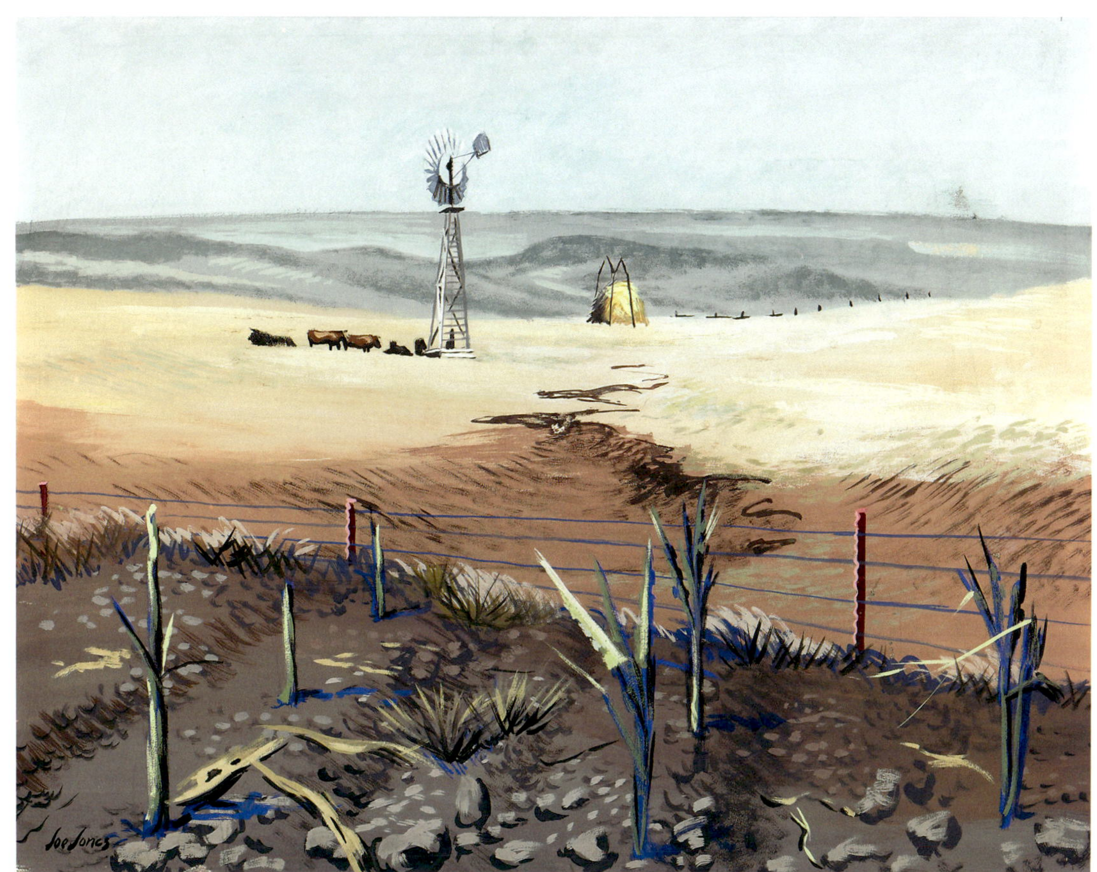

43 *Midwestern Landscape* 1936
Gouache on illustration board; 18½ × 24 in. (47 × 61 cm)
Collection of Jeanne and Rex Sinquefield

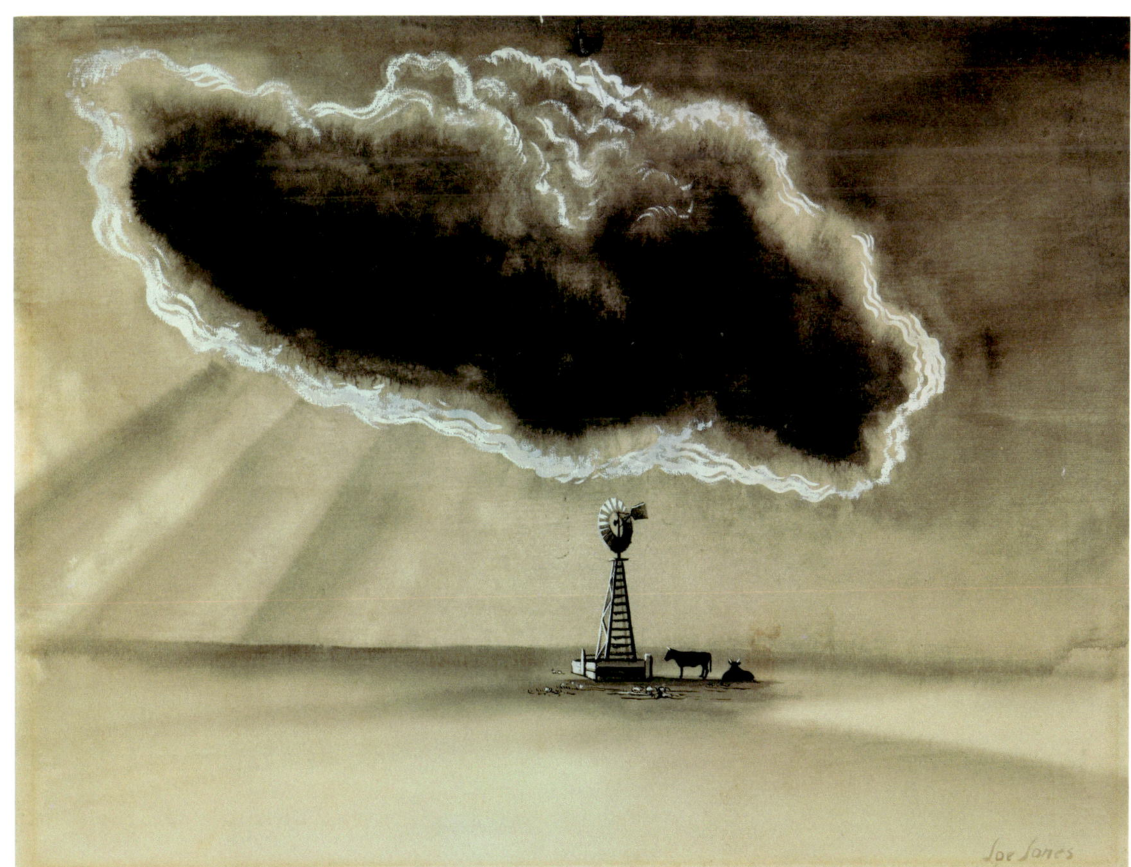

44 *Windmill and Two Bulls* 1936
Brush and ink wash, with white gouache highlights, on cream laid paper; 18 × 24 5⁄16 in. (45.7 × 61.8 cm)
Courtesy of The University Museum, Southern Illinois University Carbondale

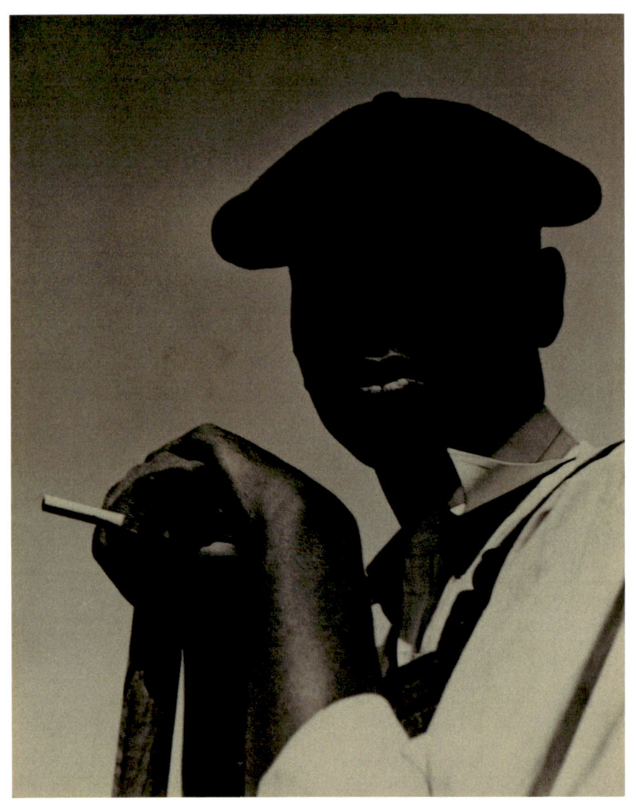

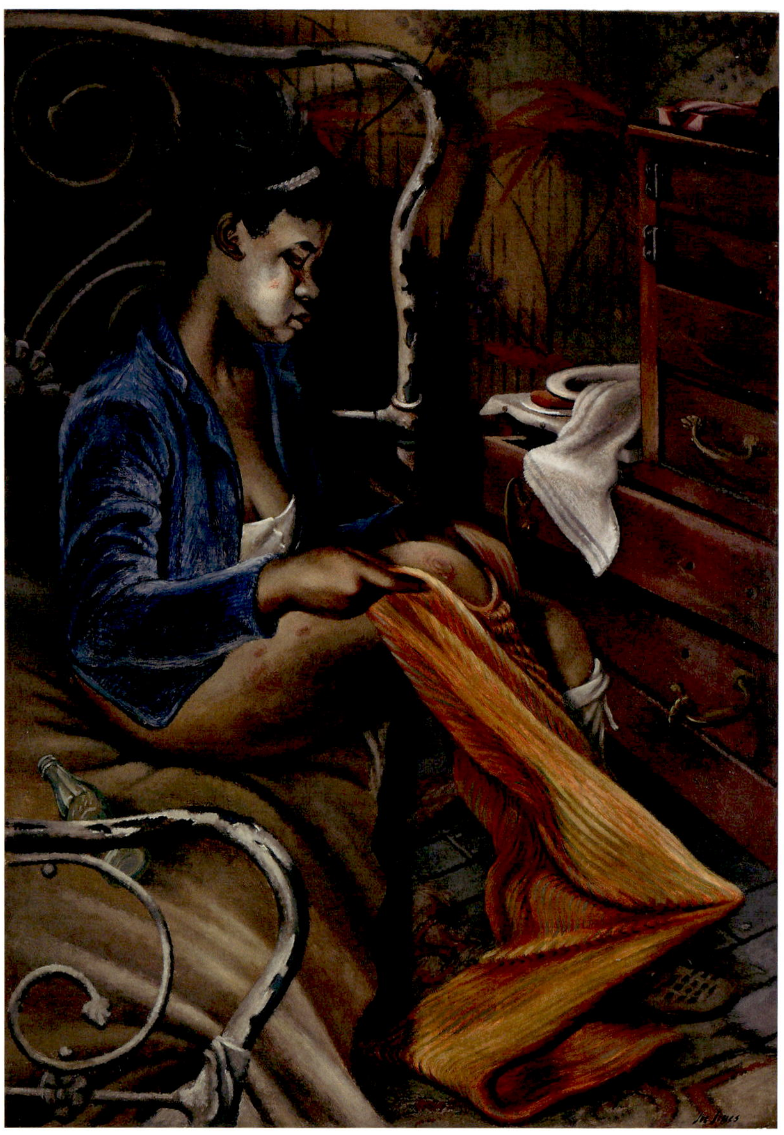

45 *PWA Worker* c. 1936
Gelatin-silver photograph; 9³⁄₁₆ × 8⅜ in.
(23.3 × 21.3 cm)
Collection of Sarah Dearry

46 *Bottle Dancer* 1936
Oil over tempera on canvas, mounted on Masonite;
54½ × 39⁹⁄₁₆ in. (138.4 × 100.5 cm)
Saint Louis Art Museum, Anonymous Gift

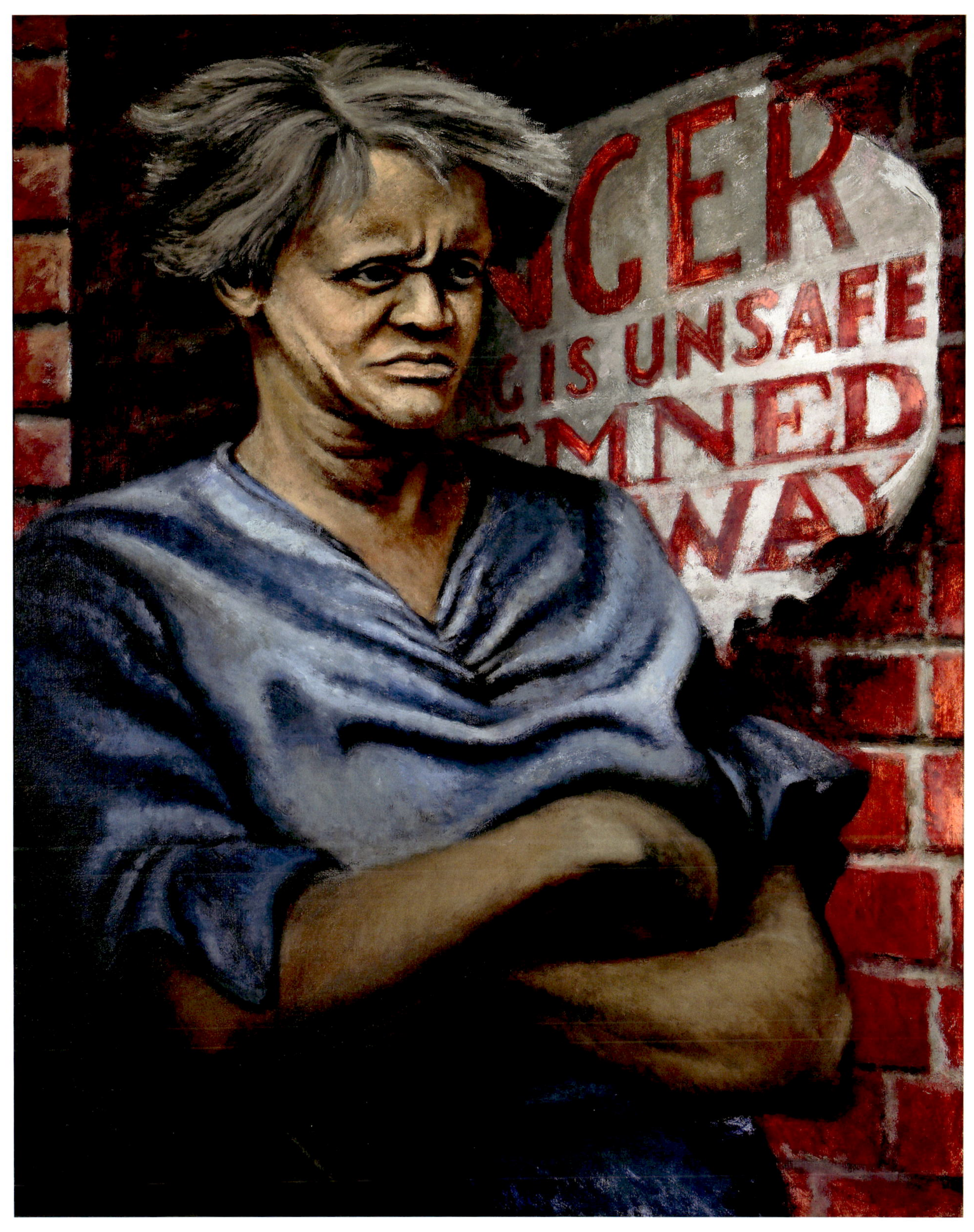

47 *Condemned* 1936
Oil on canvas, mounted on Masonite;
39 × 29 in. (99.1 × 73.7 cm)
Collection of Jeanne and Rex Sinquefield

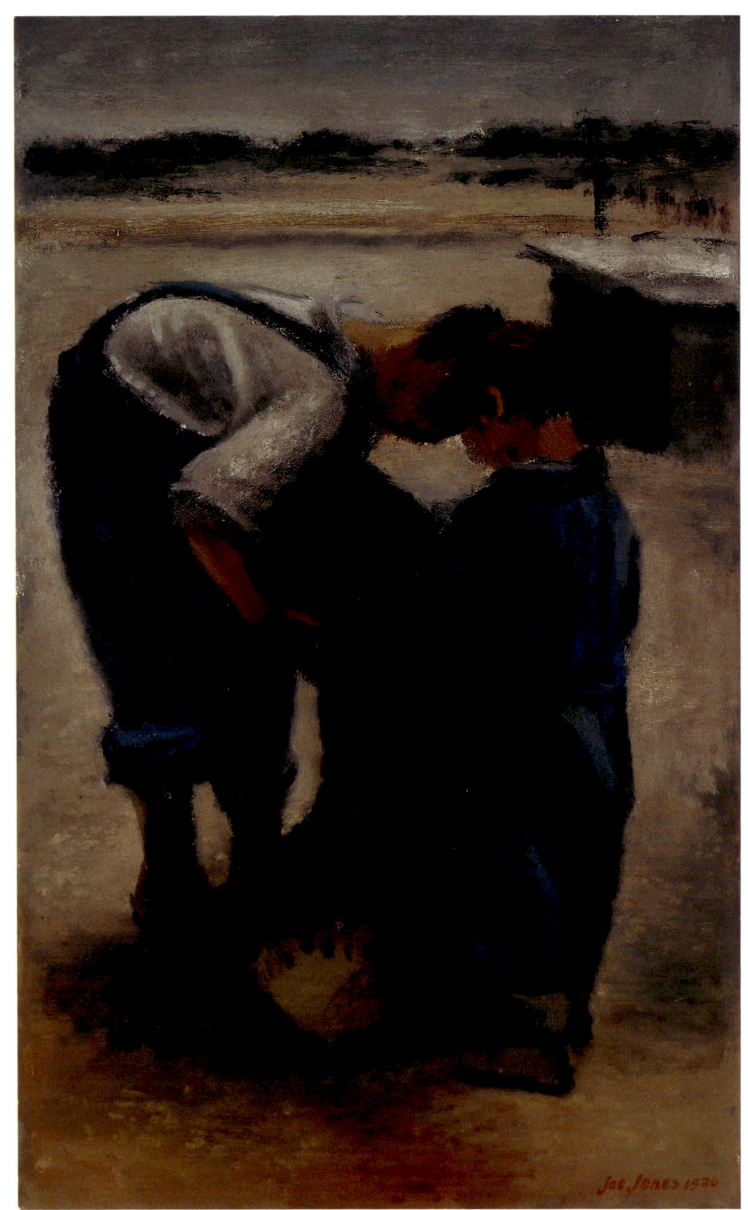

48 *To Make Our Daily Bread* 1936
Oil on Masonite; $22\frac{5}{16} \times 14\frac{5}{16}$ in. (56.7×36.4 cm)
Estate of Miss Elizabeth Green

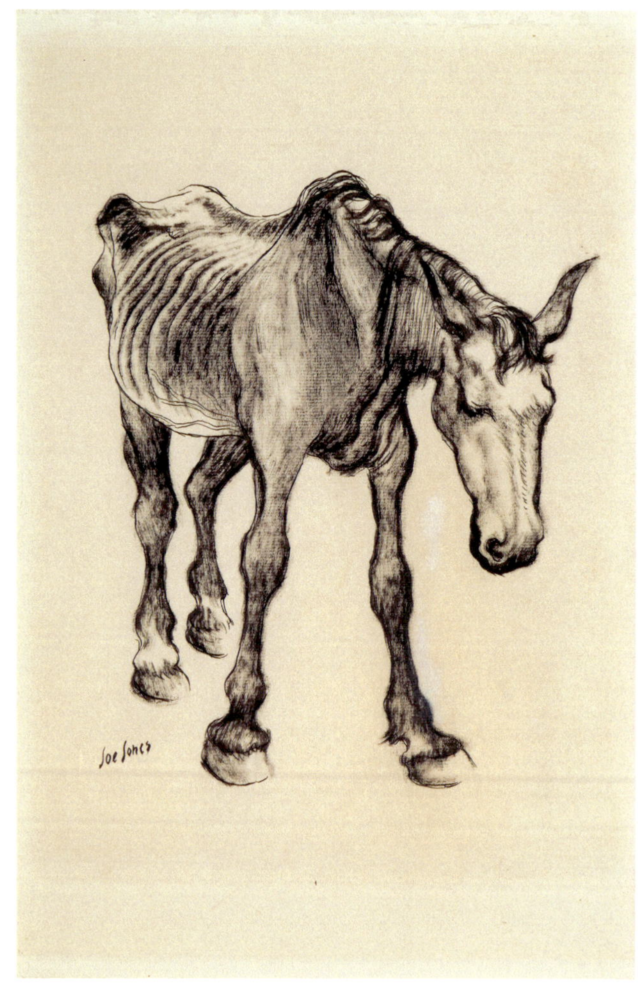

49 *On His Last Legs* 1936
Pen, brush, and ink on cream laid paper;
$17\frac{1}{8} \times 11\frac{3}{8}$ in. (43.5×28.9 cm)
Private collection

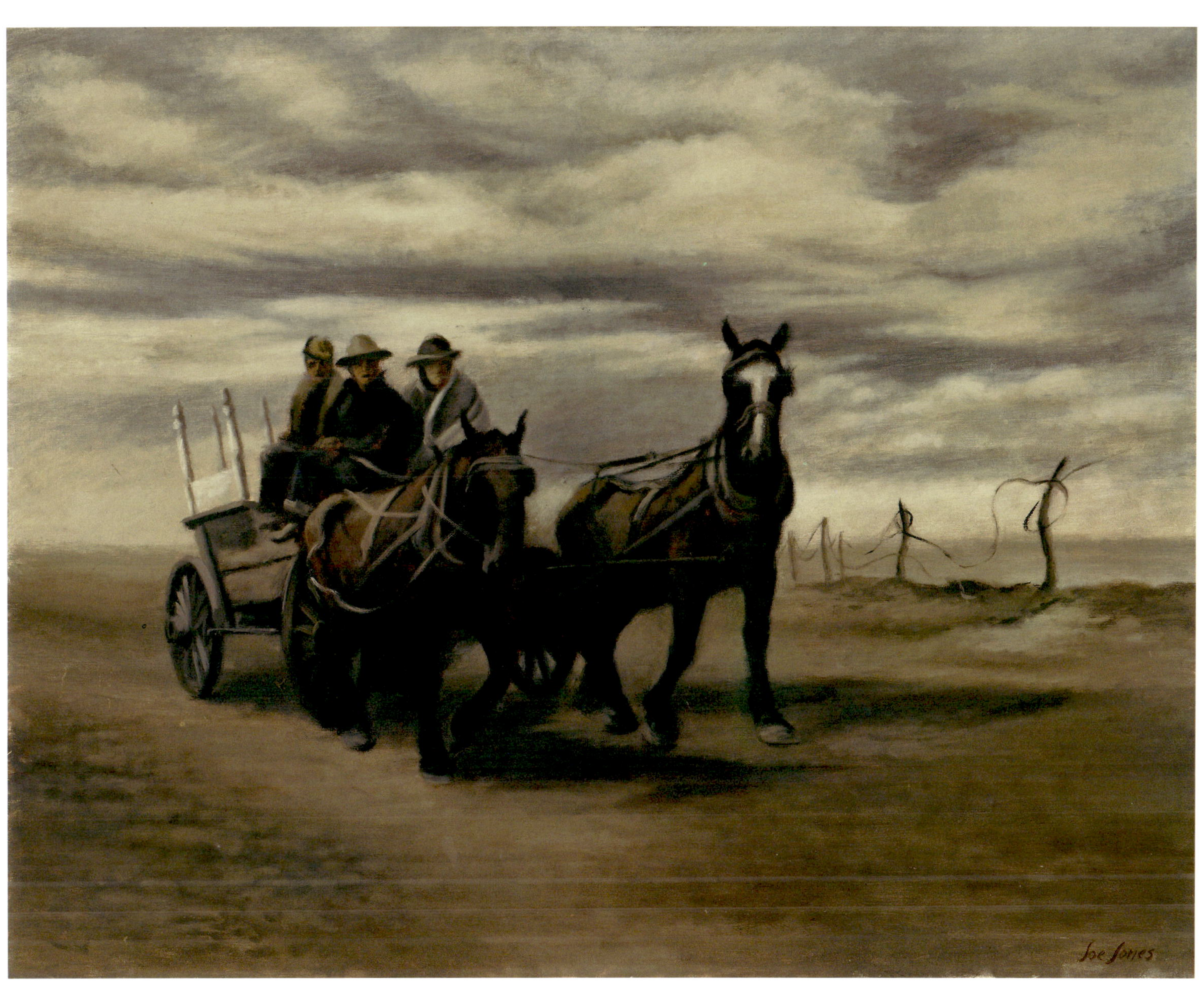

50 *Homeless Farmers (Uprooted Dirt Farmers)* 1937
Oil on canvas; 28 × 36 in. (71.1 × 91.4 cm)
The Frances Lehman Loeb Art Center, Vassar College, Poughkeepsie, New York, Gift of James F. Adams

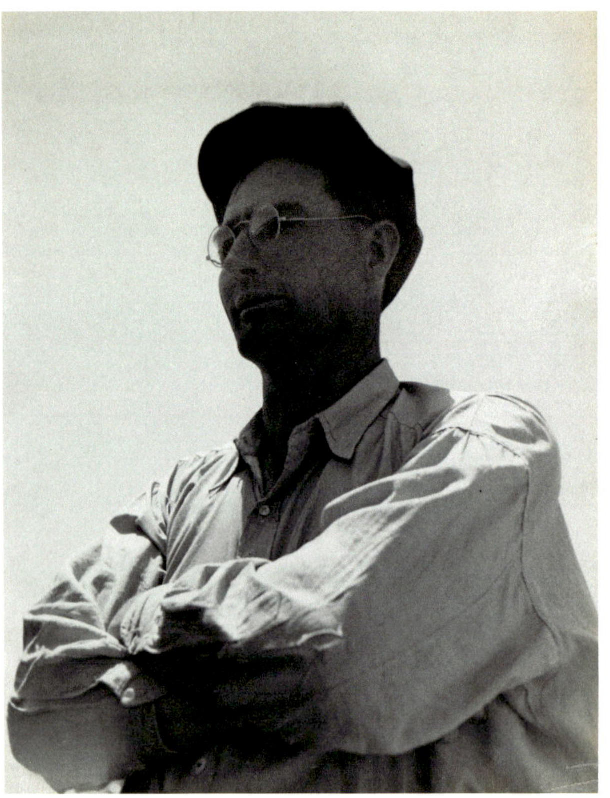

51 *WPA Worker* 1937
Gelatin-silver photograph;
9½ × 7⅜ in. (24.1 × 18.7 cm)
Jones Family Collection

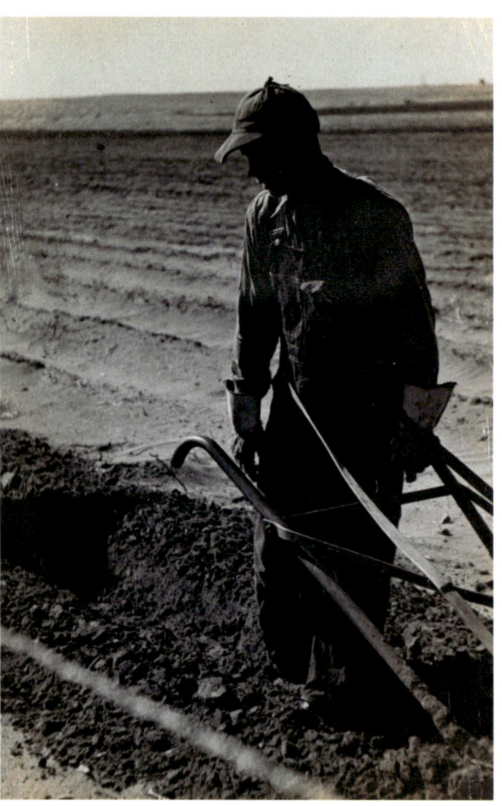

52 *Farmer with Plow* 1937
Gelatin-silver photograph;
9⅞ × 6½ in. (25.1 × 16.5 cm)
Jones Family Collection

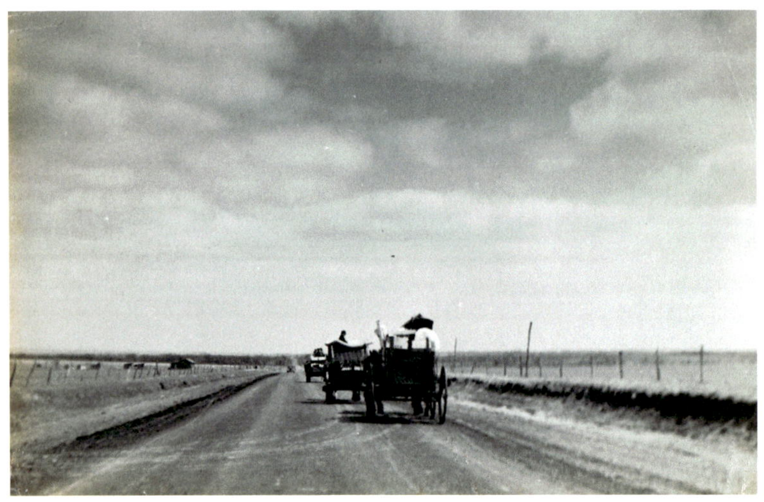

53 *Evicted Farmers* 1937
Gelatin-silver photograph;
6½ × 10⅜ in. (16.5 × 26.4 cm)
Jones Family Collection

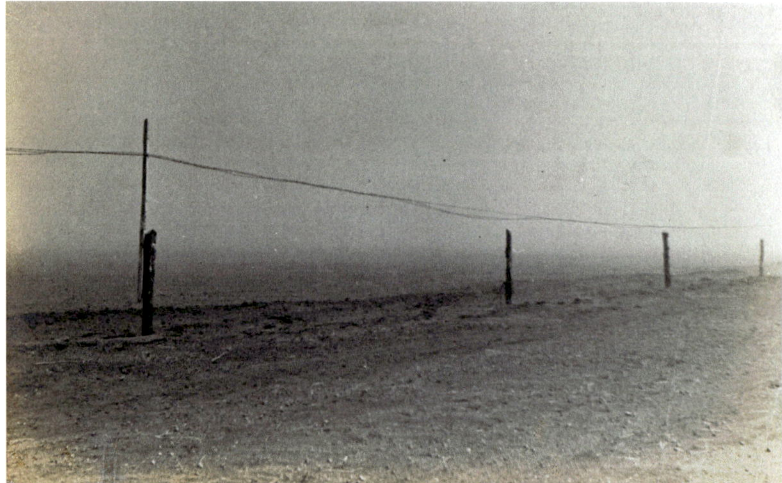

54 *Wire Fence* 1937
Gelatin-silver photograph;
6⅜ × 10⅜ in. (16.2 × 26.4 cm)
Jones Family Collection

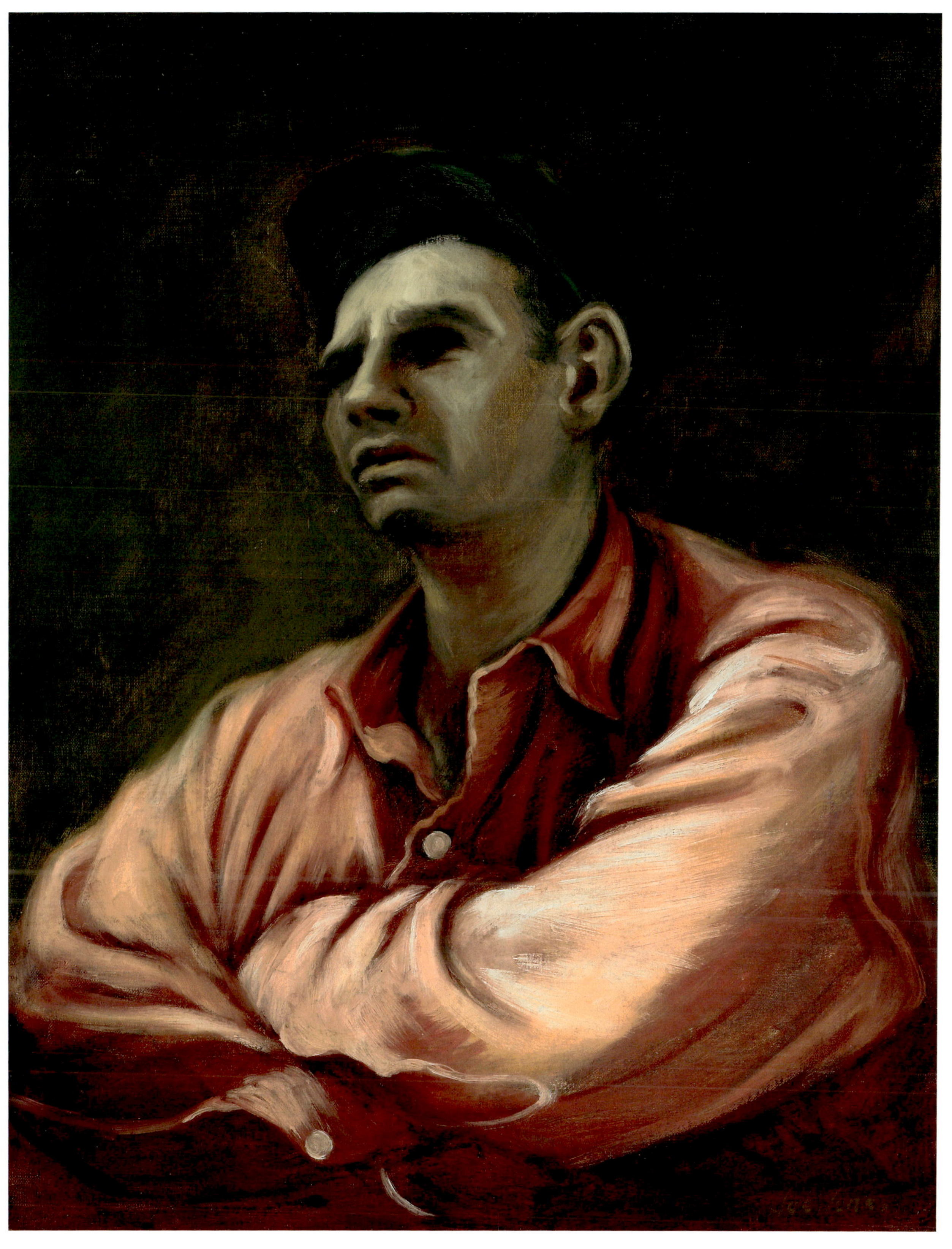

55 *A Worker Again on WPA* c. 1938
Oil on canvas; 27 × 23 in. (68.6 × 58.4 cm)
St. Louis Mercantile Library at the University of Missouri–St. Louis,
Gift of the Bruce and Barbara Feldacker Labor Art Collection

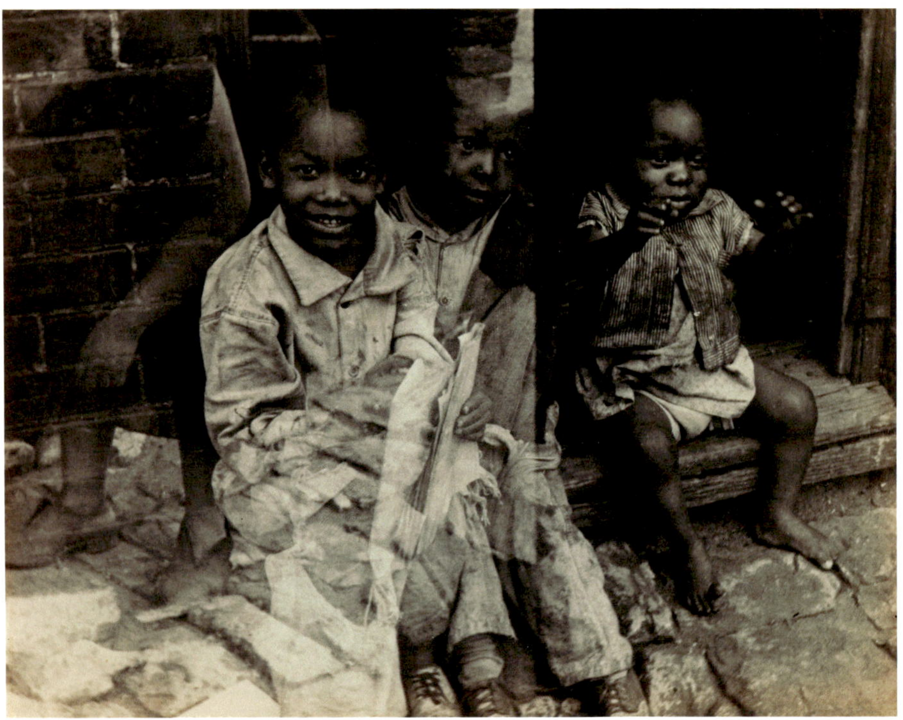

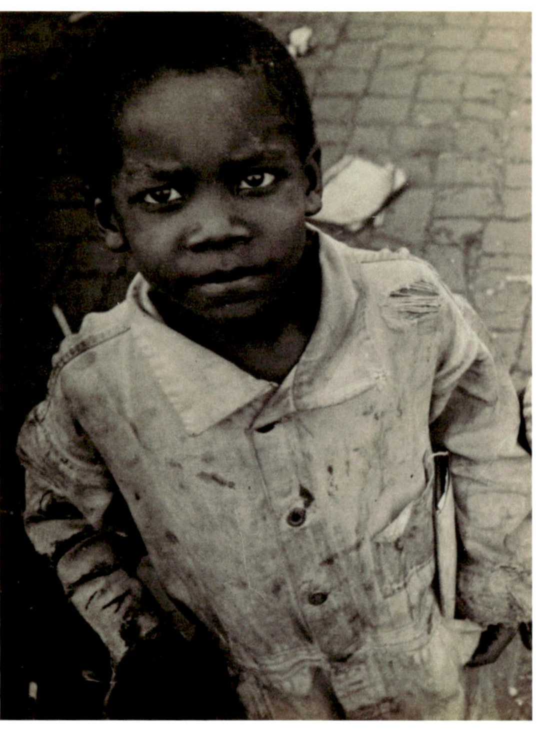

56 *They Grow and Learn to Smile* c. 1937
Gelatin-silver photograph;
11 × 14 in. (27.9 × 35.6 cm)
Collection of Sarah Dearry

57 *He Knows* c. 1937
Gelatin-silver photograph;
14 × 10⅞ in. (35.6 × 27.6 cm)
Collection of Sarah Dearry

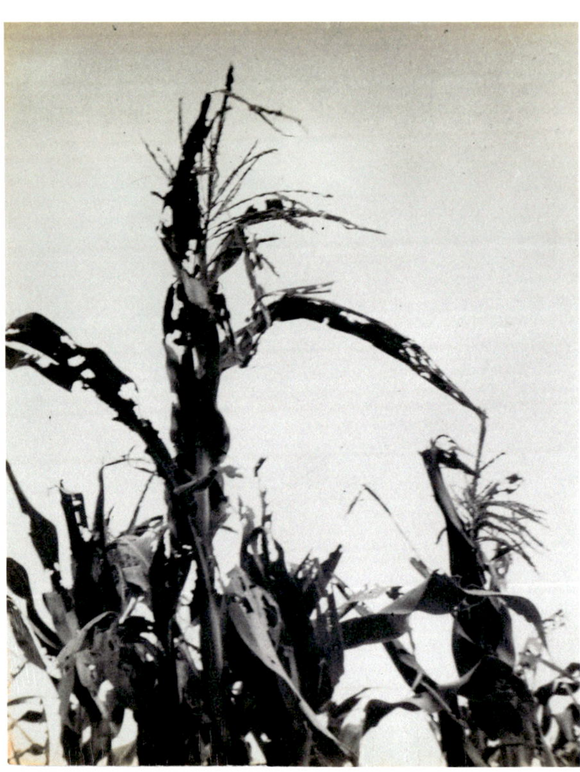

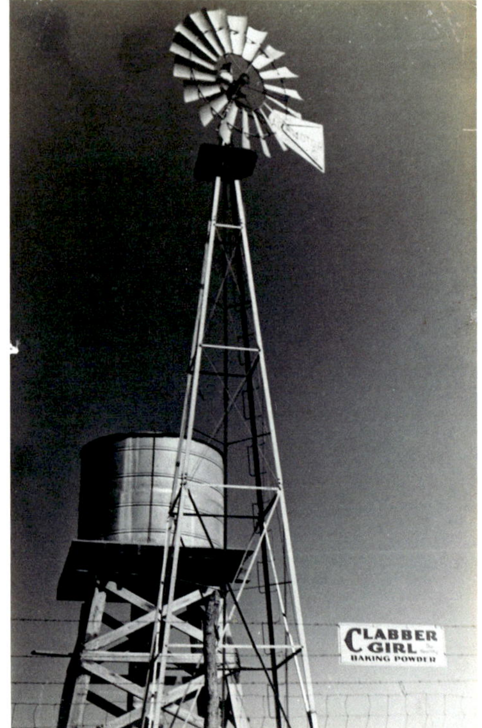

58 *Corn* 1937
Gelatin-silver photograph;
9 7/16 × 7½ in. (24 × 19.1 cm)
Jones Family Collection

59 *Windmill* 1937
Gelatin-silver photograph;
10 × 6 7/16 in. (25.4 × 16.4 cm)
Jones Family Collection

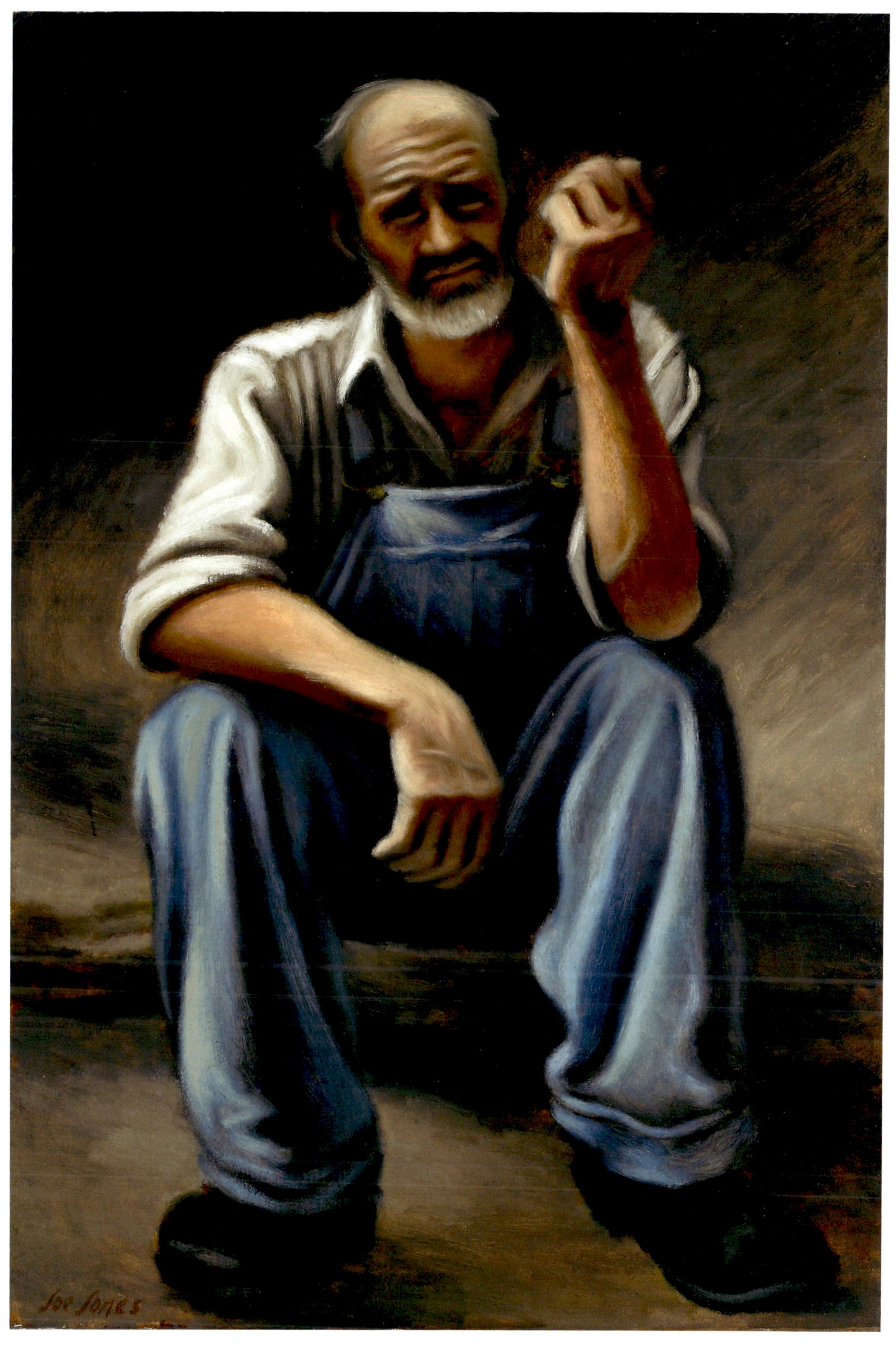

60 *Drought Farmer* c. 1937
Oil on canvas, mounted on Masonite; 20⅝ × 14¼ in. (52.4 × 36.2 cm)
Saint Louis Art Museum, Gift of Mr. and Mrs. Joseph Pulitzer, Jr.

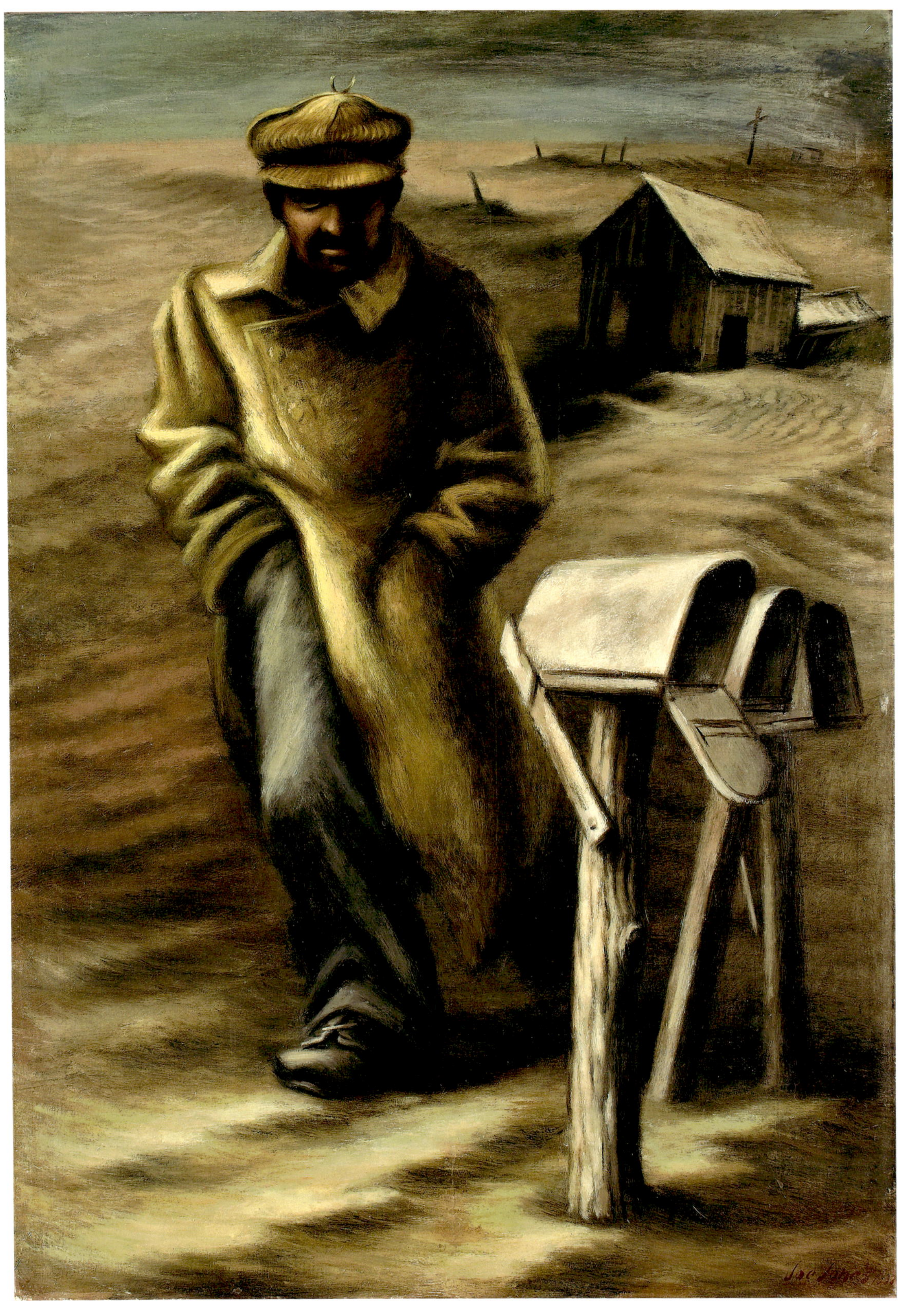

61 *Departure* 1938
Oil on canvas; 48 × 33½ in. (121.9 × 85.1 cm)
Denver Art Museum Collection, Gift of Morton D. May, Jr.

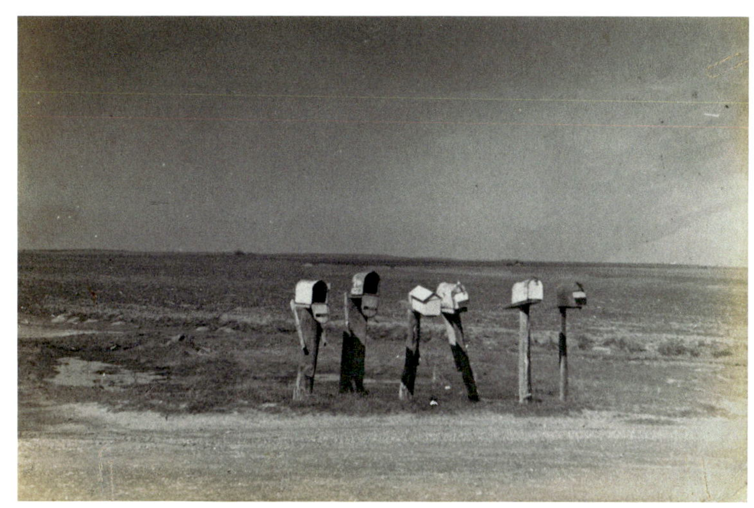

62 *Mailboxes* 1937
Gelatin-silver photograph;
6⅜ × 10 in. (16.2 × 25.4 cm)
Jones Family Collection

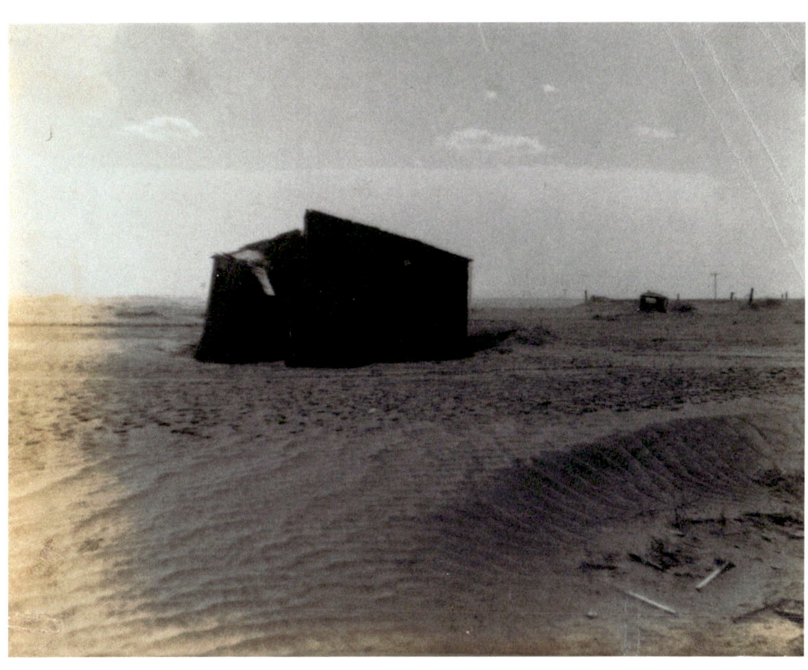

63 *Shed* 1937
Gelatin-silver photograph;
7¼ × 9¼ in. (18.4 × 23.5 cm)
Jones Family Collection

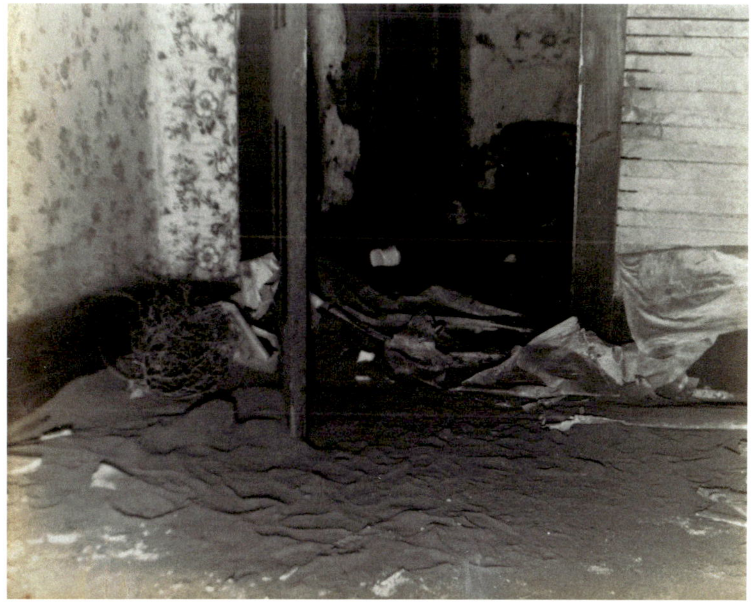

64 *Dusty Interior* 1937
Gelatin-silver photograph;
7⅜ × 9 7/16 in. (18.7 × 24 cm)
Jones Family Collection

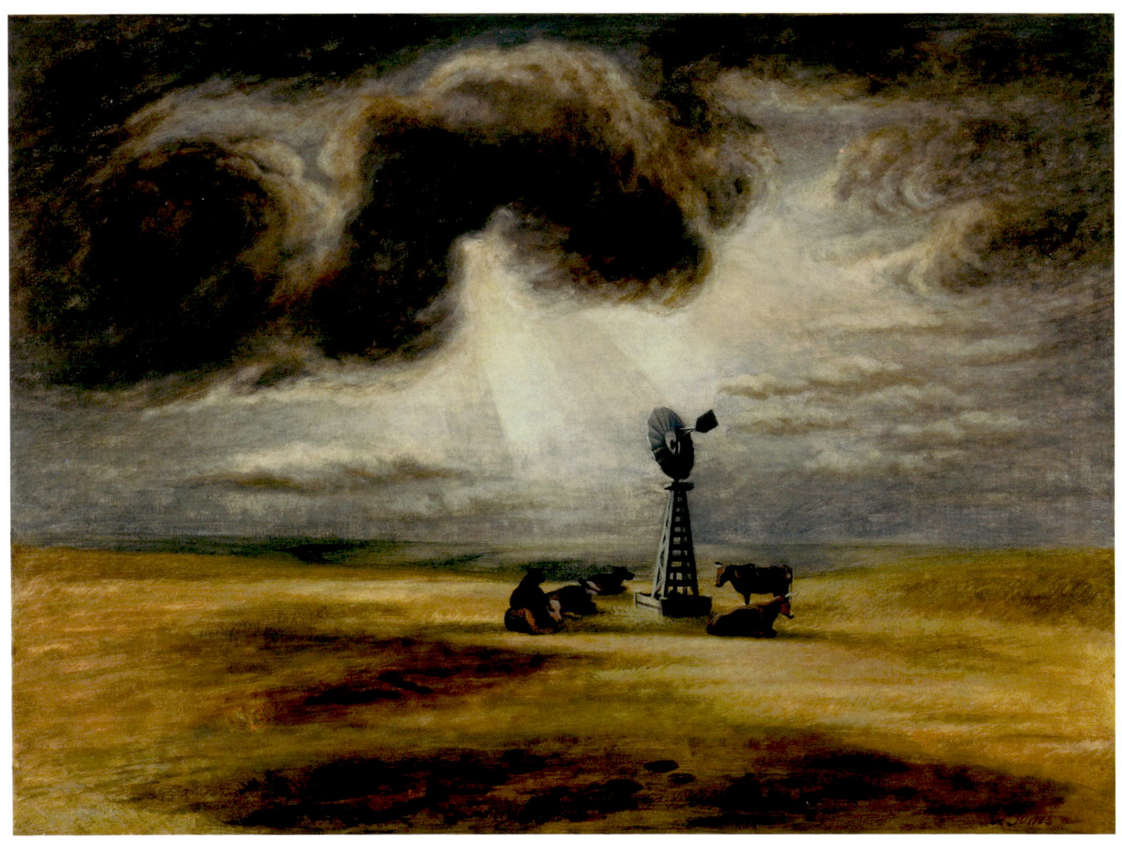

65 *Water Hole* 1936
Tempera on canvas; $25\frac{1}{2} \times 35\frac{1}{2}$ in. (64.8 × 90.2 cm)
Private collection, Courtesy of Michael Rosenfeld Gallery, LLC, New York, New York

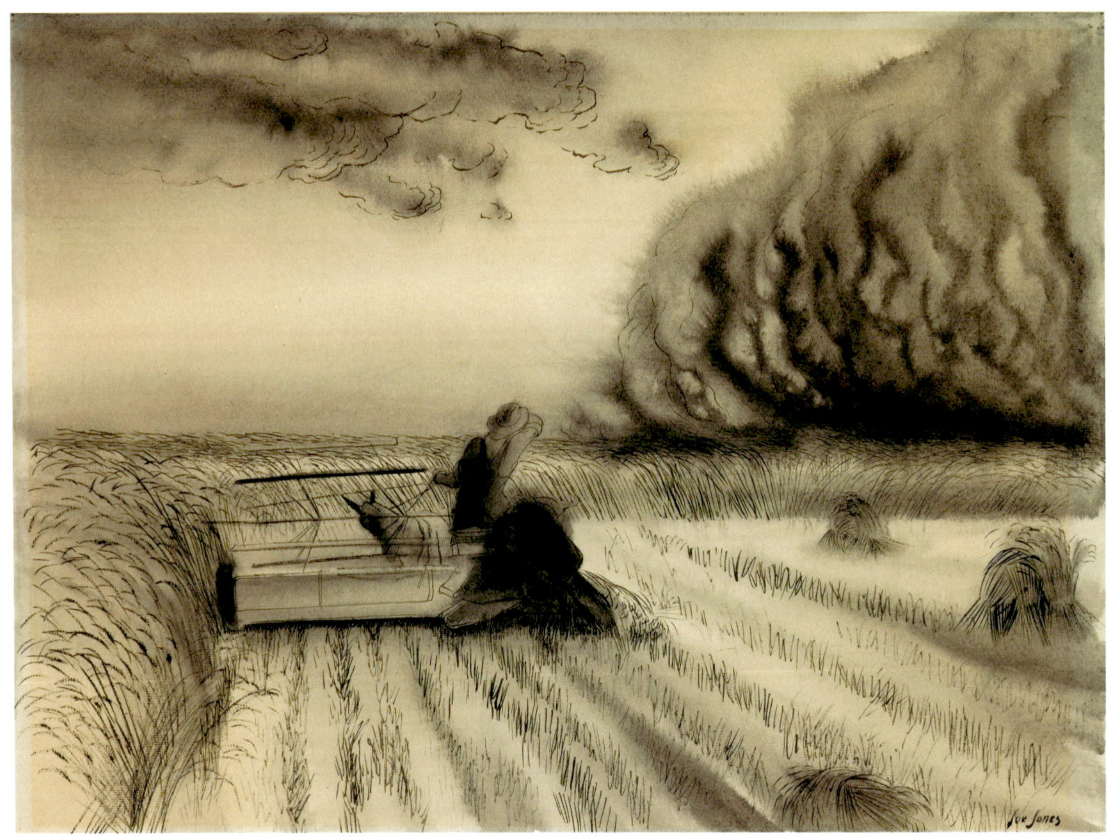

66 *Dust Storm* 1937
Brush and ink wash on cream Strathmore laid paper;
$18\frac{3}{8} \times 25$ in. (46.7 × 63.5 cm)
Collection of Ruth and Tim Wood

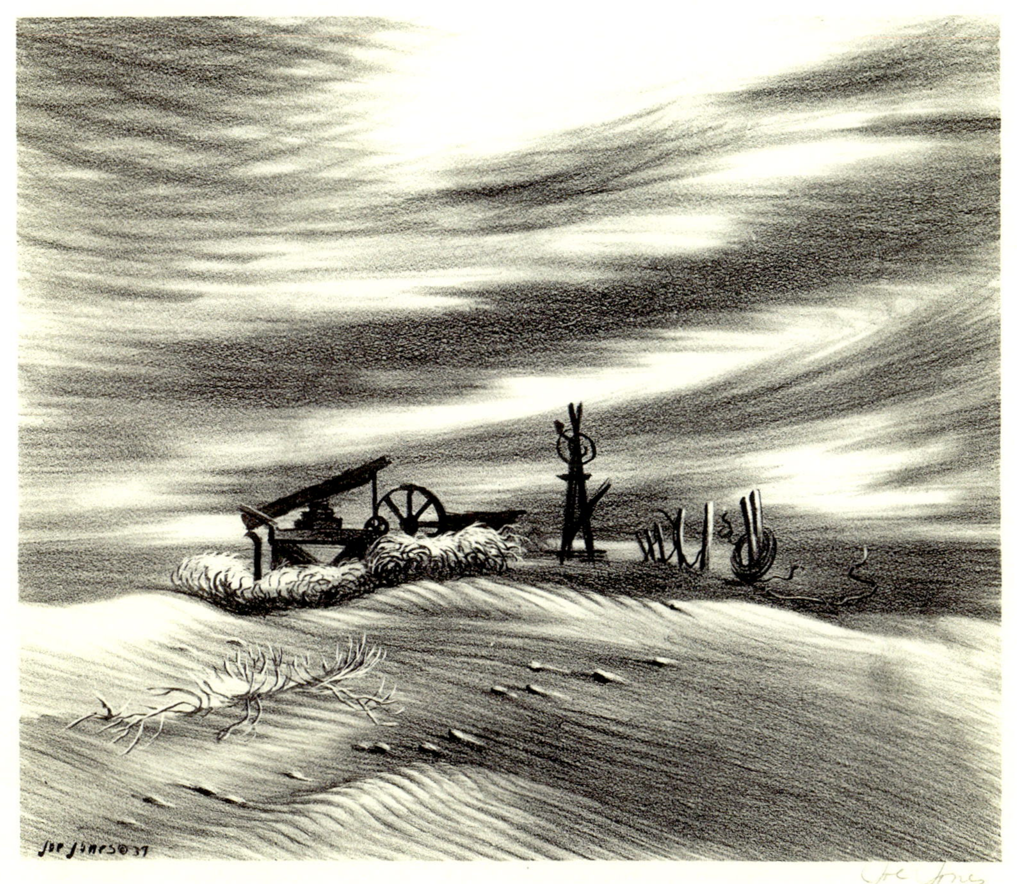

67 *Wastelands* 1937
Lithograph on off-white wove paper; image: 9⅞ × 11⅞ in. (25.1 × 30.2 cm), sheet: 12¼ × 16 in. (31.1 × 40.6 cm)
Saint Louis Art Museum, Bequest of Horace M. Swope

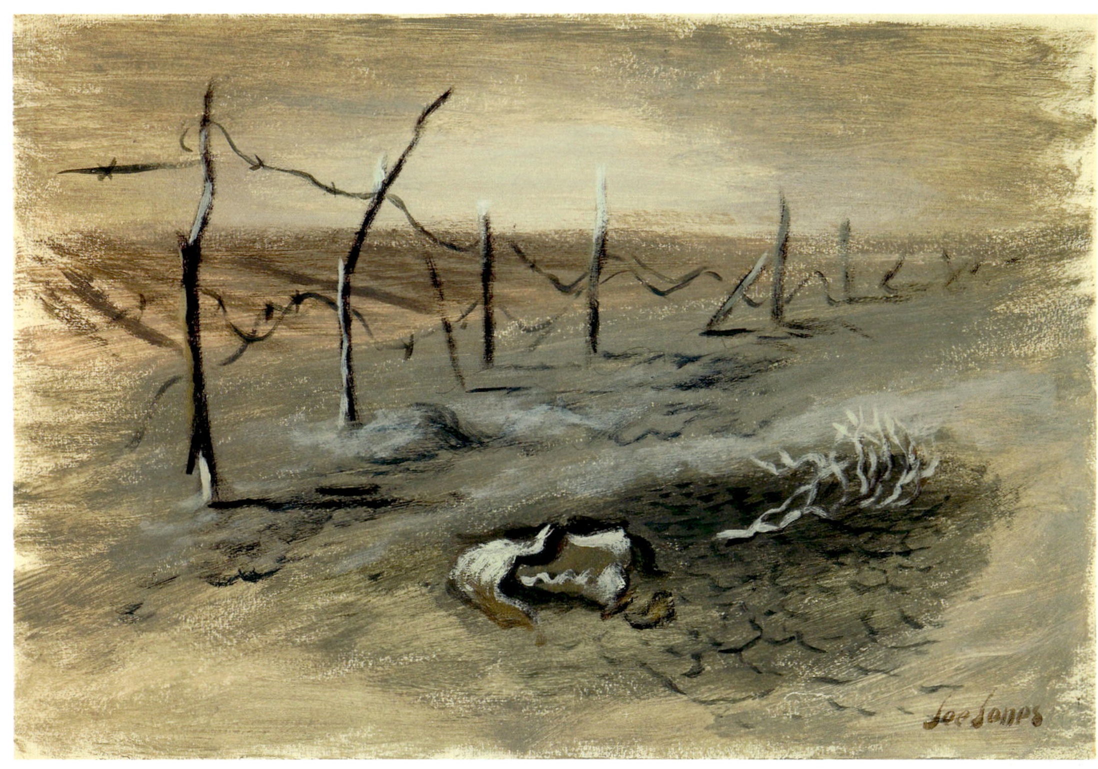

68 *Carcass* c. 1937
Casein on textured cream wove paper; 12 × 18 in. (30.5 × 45.7 cm)
Collection of Ruth and Tim Wood

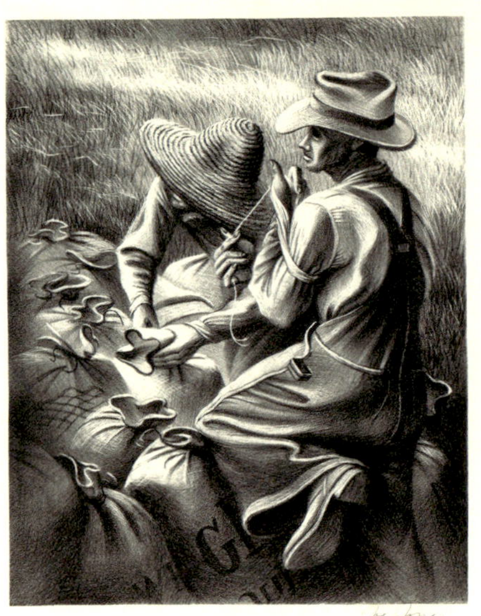

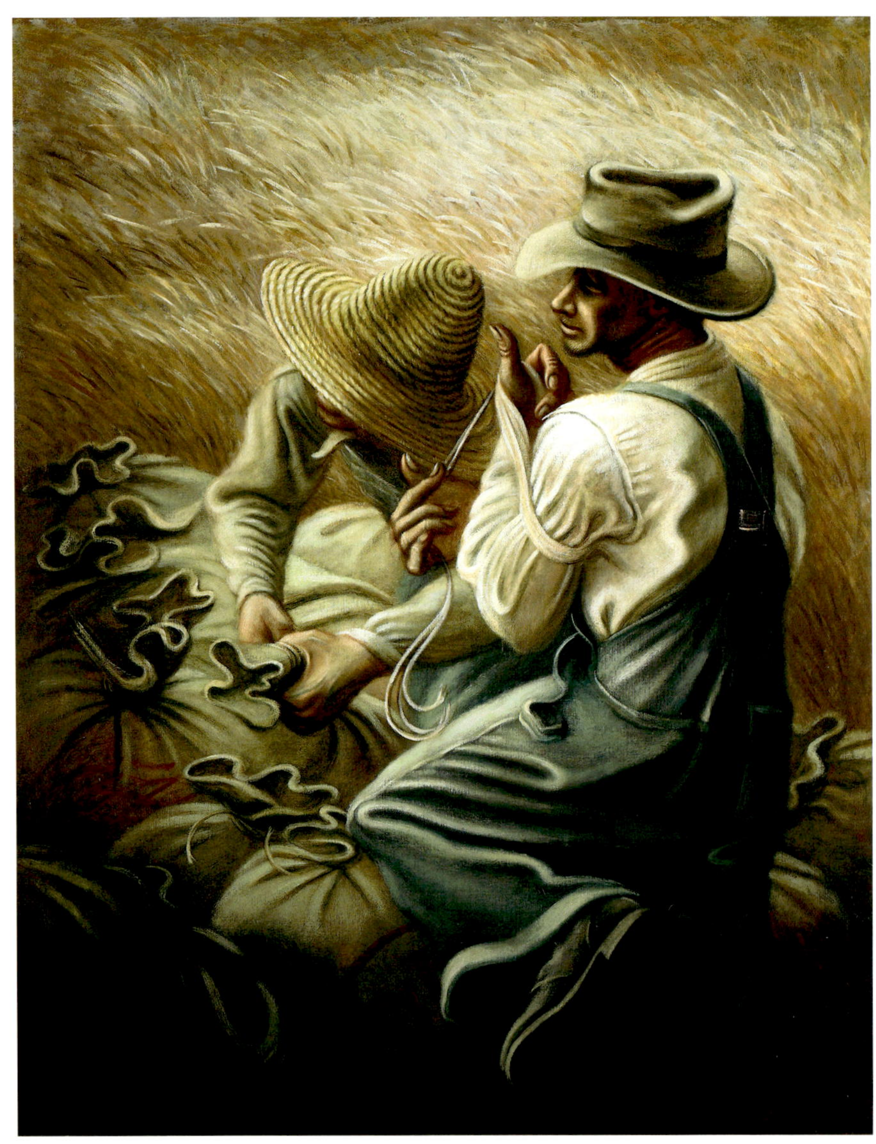

69 *Missouri Wheat Farmers* 1938
Lithograph on cream Rives wove paper;
image: 9⅞ × 8 in. (25.1 × 20.3 cm),
sheet: 16 × 11⅞ in. (40.6 × 30.2 cm)
Saint Louis Art Museum, Bequest of Horace M. Swope

70 *Missouri Wheat Farmers* 1938
Oil on canvas; 48½ × 38 in. (123.2 × 96.5 cm)
Collection of Jeanne and Rex Sinquefield

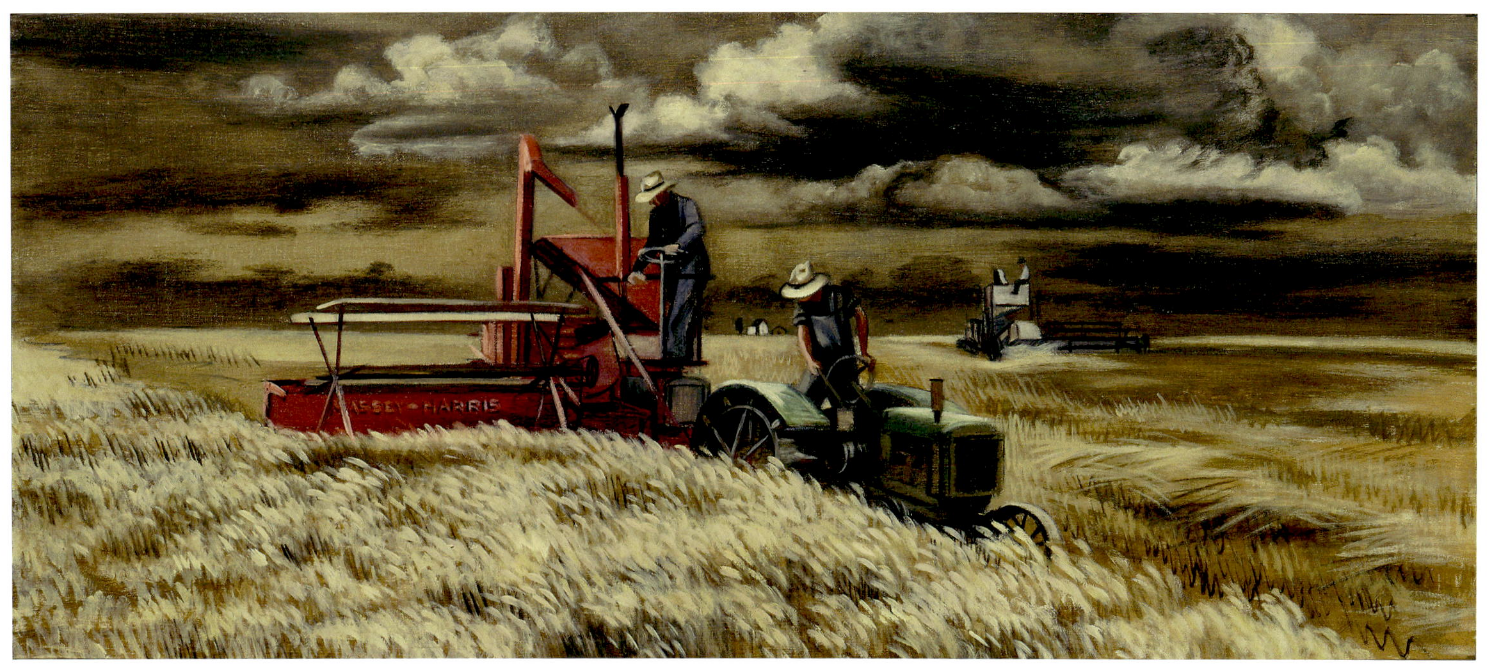

71 *Men and Wheat (Study for Post-Office Mural, Seneca, Kansas)* 1939
Oil on canvas; 15½ × 35¼ in. (39.4 × 89.5 cm)
Smithsonian American Art Museum, Washington, D.C., Transfer from the U.S. Department of the Interior, National Park Service

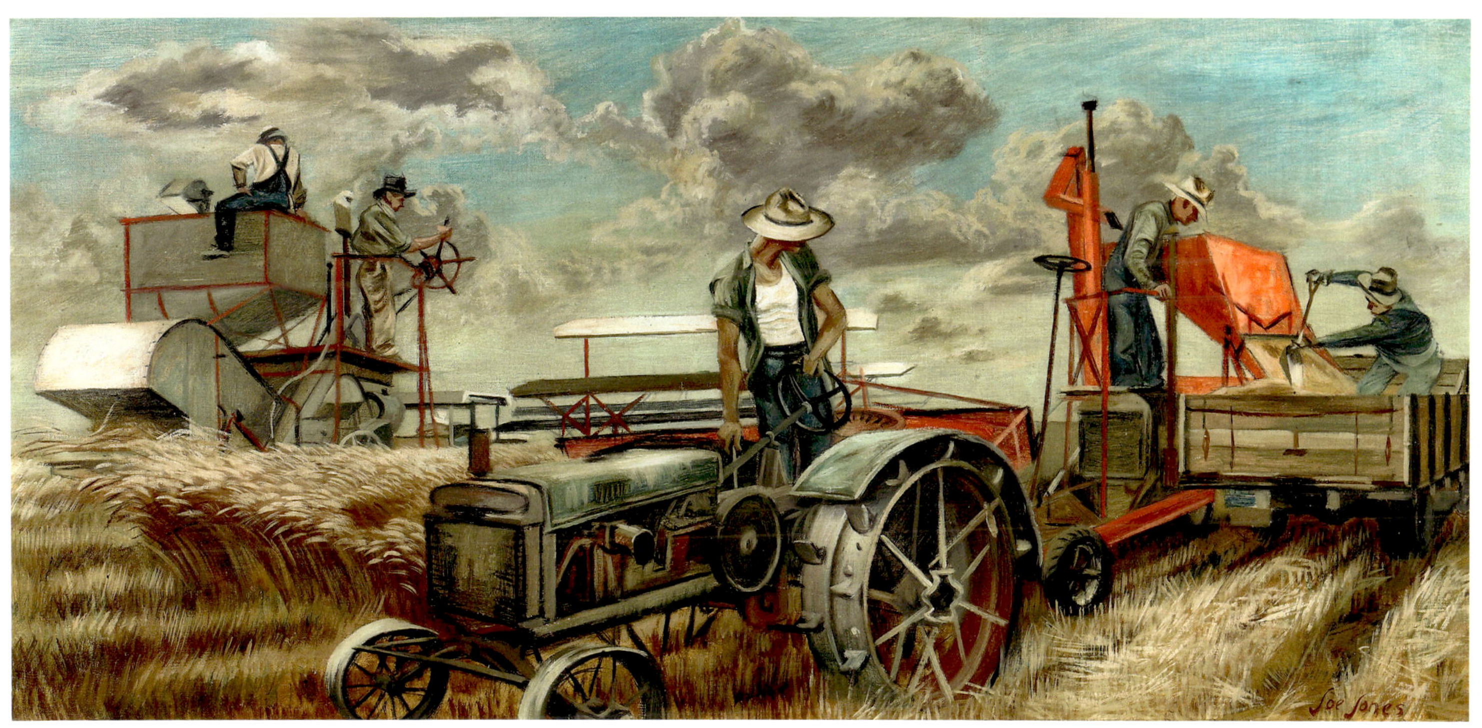

72 *Harvest Scene* c. 1939/42
Oil and tempera on canvas; 17 × 36 in. (43.2 × 91.4 cm)
Collection of Jeanne and Rex Sinquefield

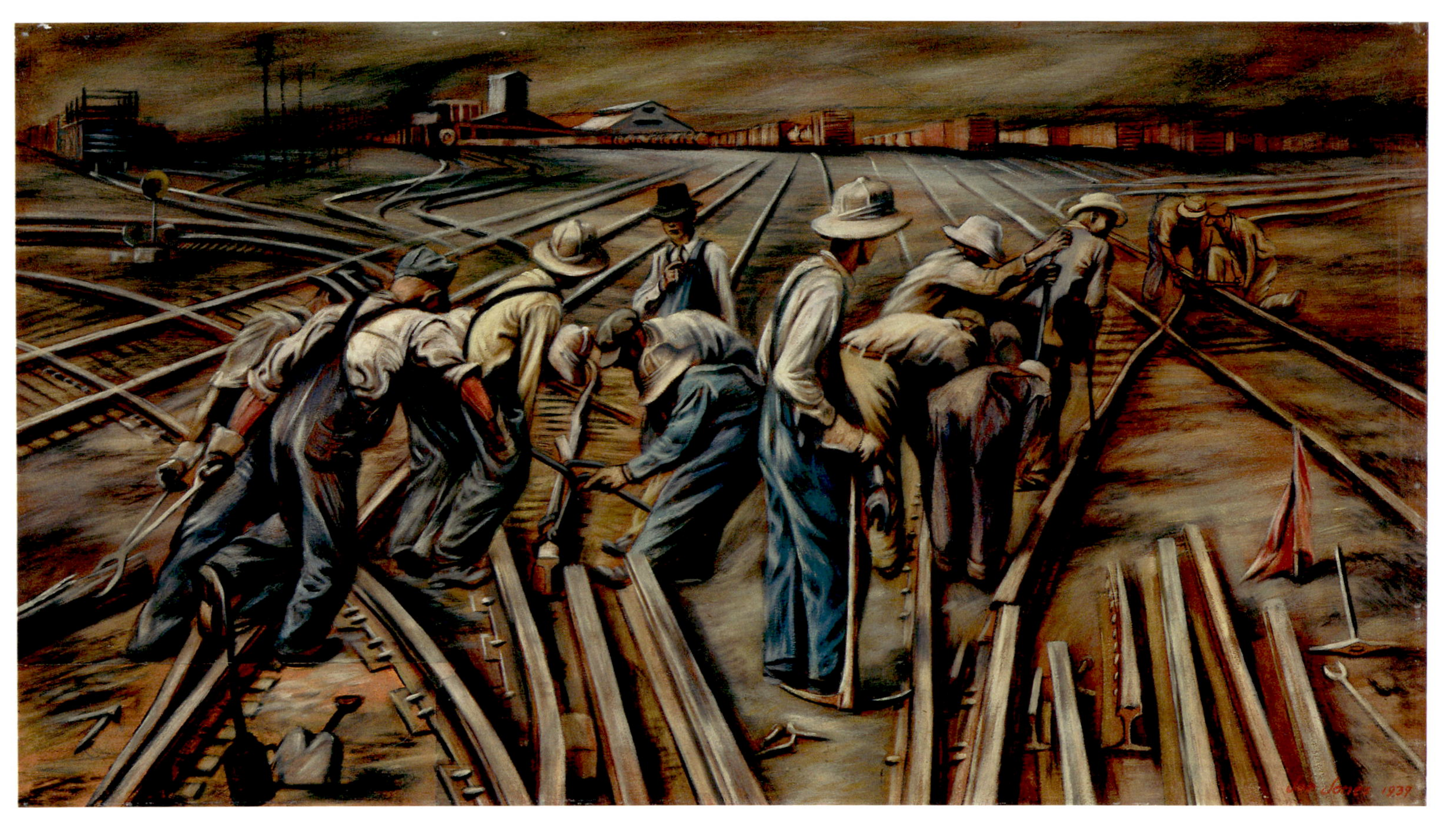

73 *Working on the Railroad* 1939
Oil on paper, mounted on Masonite; 16 × 29⅝ in. (40.7 × 75.3 cm)
Art Gallery of Hamilton, Gift of Mr. Herman H. Levy, O.B.E., 1961

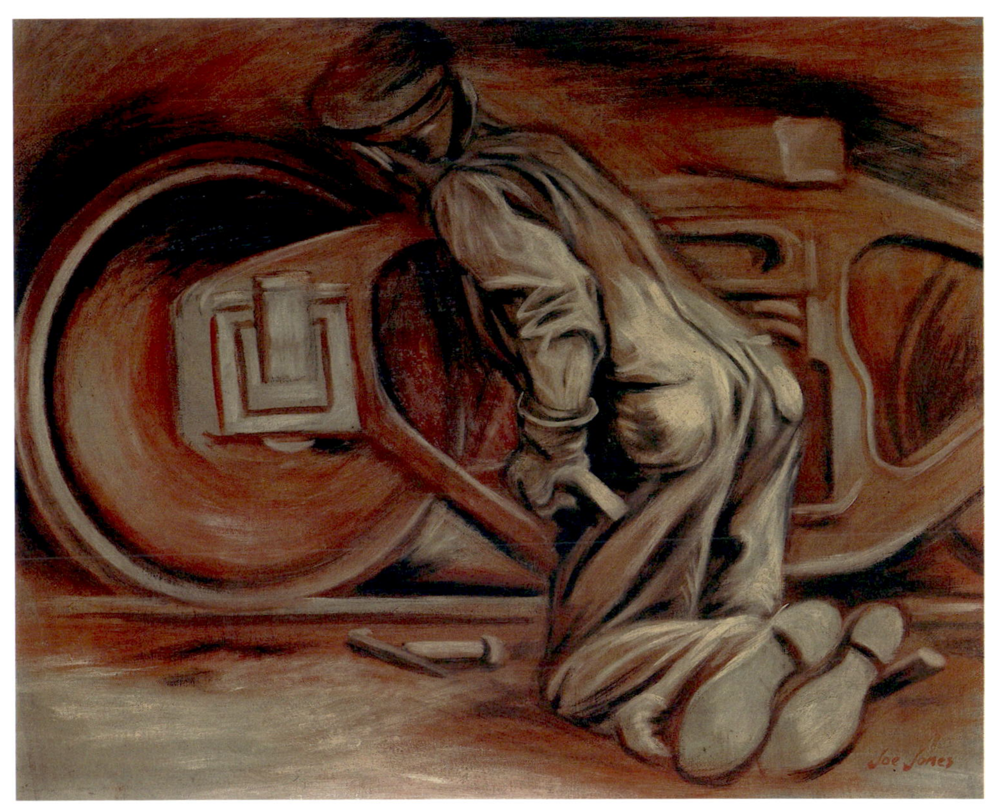

74 *Railroad Worker* c. 1937
Oil on canvas; $15\frac{7}{8} \times 20\frac{1}{16}$ in. (40.3×51 cm)
Collection of Ruth and Tim Wood

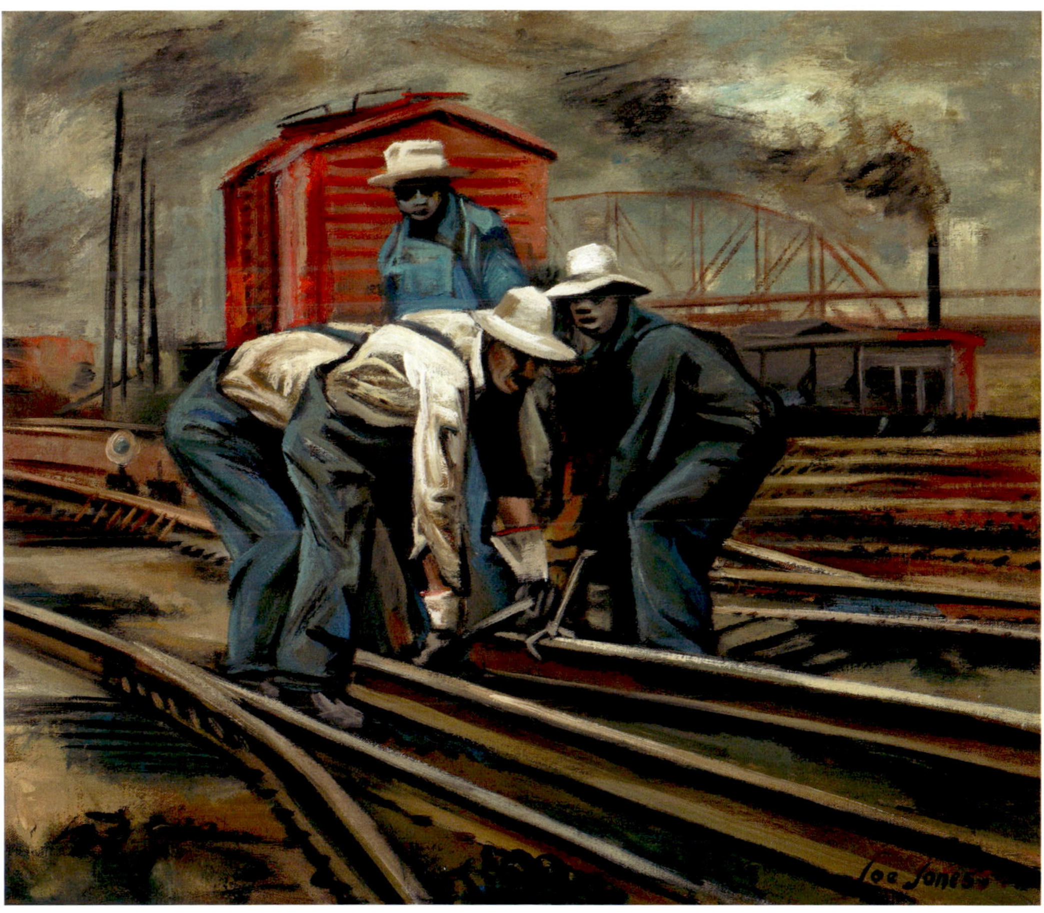

75 *Railroad Workers, St. Louis* c. 1939/40
Oil on canvas; $20\frac{1}{8} \times 24$ in. (51.1×61 cm)
Collection of Constance and Henry Christensen

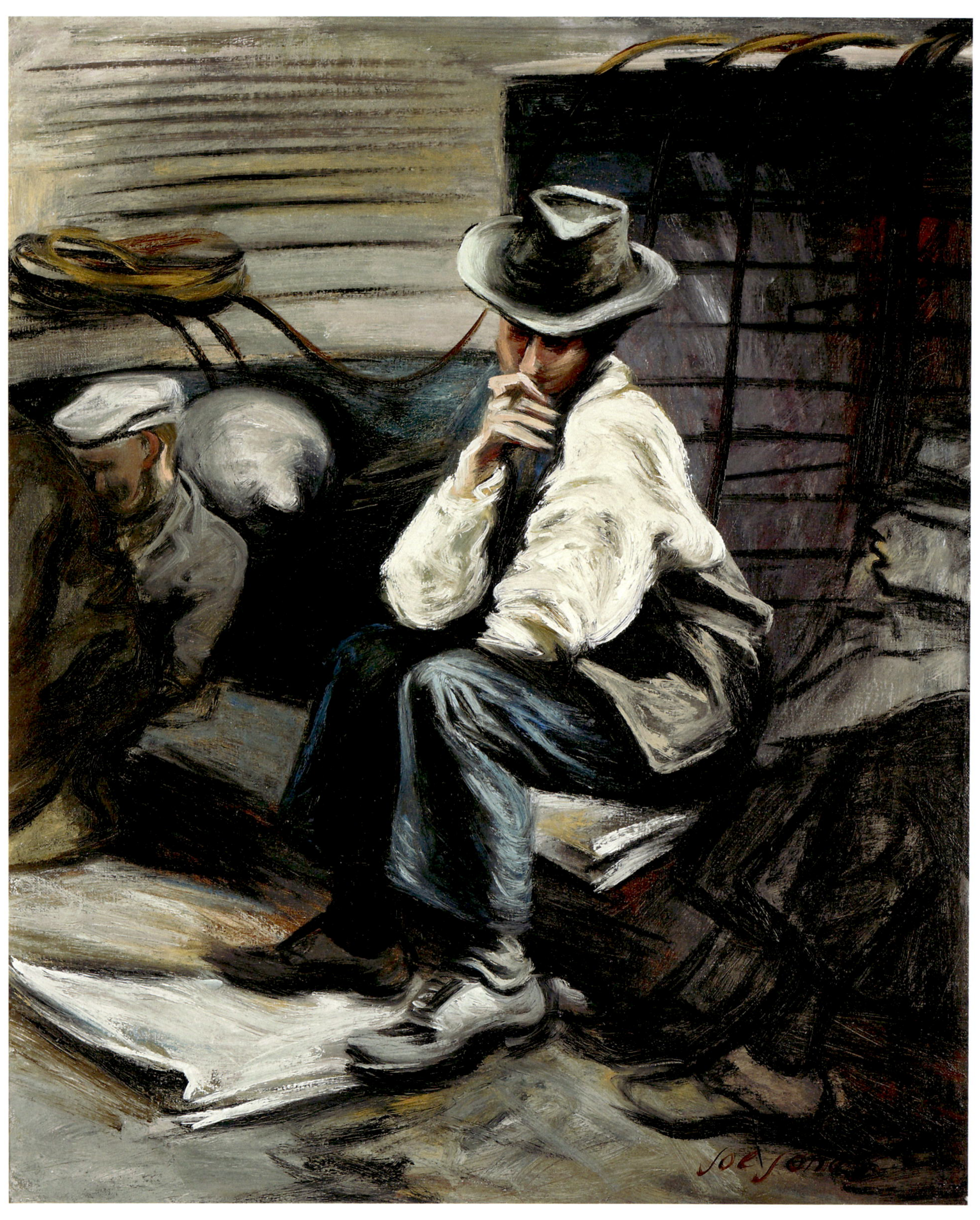

76 *Conversation* 1939
Oil on canvas; 24 × 20 in. (61 × 50.8 cm)
Private collection

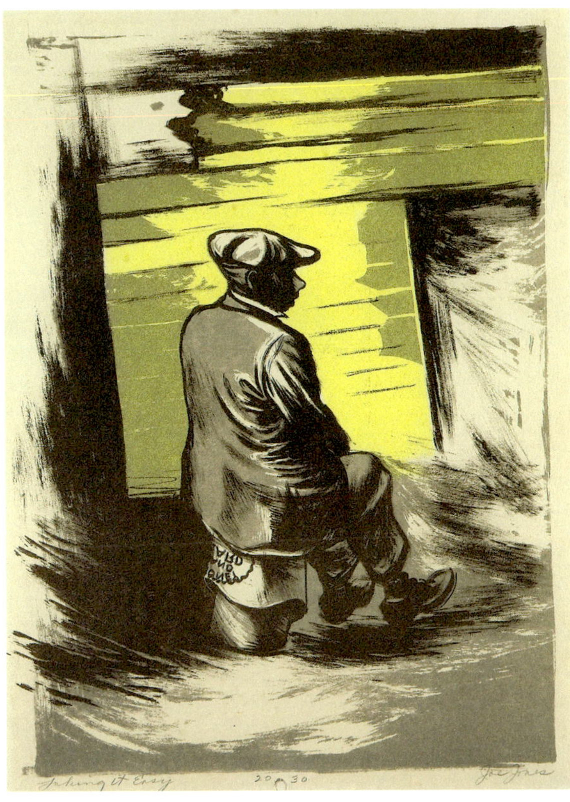

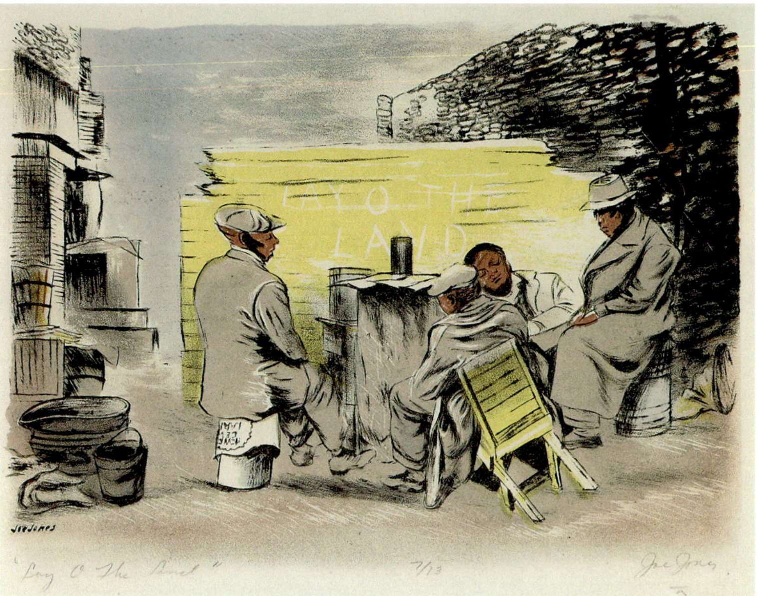

78 *Lay O' the Land* c. 1940
Color lithograph on cream wove paper;
image: 7½ × 10 in. (19.1 × 25.4 cm),
sheet: 8⅞ × 12⅜ in. (22.5 × 31.4 cm)
Collection of Raya Koren and Peter Jones

77 *Taking It Easy* c. 1940
Color lithograph on cream wove paper;
image: 11 × 8⁵⁄₁₆ in. (27.9 × 21.1 cm),
sheet: 12¹⁵⁄₁₆ × 10⅜ in. (32.9 × 26.4 cm)
Courtesy of the Missouri History Museum, St. Louis

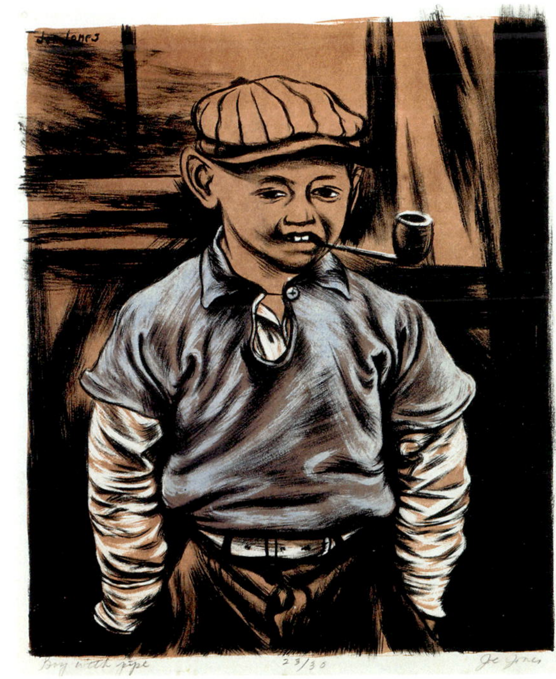

79 *Boy with Pipe*
c. 1939
Color lithograph on cream wove paper;
image: 10½ × 8 in. (26.7 × 20.3 cm),
sheet: 13 × 10⅜ in. (33 × 26.4 cm)
Collection of Jeanne and Rex Sinquefield

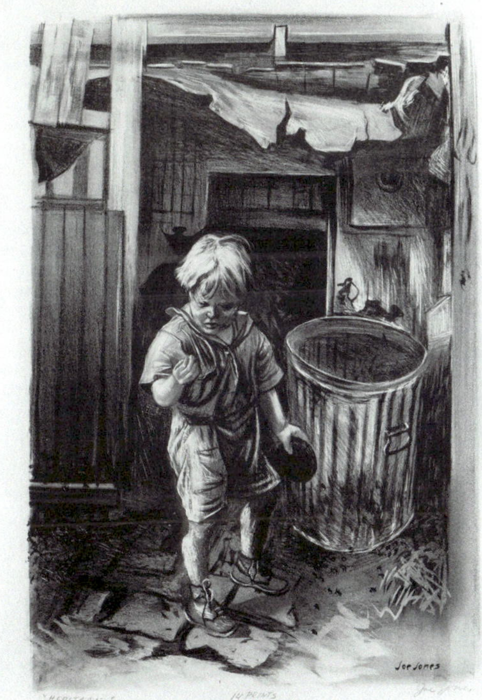

80 *Heritage* c. 1939
Lithograph on Rives wove paper;
image: 16¾ × 11¾ in. (42.5 × 29.8 cm),
sheet: 23⅛ × 15⅞ in. (58.7 × 40.3 cm)
Collection of James and Virginia Moffett

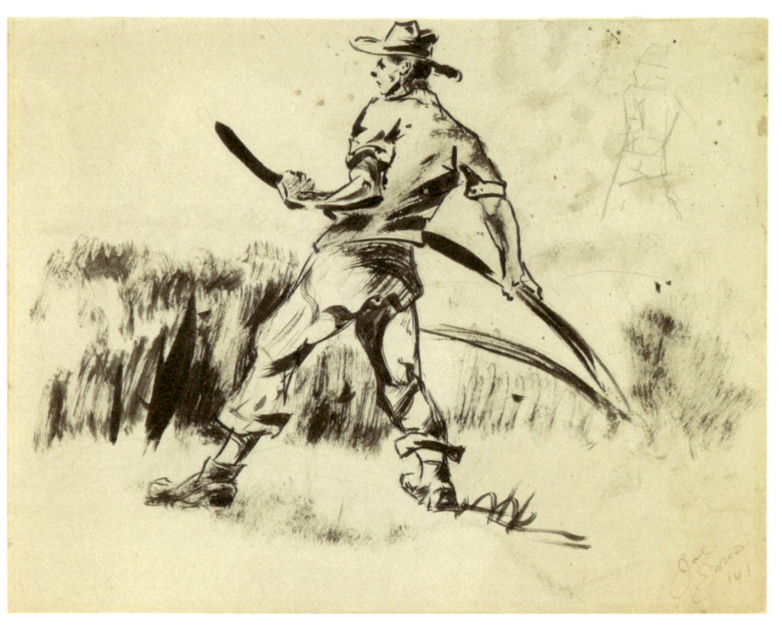

81 *Man with Scythe* 1941
India ink and graphite on cream wove paper;
10¾ × 14⅛ in. (27.3 × 35.9 cm)
Collection of Hunt and Donna Bonan

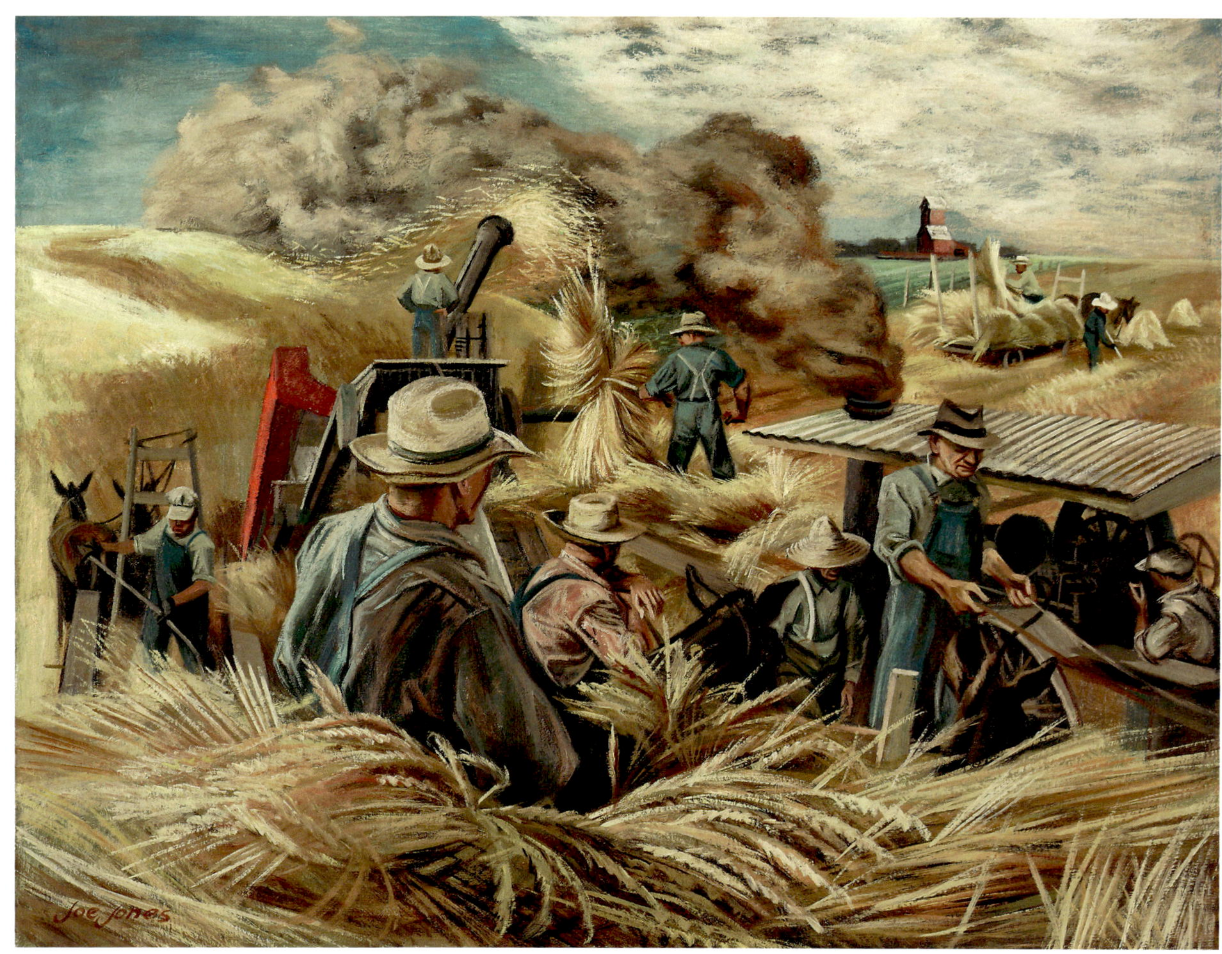

82 *Yellow Grain* c. 1942
Oil on canvas; 29½ × 40 in. (74.9 × 101.6 cm)
The Cleveland Museum of Art, Mr. and
Mrs. William H. Marlatt Fund, 1943.62

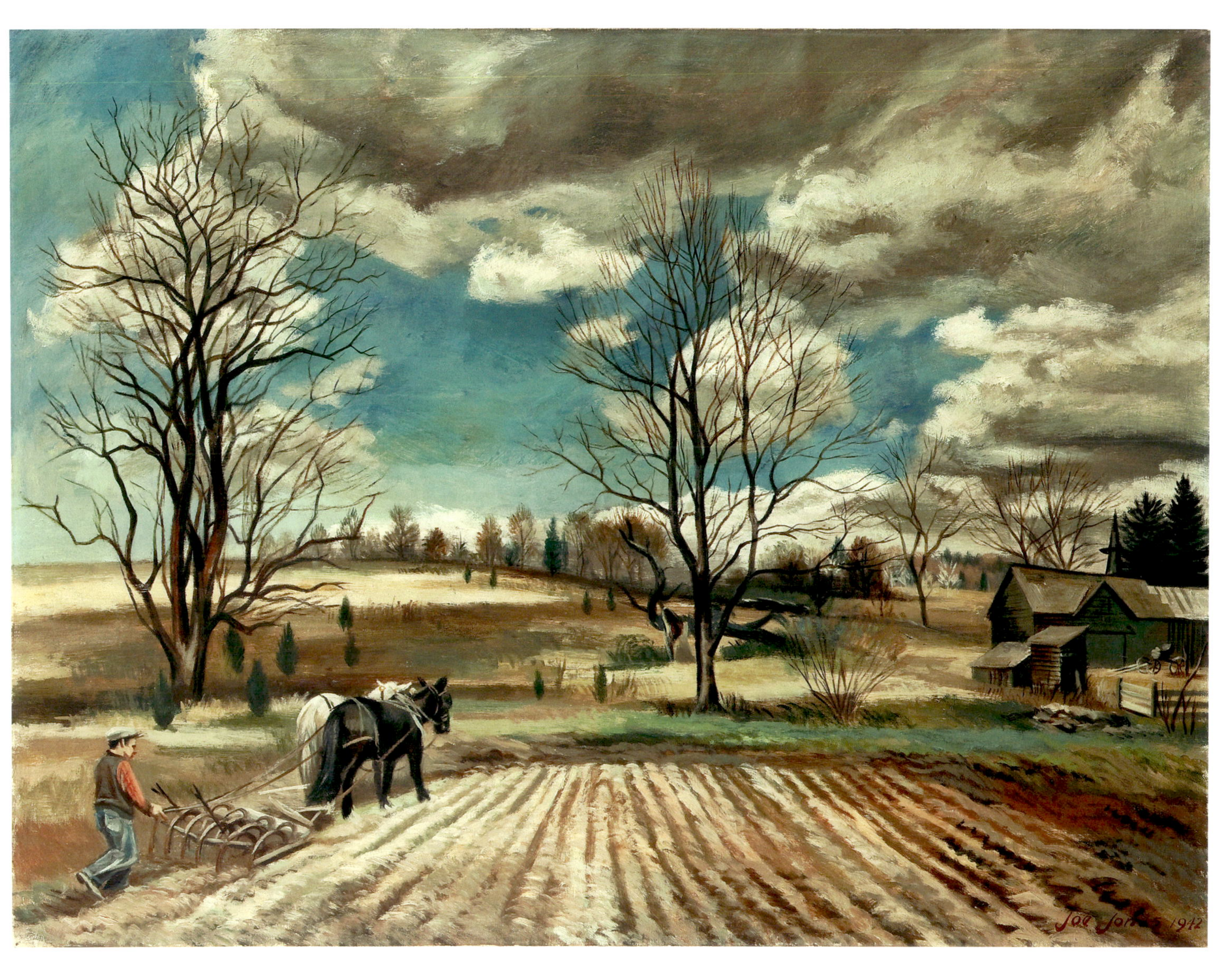

83 *Spring Plowing* 1942
Oil on canvas; 30 × 40 in. (76.2 × 101.6 cm)
Collection of the Newark Museum, Gift of
Mrs. Edith Lowenthal, 1945

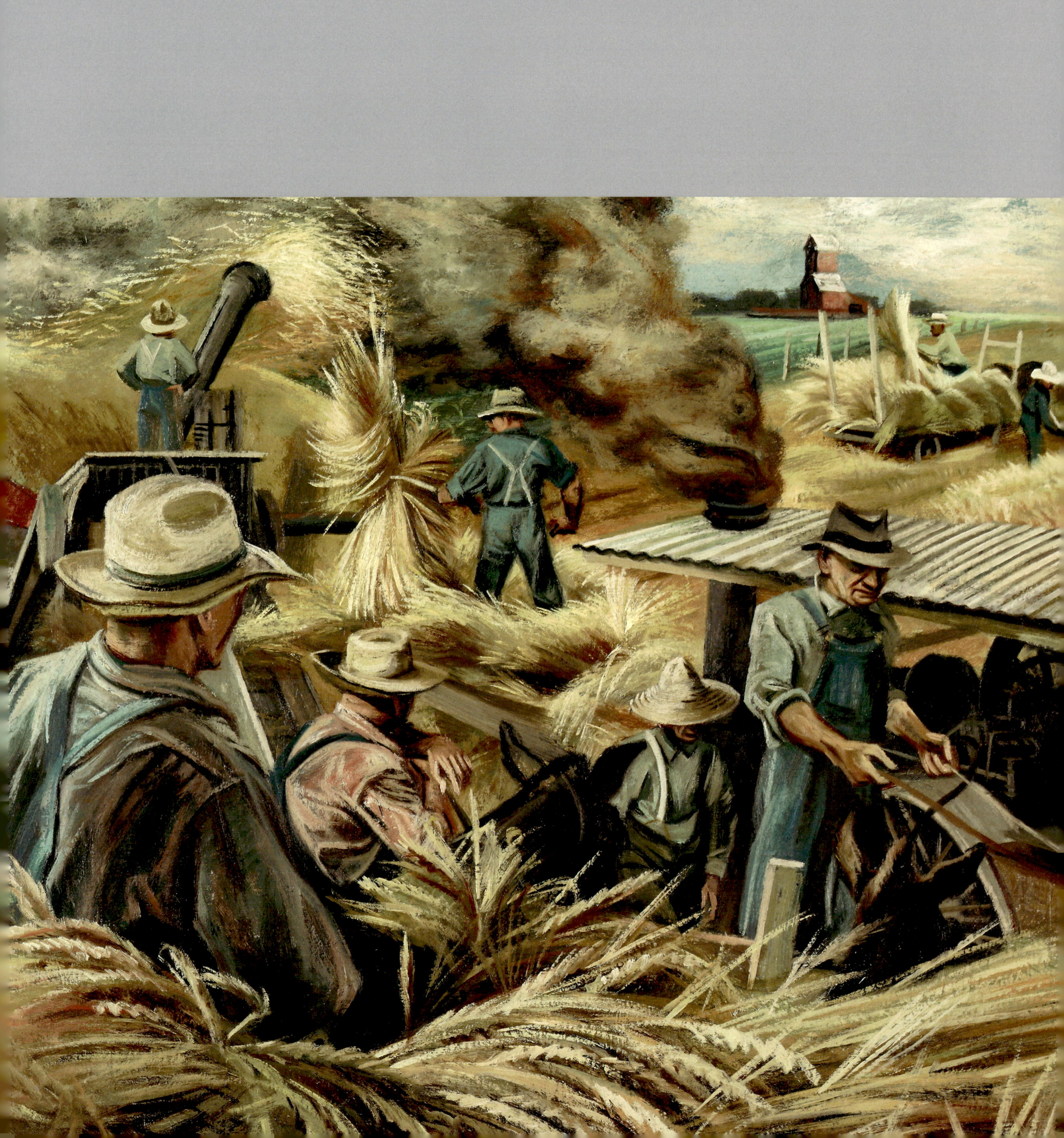

Chronology

Bryna R. Campbell

JOE JONES 1909–1963

The following abbreviations are used here:
AAA Galleries: Associated American Artists Galleries, New York
A.C.A. Gallery: American Contemporary Art Gallery, New York
CAM: City Art Museum, St. Louis
FERA: Federal Emergency Relief Administration
MMA: The Metropolitan Museum of Art, New York
MoMA: The Museum of Modern Art, New York
PWAP: Public Works of Art Project
RA: Resettlement Administration
section: Treasury Department, Section of Painting and Sculpture (until 1939), Section of Fine Arts (thereafter)
SLAG: St. Louis Artists' Guild
TRAP: Treasury Relief Art Project

All titles of works by Jones appear as listed in exhibition catalogues or other related documents. Because Jones sometimes assigned multiple titles to single works and often used the same title for more than one work, it can be difficult to identify with certainty whether or where a work exists today. Thus, all works by Jones listed here are current location unknown, unless otherwise specified. The titles of one-time exhibitions are given between quotation marks; those of annual and biannual exhibitions are not. All letters cited are in the Dr. John Green Collection, Missouri History Museum, St. Louis, unless otherwise specified.

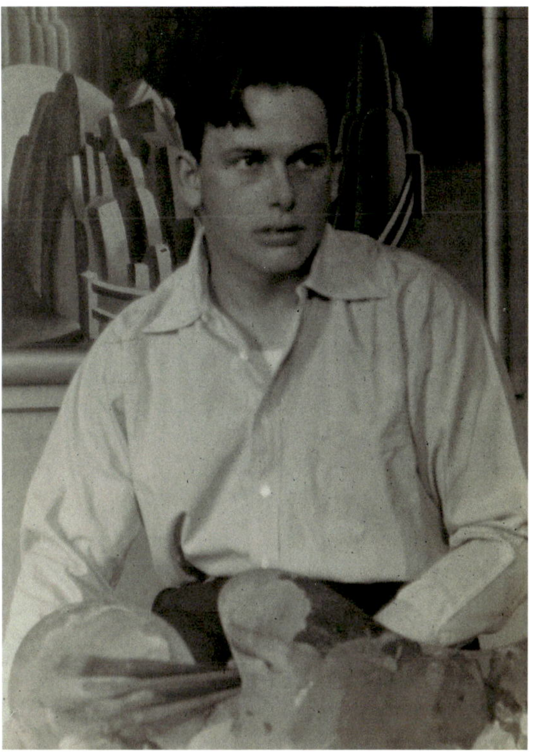

Fig. 1. Joe Jones before his painting *Aspirations* (c. 1931; location unknown), c. 1931. Courtesy of George and Dolores Friesen.

1909

Apr. 7. Joseph John Jones is born to Frank Jones (c. 1869–1939), a first-generation American of Welsh parentage; and his wife, Anna (née Roehrs; c. 1879–1964), a second-generation American of German descent. Frank Jones works as a housepainter, supporting his family on a meager income. The Joneses live at 4561 Maffitt Ave., in north St. Louis. Jones is the couple's fifth and last child. He is preceded by Robert Fenton (b. 1899), Adele (b. 1902), William Hugh (b. 1904), and Benjamin (b. 1908).

1923

Jones finishes eighth grade at Benton Grade School. After purportedly running away briefly to California, he becomes apprenticed to his housepainter father. He continues this work for the next few years, studying art in his spare time.

1927

Jones is enrolled in a decorative-painting class probably at the David Ranken, Jr., School of Mechanical Trades, where he produces sketches of ornate interior designs (see fig. 3).

1930

Mar. 30–May 1. Two works by Jones, *The Christy Plant* and *Tuscan, St. John's and Temple Israel*, appear in the *St. Louis Post-Dispatch*–sponsored Black and White Competitive Exhibition for St. Louis Scenes, at the St. Louis Artists' Guild (hereinafter SLAG).

Sept. 20–Nov. 2. Jones exhibits *Nude* in the section devoted to local artists in the Annual Exhibition of Paintings by American Artists, at the City Art Museum, St. Louis (hereinafter CAM).

Dec. 1–Jan. 10, 1931. *Marg* (or *Maarg*) (Turk, fig. 5) is exhibited in SLAG's Annual Exhibition. The painting receives the $100 L.W. Baldwin portraiture prize.

Dec. 20. At twenty-one, Jones marries Freda Sies (see Turk, fig. 8), a divorcée four years his senior. The two probably met in St. Louis's Bohemian art community; Freda is a performer of "aesthetic dance," a modern alternative to ballet and show dancing.

1931

Mar. Jones exhibits a work in the Black and White Competitive Exhibition for St. Louis Scenes, at SLAG.

May 15–June 15. *Aspirations* (see fig. 1), *Portrait of Mr. M.*, and a sculpture, *Composition*, appear in the Annual No-Jury Exhibition, sponsored by the Independent Artists of St. Louis, at the Old Courthouse. Jones joins the group around this time.

June. Jones is living in a garage with a studio space at 4490 Lindell Blvd., in St. Louis's Central West End neighborhood. His previous studios were in a warehouse and in an office building north of Forest Park, on the corner of DeBaliviere and McPherson. By September he is again living with his family.

Fall. Jones receives an honorable mention for work submitted to the summer F. Weber Co. sketch contest.

Sept. 19–Nov. 1. *Still Life* is in the section devoted to local artists in CAM's Annual Exhibition of Paintings by American Artists.

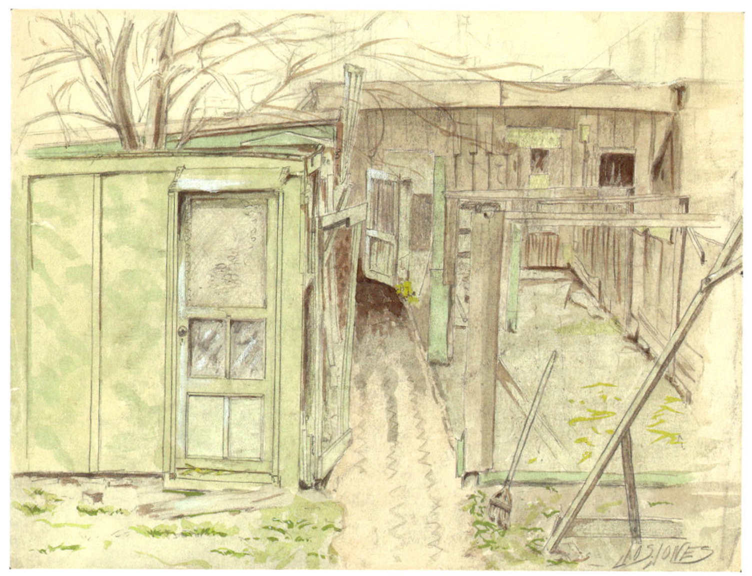

Fig. 2. Joe Jones. *Untitled*, c. 1920. Graphite (?) and watercolor (?) on paper; 9 × 12 in. (22.9 × 30.5 cm). Jones Family Collection.

Nov. Jones's first solo exhibition takes place at Mme Lisbeth Ebers Hoops's dance studio, in University City, Mo. The exhibition comprises twenty-six oils, including *Freda* (cat. 14), *Lindell Boulevard*, and *Mrs. Thomas B. Sherman* (cat. 5), and three lithographs (cats. 10, 11, 13). The exhibition closes Nov. 29.

Jones demonstrates painting to pupils of the Community School, St. Louis. The school purchases one of his paintings.

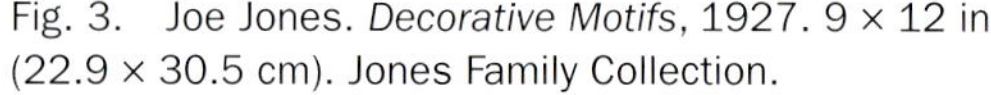

Fig. 3. Joe Jones. *Decorative Motifs*, 1927. 9 × 12 in. (22.9 × 30.5 cm). Jones Family Collection.

Nov. 13. Jones becomes a charter member of the New Hats, a by-invitation-only organization devoted to the promotion of modernism in Midwestern art.

Dec. The New Hats stages its first exhibition, at the dance studio of Mme Hoops, a club member. Jones exhibits a still life and several works from his one-person show. The exhibition closes on Dec. 26.

Jones is commissioned to execute murals for the reception room at radio station KMOX's broadcasting studio, in the new St. Louis Mart Building, at Twelfth and Spruce. His painting (see fig. 4), unveiled sometime in January 1932, features scenes of industrial St. Louis. Around this time, he is also asked to paint a modernist mural, *Wooded Landscape* (cat. 6), for the LaDue Rd. home of Mrs. Aaron Rauh, wife of the president of Rice-Stix Co.

1932

Jan. 16. The New Hats exhibition opens at a second venue, the Quincy (Ill.) Art Center, with a reception featuring music and dancing.

Mar. Jones is represented in "March Group of Contemporary Artists," an exhibition of black and white work organized by Alexandra Korsakoff-Galston, at the Newhouse Gallery, St. Louis.

Apr. 24–May 25. *Still Life*, *Alpha Portland Cement Co.*, and a drawing, *Freda*, appear in SLAG's Annual Exhibition. *Still Life* wins the $100 Otto L. Spaeth Prize for Modern Painting.

May 28–July 1. Jones's charcoal drawing *Laclede Christy* wins the $50 Francis D. Healy Prize for St. Louis scenes in the Annual Black and White Competitive Exhibition for St. Louis Scenes, at SLAG.

Aug. 15–Oct. 16. *Still Life* and *Riverfront* appear in the section devoted to local artists in CAM's Annual Exhibition of Paintings by American Artists. *Still Life* receives an honorable mention.

Oct. 15–Nov. 15. At the third Annual No-Jury Exhibition of the Independent Artists of St. Louis, held in the rotunda of the city's Old Courthouse, Jones shows a group of still lifes.

Nov. Jones participates in the second annual New Hats exhibition, at the Noonan–Kocian Gallery, St. Louis. In December the exhibition travels to two Illinois venues, the Art Center in Quincy, and the Art Museum in Springfield.

In a studio at 1049a N. Grand Blvd., in north St. Louis, Jones and artist Sheila Burlingame hold classes for advanced art students. Burlingame teaches sculpture, drawing, and woodcut; Jones teaches color, design, and lithography.

Nov. 20. Studio House—a gallery and studio space devoted to local artists—opens in St. Louis with a mixed-media exhibition of work by Jones and others.

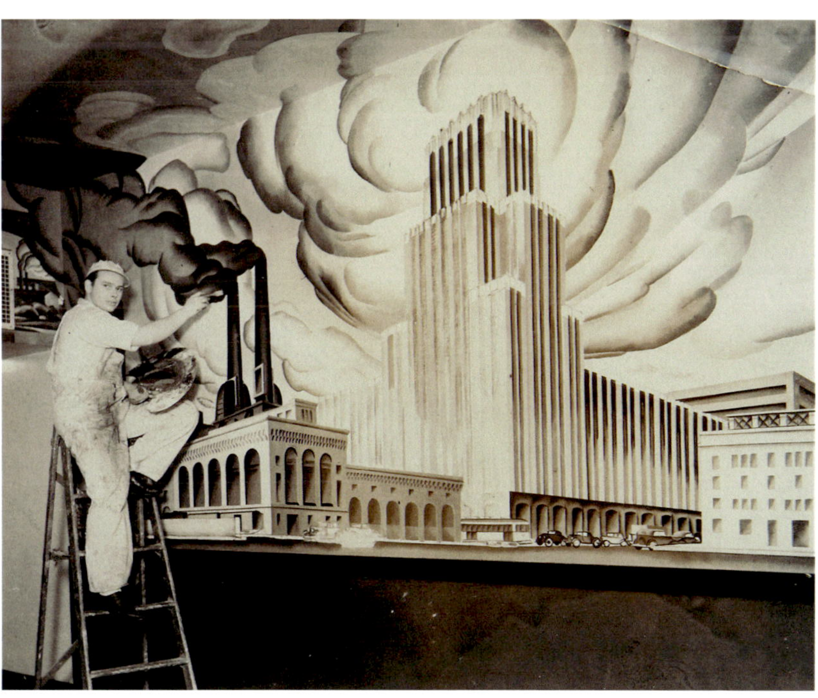

Fig. 4. Joe Jones with his mural (destroyed) for the reception room of the KMOX radio station, St. Louis, c. 1932. Courtesy of James and Karen Jones.

1933

Mid-Jan.–Feb. 15. Jones mounts a solo exhibition with twenty-eight works at SLAG, including *Alley* (cat. 23) and *Nude in a Red Robe*.

Around this time, he begins signing his works "Joe Jones" instead of "Joseph Jones" (see Signature Analysis).

Feb. Interested in Jones's artistic promise, ten prominent St. Louis citizens form the Co-operative Art Society (also known as the Joe Jones Club) to financially support the artist for a seven-month period, as well as help him arrange exhibitions of his work. They include four medical doctors: Robert Elman, Gustave Lippmann, Arthur W. Proetz, and Carliss Malone Stroud; three staff members of the *St. Louis Post-Dispatch*: the cartoonist D. R. Fitzpatrick and writers Julius H. Klyman and Clark McAdams (current president of SLAG); E. Oscar Thalinger, an artist and CAM's registrar; Israel Treiman, a lawyer and professor; and Ernest A. Weiss, a businessman.

Spring. Jones begins an important friendship with Elizabeth Green, daughter of Dr. John Green, a prominent supporter of the arts in St. Louis. Their relationship will last more than a decade (see "Elizabeth Green," p. 28).

May 15–June 2. Jones, Freda, and Green take a road trip to the East Coast, which Green details in a travel journal. They arrive in Washington, D.C., on May 19 and spend two whirlwind days visiting the Corcoran Gallery of Art, Freer Gallery of Art, Library of Congress, the Smithsonian's National Gallery, and Mt. Vernon. They then travel through the night, reaching New York on May 21.

The three spend a little over a week in Manhattan, where Jones visits several galleries and the New School of Social Research, which displays important murals by Thomas Hart Benton and José Clemente Orozco. The travelers arrive at their final destination, Provincetown, Mass., on June 2.

May 17–June 15. *Return of the Fisherman* and *Clay Mine* appear in SLAG's "Twentieth Anniversary Exhibition," at CAM. A jury that includes painter Grant Wood declares *Clay Mine* the best of the 248 works on display. Jones receives the SLAG Prize of $200.

June–Aug. Supported by Green, Jones spends about three months studying art in Provincetown. While there, he joins the American Communist Party, a turning point in his career. He commits henceforth to produce art concerned with social issues, and he executes two key political works, a sardonically titled anti-lynching painting, *American Justice* (cat. 31), and a labor-themed composition, *New Deal* (or *Capitalism*) (Walker, fig. 1).

En route home, Jones stops at the Detroit Institute of Arts to inspect Diego Rivera's newly completed mural cycle, *Detroit Industry*. Jones causes a media uproar, criticizing the Mexican artist for selling out to his wealthy patrons (Edsel and Eleanor Ford). Jones declares, "His murals of mechanized men glorify the workers in the Ford plants," instead of emphasizing their oppression.[1] Adding insult to injury, Jones uses "an old house-painter's trick": rubbing his wet thumb across the wall's surface to test the paint's integrity.[2]

Sept. 16–23. Under the auspices of the Co-operative Art Society, the Stix, Baer & Fuller Dry Goods Co. sponsors Jones's first exhibition since he declared allegiance to the Communist Party. The show features twenty-eight paintings and a group of lithographs. In the exhibition pamphlet, the artist Walt Kuhn describes Jones as "perhaps the most promising American young artist."[3]

Sept. 16–Oct. 31. *Figure*, a painting of Freda fixing her hair, is in the section devoted to local artists in CAM's Annual Exhibition of Paintings by American Artists.

Oct. Jones and Freda move into a houseboat docked on the Mississippi River at the Mound City Boat Yards, at the foot of Franklin Ave., in downtown St. Louis.

Jones's relationship with the Co-operative Art Society breaks down when the society decides to discontinue its support of his career.

Dec. With the financial support of such prominent St. Louisans as J. Lionberger Davis, Edward Mallinckrodt, Jr., and Charles Nagel, Jones begins teaching free art classes for unemployed students (see fig. 5) in the Old Courthouse, where the St. Louis Art League had been holding paid classes. Green manages the donations and expenditures. The class meets twice a week in the second-floor, southwest courtroom. About half of the twenty-five students are African American.

Contrasting his approach with that of the more academic Art League, Jones tells the *St. Louis Post-Dispatch* that he believes in giving his students the freedom to fully express themselves in art, "regardless of whether their work is a protest against the social, economic, or political conditions of the day."[4] League secretary Frank A. E. Curley disapproves of Jones's approach: "The teacher has a responsibility, and Jones is teaching an art of protest against the existing industrial and political order of the day. As for the modernistic style of painting, it's getting to a point where young artists have to use it against their own convictions, so they may get recognition in exhibitions from judges."[5]

Dec.–Jan. 1934. Jones exhibits a number of paintings and drawings, including *Tugboat*, *Clay Mine*, and *The Trestle* (on permanent loan to the Saint Louis Art Museum), in a private exhibition at Green's residence, at 4401 McPherson Ave., in St. Louis's Central West End neighborhood.

Dec. 1–Jan. 15, 1934. *American Justice* (cat. 31) appears in the Exhibition of American Painting Today at the Worcester (Mass.) Art Museum. This is the first time Jones's work is seen in the East.

Dec. 8. The Public Works of Art Project (hereinafter PWAP) is organized with a grant from Civil Works Administrator Harry L. Hopkins to the U.S. Treasury Department, with the objective of employing artists at "craftsmen's wages in the embellishment of public property with works of art."[6]

Dec. 13–Jan. 1, 1934. *Road to the Beach* (cat. 30) appears in "Painting and Sculpture from 16 American Cities," an exhibition held at the Museum of Modern Art, New York (hereinafter MoMA).

1934

Jan. 24. The Unemployed Art Class displays its first major project, a 16-×-37-foot mural (Wolfe, fig. 3) executed in chalk on beaver board, along with several individual works. Designed by Jones and executed by seven pupils, the mural focuses on local social unrest. It features scenes of labor protest, an African American baptism, and a group of industrial workers. In a Feb. 16 interview with the *St. Louis Post-Dispatch*, Jones states that the exhibition also includes "Communist propaganda—here, and there," in the form of Soviet posters and prints of Soviet art donated by a Kansas City dentist.[7]

Mar. 3. Vandals tear down the Soviet posters displayed in Jones's Old Courthouse classroom and post a notice that calls the activities taking place there un-American. The vandals, who claim to represent a Washington, D.C., agency, also leave a note threatening to destroy the mural. Subsequent newspaper reports describe them as members of the American Fascist League. Months later the city's director of public safety, George W. Chadsey, admits that he had the posters photographed and a number of them removed by city employees.

Mar. 17. Jones gives a public talk, "Art in Soviet Russia," at Baldwin Auditorium, St. Louis.

Mid- to late Apr. Green expresses concerns about the leftist activities of the Unemployed Art Class, generating tension in her friendship with Jones. The two apparently resolve their differences by late April, when Jones and Freda spend an evening at Green's home.

Late Apr. Jones opens another exhibition of work from the Unemployed Art Class.

Apr. 24–May 20. *Street Scene* (Smithsonian American Art Museum) is included in the massive "National Exhibition of Art by the Public Works of Art Project," at the Corcoran, along with photographs of the Old Courthouse mural. *Street Scene* will also appear in a second exhibition of PWAP works, at the Department of Labor, in 1935.

Late May. The Joneses' houseboat is damaged, and Freda receives minor injuries, when a set of barges breaks loose upriver and lands between their boat and the docks (see fig. 6).

Summer. The couple decides to travel by houseboat down the Mississippi. The two make it to Arkansas City, Ark., about six

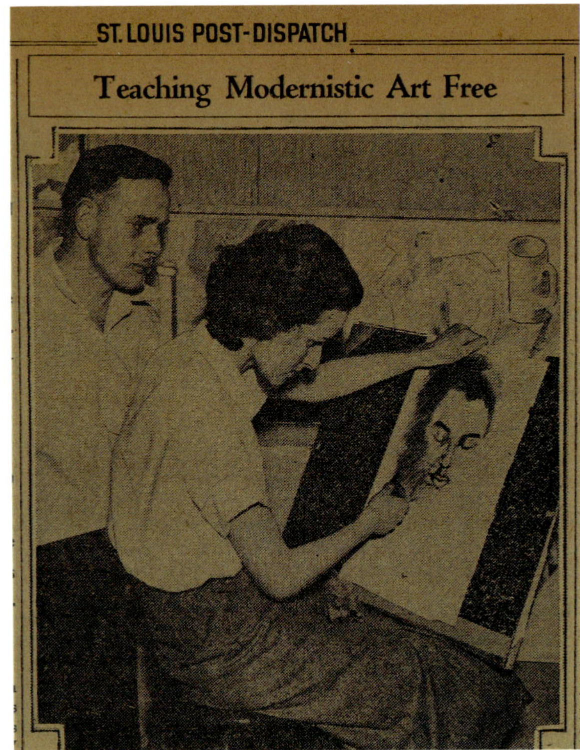
ST. LOUIS POST-DISPATCH

Teaching Modernistic Art Free

Fig. 5. "Teaching Modernistic Art Free," *St. Louis Post-Dispatch*, January 21, 1934. This photograph shows Joe Jones with Celia Schwartz, a student in his Unemployed Art Class. Courtesy of *St. Louis Post-Dispatch*.

hundred miles downriver, when the boat wears out, prohibiting further travel without expensive repairs. They remain in Arkansas for about a week before returning home by bus, thus ending their "river craze," as Jones calls it in an Aug. 29 letter to Green. They move to 303 Cedar St.

Mid–July. The Joneses visit the artists' colony in Ste. Genevieve, Mo., a French-colonial town founded around 1750. The Ste. Genevieve Artists' Colony was established in 1932 by St. Louis artists Bernard Peters, Jessie Beard Rickly, and Aimee Schweig with the goal of creating a Midwestern art center based on New England and European models, yet open enough for artists to pursue independent directions.

Fall. The Federal Emergency Relief Administration (hereinafter FERA) appoints Beatrice Bonine to assist Jones in teaching the Unemployed Art Class.

Oct. Working for PWAP, Jones begins a landscape mural for St. Louis's City Hospital. The mural is located in Division No. 8, the area designated for male tuberculosis patients. Funding for Jones falls through, and the work is eventually completed by local sculptor Ekhart Siebert.

Nov. 23. In a letter to Green, Jones lays out his extremely active work schedule. When not working on the City Hospital mural or attending to domestic tasks, he attempts to produce about "a picture a week." His evenings are even busier. On Monday nights, he studies "theoretical problems"; on Tuesday and Friday nights, he works with the Unemployed Art Class; on Wednesday nights, he attends a weekly open forum at the Old Courthouse; and on Thursday nights, he goes to political-organization meetings. Letters to Green from this period indicate tensions in his relationship with Freda.

Nov. 27–Jan. 10, 1935. *Wheat* (Walker, fig. 2) appears in the Biennial Exhibition of Contemporary American Painting at the Whitney Museum of American Art, New York.

Nov. 30. Freda is one of nine arrested for disturbing the peace at a demonstration of about one hundred Communists on the steps of St. Louis City Hall. They are protesting Mayor Bernard F. Dickmann's stance on unemployment relief. On Dec. 7, Freda is sentenced by City Judge Finnegan to six months in the workhouse and fined $500. She appeals the ruling.

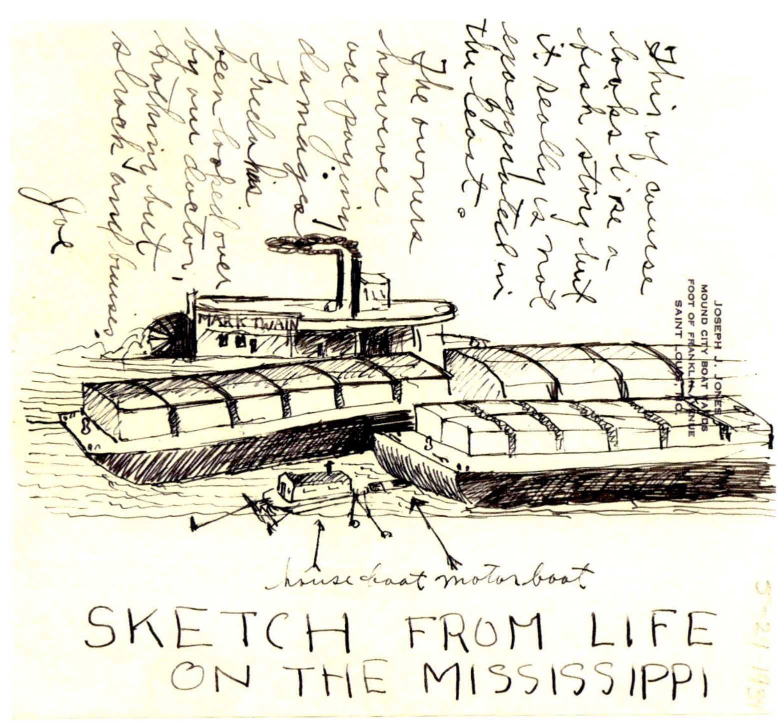

Fig. 6. Joe Jones. *Sketch from Life on the Mississippi*, 1934. Pen and ink on paper. Dr. John Green Collection, Missouri History Museum, St. Louis.

Dec. Jones is the art editor for the *Anvil*, a leftist literature magazine edited by his friend the proletarian writer Jack Conroy, author of the 1933 novel *The Disinherited*. Jones's association with the publication will end by Nov. 1935, when it can no longer afford the position.

Dec. 8. Chadsey orders Jones to vacate the premises of the Old Courthouse immediately. According to the artist, the city official believes that he has been using the Unemployed Art Class quarters as a Communist meeting place. Chadsey states that he will allow the class to continue in the space only if Jones and Freda sever their connection with the party. Jones denies the accusation: he says that there are a mere two Communists in the group—Freda and himself. The only meetings held in the room, he continues, were five forums sponsored by the Artists and Writers Union, "which were conducted respectively by a poet, a Lutheran minister, a well-known member of the Artists' Guild, a student of the theatre, and a member of the Communist Party—such of whom spoke strictly on cultural subjects."[8] In a newspaper interview, Jones likens the tone of Chadsey's accusations to Nazi fascism.[9]

According to Green, Jones is not only accused of Communist activity, but of being paid for it. In a letter written on Feb. 22, 1935, she also cites regular threats of "personal violence" made to African Americans seeking directions to the classroom, who are told that they are "not wanted in the Old Courthouse."

Dec. 14. After Jones and the members of the Unemployed Art Class refuse to leave the classroom, Chadsey orders the Old Courthouse custodian to padlock the doors and threatens to institute eviction proceedings. Class members draw up a resolution of protest, insisting that Jones remain director of the program. The entire class, now totaling thirty students, signs the document, along with FERA instructor Beatrice Bonine.

Dec. 15. A writer for the *St. Louis Star-Times* reports that he has visited the Unemployed Art Class, where he saw sketches "in the traditional art school manner," and students at work painting a still life of a green vase against a blue drape. Sympathetic to Jones's position, he writes, "Some were decidedly toil worn, but they were undoubtedly trying to draw."[10]

Dec. 21. The United Protest Committee for Civil Rights stages a mock trial of Mayor Dickmann, Judge Finnegan, Police Captain Wetzel, Relief Director Kasius, and Public Safety Director Chadsey at Hibernium Hall. Before some 150 people, they "convict" the group on five charges related to the closing of the Unemployed Art Class and the Nov. 30 demonstration during which Freda was arrested. Jones is one of eleven witnesses. Several testify to police brutality at the Nov. 30 demonstration.

1935

Jan. 4. The Artists and Writers Union displays work from the Unemployed Art Class at Union Hall, St. Louis. The exhibition, entitled "Art: Free or Dictated," occasions a symposium of the same name, and both Jones and Chadsey are invited to speak. Chadsey declines the invitation, citing another engagement.

Jan. 10. A number of prominent supporters of Jones, including Green and Ernest W. Stix, sign a petition protesting the closure of the Unemployed Art Class. They argue that Chadsey has no authority to shut down the operation because it had been managed by FERA since the fall. The effort is ultimately unsuccessful, and the room with the mural remains closed. By the end of the decade, the mural is in a state of permanent decay.

Jan. 14. Jones and Freda legally separate. Jones moves in with his parents at 9234 Arlene St., in Overland, Mo., around this time.

Feb. 4. A St. Louis judge grants Jones a divorce after he files charges of "general indignities."[11] Within days, Jones travels by bus to New York, planning to stay about a month. There he meets up with a colleague, Robert Hanna. The two rent a room at 315 W. 18th St., in Manhattan, for four dollars a day.

Feb. 8. Jones visits the Brooklyn Museum, where he sees an exhibition of American watercolors and expresses a new appreciation for the medium. He goes to the Whitney and several galleries and exhibitions throughout the week, including a mural exhibit at Grand Central Station. He writes Green that he is seeing "fifty museums a day." "Already I've seen more painting than can be digested for a long time," he declares in another letter

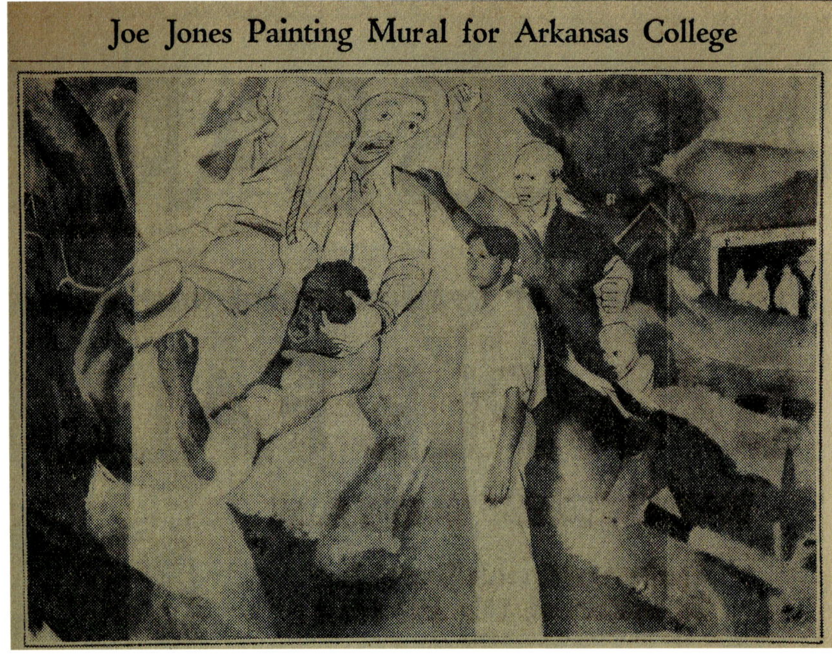
Joe Jones Painting Mural for Arkansas College

Fig. 7. "Joe Jones Painting Mural for Arkansas College," *St. Louis Post-Dispatch*, August 20, 1935. This photograph shows Joe Jones working on *The Struggle in the South*, 1935, his mural for Commonwealth College, Mena, Arkansas (see also fig. 8; Wolfe, fig. 6; and cat. 39).

(Feb. 11). "Everything I see seems to challenge me." Jones also reports plans to take a four-day-a-week lithography class.

Feb. 22. Green corresponds with Harriette F. Ryan, director of the International Institute in St. Louis, to see if the organization would be willing to provide a space for the Unemployed Art Class. After the institute turns down the request, the class disbands.

Feb. 23. Advised by CAM director Meyric Rogers, Jones contacts the Downtown and Rehn galleries in New York about a one-person show. However, as he notes in a letter to Green, the artist does not entirely trust Rogers because of what he sees as his "evasive attitude and indifference on questions of subject matter," and is unhappy about the commercial motives of the two galleries.

Feb. 26. Green sends several of Jones's works to New York at her expense.

Mar. 3. With friends Jones attends a party at the Connecticut home of an editor at Harcourt Brace and Co., where he meets several writers. "Very funny, my path seems to cross more writers than painters," he writes to Green. "I've met at least 75 writers to 20 or so painters, and very many of them I liked and will meet again."

Mar. 3–16. *Lynching* appears in "Struggle for Negro Rights," an anti-lynching exhibition comprising more than fifty prints and drawings, at the American Contemporary Art Gallery (hereinafter A.C.A. Gallery), 52 West 8th St., New York, sponsored by the John Reed Club and the Harlem-based Vanguard group (see "Anti-Lynching Activism," p. 40).

Mar. 7. Jones visits Walt Kuhn. In letters to Green, he reports spending at least five days at the Metropolitan Museum of Art (hereinafter MMA).

Mar. 12. After the Downtown and Rehn galleries show no interest in Jones's work, he begins working with the leftist A.C.A. Gallery toward a one-person exhibition in May.

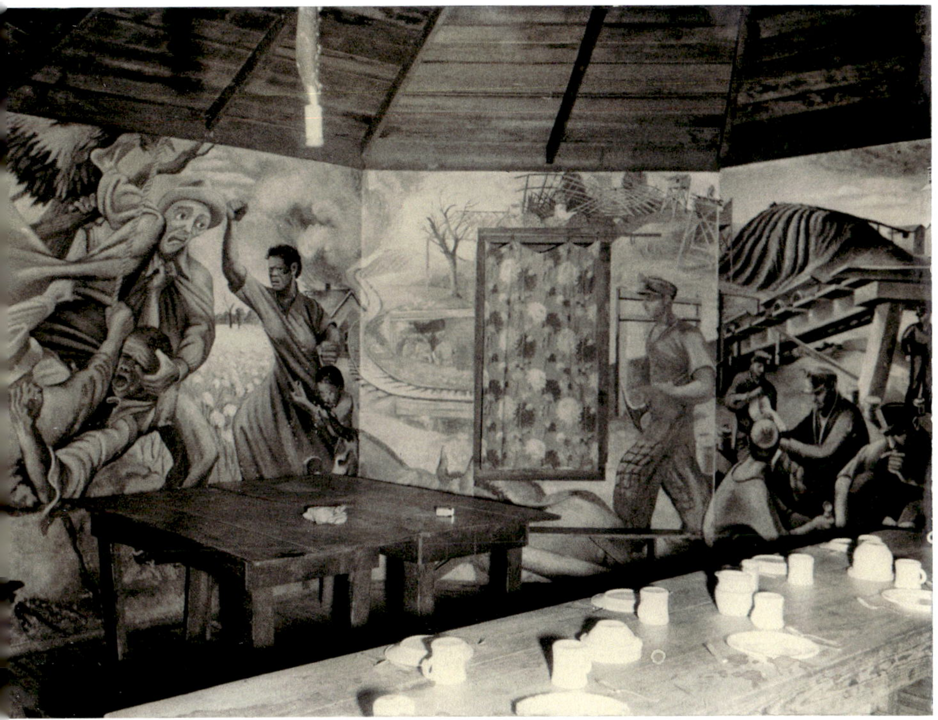

Fig. 8. Joe Jones. *The Struggle in the South*, 1935. Oil on Masonite. In situ at Commonwealth College, Mena, Arkansas. Courtesy of Jones Family.

Apr. 12. Jones returns to the St. Louis area and moves to 720 S. Main St., in nearby St. Charles.

May 7–June 12. *Apple Tree* appears in CAM's annual Paintings by Artists of St. Louis and Vicinity exhibition.

May 19–June 1. Jones's first one-person show takes place in New York at the A.C.A. Gallery. The exhibition, which features *American Justice*, *Roustabouts*, *We Demand*, *Red Earth* (cats. 31–33, 35, respectively), and other socially conscious works, is enthusiastically received.

June. The town of St. Charles, where Jones lives, experiences its worst flooding since 1903, making travel difficult. The artist takes this opportunity to photograph the destruction and flood victims.

Over the summer, Jones restores Georgia O'Keeffe's *Shell and Shingle VI* for its owner, Marguerite Kauffman Fischel (the painting is now at the Saint Louis Art Museum). Jones asks to be paid $100, but Fischel gives him only half that because she claims to have assisted in the work herself.

June 30. Jones and Green attend a performance by Paul Robeson, the noted left-wing African American singer and actor, at Loew's State Theatre, St. Louis.

July 14–Aug. 31. The overwhelming popularity of Jones's solo show prompts the A.C.A. Gallery to reopen it with additional lithographs.

Around this time, Green begins communicating with Edward B. Rowan, superintendant of the Section of Painting and Sculpture (hereinafter section), about the possibility of finding work for Jones. In a letter of August 13, Rowan suggests that he might be eligible for a new relief program, the Treasury Relief Art Project (hereinafter TRAP), charged with administering the decoration of federal buildings, for which the section has no appropriations.

July 20–Aug. 31. Jones's *Straw Stacks* (possibly cat. 36) appears in the First Annual Exhibition of Paintings by Artists West of the Mississippi, at the Colorado Springs Fine Arts Center.

Aug. 4–19. Jones is hired as a special lecturer on proletarian art and culture at the left-leaning Commonwealth College, Mena, Ark. He gives four talks there. The college asks him to paint a mural in its dining hall about the lives of Arkansas laborers.

At Commonwealth Jones meets "Mother" Ella Reeve Bloor. Bloor, a celebrated leftist labor and farmworker activist in the South, has also been invited by the college to deliver a series of lectures.

Aug. 6. On a two-day exploratory trip funded by Commonwealth College, Jones travels about three hundred miles around Arkansas, taking forty-eight photographs to use as preparatory material for the Commonwealth mural.

Late Aug. Green communicates with Olin Dows, director of the newly formed TRAP, about Jones's art. The same week, Rowan writes Jones about his eligibility for this program.

Aug. 30–Sept. 10. Jones completes his Commonwealth College mural cycle, which features striking miners and an anti-lynching scene (see figs. 7–8; Wolfe, fig. 6; and cat. 39). Shortly thereafter, he and Bloor take a road trip East, with stops in Little Rock and Memphis, and a short stay in St. Louis on Sept. 6–7. By Sept. 10, Jones is in Washington, D.C.

Sept. 11. Jones attends a dinner party with Rowan and several government officials in Washington. During his visit, he rejects an offer to work for TRAP and instead accepts a job with the Resettlement Administration (hereinafter RA) to tour small towns and depict the American scene. The position pays about $3,200 for one year's work. However, he does not take the job. In July–August 1936, the RA will employ him to travel through the Dust Bowl.

Sept. 16. Jones arrives in New York.

Sept. 21–28. *Hay*, *Wheat Field*, and *Across the Tracks* are in an A.C.A. Gallery group exhibition.

Oct. Jones signs a call for the founding of the American Artists' Congress against Fascism and War. Its goals are to discuss the role of federal-, state-, and municipal-funded art projects; art-rental policies, the economic plight of artists, the content of art, and art criticism; as well as fascism, war, racial discrimination, and the preservation of civil liberties.

Oct. 6. Jones gives a public lecture, "Painting with Social Content," at the Communist-affiliated John Reed Club School of Art, New York.

Nov. 1–Dec. 15. *Roustabouts* (cat. 32) appears in the Biennial Exhibition of American Painting Today, at the Worcester Art Museum.

Nov. 10–21. *Miners* appears in an American Artists' Congress–sponsored exhibit of graphic art at the A.C.A. Gallery. The works on display are sold at ten dollars apiece to benefit the congress.

Nov. 29–Dec. 11. *The Pool* is included in "Younger American Artists Show" at the Walker Galleries, New York.

Dec. *Dispossessed* appears in "The Capitalist Crisis," sponsored by the John Reed Club at the A.C.A. Gallery.

Jones exhibits some of his early work at the Labor Center, St. Louis, with former Unemployed Art Class students Donald MacKenzie, Terry Tiebells, and Donald Williams.

1936

Jan. 4–Feb. 16. *Apple Tree* is in the section devoted to local artists in CAM's Annual Exhibition of Paintings by American Artists.

Jan. 20–Feb. 2. Jones's one-person exhibition, "Joe Jones: Paintings of Wheat Fields," at the Walker Galleries, 108 E. 57th St., New York, garners mostly favorable reviews. The exhibition comprises fourteen works, including *Threshing No. 1* (cat. 34), and marks a shift in Jones's subject matter from social justice to agriculture, although works concerned with socio-economic issues, such as *Miners* (cat. 38), are included as well.

Feb. In articles from this time, Jones is listed as a member of the executive committee of the League of American Artists.

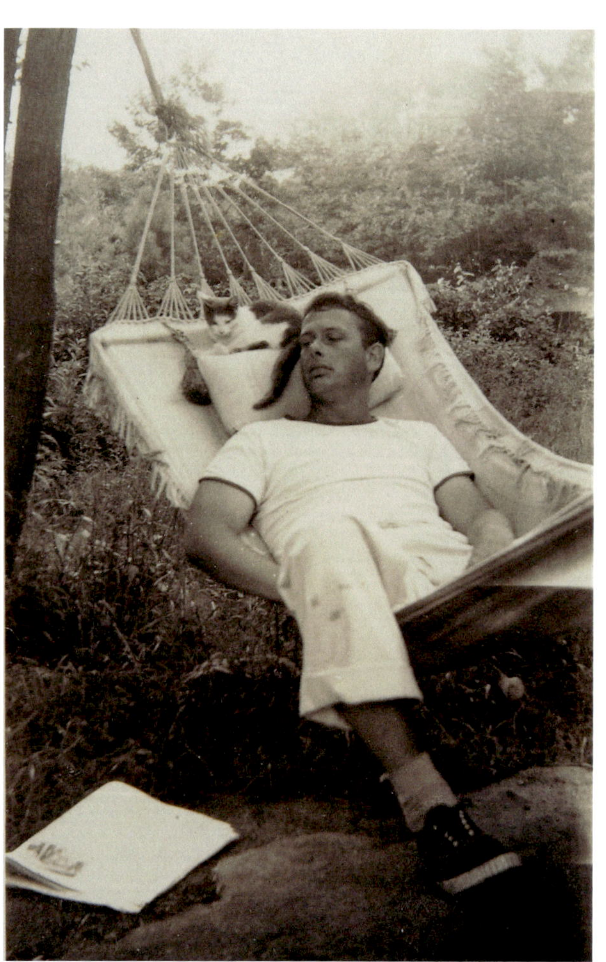

Fig. 9. Joe Jones. c. 1935. Courtesy of James and Karen Jones.

Feb. 2. The New York committee for Commonwealth College hosts "Art Frontiers: A New York Welcome to Joe Jones," at the New School for Social Research.

Feb. 5. Jones gives a talk, "Art as an Expression of the Life of the Working Class," at the Art Students' League Gallery, New York.

Feb. 9. Jones lectures in Philadelphia and sees a Vincent van Gogh exhibition at the Philadelphia Museum of Art. The show has traveled from MoMA, where it opened the previous Nov. 5.

Feb. 14. Jones delivers a speech, "Repression of Art in America," at the First American Artists' Congress, held in New York.

Late Feb. Jones returns to St. Louis, and resides with Jack Conroy at 3522 Franklin Ave.

Mar. Jones is among a group of St. Louis artists who picket SLAG for charging fees for its "Surrealist Ball."

Jones and seven other artists, including Arnold Blanch and Reginald Marsh, decline invitations to show at the Carnegie Institute, Pittsburgh, to protest its refusal to pay artists a rental fee when they are asked to loan works.

Mar. 9–Apr. 6. *Farmer with Load of Wheat* appears in SLAG's Annual Exhibition of Oil Painting and Sculpture.

Mar. 15–31. Jones shows work in a New Hats group exhibition, at the Noonan-Kocian Gallery.

Apr. 5. Jones helps to found the Vanguard Gallery and speaks at the opening reception. The new St. Louis gallery is devoted to "contemporary art with a social significance" and is partially funded by Green.

May 4–16. *Condemned* (cat. 47) and *To Make Our Daily Bread* (cat. 48) are included in "Paintings by Midwestern Artists" at the A.C.A. Gallery, an exhibition Jones has helped organize, along with fellow Missouri artists Fred Conway, E. Oscar Thalinger, James B. Turnbull, and Joseph P. Vorst.

May 6. Jones is involved in labor protests in Memphis.

May 6–31. The Junior League of Pittsburgh hosts a one-person exhibition of Jones's work, including *Wheat with Farmers* and *Threshing No. 2*, at the Junior League William Penn Galleries.

June 5. Jones is arrested and later released in Forrest City, Ark., on suspicion of encouraging cotton workers to strike, in conjunction with union organizers. Also arrested are St. Louisan Josephine Winslow Johnson (who won a Pulitzer Prize in 1935 for her novel *Now in November*) and David M. Benson, a union attorney based in Washington, D.C.

June 17–July 1. The A.C.A. exhibition "Paintings by Midwestern Artists" travels to St. Louis's Vanguard Gallery.

July 8–Aug. 17. Jones presides as one of the directors of the Ste. Genevieve Summer School of Art, along with Missouri artists Schweig and Thalinger. Benton and Turnbull are among the colony's visiting faculty that summer.

July 18–Aug. 28. Jones is employed by the RA as a Special Skills Artist.

Early Aug. Jones returns to Ste. Genevieve after spending several weeks traveling around the Dust Bowl, in the South and the Great Plains, gathering material for his RA assignment.

Sept. 6. Examples of Jones's RA work are reproduced in the *St. Louis Post-Dispatch Magazine* and *East St. Louis Journal* (*Illinois Magazine*).

Sept. 21–June 12, 1937. Jones serves as a member of the advisory board for the Marxist-leaning American Artists School, New York. Its faculty includes such artists as Philip Evergood, Louis Lozowick, Elizabeth Olds, and Raphael Soyer, among others.

Oct. 15. Jones submits a fellowship application to the Guggenheim Foundation, expressing a desire to continue the work he had begun for the RA. He intends to produce a series of paintings recording the effects of drought and erosion on Midwestern farms. Jones lists as references the artist Marsh; critics Lewis

Mumford and Edward Alden Jewell; and museum officials Lloyd Goodrich (a curator at the Whitney), Rogers, and Francis Taylor (director of MMA).

Oct. 31–Nov. 29. *Midwestern Water Hole* (or *Water Hole* [cat. 65]) and other works are included in "Protest Show: Exhibition of Paintings and Sculpture by 30 Outstanding St. Louis Artists," organized by the Campaign of the American Society of Painters, Sculptors and Gravers, Local [St. Louis] Endorsers of the Rental Policy. The exhibition is intended to protest CAM's refusal to pay rental fees to artists showing their work in the museum's annual Paintings by Artists of St. Louis and Vicinity exhibition.

Nov. *Sharecropper's Family* appears in an exhibition organized by Alan D. Gruskin of the Midtown Galleries, New York. The exhibition, held at the Gillespie Galleries, Pittsburgh, features the work of artists boycotting the Carnegie International for their rental-fee policies.

Jones contributes to "Four Cases of Mural Censorship," for *Midwest–A Review*, along with Raymond Breinin, Herbert Rosengren, and Gilbert Wilson. Jones writes about the Old Courthouse mural.

Nov. 10–Dec. 10. *Our American Farms* (cat. 42) appears in the Whitney's Biennial Exhibition of Contemporary American Painting. The painting is one of eight works the Whitney purchases that year for its permanent collection.

1937

Jan. Jones's five-part mural *The Story of the Grain* (cats. 40–41; Haggerty Museum of Art, Marquette University) is installed in the 905 Liquor Store, on Market Street in downtown St. Louis, one of a chain of taprooms owned by Morris Multin. The artist received the commission and completed the project in 1936.

Feb. Jones travels to Mexico City to attend the Congress of Revolutionary Writers and Artists. He is joined by Mack Schwab, a photographer interested in filming the lives of Mexicans.

Mar. Jones is one of six artists, including Gropper and George Grosz, selected from a pool of one thousand applicants to receive a Guggenheim Foundation fellowship. Jones plans to use the $1,800 grant to take a series of six-week trips to western Oklahoma and the southern delta in order to produce work related to sharecropping and the Dust Bowl.

Apr. 2–May 3. *Drought* appears in the Annual Exhibition of American Art at the Detroit Institute of Arts.

May. MMA purchases Jones's *Threshing No. 1* (cat. 34) for $1,000. Over the summer, the painting appears alongside twelve other recent acquisitions. (The museum will deaccession it in 1990.)

Summer. Jones visits the Ste. Genevieve Summer School of Art to meet with students.

June. Jones shows two gouache sketches of Dust Bowl farmers in the second "Exhibition of Midwestern Artists," at the A.C.A. Gallery.

June 1–Sept. 30. *Our American Farms* (cat. 42) appears in the Whitney's "Summer Exhibition 1937: Sculpture, Paintings, and Watercolors from the Permanent Collection," highlighting recent accessions.

July. *Share Cropper's Family* is in the Annual Exhibition of Paintings by Artists West of the Mississippi, at the Colorado Springs Fine Arts Center. The exhibition travels to the Denver Art Museum in September, and to the Nelson Gallery/Mary Atkins Museum, Kansas City, Mo., in October, and later to venues in Bozeman, Portland, Seattle, San Francisco, Santa Barbara, and Los Angeles.

July 7. Both Jones and Green write to the editor of the *St. Louis Star-Times* protesting Missouri's exclusion from Federal Art Project initiatives. They accuse state officials of thwarting federal efforts.

Aug. The section commissions Jones to execute a mural for the Magnolia (Ark.) Post Office. Jones travels to Magnolia to scout the location, interview town businessmen, and take photographs. He makes preliminary sketches of African American sharecroppers and children eating watermelons.

Sept. The study *Squatter's Children* appears in an exhibition of work by thirty artists at the Walker Galleries.

Jones moves to New York, citing a lack of support for the arts in Missouri. Letters from around this time list him as living in Manhattan, at 20 E. 9th St., Apt. 3.

Sept. 27. In a letter to Green, Jones confirms rumors of his romantic relationship with housing activist Jane Kauffman, daughter of the wealthy St. Louis financier Harold Kauffman (see "Jane Kauffman Wood," p. 65).

Oct. 14–Dec. 5. *Wheat with Farmer* appears in the Carnegie's International Exhibition of Paintings.

Oct. 15. Rowan informs Jones that the section has rejected his initial sketches for the Magnolia mural. Rather than a scene of children eating watermelons, Rowan prefers something like the "splendid landscapes which you did in your series of easel paintings dealing with the story of wheat."[12]

Oct. 24.–Nov. 13. The A.C.A. Gallery holds another solo show of Jones's work. *Wheat Field* and *Bottle Dancer* (or *Human Refuse*) (cat. 46) are included.

Nov. 5–Dec. 13. *Without Mother* (Balken, fig. 3) appears in the MoMA exhibition "Paintings for Paris."

Nov. 10–Dec. 12. *Wheat* is included in the Whitney's Annual Exhibition of Contemporary American Painting.

Nov. 18–Jan. 16, 1938. *Drought* is included in the Annual Exhibition of American Paintings and Sculpture at the Art Institute of Chicago.

Dec. 28. Jones applies for an extension of his Guggenheim fellowship, but his request will be turned down.

1938

A version of *We Demand* (cat. 33) appears in a 1938 calendar produced for the International Workers Order. The artist also executes the cover art for the 1938 edition of Langston Hughes's *A New Song*, published by IWO.

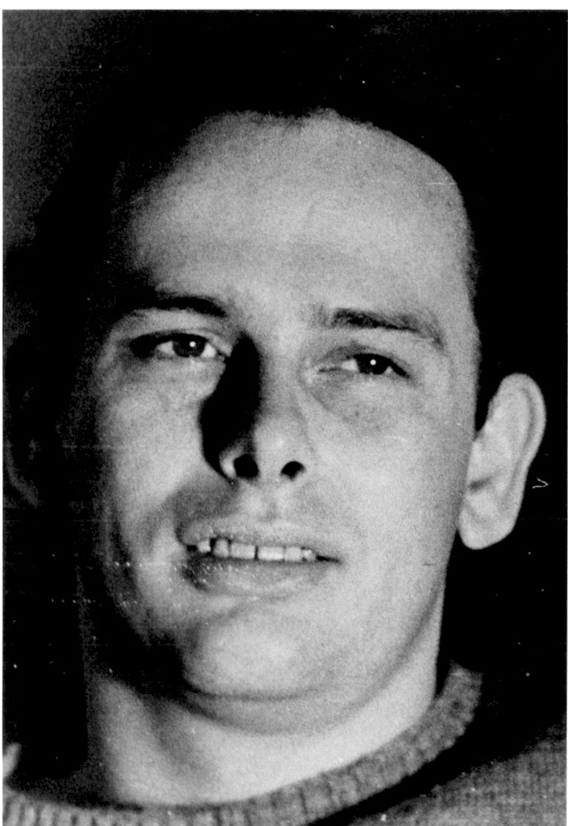

Fig. 10. Joe Jones, c. 1938. Courtesy of James and Karen Jones.

Jan. 19–Feb. 27. *Midwest Water Hole* (possibly cat. 65), appears in American Painting of Today at the Worcester Art Museum.

Feb. 5–Mar. 20. *Slum Child* and *Farmer*, both African American subjects, appear in the national section in CAM's Annual Exhibition of Paintings by American Artists.

Feb. 9. After approving his second preliminary sketch, the section contracts Jones to execute the mural *Threshing* for the Magnolia Post Office, with a deadline of Aug. 31. Jones will receive $560 for the preliminary design, cartoon, and completed mural.

May. Missing the Midwest, Jones moves back to St. Louis and resides at 3528 Franklin Ave.

May 15–July. *We Want More Pay* appears in the massive exhibition "Trois siècles d'art aux États-Unis" ("Three Centuries of Art in the United States"), organized by MoMA for the Musée du Jeu de Paume, Paris.

June. PWAP places Jones's *The Trestle* (1933) with CAM on permanent loan. Jones does not consider the composition finished. His offer to give CAM another work in its place is refused. CAM later agrees to change the painting's title to *Landscape Study—Trestle*.

July. Jones's Magnolia mural (Walker and Turk, fig. 1) is installed two months ahead of schedule.

Aug. Jones is represented in the Annual Exhibition of Paintings by Artists West of the Mississippi, which opens at the Colorado Springs Fine Arts Center and then travels to venues in Denver, New York, Cincinnati, St. Louis (CAM), Kansas City (Mo.), and Austin.

Aug. 10. Jones is among the members of the American Artists' Congress to sign an open letter to CAM opposing the use of funds to purchase an expensive, ancient Egyptian statue of a cat rather than to support work by contemporary artists.

Aug. 16–Sept. 10. *A Worker Again on WPA* (cat. 55) is in "1938: Dedicated to the New Deal," an exhibition organized to protest a decrease in funding of New Deal programs, at the A.C.A. Gallery. The show is seen at CAM from Sept. 28 to Oct. 16 and then in Nov. at the Washington, D.C., Bookshop Association Gallery.

Sept. 5–30. *Field Workers* and *Threshing* are included in "Labor in Art," an exhibition sponsored by the Baltimore Federation of Labor at the Baltimore Museum of Art.

Sept. 6. Pleased with Jones's mural for the Magnolia Post Office, the section invites him to submit designs for a four-by-twelve-foot mural for the post office in Charleston, Mo. The agency contracts Jones on Sept. 15, after accepting his design, entitled *Harvest*. He has 138 days to finish the project, for which he will be paid $670.

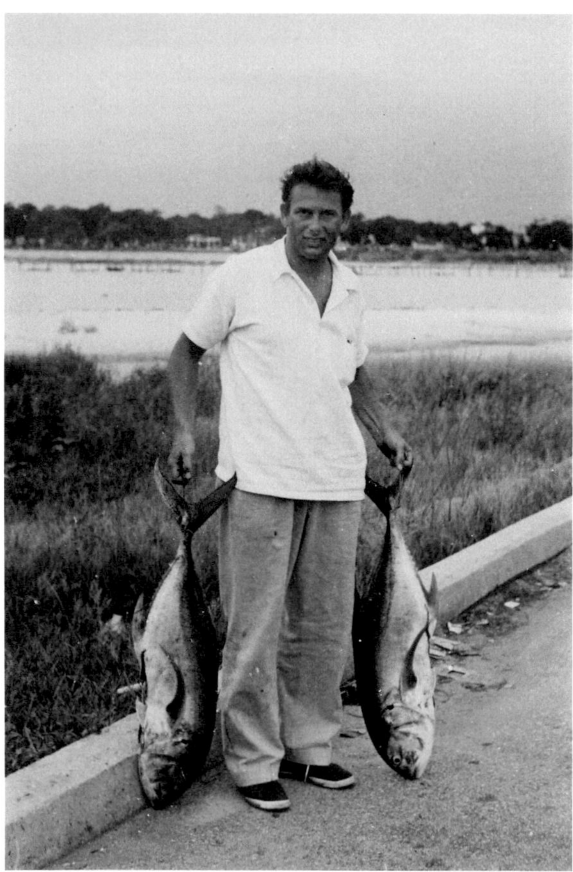

Fig. 11. Joe Jones, c. 1938. Courtesy of James and Karen Jones.

Sept. 11. In a newspaper interview with reporter John Selby, Jones names Picasso, Grosz, and Orozco as his favorite living artists; and Daumier, Delacroix, Dürer, El Greco, Rembrandt, and Rubens as his favorite deceased artists.[13]

Oct. 13–Dec. 4. *Tractor* appears in the Carnegie's International Exhibition of Paintings.

Oct. 30–Nov. 30. *Railroad Workers* is seen in CAM's annual Paintings by Artists of St. Louis and Vicinity exhibition.

Nov. *Sharecropper's Family* is included in an exhibition protesting the Carnegie International's policy on rental fees, at the Gillespie Galleries, Pittsburgh.

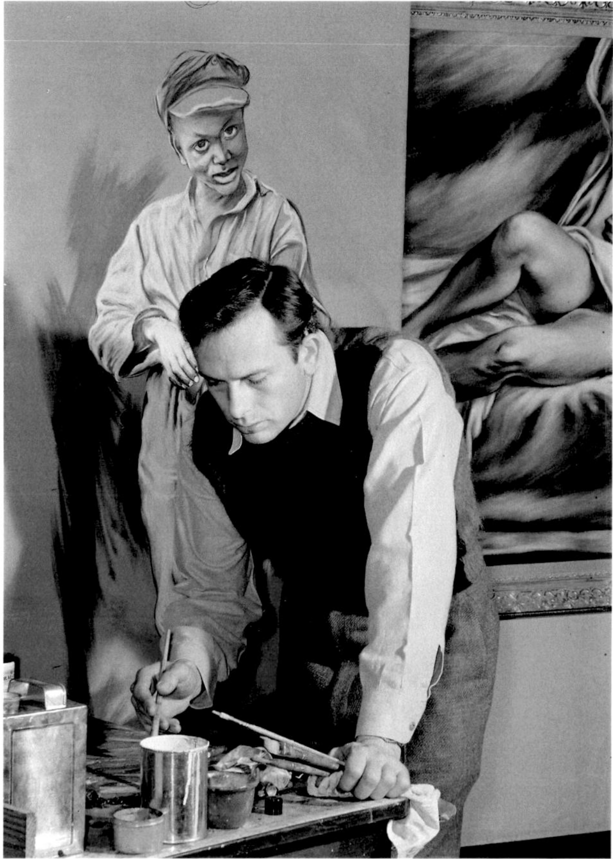

Fig. 12. Arthur Rothstein (1915–1985). *Joe Jones, Artist*, 1939. This photograph shows Jones with his paintings *Hope and Hard Times* (location unknown) and *Nude with White Robe*, Collection of Raya Koren and Peter Jones. Farm Security Administration–Office of War Information Photograph Collection, Library of Congress, Washington, D.C. LC-USF34-027047-D.

Nov. 2–Dec. 11. A self-portrait appears in the Whitney's Annual Exhibition of Contemporary American Painting.

Nov. 8. Green corresponds with Gordon B. Washburn, director of the Albright Art Gallery, Buffalo, to see if the museum is interested in being a venue for a traveling show devoted to Jones's work. The exhibition never materializes.

Nov. 8–Dec. 4. *Our American Farms* (cat. 42) appears in "Paintings by Living Americans Loaned from the Collection of the Whitney Museum of American Art," at the Museum of Modern Art Gallery, Washington, D.C.

Dec. 31–Feb. 12, 1939. *Railroad Workers* is in the section devoted to local artists in CAM's Annual Exhibition of Paintings by American Artists.

1939

Jan. 8. Jones installs the mural *Harvest* (Walker and Turk, fig. 2) in the lobby of the Charleston Post Office.

Jan. 23–Feb. 6. *Wastelands* (cat. 67) appears in an exhibition of sixteen local artists at the St. Louis Art Center. The show is organized by the regional branch of the American Artists' Congress in conjunction with a five-day symposium, "Art—A Necessity of the People," at which Jones gives a lecture, "Art and Democracy."

Feb. An exhibition at the St. Louis Art Center devoted to Jones's work features *Slum Child* and a number of preliminary sketches for his Magnolia Post Office mural.

Farmer appears in the Annual Exhibition of Paintings by Artists West of the Mississippi, organized by the Colorado Springs Fine Arts Center, at Colorado Springs, St. Louis (CAM), and Los Angeles.

Apr. The section rejects Jones's design—a depiction of railroad workers—for a mural in the post office of Wellston, a suburb north of St. Louis. Instead, it selects a much tamer subject, Lumen Winter's *Old Levee and Market at St. Louis*, a stagecoach scene set in nineteenth-century Missouri.

June. Jones travels to Anthony, Kans., to make preliminary sketches and photographs for another post-office mural commissioned by the section. He submits a rough layout for his mural design immediately after his trip, in late June.

June 4. The *St. Louis Post-Dispatch* publishes a series of photographs (see fig. 13) by Jones that represent "the seamy side of St. Louis," including images of tenements and poverty-stricken children.

July 3. The section accepts Jones's first preliminary design for the Anthony Post Office and contracts him to execute the mural,

Turning a Corner. He has a 152-day deadline and will be paid $730 for the completed project.

July 5. Jones and Green temporarily break off their friendship after arguing about the artist's clandestine affair with Grace Adams Mallinckrodt, who is married to Henry E. Mallinckrodt, grandson of St. Louis millionaire philanthropist Edward Mallinckrodt.

July 26. Local newspapers describe Jones's Anthony Post Office mural (Walker and Turk, fig. 3) as complete, over three months ahead of schedule. However, the section does not pay Jones his last two installments until he meets the requirement to submit a full-size cartoon of the mural.

Aug. *Negro Boy* (later titled *Hope and Hard Times*; see fig. 12) wins second prize in "American Art Today," at the New York World's Fair, Flushing Meadows–Corona Park, N.Y.

Sept. The lithographs *Taking It Easy* (cat. 77) and *Boy with Pipe* (cat. 79), and a sketch from the Wellston Post Office mural competition (cat. 73) are in an exhibition at CAM sponsored by the St. Louis branch of the American Artists' Congress.

Sept. 18–Oct. 7. *Missouri Wheat Farmers* (perhaps cat. 70) appears in "An American Group," the ninth-anniversary exhibition for the Associated American Artists (hereinafter AAA) Galleries, New York.

Mid-Oct. Jones is selected from the "Forty-eight State Mural Competition" to execute a mural for the Seneca (Kans.) Post Office. On Nov. 1, the section contracts with Jones to execute *Men and Wheat*. He is given a deadline of 274 days and will be paid $740 for the completed project.

Nov. 2–21. A study for Jones's Seneca Post Office mural is included in "Painting and Sculpture Designed for Federal Buildings," at the Corcoran. The exhibition honors the winners of the "Forty-eight State Mural Competition."

Nov. 12–Dec. 2. A solo show of Jones's work takes place at the A.C.A. Gallery. It features *Working on the Railroad*, *Missouri Farmers*, and sketches for the artist's post-office mural commissions. The paintings on view signal a shift in the artist's choice of medium, from oil to tempera, as well as a return to social issues.

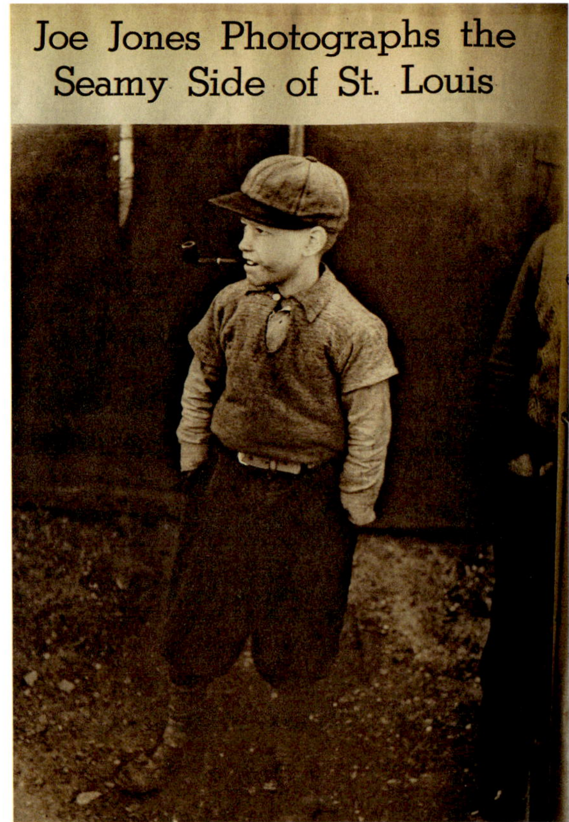

Fig. 13. "Joe Jones Photographs the Seamy Side of St. Louis." *St. Louis Post-Dispatch*, June 4, 1939.

Mid-Nov. Jones is living on Mount Airy Rd., Croton-on-Hudson, N.Y.

1940

Jan. 3. After a negotiation process that takes up late Nov. and early Dec., Jones submits a full-size cartoon for the Seneca mural that incorporates changes in details on which Rowan and the town's postmaster have insisted. The section accepts the composition.

Jan. 10–Feb. 18. *Slum Nymph* appears in the Whitney's Annual Exhibition of Contemporary American Art.

Jan. 28–Mar. 3. *Kansas Farmer* is seen in the Pennsylvania Academy of the Fine Arts' Annual Exhibition of Painting and Sculpture.

Feb. Jones writes an introduction for the A.C.A. Gallery exhibition catalogue *20 Years of Gropper*.

Feb. 2. Jones installs *Men and Wheat* (Walker and Turk, fig. 4; see also cat. 71) in the Seneca Post Office.

Feb. 27–Mar. 17. A preliminary study for Jones's Seneca mural appears in "Mural Designs for Federal Buildings from the Section of Fine Arts, Public Buildings Administration, Federal Works Agency," at the Whitney.

Mar. Jones and Green resume correspondence.

May 16–June 13. CAM's annual exhibition of works by members of the St. Louis American Artists' Congress includes Jones's *Three Men and a Tree*, an anti-lynching painting.

May 25–Sept. 29. *Blue Plate Special*, *Farmer*, and *Slum Nymph* appear at the Golden Gate International Exposition, San Francisco.

June. In a high-profile divorce trial, Jones is identified by name as Grace Adams Mallinckrodt's lover. According to court records, a private detective found the two in a cottage in Croton-on-Hudson.

Summer. Jones builds a house in Fishkill, N.Y.

Oct. 20–Nov. A one-person exhibition of Jones's oils and lithographs, including *Sharecropper's Family*, is hosted by the Washington (D.C.) Bookshop Association Gallery. Although the show is scheduled to close in mid-Nov., it remains open until the end of the month.

Oct. 15. The section invites Jones to submit a design for a mural in the post office of Dexter, Mo.

Oct. 22. Rowan informs Jones that the section is satisfied with the theme of corn for the Dexter mural, but rejects the design: "The preliminary design which you submitted does not occur to us to have been as carefully thought out as we think it should be. Frankly, it does not seem convincingly composed for the space."[14]

Oct. 24. Jones marries the recently divorced, twenty-two-year-old Grace Adams Mallinckrodt, in Morristown, N.J.

Nov. 10–30. The A.C.A. Gallery stages an exhibition of twenty-one paintings and eleven lithographs by Jones. These include some of his darkest works, such as *Luncheon*, *Slum Nymph*, and *Nothing Better to Do*—all St. Louis slum scenes.

Nov. 13. The section accepts Jones's second design for the Dexter Post Office mural, *Husking Corn*, an energetic composition of farmers cutting, husking, and shucking corn. The agency draws up a contract on Nov. 18, with a deadline of 194 days. Jones will be paid $800 for the completed project.

Nov. 27–Jan. 8, 1941. *Conversation* (cat. 76) is in the Whitney's Annual Exhibition of Contemporary American Painting.

1941

Jan. 15–Feb. 19. *Man with Rope* appears in the Whitney's Annual Exhibition of Sculpture, Watercolors, Drawings, and Prints.

Late Feb. Jones installs *Husking Corn* (Walker and Turk, fig. 5) in the Dexter Post Office. Although the section pays him in full for his work, Rowan criticizes Jones's final product, likening it to an "amusing cartoon."[15]

Jan. 26–Mar. 2. *What More Could One Ask For?* is included in the Pennsylvania Academy's Annual Exhibition of Painting and Sculpture.

Mar. 23–May 4. *Playground* is in the Corcoran's Biennial Exhibition of Contemporary American Oil Paintings.

Apr. Jones has moved from Croton-on-Hudson to Wappingers Falls, near Poughkeepsie, N.Y.

Apr. 19–27. *Threshing No. 1* (cat. 34) and *Wheat* appear in "Contemporary Painting in the United States," at MMA.

June 12. The Joneses' first child, Peter Paul Jones, is born.

Oct. 30–Jan. 4, 1942. *What More Could One Ask For?* is seen in the Annual Exhibition of American Paintings and Sculpture at the Art Institute of Chicago.

Nov. 12–Dec. 30. *Edge of the Fields* and *Playground* are included in the Whitney's Annual Exhibition of Paintings by Artists under Forty.

1942

Jan. 25–Mar. 1. Jones wins the Jennie Sesnan Medal for his painting *Harvesting* in the Pennsylvania Academy's Annual Exhibition of Painting and Sculpture.

Aug. 24. Jones flies to St. Louis and visits Green and his former student Donald MacKenzie.

Sept. 26. Jones completes his first commissioned work for the American Tobacco Co.'s Lucky Strike advertising campaign. He writes to Green that he is pleased with it, despite having to make "so many compromises."

Oct. Jones and his family are living in the house Jones built in Fishkill.

Oct. 3–22. Jones, having left the A.C.A. Gallery, has a one-person exhibition at the AAA Galleries, comprising mainly harbor scenes.

Oct. 29–Dec. 10. *Playground* appears in the Annual Exhibition of American Paintings and Sculpture at the Art Institute of Chicago.

Nov. Jones sends Green a portfolio of lithographs for a fundraising raffle for the People's Art Center, St. Louis.

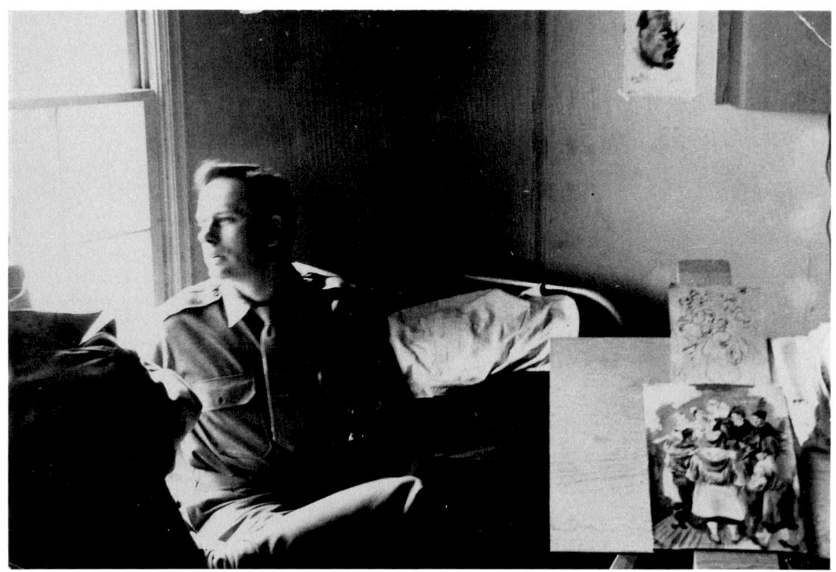

Fig. 14. Joe Jones on assignment for the War Art Unit, 1943. Courtesy of James and Karen Jones.

Around this time, Jones presents his completed painting for the Lucky Strike campaign to the American Tobacco Co.'s New York advertising agency (see Balken, fig. 10).

Nov. 18. Jones reports to Green that he has designed a war poster after observing an operation at the Vassar Hospital, Poughkeepsie. He sends her photographs of two paintings he has made of Peter, indicating a growing interest in personal subject matter. Writes Jones: "I think they say something about my life at the moment as well as indicate a development in my work."

Nov. 24–Jan. 6, 1943. *Spring Plowing* (cat. 83) is seen in the Whitney's Annual Exhibition of Contemporary American Art.

Dec. 7–Feb. 22, 1943. Jones's *Winter in Dutchess County* and *Yellow Grain* (cat. 82) appear in "Artists for Victory: An Exhibition of Contemporary American Art," at MMA.

Dec. 23–Jan. 21, 1943. *Three Men and a Tree* (Wolfe, fig. 9), an anti-lynching print, is included in "The Negro in Art," at the People's Art Center, St. Louis.

1943

Winter. Jones and his family move from Fishkill to 25 E. 10th St., in Manhattan.

Jan. 24–Feb. 28. *Orange Vendor* appears in the Pennsylvania Academy's Annual Exhibition of Painting and Sculpture.

Mar. The Cleveland Museum of Art acquires Jones's painting *Yellow Grain* (cat. 82).

Around this time, Jones finishes a poster design for Abbott Laboratories, which has been commissioning advertising work from the artist for nearly a year. On Mar. 1, Jones writes to Green that the company "gives these posters to the government free and mine is hoped to fill a need in the agricultural dept." Jones also produces a painting of Niagara Falls for the Niagara Alkali Co.

Mar. 2. Jones is assigned to Alaska as a war correspondent by the War Department's U.S. Engineer Office, as part of the official War Art Unit. He leaves in late March, traveling first to San Francisco.

Mar. 8–27. The AAA Galleries shows twenty-six paintings by Jones. They are mainly agricultural scenes, such as *Spring Plowing* (cat. 83) and *Fishkill Valley*.

Mar. 21–May 2. *Wheat* appears in the Corcoran's Biennial Exhibition of Contemporary American Oil Paintings.

May 7. Jones arrives at an undisclosed location in Alaska (see fig. 14), which he describes to Green as "beautiful and very paintable." Artists Willard Cummings, Edward Laning, Ogden Pleissner, and Henry Varnum Poor (see fig. 15) are also assigned to the Alaskan front.

July 16. Jones writes Green about visiting an Eskimo village while on assignment. "I have fallen in love with the Eskimo people, they are a sensitive and intelligent people with delightful ways and very friendly."

July 26. Jones's assignment in Alaska ends after Congress terminates the War Art Unit. He and his family spend the remainder of the summer on Martha's Vineyard.

Sept. *Life* magazine takes over the War Art project and commissions Jones to finish his Alaskan works, which are eventually donated to the federal government. He uses this opportunity to experiment with pastel over colored ink and watercolor.

Sept. 11. Jones's American Tobacco Co.–sponsored work, *Tobacco Expert*, appears in the *Saturday Evening Post*. (Balken, fig. 10).

Oct. 1. The Jones family moves to 290 W. 11th St., New York.

Oct. 14–Dec. 12. *The Falls* is in the Carnegie's annual Painting in the United States exhibition.

Nov. 23–Jan. 4, 1944. *Eskimo Women Fishing* appears in the Whitney's Annual Exhibition of Contemporary American Art.

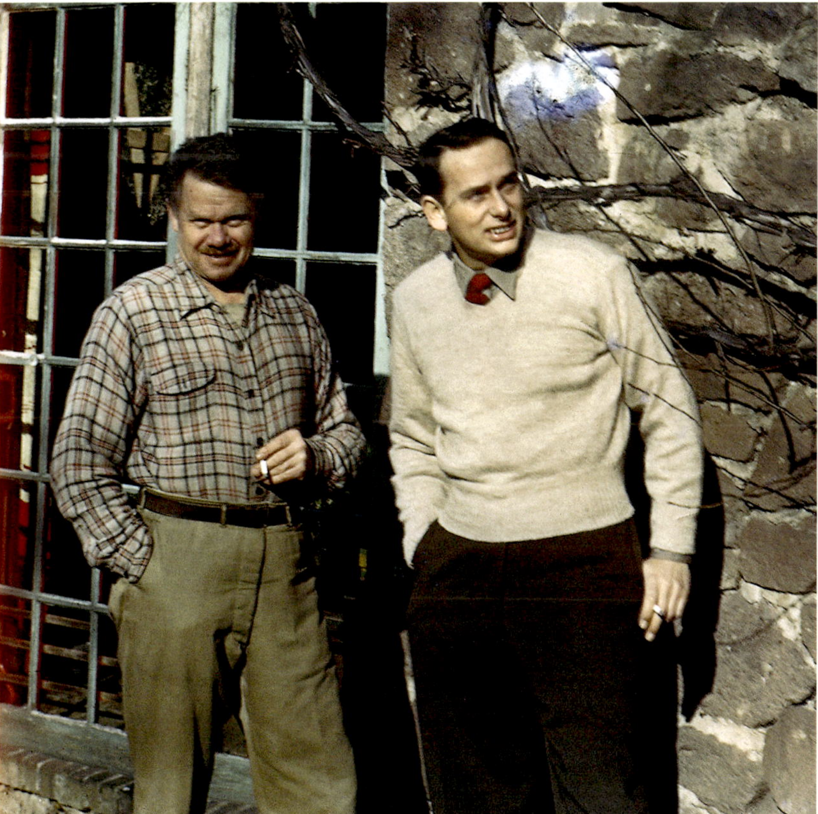

Fig. 15. Henry Varnum Poor and Joe Jones, c. 1944. Courtesy of Jones Family.

1944

Jan. 23–Feb. 27. *Dutchess County Cowboy* appears in the Pennsylvania Academy's Annual Exhibition of Painting and Sculpture.

Feb. 5–Mar. 13. *Farmer with Wheat* is in the section devoted to local artists in CAM's Annual American Painting of Today exhibition.

Feb. 8–Mar. 26. Jones's portrait of the artist Abraham Walkowitz appears in an unusual exhibition, "One Hundred Artists and Walkowitz," at the Brooklyn Museum.

Feb. 20–Mar. 19. Jones shows several oils and gouaches of Alaska in "The Army at War Art Exhibition," at the National Gallery of Art, Washington, D.C. It comprises paintings and drawings lent by the War Department.

Mar. 8–18. An Eskimo-themed work by Jones appears in the "American-British Goodwill Art Exhibition," at Grand Central Art Galleries, New York, a show arranged by the national organization Artists for Victory. The exhibition travels to the Hertford House, London, in June.

Mar. 9. Jones finishes two designs for Coca Cola's new "Americana Series" advertising campaign.

May. After a contract to purchase a house in Croton-on-Hudson falls through, the Joneses buy a five-bedroom, three-bathroom house at 9 Farragut Pl., Morristown, N.J. They move into the residence in early July, and add a studio to the house in August. The family will remain in Morristown for the rest of Jones's life.

Fall. Jones travels to Oklahoma and Montana to sketch oil fields for New Jersey Standard Oil. In collaboration with the AAA Galleries, Standard Oil hired Jones and fifteen other artists, including Benton and Adolph Dehn, to document oil production in the U.S. during the war.

Sept. 11–30. *Missouri Wheat Farmers* (cat. 69), *The Green Snake* (cat. 25). and *Pink Rocks* are in "Looking Back and Looking Ahead," an exhibition commemorating the tenth anniversary of the founding of the AAA Galleries.

Oct. 12–Dec. 10. *The Vineyard* is included in the Carnegie's annual Painting in the United States exhibition.

Oct. 26. The Joneses' second son, Timothy Adams Jones, is born.

Nov. 14–Dec. 12. Jones shows *Young Girl* in the Whitney's Annual Exhibition of Contemporary American Painting.

Dec. 18–28. "The Army at War Art Exhibition," which features numerous Alaskan works by Jones, is shown at the Art Institute of Chicago.

1945

Jan. 19–Feb. 25. *The Pink Rock* is in the Pennsylvania Academy's Annual Exhibition of Painting and Sculpture.

Jan. 22–Feb. 10. A solo show at the AAA Galleries includes works by Jones depicting scenes of Martha's Vineyard, Rockport, the Hudson River Valley, and Alaska.

Feb. 10–Mar. 12. *The Hudson* is seen in the national section of CAM's Annual Exhibition of American Paintings.

Mar. 18–Apr. 29. *Derselbe Kommandant in Profil* is included in the Corcoran's Biennial Exhibition of Contemporary American Oil Paintings.

Apr. The Dayton Institute of Art hosts a small exhibition of Jones's work in its Modern Room.

After its purchase by the Encyclopaedia Britannica Co., *Wheat Farmers* appears in "The Encyclopaedia Britannica Collection of Contemporary American Painting," an exhibition that begins at the Art Institute of Chicago and tours the country.

Apr. 11. Jones joins the Army Special Services as a private.

May 20. Jones writes that he has been assigned to the army's tank corps.

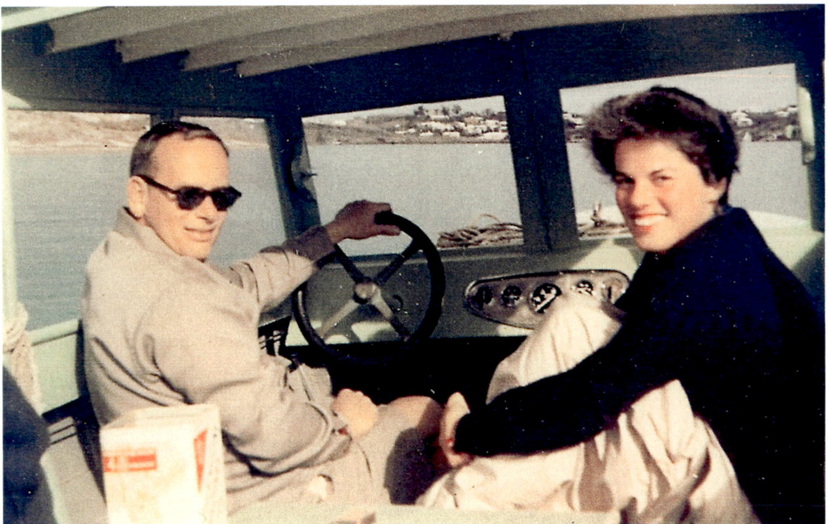

Fig. 16. Joe and Grace Jones in Bermuda, early 1950s. Courtesy of James and Karen Jones.

June–Aug. Jones suffers several illnesses that prevent him from performing his military duties. He develops a hernia while experiencing lingering effects from a bout with the mumps (which he had caught from his son Peter). By June 11, he is in the hospital with a sore throat and temperature, and he is diagnosed with gout. After a hernia operation, he improves. The medical disposition board assigns him to Fort Knox, Ky., to work as an art instructor after completing basic training.

Oct. 11–Dec. 9. Jones exhibits *Voyage into the Unknown* in the Carnegie's annual Paintings in the United States exhibition.

Nov. 7. After filing for "dependency discharge," Jones leaves the army.

Nov. 27–Jan. 10, 1946. *Mother with Infant* appears in the Whitney's Annual Exhibition of Contemporary American Painting.

Dec. 4–21. Jones receives the Carnegie Prize of $300 for *The Falls* in the Annual Exhibition of Contemporary American Painting and Sculpture, at the National Academy of Design, New York.

1946

Jan. 8–19. Jones exhibits several Standard Oil Co. commissions, including *Elk Basin* and *Removing the Drill*, in "Oil: 1940–1945," at the AAA Galleries. These paintings feature oil wells set against the dramatic landscape of the Elk Basin oil fields, near Yellowstone National Park (see Balken, fig. 8).

Feb. 5–Mar. 13. The drawing *Pink Rocks* is in the Whitney's Annual Exhibition of Contemporary American Sculpture, Watercolors, and Drawings.

Feb. 16–Mar. 19. Jones shows *Niagara Falls* in CAM's Annual Exhibition of American Paintings.

Mar. Exploring a new-found interest in natural phenomena, Jones spends a week sketching in the Carolinas. He becomes enthralled with a waterfall and stream about ten miles from his home.

Aug. The AAA Galleries in New York and Chicago stage an exhibition of work by Jones, Benton, Aaron Bohrod, Steuart Curry, and Grosz, among others.

Sept. Gimbel Brothers, a leading department-store company whose roster includes a store in Philadelphia and one in Pittsburgh, commissions fourteen artists, including Jones, to execute scenes of contemporary Pennsylvania as gifts to the state. The $100,000 project is planned in conjunction with the AAA Galleries, and is approved by Pennsylvania's governor, Edward Martin. The completed collection is scheduled to go on tour in 1947.

Oct. 1–Nov. 3. "Oil: 1940–1945," which features several works by Jones, is displayed at the Philbrook Art Center, Tulsa, sponsored by the Carter Oil Co.

Oct. 10–Dec. 8. *New York Harbor* appears in the Carnegie's annual Painting in the United States exhibition.

Nov. 1–Dec. 1. *Landscape Study—Trestle* (on permanent loan to the Saint Louis Art Museum) and *Landscape* appear in CAM's Annual Missouri Exhibition. The exhibition travels to the Nelson Gallery/Mary Atkins Museum, where it is on view Dec. 13–31.

Dec. 10–Jan. 16, 1947. *Black Rocks* is seen in the Whitney's Annual Exhibition of Contemporary American Painting.

1947

Jan. 4–22. *Vineyard* appears in the National Academy's Annual Exhibition of Contemporary American Painting, Sculpture, Watercolor, and Graphic Art.

Jan. 16. The Joneses' third child, Katharine Fairchild Jones, is born.

Jan. 26–Mar. 2. *Skate and Shark* appears in the Pennsylvania Academy's Annual Exhibition of Painting and Sculpture.

Feb. A show of Jones's work, featuring landscapes, is on view at the AAA Galleries, Chicago.

Mar. 30–May 11. *Black Rocks, No. 2* is in the Corcoran's Biennial Exhibition of Contemporary American Oil Paintings.

Fall. Jones begins teaching at Lehigh University, Bethlehem, Pa., sixty miles from his home. He makes the 120-mile round trip by car.

A work by Jones appears above the fireplace in "Idea House II," a split-level contemporary design outfitted with the latest features and appliances and intended by the Walker Art Gallery, Minneapolis, to embody its belief that a home should be considered functional art.

Oct. Lehigh University Gallery opens the academic year with a show of oils, watercolors, and drawings by Jones.

Oct. 9–Dec. 10. *Mantoloking* appears in the Carnegie's annual Painting in the United States exhibition.

Nov 10–29. The AAA Galleries stages an exhibition of Jones's work.

1948

Feb. Having become proficient at building model trains, Jones enters the annual exhibition of the New York Society of Model Engineers, at the Lackawanna Terminal, Hoboken. He wins first prize for a model locomotive and honorable mention for a model of the Morristown Terminal.

Feb. 16. Jones shows several scenes of Michigan, including *Falls at Eagle River* and *Old Mine at Hancock*, in a group exhibition of works commissioned by the J. L. Hudson Department Store through the AAA Galleries. The show, which takes place in the Detroit store's auditorium, is intended to travel throughout the state.

Mar. 25–Apr. 14. *Boat Dock* appears in the National Academy's Annual Exhibition.

Apr. 4–May 5. Jones's first West Coast show takes place at the AAA Galleries, Beverly Hills, Calif. It features twenty-six works, abstracted landscapes that critics liken to Chinese watercolors.

July. *Departure* (cat. 61), presented to the Denver Art Museum in 1946, appears at the Colorado Springs Fine Arts Center in an exhibition of recent acquisitions by American museums.

Fall. *Fortune* magazine commissions Jones to travel the Quebec–Labrador border to create a portfolio of paintings depicting the region's great iron-ore deposits.

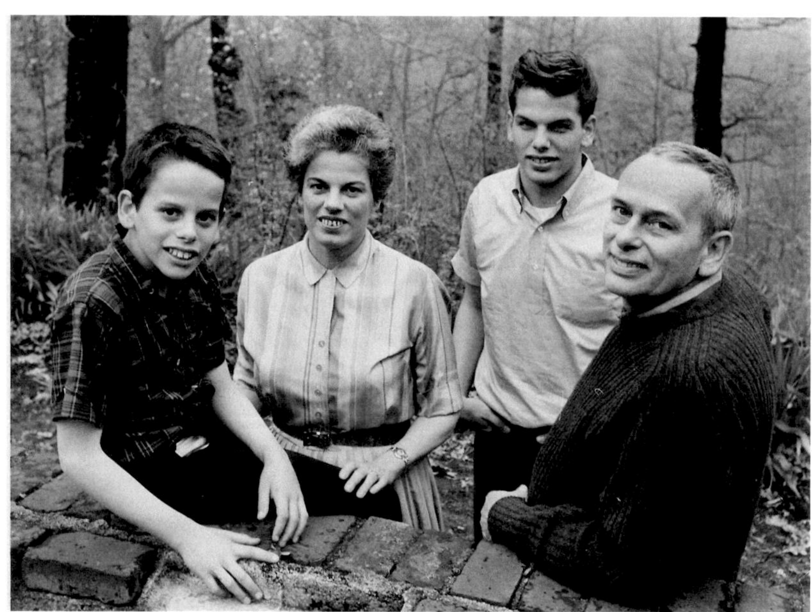

Fig. 17. James, Grace, Tim, and Joe Jones, late 1950s. Courtesy of James and Karen Jones.

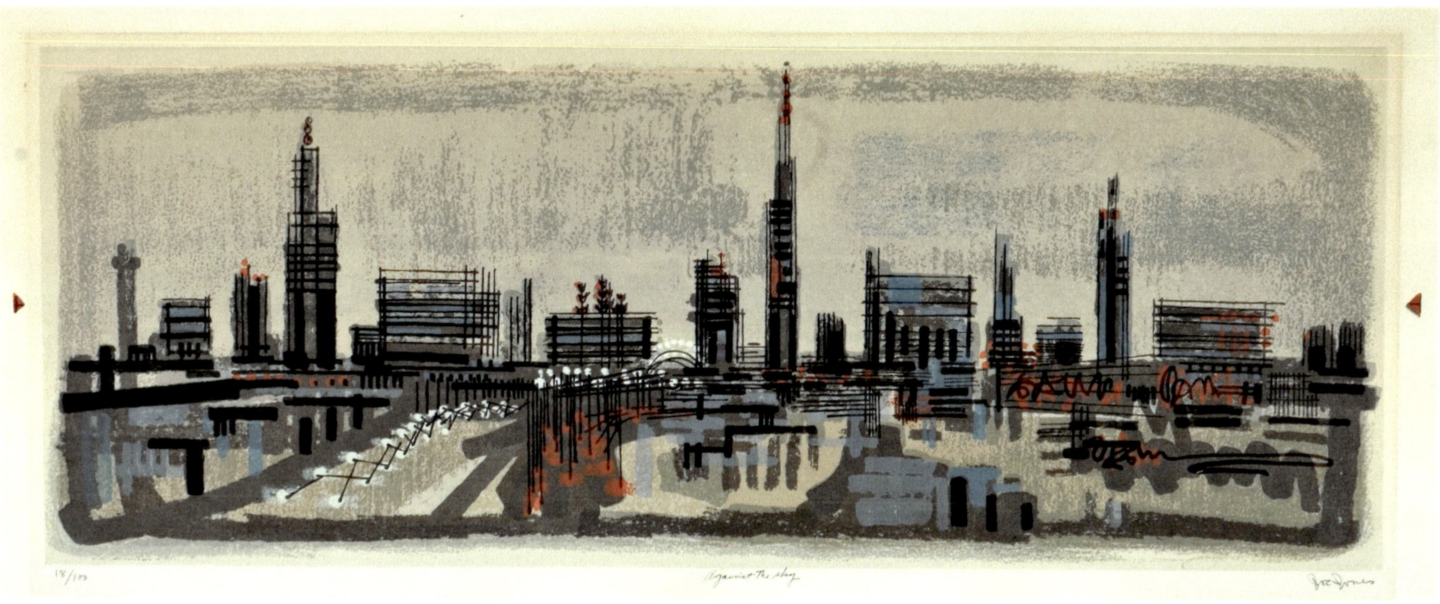

Fig. 18. Joe Jones. *Against the Sky*, c. 1950. Color silkscreen; image: 12 3⁄16 × 31 15⁄16 in. (31 × 81.2 cm); sheet: 18 7⁄16 × 37 11⁄16 in. (46.8 × 95.8 cm). Saint Louis Art Museum, Gift of Paul T. Putzel.

Sept. 20–Oct. 25. *Mexican*, a 1937 gouache owned by Green (private collection), appears in "St. Louis Collections: An Exhibition of 20th Century Art," at CAM.

Oct. 14–Dec. 12. *Coast Guard Buildings* is included in the Carnegie's annual Painting in the United States exhibition.

1949

Mar. 27–May 8. *Waterfall* appears in the Corcoran's Biennial Exhibition of Contemporary American Oil Paintings.

Apr. Jones's model railroad construction "Terminal Scene on the HO Gauge Pike" appears on the cover of the journal *Model Railroad Craftsman*.

Apr. 2–May 8. *Haverstraw*, in ink and wash, is displayed in the Whitney's Annual Exhibition of American Art.

1950

June 16. *Threshing No. 1* (cat. 34) appears in "20th Century Painters: A Special Exhibition of Oils, Water Colors, and Drawings Selected from the Collections of American Art," at MMA.

June 23. The Jones's fourth and last child, James Place Jones, is born.

1951

Apr. 1–May 13. *Road to Yacht Club* appears in the Corcoran's Biennial Exhibition of Contemporary American Oil Paintings.

Oct. Standard Oil Co. presents oil-field paintings to the Massachusetts Institute of Technology, Cambridge, Mass., including works by Jones.

Oct. 1–20. An exhibition of Jones's recent work is mounted at the AAA Galleries.

1952

Winter. Jones is a juror for the exhibition "Artists of Cincinnati" at the Cincinnati Art Museum.

Mar. 13–May 4. *Boats in the Bay* appears in the Whitney's Annual Exhibition of Contemporary American Sculpture, Watercolors, and Drawings.

July–Aug. The Philbrook Art Center organizes an exhibition of work by Jones, Benton, and others that it has received from Standard Oil Co.

Oct.–Dec. 14. *Regatta* (possibly Balken, fig. 11) appears in the Carnegie's International Exhibition of Contemporary Painting.

1953

Jan. 2–Mar. 1. *Red Nets* is included in the Pennsylvania Academy's Annual Exhibition of Painting and Sculpture.

Mar. 15–May 3. *Jersey Shore No. 2* is displayed in the Corcoran's Biennial Exhibition of Contemporary American Oil Paintings.

Apr. 9–May 29. *Haverstraw* appears in the Whitney's Annual Exhibition of Contemporary American Sculpture, Watercolors, and Drawings.

Oct. 26–Nov. 14. The AAA Galleries mounts a show of recent watercolors and drawings by Jones, including scenes of Bermuda, which Jones visited in the early 1950s (see fig. 16).

Dec. 13. Jones illustrates Margaret Mead's essay "Modern Youth in a Changing World," published in the *St. Louis Post-Dispatch*, with sketches of party- and moviegoers.

1954

Jan. 24–Feb. 28. *Boat Dock* appears in the Pennsylvania Academy's Annual Exhibition of Painting and Sculpture.

Mar. 9–Apr. 11. The Detroit Institute of Arts organizes an exhibition of work by Jones, Ben Shahn, and Charles Sheeler.

1955

Oct. 3–22. The AAA Galleries shows recent work by Jones, including four mural panels executed for the Four Aces, the quartet of passenger-cargo liners of the American Export Lines.

1956

The AAA Galleries regularly commissions Jones to make lithographs and silkscreens that are produced in large runs (from 100 to 300). Individual prints are sold through the mail at around $35 each.

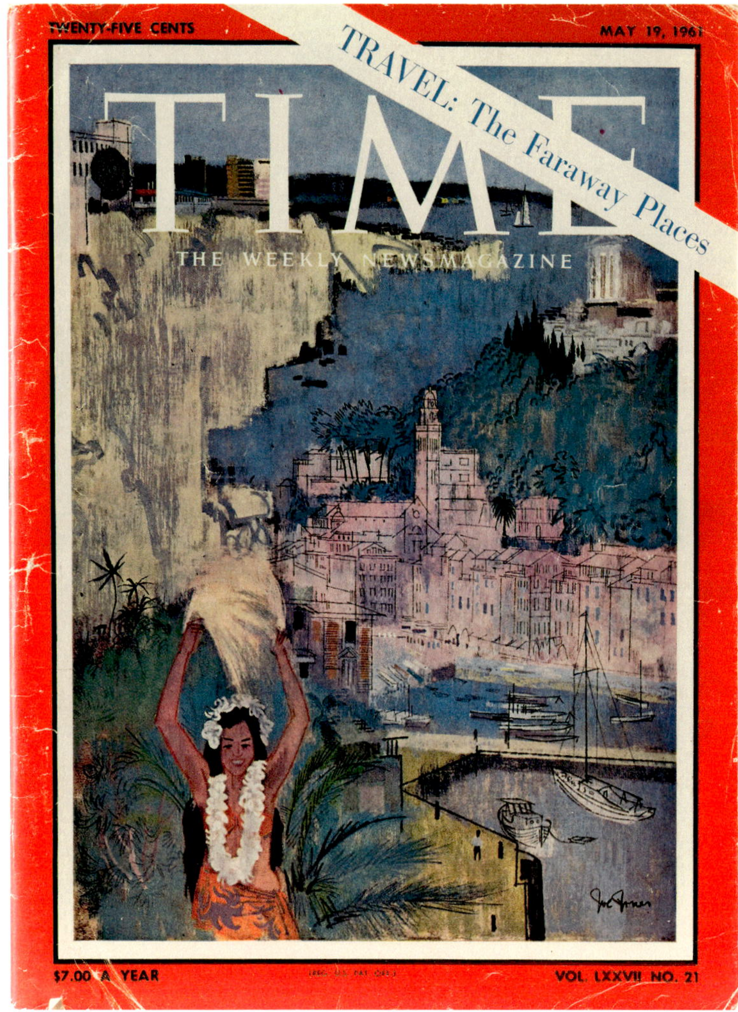

Fig. 19. Joe Jones. Cover of *Time* 77, 21 (May 19, 1961).

1957

Jan. 10. Jones writes to John Boksenbaum about his relationship with the Communist Party in the 1930s: "My political affiliations ended about *seventeen years* ago and my belief in that political party ended even before that—so in that area of referance [*sic*]—the issue is dead and I don't see what is to be accomplished by me saying I hate the Communist Party while there are so many other things I hate at least as much."[16]

1961

Jan. Jones attends funeral services for long-time A.C.A. Gallery director Herman Baron (see "Herman Baron," p. 103), one of his closest supporters and friends during the Depression.

May 19. Jones illustrates the cover of *Time* magazine (fig. 19) for an issue entitled "Travel: The Faraway Places."

Dec. 15. A Christmas-season issue of *Time* features a cover image by Jones with an abstracted, bustling scene of urban shoppers.

1962

June 11–July 1. A show of Jones's recent work is held at the Maxwell Galleries, Ltd., San Francisco.

1963

Apr. 9. Jones dies at home of a heart attack at age fifty-four. He is survived by his wife, four children, his mother, and three siblings.

Oct. 13–27. SLAG holds a memorial retrospective exhibition honoring Jones. A symposium takes place on Oct. 27 with talks by Jones's former St. Louis colleagues Fred Conway and Wallace Herndon Smith.

Oct. 29–Nov. 16. The Selected Artists Galleries, New York, organizes a memorial exhibition of Jones's work, covering the period from 1947 to his death.

NOTES

1. "Provincetown Makes Artist a Communist," *St. Louis Post-Dispatch*, Sept. 21, 1933.
2. Martin Hayden, "House Painter Artist Gives Views on Rivera Murals," *Detroit News*, n.d. (1933), St. Louis Public Library, artist's file.
3. *Joe Jones—A St. Louisan and One of America's Most Promising Young Artists*, exh. brochure (Stix, Baer & Fuller, 1933).
4. "Joe Jones Stirs up Art Row at Old Courthouse," *St. Louis Post-Dispatch*, Jan. 21, 1934.
5. Ibid.
6. *National Exhibition of Art by the Public Works of Art Project*, exh. cat. (Corcoran Gallery of Art, 1934), pp. 15, 26.
7. "Social Unrest Mural in Old Court-House," *St. Louis Post-Dispatch*, Feb. 16, 1934.
8. Joe Jones, handwritten summary of Old Courthouse controversy, Jan. 1935; Dr. John Green Collection, Missouri History Museum, St. Louis.
9. "Head of Art Class in Old Courthouse Will Oppose Ouster," *St. Louis Globe-Democrat*, Dec. 14, 1934.
10. "Chadsey Takes No Chances on Art, Fears Communism," *St. Louis Star-Times*, Dec. 15, 1934.
11. "Joe Jones, Artist, Granted Divorce," *St. Louis Globe-Democrat*, Feb. 12, 1935.
12. Edward B. Rowan to Jones, Oct. 15, 1937, Record Group 121, case files concerning embellishment of federal buildings, 1934–43; records of the Section of Fine Arts, Public Buildings Administration; Entry 133, Box 3 (Magnolia, Ark., file); National Archives, College Park, Md.
13. John Selby, "Joe Jones, House Painter, Accomplished Artist Today," *St. Louis Globe-Democrat*, Sept. 11, 1938.
14. Rowan to Jones, Oct. 22, 1940, Record Group 121 (note 12), Box 56 (Dexter, Mo., file).
15. Rowans to Jones, Apr. 4, 1941, in ibid.
16. Jones to John Boksenbaum, Jan. 10, 1957, Saint Louis Art Museum, archives.

Signature Analysis

Emily Allred

Joe Jones changed the manner in which he signed his artwork several times over the course of the 1930s. Early on he used several variations of his full name, as well as, at times, his initials. However, in 1933, the year in which he joined the Communist Party, he began to sign his art as "Joe Jones." He would continue to use this version of his name to the end of his life. In the 1930s, Jones frequently signed the lower-right corners of paintings and graphic works, though a few paintings, such as *My Mother* (c. 1932; cat. 28) and *The Green Snake* (1933; cat. 25), feature signatures at the lower left.

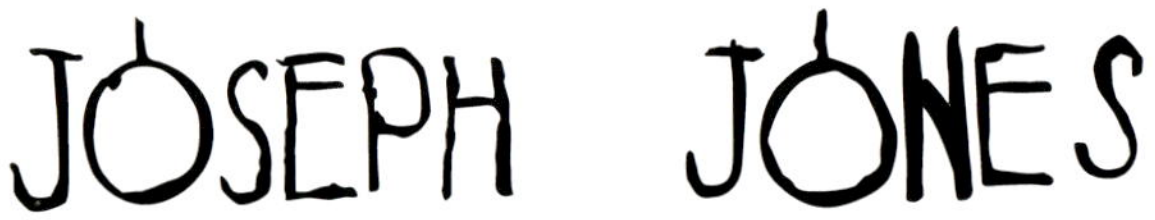

Signature 1 *Freda*, 1931 (cat. 14)
Jones used this Art Deco–influenced signature for several paintings he exhibited at his first solo show, at Madame Lisbeth Ebers Hoops's studio, University City, in 1931. It features all capital letters and J's with crossbars.

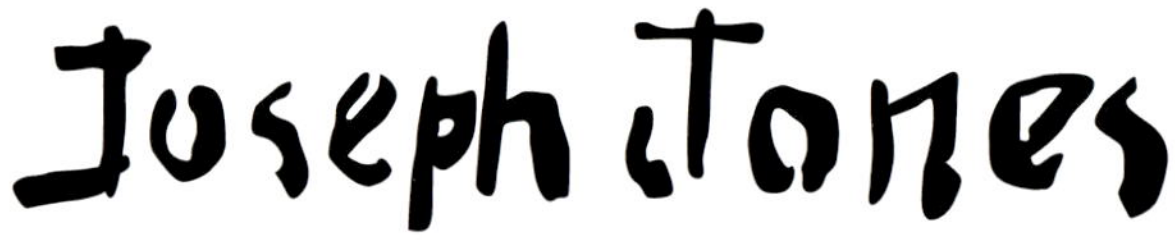

Signature 2 *Wooded Landscape*, 1931 (cat. 6)
Though this painting was executed in the same year as *Freda*, the signature it bears is somewhat more informal.

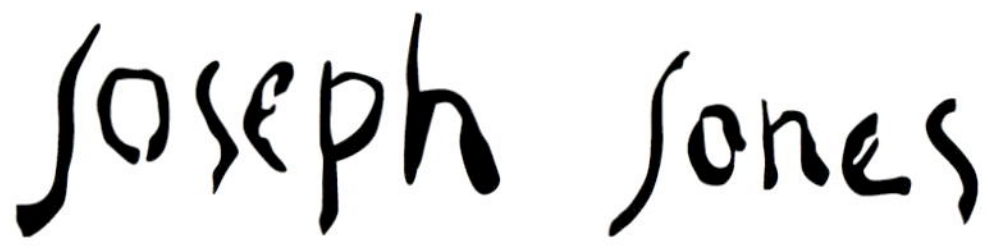

Signature 3 *Landscape*, c. 1931 (cat. 15)
This signature is closer in style to those of Jones's later career. The J's lack crossbars and resemble S's.

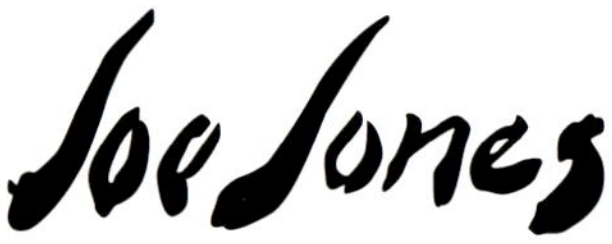

Signature 4 *Midwestern Landscape*, 1936 (cat. 43)
During the mid-to-late 1930s, Jones's signatures often featured J's with thickened arcs that extend below the baseline of the name. This painting bears the moniker adopted in 1933 and used throughout the rest of his career.

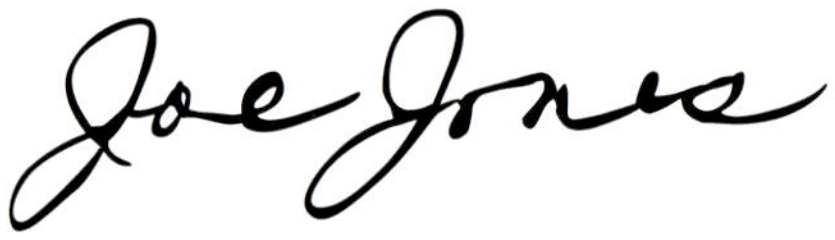

Signature 5 *Taking It Easy*, c. 1940 (cat. 77)
This is the style of signature that Jones most often used for his post-1933 prints. Some feature two signatures: one, most often printed with the image itself, and one in a cursive style, as here, inscribed by hand below the image. This signature is also similar to the way he signed his name in letters and in his late work.

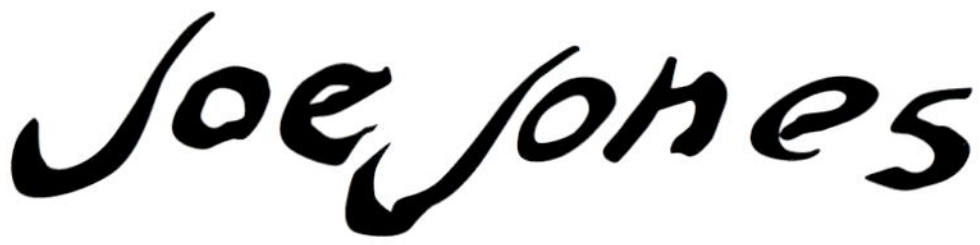

Signature 6 *Yellow Grain*, c. 1942 (cat. 82)
In the early 1940s, Jones again changed the appearance of the J's in his signature. Though earlier they resembled S's, now they look like hooks. As in the previous signatures, the arc of the J's drops below the baseline of the artist's name. The letters also lean to the right.

Selected Exhibitions, 1930–42

The following abbreviations and symbol are used here:

A.A.A. Galleries: Associated American Artists Galleries, New York

A.C.A. Gallery: American Contemporary Art Gallery, New York

CAM: City Art Museum, St. Louis

SLAG: St. Louis Artists' Guild

Asterisk (°): exhibition catalogue or brochure exists

1930

St. Louis. *St. Louis Post-Dispatch* Black and White Competitive Exhibition for St. Louis Scenes. Mar. 30–May 1. St. Louis Artists' Guild (hereinafter SLAG). / Twenty-fifth Annual Exhibition of Paintings by American Artists. Sept. 20–Nov. 2. City Art Museum (hereinafter CAM).° / Eighteenth Annual Exhibition. Dec. 1–Jan. 10, 1931. SLAG.

1931

St. Louis. *St. Louis Post-Dispatch* Black and White Competitive Exhibition for St. Louis Scenes. Mar. SLAG. / Second Annual No-Jury Exhibition. May 15–June 15. Org. by Independent Artists of St. Louis, Old Courthouse.° / F. Weber Co. sketch-contest exhibition. Summer. Old Courthouse. / Twenty-sixth Annual Exhibition of Paintings by American Artists, Sept. 19–Nov. 1. CAM.°

University City, Missouri. Exhibition by Joseph Jones. Through Nov. 29. Dance studio of Mme Lisbeth Ebers Hoops. / First exhibition of the New Hats. Through Dec. 26. Dance studio of Mme Lisbeth Ebers Hoops. Travels to Quincy (Ill.) Art Center. From Jan. 16, 1932.

1932

St. Louis. March Group of Contemporary Artists. Mar. Org. by Alexandra Korsakoff-Galston. Newhouse Gallery. / Nineteenth Annual Exhibition, Apr. 24–May 25. SLAG. / *St. Louis Post-Dispatch* Black and White Competitive Exhibition for St. Louis Scenes. May 28–July 1. SLAG. / Twenty-seventh Annual Exhibition of Painting by American Artists, Aug. 15–Oct. 16, CAM.° / Third Annual No-Jury Exhibit. Oct. 15–Nov. 15. Org. by Independent Artists of St. Louis. Old Courthouse (works selected from this exhibition are shown later at CAM). / Second Annual Exhibition of the New Hats. Nov. Noonan-Kocian Gallery. Traveled to Quincy (Ill.) Art Center. From Dec. 10. Travels to Springfield (Ill.) Art Museum. From Dec. 25. / Inaugural show of local artists. From Nov. 20. Studio House.

1933

New York. Painting and Sculpture from 16 American Cities. Dec. 11, 1933–Jan. 1, 1934. Museum of Modern Art.

St. Louis. One-person exhibition. Mid-Jan.–Feb. 15. SLAG. / Twentieth Anniversary Exhibition of SLAG. May 17–June 15. CAM.° / Paintings by Joe Jones. Sept. 16–23. Org. by the Co-operative Art Society. Stix, Baer & Fuller Dry Goods Co.° / Twenty-eighth Annual Exhibition of Paintings by American Artists. Sept. 16–Oct. 31. CAM.° / Solo exhibition of paintings and drawings. Elizabeth Green's residence, 4401 McPherson Ave. Dec.–Jan. 1934.

Worcester. Exhibition of American Painting Today. Dec. 1–Jan. 15, 1934. Worcester Art Museum.°

1934

New York. Second Biennial Exhibition of Contemporary American Painting. Nov. 27–Jan. 10, 1935. Whitney Museum of American Art.°

Washington, D.C. National Exhibition of Art by the Public Works of Art Project. Apr. 24–May 20, Corcoran Gallery of Art.

1935

Colorado Springs. First Annual Exhibition of Paintings by Artists West of the Mississippi. July 20–Aug. 31. Colorado Springs Fine Arts Center.

New York. Struggle for Negro Rights. Mar. 3–16. American Contemporary Art Gallery (hereinafter A.C.A. Gallery).° / Joe Jones. May 19–June 1 and July 14–Aug. 31. A.C.A. Gallery.° / Group show. Sept. 21–28, A.C.A. Gallery. / American Artists' Congress Graphic Art Exhibition. Nov. 10–21. A.C.A. Gallery. /

Younger American Artists Show. Nov. 29–Dec. 11. Walker Galleries. / Untitled exhibition. Dec. Marie Harriman Gallery. / The Capitalist Crisis. Dec. 1–7, A.C.A. Gallery.

St. Louis. Exhibition of Paintings by Artists of St. Louis and Vicinity. May 7– June 12. CAM. / Untitled exhibition. Dec. Labor Center.

Washington, D.C. Public Works of Art Pictures Exhibited in the United States Department of Labor. May. Department of Labor.°

Worcester. Second Biennial Exhibition of American Painting Today. Nov. 1–Dec. 15. Worcester Art Museum.°

1936

New York. Joe Jones: Paintings of Wheat Fields. Jan. 20–Feb. 2. Walker Galleries.° / Paintings by Midwestern Artists. May 4–16. A.C.A. Gallery.° Travels to Vanguard Gallery, St. Louis. June 17–July 1. / Group exhibition. July 15. Walker Galleries. / Third Biennial Exhibition of Contemporary American Painting. Nov. 10–Dec. 10. Whitney Museum of American Art.

Pittsburgh. Untitled exhibition. May 6–31. Junior League William Penn Galleries.° / Exhibition of works by artists boycotting the Carnegie Institute. Nov. Gillespie Galleries.

St. Louis. Thirtieth Annual Exhibition of Paintings by American Artists. Jan. 4–Feb. 16. CAM.° / Twenty-third Annual Exhibition of Oil Painting and Sculpture. Mar. 9–Apr 6. SLAG.° / The New Hats' Fifth Annual Exhibition of Paintings. Mar. 15–31. Noonan-Kocian Gallery.° / Protest Show: Exhibition of Paintings and Sculpture by 30 Outstanding St. Louis Artists. Oct. 31–Nov. 29. 1114 Locust St. Org. by the Campaign of the American Society of Painters, Sculptors and Gravers [against] the Rental Policy.

1937

Chicago. Forty-eighth Annual Exhibition of American Paintings and Sculpture. Nov. 18–Jan. 16, 1938. Art Institute of Chicago.°

Colorado Springs. Third Annual Exhibition of Paintings by Artists West of the Mississippi. July. Colorado Springs Fine Arts Center. Travels to Denver, Kansas City (Mo.), Bozeman, Portland, Seattle, San Francisco, Santa Barbara, and Los Angeles.

Detroit. Eighteenth Annual Exhibition of American Art. Apr. 2–May 3. Detroit Institute of Arts.°

New York. Exhibition of New Acquisitions. June. Metropolitan Museum of Art. / Exhibition of Midwestern Artists. June. A.C.A. Gallery. / Summer Exhibition 1937: Sculpture, Paintings and Watercolors from the Permanent Collection. June 1–Sept. 30. Whitney Museum of American Art.° / Group show. Sept. Walker Galleries. / Paintings by Joe Jones. Oct. 24–Nov. 13. A.C.A. Gallery. / Paintings for Paris. Nov. 5–Dec. 13. Museum of Modern Art.° / Annual Exhibition of Contemporary American Painting. Nov. 10–Dec. 12. Whitney Museum of American Art.° Second Anniversary Exhibition. Nov. 14–27. Walker Galleries.

Pittsburgh. International Exhibition of Paintings. Oct. 14–Dec.5. Carnegie Institute.°

1938

Baltimore. Labor in Art. Sept. 5–30. Baltimore Museum of Art.°

Colorado Springs. Fourth Annual Exhibition of Paintings by Artists West of the Mississippi. Aug. Colorado Springs Fine Arts Center. Travels to Denver, New York, Cincinnati, St. Louis (CAM), Kansas City (Mo.), and Austin into 1939.

Minneapolis. Third Annual Exhibition of Contemporary American Paintings. Feb. 4–28. University of Minnesota Gallery.

New York. Exhibition of American Art. June. Riverside Museum of Art. / 1938: Dedicated to the New Deal. Aug. 16–Sept. 10. A.C.A. Gallery. Traveled to St. Louis (CAM), Sept. 28–Oct. 16; and to Washington (D.C.) Bookshop Association Gallery, c. Nov. 20. / Annual Exhibition of Contemporary American Painting. Nov. 2–Dec. 11. Whitney Museum of American Art.°

Paris. Trois siècles d'art aux États-Unis. May 15–July. Org. by the Museum of Modern Art, New York. Musée du Jeu de Paume.°

Pittsburgh. International Exhibition of Paintings. Oct. 13–Dec. 4. Carnegie Institute.°

St. Louis. Thirty-second Annual Exhibition of Paintings by American Artists. Feb. 5–Mar. 20. CAM.° / Annual Exhibition of Paintings by Artists of St. Louis and Vicinity. Oct. 30–Nov. 30. CAM. / Thirty-third Annual Exhibition of Paintings by American Artists. Dec. 31–Feb. 12, 1939. CAM.°

Washington, D.C. Paintings by Living Americans Loaned from the Collection of the Whitney Museum of American Art. Nov. 8–Dec. 4, Museum of Modern Art Gallery.°

Worcester. American Painting of Today. Jan. 19–Feb. 27. Worcester Art Museum.°

1939

New York. American Art Today. Apr. 30–Oct. 31. New York World's Fair. / An American Group: Ninth Anniversary Exhibition. Sept. 18–Oct. 7. Associated American Artists Galleries (hereinafter AAA Galleries).° / Recent Paintings: Joe Jones. Nov. 12–Dec. 2. A.C.A. Gallery.°

St. Louis. Group exhibition. In conjunction with symposium "Art—A Necessity of the People." Jan. 23–Feb. 6. Org. by the St. Louis branch of the American Artists' Congress. St. Louis Art Center. / Group exhibition. June. Contemporary Art Center. / Work by Members of the St. Louis branch of the American Artists' Congress. Sept. CAM.

Washington, D.C. Painting and Sculpture Designed for Federal Buildings. Nov. 2–21. Corcoran Gallery of Art.

1940

Bloomfield Hills, Mich. Cranbook—Life [magazine] Exhibition of Contemporary American Painting. May. Cranbrook Academy of Art.

Buffalo. 60 American Paintings from the Whitney Museum. Nov. 1–Dec. 2. Albright Art Gallery.°

Cleveland. Exhibition of Contemporary American Oil Paintings. June 11–Oct. 3. Cleveland Museum of Art.°

Ithaca. Untitled exhibition. May. Cornell University.

New York. Annual Exhibition of Contemporary American Painting. Jan. 10–Feb. 18. Whitney Museum of American Art. / Mural Designs for Federal Buildings from the Section of Fine Arts, Public Buildings Administration, Federal Works Agency. Feb. 27–Mar. 17. Whitney Museum of American Art. / Joe Jones. Nov. 10–30. A.C.A. Gallery.° / Annual Exhibition of Contemporary American Painting. Nov. 27–Jan. 8, 1941. Whitney Museum of American Art.°

Philadelphia. One Hundred and Thirty-fifth Annual Exhibition of Painting and Sculpture. Jan. 28–Mar. 3. Pennsylvania Academy of the Fine Arts.°

San Francisco. Golden Gate International Exposition. May 25–Sept. 29.

St. Louis. Work by Members of the St. Louis branch of the American Artists' Congress. May 16–June 13. CAM.

Washington, D.C. Exhibition of oils and lithographs by Jones. Oct. 20–Nov. Washington Bookshop Association Gallery.

1941

Chicago. Fifty-second Annual Exhibition of American Paintings and Sculpture. Oct. 30–Jan. 4, 1942. Art Institute of Chicago.°

Cincinnati. Exhibition of Government Murals. Nov. Cincinnati Public Library.

New York. Annual Exhibition of Sculpture, Watercolors, Drawings, and Prints. Jan. 15–Feb. 19. Whitney Museum of American Art. / This Is Our City. Mar. 11–Apr. 13. Whitney Museum of American Art. / Roofs for 40 Million: An Exhibition on Housing. Apr. 9–May 1. Org. by An American Group, Inc. La Maison Française, Rockefeller Center. / Contemporary Painting in the United States. Apr. 19–27. Metropolitan Museum of Art.

Travels as Pintura contemporánea norteamericana to ten Latin American cities from May to December. / Annual Exhibition of Paintings by Artists under Forty. Nov. 12–Dec. 30. Whitney Museum of American Art.

Philadelphia. One Hundred and Thirty-sixth Annual Exhibition of Painting and Sculpture. Jan. 26–Mar. 2. Pennsylvania Academy of the Fine Arts.

Washington, D.C. Seventeenth Biennial Exhibition of Contemporary American Oil Paintings. Mar. 23–May 4. Corcoran Gallery of Art.°

1942

Chicago. Fifty-third Annual Exhibition of American Paintings and Sculpture. Oct. 29–Dec. 10. Art Institute of Chicago.°

New York. Between Two Barges. Mar. 3–31. Whitney Museum of Art.° / Joe Jones. Oct. 3–22. AAA Galleries.° / Annual Exhibition of Contemporary American Art. Nov. 24–Jan. 6, 1943. Whitney Museum of American Art.° / Artists for Victory: An Exhibition of Contemporary American Art. Dec. 7–Feb. 22, 1943. Metropolitan Museum of Art.°

Philadelphia. One Hundred and Thirty-seventh Annual Exhibition of Painting and Sculpture. Jan. 25–Mar. 1. Pennsylvania Academy of the Fine Arts.°

Richmond. Third Biennial Exhibition of Contemporary American Paintings. Mar. 4–Apr. 14. Virginia Museum of Fine Arts.°

St. Louis. The Negro in Art. Dec. 23–Jan. 21, 1943. People's Art Center.°

Terre Haute. Inaugural Show of Present Day American Paintings. Mar. 21–May 2. Swope Art Museum.°

Bibliography

SELECTED PUBLISHED WRITINGS AND ILLUSTRATIONS

The following abbreviations are used here:
AAA Galleries: Associated American Artists Galleries, New York
A.C.A. Gallery: American Contemporary Art Gallery, New York
Green Papers: Dr. John Green Collection, Missouri History Museum, St. Louis.

1928

Vagaries. "A Nordic Clown." (Nov.–Dec.), p. 9. Illustration.

1932

Saint Louis Review. "Art, Theatre, Movies." 1, 2 (Mar. 15), p. 9.

Studio Review. "Carnegie International." (Apr.). City Art Museum publicity scrapbook, Saint Louis Art Museum, archives.

1935

Art Front. "Miners." 1, 7 (Nov.), p. 5. Illustration.

1936

East St. Louis Journal (*Illinois Magazine*). "The Drouth as Seen by Joe Jones." (Sept. 6).

Johnson, Josephine. "The Arkansas Terror." *New Masses* 20, 2 (June 30), pp. 12–14. Illustrations.

Midwest–A Review. "Four Cases of Mural Censorship." 1, 1 (Nov.), pp. 17, 20.

St. Louis Post-Dispatch. "In the 'Seventh Year' of Drouth." *Magazine*. Sept. 6, p. 1. / "Pages from a Painter's Notebook." Dec. 13.

1937

New Masses. "Broun—His Guild Went C.I.O." 23, 13 (June 22), p. 14. Cartoon.

"Repression of Art in America." *Artists against War and Fascism: Papers of the First American Artists' Congress*. Introduction by Matthew Baigell and Julia Williams. Rutgers University Press, 1986. Pp. 75–77.

St. Louis Post-Dispatch. "At the Congress of Revolutionary Artists and Writers." Feb. 14.

St. Louis Star-Times. "Federal Arts Projects." Letter to the editor. July 7.

1938

Hughes, Langston. *A New Song*. International Workers Order. Frontispiece.

St. Louis Art Center. Foreword. *Savo Radulovic Paintings*. Exh. cat. Nov. 18–26 (?). Richardson Memorial Library, Saint Louis Art Museum, artist's file.

St. Louis Star-Times. "Joe Jones Commends Weber." Oct. 7.

1939

St. Louis Post-Dispatch. "Joe Jones Photographs the Seamy Side of St. Louis." June 4. Photographs.

1940

A.C.A. Gallery. "Gropper, 1940." *20 Years of Gropper*. Exh. cat. Repr. in *Social Realism: Art as a Weapon*. Edited by David Shapiro. Frederick Ungar Publishing Co., 1973.

1945

AAA Galleries. Artist's statement. *Joe Jones*. Exh. cat.

1947

AAA Galleries. Artist's statement. *Paintings by Joe Jones*. Exh. cat.

1951

AAA Galleries. Untitled poem. *Joe Jones: Recent Work*. Exh. cat.

1953

Mead, Margaret. "Modern Youth in Changing World." *St. Louis Post-Dispatch*. Dec. 13. Illustrations.

[1959]

Selected Artists Galleries. Untitled poem. *Recent Paintings by Joe Jones*. Exh. cat.

1961

Time. 77, 21 (May 19). Cover illustration. / 78, 24 (Dec. 15). Cover illustration.

SELECTED BIBLIOGRAPHY, TO 1942

1930

Art Digest. "The St. Louis Annual." 4, 20 (Sept.), p. 9.

St. Louis Globe-Democrat. "21 St. Louis Artists Chosen for Exhibit." Aug. 14.

St. Louis Post-Dispatch. "Art Museum to Show American Paintings." Aug. 14. / "American Paintings on Display Tomorrow." Sept. 19. / "Woman's Painting Wins $500 Guild Prize." Dec. 7. / "Winners of Prizes at Artists' Guild Competition." Dec. 21.

1931

Art Affairs. "Sculptors Show Merit in Exhibit of No-Jury Art." 1, 4 (May), p. 4.

Benn, Carl. "Wide Variety Exhibited by 148 Artists." *Art Affairs*. 1, 4 (May), pp. 1, 3. / "Joseph Jones Holds First One-Man Show." *St. Louis Art World*. 1, 2 (Nov.), pp. 1, 4.

Forshey, Guy. "From House Painting to Portrait Painting." *St. Louis Post-Dispatch Sunday Magazine*. June 14, p. 5.

Gottschalk, Max. "Young Artists of St. Louis in American Show." *St. Louis Art World*. 1, 1 (Oct.), pp. 1, 4.

St. Louis Art World. "Cornelia F. Maury Sketch Wins Prize." 1, 1 (Oct.), p. 1. / "Joseph Jones in University City." 1, 1 (Oct.), p. 4. / "Exhibitions." 1, 2 (Nov.), p. 2. / "'High Hats,' New Modern Group Is Organized Here." 1, 2 (Nov.), p. 3. / "Water Color Club Exhibits Works." 1, 2 (Nov.), p. 4. / "Forty Paintings in First Show of New Hats." 1, 3 (Dec.), pp. 1–3. / "Jones Commissioned to Decorate KMOX in Modern Manner." 1, 3 (Dec.).

St. Louis Globe-Democrat. "Restraint Keynote of Paintings Shown at Annual Display." Sept. 19. / "Six Oils in Exhibit of Joseph Jones Sold." Nov. 22.

St. Louis Post-Dispatch. "American Paintings to Be Exhibited Here." Sept. 18.

St. Louis Star-Times. "American Canvas Exhibit Here Has Modernistic Note." Sept. 29.

1932

Art Digest. "Art Swings to the Right in the St. Louis Annual Painting Show." 6, 20 (Sept. 1), p. 7.

Burroughs, Clyde H. "American Masters." *Saint Louis Review*. 2, 1 (Nov. 5), pp. 9–11.

Corr, Paul B. "Individuality Is Keynote of New Hats' Show." *St. Louis Art World*. 2, 3 (Nov.), p. 1.

Dawson, Frances. "Trend Towards Fundamentals Apparent in American Exhibition." *St. Louis Art World*. 2, 1 (Sept.), pp. 1–2. / "Uniformly High Quality Evident in No-Jury Show." *St. Louis Art World*. 2, 2 (Oct.), pp. 1, 6.

"The Reviewer." *Saint Louis Review*. 1, 6 (May 15), p. 2.

St. Louis Art World. "Black and Whites by St. Louisans at Newhouse Gallery." 1, 6 (Mar.), p. 1. / "Guild Annual Draws Numerous Entries." 1, 7 (Apr.), pp. 1, 4. / "New Hats to Exhibit at Kocian's Gallery." 2, 1 (Sept.), p. 1. / "Studio House Has Its Formal Opening" and untitled notice about Jones opening a studio with Sheila Burlingame. 2, 3 (Nov.), p. 2. / "Joseph Jones Exhibition to Be at Guild in January." 2, 4 (Dec.), p. 1.

St. Louis Globe-Democrat. "Works of St. Louis Artists Picked for Annual Exhibition." Aug. 7. / "American Artists' Exhibit to Open at City Museum Today." Aug. 14.

St. Louis Post-Dispatch. "New KMOX Studios Open." Jan. 13. / "Artistic House Painter Decorates Radio Station KMOX." Jan. 18. / "Artists' Guild First Prize Is Won by Ozark Farmer." May 1. / "Charles K. Gleeson Again Winner of Black and White Art Contest." May 29. / "Paintings by 28 American Masters in Show at Museum." Aug. 14. / "A St. Louis Artist Discusses His Family on Canvas." Aug. 28.

1933

Art Digest. "Joe Jones Tries to Knock Holes in Walls." 7, 10 (Feb. 15), p. 9. / "At Last, New York Gets Chance to See a Real 'National' Show." 8, 6 (Dec. 15), p. 32.

Benn, Carl. "Joe Jones' Art Goes Forward, Show Reveals." *St. Louis Art World*. 2, 5 (Jan.), p. 1.

Corr, Paul Benjamin. "Review of Art Activities of the Past Season." *St. Louis Art World*. 2, 9 (Summer), p. 2.

Dawson, Frances. "Self Portrait Exhibit One of Much Interest." *St. Louis Art World*. 2, 6 (Feb.), p. 1.

Hayden, Martin. "House Painter Artist Gives Views on Rivera Murals." *Detroit News*. N.d. St. Louis Public Library, artist's file.

Hutchings, Emily Grant. "Art and Artists." *St. Louis Globe-Democrat*. Jan. 8. / "Art and Artists." *St. Louis Globe-Democrat*. Jan. 22.

Jewell, Edward Alden. "The Realm of Art: A Nationwide Challenge." *New York Times.* Dec. 17.

Morsell, Mary. "Modern Museum Exhibits the Art of Sixteen Cities." *Art News.* 32, 12 (Dec. 23), pp. 3, 16.

"The Reviewer." "New Paintings of Joseph Jones." *Saint Louis Review.* 2, 6 (Jan. 14), p. 5.

St. Louis Art World. "Joe Jones Going to Provincetown." 2, 9 (May–June), p. 4.

St. Louis Globe-Democrat. "Society to Finance Young Artist Here." Feb. 19. / "Awards Announced in Annual Exhibit of Artists' Guild." May 28.

St. Louis Post-Dispatch. "What Young Man Thinks about Life Put on Canvas." Jan. 29. / "A Young Man with a Will." Feb. 3. / "10 Persons Pledge Aid to Struggling Artist." Feb. 19. / "Artists' Guild Award Goes to Joseph Jones." May 8. / "Young Artist's Work on Sale." Sept. 15. / "28th Exhibit of American Art Reflects Present Perplexities." Sept. 17. / "Provincetown Makes Artist a Communist." Sept. 21.

Saint Louis Review. "Art." 2, 10 (Mar. 11), p. 18.

Thalinger, Thelma Wiles. "Views and Reviews: Paintings of Joe Jones." *St. Louis Art World.* 2, 6 (Feb.), p. 4. / "Views and Reviews: Paintings of Joe Jones." *St. Louis Art World.* 2, 9 (May–June), pp. 1, 4.

1934

Cott, Perry B. "American Painting of Today." *Magazine of Art.* 27, 1 (Jan.), pp. 10–17.

Hutchings, Emily Grant. "Art and Artists." *St. Louis Globe-Democrat.* Mar. 18.

International Literature. "American Unemployed Art." 2, pp. 95–97.

Jewell, Edward Alden. "Exhibition at the Whitney Reveals Some Striking Developments in American Art." *New York Times*, Dec. 2.

Johns, Orrick. "St. Louis Artists Win." *New Masses.* 10, 10 (Mar. 6), p. 28. / "The John Reed Clubs Meet." *New Masses.* 13, 5 (Oct. 30), pp. 25–26.

Ste. Genevieve Fair Play. "Art School Notes." July 21.

Ste. Genevieve Herald. "Art Colony Notes." July 21.

St. Louis Globe-Democrat. "Mural Being Painted at City Hospital." Oct. 19. / "Eight Communists Sent to Workhouse for Disturbing Peace." Dec. 8. / "Head of Art Class in Old Courthouse Will Oppose Ouster." Dec. 14. / "Jobless Art Class Resents City Action." Dec. 15. / "Chadsey Refuses to Heed Protests of Art Students." Dec. 16. / "Civic Rights Body to Try City Officials." Dec. 17.

St. Louis Post-Dispatch. "Joe Jones Stirs up Art Row at Old Courthouse." Jan. 21. / "Social Unrest Mural in Old Court-House." Feb. 16. / "Old Courthouse Display of Soviet Art Torn Down." Mar. 5. / "Missouri Landscape Mural on City Hospital Walls." Oct. 18. / "City Hall Disturbers Sent to Workhouse." Dec. 7. / "City to Oust Artist from Old Courthouse." Dec. 13. / "Joe Jones Not Going to Move Willingly." Dec. 14. / "Unemployed Artists Protest on Lockout." Dec. 16. / "Radicals Find Mayor 'Guilty' at Mock Trial." Dec. 22. / "Exhibit by Joe Jones' Pupils." Dec. 30.

St. Louis Star-Times. "Chadsey Takes No Chances on Art, Fears Communism." Dec. 15. / "City Officials Are 'Convicted' at Mock Trial." Dec. 22.

Watson, Forbes. "A Steady Job." *Magazine of Art.* 27, 4 (Apr.), pp. 168–72.

1935

Alexander, Stephen. "Art." *New Masses.* 14, 12 (Mar. 26), p. 28. / "Art: Joe Jones." *New Masses.* 15, 9 (May 28), p. 30. / "Current Art." *New Masses.* 16, 5 (July 30), p. 27.

Art Front. "Call for an American Artists' Congress." 1, 7 (Nov.), p. 6.

Burke, Fielding. "Pelzer: 'Just Another of Those Damned Strike Towns.'" *New Masses.* 17, 5 (Oct. 29), p. 16.

Burrows, Carlyle. "A Painter of Promise." *New York Herald Tribune.* N.d. Missouri History Museum, St. Louis, artist's file.

Chicago Tribune. "Lives of Arkansas Miners and Share Croppers Depicted in Murals at College." Aug. 2.

Childs, Marquis W. "Three St. Louis Artists." *Magazine of Art.* 28, 8 (Aug.), pp. 483–88.

Commonwealth College. "Joe Jones Starts Murals at Commonwealth College." Press release. Aug. 17. Dr. John Green Collection, Missouri History Museum, St. Louis (hereinafter Green Papers).

Commonwealth College Fortnightly. "Mural in Commons Nears Completion." 11, 17 (Sept. 1.), pp. 1, 4. / "Foremost Artist on Summer Schedule." 11, 15 (Aug. 1), p. 1. / "Significant Mural to Adorn Commons." 11, 16 (Aug. 15), pp. 1, 4. All in Green Papers.

Davis, Stuart. "The Artist Today: The Standpoint of the Artists' Union." *Magazine of Art.* 28, 8 (Aug.), p. 476. Repr. in David Shapiro, ed. *Social Realism: Art as a Weapon.* Frederick Ungar Publishing Co., 1973. Pp. 111–17.

Devree, Howard. "In Galleries: Current Exhibitions and Other Events." *New York Times.* July 28. / "Briefs from a Reviewer's Notebook." *New York Times.* Dec. 1.

Jewell, Edward Alden. "Ex-House Painter in Art Show Here." *New York Times*. May 22. / "The Year in Retrospect." *New York Times*. May 26. / "Taking Stock of Local Prospects." *New York Times*. June 2. / "Younger Artists in Walker Show." *New York Times*. Nov. 30.

Kainen, Jacob. "Joe Jones, Vital Revolutionary Artist." *Daily Worker*. May 5.

Lehman, Al. "Brilliant Murals by Joe Jones Decorate Labor College Walls." *Daily Worker*. Aug. 31.

MacLeish, Archibald. "U.S. Art: 1935." *Fortune*. 7, 6 (Dec.), p. 69.

Mumford, Lewis. "The Art Galleries: In Capitulation." *New Yorker* 11, 16 (June 1), p. 57. Repr. in *Mumford on Modern Art in the 1930s*. Edited and with introduction by Robert Wojtowicz. University of California Press, 2007. Pp. 164–67.

New Masses. "American Artists' Congress: Call for an American Artists' Congress." 17, 1 (Oct. 1), p. 33.

Newsweek. "Art: Southern Labor's Story in Blue, Gray, and Fiery Red." 6, 9 (Aug. 31), p. 21.

New York Herald Tribune. "Joe Jones Made Artistic Boswell of Life in U.S." Oct. Green Papers.

New York Sun. "Two Painters Make Debuts." May 23. / "More Fall Art Displays Open." Sept. 21.

New York Times. "Footnotes on Headliners." May 26. / "Assembly to Treat of Art Instruction." June 8. / "In New York Galleries." July 14. / "Out of Town." Sept. 1. / "Art with Purpose Will Be His Theme." Oct. 5. / "Calling All Artists." Oct. 13. / "News of Art." Oct. 28. / "Contemporaries" and "Other Shows." Dec. 8.

New York World-Telegram. "Galleries Co[?]." May 25.

St. Louis Globe-Democrat. "Joe Jones, Artist, Granted Divorce." Feb. 12. / "Unknown Artist Wins Recognition with 2 Paintings." May 2. / "Art Jury Selects 49 Paintings for Exhibit Wednesday." May 5. / "Work of 36 Artists in St. Louis Area Is Exhibited Here." May 9. / "Joe Jones Assigned to Rural Painting." Oct. 8.

St. Louis Post-Dispatch. "Chadsey Can't Attend Show by Art Students He Evicted." Jan. 4. / "Display of Pictures by St. Louis Artists." May 5. / "Donald Williams and His Painting 'The Sniper.'" May 26. / "Joe Jones Painting Mural for Arkansas." Aug. 20. / "Artist Joe Jones Gets Job." Oct. 13. / "Labor Center to Show Joe Jones Paintings." N.d. Saint Louis Art Museum, archives.

St. Louis Star-Times. "A New St. Louis Author: Beamon Meacham, Whose First Successful Story Is Published Today in Star-Times." July 8.

Time. "Housepainter." 25, 22 (June 3), p. 32.

Watson, Forbes. "The Innocent Bystander." *Magazine of Art*. 28, 1 (Jan.), pp. 43–49, 61–62.

Weinstock, Clarence. "Joe Jones." *Art Front*. 1, 6 (July), p. 6.

1936

Art Digest. "Joe Jones of Missouri: A 'Success Story.'" 10, 8 (Jan. 15), p. 15. / "Joe Jones Grows." 10, 9 (Feb. 1), pp. 17, 33.

Art News. "Joe Jones Celebrates Missouri's Wheatfields." 34, 17 (Jan. 25), p. 8.

Benson, E. M. "Two Proletarian Artists: Joe Jones and William Gropper." *Magazine of Art*. 39, 3 (Mar.), p. 189.

"A Bright View of the Wheat Fields." Unidentified newspaper clipping. N.d., Missouri History Museum, St. Louis, artist's file.

Burrows, Carlyle. "Notes and Comment on Events in Art." *New York Herald Tribune*. Jan. 26.

Dalton, Mary J. "An Art Patron's Protest." Letter to the editor. *St. Louis Post-Dispatch*. Nov. 27.

Devree, Howard. "In Local Art Galleries." *New York Times*. May 10. / "The Galleries Present." *New York Times*. June 14.

Forum. "Wheat Fields: Three Scenes from the Plains." 95 (Apr.), pp. 224–25.

Freeman, Joseph. "The Battle for Art." *New Masses*. 18, 9 (Feb. 25), pp. 8, 10.

Graeme, Alice. "Artists Boycott Carnegie Show over Rental Issue." *Washington Post*. Nov. 8.

Holme, Bryan. "America." *London Studio*. 11, 61 (Apr.), pp. 111, 237–40.

Jena, Jeanette. "Junior League Shows Young Artist's Work." *Pittsburgh Post-Gazette*. May 6.

Lowe, Jeannette. "Painting and Literature at the Whitney." *Art News*. 35, 7 (Nov. 14), pp. 19–20.

Luchtemeyer, E. A. "Bolshevik Art." Letter to the editor. *St. Louis Star-Times*. Feb. 4.

Magazine of Art. "Field Notes: American Artists' Congress." 29, 3 (Mar.), pp. 192–94. / "Two Proletarian Artists: Joe Jones and Gropper." 29, 3 (Mar.), pp. 188–89.

McKenzie, Don. "When's an Artist Red?" Letter to the editor. *St. Louis Star-Times*. Feb. 2.

Mumford, Lewis. "Goya, Homer, and Jones." *New Yorker*. 11, 52 (Feb. 8), pp. 58–59. / "Looking Backward, Looking Forward." Repr. in *Mumford on Modern Art in the 1930s*. Edited and with an introduction by Robert Wojtowicz. University of California Press, 2007. Pp. 201–03.

New Masses. "Between Ourselves." 18, 8 (Feb. 18), p. 30. / "William Gropper Sees the American Artists' Congress." 18, 9 (Feb. 25), pp. 16–17.

Newsweek. "Joe Jones, Modern Worker; Francisco Goya, Ancient Rake." 7, 5 (Feb. 1), p. 28.

New York Sun. Untitled article announcing solo exhibition at Walker Galleries. Jan. 18. / "Regional Art of the West." May 7.

New York Times. "Joe Jones." Jan. 26. / "Art Brevities." Feb. 1. / "Art Notes." Feb. 4. / "Artists Spurn Bid to Carnegie Show." Mar. 9. / "Josephine Johnson Arrested in Strike." June 6. / "8 Paintings in Show Bought by Museum." Dec. 7.

New York World-Telegram. "Joe Jones Never Studied Art, but His Mine Scene Stirs Furor." Feb. 1.

Parnassus. "Artists' Congress." 8, 3 (Mar.), p. 31.

Schary, Saul. "Tendencies in American Art." Speech at second closed session at First American Artists' Congress. *Artists against War and Fascism: Papers of the First American Artists' Congress*. Introduction by Matthew Baigell and Julia Williams. Rutgers University Press, 1986. P. 148.

Ste. Genevieve Fair Play. "Art School to Open Here July 6." June 19. / "Art School to Open Here July 6." June 27. / "Art School Has Fine Enrollment as Term Begins." July 11.

St. Louis Globe-Democrat. "American Artists Open Exhibition at Art Museum Today." Jan. 4. / "Young Artists Here Selecting Paintings for New York Show." Mar. 6. / "Painting Exhibit Rounds into Shape Despite Boycott." Oct. 21. / "Artists Refused Rental Fee, to Use Vacant Storeroom." Oct. 31. / "Art Museum Firm against Rental Fee." Nov. 8.

St. Louis Post-Dispatch. "American Exhibit at City Art Museum." Jan. 4. / "Union Organizer Fined $1060 in Arkansas Strike." June 6. / "Midwest Art Display at Vanguard Gallery." June 18. / "Hostesses to Receive at Vanguard Gallery." June 21. / "Artists Insist on Fee to Exhibit Pictures." Oct. 2. / "Protest Exhibition by Artists Denied Fee." Oct. 31.

St. Louis Star-Times. "Gathering Ideas for Murals." Aug. 14. / "32 Artists of St. Louis District Represented in Paintings in City Art Museum Exhibition." Nov. 2.

Survey Graphic. "Wheat—Four Paintings." 25, 8 (Aug.), pp. 474–75.

Time. "Workers and Wheatfields." 27, 5 (Feb. 3), p. 46.

Vaughan, Malcolm. Untitled clipping. *New York American*. N.d. Missouri History Museum, St. Louis, artist's file.

Whiting, F. A., Jr. "Two Versions of American Art: Chicago and Manhattan." *Magazine of Art*. 29, 12 (Dec.), pp. 812–19, 849.

1937

American Artists Group. *Original Etchings, Lithographs and Woodcuts Published by the American Artists Group, Inc.*

Art Digest. "It Does Happen Here." 11, 14 (Apr. 15), p. 9. / "Plaudits, Bricks for Metropolitan Newcomers." 11, 13 (July 1), p. 8.

Art News. "Local Color and Stark Realism Seen by Joe Jones." 36, 1 (Oct. 30), p. 19.

Bird, Paul. "The Fortnight in New York." *Art Digest*. 12, 4 (Nov. 15), pp. 22–23.

Breuning, Margaret. "The World's Art: Pittsburgh 1937." *Parnassus*. 9, 6 (Nov.), pp. 30–34. / "Art in New York." *Parnassus*. 9, 7 (Dec.), pp. 22–28.

Burrows, Carlyle. "Notes and Comments on Events in Art." *New York Herald Tribune*. Oct. 31.

Coates, Robert M. "The Art Galleries: Ceramicists and a Modern Primitive—Joe Jones." *New Yorker*. 13, 36 (Nov. 6), pp. 43–45.

Davidson, Martha. "New Directions in Native Painting." *Art News*. 35, 31 (May 1), pp. 138–53. / "The Pantheon of Living Native Art." *Art News*. 35, 35 (May 29), pp. 9–10, 25. / "American Art at Home and Paris: Paintings for Native and Foreign Consumption in Two Shows." *Art News*. 36, 7 (Nov. 13), pp. 13–14.

Devree, Howard. "A Reviewer's Notebook: Comment on Some of the Newly Opened Group Exhibitions and One-Man Shows." *New York Times*. June 6. / "Two American Shows." *Magazine of Art*. 30, 12 (Dec.), pp. 741–43.

Genauer, Emily. "New Show Represents 30 Artists." *New York World-Telegram*. Sept. 11. / "Joe Jones Takes Rank with the Masters." *New York World-Telegram*. Oct. 30.

Jewell, Edward Allen. "American Artists Show Work Here." *New York Times*. May 29. / "Metropolitan Purchases." *New York Times*. May 30. / "Whitney Museum Arranges Show." *New York Times*. June 2. / "One-Man Shows by Benton, Biddle, and Joe Jones." *New York Times*. Oct. 31.

Kistler, Aline. "Prints of the Moment." *Prints*. 8, 2 (Dec.), pp. 90–97.

Klein, Jerome. "Art Comment: Depression Topic in Two Exhibitions." *New York Post*. June 5. / "Two Missourians Give New York Views of America." *New York Post*. Oct. 30. / "Whitney Museum Goes to Town with Americans." *New York Post*. Nov. 12.

McBride, Henry. "Paintings by Joe Jones." *New York Sun*. Oct. 30.

Metropolitan Museum of Art Bulletin. "Contemporary American Paintings." 32, 6 (June), p. 158.

New Masses. "Giotto and Gropper." 23, 4 (June 8), pp. 15–16. / "Sights and Sounds." 23, 12 (June 15), p. 29.

New York World-Telegram. "Sudden Deluge of New Art Exhibitions Takes the Critics by Surprise." June 5.

Schofield, Paul. "The Midwest Scene Comes of Age." *Parnassus*. 9, 4 (Apr.), pp. 14–15, 51.

Ste. Genevieve Fair Play. "Art School Begins Fifth Season Here." June 19.

St. Louis Globe-Democrat. "St. Louisan Invited to Artists' Congress." Jan. 2. / "$1800 Fellowship for Joe Jones." Mar. 29. / "Wins Fellowship." Mar. 29. / "Joe Jones Films." Mar. 30. / "Painter Here Breaks into Met." May 11. / "St. Louis Artist in Western Exhibit." July 12. / "Joe Jones to Move Studio to New York." Aug. 20. / "On Exhibit Here." Dec. 18.

St. Louis Post-Dispatch. "St. Louis Artist to Be Honored." Jan. 2. / "The Story of the Grain." Jan. 3. / "Guggenheim Award Won by Joe Jones." Mar. 29. / "Joe Jones—Guggenheim Fellow." Mar. 31. / "Metropolitan Buys Joe Jones Painting." May 10. / "Artist Joe Jones to Move to New York." Aug. 19. / "St. Louis and Art." Aug. 20. / "Joe Jones' Work on Calendar." Nov. 29.

Time. "Metropolitan's Moderns." 29, 23 (June 7), p. 45.

Washington Post. "Art Review of America Is Exhibited." Nov. 21.

1938

Art Digest. "Critics Sing Mournful Tune at Whitney Show." 13, 4 (Nov. 15), p. 5.

Associated American Artists. *Catalogue of Original Signed Etchings and Lithographs.*

Chomyk, Mike. "Sees Sour Grapes in Picture." Letter to the editor. *St. Louis Post-Dispatch*. Jan. 3.

Collier, F. H. "Echoes of the Streets: Why Does Good Art Move Us?" *St. Louis Globe-Democrat*. Oct. 1. / "Echoes of the Streets: Artist Jones and His Famous Tree." *St. Louis Globe-Democrat*. Oct. 7.

Devree, Howard. "New Shows: Gallery Attractions and Other Events." *New York Times*. Aug. 14. / "Activities in New York: Work of the Bureau for Blind Artists—An Exile's Etchings—Other Notes." *New York Times*. Sept. 4.

Gates, Margaret. "Unusual Art Group at Colorado Springs Center." *Washington Post*. Aug. 7.

Millier, Arthur. "Brush Strokes." *Los Angeles Times*. May 8.

New York Sun. "A Worker Again—on WPA." Aug. 20.

Selby, John. "Joe, the Boy Artist." *Hartford Courant*. Sept. 11. "Joe Jones, House Painter, Accomplished Artist Today." *Toledo Times*. Sept. 11. / "Joe Jones, Who Began as House Painter, Hailed as Promising Artist." *St. Louis Globe-Democrat*. Sept. 11. /

St. Louis Globe-Democrat. "Joe Jones' 'Trestle' at Art Museum." June 25. / "Contemporary Art Show at Museum." September 29. / "St. Louis Artists' Show Opens." Oct. 30. / "American Artists' Show at Museum." Dec. 30.

St. Louis Post-Dispatch. "Annual American Art Exhibit at Museum." Feb. 4. / "Benton and Joe Jones and St. Louis." Apr. 29. / "Joe Jones Paints a Postoffice Mural." May 29. / "Painting by Joe Jones Lent to Art Museum." June 24. / "Artists' Congress Criticizes Museum." Aug. 10. / "Left-Wing American Art at City Museum." Sept. 29. / "International Show of Art Opens Tonight." Oct. 13. / "Display of Paintings by St. Louis Artists." Oct. 30. / "Paintings by St. Louisans at Art Museum." Oct. 31. / "St. Louis Artists in New York Show." Nov. 6. / "American Artists' Exhibit at Museum." Dec. 30.

St. Louis Star-Times. "Art Museum Gets 'The Trestle' by Artist Joe Jones." June 24. / "Joe Jones' Work in City Art Museum." June 24. / "New Modern Art Works on Display at City Museum." Sept. 29. / "At St. Louis Artists' Exhibit." Oct. 31.

Sweeney, James Johnston. "Carnegie International 1938." *Parnassus*. 10, 6 (Nov.), pp. 13–18.

Washington Post. "Vain Groping in Bookshop Art Exhibition." Nov. 20.

Watson, Jane. "Baltimore Museum's 'Labor in Art' Collection One of Few to Show Quality as Well as 'Theme.'" *Washington Post*. Sept. 18.

1939

Architectural Forum. "Forty-eight State Mural Competition Winners." 71, 6 (Dec.), p. 40.

Art Digest. "These Painters and Sculptors Passed the Jury." 13, 17 (June 1), p. 33. / "Winners in Government's '48-States Competition' Shown at Corcoran." 14, 4 (Nov. 15), p. 12. / "Joe Jones Matures." 14, 5 (Dec. 1), p. 12.

Art News. "Wheat Fields and Slums in Jones' Adept Style." 38, 8 (Nov. 25), p. 13.

Burke, Harry H. "Spring Features Painting Exhibit." *St. Louis Globe-Democrat.* May 31.

Charleston (Mo.) *Enterprise-Courier*. "Mural Painting Costing $670 for Post Office." Jan. 12.

Cheney, Martha Candler. *Modern Art in America*. Whittlesey House.

Coates, Robert M. "The Art Galleries: Picasso—Cézanne—Some Americans." *New Yorker*. 15, 40 (Nov. 25), pp. 44, 46–47.

Craven, Thomas, ed. *A Treasury of American Prints: A Selection of One Hundred Etchings and Lithographs by the Foremost Living Artists*. Simon and Schuster.

Devree, Howard. "A Reviewer's Notebook: Many Shows." *New York Times*. Nov. 19. / "Taubes and Joe Jones." *Magazine of Art*. 32, 12 (Dec.), pp. 716–17, 729–30.

Fuerbringer, Otto. "No More Regionalism in American Art." *St. Louis Post-Dispatch*. Feb. 5.

Hall, W. S. *Eyes on America: The United States as Seen by Her Artists*. Studio Publications, Inc.

Magazine of Art. "Forty-eight State Competition." 32, 11 (Nov.), p. 659.

McCausland, Elizabeth. "Living American Art." *Parnassus*. 11, 5 (May), pp. 16–25.

Mok, Michael. "Oliver Twist Makes Good." *New York Post*. Nov. 10.

New York Times. "Favorite Art Picked by Visitors at Fair." Aug. 17. / "They Know What They Like." Aug. 27. / "Art Show in the Making." Sept. 3.

New York World-Telegram. "Joe Jones and Carter in Fine One-Man Shows." Nov. 18.

Parnassus. Announcement (Jones is one of several artists being considered for a monographic series). 11, 7 (Nov.), pp. 36–37.

Pencil Points. "Mural Awards." 20, 12 (Dec. suppl.), pp. 42–44.

St. Louis Globe-Democrat. "Symposium on Art." Jan. 18. / "Painting Exhibit Opened Here." Feb. 2. / "19 St. Louis Art Works to Be Shown at World's Fair." Feb. 17. / "Design for Wellston Post Office Mural." Apr. 14. / "Joe Jones Completes Post Office Mural." July 27. / "St. Louis Artists to Paint Murals." Oct. 26.

St. Louis Post-Dispatch. "Mural by Joe Jones for Charleston, Mo." Jan. 5. / "16 St. Louis Artists to Display Work." Jan. 22. / "St. Louis Art Show." Jan. 23. / "St. Louis Art for Fair." Feb. 17. / "St. Louis Art Museum's Regional Exhibit." Feb. 19. / Untitled review of St. Louis Art Center exhibition. Feb. 19. / "Joe Jones Completes His Seventh Mural." July 26. / "Artist Joe Jones Assails Art Museum 'Dictatorship.'" Aug. 27. / "Old Courthouse, City's Gift to U.S., Battered Within, Decayed Without." Dec. 8.

St. Louis Star-Times. "Joe Jones Completes Mural for Post Office." July 26.

Time. "Art: Year." 26, 1 (Jan. 3), p. 28.

Watson, Forbes. *American Painting Today*. American Federation of Arts.

1940

Berryman, Florence S. "Downtrodden Give Theme for Artist's Collection." *Washington Sunday Star*. Oct. 20.

Block, Maxine, ed. "Jones, Joe." *Current Biography*. H. W. Wilson.

Burke, Harry. "Museum Hangs Swope Prints." *St. Louis Post-Dispatch*. May 10.

Carline, Richard. "Fine Art in Modern America." *London Studio*. 120, 570 (Sept.), pp. 66–75.

Graeme, Alice. "Many Art Week Exhibitions to Remain Open." *Washington Post*. Dec. 1.

L., J. "Joe Jones' Artistic Growth Surveyed." *Art News*. 39, 8 (Nov. 23), p. 12.

New York Sun. Untitled review of 1940 A.C.A. Gallery solo exhibition. Nov. 16.

New York World-Telegram. "New Qualities Appear in Joe Jones' Paintings." Nov. 16.

"Postal Mural Here; It's Nice." [Seneca, Kans., newspaper]. Feb. 6 (?). Record Group 121, Entry 133; case files concerning embellishment of federal buildings, 1934–43; records of the Section of Fine Arts, Public Buildings Administration, Box 24 (Seneca, Kans., file). National Archives, College Park, Md.

St. Louis Globe-Democrat. "Tells of Raid in Mallinckrodt Suit." June 14.

St. Louis Post-Dispatch. "City Museum Exhibit by St. Louis Artists." May 16. / "Joe Jones Named in Mallinckrodt Divorce Trial." June 14. / "Joe Jones to Marry Divorcee in East." Oct. 20. / "Joe Jones Has Show." Nov. 18.

St. Louis Star-Times. "Joe Jones Named in Mallinckrodt Divorce Charge." June 14.

Time. "20 Years of Gropper." 25, 8 (Feb. 19), p. 41.

Washington Post. "Calendar of Art Exhibitions in District." Oct. 20. / "Jones' Work to Be on View at Bookshop." Oct. 27.

Wehle, Harry B. "National Art Week and the Museum: Trends in American Painting." *Metropolitan Museum of Art Bulletin*. 35, 11, pt. 2 (Nov.), pp. 5–13.

Who's Who in American Art. Ed. by Charlotte Ball. Vol. 3, p. 279. American Federation of Arts.

1941

Cincinnati Enquirer. ["Photographs of Murals and Sculpture."] Nov. 16.

Lindstrom, Charles. "American Art and the Tyranny of the Practical." *Pacific Art Review*. 1, 3–4 (Winter 1941–42), pp. 2–7.

1942

Art Digest. "Ten Thousand Artists Unite for Victory." 16, 9 (Feb. 1), p. 17. / "The Arizona Plan." 17, 6 (Dec. 15), p. 11.

Art News. "Two Annuals, Two Methods: Philly, St. Louis." 41, 1 (Feb. 15–28), p. 31.

Fisher, Katherine. "Self-Taught, Joe Jones Has Achieved Wide Distinction in His Art Work." *Hudson Valley Courier*. June 28.

Kansas City Star. "Harvesting." Feb. 8.

New York World-Telegram. "Turnbull's New Pictures and Other Solo Exhibits." May 23.

St. Louis Post-Dispatch. "Prize Painting." Feb. 4.

Watson, Jane. "News and Comment." *Magazine of Art*. 35, 2 (Feb.), pp. 74–76, 78–80, 83.

SELECTED BIBLIOGRAPHY, POST–1942

American Artist. "Presenting Joe Jones." 11 (Apr. 1947), pp. 40–41.

Anchorage Museum of History and Art. *Drawing the Lines of Battle: Military Art of World War II Alaska*. Exh. cat. Essay by Lynn K. Binek. 1989.

Associated American Artists. *Collector's World*. 56, 1 ([1956]).

Balken, Debra Bricker. *After Many Springs: Regionalism, Modernism and the Midwest*. Exh. cat. Des Moines Art Center/Yale University Press. 2009.

Barter, Judith A., and Lynn E. Springer. *Currents of Expansion: Painting in the Midwest, 1820–1940*. Exh. cat. Saint Louis Art Museum. 1977.

Beckham, Sue Bridwell. *Depression Post Office Murals and Southern Culture: A Gentle Reconstruction*. University of Louisiana. 1989.

Brayman, Walter Witherspoon. "Art and Politics: The Radical Artists' Movement, 1926–1945." Ph.D. diss. University of Missouri. 1973.

Breuning, Margaret. "Joe Jones Gains in Creative Power." *Art Digest*. 19, 9 (Feb. 1, 1945), p. 17.

Craven, Thomas. "American Painting." *Studio*. 127, 615 (June 1944), pp. 127, 170–84.

Dorrill, Lisa. "Picturing the Dirty Thirties: Paintings and Prints of the Dust Bowl." Ph.D. diss. University of Kansas. 1998.

Georgia Museum of Art. *Coming Home: American Paintings 1930–1950 from the Schoen Collection*. Exh. cat. Essay by Erika Doss. 2003. / *The American Scene on Paper: Prints and Drawings from the Schoen Collection*. Exh. cat. Essay by Harry Katz. 2008.

Haggerty Museum of Art, Marquette University. *Joe Jones & J. B. Turnbull: Visions of the Midwest in the 1930s*. Exh. cat. Essay by Karal Ann Marling. 1987. / *Against the Grain: A New Look at Joe Jones and J. B. Turnbull's 1930s Liquor Store Murals*. Exh. cat. Intro. by James Scarborough. 1995.

Hemingway, Andrew. *Artists on the Left: American Artists and the Communist Movement, 1926–1956*. Yale University Press, 2002.

Iarocci, Louisa. "A *View of St. Louis* by Joseph James Jones." May 3, 1990. Unpub. MS. Missouri History Museum, St. Louis, artist's file. / "The Changing American Landscape: The Art and Politics of Joe Jones." *Gateway Heritage*. 12, 2 (Fall 1991), pp. 68–75.

Johns, Orrick. *Time of Our Lives: The Story of My Father and Myself*. Stackpole Sons, 1937. Reprint: Octagon Books, 1973.

Kerr, Scott, and R. H. Dick. *An American Art Colony: The Art and Artists of Ste. Genevieve, Missouri, 1930–1940*. McCaughen and Burr Press. 2004.

Kinsey, Joni L. *Plain Pictures: Images of the American Prairie*. Exh. cat. Smithsonian Institution Press. 1996.

Marling, Karal Ann. *Wall-to-Wall America: A Cultural History of Post-Office Murals in the Great Depression*. University of Minnesota Press. 1982. / "Joe Jones: Regionalist, Communist, Capitalist." *Journal of Decorative and Propaganda Arts*. 4 (Spring 1987), pp. 46–59.

McKinzie, Richard D. *The New Deal for Artists*. Princeton University Press, 1973.

Monroe, Gerald M. "Art Front." *Archives of American Art Journal*. 13, 3 (1973), pp. 13–19.

Munson-Williams-Proctor Arts Institute. *Order and Enigma: American Art between the Two Wars*. Exh. cat. Essay by Sarah Clark-Langager. 1984.

New York Times. "Joe Jones, Artist Noted for Murals." Apr. 10, 1963.

New York World-Telegram. "Joe Jones Switches from Grimness to Fantasy." Jan. 27, 1945.

Packman, Victor. *Turnbull 1910–1976, Jones 1909–1963*. 1977.

Park, Marlene, and Gerald E. Markowitz. *Democratic Vistas: Post Offices and Public Art in the New Deal*. Temple University Press. 1984.

Pearson, Ralph M. *Experiencing American Pictures*. Harper and Bros. 1943.

Peeler, David P. "America's Depression Culture: Social Art and Literature of the 1930s." Ph.D. diss. University of Wisconsin–Madison. 1980.

Philbrook Art Center. *Oil, 1940–1945: A Selection of Documentary Paintings from the Collection of Standard Oil Co. (New Jersey)*. Exh. cat. 1946.

Pohl, Frances. *In the Eye of the Storm: An Art of Conscience, 1930–1970. Selections from the Collection of Philip J. and Suzanne Schiller*. Exh. cat. Pomegranate Artbooks. 1995.

Purcell, Winifred. "Back from Pix Works at Labrador, Local Man Now Building Locomotives." *Morristown Daily Record*. Dec. 23, 1948.

Richardson, E. P. *Ben Shahn Charles Sheeler Joe Jones*. Exh. cat. Detroit Institute of Arts. 1954.

Rogers, James G., Jr. *The Ste. Genevieve Artists' Colony and Summer School of Art, 1932–1941*. Foundation for Restoration of Ste. Genevieve. 1998.

Salpeter, Harry. "The New Mister Joe Jones." *Esquire*. 23, 6 (June 1945), pp. 82, 118.

Seevers, Helen. "Blue Lantern Bohemians." *St. Louis Post-Dispatch*. Apr. 3, 1969.

Stearns, Robert, ed. *Illusions of Eden: Visions of the American Heartland*. Arts Midwest. 2000.

Time. "Angry Man Calms Down." 58, 17 (Oct. 22, 1951), p. 21.

Wells, Richard D. "Elizabeth Green: A Patronage Portrait." Ph.D. diss. St. Louis University. 1985.

Wiegand, Shirley, and Wayne Wiegand. *Books on Trial: Red Scare in the Heartland*. University of Oklahoma Press. 2007.

Wixson, Douglas. *Worker-Writer in America: Jack Conroy and the Tradition of Midwestern Literary Radicalism, 1898–1990*. University of Illinois Press. 1994.

Woo, William F. "Softening of a Hard-Boiled Artist." *St. Louis Post-Dispatch*. May 5, 1963.

Woodward, Kesler E. *Painting in the North: Alaskan Art in the Anchorage Museum of History and Art*. University of Washington Press. 1993.

JOE JONES: SELECTED ARCHIVAL RESOURCES

Papers, letters, journals, other documents

American Contemporary Art (A.C.A.). Gallery Records, 1917–63. Archives of American Art, Smithsonian Institution, Washington, D.C.

Baron, Herman. Papers, 1937–67. Archives of American Art, Smithsonian Institution, Washington, D.C.

Chidsey, G. Alan. "Joe Jones." Scrapbook of Jones clippings. D. Wigmore, New York.

Conroy, Jack. Papers. Midwest Manuscript Collection. Newberry Library, Chicago.

John Simon Guggenheim Memorial Foundation, New York. Archives. Joe Jones's application for a grant and correspondence. Referenced with permission of the heirs of Joe Jones.

Green, Dr. John, Collection. Correspondence between Joe Jones and Elizabeth Green and others, and between Elizabeth Green and others. Missouri History Museum, St. Louis.

Jones, Joe. Artist's files. Missouri History Museum, St. Louis. / Richardson Memorial Library, Saint Louis Art Museum. / St. Louis Public Library.

Martyl (Schweig Langsdorf). Papers. Archives of American Art, Smithsonian Institution, Washington, D.C.

National Archives, College Park, Md. Records related to Jones's post-office mural commissions. Record Group 121, case files concerning embellishment of federal buildings, 1934–43; Records of the Section of Fine Arts, Public Buildings Administration; Entry 133, Boxes 3, 24, 32, and 56. / Record Group 96, Records of the Farmers Home Administration, 1918–1975; General correspondence from the Washington office, Heading 986 (Special Skills, correspondence by name), Box 67.

Saint Louis Art Museum. Archives. Directors' Correspondence. / Richardson Memorial Library. "St. Louis Artists' Guild Prizes 1914–1933." / Richardson Memorial Library. *St. Louis Art World* 1, 1–2, 9; Oct. 1931–Summer 1933.

Saint Louis Review 1, 1–2, 15; Mar. 1, 1932–May 20, 1933. Missouri History Museum, St. Louis.

Turnbull, James Baare. Papers. Woodstock (New York) Artists Association and Museum. Archives.

Vagaries, 1928 and undated issues. Missouri History Museum, St. Louis.

Worcester (Mass.) Art Museum. Correspondence, Director's Office.

Oral histories

Friesen, George and Dolores. Interviewed by Andrew Walker, Oct. 6, 2008. Saint Louis Art Museum. Archives.

Martyl (Schweig Langsdorf). Interviewed by Betty Blum, 2007. Ryerson and Burnham Libraries, The Art Institute of Chicago. / Interviewed by Andrew Walker, Feb. 12 and Nov. 3, 2009 (video). Saint Louis Art Museum. Archives.

Stix, Ernest and Judith. Interviewed by Andrew Walker and Janeen Turk, Oct. 5, 2009. Saint Louis Art Museum. Archives.

Wood, Timothy. Interviewed by Andrew Walker, July 20, 2008. Saint Louis Art Museum. Archives.

Photography Credits

All works by Joe Jones © Heirs of Joe Jones

16 Duchamp: 1950 © 2010 Artists Rights Society (ARS), New York / ADAGP, Paris / Succession Marcel Duchamp

17 St. Louis Post-Dispatch: © 2010 Artists Rights Society (ARS), New York / ADAGP, Paris
Lempicka: © 2010 Artists Rights Society (ARS), New York / ADAGP, Paris

24 O'Keeffe: © 2010 Georgia O'Keeffe Museum / Artists Rights Society (ARS), New York; Photo Credit: Georgia O'Keeffe Museum, Santa Fe / Art Resource, N.Y.

25 O'Keeffe: © 2010 Georgia O'Keeffe Museum / Artists Rights Society (ARS), New York

26 Lozowick: © Estate of Louis Lozowick

39 Benton: © AXA Gallery

47 Soyer: © Estate of Raphael Soyer

61 Pollock: © Charles Pollock Archives, Paris, France

62 Shahn: Art © Estate of Ben Shahn / Licensed by VAGA, New York, N.Y.; Digital Image © The Museum of Modern Art / Licensed by SCALA / Art Resource, N.Y.

63 Pollock: © Charles Pollock Archives, Paris, France

66 Hogue: © Olivia Hogue Mariño and Amalia Mariño

67 Gropper: © Estate of William Gropper; Reprinted with permission from the August 21, 1937 issue of *The Nation*.

71 Jones (Denver): Photography courtesy of the Denver Art Museum

73 Gropper: © Estate of William Gropper
Cortor: © Eldzier Cortor; Courtesy of Michael Rosenfeld Gallery, LLC, New York, N.Y.

83 Schweig: © Martin Schweig and Martyl

86 Vorst: © Carl Vorst

91 Vorst: © Carl Vorst

95 © Martyl

101 Evergood: Photography by Lee Stalsworth.

105 Benton: Art © T. H. Benton and R. P. Benton Testamentary Trusts / UMB Bank Trustee / Licensed by VAGA, New York, N.Y.

107 Benton: Art © T. H. Benton and R. P. Benton Testamentary Trusts / UMB Bank Trustee / Licensed by VAGA, New York, N.Y.

108 Davis: Art © Estate of Stuart Davis / Licensed by VAGA, New York, N.Y.

153 Jones: Digital restoration by Nick Smith

156 Jones: Photograph by Geoffrey Clements

166 Jones: Photography courtesy of the Denver Art Museum

202 TIME Magazine: From TIME, May 19, 1961 © 1961 TIME, Inc. All rights reserved. Used by permission and protected by the Copyright Laws of the United States. The printing, copying, redistribution, or retransmission of the Material without express written permission is prohibited.

204 Graphics by Nick Smith

Index

Italicized page references refer to figure illustrations. Boldface page references refer to catalogue plates. Endnotes are indicated with "n" followed by the endnote number.